U.S. Department of Justice

OVERVIEW OF THE PRIVACY ACT OF 1974

2012 Edition

Office of Privacy and Civil Liberties
U.S. Department of Justice

Director
Joo Y. Chung

For sale by the Superintendent of Documents, U.S. Government Printing Office
Internet: bookstore.gpo.gov Phone: toll free (866) 512-1800; DC area (202) 512-1800
Fax: (202) 512-2104 Mail: Stop IDCC, Washington, DC 20402-0001

ISBN 978-0-16-091446-1

UNITED STATES DEPARTMENT OF JUSTICE
OVERVIEW OF THE PRIVACY ACT OF 1974

2012 Edition

Preface

The "Overview of the Privacy Act of 1974," prepared by the Department of Justice's Office of Privacy and Civil Liberties (OPCL), is a discussion of the Privacy Act's disclosure prohibition, its access and amendment provisions, and its agency recordkeeping requirements. Tracking the provisions of the Act itself, the Overview provides reference to and legal analysis of court decisions interpreting the Act's provisions. The Overview is not intended to provide policy guidance, as that role statutorily rests with the Office of Management and Budget (OMB), 5 U.S.C. § 552a(v). However, where OMB has issued policy guidance on particular provisions of the Act, citation to such guidance is provided in the Overview. The 2012 edition of the Overview was issued electronically and sent for publication in September 2012 and includes cases through July 2012. The Overview is scheduled to be revised again in 2014.

OPCL is very pleased to provide this updated revision of the Overview, and could not have done so without the commitment of OPCL's small but dedicated staff. OPCL would particularly like to recognize: the written and editorial contributions of OPCL attorney Joseph R. Lullo, who carefully shepherded the publication of this edition from beginning to end; the written and editorial assistance of its former volunteer intern Kevin W. Ohlhausen; the management of the publication process by its program specialist Pamela A. Moye; and last, but certainly not least, the invaluable written and editorial contributions of its former Director, Kirsten J. Moncada, who led this edition to completion before her departure from the Department of Justice. The 2012 edition of the Overview is specifically dedicated to her. Without the valuable assistance of these individuals, the completion of this endeavor would not have been possible.

Joo Y. Chung
Director
Office of Privacy and Civil Liberties

OVERVIEW OF THE PRIVACY ACT OF 1974

TABLE OF CONTENTS

INTRODUCTION 1

LEGISLATIVE HISTORY 1

ROLE OF THE PRIVACY PROTECTION STUDY COMMISSION 1

ROLE OF THE OFFICE OF MANAGEMENT AND BUDGET 2

COMPUTER MATCHING 3

POLICY OBJECTIVES 4

DEFINITIONS 4
    A.   Agency 4
    B.   Individual 14
    C.   Maintain 17
    D.   Record 17
    E.   System of Records 28
        1)   Disclosure: Subsection (b) 34
        2)   Access and Amendment: Subsections (d)(1) and (d)(2) 46
        3)   Other Aspects 48

CONDITIONS OF DISCLOSURE TO THIRD PARTIES 52
    A.   The "No Disclosure Without Consent" Rule 52
    B.   Twelve Exceptions to the "No Disclosure Without Consent" Rule 65
        1)   5 USC § 552a(b)(1) ("need to know" within agency) 65
        2)   5 USC § 552a(b)(2) (required FOIA disclosures) 74
        3)   5 USC § 552a(b)(3) (routine uses) 79
        4)   5 USC § 552a(b)(4) (Bureau of the Census) 94
        5)   5 USC § 552a(b)(5) (statistical research) 95
        6)   5 USC § 552a(b)(6) (National Archives) 95
        7)   5 USC § 552a(b)(7) (law enforcement request) 96
        8)   5 USC § 552a(b)(8) (health or safety of an individual) 97
        9)   5 USC § 552a(b)(9) (Congress) 97
        10) 5 USC § 552a(b)(10) (Government Accountability Office) 98
        11) 5 USC § 552a(b)(11) (court order) 98
        12) 5 USC § 552a(b)(12) (Debt Collection Act) 109

ACCOUNTING OF CERTAIN DISCLOSURES 109

INDIVIDUAL'S RIGHT OF ACCESS 112

INDIVIDUAL'S RIGHT OF AMENDMENT 122

AGENCY REQUIREMENTS 123
   A. 5 USC § 552a(e)(1) 123
   B. 5 USC § 552a(e)(2) 124
   C. 5 USC § 552a(e)(3) 128
   D. 5 USC § 552a(e)(4) 132
   E. 5 USC § 552a(e)(5) 133
   F. 5 USC § 552a(e)(6) 145
   G. 5 USC § 552a(e)(7) 146
   H. 5 USC § 552a(e)(8) 154
   I. 5 USC § 552a(e)(9) 155
   J. 5 USC § 552a(e)(10) 155
   K. 5 USC § 552a(e)(11) 157

AGENCY RULES 157
   A. 5 USC § 552a(f)(1) 157
   B. 5 USC § 552a(f)(2) 158
   C. 5 USC § 552a(f)(3) 158
   D. 5 USC § 552a(f)(4) 161
   E. 5 USC § 552a(f)(5) 161

CIVIL REMEDIES 161
   A. Amendment Lawsuits under (g)(1)(A) 168
   B. Access Lawsuits under (g)(1)(B) 180
   C. Damages Lawsuits under (g)(1)(C) 186
   D. Damages Lawsuits under (g)(1)(D) 201
   E. Principles Applicable to Damages Lawsuits 210
      1) Intentional/Willful Standard 210
      2) Actual Damages 224
   F. Principles Applicable to All Privacy Act Civil Actions 231
      1) Attorney Fees and Costs 231
      2) Jurisdiction and Venue 236
      3) Statute of Limitations 239
      4) Jury Trial 259

CRIMINAL PENALTIES 260

TEN EXEMPTIONS 261
   A. One Special Exemption -- 5 USC § 552a(d)(5) 261
   B. Two General Exemptions -- 5 USC § 552a(j)(1) and (j)(2) 263
   C. Seven Specific Exemptions -- 5 USC § 552a(k) 275
      1) 5USC § 552a(k)(1) 276
      2) 5 USC § 552a(k)(2) 277
      3) 5 USC § 552a(k)(3) 284
      4) 5 USC § 552a(k)(4) 284
      5) 5 USC § 552a(k)(5) 284
      6) 5 USC § 552a(k)(6) 288
      7) 5 USC § 552a(k)(7) 289

SOCIAL SECURITY NUMBER USAGE 289

GOVERNMENT CONTRACTORS 294

MAILING LISTS 295

MISCELLANEOUS PROVISIONS 296

TEXT OF THE PRIVACY ACT OF 1974 299

OVERVIEW OF THE PRIVACY ACT

INTRODUCTION

The Privacy Act of 1974, 5 U.S.C. § 552a (2006), which has been in effect since September 27, 1975, can generally be characterized as an omnibus "code of fair information practices" that attempts to regulate the collection, maintenance, use, and dissemination of personal information by federal executive branch agencies. However, the Act's imprecise language, limited legislative history, and somewhat outdated regulatory guidelines have rendered it a difficult statute to decipher and apply. Moreover, even after more than thirty-five years of administrative and judicial analysis, numerous Privacy Act issues remain unresolved or unexplored. Adding to these interpretational difficulties is the fact that many earlier Privacy Act cases are unpublished district court decisions. A particular effort is made in this "Overview" to clarify the existing state of Privacy Act law while at the same time highlighting those controversial, unsettled areas where further litigation and case law development can be expected.

LEGISLATIVE HISTORY

The entire legislative history of the Privacy Act is contained in a convenient, one-volume compilation. See House Comm. on Gov't Operations and Senate Comm. on Gov't Operations, 94th Cong., 2d Sess., Legislative History of the Privacy Act of 1974 – S. 3418 (Pub. L. No. 93-579) Source Book on Privacy (1976) [hereinafter Source Book], available at http://www.loc.gov/rr/frd/Military_Law/pdf/LH_privacy_act-1974.pdf. The Act was passed in great haste during the final week of the Ninety-Third Congress. No conference committee was convened to reconcile differences in the bills passed by the House and Senate. Instead, staffs of the respective committees – led by Senators Ervin and Percy, and Congressmen Moorhead and Erlenborn – prepared a final version of the bill that was ultimately enacted. The original reports are thus of limited utility in interpreting the final statute; the more reliable legislative history consists of a brief analysis of the compromise amendments – entitled "Analysis of House and Senate Compromise Amendments to the Federal Privacy Act" – prepared by the staffs of the counterpart Senate and House committees and submitted in both the House and Senate in lieu of a conference report. See 120 Cong. Rec. 40,405-09, 40,881-83 (1974), reprinted in Source Book at 858-68, 987-94, available at http://www.loc.gov/rr/frd/Military_Law/pdf/LH_privacy_act-1974.pdf.

ROLE OF THE PRIVACY PROTECTION STUDY COMMISSION

Section 5 of the original Privacy Act established the "U.S. Privacy Protection Study Commission" to evaluate the statute and to issue a report containing recommendations for its improvement. The Commission issued its final report and ceased operation in 1977. See U.S. Privacy Protection Study Commission, Personal Privacy in an Information Society (1977) [hereinafter Privacy Commission Report], available at http://epic.org/privacy/ppsc1977report. See generally Doe v. Chao, 540 U.S. 615, 622-23 (2004) (looking to mandate and recommendation of Privacy Protection Study Commission in connection with legislative history to interpret Privacy Act damages provision).

OVERVIEW OF THE PRIVACY ACT

ROLE OF THE OFFICE OF MANAGEMENT AND BUDGET

Subsection (v) of the Privacy Act requires the Office of Management and Budget (OMB) to: (1) "develop and, after notice and opportunity for public comment, prescribe guidelines and regulations for the use of agencies in implementing" the Act; and (2) "provide continuing assistance to and oversight of the implementation" of the Act by agencies. 5 U.S.C. § 552a(v).

The vast majority of OMB's Privacy Act Guidelines [hereinafter OMB Guidelines] are published at 40 Fed. Reg. 28,948-78 (July 9, 1975), available at http://www.whitehouse.gov/sites/default/files/omb/assets/omb/inforeg/implementation_guidelines.pdf. However, these original guidelines have been supplemented in particular subject areas over the years. See 40 Fed. Reg. 56,741-43 (Nov. 21, 1975), available at http://www.whitehouse.gov/sites/default/files/omb/assets/omb/inforeg/implementation1974.pdf ("system of records" definition, routine use and intra-agency disclosures, consent and Congressional inquiries, accounting of disclosures, amendment appeals, rights of parents and legal guardians, relationship to Freedom of Information Act (FOIA)); 48 Fed. Reg. 15,556-60 (Apr. 11, 1983), available at http://www.whitehouse.gov/sites/default/files/omb/assets/omb/inforeg/guidance1983.pdf (relationship to Debt Collection Act); 52 Fed. Reg. 12,990-93 (Apr. 20, 1987), available at http://www.whitehouse.gov/sites/default/files/omb/assets/omb/inforeg/guidance_privacy_act.pdf ("call detail" programs); 54 Fed. Reg. 25,818-29 (June 19, 1989), available at http://www.whitehouse.gov/sites/default/files/omb/inforeg/final_guidance_p1100-503.pdf (computer matching); 56 Fed. Reg. 18,599-601 (proposed Apr. 23, 1991), available at http://www.whitehouse.gov/sites/default/files/omb/assets/omb/inforeg/computer_amendments1991.pdf (computer matching); 61 Fed. Reg. 6,428, 6,435-39 (Feb. 20, 1996) ("Federal Agency Responsibilities for Maintaining Records About Individuals"), available at http://www.whitehouse.gov/omb/circulars_a130_a130appendix_i. See also, e.g., OMB Circular No. A-130 – Memorandum for Heads of Executive Departments and Agencies, Subject: Management of Federal Information Resources, 61 Fed. Reg. 6428 (Feb. 20, 1996), as amended, 65 Fed. Reg. 77,677 (Dec. 12, 2000), available at http://www.whitehouse.gov/omb/Circulars_a130_a130trans4.pdf.

As a general rule, the OMB Guidelines are entitled to the deference usually accorded the interpretations of the agency that has been charged with the administration of a statute. See Sussman v. U.S. Marshals Serv., 494 F.3d 1106, 1120 (D.C. Cir. 2007). In Sussman, the Court of Appeals for the District of Columbia Circuit discussed this standard: "Congress explicitly tasked the OMB with promulgating guidelines for implementing the Privacy Act, and we therefore give the OMB Guidelines 'the deference usually accorded interpretation of a statute by the agency charged with its administration.'" Id. (citing Albright v. United States, 631 F.2d 915, 920 n.5 (D.C. Cir. 1980)) (citation omitted). With regard to the 1975 guidelines, the court stated: "The OMB apparently invited no public comment prior to publishing its guidelines, and after we decided Albright, Congress pointedly replaced its original grant of authority to the OMB with one that expressly required the OMB to respect such procedural niceties before its guidelines could be binding. But Congress made clear the

OVERVIEW OF THE PRIVACY ACT

change was not meant to disturb existing guidelines. Hence, the old OMB Guidelines still deserve the same level of deference they enjoyed prior to the 1998 amendment." Sussman, 494 F.3d at 1120 n.8 (citations omitted). Numerous cases have applied this standard of deference. See, e.g., Maydak v. United States, 363 F.3d 512, 518 (D.C. Cir. 2004); Henke v. U.S. Dep't of Commerce, 83 F.3d 1453, 1460 n.12 (D.C. Cir. 1996); Quinn v. Stone, 978 F.2d 126, 133 (3d Cir. 1992); Baker v. Dep't of the Navy, 814 F.2d 1381, 1383 (9th Cir. 1987); Perry v. FBI, 759 F.2d 1271, 1276 n.7 (7th Cir. 1985), rev'd en banc on other grounds, 781 F.2d 1294 (7th Cir. 1986); Bartel v. FAA, 725 F.2d 1403, 1408 n.9 (D.C. Cir. 1984); Smiertka v. U.S. Dep't of the Treasury, 604 F.2d 698, 703 n.12 (D.C. Cir. 1979); Rogers v. U.S. Dep't of Labor, 607 F. Supp. 697, 700 n.2 (N.D. Cal. 1985); Sanchez v. United States, 3 Gov't Disclosure Serv. (P-H) ¶ 83,116, at 83,709 (S.D. Tex. Sept. 10, 1982); Golliher v. USPS, 3 Gov't Disclosure Serv. (P-H) ¶ 83,114, at 83,703 (N.D. Ohio June 10, 1982); Greene v. VA, No. C-76-461-S, slip op. at 6-7 (M.D.N.C. July 3, 1978); Daniels v. FCC, No. 77-5011, slip op. at 8-9 (D.S.D. Mar. 15, 1978); see also Martin v. Office of Special Counsel, 819 F.2d 1181, 1188 (D.C. Cir. 1987) (OMB interpretation is "worthy of our attention and solicitude"). However, a few courts have rejected particular aspects of the OMB Guidelines as inconsistent with the statute. See Doe v. Chao, 540 U.S. at 62 n.11 (disagreeing with dissent's reliance on OMB interpretation of damages provision and stating that Court does "not find its unelaborated conclusion persuasive"); Scarborough v. Harvey, 493 F. Supp. 2d 1, 13-14 n.28 (D.D.C. 2007) (personal/entrepreneurial distinction); Henke v. U.S. Dep't of Commerce, No. 94-0189, 1996 WL 692020, at *2-3 (D.D.C. Aug. 19, 1994) (same), aff'd on other grounds, 83 F.3d 1445 (D.C. Cir. 1996); Kassel v. VA, No. 87-217-S, slip op. at 24-25 (D.N.H. Mar. 30, 1992) (subsection (e)(3)); Saunders v. Schweiker, 508 F. Supp. 305, 309 (W.D.N.Y. 1981) (same); Metadure Corp. v. United States, 490 F. Supp. 1368, 1373-74 (S.D.N.Y. 1980) (subsection (a)(2)); Fla. Med. Ass'n v. HEW, 479 F. Supp. 1291, 1307-11 (M.D. Fla. 1979) (same); Zeller v. United States, 467 F. Supp. 487, 497-99 (E.D.N.Y. 1979) (same).

COMPUTER MATCHING

The Computer Matching and Privacy Protection Act of 1988 (Pub. L. No. 100-503) amended the Privacy Act to add several new provisions. See 5 U.S.C. § 552a(a)(8)-(13), (e)(12), (o), (p), (q), (r), (u) (2006). These provisions add procedural requirements for agencies to follow when engaging in computer-matching activities; provide matching subjects with opportunities to receive notice and to refute adverse information before having a benefit denied or terminated; and require that agencies engaged in matching activities establish Data Protection Boards to oversee those activities. These provisions became effective on December 31, 1989. OMB's guidelines on computer matching should be consulted in this area. See 54 Fed. Reg. 25,818-29 (June 19, 1989).

Subsequently, Congress enacted the Computer Matching and Privacy Protection Amendments of 1990 (Pub. L. No. 101-508), which further clarified the due process provisions found in subsection (p). OMB's proposed guidelines on these amendments appear at 56 Fed. Reg. 18,599-601 (proposed Apr. 23, 1991), available at http://www.whitehouse.gov/sites/default/files/omb/assets/omb/inforeg/computer_amendments1991.pdf.

OVERVIEW OF THE PRIVACY ACT

The highly complex and specialized provisions of the Computer Matching and Privacy Protection Act of 1988 and the Computer Matching and Privacy Protection Amendments of 1990 are not further addressed herein. For guidance on these provisions, agencies should consult the OMB Guidelines, cited above.

POLICY OBJECTIVES

Broadly stated, the purpose of the Privacy Act is to balance the government's need to maintain information about individuals with the rights of individuals to be protected against unwarranted invasions of their privacy stemming from federal agencies' collection, maintenance, use, and disclosure of personal information about them. The historical context of the Act is important to an understanding of its remedial purposes. In 1974, Congress was concerned with curbing the illegal surveillance and investigation of individuals by federal agencies that had been exposed during the Watergate scandal. It was also concerned with potential abuses presented by the government's increasing use of computers to store and retrieve personal data by means of a universal identifier – such as an individual's social security number. The Act focuses on four basic policy objectives:

(1)   To restrict <u>disclosure</u> of personally identifiable records maintained by agencies.

(2)   To grant individuals increased rights of <u>access</u> to agency records maintained on themselves.

(3)   To grant individuals the right to seek <u>amendment</u> of agency records maintained on themselves upon a showing that the records are not accurate, relevant, timely, or complete.

(4)   To establish a code of "<u>fair information practices</u>" which requires agencies to comply with statutory norms for collection, maintenance, and dissemination of records.

DEFINITIONS

A. Agency

"any Executive department, military department, Government corporation, Government controlled corporation, or other establishment in the executive branch of the [federal] Government (including the Executive Office of the President), or any independent regulatory agency." 5 U.S.C. § 552a(1) (incorporating 5 U.S.C. § 552(f) (2006), which in turn incorporates 5 U.S.C. § 551(1) (2006)).

OVERVIEW OF THE PRIVACY ACT

Comment:

The Privacy Act – like the Freedom of Information Act (FOIA), 5 U.S.C. § 552 – applies only to a federal "agency." See OMB Guidelines, 40 Fed. Reg. 28,948, 28,950-51 (July 9, 1975), available at http://www.whitehouse.gov/sites/default/files/omb/assets/omb/inforeg/implementation_guidelines.pdf; 120 Cong. Rec. 40,408 (1974), reprinted in Source Book at 866, available at http://www.loc.gov/rr/frd/Military_Law/pdf/LH_privacy_act-1974.pdf (indicating intent that Act apply to Postal Service, Postal Rate Commission, and government corporations or government-controlled corporations); 120 Cong. Rec. 36,967 (1974), reprinted in Source Book at 958, available at http://www.loc.gov/rr/frd/Military_Law/pdf/LH_privacy_act-1974.pdf (indicating intent that term "agency" be given "its broadest statutory meaning," and, giving example of Department of Justice as an "agency," recognizing propriety of subsection (b)(1) "need to know" disclosures between its various components); see also, e.g., In re Sealed Case, 551 F.3d 1047, 1049-50 (D.C. Cir. 2009) (concluding that "the Privacy Act's definition of agency includes federally recognized National Guard units at all times" and not solely when the unit is on active federal duty); United States v. Jackson, 381 F.3d 984, 989-90 (10th Cir. 2004) (citing Ehm, infra, and holding that Amtrak is not an "agency"); NLRB v. USPS, 841 F.2d 141, 144 n.3 (6th Cir. 1988) (Postal Service is an "agency" because it is an "independent establishment of the executive branch"); Ehm v. Nat'l R.R. Passenger Corp., 732 F.2d 1250, 1252-55 (5th Cir. 1984) (Amtrak held not to constitute a "Government-controlled corporation"); Iqbal v. FBI, No. 3:11-cv-369, 2012 WL 2366634, at *4 (M.D. Fla. June 21, 2012) (declining to dismiss "just because the Plaintiff brought his claims against the FBI instead of the Department of Justice"); Cloonan v. Holder, 768 F. Supp. 2d 154, 162 (D.D.C. 2011) ("[N]aming components as defendants under the Privacy Act is appropriate since the statute's plain language is clear that 'an agency need not be a cabinet-level agency such as the DOJ to be liable.'" (quoting Lair v. Dep't of Treasury, No. 03 Civ. 827, 2005 WL 645228 (D.D.C. Mar. 21, 2005))); Thompson v. Dep't of State, 400 F. Supp. 2d 1, 21-22 (D.D.C. 2005) (finding Foreign Service Grievance Board to be an "agency" because it "consists of members appointed exclusively by an executive department, administers federal statutes, promulgates regulations, and adjudicates the rights of individuals"); Mumme v. U.S. Dep't of Labor, 150 F. Supp. 2d 162, 169 (D. Me. 2001) ("[A] claimant bringing a Privacy Act claim must bring suit against a particular agency, not the entire United States."), aff'd, No. 01-2256 (1st Cir. June 12, 2002). But cf. Shannon v. Gen. Elec. Co., 812 F. Supp. 308, 313, 315 n.5 (N.D.N.Y. 1993) ("no dispute" that GE falls within definition of "agency" subject to requirements of Privacy Act where, pursuant to contract, it operated Department of Energy-owned lab under supervision, control, and oversight of Department

OVERVIEW OF THE PRIVACY ACT

and where by terms of contract GE agreed to comply with Privacy Act).

With regard to the White House, all the courts that have considered the issue have held that those components of the Executive Office of the President whose sole function is to advise and assist the President are not "agencies" for purposes of the Privacy Act. See Alexander v. FBI, 456 F. App'x 1, 2 (D.C. Cir. 2011) (per curiam), aff'g 691 F. Supp. 2d 182 (D.D.C. 2010) (determining that prior interpretation to the contrary in an earlier holding in the case (971 F. Supp. 603, 606-07 (D.D.C. 1997)) was "no longer the correct one"); Dale v. Executive Office of the President, 164 F. Supp. 2d 22, 25-26 (D.D.C. 2001); Trulock v. DOJ, No. 00-2234, slip op. at 7 (D.D.C. Sept. 18, 2001); Tripp v. Executive Office of the President, 200 F.R.D. 140, 142-46 (D.D.C. 2001), appeal dismissed per curiam, No. 01-5189, 2001 WL 1488614 (D.C. Cir. Oct. 17, 2001); Broaddrick v. Executive Office of the President, 139 F. Supp. 2d 55, 60 (D.D.C. 2001), aff'd per curiam, No. 01-5178 (D.C. Cir. May 1, 2002); Flowers v. Executive Office of the President, 142 F. Supp. 2d 38, 41-43 (D.D.C. 2001); Jones v. Executive Office of the President, 167 F. Supp. 2d 10, 13-20 (D.D.C. 2001); Sculimbrene v. Reno, 158 F. Supp. 2d 26, 35-36 (D.D.C. 2001); Schwarz v. U.S. Dep't of Treasury, 131 F. Supp. 2d 142, 147-48 (D.D.C. 2000), summary affirmance granted, No. 00-5453 (D.C. Cir. May 10, 2001); Falwell v. Executive Office of the President, 113 F. Supp. 2d 967, 968-70 (W.D. Va. 2000); Barr v. Executive Office of the President, No. 99-CV-1695, 2000 WL 34024118, at *3 (D.D.C. Aug. 9, 2000). In fact, the Court of Appeals for the D.C. Circuit has observed that "Congress did not inadvertently omit the Offices of the President and Vice President from the Privacy Act's disclosure requirements." Wilson v. Libby, 535 F.3d 697, 708 (D.C. Cir. 2008).

Note also that federal entities outside of the executive branch, such as a federal district court, see Goddard v. Whitmer, No. 09-CV-404, 2010 WL 116744, at *2 (E.D. Ky. Jan. 6, 2010), Cobell v. Norton, 157 F. Supp. 2d 82, 86 & n.6 (D.D.C. 2001), a grand jury, see Standley v. DOJ, 835 F.2d 216, 218 (9th Cir. 1987); United States v. Richardson, No. 3:2001-10, 2007 U.S. Dist. LEXIS 77, at *3 (W.D. Pa. Jan. 3, 2007), a probation office, see Kates v. King, No. 12-1835, 2012 WL 2583374, at *2 (3d Cir. July 5, 2012) (per curiam); United States v. Bullard, 337 F. App'x 215, 216 n.1 (3d Cir. 2009) (per curiam); Fuller-Avent v. U.S. Prob. Office, 226 F. App'x 1, 2 (D.C. Cir. 2006); Schwartz v. DOJ, No. 95-6423, 1996 WL 335757, at *1 (2d Cir. June 6, 1996); Morris v. U.S. Prob. Servs., 723 F. Supp. 2d 225, 227 (D.D.C. 2010); Bowles v. BOP, No. 08 CV 9591, 2010 WL 23326, at *3 (S.D.N.Y. Jan. 5, 2010); Jackson v. DOJ, No. 09-0846, 2009 WL 5205421, at *4 (D. Minn. Dec. 23, 2009); Kyles v. Kaufman, No. 08-4169, 2008 WL 4906141, at *1 (D.S.D. Nov. 14, 2008); Harrell v. BOP, No. 99-1619, slip op. at 6 (W.D. Okla. Mar. 5, 2001), aff'd on other grounds sub nom. Harrell v.

OVERVIEW OF THE PRIVACY ACT

Fleming, 285 F.3d 1292 (10th Cir. 2002); Callwood v. Dep't of Prob. of the V.I., 982 F. Supp. 341, 343 (D.V.I. 1997), or a federal bankruptcy court, see In re Adair, 212 B.R. 171, 173 (Bankr. N.D. Ga. 1997), are not subject to the Act. Similarly, the Smithsonian Institution, although having many "links" with the federal government, "is not an agency for Privacy Act purposes." Dong v. Smithsonian Inst., 125 F.3d 877, 879-80 (D.C. Cir. 1997); see also Dodge v. Trs. of Nat'l Gallery of Art, 326 F. Supp. 2d 1, 10-11 (D.D.C. 2004) (finding that "the National Gallery is a Smithsonian Museum" and explaining that "Smithsonian Museums . . . are not subjected to the limitations of the Privacy Act because they do not fall within the definition of an 'agency'").

State and local government agencies are not covered by the Privacy Act. See, e.g., N'Jai v. Piitsburgh Bd. of Public Educ., No. 11-3320, 2012 WL 2019186, at *2 (3d Cir. June 6, 2012) (per curiam); Spurlock v. Ashley County, 281 F. App'x 628, 629 (8th Cir. 2008); Schmitt v. City of Detroit, 395 F.3d 327, 331 (6th Cir. 2005); Perez-Santos v. Malave, 23 F. App'x 11, 12 (1st Cir. 2001) (per curiam); Dittman v. California, 191 F.3d 1020, 1026, 1029 (9th Cir. 1999); Ortez v. Washington County, Or., 88 F.3d 804, 811 (9th Cir. 1996); Brown v. Kelly, No. 93-5222, 1994 WL 36144, at *1 (D.C. Cir. Jan. 27, 1994) (per curiam); Monk v. Teeter, No. 89-16333, 1992 WL 1681, at *2 (9th Cir. Jan. 8, 1992); Davidson v. Georgia, 622 F.2d 895, 896 (5th Cir. 1980); Dean v. City of New Orleans, No. 11-2209, 2012 WL 2564954, at *14 (E.D. La. July 2, 2012); Oliver v. Garfield County Det. Facility, No. CIV-10-1281, 2012 WL 668802, at *3 (W.D. Okla. Feb. 8, 2012); Goins v. Beard, No. 09-1223, 2011 U.S. Dist. LEXIS 104442, at *28 (W.D. Pa. Sept. 15, 2011); Ervin v. Cal. Dep't of Corr. & Rehab., No. 1:10-cv-01859, 2011 WL 3503181, at *5 (E.D. Cal. Aug. 10, 2011); Omegbu v. United States, No. 10-C-765, 2011 WL 2912703, at *5 (E.D. Wis. July 18, 2011); Roggio v. City of Gardner, No. 10-40076, 2011 WL 1303141, at *7 (D. Mass. Mar. 30, 2011); Terry v. Town of Morristown, No. 06-1788, 2010 WL 3906938, at *6 (D.N.J. Sept. 30, 2010); Manuel v. City of Philadelphia, No. 10-2690, 2010 WL 3566767, at *9 (E.D. Pa. Sept. 14, 2010); Prepetit v. Gov't of D.C., No. 09 2183, 2009 WL 4405756, at *1 (D.D.C. Nov. 19, 2009); Study v. United States, No. 3:08cv493, 2009 WL 2340649, at *2 (N.D. Fla. July 24, 2009); Rouse v. City of New York, No. 08CV7419, 2009 WL 1532054, at *13 (S.D.N.Y. June 2, 2009); Banda v. Camden County Bd. of Chosen Freeholders, No. 08-5115, 2009 WL 1561442, at *2 (D.N.J. May 29, 2009); Willis v. DOJ, 581 F. Supp. 2d 57, 67-68 (D.D.C. 2008); Barickman v. Bumgardner, No. 1:07CV134, 2008 WL 2872712, at *3 (N.D. W. Va. July 22, 2008); Gero v. Vt. Dep't of Corr., No. 1:07-CV-145, 2008 WL 2439891, at *1 (D. Vt. June 16, 2008); Walsh v. Krantz, No. 1:07-CV-0616, 2008 WL 2329130, at *5 (M.D. Pa. June 4, 2008); Dewille v. Ohio, No. 3:07cv3888, 2008 WL 440384, at *1 (N.D. Ohio Feb. 13, 2008);

OVERVIEW OF THE PRIVACY ACT

Sturkey v. Ozmint, No. 8:07-1502, 2008 WL 373610, at *1 (D.S.C. Feb. 7, 2008); Allen v. Woodford, No. 05-1104, 2007 WL 309945, at *9 (E.D. Cal. Jan. 30, 2007); Lawson v. Baxter, No. 4:06-CV-109, 2006 WL 3004069, at *3 (W.D. Mich. Oct. 20, 2006); Gabbard v. Hall County, No. 7:06-CV-37, 2006 U.S. Dist. LEXIS 56662, at *4-5 (M.D. Ga. Aug. 14, 2006); Brandt v. La Grange, No. 2:06 CV 1, 2006 WL 2120383, at *3 (E.D. Mo. July 27, 2006); Pitts v. Perkins Local Sch. Bd. of Educ., No. 1:05-CV-2226, 2006 WL 1050675, at *1 (N.D. Ohio Apr. 19, 2006); Fetzer v. Cambria County Human Servs., 384 F. Supp. 2d 813, 816 (W.D. Pa. 2005); Cassidy v. Rubitschun, No. 105-CV-350, 2005 WL 1335148, at *5 (W.D. Mich. June 2, 2005); Villa v. Vill. of Elmore, No. 3:02CV7357, 2002 WL 31728970, at *5 (N.D. Ohio Dec. 3, 2002), appeal dismissed sua sponte as untimely, No. 03-3034 (6th Cir. Mar. 28, 2003); Daniel v. Safir, 175 F. Supp. 2d 474, 481 (E.D.N.Y. 2001) (although characterizing claims as under FOIA, dismissing Privacy Act claims against local agency), aff'd, 42 F. App'x 528 (2d Cir. 2002); Atamian v. Ellis, No. 00-797, 2001 WL 699016, at *3 (D. Del. June 19, 2001), aff'd, 35 F. App'x 356 (3d Cir. 2002) (unpublished table decision); Lampkin v. N.Y. City Dep't of Prob., No. 00 Civ. 7165, 2001 WL 210362, at *2 (S.D.N.Y. Feb. 28, 2001); Markun v. Hillsborough County Dep't of Corr., No. 97-208, 1999 WL 813949, at *1 (D.N.H. Sept. 17, 1999); McClain v. DOJ, No. 97 C 0385, 1999 WL 759505, at *2 (N.D. Ill. Sept. 1, 1999), aff'd, 17 F. App'x 471 (7th Cir. 2001); Ferguson v. Ala. Criminal Justice Info. Ctr., 962 F. Supp. 1446, 1446-47 (M.D. Ala. 1997); Williams v. District of Columbia, No. 95CV0936, 1996 WL 422328, at *2-3 (D.D.C. July 19, 1996); Martinson v. Violent Drug Traffickers Project, No. 95-2161, 1996 WL 411590, at *1-2 (D.D.C. July 11, 1996), summary affirmance granted, No. 96-5262 (D.C. Cir. Sept. 22, 1997); Mamarella v. County of Westchester, 898 F. Supp. 236, 237-38 (S.D.N.Y. 1995); Connolly v. Beckett, 863 F. Supp. 1379, 1383-84 (D. Colo. 1994); MR by RR v. Lincolnwood Bd. of Educ., Dist. 74, 843 F. Supp. 1236, 1239-40 (N.D. Ill. 1994), aff'd sub nom. Rheinstrom v. Lincolnwood Bd. of Educ., Dist. 74, No. 94-1357, 1995 U.S. App. LEXIS 10781 (7th Cir. May 10, 1995); Malewich v. USPS, No. 91-4871, slip op. at 19 (D.N.J. Apr. 8, 1993), aff'd, 27 F.3d 557 (3d Cir. 1994) (unpublished table decision); Shields v. Shetler, 682 F. Supp. 1172, 1176 (D. Colo. 1988); Ryans v. N.J. Comm'n, 542 F. Supp. 841, 852 (D.N.J. 1982). But cf. Reno v. United States, No. 4-94CIV243, 1995 U.S. Dist. LEXIS 12834, at *6 (W.D.N.C. Aug. 14, 1995) (holding national guard to be a state entity in case decided prior to In re Sealed Case, 551 F.3d 1047, 1049-50 (D.C. Cir. 2009), which held that all federally recognized national guard units, whether on active status or not, are "agencies"). Additionally, neither federal funding nor regulation converts such entities into covered agencies. See St. Michaels Convalescent Hosp. v. California, 643 F.2d 1369, 1373 (9th Cir. 1981); Adelman v. Discover Card Servs., 915 F. Supp. 1163, 1166 (D. Utah 1996). The Act likewise does not

OVERVIEW OF THE PRIVACY ACT

apply to tribal entities. See Stevens v. Skenandore, No. 99-2611, 2000 WL 1069404, at *1 (7th Cir. Aug. 1, 2000) (no right of action against tribal officials under Privacy Act).

Similarly, private entities are not subject to the Act. See Johnson v. Mel Foster Co. Ins., No. 12-1486, 2012 WL 2892346, at *1 (8th Cir. July 16, 2012) (per curiam); KGV Easy Leasing Corp. v. Leavitt, 413 F. App'x 966, 968 (9th Cir. 2011); Chimarev v. TD Waterhouse Investor Servs., 99 F. App'x 259, 261-62 (2d Cir. 2004); McLeod v. VA, 43 F. App'x 70, 71 (9th Cir. 2002); Sharwell v. Best Buy, No. 00-3206, 2000 WL 1478341, at *2 (6th Cir. Sept. 26, 2000); Sutton v. Providence St. Joseph Med. Ctr., 192 F.3d 826, 844 (9th Cir. 1999); Mitchell v. G.E. Am. Spacenet, No. 96-2624, 1997 WL 226369, at *1 (4th Cir. May 7, 1997); Gilbreath v. Guadalupe Hosp. Found., 5 F.3d 785, 791 (5th Cir. 1993); Cintron-Garcia v. Supermercados Econo, Inc., 818 F. Supp. 2d 500, 510 (D.P.R. 2011); Chapman v. Wright Transp., No. CA 11-0097, 2011 U.S. Dist. LEXIS 96913, at *6 n.4 (S.D. Ala. Aug. 10, 2011); Ariatti-Mangum v. Korb, No. 1:11-CV-149, 2011 U.S. Dist. LEXIS 58834, at *2-3 (D. Idaho June 1, 2011); Brooks v. AAA Cooper Transp., 781 F. Supp. 2d 472, 487-88 (S.D. Tex. 2011); Nouri v. TCF Bank, No. 10-12436, 2011 WL 836764, at *4 (E.D. Mich. Mar. 9, 2011); DeConcini Family Trust v. Home Fed. Bank, No. 2:10-CV-258, 2011 WL 635257, at *1 (D. Utah Feb. 11, 2011); Wilkerson v. H & S Lee, Inc., No. CV609-033, 2010 WL 2942635, at *2 (S.D. Ga. June 22, 2010), aff'd per curiam, 438 F. App'x 769 (11th Cir. 2011); Surgick v. Cirella, No. 09-cv-3807, 2010 WL 2539418, at *5 (D.N.J. June 15, 2010); Fox v. Cal. Franchise Tax Bd., No. 08-cv-01047, 2010 WL 56094, at *6 (D. Colo. Jan. 5, 2010); Tyree v. Hope Village, Inc., 677 F. Supp. 2d 109, 110 (D.D.C. 2009); Johnson v. Homeownership Pres. Found., No. 09-600, 2009 WL 6067018, at *8-9 (D. Minn. Dec. 18, 2009); Lucido v. Mueller, No. 08-15269, 2009 WL 3190368, at *5-6 (E.D. Mich. Sept. 29, 2009); Lengerich v. Columbia Coll., 633 F. Supp. 2d 599, 607-08 (N.D. Ill. 2009); Shi v. Cent. Ariz. Coll., No. 08-80131, 2008 WL 4001795, at *1 (N.D. Cal. Aug. 27, 2008); Wilson v. Benedict Coll., No. 3:05-3614, 2006 WL 2433794, at *4-5 (D.S.C. Aug. 21, 2006); McCullough v. BOP, No. 05CV374, 2006 WL 667166, at *1 (D.D.C. Mar. 15, 2006); Piper v. R.J. Corman R.R. Group, No. 05-CV-104, 2005 WL 1523566, at *8 (E.D. Ky. June 28, 2005); Locke v. MedLab/Gen. Chem., No. 99-2137, 2000 WL 127111 (E.D. Pa. Feb. 3, 2000); Payne v. EEOC, No. 99-270, slip op. at 2-3 (D.N.M. July 7, 1999), aff'd, No. 00-2021, 2000 WL 1862659, at *2 (10th Cir. Dec. 20, 2000); Davis v. Boston Edison Co., No. 83-1114-2, 1985 U.S. Dist. LEXIS 23275 (D. Mass. Jan. 21, 1985); Friedlander v. USPS, No. 84-773, slip op. at 5-6 (D.D.C. Oct. 16, 1984); Marshall v. Park Place Hosp., 3 Gov't Disclosure Serv. (P-H) ¶ 83,088, at 83,057 (D.D.C. Feb. 25, 1983); see also Bybee v. Pirtle, No. 96-5077, 1996 WL 596458, at *1 (6th Cir. Oct. 16, 1996)

OVERVIEW OF THE PRIVACY ACT

(appellant did not state claim under Privacy Act because it does not apply to individuals who refused to hire him due to his failure to furnish his social security number or fill out W-4 forms for income tax purposes); Steadman v. Rocky Mountain News, No. 95-1102, 1995 U.S. App. LEXIS 34986, at *4 (10th Cir. Dec. 11, 1995) (Privacy Act claims "cannot be brought against defendant because defendant is not a governmental entity"); United States v. Mercado, No. 94-3976, 1995 U.S. App. LEXIS 2054, at *3-4 (6th Cir. Jan. 31, 1995) (appellant's retained defense counsel is not an "agency"). Additionally, neither federal funding nor regulation renders such private entities subject to the Act. See Burch v. Pioneer Credit Recovery, Inc., 551 F.3d 122, 125 (2d Cir. 2008); Unt v. Aerospace Corp., 765 F.2d 1440, 1448 (9th Cir. 1985); Huertas v. U.S. Dep't of Educ., No. 08-3959, 2009 WL 3165442, at *5 (D.N.J. Sept. 28, 2009); United States v. Haynes, 620 F. Supp. 474, 478-79 (M.D. Tenn. 1985); Dennie v. Univ. of Pittsburgh Sch. of Med., 589 F. Supp. 348, 351-52 (D.V.I. 1984), aff'd, 770 F.2d 1068 (3d Cir. 1985) (unpublished table decision); see also United States v. Miller, 643 F.2d 713, 715 n.1 (10th Cir. 1981) (finding that definition of "agency" does not encompass national banks); Boggs v. Se. Tidewater Opportunity Project, No. 2:96cv196, 1996 U.S. Dist. LEXIS 6977, at *5-9 (E.D. Va. May 22, 1996) (rejecting plaintiff's argument concerning entity's acceptance of federal funds and stating that "[i]t is well settled that the Administrative Procedures [sic] Act, 5 U.S.C. § 551 . . . applies only to Federal agencies").

An exception to this rule, however, is the social security number usage restrictions, contained in section 7 of the Privacy Act, which do apply to federal, state, and local government agencies. (Section 7, part of Pub. L. No. 93-579, can be found at 5 U.S.C. § 552a note (Disclosure of Social Security Number).) This special provision is discussed below under "Social Security Number Usage."

A civil action under the Privacy Act is properly filed against an "agency" only, not against an individual, a government official, an employee, or the United States. See, e.g., Kates v. King, No. 12-1835, 2012 WL 2583374, at *2 (3d Cir. July 5, 2012) (per curiam); Flores v. Fox, 394 F. App'x 170, 172 (5th Cir. 2010) (per curiam); Jones v. Luis, 372 F. App'x 967, 969 (11th Cir. 2010) (per curiam); Weinberger v. Grimes, No. 07-6461, 2009 WL 331632, at *8 (6th Cir. Feb. 10, 2009); Alexander v. Washington Gas Light Co., No. 06-7040, 2006 WL 3798858, at *1 (D.C. Cir. Aug. 24, 2006); Martinez v. BOP, 444 F.3d 620, 624 (D.C. Cir. 2006); Pennyfeather v. Tessler, 431 F.3d 54, 55 (2d Cir. 2005); Connelly v. Comptroller of the Currency, 876 F.2d 1209, 1215 (5th Cir. 1989); Petrus v. Bowen, 833 F.2d 581, 582-83 (5th Cir. 1987); Schowengerdt v. Gen. Dynamics Corp., 823 F.2d 1328, 1340 (9th Cir. 1987); Hewitt v. Grabicki, 794 F.2d 1373, 1377 & n.2 (9th Cir. 1986); Unt, 765 F.2d at 1447; Brown-Bey v. United States, 720 F.2d 467, 469 (7th

OVERVIEW OF THE PRIVACY ACT

Cir. 1983); Windsor v. The Tennessean, 719 F.2d 155, 159-60 (6th Cir. 1983); Bruce v. United States, 621 F.2d 914, 916 n.2 (8th Cir. 1980); Parks v. IRS, 618 F.2d 677, 684 (10th Cir. 1980); Lange v. Taylor, 5:10-CT-3097, 2012 WL 255333, at *3 (E.D.N.C. Jan. 27, 2012); Earle v. Holder, 815 F. Supp. 2d 176, 180 (D.D.C. 2011), aff'd per curiam, No. 11-5280, 2012 WL 1450574 (D.C. Cir. Apr. 20, 2012); Dillingham v. Schofield, No. 2:11-CV-07, 2011 WL 3664470, at *9 (E.D. Tenn. Aug. 19, 2011); Lim v. United States, No. 10-2574, 2011 WL 2650889, at *8 (D. Md. July 5, 2011); Bradley v. Mason, No. 1:11 CV 17, 2011 WL 2470297, at *4 (N.D. Ohio June 20, 2011); Brown v. Prince George's Hosp., No. 09cv295, 2011 WL 2413344, at *4 (D. Md. June 9, 2011); Chandler v. James, 783 F. Supp. 2d 33, 41 (D.D.C. 2011); Blanton v. Warden, No. 7:10-cv-00552, 2011 WL 1226010, at *3 (W.D. Va. Mar. 30, 2011); Bailey v. Fulwood, 780 F. Supp. 2d 20, 27 (D.D.C. 2011); Hackett v. New Jersey, No. 10-2547, 2010 WL 4553526, at *2 (D.N.J. Nov. 3, 2010); Off v. U.S. Gov'ts, No. 2:09-CV-01525, 2010 WL 3862097, at *3 (D. Nev. Sept. 27, 2010), aff'd on other grounds sub nom. Off v. United States, No. 10-17389, 2012 WL 1436712 (9th Cir. Apr. 26, 2012); James v. Tejera, No. 5:10-cv-048, 2010 WL 3324833, at *1 (M.D. Fla. Aug. 23, 2010); Goodwin v. Johnson, No. 8:10CV40, 2010 WL 1500872, at *3 (D. Neb. Apr. 14, 2010); Hollins v. Cross, No. 1:09cv75, 2010 WL 1439430, at *3 (N.D. W. Va. Mar. 17, 2010); Hill v. United States, No. 5:09CV19, 2010 WL 391627, at *3 (N.D. W. Va. Jan. 26, 2010); Truesdale v. DOJ, 657 F. Supp. 2d 219, 227 (D.D.C. 2009); Jackson v. BOP, 657 F. Supp. 2d 176, 178-79 (D.D.C. 2009); Goodwin v. Omaha Hous. Auth., No. 8:09CV205, 2009 WL 2581549, at *3 (D. Neb. Aug. 17, 2009); Capobianco v. Geithner, No. 09-1656, 2009 WL 2370443, at *1 n.3 (E.D. Pa. July 28, 2009); Walker v. Gambrell, 647 F. Supp. 2d 529, 536 (D. Md. 2009); Flanory v. Bonn, No. 2:08-cv-108, 2009 WL 33472, at *2 (W.D. Mich. Jan. 5, 2009); Jennings v. BOP, No. 081475, 2008 WL 3983115, at *1 (D.D.C. Aug. 26, 2008); Arsendorf v. Everson, No. 07-2703, 2008 WL 2229745, at *4 (S.D. Tex. May 27, 2008); Rainge-El v. Brill, No. 05-01831, 2008 WL 511760, at *9 (D. Colo. Feb. 22, 2008); Lewis v. Frazier, No. 07-0961, 2007 WL 2894255, at *1 (E.D. Cal. Oct. 3, 2007); Banks v. Partyka, No. 07-0331, 2007 WL 2693180, at *3 (W.D. Okla. Sept. 11, 2007); Joseph v. Cole, No. 5:07-CV-225, 2007 WL 2480171, at *1 (M.D. Ga. Aug. 27, 2007); Al-Beshrawi v. Arney, No. 5:06CV2114, 2007 WL 1245845, at *4 (N.D. Ohio Apr. 27, 2007); Kemp v. Grippen, 06-C-0076, 2007 WL 870123, at *6 (E.D. Wis. Mar. 20, 2007); Cummings v. Malone, No. 06-5442, 2006 WL 3694592, at *3 (D.N.J. Dec. 12, 2006); Thomas v. Ashcroft, No. 3:CV-05-0090, 2006 WL 860136, at *4 (M.D. Pa. Mar. 30, 2006); Corey v. McNamara, 409 F. Supp. 2d 1225, 1229 (D. Nev. 2006), aff'd, 265 F. App'x 555 (9th Cir. 2008); Afshar v. Everitt, No. 04-1104, 2005 WL 2898019, at *3 (W.D. Mo. Oct. 31, 2005); Swartz v. IRS, No. 05-72215, 2005 WL 3278026, at *4 (E.D. Mich. Oct. 26, 2005); Fetzer

OVERVIEW OF THE PRIVACY ACT

v. Cambria County Human Servs., 384 F. Supp. 2d 813, 816 (W.D. Pa. 2005); Benham v. Rice, No. 0301127, 2005 WL 691871, at *4 (D.D.C. Mar. 24, 2005); House v. Gutierrez, No. Civ.A. 04-1796, 2005 WL 405449, at *1 (D.D.C. Feb. 18, 2005); Burns v. Potter, 334 F. Supp. 2d 13, 20-21 (D. Mass. 2004); Buckles v. Indian Health Serv., 268 F. Supp. 2d 1101, 1102 (D.N.D. 2003); Stokes v. Barnhart, 257 F. Supp. 2d 288, 299 (D. Me. 2003); Mandel v. OPM, 244 F. Supp. 2d 146, 153 (E.D.N.Y. 2003), aff'd on other grounds, 79 F. App'x 479 (2d Cir. 2003); Mumme v. U.S. Dep't of Labor, 150 F. Supp. 2d 162, 169 (D. Me. 2001), aff'd, No. 01-2256 (1st Cir. June 12, 2002); Payne v. EEOC, No. 99-270, slip op. at 2 (D.N.M. July 7, 1999), aff'd, No. 00-2021, 2000 WL 1862659, at *2 (10th Cir. Dec. 20, 2000); Armstrong v. BOP, 976 F. Supp. 17, 23 (D.D.C. 1997), summary affirmance granted, No. 97-5208, 1998 WL 65543 (D.C. Cir. Jan. 30, 1998); Claasen v. Brown, No. 94-1018, 1996 WL 79490, at *3-4 (D.D.C. Feb. 16, 1996); Lloyd v. Coady, No. 94-5842, 1995 U.S. Dist. LEXIS 2490, at *3-4 (E.D. Pa. Feb. 28, 1995), upon consideration of amended complaint, 1995 U.S. Dist. LEXIS 6258, at *3 n.2 (E.D. Pa. May 9, 1995); Hill v. Blevins, No. 3-CV-92-0859, slip op. at 4-5 (M.D. Pa. Apr. 12, 1993), aff'd, 19 F.3d 643 (3d Cir. 1994) (unpublished table decision); Malewicht, No. 91-4871, slip op. at 19; Sheptin v. DOJ, No. 91-2806, 1992 U.S. Dist. LEXIS 6221, at *5-6 (D.D.C. Apr. 30, 1992); Williams v. McCausland, 791 F. Supp. 992, 1000 (S.D.N.Y. 1992); Mittleman v. U.S. Treasury, 773 F. Supp. 442, 450 (D.D.C. 1991); Stephens v. TVA, 754 F. Supp. 579, 580 n.1 (E.D. Tenn. 1990); B.J.R.L. v. Utah, 655 F. Supp. 692, 696-97 (D. Utah 1987); Dennie, 589 F. Supp. at 351-53; Gonzalez v. Leonard, 497 F. Supp. 1058, 1075-76 (D. Conn. 1980). See also Bavido v. Apfel, 215 F.3d 743, 747 (7th Cir. 2000) (finding that Social Security Administration Commissioner was not proper party defendant, but that SSA had waived any objection as to naming of proper party agency defendant); Gordon v. Gutierrez, No. 1:06cv861, 2006 WL 3760134, at *3 (E.D. Va. Dec. 14, 2006) ("[C]ourts have consistently declined to imply a Bivens-style right of action against individual officers for conduct that would be actionable under the Privacy Act."); cf. Stewart v. FBI, No. 97-1595, 1999 U.S. Dist. LEXIS 21335, at *15-22 (D. Or. Dec. 10, 1999) (magistrate's recommendation) (actions of two Air Force officers assigned to other agencies were not attributable to Air Force; neither were their actions attributable to State Department, because although they both physically worked at embassy and ambassador had supervisory responsibility over all executive branch agency employees, neither reported to State Department or ambassador), adopted, 2000 U.S. Dist. LEXIS 2954 (D. Or. Mar. 15, 2000). One court also noted, though, that while of course a Privacy Act action "must be maintained against an agency," it is "unaware of any authority which requires the Plaintiffs to specifically name, either as an individual defendant or within the body of a complaint, each and every agency employee who may have contributed to an

OVERVIEW OF THE PRIVACY ACT

alleged Privacy Act violation." Buckles v. Indian Health Serv., 305 F. Supp. 2d 1108, 1112 (D.N.D. 2004).

The District Court for the District of Columbia has explained that "[i]n order for an agency to be liable for a Privacy Act violation allegedly committed by one of its employees, the responsible agency employee must have been acting within the scope of his or her employment." Convertino v. DOJ, 769 F. Supp. 2d 139, 147 (D.D.C. 2011) ("Therefore, even if [plaintiff] could prove that the leak must have come from a DOJ employee – which he cannot – his claim would fail because no reasonable fact-finder could conclude that any such DOJ employee was acting within the scope of his or her employment at the time of the leak."), rev'd and remanded on other grounds, No. 11-5133, 2012 WL 2362591 (D.C. Cir. June 22, 2012) (reversing district court's summary judgment and ruling that district court committed abuse of discretion in denying appellant's motion to stay summary judgment to allow for further discovery).

Some courts have held that the head of an agency, if sued in his or her official capacity, can be a proper party defendant under the Privacy Act. See Hampton, No. 93-0816, slip op. at 8, 10-11 (D.D.C. June 30, 1995); Jarrell v. Tisch, 656 F. Supp. 237, 238 (D.D.C. 1987); Diamond v. FBI, 532 F. Supp. 216, 219-20 (S.D.N.Y. 1981), aff'd, 707 F.2d 75 (2d Cir. 1983); Nemetz v. Dep't of the Treasury, 446 F. Supp. 102, 106 (N.D. Ill. 1978); Rowe v. Tennessee, 431 F. Supp. 1257, 1264 (M.D. Tenn. 1977), vacated on other grounds, 609 F.2d 259 (6th Cir. 1979); see also Walker v. Gambrell, 647 F. Supp. 2d at 536 (construing pro se plaintiff's suit against Treasury secretary "as a suit against the Department of the Treasury" partly because "pleadings of pro se plaintiffs are to be construed liberally"); cf. Cloonan, 768 F. Supp. 2d at 162 ("find[ing] that plaintiff's error in naming only individual defendants was harmless" because "[o]n its face, the Complaint makes clear that in naming former attorney general Michael Mukasey, plaintiff was naming the Department of Justice as a defendant" and because complaint named Attorney General only in his official capacity). Further, leave to amend a complaint to substitute a proper party defendant ordinarily is freely granted where the agency is on notice of the claim. See, e.g., Reyes v. Supervisor of DEA, 834 F.2d 1093, 1097 (1st Cir. 1987); Petrus v. Bowen, 833 F.2d at 583. But cf. Doe v. Rubin, No. 95-CV-75874, 1998 U.S. Dist. LEXIS 14755, at *9 (E.D. Mich. Aug. 10, 1998) (granting summary judgment for defendant where plaintiff had named Secretary of the Treasury as sole defendant and had filed no motion to amend).

Note that a prosecution enforcing the Privacy Act's criminal penalties provision, 5 U.S.C. § 552a(i) (see "Criminal Penalties" discussion, below), would of course properly be filed against an individual. See Stone v. Def.

OVERVIEW OF THE PRIVACY ACT

Investigative Serv., 816 F. Supp. 782, 785 (D.D.C. 1993) ("Under the Privacy Act, this Court has jurisdiction over individually named defendants only for unauthorized disclosure in violation of 5 U.S.C. § 552a(i)."); see also Hampton v. FBI, No. 93-0816, slip op. at 8, 10-11 (D.D.C. June 30, 1995) (citing Stone).

B. Individual

"a citizen of the United States or an alien lawfully admitted for permanent residence." 5 U.S.C. § 552a(a)(2).

Comment:

Compare this definition with the FOIA's much broader "any person" definition (5 U.S.C. § 552(a)(3) (2006)). See, e.g., Fares v. INS, No. 94-1339, 1995 WL 115809, at *4 (4th Cir. 1995) (per curiam) ("[Privacy] Act only protects citizens of the United States or aliens lawfully admitted for permanent residence."); Raven v. Panama Canal Co., 583 F.2d 169, 170-71 (5th Cir. 1978) (same as Fares, and comparing "use of the word 'individual' in the Privacy Act, as opposed to the word 'person,' as more broadly used in the FOIA"); Rojas-Vega v. Cejka, No. 09CV2489, 2010 WL 1541369, at *3 (S.D. Cal. Apr. 15, 2010) (dismissing access claim brought by plaintiff whose "lawful U.S. resident alien status was revoked" because plaintiff "cannot state a claim for a benefit that he is clearly not entitled to under the Privacy Act"; "Congress purposely limited the Privacy Act in this manner, in contrast to FOIA."); Cudzich v. INS, 886 F. Supp. 101, 105 (D.D.C. 1995) (A plaintiff whose permanent resident status had been revoked "is not an 'individual' for the purposes of the Privacy Act. . . . Plaintiff's only potential access to the requested information is therefore under the Freedom of Information Act.").

Deceased individuals do not have any Privacy Act rights, nor do executors or next-of-kin. See OMB Guidelines, 40 Fed. Reg. 28,948, 28,951 (July 9, 1975), available at http://www.whitehouse.gov/sites/default/files/omb/assets/omb/inforeg/implementation_guidelines.pdf; see also Monk v. Teeter, No. 89-16333, 1992 WL 1681, at *2 (9th Cir. Jan. 8. 1992); Crumpton v. United States, 843 F. Supp. 751, 756 (D.D.C. 1994), aff'd on other grounds sub nom. Crumpton v. Stone, 59 F.3d 1400 (D.C. Cir. 1995); cf. Flores v. Fox, 394 F. App'x 170, 171-72 (5th Cir. 2010) (per curiam) ("[Plaintiff's] claim for injunctive relief to correct his prison records . . . is mooted by his death.").

Corporations and organizations also do not have any Privacy Act rights. See St. Michaels Convalescent Hosp. v. California, 643 F.2d 1369, 1373 (9th

OVERVIEW OF THE PRIVACY ACT

Cir. 1981); OKC v. Williams, 614 F.2d 58, 60 (5th Cir. 1980); Dresser Indus. v. United States, 596 F.2d 1231, 1237-38 (5th Cir. 1980); Cell Assocs. v. NIH, 579 F.2d 1155, 1157 (9th Cir. 1978); Stone v. Exp.-Imp. Bank of the United States, 552 F.2d 132, 137 n.7 (5th Cir. 1977); Falwell v. Executive Office of the President, 158 F. Supp. 2d 734, 736, 739 n.3 (W.D. Va. 2001); Comm. in Solidarity v. Sessions, 738 F. Supp. 544, 547 (D.D.C. 1990), aff'd on other grounds, 929 F.2d 742 (D.C. Cir. 1991); United States v. Haynes, 620 F. Supp. 474, 478-79 (M.D. Tenn. 1985); Utah-Ohio Gas & Oil, Inc. v. SEC, 1 Gov't Disclosure Serv. (P-H) ¶ 80,038, at 80,114 (D. Utah Jan. 9, 1980); see also OMB Guidelines, 40 Fed. Reg. at 28,951, available at http://www.whitehouse.gov/sites/default/files/omb/assets/ omb/inforeg/implementation_guidelines.pdf. But cf. Recticel Foam Corp. v. DOJ, No. 98-2523, slip op. at 11-15 (D.D.C. Jan. 31, 2002) (issuing novel ruling that corporation had standing to bring action under Administrative Procedure Act to enjoin agency from disclosing investigative information about company; "[T]he fact that Congress did not create a cause of action for corporations under the Privacy Act does not necessarily mean that Recticel's interests do not fall within the 'zone of interests' contemplated by that Act. It is sufficient for a standing analysis that Plaintiffs' interests 'arguably' fall within the zone of interests contemplated by the statute."), appeal dismissed, No. 02-5118 (D.C. Cir. Apr. 25, 2002).

The OMB Guidelines suggest that an individual has no standing under the Privacy Act to challenge agency handling of records that pertain to him solely in his "entrepreneurial" capacity. OMB Guidelines, 40 Fed. Reg. at 28,951, available at http://www.whitehouse.gov/sites/default/files/ omb/assets/omb/inforeg/implementation_guidelines.pdf (quoting legislative history and stating that it "suggests that a distinction can be made between individuals acting in a personal capacity and individuals acting in an entrepreneurial capacity (e.g., as sole proprietors) and that th[e] definition [of 'individual'] (and, therefore, the Act) was intended to embrace only the former"). However, there is a split of authority concerning OMB's personal/entrepreneurial distinction as applied to an individual. Compare Shermco Indus. v. Sec'y of the U.S. Air Force, 452 F. Supp. 306, 314-15 (N.D. Tex. 1978) (accepting distinction), rev'd & remanded on other grounds, 613 F.2d 1314 (5th Cir. 1980), and Daniels v. FCC, No. 77-5011, slip op. at 8-9 (D.S.D. Mar. 15, 1978) (same), with Rice v. United States, 245 F.R.D. 3, 5-6 (D.D.C. 2007) (rejecting distinction without referencing OMB Guidelines and observing that "the line between personal and business information is blurred for farmers, ranchers, and other family-owned businesses"); Scarborough v. Harvey, 493 F. Supp. 2d 1, 15 n.28 (D.D.C. 2007) (rejecting distinction); Henke v. Dep't of Commerce, No. 94-189, 1995 WL 904918, at *2 (D.D.C. May 26, 1995) (same), vacated & remanded on other grounds, 83 F.3d 1453 (D.C. Cir. 1996); Henke v. U.S. Dep't of

OVERVIEW OF THE PRIVACY ACT

Commerce, No. 94-0189, 1996 WL 692020, at *2-3 (D.D.C. Aug. 19, 1994) (same), aff'd on other grounds, 83 F.3d 1445 (D.C. Cir. 1996); Metadure Corp. v. United States, 490 F. Supp. 1368, 1373-74 (S.D.N.Y. 1980) (same); Fla. Med. Ass'n v. HEW, 479 F. Supp. 1291, 1307-11 (M.D. Fla. 1979) (same); and Zeller v. United States, 467 F. Supp. 487, 496-99 (E.D.N.Y. 1979) (same). Cf. St. Michaels Convalescent Hosp., 643 F.2d at 1373 (stating that "sole proprietorships[] are not 'individuals' and thus lack standing to raise a claim under the Privacy Act").

Privacy Act rights are personal to the individual who is the subject of the record and cannot be asserted derivatively by others. See, e.g., Parks v. IRS, 618 F.2d 677, 684-85 (10th Cir. 1980) (union lacks standing to sue for damages to its members); Word v. United States, 604 F.2d 1127, 1129 (8th Cir. 1979) (criminal defendant lacks standing to allege Privacy Act violations regarding use at trial of medical records concerning third party); Dresser Indus., 596 F.2d at 1238 (company lacks standing to litigate employees' Privacy Act claims); Raley v. Astrue, No. 2:11cv555, 2012 WL 2368609, at *8 (M.D. Ala. June 21, 2012) ("Plaintiff brings a claim on behalf of the individuals whose information she received and Plaintiff lacks standing to do so."); Lorenzo v. United States, 719 F. Supp. 2d 1208, 1215-16 (S.D. Cal. 2010) (plaintiff lacks standing to pursue claim for recovery for adverse effects she suffered based on disclosure of her husband's record); Research Air, Inc. v. Kempthorne, 589 F. Supp. 2d 1, 11 (D.D.C. 2008) (individual's attorney has no Privacy Act rights to request documents relating to client absent the client's consent); Sirmans v. Caldera, 27 F. Supp. 2d 248, 250 (D.D.C. 1998) (plaintiffs "may not object to the Army's failure to correct the records of other officers"); Shulman v. Sec'y of HHS, No. 94 CIV. 5506, 1997 WL 68554, at *1, 3 (S.D.N.Y. Feb. 19, 1997) (plaintiff had no standing to assert any right that might have belonged to former spouse), aff'd, No. 96-6140 (2d Cir. Sept. 3, 1997); Harbolt v. DOJ, No. A-84-CA-280, slip op. at 2 (W.D. Tex. Apr. 29, 1985) (prisoner lacks standing to assert Privacy Act claims of other inmates regarding disclosure of their records to him); Abramsky v. U.S. Consumer Prod. Safety Comm'n, 478 F. Supp. 1040, 1041-42 (S.D.N.Y. 1979) (union president cannot compel release of records pertaining to employee's termination); Attorney Gen. of the United States v. Irish N. Aid Comm., No. 77-700, 1977 U.S. Dist. LEXIS 13581, at *12 (S.D.N.Y. Oct. 7, 1977) (committee lacks standing to sue in representative capacity). But see Nat'l Fed'n of Fed. Employees v. Greenberg, 789 F. Supp. 430, 433 (D.D.C. 1992) (union has associational standing because members whose interests union seeks to represent would themselves have standing), vacated & remanded on other grounds, 983 F.2d 286 (D.C. Cir. 1993).

Note, however, that the parent of any minor, or the legal guardian of an

OVERVIEW OF THE PRIVACY ACT

incompetent, may act on behalf of that individual. See 5 U.S.C. § 552a(h); see also Gula v. Meese, 699 F. Supp. 956, 961 (D.D.C. 1988); cf. Maldonado Guzman v. Massanari, No. 00-2410, slip op. at 6-7 (D.P.R. Aug. 10, 2001) (holding that plaintiff had no avenue of relief in obtaining information about his emancipated daughter under Privacy Act because he did not provide documentation required by agency regulations to verify any relationship as her legal guardian), subsequent related opinion sub nom. Maldonado Guzman v. SSA, 182 F. Supp. 2d 216 (D.P.R. 2002). The OMB Guidelines note that subsection (h) is "discretionary and that individuals who are minors are authorized to exercise the rights given to them by the Privacy Act or, in the alternative, their parents or those acting in loco parentis may exercise them in their behalf." OMB Guidelines, 40 Fed. Reg. at 28,970, available at http://www.whitehouse.gov/sites/default/files/omb/assets/omb/inforeg/implementation_guidelines.pdf; see also OMB Guidelines, 40 Fed. Reg. 56,741, 56,742 (Nov. 21, 1975), available at http://www.whitehouse.gov/sites/default/files/omb/assets/omb/inforeg/implementation1974.pdf (noting that "[t]here is no absolute right of a parent to have access to a record about a child absent a court order or consent").

C. Maintain

"maintain, collect, use or disseminate." 5 U.S.C. § 552a(a)(3).

Comment:

This definition embraces various activities with respect to records and has a meaning much broader than the common usage of the term. See OMB Guidelines, 40 Fed. Reg. 28,948, 28,951 (July 9, 1975), available at http://www.whitehouse.gov/sites/default/files/omb/assets/omb/inforeg/implementation_guidelines.pdf; see also, e.g., Albright v. United States, 631 F.2d 915, 918-20 (D.C. Cir. 1980) (analyzing scope of term "maintain" in context of subsection (e)(7) challenge to record describing First Amendment-protected activity and stating that "the Act clearly prohibits even the mere collection of such a record, independent of the agency's maintenance, use or dissemination of it thereafter").

D. Record

"any item, collection, or grouping of information about an individual that is maintained by an agency, including, but not limited to, his education, financial transactions, medical history, and criminal or employment history and that contains his name, or the identifying number, symbol, or other identifying particular assigned to the individual, such as a finger or voice print or a photograph." 5 U.S.C. § 552a(a)(4).

OVERVIEW OF THE PRIVACY ACT

Comment:

To qualify as a Privacy Act "record," the information must identify an individual. Compare Reuber v. United States, 829 F.2d 133, 142 (D.C. Cir. 1987) (letter reprimanding individual sent to and disclosed by agency was "record" because it clearly identified individual by name and address), with Robinson v. U.S. Dep't of Educ., No. 87-2554, 1988 WL 5083, at *1 (E.D. Pa. Jan. 20, 1988) (letter describing individual's administrative complaint was not "record" because it did not mention his name). See also Albright v. United States, 631 F.2d 915, at 920 (D.C. Cir. 1980) (subsection (e)(7) case holding that a videotape of a meeting constituted a "record" and stating that "[a]s long as the tape contains a means of identifying an individual by picture or voice, it falls within the definition of a 'record' under the Privacy Act"); Fleming v. U.S. R.R. Ret. Bd., No. 01 C 6289, 2002 WL 252459, at *2 (N.D. Ill. Feb. 21, 2002) (citing Robinson and holding that a summary of an investigation of plaintiff that was disclosed in a semi-annual report to Congress did not identify plaintiff and thus did not constitute a "record" because disclosure "would have identified plaintiff only to an individual who had other information that would have caused that individual to infer from the report that plaintiff was the subject of the investigation"); cf. Speaker v. HHS Ctrs. for Disease Control & Prevention, 623 F.3d 1371, 1383-87 (11th Cir. 2010) (where complaint sufficiently alleged that agency itself made disclosure of plaintiff's identity, stating that, "we do not need to reach, for Rule 12(b)(6) purposes, the legal issues of whether the CDC disclosed enough, or the requisite type of, identifying particulars to constitute a Privacy Act violation, which in turn caused the press to identify him"); Cacho v. Chertoff, No. 06-00292, 2006 WL 3422548, *6 n.3 (D.D.C. Nov. 28, 2006) (declining to decide "the novel issue of whether a disclosure of the absence of information from a system of records can constitute the disclosure of a record"; however, given that plaintiff deliberately did not report his health problems, "accepting plaintiff's characterization of his failure to report them as itself constituting a record that is afforded protection by the Privacy Act would stretch the meaning of the statute beyond its intended purpose").

The OMB Guidelines state that the term "record" means "any item of information about an individual that includes an individual identifier," OMB Guidelines, 40 Fed. Reg. 28,948, 28,951 (July 9, 1975), available at http://www.whitehouse.gov/sites/default/files/omb/assets/omb/inforeg/implementation_guidelines.pdf (emphasis added), and "'can include as little as one descriptive item about an individual,'" id. at 28,952 (quoting legislative history appearing at 120 Cong. Rec. 40,408, 40,883 (1974), reprinted in Source Book at 866, 993, available at http://www.loc.gov/rr/frd/Military_Law/pdf/LH_privacy_act-1974.pdf.

OVERVIEW OF THE PRIVACY ACT

Several courts of appeals have articulated tests for determining whether an item qualifies as a "record" under the Privacy Act, resulting in different tests for determining "record" status:

(1) Consistent with the OMB Guidelines, the Courts of Appeals for the Second and Third Circuits have broadly interpreted the term "record." See Bechhoefer v. DEA, 209 F.3d 57 (2d Cir. 2000); Quinn v. Stone, 978 F.2d 126 (3d Cir. 1992). The Third Circuit held that the term "record" "encompass[es] any information about an individual that is linked to that individual through an identifying particular" and is not "limited to information which taken alone directly reflects a characteristic or quality." Quinn v. Stone, 978 F.2d at 133 (out-of-date home address on roster and time card information held to be records covered by Privacy Act). The Second Circuit, after analyzing the tests established by the other courts of appeals, adopted a test "much like the Third Circuit's test." Bechhoefer, 209 F.3d at 60. The Second Circuit did so for three reasons: First, it found the Third Circuit's test to be "most consistent with the 'broad terms' . . . of the statutory definition," id.; second, it found the Third Circuit's test to be the only one consistent with the Supreme Court's decision in DOD v. FLRA, 510 U.S. 487, 494 (1994), which held that federal civil service employees' home addresses qualified for protection under the Privacy Act, Bechhoefer, 209 F.3d at 61; and, finally, it found the Third Circuit's test to be supported by the legislative history of the Privacy Act and by the guidelines issued by OMB, id. at 61-62. Emphasizing that "the legislative history makes plain that Congress intended 'personal information' . . . to have a broad meaning," the Second Circuit held that the term "record" "has 'a broad meaning encompassing,' at the very least, any personal information 'about an individual that is linked to that individual through an identifying particular.'" Id. at 62 (quoting Quinn and holding that letter containing Bechhoefer's name and "several pieces of 'personal information' about him, including his address, his voice/fax telephone number, his employment, and his membership in [an association]," was record covered by Privacy Act).

Other courts have also applied a broad interpretation of the term "record." See, e.g., Williams v. VA, 104 F.3d 670, 673-74 (4th Cir. 1997) (citing Quinn, inter alia, and stating that "[w]hether the Tobey court's distinction [(discussed below)] be accepted, the legislative history of the Act makes it clear that a 'record' was meant to 'include as little as one descriptive item about an

[19]

OVERVIEW OF THE PRIVACY ACT

individual,'" and finding that "draft" materials qualified as "records" because they "substantially pertain to Appellant," "contain 'information about' [him], as well as his 'name' or 'identifying number,'" and "do more than merely apply to him" (quoting legislative history, Source Book at 866)); Unt v. Aerospace Corp., 765 F.2d 1440, 1449-50 (9th Cir. 1985) (Ferguson, J., dissenting) (opining that majority's narrow interpretation of term "record" (discussed below) "is illogical, contrary to the legislative intent, and defies the case laws' consistent concern with the actual effect of a record on a person's employment when assessing that record's nature or subject"); Sullivan v. USPS, 944 F. Supp. 191, 196 (W.D.N.Y. 1996) (finding that disclosure to job applicant's employer of fact that applicant had applied for employment with Postal Service constituted disclosure of "record" under Privacy Act; although no other information was disclosed from application, rejecting Postal Service's attempt to distinguish between disclosing fact of record's existence and disclosing information contained in record, as applicant's name was part of information contained in application and Postal Service disclosed that particular applicant by that name had applied for employment).

(2)   The Courts of Appeals for the Ninth and Eleventh Circuits have limited Privacy Act coverage by adopting a narrow construction of the term "record" -- requiring that in order to qualify, the information "must reflect some quality or characteristic of the individual involved." Boyd v. Sec'y of the Navy, 709 F.2d 684, 686 (11th Cir. 1983) (per curiam) (although stating narrow test, finding that memorandum reflecting "Boyd's failure to follow the chain of command and his relationship with management" qualified as Privacy Act record); accord Unt v. Aerospace Corp., 765 F.2d 1440, 1448-49 (9th Cir. 1985) (letter written by employee – containing allegations of mismanagement against corporation that led to his dismissal – held not his "record" because it was "about" corporation and reflected "only indirectly on any quality or characteristic" of employee).

(3)   The Courts of Appeals for the District of Columbia and Fifth Circuits have taken another approach to interpreting the term "record." See Pierce v. Dep't of Air Force, 512 F.3d 184, 188 (5th Cir. 2007); Tobey v. NLRB, 40 F.3d 469, 471 (D.C. Cir. 1994). The D.C. Circuit held that in order to qualify as a "record," the information "must both be 'about' an individual and include his name or other identifying particular." Tobey, 40 F.3d at 471.

OVERVIEW OF THE PRIVACY ACT

Examining the Third Circuit's statement in Quinn that information could qualify as a record "'if that piece of information were linked with an identifying particular (or was itself an identifying particular),'" the D.C. Circuit rejected the Third Circuit's interpretation "[t]o the extent that . . . [it] fails to require that information both be 'about' an individual and be linked to that individual by an identifying particular." Id. On the other hand, the D.C. Circuit rejected "as too narrow the Ninth and Eleventh Circuits' definitions" in Unt and Boyd, and stated that: "So long as the information is 'about' an individual, nothing in the Act requires that it additionally be about a 'quality or characteristic' of the individual." Tobey, 40 F.3d at 472. Ultimately, the D.C. Circuit, "[w]ithout attempting to define 'record' more specifically than [necessary] to resolve the case at bar," held that an NLRB computer system for tracking and monitoring cases did not constitute a system of records, because its files contained no information "about" individuals, despite the fact that the case information contained the initials or identifying number of the field examiner assigned to the case. Id. at 471-73. Although the court recognized that the case information could be, and apparently was, used in connection with other information to draw inferences about a field examiner's job performance, it stated that that "does not transform the [computer system] files into records about field examiners." Id. at 472-73. For other D.C. Circuit and D.C. District Court cases, see for example Sussman v. U.S. Marshals Serv., 494 F.3d 1106, 1121 (D.C. Cir. 2007) ("[the record] must actually describe him in some way"); Houghton v. U.S. Dep't of State, No. 11-0869, 2012 WL 2855868 at *10-11 (D.D.C. July 12, 2012) (following standard set in Tobey and determining transcripts at issue were not "about" plaintiff but rather "about a Memorandum of Understanding [between governments]" and "[e]ven the parts of the transcripts that mention [plaintiff] are about a letter he wrote that was published . . . not about him"; "the mere fact that the transcripts contain reference to or quote from plaintiff's written work is not sufficient to make it a record"); Aguirre v. SEC, 671 F. Supp. 2d 113, 121-22 (D.D.C. 2009) (following Sussman and determining that "records of an investigation of [plaintiff's] allegation that the SEC 'fired [him] for questioning' the decision to give 'preferential treatment to one of Wall Street's elite'" was sufficient to allege "that the records describe the reasons for [plaintiff's] termination" and therefore "at the very least, plausible that these records . . . describe him in some way"); Hatfill v. Gonzalez, 505 F. Supp. 2d 33, 35-39 (D.D.C. 2007) (concluding that information in news articles and

OVERVIEW OF THE PRIVACY ACT

reports concerning plaintiff's suspected involvement in criminal activity were "records"); Scarborough v. Harvey, 493 F. Supp. 2d 1, 15-16 (D.D.C. 2007) (documents naming individual plaintiffs and describing their involvement in allegedly criminal activities were "about" plaintiffs and therefore were not excluded from definition of "records," even if these activities were undertaken in connection with plaintiffs' businesses); Leighton v. CIA, 412 F. Supp. 2d 30, 38-39 (D.D.C. 2006) (finding that information contained in a magazine column, which did not name plaintiff contractor or contain an identifier but did state that "the CIA is looking at contractors and suspended two in June for talking to the press," was not "about" plaintiff); Roberts v. DOJ, 366 F. Supp. 2d 13, 26 (D.D.C. 2005) (finding that FBI director's public response to IG report investigating plaintiff's allegations of FBI wrongdoing was not "about" plaintiff; rather, it was an examination of the "validity of public allegations of misconduct lodged against [the FBI]"); Tripp v. DOD, 193 F. Supp. 2d 229, 236 (D.D.C. 2002) (citing Tobey and stating that salary information for position for which plaintiff had applied "is not 'about' plaintiff – the fact that she could receive that salary had she been chosen for the position does not convert this into information 'about' plaintiff"); Voinche v. CIA, No. 98-1883, 2000 U.S. Dist. LEXIS 14291, at *8, 11-12 (D.D.C. Sept. 27, 2000) (citing Tobey and Fisher, infra, and finding that records regarding plaintiff's administrative appeal concerning a prior access request and the case files of plaintiff's prior Freedom of Information Act litigation, "while identifying plaintiff by name, are not 'about' the plaintiff, but rather are 'about' the administrative appeal and prior litigation under the FOIA"); Fisher v. NIH, 934 F. Supp. 464, 466-67, 469-72 (D.D.C. 1996) (following Tobey and finding that information in database about articles published in scientific journals that contained bibliographic information including title of article and publication, name and address of author, and summary of article and also included annotation "[scientific misconduct – data to be reanalyzed]," provides "information 'about' the article described in each file and does not provide information 'about' [the author]," even though information "could be used to draw inferences or conclusions about [the author]"; "The fact that it is possible for a reasonable person to interpret information as describing an individual does not mean the information is about that individual for purposes of the Privacy Act."), summary affirmance granted, No. 96-5252 (D.C. Cir. Nov. 27, 1996); Henke v. U.S. Dep't of Commerce, No. 94-0189, 1996 WL 692020, at *3 (D.D.C. Aug. 19, 1994) (holding that names of four reviewers who evaluated

OVERVIEW OF THE PRIVACY ACT

grant applicant's proposal are applicant's "records" under Privacy Act), aff'd on other grounds, 83 F.3d 1445 (D.C. Cir. 1996); Doe v. DOJ, 790 F. Supp. 17, 22 (D.D.C. 1992) (applying Nolan, infra, and alternatively holding that "names of agents involved in the investigation are properly protected from disclosure"); Topuridze v. FBI, No. 86-3120, 1989 WL 11709, at *2 (D.D.C. Feb. 6, 1989) (citing Unt with approval and holding that letter written about requester, authored by third party, cannot be regarded as third party's record; it "does not follow that a document reveals some quality or characteristic of an individual simply by virtue of the individual having authored the document"), reconsideration denied sub nom. Topuridze v. USIA, 772 F. Supp. 662, 664-65 (D.D.C. 1991) (after in camera review, although reaffirming that "[i]n order to be about an individual a record must 'reflect some quality or characteristic of the individual involved,'" stating that document "may well be 'about' the author," as it discussed author's family status, employment, and fear of physical retaliation if letter were disclosed to plaintiff, and ultimately ruling that it need not reach issue of whether or not letter was "about" author and denying reconsideration on ground that letter was without dispute about subject/plaintiff); and Shewchun v. U.S. Customs Serv., No. 87-2967, 1989 WL 7351, at *1 (D.D.C. Jan. 11, 1989) (letter concerning agency's disposition of plaintiff's merchandise "lacks a sufficient informational nexus with [plaintiff] (himself, as opposed to his property) to bring it within the definition of 'record'").

Agreeing with Tobey, the Fifth Circuit concluded that information must both be "about" an individual and contain an identifying particular assigned to that individual to qualify as a "record." See Pierce, 512 F.3d at 188. In Pierce, the Fifth Circuit explained that "[a]lthough the Privacy Act protects more than just documents that contain a person's name, it does not protect documents that do not include identifying particulars." Id. at 187. In determining whether a "final response letter" and "summary report of investigation" containing only "duty titles" constituted "records," the court concluded that in that case, where the duty titles did "not pertain to one and only one individual," they did not qualify as "identifying particulars" and thus, did not qualify as records under the Act. Id. at 187-88. However, the court also recognized that "where duty titles pertain to one and only one individual . . . duty titles may indeed be 'identifying particulars' as that term is used in the definition of 'record' in the Privacy Act." Id.

Several other courts have limited Privacy Act coverage by applying narrow

OVERVIEW OF THE PRIVACY ACT

constructions of the term "record." See, e.g., Counce v. Nicholson, No. 3:06cv00171, 2007 WL 1191013, at *15 (M.D. Tenn. Apr. 18, 2007) (concluding that "email contain[ing] information regarding a potential presentation on bullying that [plaintiff's] supervisors directed her to submit for their review" was not a "record"); Lapka v. Chertoff, No. 05-C-668, 2006 WL 3095668, at *6-7 (N.D. Ill. Oct. 30, 2006) (citing Unt and explaining that "[u]nder the Privacy Act, records that are generated in response to a complaint are not records about the complainant but rather are considered records about the accused"); Hassell v. Callahan, No. 97-0037-B, slip op. at 3-5 (W.D. Va. Aug. 7, 1997) (finding that public sign-up sheet that asked for name of claimant and name of his representative for disability benefits did not constitute "record"; stating that "this court is not inclined to lump the name of a person's representative within the same category as information regarding his medical or financial history"); Wolde-Giorgis v. United States, No. 94-254, slip op. at 5-6 (D. Ariz. Dec. 9, 1994) (citing Unt with approval and holding that Postal Service claim form and information concerning estimated value of item sent through mail was "not a 'record' within the meaning of the [Privacy Act]" because it "disclosed no information about the plaintiff" and did not reflect any "'quality or characteristic' concerning the plaintiff"), aff'd, 65 F.3d 177 (9th Cir. 1995) (unpublished table decision); Ingerman v. IRS, No. 89-5396, slip op. at 6 (D.N.J. Apr. 3, 1991) ("An individual's social security number does not contain his name, identifying number or other identifying particular. . . . [A] social security number is the individual's identifying number, and therefore, it cannot qualify as a record under . . . the Privacy Act."), aff'd, 953 F.2d 1380 (3d Cir. 1992) (unpublished table decision); Nolan v. DOJ, No. 89-A-2035, 1991 WL 36547, at *10 (D. Colo. Mar. 18, 1991) (names of FBI special agents and other personnel held not requester's "record" and therefore "outside the scope of the [Privacy Act]"), aff'd, 973 F.2d 843 (10th Cir. 1992); Blair v. U.S. Forest Serv., No. A85-039, slip op. at 4-5 (D. Alaska Sept. 24, 1985) ("Plan of Operation" form completed by plaintiff held not his "record" as it "reveals nothing about his personal affairs"), appeal dismissed, No. 85-4220 (9th Cir. Apr. 1, 1986); Windsor v. A Fed. Executive Agency, 614 F. Supp. 1255, 1260-61 (M.D. Tenn. 1983) (record includes only sensitive information about individual's private affairs), aff'd, 767 F.2d 923 (6th Cir. 1985) (unpublished table decision); Cohen v. U.S. Dep't of Labor, 3 Gov't Disclosure Serv. (P-H) ¶ 83,157, at 83,791 (D. Mass. Mar. 21, 1983) (record includes only "personal" information); AFGE v. NASA, 482 F. Supp. 281, 282-83 (S.D. Tex. 1980) (determining that sign-in/sign-out sheet was not "record" because, standing alone, it did not reveal any "substantive information about the employees"); Houston v. U.S. Dep't of the Treasury, 494 F. Supp. 24, 28 (D.D.C. 1979) (same as Cohen); see also Drake v. 136th Airlift Wing, Tex. Air Nat'l Guard, No. 3:98-CV-1673D, 1998 WL 872915, at *1-2 (N.D. Tex. Nov. 30, 1998) (stating that

OVERVIEW OF THE PRIVACY ACT

list of names of witnesses is not record, as it "does not include personal information regarding any particular individual"), aff'd, 209 F.3d 718 (5th Cir. 2000) (unpublished table decision); Benson v. United States, No. 80-15-MC, slip op. at 4 (D. Mass. June 12, 1980) (permitting withholding of OPM investigator's name where identities of informants were properly excised under subsection (k)(5)); cf. Brancheau v. Sec'y of Labor, No. 6:11-cv-1416, 2011 WL 4105047, at *2 (M.D. Fla. Sept. 15, 2011) (although quoting Act's definition of "record" as including "photograph," nevertheless going on to state that, "it appears highly unlikely" that "video recordings and photographs depicting such things as [individual's] death and the efforts to rescue her and recover her body" qualify as "records"); Vinzant v. United States, No. 2:06-cv-10561, 2010 WL 2674609, at *6-7 (E.D. La. June 30, 2010) (expressing "doubt that any Privacy Act 'record' would need to be produced to comply with [plaintiff's] interrogatory . . . seek[ing] production of 'all contact information that . . . relate[s] to any and all listed inmate witnesses'" because interrogatory could be restricted and disclosure could be by a separate writing rather than a formal "record," but "look[ing] beyond this issue, because the information sought implies a privacy concern no matter what form of transmission the government may choose or the court may order").

For a further illustration of conflicting views concerning the meaning of the term "record" in the subsection (d)(1) access context, compare Voelker v. IRS, 646 F.2d 332, 334 (8th Cir. 1981) (requiring agency to provide individual with access to his entire record, even though some information in that record "pertained" to third party), with Sussman v. U.S. Marshals Serv., 494 F.3d 1106, 1121 n.9 (interpreting subsection (d)(1) "to give parties access only to their own records, not to all information pertaining to them that happens to be contained in a system of records"; "For an assemblage of data to qualify as one of [plaintiff's] records, it must not only contain his name or other identifying particulars but also be about him"), Aguirre v. SEC, 671 F. Supp. 2d 113, 121 (D.D.C. 2009), Nolan v. DOJ, No. 89-A-2035, 1991 WL 36547, at *3 (D. Colo. Mar. 18, 1991), aff'd, 973 F.2d 843 (10th Cir. 1992), and DePlanche v. Califano, 549 F. Supp. 685, 693-98 (W.D. Mich. 1982). These important cases are further discussed below under "Individual's Right of Access."

One district court, in a case concerning the Privacy Act's subsection (b)(3) routine use exception, has held that a plaintiff may choose which particular "item of information" (one document) contained within a "collection or grouping of information" disclosed (a prosecutive report indicating a potential violation of law) to denominate as a "record" and challenge as wrongfully disclosed. Covert v. Harrington, 667 F. Supp. 730, 736-37 (E.D. Wash. 1987), aff'd on other grounds, 876 F.2d 751 (9th Cir. 1989).

OVERVIEW OF THE PRIVACY ACT

Purporting to construe the term "record" narrowly, the district court in Covert ruled that the Department of Energy's routine use – 47 Fed. Reg. 14,333 (Apr. 2, 1982) (permitting disclosure of relevant records where "a record" indicates a potential violation of law) – did not permit its Inspector General to disclose personnel security questionnaires to the Justice Department for prosecution because the questionnaires themselves did not reveal a potential violation of law on their face. 667 F. Supp. at 736-37. Covert is discussed further under "Conditions of Disclosure to Third Parties," "Agency Requirements," and "Civil Remedies," below.

Note also that purely private notes – such as personal memory refreshers – are generally regarded as not subject to the Privacy Act because they are not "agency records." See Johnston v. Horne, 875 F.2d 1415, 1423 (9th Cir. 1989); Bowyer v. U.S. Dep't of the Air Force, 804 F.2d 428, 431 (7th Cir. 1986); Boyd v. Sec'y of the Navy, 709 F.2d 684, 686 (11th Cir. 1983) (per curiam); Harmer v. Perry, No. 95-4197, 1998 WL 229637, at *3 (E.D. Pa. Apr. 28, 1998), aff'd, No. 98-1532 (3d Cir. Jan. 29, 1999); Sherwin v. Dep't of Air Force, No. 90-34-CIV-3, slip op. at 2-7 (E.D.N.C. Apr. 15, 1992), aff'd, 37 F.3d 1495 (4th Cir. 1994) (unpublished table decision); Glass v. U.S. Dep't of Energy, No. 87-2205, 1988 WL 118408, at *1 (D.D.C. Oct. 29, 1988); Mahar v. Nat'l Parks Serv., No. 86-0398, slip op. at 16-17 (D.D.C. Dec. 23, 1987); Kalmin v. Dep't of the Navy, 605 F. Supp. 1492, 1494-95 (D.D.C. 1985); Machen v. U.S. Army, No. 78-582, slip op. at 4 (D.D.C. May 11, 1979); see also OMB Guidelines, 40 Fed. Reg. at 28,952, available at (http://www.whitehouse.gov/sites/default/files/omb/assets/omb/inforeg/implementation_guidelines.pdf) ("Uncirculated personal notes, papers and records which are retained or discarded at the author's discretion and over which the agency exercises no control or dominion (e.g., personal telephone lists) are not considered to be agency records within the meaning of the Privacy Act."); cf. System of Records Notice, Employee Performance File System Records (OPM/GOVT-2), 71 Fed. Reg. 35347, 35348 (June 19, 2006) ("[W]hen supervisors/managers retain personal 'supervisory' notes, i.e., information on employees that the agency exercises no control [over] and does not require or specifically describe in its performance system, which remain solely for the personal use of the author and are not provided to any other person, and which are retained or discarded at the author's sole discretion, such notes are not subject to the Privacy Act and are, therefore, not considered part of this system."); FOIA Update, Vol. V, No. 4, at 3 ("OIP Guidance: 'Agency Records' vs. 'Personal Records'") (analyzing concepts of agency records and personal records under FOIA), available at http://www.justice.gov/oip/foia_updates/Vol_V_4/page5.htm.

However, in Chapman v. NASA, 682 F.2d 526, 529 (5th Cir. 1982), the Court of Appeals for the Fifth Circuit, relying on the fair recordkeeping

OVERVIEW OF THE PRIVACY ACT

duties imposed by subsection (e)(5), ruled that private notes may "evanesce" into records subject to the Act when they are used to make a decision on the individual's employment status well after the evaluation period for which they were compiled. See also Lawrence v. Dole, No. 83-2876, slip op. at 5-6 (D.D.C. Dec. 12, 1985) ("[a]bsent timely incorporation into the employee's file, the private notes may not be used as a basis for an adverse employment action"); Thompson v. Dep't of Transp. U.S. Coast Guard, 547 F. Supp. 274, 283-84 (S.D. Fla. 1982) (timeliness requirement of subsection (e)(5) is met where private notes upon which disciplinary action is based are placed in a system of records "contemporaneously with or within a reasonable time after an adverse disciplinary action is proposed"); cf. Risch v. Henderson, 128 F. Supp. 2d 437, 441 (E.D. Mich. 1999) (stating that "another person's witnessing of a personal note converts it to a Level 2 – Supervisor's Personnel Record, and therefore it is properly maintained under the Privacy Act" in a system of records in accordance with the agency manual). But cf. Sherwin, No. 90-34-CIV-3, slip op. at 2-7 (E.D.N.C. Apr. 15, 1992) (distinguishing Chapman and finding that notes of telephone conversations between two of plaintiff's supervisors concerning plaintiff were not "agency 'records'" because plaintiff was "well aware of the general content" of notes, "essence" of notes was incorporated in agency's records, "private notes played no role" in plaintiff's discharge, and although some of notes were shared between two supervisors, "they remained personal notes at all times").

Note that publicly available information, such as newspaper clippings or press releases, can constitute a "record." See Clarkson v. IRS, 678 F.2d 1368, 1372 (11th Cir. 1982) (permitting subsection (e)(7) challenge to agency's maintenance of newsletters and press releases); Krieger v. DOJ, 529 F. Supp. 2d 29, 51 (D.D.C. 2008) (same as to copies of plaintiff's speech announcements and publicly filed court complaint); Murphy v. NSA, 2 Gov't Disclosure Serv. (P-H) ¶ 81,389, at 82,036-37 (D.D.C. Sept. 29, 1981) (same as to newspaper clippings); see also OMB Guidelines, 40 Fed. Reg. 56,741, 56,742 (Nov. 21, 1975), available at http://www.whitehouse.gov/sites/default/files/omb/assets/omb/inforeg/implementation1974.pdf ("Collections of newspaper clippings or other published matter about an individual maintained other than in a conventional reference library would normally be a system of records."); cf. Gerlich v. DOJ, 659 F. Supp. 2d 1, 12-16 (D.D.C. 2009) (concluding without discussing that "printouts" of "Internet searches regarding [job] candidates' political and ideological affiliations" constituted "records"); Fisher, 934 F. Supp. at 469 (discussing difference between definition of "record" for purposes of FOIA and statutory definition under Privacy Act and rejecting argument, based on FOIA case law, that "library reference materials" are not covered by Privacy Act).

OVERVIEW OF THE PRIVACY ACT

One court has relied on non-Privacy Act case law concerning grand jury records to hold that a grand jury transcript, "though in possession of the U.S. Attorney, is not a record of the Justice Department within the meaning of the Privacy Act." Kotmair v. DOJ, No. S 94-721, slip op. at 1 (D. Md. July 12, 1994) (citing United States v. Penrod, 609 F.2d 1092, 1097 (4th Cir. 1979), for above proposition, but then confusingly not applying same theory to analysis of FOIA accessibility), aff'd, 42 F.3d 1386 (4th Cir. 1994) (unpublished table decision).

The Privacy Act – like the FOIA – does not require agencies to create records that do not exist. See DeBold v. Stimson, 735 F.2d 1037, 1041 (7th Cir. 1984); Perkins v. IRS, No. 86-CV-71551, slip op. at 4 (E.D. Mich. Dec. 16, 1986); see also, e.g., Villanueva v. DOJ, 782 F.2d 528, 532 (5th Cir. 1986) (rejecting argument that the FBI was required to "find a way to provide a brief but intelligible explanation for its decision . . . without [revealing exempt information]"). But compare May v. Dep't of the Air Force, 777 F.2d 1012, 1015-17 (5th Cir. 1985) (singularly ruling that "reasonable segregation requirement" obligates agency to create and release typewritten version of handwritten evaluation forms so as not to reveal identity of evaluator under exemption (k)(7)), with Church of Scientology W. United States v. IRS, No. CV-89-5894, slip op. at 4 (C.D. Cal. Mar. 5, 1991) (FOIA decision rejecting argument based upon May, and holding that agency is not required to create records).

E. **System of Records**

"a group of any records under the control of any agency from which information is retrieved by the name of the individual or by some identifying number, symbol, or other identifying particular assigned to the individual." 5 U.S.C. § 552a(a)(5).

Comment:

The OMB Guidelines explain that a system of records exists if: (1) there is an "indexing or retrieval capability using identifying particulars [that is] built into the system"; and (2) the agency "does, in fact, retrieve records about individuals by reference to some personal identifier." OMB Guidelines, 40 Fed. Reg. 28,948, 28,952 (July 9, 1975), available at http://www.whitehouse.gov/sites/default/files/omb/assets/omb/inforeg/imple mentation_guidelines.pdf. The Guidelines state that the "is retrieved by" criterion "implies that the grouping of records under the control of an agency is accessed by the agency by use of a personal identifier; not merely that a capability or potential for retrieval exists." Id. (emphasis added).

OVERVIEW OF THE PRIVACY ACT

It is important to note that by its very terms the statute includes as personal identifiers items beyond the perhaps most commonly used name and social security number. As the Court of Appeals for the District of Columbia Circuit pointed out when considering a "photo file":

> Recall that a system of records is "a group of any records . . . from which information is retrieved by the name of the individual or by some identifying number, symbol, or <u>other identifying particular assigned to the individual</u>." 5 U.S.C. § 552a(a)(5) (emphasis added). The term "record" includes "any item . . . about an individual . . . that contains his name, or the identifying number, symbol, or other identifying particular assigned to the individual, such as a finger or voice print <u>or a photograph</u>." <u>Id.</u> § 552a(a)(4) (emphasis added). Under the Act's plain language, then, a "system of records" may be a group of any records retrieved by an identifying particular such as a photograph. In other words, the personal identifier may be the photograph itself.

<u>Maydak v. United States</u>, 363 F.3d 512, 519-20 (D.C. Cir. 2004) (remanding case to district court to determine whether prisons' compilation of photographs constitutes system of records), <u>on remand</u> No. 1:97-cv-02199, slip op. at 2-4 (D.D.C. Mar. 30, 2006) ("Searching through a box or collection of unidentified photos with the hope of recognizing an inmate does not fit the definition because the photos are not 'retrieved' by any 'assigned' personal identifier."), <u>aff'd in part on other grounds, vacated in nonpertinent part</u>, 630 F.3d 166, 179 (D.C. Cir. 2010) (electing to "simply assume, without deciding, that BOP's review and retention of the duplicate photos constituted a 'system of records'" and to "focus on whether Government officials acted intentionally or willfully to violate appellants' rights under the Act"). But see <u>Ingerman v. IRS</u>, No. 89-5396, slip op. at 6 (D.N.J. Apr. 3, 1991) ("An individual's social security number does not contain his name, identifying number, or other identifying particular. . . . [A] social security number <u>is</u> the individual's identifying number, and therefore, it cannot qualify as a record under . . . the Privacy Act."), <u>aff'd</u>, 953 F.2d 1380 (3d Cir. 1992) (unpublished table decision).

The D.C. Circuit also addressed the "system of records" definition in <u>Henke v. U.S. Department of Commerce</u>, 83 F.3d 1453 (D.C. Cir. 1996), and noted that "the OMB guidelines make it clear that it is not sufficient that an agency has the <u>capability</u> to retrieve information indexed under a person's name, but the agency must <u>in fact</u> retrieve records in this way in order for a system of

OVERVIEW OF THE PRIVACY ACT

records to exist." Id. at 1460 n.12; see also Elec. Privacy Info. Ctr. v. DHS, 653 F.3d 1, 8 (D.C. Cir. 2011) ("Even if . . . the TSA has the ability to combine various sources of information and then to link names to the images produced using [advanced imaging technology], [the petitioners'] Privacy Act claim still fails because they offer no reason to believe the TSA has in fact done that." (citing Henke)); Chang v. Dep't of the Navy, 314 F. Supp. 2d 35, 41 (D.D.C. 2004) ("[A]n agency's failure to acknowledge that it maintains a system of records will not protect the agency from statutory consequences if there is evidence that the agency in practice retrieves information about individuals by their names or personal identifiers. . . . [H]owever, mere retrievability – that is, the capability to retrieve – is not enough.").

The highly technical "system of records" definition is perhaps the single most important Privacy Act concept, because (with some exceptions discussed below) it makes coverage under the Act dependent upon the method of retrieval of a record rather than its substantive content. See Baker v. Dep't of the Navy, 814 F.2d 1381, 1384 (9th Cir. 1987) (noting the "overwhelming support for using a record's method of retrievability to determine the scope of accessibility"); Shannon v. Gen. Elec. Co., 812 F. Supp. 308, 321 (N.D.N.Y. 1993) (method of retrieval rather than substantive content controls determination of whether record is in a system of records); see also Mata v. McHugh, No. 10-cv-838, 2012 WL 2376285, at *6 (W.D. Tex. Jun. 22, 2012) (finding that "[p]laintiff's resume was retrieved by his job description, not his name, and is thus not a record in a system of records"); Krieger v. DOJ, 529 F. Supp. 2d 29, 44-46 (D.D.C. 2008) ("That several of the documents do not fit th[e] description [of the label used to retrieve them] does not mean that [an agency employee] has intentionally evaded the provisions of the Privacy Act, as an agency employee seeking to find records relating to [plaintiff] would have to individually review each document to locate records associated with him – hardly a characterization of an 'actual practice of retrieval by name.' . . . Because the agency's press releases are actually retrieved by date and not by individual identifier, they cannot be characterized as included within a system of records." (quoting McCready v. Nicholson, 465 F.3d 1, 11 (D.C. Cir. 2006))); Lee v. DOJ, No. 04-1013, 2007 WL 2852538, *9-10 (W.D. Pa. Sept. 27, 2007) (concluding that plaintiff's wrongful disclosure claim must fail because record at issue was "retrieved by the name of the fugitive," not by plaintiff's name); Artz v. United States, No. 3:05-CV-51, 2007 WL 1175512, at *5 (D.N.D. Apr. 20, 2007) (although report named plaintiffs, it was not contained in a "system of records" because it was retrieved by date, not by plaintiffs' names); Lee v. Geren, 480 F. Supp. 2d 198, 207 (D.D.C. Mar. 29, 2007) (citing Henke and finding that record was not maintained in a system of records because record was retrieved by log number that was "unrelated to specific individuals");

OVERVIEW OF THE PRIVACY ACT

Smith v. Henderson, No. C-99-4665, 1999 WL 1029862, at *5 (N.D. Cal. Oct. 29, 1999) (applying Henke and finding that "locked drawer containing a file folder in which [were] kept . . . notes or various other pieces of paper relating to special circumstances hires" did not constitute a system of records because the agency "did not utilize the drawer to systematically file and retrieve information about individuals indexed by their names"), aff'd sub nom. Smith v. Potter, 17 F. App'x 731 (9th Cir. 2001); Crumpton v. United States, 843 F. Supp. 751, 755-56 (D.D.C. 1994) (although records disclosed to press under FOIA contained information about plaintiff, they were not retrieved by her name and therefore Privacy Act did not apply), aff'd on other grounds sub nom. Crumpton v. Stone, 59 F.3d 1400 (D.C. Cir. 1995). Indeed, a major criticism of the Privacy Act is that it can easily be circumvented by not filing records in name-retrieved formats. See Privacy Commission Report at 503-04 & n.7, available at http://epic.org/privacy/ppsc1977report. A recognition of this potential for abuse has led some courts to relax the "actual retrieval" standard in particular cases (examples in cases cited below). Moreover, certain subsections of the Act (discussed below) have been construed to apply even to records not incorporated into a "system of records."

Even in the context of computerized information, courts that have considered the issue have held that retrievability alone is insufficient to satisfy the system of records "retrieved by" requirement. See York v. McHugh, No. 09-075, 2012 WL 1014503, at *1, *9 (D.D.C. Mar. 27, 2012) (where agency stored electronic documents containing plaintiff's medical information in "shared network drive" accessible to other employees, ruling that shared drive did not constitute system of records even though this method of storage "allowed [plaintiff] to discover the files by searching the shared [] drive for [her name]"; "The fact that some documents were labeled with [plaintiff's] name does not convert the shared . . . drive into a system of records, particularly where there is no evidence that the agency used the shared drive to retrieve the personal information by personal identifiers and the drive was not created for employees to do so."); Krieger, 529 F. Supp. 2d at 42-44, 45-46 (finding that plaintiff "offers no facts suggesting that [emails] would have been indexed by name, or that an electronic folder existed that grouped emails related to him by name or other identifier" and noting that "a search function does not a system of records make"); Chang, 314 F. Supp. 2d at 41 (applying Henke, rejecting plaintiff's assertion that document was retrievable by searching within the computer files of the relevant officers, and stating that "[p]laintiff's assertion that it is 'technically possible' to retrieve the [document] by searching for [plaintiff's] name is insufficient to meet the requirement that the data was retrieved in such a manner"); Fisher v. NIH, 934 F. Supp. 464, 472-73 (D.D.C. 1996) (applying Henke and stating: "[T]he primary practice and policy of the agency [during the time of the alleged disclosures] was to index and retrieve the investigatory files by the name of the institution in which the alleged misconduct occurred, rather than by the name of the individual scientist accused of committing the misconduct. The fact that it was possible to use plaintiff's name to identify a file containing information about the plaintiff is irrelevant."), summary affirmance granted, No. 96-5252 (D.C. Cir. Nov. 27, 1996); Beckette v. USPS, No. 88-802, slip op. at 19-22 (E.D. Va. July 3, 1989) (Although the plaintiff demonstrated that the agency "could retrieve . . . records by way of an individual's name or other personal identifier," that fact "does not make those records a Privacy Act system of records. The relevant inquiry is whether the records or the information they contain are [in fact] retrieved by name or other personal identifier.").

Indeed, the issue in Henke was whether or not computerized databases that contained information concerning technology grant proposals submitted by businesses constituted a "system of records" as to individuals listed as the "contact persons" for the grant applications, where the agency had acknowledged that "it could theoretically retrieve information by the name of the contact person." Id. at 1457-58. The D.C. Circuit looked to Congress's use of the words "is retrieved" in the statute's definition of a system of records and focused on whether the agency "in practice" retrieved information. Id. at 1459-61. The court held that "in determining whether an agency maintains a system of records keyed to individuals, the court should view the entirety of the situation, including the agency's function, the purpose for which the information was gathered, and the agency's actual retrieval practice and policies." Id. at 1461. Regarding the purpose for which the information was gathered, the court drew a distinction between information gathered for investigatory purposes and information gathered for administrative purposes. Id. at 1461. The court stated that where information is compiled about individuals "primarily for investigatory purposes, Privacy Act concerns are at their zenith, and if there is evidence of even a few retrievals of information keyed to individuals' names, it may well be the case that the agency is maintaining a system of records." Id. Applying this test, the D.C. Circuit determined that the agency did "not maintain a system of records keyed to individuals listed in the contact person fields of its databases" because the agency's "purpose in requesting the name of a technical contact [was] essentially administrative and [was] not even necessary for the conduct of the [program's] operations," nor was there "any evidence that the names of contact persons [were] used regularly or even frequently to obtain information about those persons." Id. at 1456, 1461-62.

Several courts have followed Henke insofar as it calls on them to "view the entirety of the situation, including the agency's function, the purpose for which the information was gathered, and the agency's actual retrieval

OVERVIEW OF THE PRIVACY ACT

practice and policies" in determining "whether an agency maintains a system of records keyed to individuals." Id. at 1461. See Maydak, 363 F.3d at 520 (quoting Henke and remanding case to district court to determine whether prisons' compilation of photographs constitutes system of records and instructing district court to "take into account 'the entirety of the situation, including the agency's function, the purpose for which the information was gathered, and the agency's actual retrieval practices and policies'"); Pippinger v. Rubin, 129 F.3d 519, 526-27 (10th Cir. 1997) (finding approach in Henke "instructive" and holding that under "a properly 'narrow' construction of 5 U.S.C. § 552a(a)(5)," an IRS database containing an "abstraction" of information from two existing Privacy Act systems did not constitute a new system of records because it could be "accessed only by the same users, and only for the same purposes, as those published in the Federal Register for the original 'system[s] of records'"); Sussman v. U.S. Marshals Serv., 657 F. Supp. 2d 25, 27-28 (D.D.C. 2009) ("Given the function of the Marshals Service, Privacy Act concerns are at their zenith. . . . [T]he Marshals Service's declarations do not establish a record that sufficiently explains the purpose for which all of the information on Sussman was gathered, or its actual retrieval practice and policies for the information maintained in various locations on Sussman[.]"), on remand from 494 F.3d 1106 (D.C. Cir. 2007); Koenig v. Dep't of Navy, No. 05-35, 2005 WL 3560626, at *4 (S.D. Tex. Dec. 29, 2005) ("[A]lthough neither party presented any evidence regarding where or in what manner the request for medical leave was kept, common sense and experience in an office setting lead to the conclusion that the record was most likely either kept in a file with the plaintiff's name on it, or entered into her leave record, which also would have been accessible by her name or social security number."); Doe v. Veneman, 230 F. Supp. 2d 739, 752 (W.D. Tex. 2002) (quoting language from Henke regarding "even a few retrievals," and determining that noninvestigatory information "f[e]ll within the ambit of the Privacy Act" where information could "be retrieved by personal identifiers" and information was maintained in "single data repository from which more than 200 different types of reports [we]re generated," all from the raw data entered into the system), aff'd in pertinent part, rev'd & remanded on other grounds, 380 F.3d 807 (5th Cir. 2004); Walker v. Ashcroft, No. 99-2385, slip op. at 17-18 (D.D.C. Apr. 30, 2001) (alternative holding) (applying Henke and finding no evidence that the FBI "independently collected, gathered or maintained" a document containing plaintiff's prescription drug information given to the FBI by a state investigator, or that the FBI "could, in practice, actually retrieve the record by reference to [plaintiff's] name"), summary affirmance granted on other grounds, No. 01-5222, 2002 U.S. App. LEXIS 2485 (D.C. Cir. Jan. 25, 2002); Alexander v. FBI, 193 F.R.D. 1, 6-8 (D.D.C. 2000) (applying Henke and finding that the agency maintained a system of records, considering the "purpose for which the information was

OVERVIEW OF THE PRIVACY ACT

gathered and the ordinary retrieval practices and procedures"), mandamus denied per curiam sub nom. In re: Executive Office of the President, 215 F.3d 20 (D.C. Cir. 2000). But cf. Williams v. VA, 104 F.3d 670, 674-77 & n.4 (4th Cir. 1997) (although remanding case for further factual development as to whether records were contained within system of records, and noting that it was "express[ing] no opinion on the Henke court's rationale when applied to circumstances where a plaintiff seeks to use retrieval capability to transform a group of records into a 'system of records,' as in Henke," nevertheless finding the "narrow Henke rationale . . . unconvincing" in circumstances before the court where there "appear[ed] to exist already a formal system of records," where "published characteristics of the agency's formal system of records ha[d] not kept current with advances in and typical uses of computer technology," and where record was "poorly developed" on such point).

Note also that the "practice of retrieval by name or other personal identifier must be an agency practice to create a system of records and not a 'practice' by those outside the agency." McCready v. Nicholson, 465 F.3d 1, 13 (D.C. Cir. 2006) (holding that agency's public Web site, which was not used by agency personnel to retrieve information by personal identifier, did not constitute a "system of records"). See also Yonemoto v. VA, No. 06-00378, 2007 WL 1310165, at *5-6 (D. Haw. May 2, 2007) ("[I]t was not the agency, but the public who caused [information contained in e-mails] to be retrieved. Just because an agency is capable of retrieving the information, and just because it does so to comply with a FOIA request, does not mean that the information is maintained in a Privacy Act 'system of records.'"), appeal dismissed as moot, 305 F. App'x 333 (9th Cir. 2008); Freeman v. EPA, No. 02-0387, 2004 WL 2451409, at *11-12 (D.D.C. Oct. 25, 2004) (explaining that because an agency's search for records pursuant to a FOIA request "will normally trigger a search beyond the narrow confines of a Privacy Act system of records," it is not conclusive as to whether any responsive records would be "retrieved by [plaintiff's] name or some other identifying particular assigned to the individual" (internal quotation marks omitted)).

1. **Disclosure: Subsection (b)**

   Subsection (b) prohibits the disclosure only of records that are retrieved from a system of records. 5 U.S.C. § 552a(a)(5), (b); see also, e.g., Paige v. DEA, 665 F.3d 1355, 1359-61 (D.C. Cir. 2012) (where DEA obtained video of agent accidentally shooting himself in leg, produced multiple copies of video, and allegedly disclosed one or more copies, all before incorporating video into system of records, ruling for agency because "no system of records existed from which information was in fact retrieved by [agent's] name or other personal

OVERVIEW OF THE PRIVACY ACT

identifier until [a DEA] program analyst opened the [office] file" at headquarters days after alleged disclosure; adding that "disclosure of the [copy] was not prohibited under the Privacy Act simply because the [original version] subsequently became a 'record which is contained in a system of records'"); White v. Schafer, 738 F. Supp. 2d 1121, 1139 (D. Colo. 2010) (plaintiff who claimed that agency disclosed report of investigation in violation of subsection (b) failed to show that report was ever contained in "system of records" because she put forth no evidence concerning agency's method of retrieving report), aff'd, 435 F. App'x 764 (10th Cir. 2011); Krueger v. Mansfield, No. 06C3322, 2008 WL 2271493, at *7 (N.D. Ill. May 30, 2008) (unless a record is contained in a system of records, its disclosure does not fall within the Privacy Act's prohibition); Bechhoefer v. DOJ, 179 F. Supp. 2d 93, 95-101 (W.D.N.Y. 2001) (finding that the disclosed record "never became part of a system of records" where DEA agent had "stuck it in his desk drawer along with a number o[f] other miscellaneous documents, and later retrieved it from that drawer, from his own memory and personal knowledge of where he kept it"; noting, too, that plaintiff's claim that agent may have looked at plaintiff's name on record to retrieve it from drawer "confuses retrieving a document with identifying the document. If one is looking for a letter from a particular person, one will probably look at the name on the letter in order to identify it as the letter being sought. If that letter is in a stack of unrelated, miscellaneous documents, however, it cannot be said to be contained within a group of records organized in such a fashion that information can be retrieved by an individual's name."), aff'd, 312 F.3d 563, 567-68 & n.1 (2d Cir. 2002) (affirming on ground that "an assortment of papers excluded from the agency's formal files because they are deemed not relevant to the agency's mission and left in a desk drawer are not part of the agency's system of records, to which the obligations of the Act apply," and accordingly finding no need to consider agency's further argument concerning single instance of retrieval by individual's name); Barhorst v. Marsh, 765 F. Supp. 995, 999-1000 (E.D. Mo. 1991) (claim under subsection (b) dismissed on alternative grounds where record retrieved by job announcement number, not by individual's name; noting that "'mere potential for retrieval' by name or other identifier is insufficient to satisfy the 'system of records' requirement" (quoting Fagot v. FDIC, 584 F. Supp. 1168, 1175 (D.P.R. 1984), aff'd in part & rev'd in part, 760 F.2d 252 (1st Cir. 1985) (unpublished table decision))); cf. Corey v. McNamara, 265 F. App'x 555, 556 (9th Cir. 2008) (finding that plaintiff "offered no evidence to counter the USPS' evidence that [plaintiff's] documentation, the disclosure of which forms the basis

OVERVIEW OF THE PRIVACY ACT

of [his] federal action, is not part of the USPS 'system of records'"); Gadd v. United States, No. 4:08CV04229, 2010 WL 60953, at *11 (E.D. Ark. Jan. 5, 2010) (where plaintiff, an agency employee, had "supplied [the agency with] three documents from [his doctor] in support of his request for accommodation" and alleged that agency improperly disclosed the records, explaining that plaintiff "was the source of the medical records in dispute here"; "There is no allegation or evidence that defendants disclosed documents they initially obtained from a system of records."), aff'd per curiam, 392 F. App'x 503 (8th Cir. 2010); Smith v. BOP, No. 05-1824, 2006 WL 950372, at *3 (D. Md. Apr. 11, 2006) (dismissing claim for improper disclosure of letter plaintiff sent to her inmate husband because claim related to "a single item of correspondence," and explaining that "the court can find no basis in the Privacy Act for the conclusion that the Act's elaborate record-keeping and notice requirements apply in such circumstances"). But see Wall v. IRS, No. 1:88-CV-1942, 1989 U.S. Dist. LEXIS 9427, at *4-7 (N.D. Ga. July 5, 1989) (because agency official retrieved applicant's folder by name from file maintained under vacancy announcement number, records were kept within "system of records" and thus subsection (b) was applicable).

Several courts have stated that the first element a plaintiff must prove in a wrongful disclosure suit is that the information disclosed is a record within a system of records. See Quinn v. Stone, 978 F.2d 126, 131 (3d Cir. 1992); Feldman v. CIA, 797 F. Supp. 2d 29, 38 (D.D.C. 2011); Cloonan v. Holder, 768 F. Supp. 2d 154, 163 (D.D.C. 2011); Banks v. Butler, No. 5:08cv336, 2010 WL 4537902, at *6 (S.D. Miss. Sept. 23, 2010) (magistrate's recommendation), adopted, 2010 WL 4537909 (S.D. Miss. Nov. 2, 2010); White v. Schafer, 738 F. Supp. 2d at 1139; Walker v. Gambrell, 647 F. Supp. 2d 529, 536 (D. Md. 2009); Doe v. U.S. Dep't of Treasury, 706 F. Supp. 2d 1, 6 (D.D.C. 2009); Armstrong v. Geithner, 610 F. Supp. 2d 66, 70-71 (D.D.C. 2009); Shutte v. IRS, No. 08-CV-2013, 2008 WL 2114920, at *2 (N.D. Iowa May 19, 2008); Kinchen v. USPS, No. 90-1180, slip op. at 5 (W.D. Tenn. June 17, 1994); Hass v. U.S. Air Force, 848 F. Supp. 926, 932 (D. Kan. 1994); Swenson v. USPS, No. S-87-1282, 1994 U.S. Dist. LEXIS 16524, at *14-15 (E.D. Cal. Mar. 10, 1994); see also Davis v. Runyon, No. 96-4400, 1998 WL 96558, at *4-5 (6th Cir. Feb. 23, 1998) (affirming district court's dismissal of Privacy Act wrongful disclosure claim where appellant had failed to allege any facts as to whether "'information' was a 'record' contained in a 'system of records,'" whether it was "disclos[ed] within the meaning of the Act," whether disclosure had "adverse effect," or whether disclosure was "willful or intentional"); Doe v. U.S. Dep't of the

OVERVIEW OF THE PRIVACY ACT

Interior, No. 95-1665, slip op. at 2-5 (D.D.C. Mar. 11, 1996) (alleged disclosure that plaintiff was HIV positive and had been treated for AIDS-related illnesses was not violation of Privacy Act because "[w]hile it appears to be true that some breach in confidentiality occurred . . . plaintiff cannot show that the breach stemmed from an improper disclosure of plaintiff's personnel records"); Mittleman v. U.S. Dep't of the Treasury, 919 F. Supp. 461, 468 (D.D.C. 1995) ("statement of general provisions of law" that was "not a disclosure of information retained in the [agency's] records on plaintiff . . . does not implicate the general nondisclosure provisions of the Privacy Act"), aff'd in part & remanded in part on other grounds, 104 F.3d 410 (D.C. Cir. 1997). But cf. Doe v. USPS, 317 F.3d 339, 342-43 (D.C. Cir. 2003) (ruling that genuine issues of material fact as to whether plaintiff's supervisor told co-workers about his HIV status and whether supervisor learned of that status from plaintiff's Privacy Act-protected Family and Medical Leave Act form precluded summary judgment for agency on plaintiff's claim for wrongful disclosure even though "evidence of retrieval [wa]s purely circumstantial"; "[B]ecause plaintiffs can rarely produce direct evidence that the government has disclosed confidential information obtained from their private records, requiring such evidence would eviscerate the protections of the Privacy Act.").

In fact, the Court of Appeals for the First Circuit has held that a complaint that fails to allege a disclosure from a "system of records" is facially deficient. Beaulieu v. IRS, 865 F.2d 1351, 1352 (1st Cir. 1989); see also Zahedi v. DOJ, No. 10-694, 2011 WL 1872206, at *4 (D. Or. May 16, 2011); Al-Dahir v. Hamlin, No. 10-2571, 2011 WL 1666894, at *4 (D. Kan. May 3, 2011); Del Fuoco v. O'Neill, No. 8:09-CV-1262, 2011 WL 601645, at *9-10 & n.13 (M.D. Fla. Feb. 11, 2011); Thomas v. USPS, No. 3:10-CV-1091, slip op. at 7-8 (N.D. Tex. Nov. 3, 2010); Mumme v. U.S. Dep't of Labor, 150 F. Supp. 2d 162, 175 (D. Me. 2001), aff'd, No. 01-2256 (1st Cir. June 12, 2002); Whitson v. Dep't of the Army, No. SA-86-CA-1173, slip op. at 8-12 (W.D. Tex. Feb. 25, 1988); Bernson v. ICC, 625 F. Supp. 10, 13 (D. Mass. 1984). However, other courts, including the Court of Appeals for the District of Columbia Circuit, have not held pleadings in Privacy Act cases to such a strict standard. See Krieger v. Fadely, 211 F.3d 134, 136-37 (D.C. Cir. 2000) (holding that complaint that alleged wrongful disclosure of records "subject to protection under the Privacy Act" thereby "alleged the essential elements of [plaintiff's] claim and put the government on notice," and that "[n]othing more was required to survive a motion to dismiss for failure to state a claim"; "If his lawsuit went forward, there would

OVERVIEW OF THE PRIVACY ACT

come a time when [plaintiff] would have to identify the particular records [defendant] unlawfully disclosed. But that point surely was not as early as the pleading stage."); Feldman, 797 F. Supp. 2d at 41 (stating that Circuit case law did not require that plaintiff allege full details of a disclosure at the pleading stage and explaining that "in the typical case, a plaintiff can hardly be expected to know the full details behind an improper disclosure prior to discovery, since those details are most likely to be under the control of the defendant"); Tripp v. DOD, 219 F. Supp. 2d 85, 89-91 (D.D.C. 2002) (where complaint "alleged that during a specific time period a specific defendant repeatedly released information about plaintiff to the press and public that is contained in a Privacy Act system of records, including but not limited to the contents of plaintiff's security forms and other personnel files," following Krieger to hold that Federal Rule of Civil Procedure 8 "does not require plaintiff to plead facts to further elaborate which records were released, by which DOD officials, to which members of the press or public, or on which specific dates"); Tripp v. DOD, 193 F. Supp. 2d 229, 237 (D.D.C. 2002) (following Krieger and "the liberal pleading standard permitted by the Federal Rules of Civil Procedure"); Johnson v. Rinaldi, No. 1:99CV170, 2001 U.S. Dist. LEXIS 9833, at *16-18 (M.D.N.C. Apr. 13, 2001) (stating that the "Federal Rules of Civil Procedure require only that the complaint put Defendants on notice" and that the plaintiff "need not use the exact words 'record' or 'system of records' or state facts sufficient to show that the documents in dispute meet those legal definitions"); cf. Sterling v. United States, 798 F. Supp. 47, 49 (D.D.C. 1992) (individual is "not barred from stating a claim for monetary damages [under (g)(1)(D)] merely because the record did not contain 'personal information' about him and was not retrieved through a search of indices bearing his name or other identifying characteristics"), subsequent related opinion, Sterling v. United States, 826 F. Supp. 570, 571-72 (D.D.C. 1993), summary affirmance granted, No. 93-5264 (D.C. Cir. Mar. 11, 1994).

It is not enough, however, for a plaintiff claiming that an agency disclosed information about the plaintiff in violation of subsection (b) to show that the information was contained in any system of records maintained by the agency. See Sussman v. U.S. Marshals Serv., 494 F. 3d 1106, 1123 (D.C. Cir. 2007). Rather, the plaintiff "must show [that] the [agency] improperly disclosed materials located in records retrievable by [the plaintiff's] name as opposed to someone else's name." Id. The plaintiff in Sussman had alleged that the agency disclosed information about him in violation of subsection (b). See

OVERVIEW OF THE PRIVACY ACT

id. The Marshals Service did "not deny[] the materials were in a system of records" but pointed out that "'[t]he information was not maintained in a system of records retrievable by [the plaintiff's] name, but by [another individual's] name.'" Id. Reasoning in part that it "must construe § 552a(g)(1)(D)'s waiver of sovereign immunity narrowly," the Court of Appeals for the District of Columbia Circuit held that "for his action to survive, [the plaintiff] must present evidence that materials from records about him, which the [agency] retrieved by his name, were improperly disclosed." Id.

Furthermore, information taken from a protected record in a system of records, but subsequently incorporated into a record that is not maintained in a system of records, can nonetheless itself become a protected record. See e.g., Jacobs v. Nat'l Drug Intelligence Ctr., 423 F.3d 512, 516-519 (5th Cir. 2005) (ruling that disclosure of executive summary, which was not retrieved by plaintiff's name but was created from information in a system of records that was so retrieved, was from a system of records); see also Bartel v. FAA, 725 F.2d 1403, 1407-09 (D.C. Cir. 1984) (finding that letters that did not qualify as covered "records," but that communicated sensitive information contained in report of investigation, which was a "record" maintained in a "system of records," triggered disclosure provisions of the Act; "[A]n absolute policy of limiting the Act's coverage to information physically retrieved from a record would make little sense in terms of [the Privacy Act's] underlying purpose."); Chang v. Dep't of the Navy, 314 F. Supp. 2d 35, 41 (D.D.C. 2004) (although it was undisputed that the documents at issue (a press release and "information paper" containing details of plaintiff's non-judicial punishment) were not retrieved from a system of records, nonetheless looking beneath the press release and "information paper" and finding that information from a system of records had been disclosed, because the "underlying documents, from which the documents were compiled, were contained in a system of records"). Similarly, the Court of Appeals for the First Circuit has held that "the unauthorized disclosure by one agency of protected information obtained from a record in another agency's system is a prohibited disclosure under the Act, unless the disclosure falls within the statutory exceptions." Orekoya v. Mooney, 330 F.3d 1, 6-7 (1st Cir. 2003); Doe v. U.S. Dep't of Treasury, 706 F. Supp. 2d at 6 ("[T]he Privacy Act only covers disclosures of information which was either directly or indirectly retrieved from a system of records." (quoting Fisher v. NIH, 934 F. Supp. 464, 473 (D.D.C. 1996))). In Orekoya, the First Circuit, although ultimately affirming the district court on other grounds, disagreed with the district court's

OVERVIEW OF THE PRIVACY ACT

determination that such a disclosure was not a violation of the Privacy Act, and it stated that the language of the Privacy Act "does not support the view that an agency may immunize itself from liability by obtaining information from a different agency's system of records and then saying its further unauthorized disclosure is protected because its own system of records was not the original source." Id.

Although subsection (b) "does not specifically require that the information disclosed be retrieved directly from" a record contained in a system of records, "courts generally apply some type of retrieval requirement to give effect to the meaning and purpose of the Privacy Act." Doe v. VA, 519 F.3d 456, 464 (8th Cir. 2008) (Hansen, J., concurring); see also, e.g., Armstrong v. Geithner, 608 F.3d 854, 857 (D.C. Cir. 2010) ("To be actionable . . . a disclosure generally must be the result of someone having actually retrieved the 'record' from th[e] 'system of records'; the disclosure of information is not ordinarily a violation 'merely because the information happens to be contained in the records.'" (quoting Bartel v. FAA, 725 F.2d 1403, 1408 (D.C. Cir. 1984))); Doe v. VA, 519 F.3d at 461 ("'[T]he only disclosure actionable under section 552a(b) is one resulting from a retrieval of the information initially and directly from the record contained in the system of records.'" (quoting Olberding v. DOD, 709 F.2d 621, 622 (8th Cir. 1983))); Cloonan, 768 F. Supp. 2d at 164 (explaining that the "definition [of 'system of records'] – which incorporates the requirement that information 'is retrieved' – has given rise to the so-called 'retrieval rule' under the Privacy Act"). Thus, it has frequently been held that subsection (b) is not violated when a dissemination is made on the basis of knowledge acquired independent of actual retrieval from an agency's system of records (such as a disclosure purely from memory), regardless of whether the identical information also happens to be contained in the agency's systems of records. The leading case articulating the "actual retrieval" and "independent knowledge" concepts is Savarese v. HEW, 479 F. Supp. 304, 308 (N.D. Ga. 1979), aff'd, 620 F.2d 298 (5th Cir. 1980) (unpublished table decision), in which the court ruled that for a disclosure to be covered by subsection (b), "there must have initially been a retrieval from the system of records which was at some point a source of the information." 479 F. Supp. at 308. In adopting this stringent "actual retrieval" test, the court in Savarese reasoned that a more relaxed rule could result in excessive governmental liability, or an unworkable requirement that agency employees "have a pansophic recall concerning every record within every system of records within the agency." Id.

OVERVIEW OF THE PRIVACY ACT

There are numerous subsection (b) cases that follow Savarese and apply the "actual retrieval" and "independent knowledge" concepts in varying factual situations. See, e.g., Doe v. VA, 519 F.3d 456, 460-63 (8th Cir. 2008); Kline v. HHS, 927 F.2d 522, 524 (10th Cir. 1991); Manuel v. VA Hosp., 857 F.2d 1112, 1119-20 (6th Cir. 1988); Thomas v. U.S. Dep't of Energy, 719 F.2d 342, 344-46 (10th Cir. 1983); Olberding v. DOD, 564 F. Supp. 907, 913 (S.D. Iowa 1982), aff'd per curiam, 709 F.2d 621 (8th Cir. 1983); Boyd v. Sec'y of the Navy, 709 F.2d 684, 687 (11th Cir. 1983) (per curiam); Doyle v. Behan, 670 F.2d 535, 538-39 & n.5 (5th Cir. 1982) (per curiam); Hanley v. DOJ, 623 F.2d 1138, 1139 (6th Cir. 1980) (per curiam); Doe v. U.S. Dep't of Treasury, 706 F. Supp. 2d at 9-11 (D.D.C. 2009); Tarullo v. Def. Contract Audit Agency, 600 F. Supp. 2d 352, 360-61 (D. Conn. 2009); Balbinot v. United States, 872 F. Supp. 546, 549-51 (C.D. Ill. 1994); Coakley v. U.S. Dep't of Transp., No. 93-1420, 1994 U.S. Dist. LEXIS 21402, at *2-3 (D.D.C. Apr. 7, 1994); Swenson, 1994 U.S. Dist. LEXIS 16524, at *19-22; Gibbs v. Brady, 773 F. Supp. 454, 458 (D.D.C. 1991); McGregor v. Greer, 748 F. Supp. 881, 885-86 (D.D.C. 1990); Avant v. USPS, No. 88-T-173-S, slip op. at 4-5 (M.D. Ala. May 4, 1990); Howard v. Marsh, 654 F. Supp. 853, 855 (E.D. Mo. 1986); Krowitz v. USDA, 641 F. Supp. 1536, 1545 (W.D. Mich. 1986), aff'd, 826 F.2d 1063 (6th Cir. 1987) (unpublished table decision); Blanton v. DOJ, No. 82-0452, slip op. at 4-5 (D.D.C. Feb. 17, 1984); Sanchez v. United States, 3 Gov't Disclosure Serv. (P-H) ¶ 83,116, at 83,708-09 (S.D. Tex. Sept. 10, 1982); Golliher v. USPS, 3 Gov't Disclosure Serv. (P-H) ¶ 83,114, at 83,703 (N.D. Ohio June 10, 1982); Thomas v. U.S. Dep't of the Navy, No. C81-0654-L(A), slip op. at 2-3 (W.D. Ky. Nov. 4, 1982), aff'd, 732 F.2d 156 (6th Cir. 1984) (unpublished table decision); Balk v. U.S. Int'l Commc'ns Agency, No. 81-0896, slip op. at 2-4 (D.D.C. May 7, 1982), aff'd, 704 F.2d 1293 (D.C. Cir. 1983) (unpublished table decision); Johnson v. U.S. Dep't of the Air Force, 526 F. Supp. 679, 681 (W.D. Okla. 1980), aff'd, 703 F.2d 583 (Fed. Cir. 1981) (unpublished table decision); Carin v. United States, 1 Gov't Disclosure Serv. (P-H) ¶ 80,193, at 80,491-92 (D.D.C. Aug. 5, 1980); Jackson v. VA, 503 F. Supp. 653, 655-57 (N.D. Ill. 1980); King v. Califano, 471 F. Supp. 180, 181 (D.D.C. 1979); Greene v. VA, No. C-76-461-S, slip op. at 6-7 (M.D.N.C. July 3, 1978); see also Armstrong, 608 F.3d at 858-60 (affirming district court finding that plaintiff had failed to establish that information disclosed had been retrieved from a record in a system of records where agency employee disclosed information regarding investigation of plaintiff from independent sources – her own "'observations and speculation' or 'those of others,' or information 'from the rumor mill'"); Cloonan,

OVERVIEW OF THE PRIVACY ACT

768 F. Supp. 2d at 169 ("[O]n its face, the language of the . . . letter is replete with references to 'the record' and 'documentation' from which a reasonable juror could conclude that the preparer of the document did in fact review, and is referring to, agency records."); Drapeau v. United States, No. Civ. 04-4091, 2006 WL 517646, at *6-7 (D.S.D. Mar. 1, 2006) (agency employees who disclosed information regarding plaintiff's dismissal for rules violation did not obtain that information from record in system of records but rather from employee who had observed violation); Finnerty v. USPS, No. 03-558, 2006 WL 54345, at *11-13 (D.N.J. Jan. 9, 2006) ("The fact that the memorandum documenting [a witness'] observations may have been simultaneously circulated to recipients and directed to a file and thereafter maintained as a 'record' in a 'system of records' does not change the fact that [the witness'] source of the information was his own observation, and not a retrieval of information from a system of records."); Krieger v. Fadely, 199 F.R.D. 10, 13 (D.D.C. 2001) (ruling that discovery request seeking all communications that supervisor had with anyone, irrespective of any relation between communication and Privacy Act-protected record, was overbroad, and stating that Privacy Act "does not create a monastic vow of silence which prohibits governmental employees from telling others what they saw and heard merely because what they saw or heard may also be the topic of a record in a protected file"); Fisher v. NIH, 934 F. Supp. 464, 473-74 (D.D.C. 1996) (plaintiff failed to demonstrate that individuals who disclosed information learned it from investigatory file or through direct involvement in investigation), summary affirmance granted, No. 96-5252 (D.C. Cir. Nov. 27, 1996); Viotti v. U.S. Air Force, 902 F. Supp. 1331, 1338 (D. Colo. 1995) ("Section 552a(b) contemplates a 'system of records' as being the direct or indirect source of the information disclosed" and although agency employee admitted disclosure of information to press "based on personal knowledge," plaintiff "was obligated to come forward with some evidence indicating the existence of a triable issue of fact as to the identity of the 'indirect' source" of disclosure to press), aff'd, 153 F.3d 730 (10th Cir. 1998) (unpublished table decision); Mittleman, 919 F. Supp. at 469 (although no evidence indicated that there had been disclosure of information about plaintiff, even assuming there had been, information at issue would not have been subject to restrictions of Privacy Act because "it was a belief . . . derived from conversations . . . and which was acquired independent from a system of records"); Doe v. U.S. Dep't of the Interior, No. 95-1665, slip op. at 4-5 (D.D.C. Mar. 11, 1996) (where plaintiff could "not show that the breach [in confidentiality] stemmed from an improper disclosure of

OVERVIEW OF THE PRIVACY ACT

[his] records," stating further that "[t]his is especially true in light of the fact that several other employees knew of, and could have told . . . of, plaintiff's illness"); Stephens v. TVA, 754 F. Supp. 579, 582 (E.D. Tenn. 1990) (comparing Olberding and Jackson and noting "confusion in the law with respect to whether the Privacy Act bars the disclosure of personal information obtained indirectly as opposed to directly from a system of records"); cf. Feldman, 797 F. Supp. 2d at 41 ("[W]hile the res ipsa loquitur inference invoked in Armstrong was inadequate to sustain a Privacy Act claim on the merits, a plaintiff's reliance on such an inference at the pleading stage may be sufficient to survive a motion to dismiss, depending on the facts alleged."); Rice v. United States, 166 F.3d 1088, 1092 n.4 (10th Cir. 1999) (in action for wrongful disclosure in violation of tax code, noting that plaintiff similarly had no Privacy Act claim for IRS's disclosure in press releases of information regarding plaintiff's criminal trial and conviction because information disclosed was procured by agency public affairs officer through review of indictment and attendance at plaintiff's trial and sentencing); Smith v. Henderson, No. C-96-4665, 1999 WL 1029862, at *6-7 (N.D. Cal. Oct. 29, 1999) (although finding no evidence of existence of written record retrieved from system of records, finding further that alleged disclosure was made from information "obtained independently of any system of records"), aff'd sub nom. Smith v. Potter, 17 F. App'x 731 (9th Cir. 2001).

However, the Court of Appeals for the District of Columbia Circuit, in Bartel v. FAA, 725 F.2d 1403, 1408-11 (D.C. Cir. 1984), held that the "actual retrieval" standard is inapplicable where a disclosure is undertaken by agency personnel who had a role in creating the record that contains the released information. In other words, the "independent knowledge" defense is not available to such agency personnel. See id. This particular aspect of Bartel has been noted with approval by several other courts. See Manuel, 857 F.2d at 1120 & n.1; Longtin v. DOJ, No. 06-1302, 2006 WL 2223999, at *3 (D.D.C. Aug. 3, 2006) (following Bartel and finding that requested disclosure of records concerning third-party criminal case by official who had role in creating records would violate Privacy Act, and therefore denying plaintiff's "Touhy" request); Stokes v. SSA, 292 F. Supp. 2d 178, 181 (D. Me. 2003) ("[A]gency employees who . . . create or initiate records are not shielded from the Privacy Act merely because they do not have to consult or retrieve those records before disclosing the information that they contain."); Pilon v. DOJ, 796 F. Supp. 7, 12 (D.D.C. 1992) (denying agency's motion to dismiss or alternatively for summary judgment where information

OVERVIEW OF THE PRIVACY ACT

"obviously stem[med] from confidential Department documents and oral statements derived therefrom"); Kassel v. VA, 709 F. Supp. 1194, 1201 (D.N.H. 1989); Cochran v. United States, No. 83-216, slip op. at 9-13 (S.D. Ga. July 2, 1984), aff'd, 770 F.2d 949 (11th Cir. 1985); Fitzpatrick v. IRS, 1 Gov't Disclosure Serv. (P-H) ¶ 80,232, at 80,580 (N.D. Ga. Aug. 22, 1980), aff'd in part, vacated & remanded in part, on other grounds, 665 F.2d 327 (11th Cir. 1982); cf. Armstrong, 608 F.3d at 857-60 (where agency employee had filed complaint triggering investigation of co-worker, sent letters disclosing information about investigation to another agency, and based letters in part on her initial complaint, explaining that "[t]he exception we suggested in Bartel does not extend to this case, in which [employee who disclosed information] neither acquired the information contained in her initial complaint in any way related to a record, as an investigator might have done, nor used the record in her work for the agency"); Cloonan, 768 F. Supp. 2d at 156, 165-67 (Bartel exception held "inapplicable" where plaintiff's supervisor, who had been "involved in several interagency complaints and proceedings" with plaintiff, disclosed information critical of plaintiff's performance because "[t]here is no evidence upon which the Court can conclude that any information [disclosed by supervisor] was learned by [supervisor] during the course of any investigation that he ordered, undertook or oversaw"); Doe v. U.S. Dep't of Treasury, 706 F. Supp. 2d at 8-9 (declining to apply Bartel exception where IRS employee disclosed information about investigation, which he had acquired from a press release and from his own involvement in investigation, because he did not "institute" investigation, did not have a "primary role in creating and using" the information, and did not acquire the information from a "record-related role"); Krieger v. DOJ, 529 F. Supp. 2d 29, 48 (D.D.C. 2008) (distinguishing Bartel, and finding no wrongful disclosures); Carlson v. GSA, No. 04-C-7937, 2006 WL 3409150, at *3-4 (N.D. Ill. Nov. 21, 2006) (supervisor's email detailing employee's settlement of his wrongful termination claims was a "'communication' of a protected 'record'" even though supervisor, who conducted investigation that resulted in the settlement, "compiled the email from his own memory"). But cf. Abernethy v. IRS, 909 F. Supp. 1562, 1570 (N.D. Ga. 1995) (holding that alleged statements made to other IRS employees that plaintiff was being investigated pertaining to allegations of EEO violations, assuming they were in fact made, did not violate the Act "because information allegedly disclosed was not actually retrieved from a system of records" even though individual alleged to have made such statements was same individual who ordered investigation), aff'd per curiam, No. 95-9489 (11th Cir. Feb. 13, 1997).

In particular, the Court of Appeals for the Ninth Circuit held that an Administrative Law Judge for the Department of Health and Human Services violated the Privacy Act when he stated in an opinion that one of the parties' attorneys had been placed on a Performance Improvement Plan (PIP) while he was employed at HHS – despite the fact that there was no actual retrieval by the ALJ – because, as the creator of the PIP, the ALJ had personal knowledge of the matter. Wilborn v. HHS, 49 F.3d 597, 600-02 (9th Cir. 1995). The Ninth Circuit noted the similarity of the facts to those of Bartel and held that "'independent knowledge,' gained by the creation of records, cannot be used to sidestep the Privacy Act." Id. at 601. Additionally, it rejected the lower court's reasoning that not only was there no retrieval, but there was no longer a record capable of being retrieved because as the result of a grievance action, all records relating to the PIP had been required to be expunged from the agency's records and in fact were expunged by the ALJ himself. Id. at 599-602. The Ninth Circuit found the district court's ruling "inconsistent with the spirit of the Privacy Act," and stated that the "fact that the agency ordered expungement of all information relating to the PIP makes the ALJ's disclosure, if anything, more rather than less objectionable." Id. at 602.

The Court of Appeals for the Eighth Circuit, however, has twice taken a narrow view of the "actual retrieval" standard. In a per curiam decision in Olberding v. U.S. Department of Defense, 709 F.2d 621 (8th Cir. 1983), the court ruled that information orally disclosed by a military psychiatrist to the plaintiff's commanding general, revealing the results of the plaintiff's examination – which had not yet been put in writing – was not retrieved from a "record." Id. at 621 (adopting reasoning of trial court, which found that the conversation took place before the report was written, 564 F. Supp. 907, 910 (S.D. Iowa 1982)). Subsequently, in Doe v. Department of Veterans Affairs, 519 F.3d 456 (8th Cir. 2008), the court ruled that there was no actual retrieval from a record where a VA physician revealed an employee's HIV status and marijuana use to a union representative because the physician recalled the information exclusively from discussions during employee's medical appointments, not from any subsequent review of his medical notes. Id. at 459-62. Although the court purported to distinguish Bartel and Wilborn, id. at 462-63, Judge Hanson stated in his concurring opinion that were he not bound by Olberding, he would adopt a

OVERVIEW OF THE PRIVACY ACT

"scrivener's exception" in order to "justify an exception to the general retrieval rule, particularly where 'a mechanical application of the rule would thwart, rather than advance, the purpose of the Privacy Act.'" Id. at 464-65 (quoting Wilborn, 49 F.3d at 600).

2. **Access and Amendment: Subsections (d)(1) and (d)(2)**

One of Congress's underlying concerns in narrowly defining a "system of records" appears to have been efficiency – i.e., a concern that any broader definition would require elaborate cross-references among records and/or burdensome hand-searches for records. See OMB Guidelines, 40 Fed. Reg. at 28,957, available at http://www.whitehouse.gov/sites/default/files/omb/assets/omb/inforeg/implementation_guidelines.pdf; see also Baker v. Dep't of the Navy, 814 F.2d 1381, 1385 (9th Cir. 1987); Carpenter v. IRS, 938 F. Supp. 521, 522-23 (S.D. Ind. 1996).

Consistent with OMB's guidance, numerous courts have held that, under subsection (d)(1), an individual has no Privacy Act right of access to his record if it is not indexed and retrieved by his name or personal identifier. See Bettersworth v. FDIC, 248 F.3d 386, 391-92 (5th Cir. 2001); Gowan v. U.S. Dep't of the Air Force, 148 F.3d 1182, 1191 (10th Cir. 1998); Williams v. VA, 104 F.3d 670, 673 (4th Cir. 1997); Henke v. U.S. Dep't of Commerce, 83 F.3d 1453, 1458-62 (D.C. Cir. 1996); Manuel v. VA Hosp., 857 F.2d 1112, 1116-17 (6th Cir. 1988); Baker, 814 F.2d at 1383-84; Cuccaro v. Sec'y of Labor, 770 F.2d 355, 360-61 (3d Cir. 1985); Wren v. Heckler, 744 F.2d 86, 89 (10th Cir. 1984); Augustus v. McHugh, No. 02-2545, 2011 WL 5841468, at *6-8 (D.D.C. Nov. 22, 2011); Jackson v. Shinseki, No. 10-cv-02596, 2011 WL 3568025, at *6 (D. Colo. Aug. 9, 2011); McCready v. Principi, 297 F. Supp. 2d 178, 188 (D.D.C. 2003), rev'd in part on other grounds sub nom. McCready v. Nicholson, 465 F.3d 1 (D.C. Cir. 2006); Springmann v. U.S. Dep't of State, No. 93-1238, slip op. at 9 n.2 (D.D.C. Apr. 21, 1997); Fuller v. IRS, No. 96-888, 1997 WL 191034, at *3-5 (W.D. Pa. Mar. 4, 1997); Carpenter, 938 F. Supp. at 522-23; Quinn v. HHS, 838 F. Supp. 70, 76 (W.D.N.Y. 1993); Shewchun v. U.S. Customs Serv., No. 87-2967, 1989 WL 7351, at *2 (D.D.C. Jan. 11, 1989); Bryant v. Dep't of the Air Force, No. 85-4096, slip op. at 4 (D.D.C. Mar. 31, 1986); Fagot v. FDIC, 584 F. Supp. 1168, 1174-75 (D.P.R. 1984), aff'd in part & rev'd in part, 760 F.2d 252 (1st Cir. 1985) (unpublished table decision); Grachow v. U.S. Customs Serv., 504 F. Supp. 632, 634-36 (D.D.C. 1980); Smiertka v. U.S. Dep't of the Treasury, 447 F. Supp. 221, 228 (D.D.C. 1978), remanded on other grounds, 604 F.2d 698

OVERVIEW OF THE PRIVACY ACT

(D.C. Cir. 1979); see also OMB Guidelines, 40 Fed. Reg. at 28,957 (giving examples).

Likewise, with regard to amendment, several courts have ruled that where an individual's record is being maintained allegedly in violation of subsection (e)(1) or (e)(5), the individual has no Privacy Act right to amend his record, under subsection (d)(2), if it is not indexed and retrieved by his name or personal identifier. See Baker, 814 F.2d at 1384-85 ("the scope of accessibility and the scope of amendment are coextensive"); Seldowitz v. Office of the IG of the U.S. Dep't of State, No. 99-1031, slip op. at 19-23 (E.D. Va. June 21, 2002), aff'd per curiam, 95 F. App'x 465 (4th Cir. 2004); Pototsky v. Dep't of the Navy, 717 F. Supp. 20, 22 (D. Mass. 1989) (following Baker), aff'd per curiam, 907 F.2d 142 (1st Cir. 1990) (unpublished table decision); see also Clarkson v. IRS, 678 F.2d 1368, 1376-77 (11th Cir. 1982) (although finding that subsections (e)(1) and (e)(5) apply only to records contained in a system of records, "find[ing] it both necessary and appropriate to construe the plain meaning of the language of subsections (d)(2) and (d)(3) to authorize the amendment or expungement of all records which are maintained in violation of subsection (e)(7)"). But cf., e.g., McCready v. Nicholson, 465 F.3d 1, 10-12 (D.C. Cir. 2006) (holding that subsection (g)(1)(C), the civil remedy provision for violations of subsection (e)(5), "applies to any record, and not [just] any record within a system of records" (internal quotation marks omitted)), discussed, below, under "Other Aspects."

However, with respect to access under subsection (d)(1), and amendment under subsection (d)(2), several courts have cautioned that an agency's purposeful filing of records in a non-name-retrieved format, in order to evade those provisions, will not be permitted. See, e.g., Pototsky v. Dep't of the Navy, No. 89-1891, slip op. at 2 (1st Cir. Apr. 3, 1990) (per curiam); Baker, 814 F.2d at 1385; Kalmin v. Dep't of the Navy, 605 F. Supp. 1492, 1495 n.5 (D.D.C. 1985); see also Manuel, 857 F.2d at 1120 ("The Court does not want to give a signal to federal agencies that they should evade their responsibility to place records within their 'system of records' in violation of the [Act].").

Following the rationale of the Fifth Circuit Court of Appeals in Chapman v. NASA, 682 F.2d 526, 529 (5th Cir. 1982), several courts have recognized a subsection (e)(5) duty to incorporate records into a system of records (thus making them subject to access and amendment) where such records are used by the agency in taking an adverse action against the individual. See MacDonald v. VA, No.

87-544-CIV-T-15A, slip op. at 2-5 (M.D. Fla. Feb. 8, 1988); Lawrence v. Dole, No. 83-2876, slip op. at 5-6 (D.D.C. Dec. 12, 1985); Waldrop v. U.S. Dep't of the Air Force, 3 Gov't Disclosure Serv. (P-H) ¶ 83,016, at 83,453 (S.D. Ill. Aug. 5, 1981); Nelson v. EEOC, No. 83-C-983, slip op. at 6-11 (E.D. Wis. Feb. 14, 1984); cf. Manuel, 857 F.2d at 1117-19 (no duty to place records within system of records where records "are not part of an official agency investigation into activities of the individual requesting the records, and where the records requested do not have an adverse effect on the individual"). But cf. Horowitz v. Peace Corps, 428 F.3d. 271, 280-81 (D.C. Cir. 2005) (denying plaintiff access to draft Administrative Separation Report (ASR) that was not in "system of records" where "Peace Corps's regulations dictate that an ASR should not be maintained in the agency's records if a volunteer resigns prior to an official decision to administratively separate him" and "the Peace Corps's manual states that an ASR should not even be completed if a volunteer resigns before such a decision is made" and since plaintiff "resigned before any final decision was made, the report was never completed and pursuant to the procedure specified by the manual was not maintained in the Peace Corps's official files"; "[n]or has [plaintiff] shown that [the agency] nevertheless placed the draft ASR in a 'system of records'" as the draft ASR was stored in Peace Corps's Country Director's safe and plaintiff "has not shown that files in the safe are, in practice, retrieved by individuals' names"); Gowan v. Dep't of the Air Force, No. 90-94, slip op. at 7, 11, 13, 16, 30, 33 (D.N.M. Sept. 1, 1995) (although ultimately finding access claim moot, stating that "personal notes and legal research" in file "marked 'Ethics'" that was originally kept in desk of Deputy Staff Judge Advocate but that was later given to Criminal Military Justice Section and used in connection with court martial hearing were not in system of records for purposes of either Privacy Act access or accuracy lawsuit for damages), aff'd, 148 F.3d 1182, 1191 (10th Cir. 1998) (concluding that "the word 'Ethics' was not a personal identifier" and stating that it did "not find the district court's rulings regarding those documents to be clearly erroneous").

3. **Other Aspects**

The "system of records" threshold requirement is not necessarily applicable to all subsections of the Act. See OMB Guidelines, 40 Fed. Reg. at 28,952, available at http://www.whitehouse.gov/sites/default/files/omb/assets/omb/inforeg/implementation_guidelines.pdf (system of records definition "limits the applicability of some of the provisions of the Act") (emphasis added). But see Privacy

OVERVIEW OF THE PRIVACY ACT

Commission Report at 503-04, available at http://epic.org/privacy/ppsc1977report (assuming that definition limits entire Act); cf. Henke v. U.S. Dep't of Commerce, 83 F.3d 1453, 1459 (D.C. Cir. 1996) ("[T]he determination that a system of records exists triggers virtually all of the other substantive provisions of the Privacy Act."); McCready v. Principi, 297 F. Supp. 2d 178, 185 (D.D.C. 2003) ("For almost all circumstances, the Act extends only to those records that are in a 'system of records' which is a specific term of art."), aff'd in part & rev'd in part sub nom. McCready v. Nicholson, 465 F.3d 1 (D.C. Cir. 2006).

Primarily, in Albright v. United States, 631 F.2d 915, 918-20 (D.C. Cir. 1980), the Court of Appeals for the District of Columbia Circuit held that subsection (e)(7) – which restricts agencies from maintaining records describing how an individual exercises his First Amendment rights – applies even to records not incorporated into a system of records. Albright involved a challenge on subsection (e)(7) grounds to an agency's maintenance of a videotape – kept in a file cabinet in an envelope that was not labeled by any individual's name – of a meeting between a personnel officer and agency employees affected by the officer's job reclassification decision. Id. at 918. Relying on both the broad definition of "maintain," 5 U.S.C. § 552a(a)(3), and the "special and sensitive treatment accorded First Amendment rights," the D.C. Circuit held that the mere collection of a record regarding those rights could be a violation of subsection (e)(7), regardless of whether the record was contained in a system of records retrieved by an individual's name or personal identifier. Id. at 919-20; see also Maydak v. United States, 363 F.3d 512, 516, 518-19 (D.C. Cir. 2004) (reaffirming holding in Albright).

Albright's broad construction of subsection (e)(7) has been adopted by several other courts. See MacPherson v. IRS, 803 F.2d 479, 481 (9th Cir. 1986); Boyd v. Sec'y of the Navy, 709 F.2d 684, 687 (11th Cir. 1983); Clarkson, 678 F.2d at 1373-77; Fagot, 584 F. Supp. at 1175; Gerlich v. DOJ, 659 F. Supp. 2d 1, 13-15 (D.D.C. 2009). Further, the Court of Appeals for the Eleventh Circuit in Clarkson, 678 F.2d at 1375-77, held that, at least with respect to alleged violations of subsection (e)(7), the Act's amendment provision (subsection (d)(2)) also can apply to a record not incorporated into a system of records. However, Judge Tjoflat's concurring opinion in Clarkson intimated that something more than a bare allegation of a subsection (e)(7) violation would be necessary in order for an agency to be obligated to search beyond its systems of records for potentially offensive materials. Id. at 1378-79.

OVERVIEW OF THE PRIVACY ACT

In <u>McCready v. Nicholson</u>, 465 F.3d 1, 10-12 (D.C. Cir. 2006), the D.C. Circuit went even further and held that the terms of subsection (g)(1)(C) – the judicial remedy provision for subsection (e)(5) violations – "[do] not incorporate or otherwise refer to the Act's definition of a 'system of records' found in § 552a(a)(5)." The Court of Appeals stated that the "distinction between a claim that requires a system of records and a claim under § 552a(g)(1)(C) that does not require a system of records makes perfect sense." <u>Id.</u> Unlike other types of Privacy Act claims, which are shielded by the system of records definition in order to avoid "costly fishing expeditions," the Court of Appeals reasoned, subsection (g)(1)(C) claims do not implicate "[t]his legitimate concern with preserving an agency's resources" because "an individual and an agency already have identified the record at issue, that record is therefore easily retrieved, and the only issue is the accuracy of the record." <u>Id.</u> <u>See also</u> <u>Gerlich</u>, 659 F. Supp. 2d at 15-16 (relying on <u>McCready v. Nicholson</u> to conclude that the system of records requirement did not apply to plaintiffs' claim under subsections (e)(5) and (g)(1)(C)).

Some district courts have similarly extended the coverage of other Privacy Act provisions to records that are not maintained in a system of records. <u>See</u> <u>Connelly v. Comptroller of the Currency</u>, 673 F. Supp. 1419, 1424 (S.D. Tex. 1987) (construing "any record" language contained in 5 U.S.C. § 552a(g)(1)(C) to permit a damages action arising from an allegedly inaccurate record that was not incorporated into a system of records), <u>rev'd on other grounds</u>, 876 F.2d 1209 (5th Cir. 1989); <u>Reuber v. United States</u>, No. 81-1857, slip op. at 5 (D.D.C. Oct. 27, 1982) (relying on <u>Albright</u> for proposition that subsections (d)(2), (e)(1)-(2), (e)(5)-(7), and (e)(10) all apply to a record not incorporated into a system of records), <u>partial summary judgment denied</u> (D.D.C. Aug. 15, 1983), <u>partial summary judgment granted</u> (D.D.C. Apr. 13, 1984), <u>subsequent decision</u> (D.D.C. Sept. 6, 1984), <u>aff'd on other grounds</u>, 829 F.2d 133 (D.C. Cir. 1987); <u>cf.</u> <u>Fiorella v. HEW</u>, 2 Gov't Disclosure Serv. (P-H) ¶ 81,363, at 81,946 n.1 (W.D. Wash. Mar. 9, 1981) (noting that subsections (e)(5) and (e)(7) "are parallel in structure and would seem to require the same statutory construction").

However, the Court of Appeals for the District of Columbia Circuit has declined to extend the holding in <u>Albright</u> to certain other subsections of § 552a(e). <u>See</u> <u>Maydak v. United States</u>, 363 F.3d 512, 517-19 (D.C. Cir. 2004). In <u>Maydak</u>, the Court of Appeals held that in accordance with the OMB Guidelines, the requirements contained in subsections (e)(1), (2), (3), and (10) are "triggered only

OVERVIEW OF THE PRIVACY ACT

if the records are actually incorporated into a system of records." Id. The D.C. Circuit explained that it reached a different conclusion as to subsection (e)(7) in Albright because of "'Congress'[s] own special concern for the protection of First Amendment rights,'" id. at 518 (quoting Albright, 631 F.2d at 919), and it went on to state that "at least in comparison to the other subsections at issue, subsection 552a(e)(7) proves the exception rather than the rule," id. at 519. See also Augustus v. McHugh, No. 02-2545, 2011 WL 5841468, at *8-10 (D.D.C. Nov. 22, 2011) (rejecting claims alleging violations of subsections (e)(2), (e)(4), and (e)(10), and Army regulations implementing (e)(3), because plaintiff failed to show that records at issue were contained in system of records); Gerlich, 659 F. Supp. 2d at 16 ("[S]ubsections (e)(1), (e)(2), (e)(6), (e)(9), and (e)(10) . . . only apply to records that are contained within a 'system of records.'"); Krieger v. DOJ, 529 F. Supp. 2d 29, 50-56 (D.D.C. 2008) (finding that subsections (e)(1), (4), (6), (9), and (10) apply only to records contained in a system of records); cf. Thompson v. Dep't of State, No. 03-2227, 400 F. Supp. 1, 12 (D.D.C. 2005) (following Maydak and observing that "[i]t is not at all clear that subsection (e)(2) applies where the requested information never becomes part of [the] system"), aff'd 210 F. App'x 5 (D.C. Cir. 2006).

Other courts have also declined to follow Albright and have limited the applicability of the Privacy Act requirements that are contained in subsections other than (e)(7) to records that are maintained in a system of records. See, e.g., Gowan v. U.S. Dep't of the Air Force, 148 F.3d 1182, 1192 (10th Cir. 1998) (holding that appellant "ha[d] no § 552a(e)(5) cause of action" for maintenance of report that was not maintained in system of records); Clarkson, 678 F.2d at 1377 (declining to extend Albright rationale to subsections (e)(1) and (e)(5)); Bettersworth v. FDIC, No. A-97-CA-624, slip op. at 10 (W.D. Tex. Feb. 1, 2000) (magistrate's recommendation) (recognizing holding in Connelly, but noting that both subsections (d)(1) and (g)(1)(C) contain same "system of records" language, and stating that court is "unpersuaded that Congress intended any other meaning than what has previously been applied"), adopted (W.D. Tex. Feb. 17, 2000), aff'd on other grounds, 248 F.3d 386 (5th Cir. 2001); Felsen v. HHS, No. CCB-95-975, slip op. at 61-62, 65 (D. Md. Sept. 30, 1998) (granting defendants summary judgment on alternative ground that subsection (e)(2) is inapplicable to records not included in system of records); Barhorst, 765 F. Supp. at 999-1000 (dismissing, on alternative grounds, Privacy Act claims under subsections (b), (e)(1)-(3), (e)(5)-(6), and (e)(10) because of finding that information was not in system of records; information was

OVERVIEW OF THE PRIVACY ACT

retrieved by job announcement number, not by name or other identifying particular).

Albright and its progeny establish that the "system of records" limitation on the scope of the Act is not uniformly applicable to all of the statute's subsections. As is apparent from the above discussion, there has been some uncertainty about which particular subsections of the statute are limited to records contained in a "system of records."

CONDITIONS OF DISCLOSURE TO THIRD PARTIES

A. The "No Disclosure Without Consent" Rule

"No agency shall disclose any record which is contained in a system of records by any means of communication to any person, or to another agency, except pursuant to a written request by, or with the prior written consent of, the individual to whom the record pertains [subject to 12 exceptions]." 5 U.S.C. § 552a(b).

Comment:

A "disclosure" can be by any means of communication – written, oral, electronic, or mechanical. See OMB Guidelines, 40 Fed. Reg. 28,948, 28,953 (July 9, 1975), available at http://www.whitehouse.gov/sites/default/files/omb/assets/omb/inforeg/implementation_guidelines.pdf; see also, e.g., Speaker v. HHS Ctrs. for Disease Control & Prevention, 623 F.3d 1371, 1382 n.11 (11th Cir. 2010) ("Numerous courts have held that the Privacy Act protects against improper oral disclosures."); Jacobs v. Nat'l Drug Intelligence Ctr., 423 F.3d 512, 517-19 (5th Cir. 2005) (rejecting argument that "the [Privacy Act] only protects against the disclosure of a physical document that is contained in a system of records" and holding that "damaging information . . . taken from a protected record and inserted into a new document, which was then disclosed without the plaintiff's consent," violated subsection (b) because "the new document is also a protected record"); Orekoya v. Mooney, 330 F.3d 1, 6 (1st Cir. 2003) ("The Privacy Act prohibits more than dissemination of records themselves, but also 'nonconsensual disclosure of any information that has been retrieved from a protected record.'" (quoting Bartel v. FAA, 725 F.2d at 1408)); Cloonan v. Holder, 768 F. Supp. 2d 154, 163 (D.D.C. 2011) ("[T]he Privacy Act goes beyond the mere dissemination of the physical records to prohibit 'nonconsensual disclosure of any information that has been retrieved from a protected record.'" (quoting Bartel v. FAA, 725 F.2d at 1408)); Chang v. Dep't of the Navy, 314 F. Supp. 2d 35, 41 n.2 (D.D.C. 2004) ("[D]isclosure

OVERVIEW OF THE PRIVACY ACT

encompasses release of the contents of a record 'by any means of communication,' 5 U.S.C. § 552a(b), and not just 'the mere physical dissemination of records (or copies).'" (quoting Bartel, 725 F.2d at 1408)). Further, disclosure under the Privacy Act "may be either the transfer of a record or the granting of access to a record." OMB Guidelines, 40 Fed. Reg. 28948, 28953 (July 9, 1975), available at http://www.whitehouse.gov/sites/default/files/omb/assets/omb/inforeg/implementation_guidelines.pdf; see also Wilkerson v. Shinseki, 606 F.3d 1256, 1268 (10th Cir. 2010) (interpreting disclosure under the Privacy Act "liberally to include not only the physical disclosure of the records, but also the accessing of private records").

A plaintiff has the burden of demonstrating that a disclosure by the agency has occurred. See, e.g., Askew v. United States, 680 F.2d 1206, 1209-11 (8th Cir. 1982); Zerilli v. Smith, 656 F.2d 705, 715-16 (D.C. Cir. 1981); cf. Luster v. Vilsack, 667 F.3d 1089, 1097-98 (10th Cir. 2011) (rejecting appellant's contention that "mere transmission of the documents to a fax machine at which unauthorized persons might have viewed the documents constitutes a prohibited disclosure"; affirming district court's ruling that appellant "failed to establish a prohibited disclosure"; and stating: "As the district court noted, [appellant] cites 'no authority to suggest that the possibility that a record might be revealed to unauthorized readers by negligent or reckless transmission is sufficient to constitute a prohibited disclosure under the Act,' . . . nor have we found any authority so holding."); Whyde v. Rockwell Int'l Corp., 101 F. App'x 997, 1000 (6th Cir. 2004) (holding that "the fact that [a company] somehow came into possession of documents that might have been included in plaintiff's personnel file . . . gives rise only to a metaphysical doubt as to the existence of a genuine issue of material fact" and that "[u]nder the circumstances, the district court properly granted summary judgment for the [agency]"); Brown v. Snow, 94 F. App'x 369, at *3 (7th Cir. 2004) (ruling that district court grant of summary judgment was proper where no evidence was found that record was disclosed, and stating that "burden is on the plaintiff at the summary judgment stage to come forward with specific evidence"); Lennon v. Rubin, 166 F.3d 6, 10-11 (1st Cir. 1999) (where agency employee testified that, despite memorandum indicating otherwise, she had disclosed information only within agency, and where plaintiff responded that whether his file was reviewed by other individuals is question of fact he "want[ed] decided by a fact finder, 'not an affidavit,'" stating that such "arguments misapprehend [plaintiff's] burden at the summary judgment stage"); Russell v. Potter, No. 3:08-CV-2272, 2011 WL 1375165, at *9 (N.D. Tex. Mar. 4, 2011) (holding that plaintiff cannot prove a disclosure violation where "the only agency involved, the Postal Service, received rather than 'disclosed' the information in question"); Collins v. FBI, No. 10-cv-03470, 2011 WL 1627025, at *7

OVERVIEW OF THE PRIVACY ACT

(D.N.J. Apr. 28, 2011) (dismissing claim and stating that plaintiff's "conclusory allegations" of unlawful disclosure, "without identifying or describing who acted against Plaintiff or what the person did, is insufficient"); Roggio v. FBI, No. 08-4991, 2009 WL 2460780, at *2 (D.N.J. Aug. 11, 2009) (concluding that plaintiffs "fail[ed] to allege sufficient facts supporting that the FBI, as opposed to some other law enforcement body, disclosed [one plaintiff's] rap sheet" on the Internet, where plaintiffs "base[d] their allegation on . . . the mere fact that [a particular Internet] posting contained some expunged information"), reconsideration denied, No. 08-4991, 2009 WL 2634631 (D.N.J. Aug. 26, 2009); Walia v. Chertoff, No. 06-cv-6587, 2008 WL 5246014, at *11 (E.D.N.Y. Dec. 17, 2008) (concluding that plaintiff failed to make out a prima facie case under subsection (b) of the Privacy Act because plaintiff alleged merely that records were accessible to other individuals in an office, rather than that they were actually disclosed); Buckles v. Indian Health Serv., 310 F. Supp. 2d 1060, 1068 (Mar. 3, 2004) (finding that plaintiffs failed to "prove, by preponderance of the evidence, that IHS disclosed protected information" where plaintiffs did not "have personal knowledge that [the memorandum was disclosed]" and witnesses at trial denied disclosing or receiving memorandum); Meldrum v. USPS, No. 5:97CV1482, slip op. at 11 (N.D. Ohio Jan. 21, 1999) (finding lack of evidence that disclosure occurred where plaintiff alleged that, among other things, file had been left in unsecured file cabinet), aff'd per curiam, No. 99-3397, 2000 WL 1477495, at *2 (6th Cir. Sept. 25, 2000). But cf. Speaker, 623 F.3d at 1386 (finding plaintiff's complaint sufficient to survive summary judgment because he "need not prove his case on the pleadings" but rather "must merely provide enough factual material to raise a reasonable inference, and thus a plausible claim, that the CDC was the source of the disclosures"); Ciralsky v. CIA, 689 F. Supp. 2d 141, 156-57 (D.D.C. 2010) (concluding that the plaintiff's allegation of CIA disclosure to unidentified government officials, who were unrelated to the handling of plaintiff's case, was "not unacceptably vague" and need not include identities of alleged recipients for CIA to "understand Plaintiff's charge"); Tolbert-Smith v. Chu, 714 F. Supp. 2d 37, 43 (D.D.C. 2010) (ruling that plaintiff had stated a claim for relief under the Privacy Act where plaintiff "pled that a member of [agency] management placed records referring and relating to her disability on a server accessible by other federal employees and members of the public").

One district court has concluded that when an agency destroys evidence in order to undermine the plaintiff's ability to prove that a disclosure occurred, there will be an adverse inference against the agency. See Beaven v. DOJ, No. 03-84, 2007 WL 1032301, at *17 (E.D. Ky. Mar. 30, 2007) ("whether by use of adverse inference" or "by a preponderance of the evidence" showing that "the officials who inspected the folder found evidence that an

OVERVIEW OF THE PRIVACY ACT

inmate had tampered with it," finding that a "disclosure" occurred and concluding, therefore, that agency violated the Privacy Act), aff'd in part, rev'd in part & remanded, on other grounds, 622 F.3d 540 (6th Cir. 2010).

It has frequently been held that a "disclosure" under the Privacy Act does not occur if the communication is to a person who is already aware of the information. See, e.g., Quinn v. Stone, 978 F.2d 126, 134 (3d Cir. 1992) (dictum); Kline v. HHS, 927 F.2d 522, 524 (10th Cir. 1991); Hollis v. U.S. Dep't of the Army, 856 F.2d 1541, 1545 (D.C. Cir. 1988); Reyes v. DEA, 834 F.2d 1093, 1096 n.1 (1st Cir. 1987); Schowengerdt v. Gen. Dynamics Corp., 823 F.2d 1328, 1341 (9th Cir. 1987); Pellerin v. VA, 790 F.2d 1553, 1556 (11th Cir. 1986); FDIC v. Dye, 642 F.2d 833, 836 (5th Cir. 1981); Ash v. United States, 608 F.2d 178, 179 (5th Cir. 1979); Barry v. DOJ, 63 F. Supp. 2d 25, 26-28 (D.D.C. 1999); Sullivan v. USPS, 944 F. Supp. 191, 196 (W.D.N.Y. 1996); Viotti v. U.S. Air Force, 902 F. Supp. 1331, 1337 (D. Colo. 1995), aff'd, 153 F.3d 730 (10th Cir. 1998) (unpublished table decision); Abernethy v. IRS, 909 F. Supp. 1562, 1571 (N.D. Ga. 1995), aff'd per curiam, No. 95-9489 (11th Cir. Feb. 13, 1997); Kassel v. VA, 709 F. Supp. 1194, 1201 (D.N.H. 1989); Krowitz v. USDA, 641 F. Supp. 1536, 1545 (W.D. Mich. 1986), aff'd, 826 F.2d 1063 (6th Cir. 1987) (unpublished table decision); Golliher v. USPS, 3 Gov't Disclosure Serv. ¶ 83,114, at 83,702 (N.D. Ohio June 10, 1982); King v. Califano, 471 F. Supp. 180, 181 (D.D.C. 1979); Harper v. United States, 423 F. Supp. 192, 197 (D.S.C. 1976); see also Hoffman v. Rubin, 193 F.3d 959, 966 (8th Cir. 1999) (no Privacy Act violation found where agency disclosed same information in letter to journalist that plaintiff himself had previously provided to journalist; plaintiff "waiv[ed], in effect, his protection under the Privacy Act"); Mudd v. U.S. Army, No. 2:05-cv-137, 2007 WL 4358262, at *5 (M.D. Fla. Dec. 10, 2007) (finding no "disclosure" where agency posted statement of admonishment of plaintiff on its Web site because by time of posting, plaintiff had been quoted in newspaper as saying he received letter of admonishment, another newspaper article had referred to letter, and plaintiff had testified before Congress regarding letter; also finding no "disclosure" of report where agency provided link to report on its Web site because "at the time the [agency's] link was provided, the entire [report] had been the subject of a press release and news conference by a separate and independent agency . . . and had been released to the media by the same"); Schmidt v. VA, 218 F.R.D. 619, 630 (E.D. Wis. 2003) ("defin[ing] the term 'disclose' to mean the placing into the view of another information which was previously unknown"); Loma Linda Cmty. Hosp. v. Shalala, 907 F. Supp. 1399, 1404-05 (C.D. Cal. 1995) (policy underlying Privacy Act of protecting confidential information from disclosure not implicated by release of information health care provider had already received through patients' California "Medi-Cal" cards); Owens v. MSPB, No. 3-83-0449-R, slip op. at

OVERVIEW OF THE PRIVACY ACT

2-3 (N.D. Tex. Sept. 14, 1983) (mailing of agency decision affirming employee's removal to his former attorney held not a "disclosure" as "attorney was familiar with facts of [employee's] claim" and "no new information was disclosed to him"); cf. Pippinger v. Rubin, 129 F.3d 519, 532-33 (10th Cir. 1997) (finding no evidence that disclosure "could possibly have had 'an adverse effect'" on plaintiff where recipient "had been privy to every event described in [plaintiff's] records at the time the event occurred"); Leighton v. CIA, 412 F. Supp. 2d 30, 39 (D.D.C. 2006) (citing Hollis and expressing doubt as to whether the disclosure at issue "has presented any new information to those in the intelligence community"); Jones v. Runyon, 32 F. Supp. 2d 873, 876 (N.D. W. Va. 1998) (although finding disclosure to credit reporting service valid under routine use exception, stating further that information disclosed was already in possession of recipient and that other courts had held that Privacy Act is not violated in such cases), aff'd, 173 F.3d 850 (4th Cir. 1999) (unpublished table decision).

However, the Court of Appeals for the District of Columbia Circuit clarified that this principle does not apply to all disseminations of protected records to individuals with prior knowledge of their existence or contents. Pilon v. DOJ, 73 F.3d 1111, 1117-24 (D.C. Cir. 1996). In Pilon, the D.C. Circuit held that the Justice Department's transmission of a Privacy Act-protected record to a former employee of the agency constituted a "disclosure" under the Privacy Act, even though the recipient had come "into contact with the [record] in the course of his duties" while an employee. Id. The court's "review of the Privacy Act's purposes, legislative history, and integrated structure convince[d it] that Congress intended the term 'disclose' to apply in virtually all instances to an agency's unauthorized transmission of a protected record, regardless of the recipient's prior familiarity with it." Id. at 1124.

In an earlier case, Hollis v. U.S. Department of the Army, 856 F.2d 1541 (D.C. Cir. 1988), the D.C. Circuit had held that the release of a summary of individual child-support payments previously deducted from plaintiff's salary and sent directly to his ex-wife, who had requested it for use in pending litigation, was not an unlawful disclosure under the Privacy Act as she, being the designated recipient of the child-support payments, already knew what had been remitted to her. Id. at 1545. In Pilon, the D.C. Circuit reconciled its opinion in Hollis by "declin[ing] to extend Hollis beyond the limited factual circumstances that gave rise to it," 73 F.3d at 1112, 1124, and holding that:

> [A]n agency's unauthorized release of a protected record does constitute a disclosure under the Privacy Act except

[56]

in those rare instances, like Hollis, where the record merely reflects information that the agency has previously, and lawfully, disseminated outside the agency to the recipient, who is fully able to reconstruct its material contents.

Id. at 1124; cf. Osborne v. USPS, No. 94-30353, slip op. at 2-4, 6-11 (N.D. Fla. May 18, 1995) (assuming without discussion that disclosure of plaintiff's injury-compensation file to retired employee who had prepared file constituted "disclosure" for purposes of Privacy Act).

Whether the disclosure of information that is readily accessible to the public constitutes a "disclosure" under the Privacy Act is an issue that has been decided differently by the courts that have considered it. A few courts have extended the principle that there is no "disclosure" to rule that the release of previously published or publicly available information is not a Privacy Act "disclosure" – regardless of whether the particular persons who received the information were aware of the previous publication. See FDIC v. Dye, 642 F.2d at 836; Lee v. Dearment, No. 91-2175, 1992 WL 119855, at *2 (4th Cir. June 3, 1992); Banks v. Butler, No. 5:08cv336, 2010 WL 4537902, at *6 (S.D. Miss. Sept. 23, 2010); Drennon-Gala v. Holder, No. 1:08-CV0321G, 2011 WL 1225784, at *8 (N.D. Ga. Mar. 30, 2011); Smith v. Cont'l Assurance Co., No. 91-C-0963, 1991 WL 164348, at *5 (N.D. Ill. Aug. 22, 1991); Friedlander v. USPS, No. 84-0773, slip op. at 8 (D.D.C. Oct. 16, 1984); King, 471 F. Supp. at 181; cf. Sierra Pac. Indus. v. USDA, No. 11-1250, 2012 WL 245973, at *4 (E.D. Cal. Jan. 25, 2012) (finding that the Privacy Act did not require it to seal documents where "substance of the information . . . [was] already in the public record in one form or another"). Other courts, however, have held that the release of information that is "merely readily accessible to the public" does constitute a disclosure under subsection (b). See, e.g., Quinn v. Stone, 978 F.2d 126, 134 (3d Cir. 1992); see also Gowan v. U.S. Dep't of the Air Force, 148 F.3d 1182, 1193 (10th Cir. 1998) ("adopt[ing] the Third Circuit's reasoning [in Quinn] and hold[ing] that an agency may not defend a release of Privacy Act information simply by stating that the information is a matter of public record"); Scarborough v. Harvey, 493 F. Supp. 2d 1, 15-16 n.29 (D.D.C. 2007) (agreeing with Quinn and concluding that "the unqualified language of the Privacy Act," which protects an individual's "criminal . . . history," does not exclude information that is readily accessible to the public); cf. Wright v. FBI, 241 F. App'x 367, 369 (9th Cir. 2007) (noting that "the issue of whether a Privacy Act claim can be based on a defendant's disclosure of information previously disclosed to the public is a matter of first impression both in this Circuit and in the Seventh Circuit, where the underlying action is pending," and directing district court to stay proceedings until plaintiff

OVERVIEW OF THE PRIVACY ACT

"obtains from the district court . . . an order defining the scope of his claims and, potentially, stating that court's position on whether the Privacy Act applies to information previously disclosed to the public"); Doe v. Herman, No. 297CV00043, 1999 WL 1000212, at *11 (W.D. Va. Oct. 29, 1999) (magistrate's recommendation) (agreeing with Quinn in dictum), adopted in pertinent part & rev'd in other part (W.D. Va. July 24, 2000), aff'd in part, rev'd in part, & remanded, on other grounds sub nom. Doe v. Chao, 306 F.3d 170 (4th Cir. 2002), aff'd, 540 U.S. 614 (2004); Pilon v. DOJ, 796 F. Supp. 7, 11-12 (D.D.C. 1992) (rejecting argument that information was already public and therefore could not violate Privacy Act where agency had republished statement that was previously publicly disavowed as false by agency).

The D.C. Circuit's opinions in Hollis and Pilon, both discussed above, provide some insight into its view of this issue. In Hollis, the D.C. Circuit had recognized in dictum that other courts had held that the release of previously published material did not constitute a disclosure, and perhaps had indicated a willingness to go that far. Hollis, 856 F.2d at 1545 (holding that a disclosure did not violate the Privacy Act because the recipient of the information already was aware of it, but stating that "[o]ther courts have echoed the sentiment that when a release consists merely of information to which the general public already has access, or which the recipient of the release already knows, the Privacy Act is not violated"). However, the D.C. Circuit's subsequent holding in Pilon appears to foreclose such a possibility. In Pilon, the D.C. Circuit further held that even under the narrow Hollis interpretation of "disclose," the agency would not be entitled to summary judgment because it had "failed to adduce sufficient evidence that [the recipient of the record] remembered and could reconstruct the document's material contents in detail at the time he received it." 73 F.3d at 1124-26. Nevertheless, the D.C. Circuit in Pilon noted that "[t]his case does not present the question of whether an agency may . . . release a document that has already been fully aired in the public domain through the press or some other means" but that "the Privacy Act approves those disclosures that are 'required' under the [FOIA] . . . and that under various FOIA exemptions, prior publication is a factor to be considered in determining whether a document properly is to be released." Id. at 1123 n.10; see also Barry v. DOJ, 63 F. Supp. 2d 25, 27-28 (D.D.C. 1999) (distinguishing Pilon and finding no disclosure where agency posted Inspector General report on Internet Web site, after report had already been fully released to media by Congress and had been discussed in public congressional hearing, even though some Internet users might encounter report for first time on Web site). Furthermore, though, and consistent with the D.C. Circuit's note in Pilon, one might argue that to say that no "disclosure" occurs for previously published or public information is at least somewhat inconsistent with the

OVERVIEW OF THE PRIVACY ACT

Supreme Court's decision in U.S. Department of Justice v. Reporters Committee for Freedom of the Press, 489 U.S 749, 762-71 (1989), which held that a privacy interest can exist, under the FOIA, in publicly available – but "practically obscure" – information, such as a criminal history record. Cf. Finley v. NEA, 795 F. Supp. 1457, 1468 (C.D. Cal. 1992) (alleged disclosure of publicly available information states claim for relief under Privacy Act; recognizing Reporters Committee).

On a related point, the Court of Appeals for the Ninth Circuit held in a subsection (b) case that the single publication rule applies with respect to continuous postings of information on an agency's Web site. See Oja v. U.S. Army Corp. of Engineers, 440 F.3d 1122, 1130-33 (9th Cir. 2006) (holding that agency's continuous posting of personal information was one disclosure for Privacy Act purposes rather than separate disclosures giving rise to separate causes of action). However, the Court of Appeals ruled that with regard to "the same private information at a different URL address [within the same Web site] . . . that disclosure constitutes a separate and distinct publication – one not foreclosed by the single publication rule – and [the agency] might be liable for a separate violation of the Privacy Act." Id. at 1133-34.

The legislative history indicates that "a court is not defined as an 'agency' nor is it intended to be a 'person' for purposes of [the Privacy Act]," and that the Act was "not designed to interfere with access to information by the courts." 120 Cong. Rec. 36,967 (1974), reprinted in Source Book at 958-59, available at http://www.loc.gov/rr/frd/Military_Law/pdf/LH_privacy_act-1974.pdf. However, the public filing of records with a court, during the course of litigation, does constitute a subsection (b) disclosure. See Laningham v. U.S. Navy, No. 83-3238, slip op. at 2-3 (D.D.C. Sept. 25, 1984), summary judgment granted (D.D.C. Jan. 7, 1985), aff'd per curiam, 813 F.2d 1236 (D.C. Cir. 1987); Citizens Bureau of Investigation v. FBI, No. 78-60, slip op. at 2-3 (N.D. Ohio Dec. 14, 1979). Accordingly, any such public filing must be undertaken with written consent or in accordance with either the subsection (b)(3) routine use exception or the subsection (b)(11) court order exception, both discussed below. See generally Krohn v. DOJ, No. 78-1536, slip op. at 3-11 (D.D.C. Mar. 19, 1984) (finding violation of Privacy Act where agency's disclosure of records as attachments to affidavit in FOIA lawsuit "did not fall within any of the exceptions listed in Section 552a"), reconsideration granted & vacated in nonpertinent part (D.D.C. Nov. 29, 1984) (discussed below).

Often during the course of litigation, an agency will be asked to produce Privacy Act-protected information pursuant to a discovery request by an opposing party. An agency in receipt of such a request must object on the

OVERVIEW OF THE PRIVACY ACT

ground that the Privacy Act prohibits disclosure. See Golez v. Potter, No. 09-cv-965, 2011 WL 6002612, at *1-2 (S.D. Cal. Nov. 29, 2011) ("The exceptions allowed in the Privacy Act of 1974 are not applicable here. . . . Accordingly, the Privacy Act . . . precludes the [agency] from complying with Plaintiff's discovery request."); Johnson v. United States, No. C 10-00647, 2011 WL 2709871, at *3 (N.D. Cal. July 12, 2011) (ruling that "medical records of non-parties are not discoverable absent the written permission of those individuals" in accordance with 5 U.S.C. § 552a(b)). Although courts have unanimously held that the Privacy Act does not create a discovery privilege, see Laxalt v. McClatchy, 809 F.2d 885, 888-90 (D.C. Cir. 1987); Weahkee v. Norton, 621 F.2d 1080, 1082 (10th Cir. 1980); Ala. & Gulf Coast Ry. v. United States, No. CA 10-0352, 2011 WL 1838882, at *3 (S.D. Ala. May 13, 2011); Forrest v. United States, No. 95-3889, 1996 WL 171539, at *2 (E.D. Pa. Apr. 11, 1996); Ford Motor Co. v. United States, 825 F. Supp. 1081, 1083 (Ct. Int'l Trade 1993); Clavir v. United States, 84 F.R.D. 612, 614 (S.D.N.Y. 1979); cf. Baldrige v. Shapiro, 455 U.S. 345, 360-62 (1982) (Census Act confidentiality provisions constitute privilege because they "embody explicit congressional intent to preclude all disclosure"), an agency can disclose Privacy Act-protected records only as permitted by the Act. The most appropriate method of disclosure in this situation is pursuant to a subsection (b)(11) court order. See generally Doe v. DiGenova, 779 F.2d 74 (D.C. Cir. 1985); Doe v. Stephens, 851 F.2d 1457 (D.C. Cir. 1988) (both discussed below under subsection (b)(11)). Indeed, the courts that have rejected the Privacy Act as a discovery privilege have pointed to subsection (b)(11)'s allowance for court-ordered disclosures in support of their holdings. See Laxalt, 809 F.2d at 888-89; Weahkee, 621 F.2d at 1082; Hernandez v. United States, No. 97-3367, 1998 WL 230200, at *2-3 (E.D. La. May 6, 1998); Forrest, 1996 WL 171539, at *2; Ford Motor Co., 825 F. Supp. at 1082-83; Clavir, 84 F.R.D. at 614; cf. Alford v. Todco, No. CIV-88-731E, slip op. at 4-5 (W.D.N.Y. June 12, 1990) ("Even assuming the Privacy Act supplies a statutory privilege . . . the plaintiff has waived any such privilege by placing his physical condition at issue."; ordering production of records); Tootle v. Seaboard Coast Line R.R., 468 So. 2d 237, 239 (Fla. Dist. Ct. App. 1984) (recognizing that privacy interests in that case "must give way to the function of the discovery of facts" and that subsection (b)(11) provides the mechanism for disclosure).

On the other hand, when an agency wishes to make an affirmative disclosure of information during litigation it may either rely on a routine use permitting such disclosure or seek a court order. Because the Privacy Act does not constitute a statutory privilege, agencies need not worry about breaching or waiving such a privilege when disclosing information pursuant to subsections (b)(3) or (b)(11). Cf. Mangino v. Dep't of the Army, No. 94-2067, 1994 WL 477260, at *5-6 (D. Kan. Aug. 24, 1994) (finding that

OVERVIEW OF THE PRIVACY ACT

disclosure to court was appropriate pursuant to agency routine use and stating that to extent Privacy Act created privilege, such privilege was waived by plaintiff when he placed his records at issue through litigation); Lemasters v. Thomson, No. 92 C 6158, 1993 U.S. Dist. LEXIS 7513, at *3-8 (N.D. Ill. June 3, 1993) (same finding as in Mangino, despite fact that "court ha[d] not located" applicable routine use). For further discussions of disclosures during litigation, see the discussions of subsections (b)(3) and (b)(11), below.

By its own terms, subsection (b) does not prohibit an agency from releasing to an individual his own record, contained in a system of records retrieved by his name or personal identifier, in response to his "first-party" access request under subsection (d)(1). Cf. Weatherspoon v. Provincetowne Master Owners Ass'n., No. 08-cv-02754, 2010 WL 936109, at *3 (D. Colo. Mar. 15, 2010) (Where plaintiff had been ordered in discovery to produce her mental health records in her emotional distress suit, finding that even though records were maintained by a federal agency (the Veterans Administration), there would be no improper disclosure because "the VA will disclose Plaintiff's mental health records to her, so that she can transmit copies of them to defense counsel. Thus, disclosure by the VA to an 'unauthorized party' is not involved."). However, as is discussed below under "Individual's Right of Access," one exception to this point could conceivably arise in the first-party access context where a record is also about another individual and is "dually retrieved." Subsection (b) also explicitly authorizes disclosures made with the prior written consent of the individual. See, e.g., Taylor v. Potter, No. 02-1552, 2004 WL 422664, at *1-2 (D. Del. Mar. 4, 2004) (finding it to be "clear from the documents attached to Plaintiff's complaint that she provided prior written consent . . . for her medical records to be disclosed"); Scherer v. Hill, No. 02-2043, 2002 U.S. Dist. LEXIS 17872, at *6-8 (D. Kan. Sept. 17, 2002) (finding plaintiff's argument that agency violated his privacy by sending photographs of his skin condition to United States Attorney rather than directly to him to be "frivolous," as "[h]e specifically asked the 'US Attorney and the Veterans Administration' to produce the photographs" in his motion to compel, and the "Privacy Act does not prohibit the consensual disclosure of photographs or documents by an agency"); cf. Stokes v. SSA, 292 F. Supp. 2d 178, 181 (D. Me. 2003) ("The Privacy Act does not prevent an agency employee from discussing the contents of a protected record with the person to whom the record pertains."; finding that statement directed at the subject of the record "did not become the kind of 'disclosure' for which the Privacy Act requires written consent merely because [a third party] overheard it," especially given that the individual gave the employee consent to continue the interview in the third party's presence and thereby, in accordance with the agency regulation, "affirmatively authorized [the third party's] presence during this

OVERVIEW OF THE PRIVACY ACT

discussion").

Additionally, although it may seem self-evident, the fact pattern in one case caused a court to explicitly hold that an agency cannot be sued for disclosures that an individual makes himself. Abernethy v. IRS, 909 F. Supp. 1562, 1571 (N.D. Ga. 1995) (plaintiff had informed employees that he was being removed from his position as their supervisor and disclosed reason for his removal).

One district court has declined to "recognize a new exception to [subsection (b) of the Privacy Act] based on California public policy to protect persons investigating acts of child abuse." Stafford v. SSA, 437 F. Supp. 2d 1113, 1121 (N.D. Cal. 2006). In Stafford, a Social Security Administration employee disclosed to California Child Protective Services "the precise diagnosis of mental illness on which the SSA had made its determination that [the suspected child abuser] was disabled and thus eligible for benefits." Id. at 1116. The suspect brought a subsection (b)/(g)(1)(D) claim against the agency. Id. at 1114. The agency argued that the court should recognize a new exception because "[t]he public interest in detecting and eradicating child abuse is so strong that under California state law, malicious acts or acts taken without probable cause by investigators such as [the Child Protective Services employee] are immunized." Id. at 1121. The court explained that "Congress enacted the Privacy Act as a limitation on the sharing of private information among government agencies to further what it determined was an important public policy" and stated that "[t]he Court cannot create an exception to a federal statute based on state policy." Id.

The Act does not define "written consent." Implied consent, however, is insufficient. See Taylor v. Orr, No. 83-0389, 1983 U.S. Dist. LEXIS 20334, at *6 n.6 (D.D.C. Dec. 5, 1983) (in addressing alternative argument, stating that: "Implied consent is never enough" as the Act's protections "would be seriously eroded if plaintiff's written submission of [someone's] name were construed as a voluntary written consent to the disclosure of her [medical] records to him"); cf. Milton v. DOJ, 783 F. Supp. 2d 55, 59 (D.D.C. 2011) (in context of Freedom of Information Act claim, rejecting plaintiff's argument that his privacy waiver to permit BOP to monitor his telephone calls impliedly extended to any party who accepted his calls; "[A] protected privacy interest can be waived only by the person whose interest is affected, . . . and [plaintiff] has not produced Privacy Act waivers from the individuals with whom he spoke on the telephone."); Baitey v. VA, No. 8:CV89-706, slip op. at 5 (D. Neb. June 21, 1995) (concluding that "at a minimum, the phrase 'written consent' necessarily requires either (1) a medical authorization signed by [plaintiff] or (2) conduct which, coupled with the unsigned authorization, supplied the necessary written consent for the

OVERVIEW OF THE PRIVACY ACT

disclosure"). But cf. Pellerin v. VA, 790 F.2d 1553, 1556 (11th Cir. 1986) (applying doctrine of "equitable estoppel" to bar individual from complaining of disclosure of his record to congressmen "when he requested their assistance in gathering such information") (distinguished in Swenson v. USPS, 890 F.2d 1075, 1077-78 (9th Cir. 1989)); Del Fuoco v. O'Neill, No. 8:09-CV-1262, 2011 WL 601645, at *10 (M.D. Fla. Feb. 11, 2011) (Where regulation mandated that DOJ furnish plaintiff's termination letter to MSPB, noting that it was plaintiff's appeal to MSPB that triggered the disclosure, "which did not require Plaintiff's consent, which is implied by virtue of his appeal."); Jones v. Army Air Force Exchange Serv. (AAFES), No. 3:00-CV-0535, 2002 WL 32359949, at *5 (N.D. Tex. Oct. 17, 2002) (with respect to plaintiff's claim that AAFES disclosed protected information to congressional offices in violation of the Privacy Act, finding plaintiff to be "estopped from asserting such a claim because AAFES released the information pursuant to congressional office inquiries that were initiated at Plaintiff's request").

The OMB Guidelines caution that "the consent provision was not intended to permit a blanket or open-ended consent clause, i.e., one which would permit the agency to disclose a record without limit," and that, "[a]t a minimum, the consent clause should state the general purposes for, or types of recipients [to,] which disclosure may be made." 40 Fed. Reg. at 28,954, available at http://www.whitehouse.gov/sites/default/files/omb/assets/omb/inforeg/implementation_guidelines.pdf. See also Perry v. FBI, 759 F.2d 1271, 1276 (7th Cir. 1985) (upholding disclosure because release was "not so vague or general that it is questionable whether [plaintiff] knew what he was authorizing or whether the [agency] knew what documents it could lawfully release"), rev'd en banc on other grounds, 781 F.2d 1294 (7th Cir. 1986). For other cases in which courts have approved disclosures made pursuant to consent, see Elnashar v. DOJ, 446 F.3d 792, 795 (8th Cir. 2006) (plaintiff's signed release "authoriz[ing] representatives of [a human rights organization] to obtain and examine copies of all documents and records contained by the Federal Bureau of Investigation . . . pertaining to [plaintiff]" constituted his subsection (b) consent for FBI to disclose "that it had records which were responsive to the request for records and that records were contained in the 'PENTBOMB' investigation"); United States v. Rogers, No. 10-00088, 2010 WL 5441935, at *1 (S.D. Ala. Dec. 28, 2010) ("Despite the representation that the BOP needs a court order to release the records subpoenaed, if defendant is willing to make a written request to the BOP for his own records and give written consent for their release to his defense counsel, the Court sees no reason why an order is necessary."); Roberts v. U.S. Dep't of Transp., No. 02-CV-4414, 2006 WL 842401, at *8, *2 (E.D.N.Y. Mar. 28, 2006) (plaintiff's signed SF 171, which "explicitly stated that [plaintiff] 'consent[ed] to the release of information about [his]

OVERVIEW OF THE PRIVACY ACT

ability and fitness for Federal employment . . . to . . . authorized employees of the Federal Government,'" authorized disclosure of plaintiff's medical records by agency who previously employed him to agency considering employing him in order to "assist [the latter agency] in determining whether the employee is capable of performing the duties of the new position"); and Thomas v. VA, 467 F. Supp. 458, 460 n.4 (D. Conn. 1979) (consent held adequate because it was both agency- and record-specific); cf. Tarullo v. Def. Contract Audit Agency, 600 F. Supp. 2d 352, 360-61 (D. Conn. 2009) (Where "[t]he forms in question have sections that must be filled out by training officers and school officials from the training facility, . . . the forms themselves put the Plaintiff on notice that they (and hence their contents) would be disclosed. . . . Yet, the Plaintiff supplied his SSN. As a result, he voluntarily disclosed his SSN" to the training facility.); Wiley v. VA, 176 F. Supp. 2d 747, 751-56 (E.D. Mich. 2001) (accepting written release signed by plaintiff in connection with application for employment that broadly authorized employer to corroborate and obtain information about plaintiff's background, without reference to particular time frame, as valid consent under Privacy Act to authorize disclosure of all 466 pages of plaintiff's VA claims file to employer to be used in connection with union grievance proceeding, even though release was signed eight years prior to disclosure; stating further that "[p]laintiff might well have forfeited his Privacy Act protection through his own selective disclosure of and reference to his VA records").

For cases in which courts have found consent clauses to be inadequate to authorize disclosure, see Schmidt v. U.S. Air Force, No. 06-3069, 2007 WL 2812148, at *8 (C.D. Ill. Sept. 30, 2007) (issuance of press release and posting of complete text of plaintiff's reprimand on agency Web site was outside scope of plaintiff's signed waiver, which was limited to "a press release announcing the conclusion of the case"); Fattahi v. ATF, 186 F. Supp. 2d 656, 660 (E.D. Va. 2002) (consent providing that the information on an application "may be disclosed to members of the public in order to verify the information on the application when such disclosure is not prohibited by law" was "a mere tautology: plaintiff consented to no more than that ATF may disclose information except in cases where that disclosure is prohibited"); Doe v. Herman, No. 297CV00043, 1999 WL 100012, at *9 (W.D. Va. Oct. 29, 1999) (magistrate's recommendation) (rejecting argument that when plaintiffs provided their social security numbers for purpose of determining eligibility for and amount of benefits payable, they consented to use of those numbers as identifiers on multi-captioned hearing notices sent to numerous other individuals and companies as well as to publication of numbers in compilations of opinions), adopted in pertinent part & rev'd in other part (W.D. Va. July 24, 2000), aff'd in part, rev'd in part, & remanded, on other grounds sub nom. Doe v. Chao, 306

OVERVIEW OF THE PRIVACY ACT

F.3d 170 (4th Cir. 2002), aff'd, 540 U.S. 614 (2004); AFGE v. U.S. R.R. Ret. Bd., 742 F. Supp. 450, 457 (N.D. Ill. 1990) (SF-86 "release form" held overbroad and contrary to subsection (b)); and Doe v. GSA, 544 F. Supp. 530, 539-41 (D. Md. 1982) (authorization which was neither record- nor entity-specific was insufficient under GSA's own internal interpretation of Privacy Act); cf. Taylor, No. 83-0389, 1983 U.S. Dist. LEXIS 20334, at *6 n.6 (D.D.C. Dec. 5, 1983) (in addressing alternative argument, stating: "It is not unreasonable to require that a written consent to disclosure address the issue of such disclosure and refer specifically to the records permitted to be disclosed.").

In light of the D.C. Circuit's decision in Summers v. U.S. Department of Justice, 999 F.2d 570, 572-73 (D.C. Cir. 1993), agencies whose regulations require that privacy waivers be notarized to verify identity must also accept declarations in accordance with 28 U.S.C. § 1746 (2006) (i.e., an unsworn declaration subscribed to as true under penalty of perjury). See, e.g., 28 C.F.R. § 16.41(d) (2012) (Department of Justice regulation regarding verification of identity).

B. Twelve Exceptions to the "No Disclosure Without Consent" Rule

Note that with the exception of disclosures under subsection (b)(2) (see the discussion below), disclosures under the following exceptions are permissive, not mandatory. See OMB Guidelines, 40 Fed. Reg. at 28,953, available at http://www.whitehouse.gov/sites/default/files/omb/assets/omb/inforeg/implementation_guidelines.pdf.

1. 5 U.S.C. § 552a(b)(1) ("need to know" within agency)

"to those officers and employees of the agency which maintains the record who have a need for the record in the performance of their duties."

Comment:

This "need to know" exception authorizes the intra-agency disclosure of a record for necessary, official purposes. See OMB Guidelines, 40 Fed. Reg. 28,948, 28,950-01, 28,954 (July 9, 1975), available at http://www.whitehouse.gov/sites/default/files/omb/assets/omb/inforeg/implementation_guidelines.pdf. The Privacy Act's legislative history indicates an intent that the term "agency" be given "its broadest statutory meaning," and it recognizes the propriety of "need to know" disclosures between various components of large agencies. See 120 Cong. Rec. 36,967 (1974), reprinted in Source Book at 958,

OVERVIEW OF THE PRIVACY ACT

available at http://www.loc.gov/rr/frd/Military_Law/pdf/LH_ privacy_act-1974.pdf (recognizing propriety of "need to know" disclosures between Justice Department components); see also Sussman v. U.S. Marshals Serv., 808 F. Supp. 2d 192, 196-204 (D.D.C. 2011) (extensively analyzing disclosure between USMS and FBI under subsection (b)(1); recognizing that "[a]lthough the USMS and FBI may themselves be considered agencies, they are also components of DOJ, which is itself an agency," and that disclosures "qualif[ied] as intra-agency disclosures" and were permitted under (b)(1)); Lora v. DOJ, No. 00-3072, slip op. at 14-15 (D.D.C. Apr. 9, 2004) (citing subsection (b)(1) and legislative history, and finding plaintiff's argument that Privacy Act violation occurred when INS, then component of Department of Justice, released documents to prosecutor to be without merit); Walker v. Ashcroft, No. 99-2385, slip op. at 18-20 & n.6 (D.D.C. Apr. 30, 2001) (alternative holding) (finding that disclosures from FBI field office to FBI Headquarters and then to Department of Justice prosecutors were "proper under the 'need to know' exception"; "FBI employees and federal prosecutors are considered employees of the same agency, namely the Department of Justice."), summary affirmance granted, No. 01-5222, 2002 U.S. App. LEXIS 2485, at *2 (D.C. Cir. Jan. 25, 2002); cf. Sutera v. TSA, 708 F. Supp. 2d 304, 318 (E.D.N.Y. 2010) (where agency sent plaintiff's urine sample to private lab, stating that "[f]or testing purposes a private laboratory is necessarily treated as part of the agency"); Freeman v. EPA, No. 02-0387, 2004 WL 2451409, at *4-5 (D.D.C. Oct. 25, 2004) (finding that disclosure of plaintiffs' drug testing schedules and results by EPA IG to an EPA-hired DOD investigator did not violate Act because "according to the OMB Guidelines, an agency that hires a member of another agency to serve in a temporary task force or similar, cross-designated function can share otherwise protected information with that hired person and still satisfy exception (b)(1)").

Intra-agency disclosures for improper purposes will not be condoned. See, e.g., Parks v. IRS, 618 F.2d 677, 680-81 & n.1 (10th Cir. 1980) (publication of names of employees who did not purchase savings bonds, "for solicitation purposes," held improper); Carlson v. GSA, No. 04-C-7937, 2006 WL 3409150, at *3-4 (N.D. Ill. Nov. 21, 2006) (explaining that a supervisor's e-mail to employees that explained the reasons for plaintiff's termination does not fall within need to know exception because supervisor "encouraged [employees] to share [the e-mail] without restriction" and because supervisor "express[ed] his personal satisfaction with [employee's] termination" in e-mail); MacDonald v. VA, No. 87-544-CIV-T-15A, slip op. at 8-9 (M.D.

OVERVIEW OF THE PRIVACY ACT

Fla. July 28, 1989) (disclosure of counseling memorandum in "callous attempt to discredit and injure" employee held improper); Koch v. United States, No. 78-273T, slip op. at 1-2 (W.D. Wash. Dec. 30, 1982) (letter of termination posted in agency's entrance hallway held improper); Smigelsky v. USPS, No. 79-110-RE, slip op. at 3-4 (D. Or. Oct. 1, 1982) (publication of employees' reasons for taking sick leave held improper); Fitzpatrick v. IRS, 1 Gov't Disclosure Serv. (P-H) ¶ 80,232, at 80,580 (N.D. Ga. Aug. 22, 1980) (disclosure of fact that employee's absence was due to "mental problems" held improper; "quelling rumors and gossip [and] satisfying curiosity is not to be equated with a need to know"), aff'd in part, vacated & remanded in part, on other grounds, 665 F.2d 327 (11th Cir. 1982); see also Bigelow v. DOD, 217 F.3d 875, 879 (D.C. Cir. 2000) (Tatel, J., dissenting) (interpreting DOD regulations to find that supervisor did not have official need to review personnel security file of individual he supervised); Boyd v. Snow, 335 F. Supp. 2d 28, 38-39 (D.D.C. 2004) (explaining that where there are "serious questions" as to whether plaintiff's rebuttal statement to her performance evaluation was disclosed to certain personnel in plaintiff's office pursuant to a "need to know," agency will not prevail on summary judgment); Vargas v. Reno, No. 99-2725, slip op. at 3, 12-13 (W.D. Tenn. Mar. 31, 2000) (denying summary judgment where no evidence was submitted to show that information about plaintiff that was disclosed to Inspector General agent in course of investigating another employee was disclosed based on agent's "need to know"); cf. Berry v. Henderson, No. 99-283-P-C, 2000 WL 761896, at *1, 3 (D. Me. May 8, 2000) (finding that agency's examination of personnel and medical records within its possession in connection with its defense in Title VII case did not satisfy subsection (b)(1) and constituted violation of Privacy Act, despite fact that agency did not contend that disclosure was proper under subsection (b)(1)).

The cases are replete with examples of proper intra-agency "need to know" disclosures. See, e.g., Coburn v. Potter, 329 F. App'x 644, 645 (7th Cir. 2009) ("It is enough that the persons to whom disclosure is made are employees of the agency that maintains the records and that those employees have a need for access; disclosure under this subsection is not limited to the employees responsible for maintaining the records."); Bigelow v. DOD, 217 F.3d 875, 876-78 (D.C. Cir. 2000) (review of plaintiff's personnel file by immediate supervisor in connection with supervisor's "continuing duty to make sure that [plaintiff] was worthy of trust"; supervisor "had a need to examine the file in view of the doubts that had been raised in his mind about [plaintiff] and [plaintiff's] access to the country's top secrets"); Lennon v. Rubin, 166 F.3d 6, 10 (1st Cir. 1999) (citing subsection (b)(1) and finding that district court correctly granted summary judgment to defendant where, despite memorandum indicating intent to distribute information to task force that included individuals from outside agency, agency employee testified that she actually gave information only to member who was agency employee and recipient employee declared that she had never given information to other task force members); Hudson v. Reno, 130 F.3d 1193, 1206-07 (6th Cir. 1997) (disclosure of plaintiff's performance evaluation to individual who typed it originally, for retyping); Pippinger v. Rubin, 129 F.3d 519, 529-31 (10th Cir. 1997) (disclosure of identity of investigation's subject by supervisor investigating allegations of employee misconduct to staff members to assist in investigation; disclosure to agency attorney charged with defending agency's actions in related MSPB proceeding against another individual); Mount v. USPS, 79 F.3d 531, 533-34 (6th Cir. 1996) (disclosure of information in plaintiff's medical records to other employees "with responsibilities for making employment and/or disciplinary decisions regarding plaintiff"; "In light of the questions surrounding plaintiff's mental stability, each had at least an arguable need to access the information in plaintiff's medical records."); Britt v. Naval Investigative Serv., 886 F.2d 544, 549 n.2 (3d Cir. 1989) (disclosure of investigative report to commanding officer approved "since the Reserves might need to reevaluate Britt's access to sensitive information or the level of responsibility he was accorded"); Covert v. Harrington, 876 F.2d 751, 753-54 (9th Cir. 1989) (disclosure of security questionnaires to Inspector General for purpose of detecting fraud); Daly-Murphy v. Winston, 837 F.2d 348, 354-55 (9th Cir. 1988) (disclosure of letter suspending doctor's clinical privileges to participants in peer-review proceeding); Lukos v. IRS, No. 86-1100, 1987 WL 36354, at *1-2 (6th Cir. Feb. 12, 1987) (disclosure of employee's arrest record to supervisor for purpose of evaluating his conduct and to effect discipline); Howard v. Marsh, 785 F.2d 645, 647-49 (8th Cir. 1986) (disclosure of employee's personnel records to agency attorney and personnel specialist for purpose of preparing response to discrimination complaint); Hernandez v. Alexander, 671 F.2d 402, 410 (10th Cir. 1982) (disclosure of employee's EEO files to personnel advisors for purpose of determining whether personnel action should be taken against employee); Grogan v. IRS, 3 Gov't Disclosure Serv. (P-H) ¶ 82,385, at 82,977-78 (4th Cir. Mar. 22, 1982) (disclosure of questionable income tax returns prepared by professional tax preparer while he was IRS employee to IRS examiners for purpose of alerting them to possible irregularities);

OVERVIEW OF THE PRIVACY ACT

Beller v. Middendorf, 632 F.2d 788, 798 n.6 (9th Cir. 1980) (disclosure of record revealing serviceman's homosexuality by Naval Investigative Service to commanding officer for purpose of reporting "a ground for discharging someone under his command"); Middlebrooks v. Mabus, No. 1:11cv46, 2011 WL 4478686, at *6-7 (E.D. Va. Sept. 23, 2011) (disclosure to "small group of senior employees" who were "required 'to perform their job of legal oversight for the agency'" and "determine proper compliance with disclosure regulations"); Drennon-Gala v. Holder, No. 1:08-CV-321G, 2011 WL 1225784, at *5 (N.D. Ga. Mar. 30, 2011) (disclosure of plaintiff's workers compensation file to agency officials investigating allegations "directly related to misconduct involving [plaintiff's] worker's compensation claim"); Sutera, 708 F. Supp. 2d at 318 (in response to plaintiff's assertion that agency's "statement that he had failed a drug test violated the Privacy Act" (although he had failed to specify to whom the statement was made), recognizing that "[TSA Disciplinary Review Board] officials, the Medical Review Officer, and the deciding official are all agency employees responsible for making employment decisions regarding plaintiff" and "[t]heir communications are within the Privacy Act's 'need-to-know' exception"); Doe v. DOJ, 660 F. Supp. 2d 31, 45-46 (D.D.C. 2009) (disclosure of plaintiff AUSA's mental state to DOJ security personnel, who "needed . . . to assess his trustworthiness and make related personnel decisions about his eligibility for security clearance," to acting U.S. Attorney and division chief, who "[a]s plaintiff's supervisors . . . were responsible for ensuring that the [office] was operating safely," and to an EOUSA attorney, who was "entitled to access the records because he represented DOJ in various pending disciplinary matters against plaintiff at the time" (internal quotation marks omitted)); Gamble v. Dep't of Army, 567 F. Supp. 2d 150, 156 (D.D.C. 2008) (disclosure to plaintiff's commanding officer of past allegations of sexual misconduct by plaintiff in the context of investigation of new allegations of same); Shayesteh v. Raty, No. 02:05-CV-85TC, 2007 WL 2317435, at *4-5 (D. Utah Aug. 7, 2007) (disclosure for purpose of "pursu[ing] forfeiture of funds . . . [is] a task clearly within [employees'] duties as federal law enforcement officers"); Thompson v. Dep't of State, 400 F. Supp. 2d 1, 20 (D.D.C. 2005) (disclosure of investigative report to agency's Office of Civil Rights to determine "whether plaintiff's supervisor was promoting plaintiff's career to the detriment of the office and other employees because of a romantic relationship" was "relevant to the agency's compliance with EEO regulations"); Roberts v. DOJ, 366 F. Supp. 2d 13, 26-28 (D.D.C. 2005) (disclosure of results of investigation by OPR to FBI was "entirely appropriate" because FBI

OVERVIEW OF THE PRIVACY ACT

referred matter to OPR for investigation and because FBI had duty to respond to plaintiff, who had requested that FBI look into matter; dismissing claim because "OPR was entitled to share information regarding the results of its investigation" with agency that was the subject of its investigation); Lucas v. SBA, No. 03-2617, 2005 WL 613574, at *1 (D.D.C. Mar. 16, 2005) (disclosure of plaintiff's personnel file to employee outside plaintiff's chain of command "in the course of an internal investigation of a third party's complaint" was appropriate under "need to know" exception); Buckles v. Indian Health Serv., 305 F. Supp. 2d 1108, 1111 (D.N.D. 2004) (disclosure of employees' medical records by employer's health facility to risk management team – due to concerns that employees were illegally receiving prescription drugs – was proper because it conformed with facility's protocol to discuss issues of potential wrongdoing with upper management); McCready v. Principi, 297 F. Supp. 2d 178, 197 n.11 (D.D.C. 2003) (although not specifically citing subsection (b)(1), finding that "limited distribution of [a memorandum concerning plaintiff] to those [within the agency] with a legitimate need to know did not violate [plaintiff's] rights under the Privacy Act"), aff'd in part, rev'd in part, & remanded in part, all on other grounds sub nom. McCready v. Nicholson, 465 F.3d 1 (D.C. Cir. 2006); Schmidt v. VA, 218 F.R.D. 619, 631 (E.D. Wis. 2003) (although finding no evidence of disclosure, even presuming disclosure took place finding that "VA personnel need to have access to the entire [social security number] of persons accessible through the [Computerized Patient Records System] to avoid misidentification"); Hanna v. Herman, 121 F. Supp. 2d 113, 123-24 (D.D.C. 2000) (disclosure of information by agency official about plaintiff's demotion to another supervisor was covered by "need to know" exception even though that supervisor was not within same office), summary affirmance granted sub nom. Hanna v. Chao, No. 00-5433 (D.C. Cir. Apr. 11, 2001); Khalfani v. VA, No. 94-CV-5720, 1999 WL 138247, at *7-8 (E.D.N.Y. Mar. 10, 1999) (disclosure of plaintiff's medical records within VA so that his supervisor could document his request for medical leave and determine level of work he could perform), appeal dismissed for appellant's failure to comply with scheduling order, No. 99-6157 (2d Cir. Oct. 10, 2000); Blazy v. Tenet, 979 F. Supp. 10, 26 (D.D.C. 1997) (disclosure of status of plaintiff's security investigation to his supervisor and disclosure of records needed by members of Employee Review Panel responsible for assessing plaintiff's employment performance and prospects), summary affirmance granted, No. 97-5330, 1998 WL 315583 (D.C. Cir. May 12, 1998); Porter v. USPS, No. CV595-30, slip op. at 23-24 (S.D. Ga. July 24,

OVERVIEW OF THE PRIVACY ACT

1997) (disclosure of employee's medical records to supervisory personnel in order to "figure out exactly what level of duty [employee] was fit and able to perform"), aff'd, 166 F.3d 352 (11th Cir. 1998) (unpublished table decision); Jones v. Dep't of the Air Force, 947 F. Supp. 1507, 1515-16 (D. Colo. 1996) (Air Force investigator's review of plaintiff's medical and mental health records and publication of statements about the records in report of investigation compiled in preparation for plaintiff's court-martial, which was distributed to certain Air Force personnel); Viotti v. U.S. Air Force, 902 F. Supp. 1331, 1337 (D. Colo. 1995) (disclosure by general to academic department staff that he was removing acting head of department because he had lost confidence in his leadership; subsequent disclosure by new head of department to department staff of same information regarding removal of prior department head), aff'd, 153 F.3d 730 (10th Cir. 1998) (unpublished table decision); Abernethy v. IRS, 909 F. Supp. 1562, 1570-71 (N.D. Ga. 1995) ("[investigatory] panel's review of Plaintiff's performance appraisals was not a violation of the Privacy Act because the members had a need to know the contents of the appraisals"; member of the panel that recommended that plaintiff be removed from management in response to an EEO informal class complaint "had a need to know the contents of the [EEO] complaint file"), aff'd per curiam, No. 95-9489 (11th Cir. Feb. 13, 1997); Magee v. USPS, 903 F. Supp. 1022, 1029 (W.D. La. 1995) (disclosure of employee's medical report following fitness-for-duty examination to Postmaster of Post Office where employee worked to determine whether employee could perform essential functions of job and to Postmaster's supervisor who was to review Postmaster's decision), aff'd, 79 F.3d 1145 (5th Cir. 1996) (unpublished table decision); McNeill v. IRS, No. 93-2204, 1995 U.S. Dist. LEXIS 2372, at *8 (D.D.C. Feb. 7, 1995) (disclosures made to Treasury Department's Equal Employment Opportunity (EEO) personnel in course of their investigation of EEO allegations initiated by plaintiff); Harry v. USPS, 867 F. Supp. 1199, 1206 (M.D. Pa. 1994) (disclosure from one internal subdivision of Postal Service to another – the Inspection Service (Inspector General) – which was conducting an investigation), aff'd sub nom. Harry v. USPS, 60 F.3d 815 (3d Cir. 1995) (unpublished table decision); Hass v. U.S. Air Force, 848 F. Supp. 926, 932 (D. Kan. 1994) (disclosure of mental health evaluation to officers who ultimately made decision to revoke plaintiff's security clearance and discharge her); Lachenmyer v. Frank, No. 88-2414, slip op. at 3-4 (C.D. Ill. July 16, 1990) (disclosure of investigative report, referencing employee's admission that he had been treated for alcohol abuse, to supervisor); Williams v. Reilly, 743 F. Supp. 168, 175 (S.D.N.Y. 1990)

OVERVIEW OF THE PRIVACY ACT

(admission of drug use disclosed by the Naval Investigative Service to plaintiff's employer, the Defense Logistics Agency); Bengle v. Reilly, No. 88-587, 1990 U.S. Dist. LEXIS 2006, at *21 (D.D.C. Feb. 28, 1990) (disclosure to personnel consulted by employee's supervisors in order to address employee's complaints); Glass v. U.S. Dep't of Energy, No. 87-2205, 1988 WL 118408, at *1 (D.D.C. Oct. 29, 1988) (disclosure to "officials or counsel for the agency for use in the exercise of their responsibility for management of the agency or for defense of litigation initiated by plaintiff"); Krowitz v. USDA, 641 F. Supp. 1536, 1545-46 (W.D. Mich. 1986) (details of employee's performance status disclosed to other personnel who were assigned to assist plaintiff), aff'd, 826 F.2d 1063 (6th Cir. 1987) (unpublished table decision); Marcotte v. Sec'y of Def., 618 F. Supp. 756, 763 (D. Kan. 1985) (disclosure of "talking paper" chronicling officer's attempts to correct effectiveness ratings to Inspector General for purpose of responding to officer's challenge to "staff advisories"); Nutter v. VA, No. 84-2392, slip op. at 8-9 (D.D.C. July 9, 1985) (disclosure of record reflecting employee's impending indictment to personnel responsible for responding to public and press inquiries); Brooks v. Grinstead, 3 Gov't Disclosure Serv. (P-H) ¶ 83,054, at 83,551-53 (E.D. Pa. Dec. 12, 1982) (disclosure of employee's security file to supervisor for purpose of ascertaining employee's trustworthiness); Carin v. United States, 1 Gov't Disclosure Serv. (P-H) ¶ 80,193, at 80,492 & n.1 (D.D.C. Aug. 5, 1980) (disclosure of employee's EEO complaint to other employees during grievance process); Lydia R. v. U.S. States Army, No. 78-069, slip op. at 3-6 (D.S.C. Feb. 28, 1979) (disclosure of derogatory information from employee's file to officer for purpose of determining appropriateness of assigning employee to particular position); cf. Cacho v. Chertoff, No. 06-00292, 2006 WL 3422548, *4-7 (D.D.C. Nov. 28, 2006) (finding plaintiff's argument alleging improper access of information irrelevant to (b)(1) analysis; "What matters then is the 'need to know' of the agency official who received the disclosure, not the authority of the agency official who made the disclosure."); Gill v. DOD, 92 M.S.P.R. 23, 31-32 (2002) (finding that agency failed to establish that appellant's disclosure to EEO counselor of other employees' records was unauthorized, as disclosure appeared to fall within (b)(1) exception, where appellant provided records at request of EEO counselor in support of appellant's claim that she was disparately treated).

Although subsection (b)(1) permits disclosure only to "those officers and employees of the agency which maintains the record," some courts have upheld disclosures to contractors who serve the function

OVERVIEW OF THE PRIVACY ACT

of agency employees. See Mount v. USPS, 79 F.3d 531, 532-34 (6th Cir. 1996) (concluding disclosure of plaintiff's medical files to "a physician under contract with the USPS" who had "responsibilities for making employment and/or disciplinary decisions regarding plaintiff" had some basis in the need to know exception); Gard v. U.S. Dep't of Educ., 789 F. Supp. 2d 96, 110 (D.D.C. 2011) (finding a permissible intra-agency disclosure where information was disclosed to an "'occupational medicine consultant' under contract with" the Department of Education for purposes of evaluating employee's risk to coworkers); Ciralsky v. CIA, 689 F. Supp. 2d 141, 155 (D.D.C. 2010) (holding that disclosures to private contractors hired to investigate certain allegations, including plaintiff's, were permissible intra-agency disclosures); Sutera, 708 F. Supp. 2d at 318 (finding an intra-agency disclosure where a medical sample was sent to an outside laboratory because "[f]or testing purposes a private laboratory is necessarily treated as part of the agency"); Coakley v. U.S. Dep't of Transp., No. 93-1420, 1994 U.S. Dist. LEXIS 21402, at *3-4 (D.D.C. Apr. 7, 1994) (holding that an EEO investigator who was an independent contractor "must be considered an employee of DOT for Privacy Act purposes" and that the disclosure of information by a former DOT employee to that contractor, "[g]iven that the disclosure in question occurred in connection with an official agency investigation . . . must be considered an intra-agency communication under the Act"); Hulett v. Dep't of the Navy, No. TH 85-310-C, slip op. at 3-4 (S.D. Ind. Oct. 26, 1987) (disclosure of medical and personnel records to contractor/psychiatrist for purpose of assisting him in performing "fitness for duty" examination), aff'd, 866 F.2d 432 (7th Cir. 1988) (unpublished table decision); cf. Gill v. DOD, 92 M.S.P.R. at 32 n.7 (in case before the MSPB where the agency was in the unusual position of having to establish a violation of the Privacy Act in order to defend its disciplinary action against plaintiff for wrongful disclosure, finding that although the record indicated that the EEO counselor to whom the disclosure was made "was employed by a contractor, rather than directly by the agency . . . the EEO counselor was performing an administrative function for which the agency was responsible, and the agency ha[d] not argued nor established that the EEO counselor was not an officer or employee of the agency for the purposes of 5 U.S.C. § 552a(b)(1)," and stating further that "[i]t is clear that, for particular purposes, the Privacy Act provides that any government contractor and any employee of such contractor shall be considered an employee of an agency" (citing 5 U.S.C. § 552a(m))). Another court, however, has held to the contrary on facts nearly identical to those in Hulett. Taylor v. Orr, No. 83-0389, 1983 U.S. Dist. LEXIS 20334, at *7-10

OVERVIEW OF THE PRIVACY ACT

(D.D.C. Dec. 5, 1983); cf. Appendix I to OMB Circular No. A-130 – Federal Agency Responsibilities for Maintaining Records About Individuals, 61 Fed. Reg. 6428, 6439 (Feb. 20, 1996), as amended, 65 Fed. Reg. 77,677 (Dec. 12, 2000), available at http://www.whitehouse.gov/omb/circulars_a130_a130appendix_i (directing agencies that provide by contract for the operation of a system of records to "review the [system] notice to ensure that it contains a routine use . . . permitting disclosure to the contractor and his or her personnel"). See generally OMB Guidelines, 40 Fed. Reg. at 28,954, available at http://www.whitehouse.gov/sites/default/files/omb/assets/omb/inforeg/implementation_guidelines.pdf (noting that "movement of records between personnel of different agencies may in some instances be viewed as intra-agency disclosures if that movement is in connection with an inter-agency support agreement").

2.   5 U.S.C. § 552a(b)(2) (required FOIA disclosure)

"required under section 552 of this title."

Comment:

The point of this exception is that the Privacy Act never prohibits a disclosure that the Freedom of Information Act actually requires. See News-Press v. DHS, 489 F.3d 1173, 1189 (11th Cir. 2007) ("The net effect of the interaction between the two statutes is that where the FOIA requires disclosure, the Privacy Act will not stand in its way, but where the FOIA would permit withholding under an exemption, the Privacy Act makes such withholding mandatory upon the agency."); Greentree v. U.S. Customs Serv., 674 F.2d 74, 79 (D.C. Cir. 1982) (subsection (b)(2) "represents a Congressional mandate that the Privacy Act not be used as a barrier to FOIA access").

Thus, if an agency is in receipt of a FOIA request for information about an individual that is contained in a system of records and that is not properly withholdable under any FOIA exemption, then it follows that the agency is "required under Section 552 of this title" to disclose the information to the FOIA requester. This would be a required subsection (b)(2) disclosure. However, if a FOIA exemption – typically, Exemption 6 or Exemption 7(C) – applies to a Privacy Act-protected record, the Privacy Act prohibits an agency from making a "discretionary" FOIA release because that disclosure would not be "required" by the FOIA within the meaning of subsection (b)(2). See, e.g., DOD v. FLRA, 510 U.S. 487, 502

OVERVIEW OF THE PRIVACY ACT

(1994); U.S. Dep't of the Navy v. FLRA, 975 F.2d 348, 354-56 (7th Cir. 1992); DOD v. FLRA, 964 F.2d 26, 30 n.6 (D.C. Cir. 1992); Andrews v. VA, 838 F.2d 418, 422-24 & n.8 (10th Cir. 1988); Citizens for Responsibility and Ethics in Washington v. Nat'l Indian Gaming Comm'n, 467 F. Supp. 2d 40, 54-55 (D.D.C. 2006); Robbins v. HHS, No. 1:95-cv-3258, slip op. at 2-9 (N.D. Ga. Aug. 13, 1996), aff'd, No. 96-9000 (11th Cir. July 8, 1997); Kassel v. VA, 709 F. Supp. 1194, 1199-1200 (D.N.H. 1989); Howard v. Marsh, 654 F. Supp. 853, 855-56 (E.D. Mo. 1986); Fla. Med. Ass'n v. HEW, 479 F. Supp. 1291, 1305-07 (M.D. Fla. 1979); Providence Journal Co. v. FBI, 460 F. Supp. 762, 767 (D.R.I. 1978), rev'd on other grounds, 602 F.2d 1010 (1st Cir. 1979); Phila. Newspapers, Inc. v. DOJ, 405 F. Supp. 8, 10 (E.D. Pa. 1975); see also OMB Guidelines, 40 Fed. Reg. 28,948, 28,954 (July 9, 1975), available at http://www.whitehouse.gov/sites/default/files/omb/assets/omb/inforeg/implementation_guidelines.pdf.

In U.S. Department of Justice v. Reporters Committee for Freedom of the Press, 489 U.S. 749, 762-75 (1989), the Supreme Court significantly expanded the breadths of FOIA Exemptions 6 and 7(C). The Court ruled that a privacy interest may exist in publicly available information – such as the criminal history records (rap sheets) there at issue – where the information is "practically obscure." Id. at 764-71. Even more significantly, the Court held that the identity of the FOIA requester, and any socially useful purpose for which the request was made, are not to be considered in evaluating whether the "public interest" would be served by disclosure. Id. at 771-75. The Court determined that the magnitude of the public interest side of the balancing process can be assessed only by reference to whether disclosure of the requested records directly advances the "core purpose" of the FOIA – to shed light on the operations and activities of the government. Id. at 774-75.

In light of Reporters Committee, personal information of the sort protected by the Privacy Act is less likely to be "required" to be disclosed under the FOIA, within the meaning of subsection (b)(2). Specifically, where an agency determines that the only "public interest" that would be furthered by a disclosure is a nonqualifying one under Reporters Committee (even where it believes that disclosure would be in furtherance of good public policy generally), it may not balance in favor of disclosure under the FOIA and therefore disclosure will be prohibited under the Privacy Act – unless authorized by another Privacy Act exception or by written consent. See, e.g., DOD v. FLRA, 510 U.S. at 497-502 (declining to "import

OVERVIEW OF THE PRIVACY ACT

the policy considerations that are made explicit in the Labor Statute into the FOIA Exemption 6 balancing analysis" and, following the principles of Reporters Committee, holding that home addresses of bargaining unit employees are covered by FOIA Exemption 6 and thus that Privacy Act "prohibits their release to the unions"); Schwarz v. INTERPOL, No. 94-4111, 1995 U.S. App. LEXIS 3987, at *4-7 & n.2 (10th Cir. Feb. 28, 1995) (balancing under Reporters Committee and holding that individual clearly has protected privacy interest in avoiding disclosure of his whereabouts to third parties; disclosure of this information would not "contribute anything to the public's understanding of the operations or activities of the government"; and thus any information was exempt from disclosure under FOIA Exemption 7(C) and does not fall within Privacy Act exception (b)(2)); FLRA v. U.S. Dep't of Commerce, 962 F.2d 1055, 1059 (D.C. Cir. 1992) (Privacy Act prohibits disclosure of identities of individuals who received outstanding or commendable personnel evaluations, as such information falls within FOIA Exemption 6); Doe v. Veneman, 230 F. Supp. 2d 739, 748-52 (W.D. Tex. 2002) (in reverse FOIA lawsuit where information regarding government program for protection of livestock using livestock-protection collars already had been released, finding that no personally identifying information about particular ranchers and farmers participating in program "could shed any further light on workings of the [program]," that information thus was protected by FOIA Exemption 6, and that its disclosure therefore was prohibited by the Privacy Act), aff'd in part, rev'd in part, on other grounds, 380 F.3d 807 (5th Cir. 2004); Fort Hall Landowners Alliance, Inc. v. BIA, No. CV-99-00052-E-BLW, slip op. at 7-14 (D. Idaho Mar. 17, 2000) (finding that document that "contains only names and addresses . . . does not provide information shedding light on how the BIA is performing its duties," and that "[h]aving determined that disclosure of the information is not required by FOIA . . . the Privacy Act prohibits disclosure of the information"); Burke v. DOJ, No. 96-1739, 1999 WL 1032814, at *3-5 (D.D.C. Sept. 30, 1999) (stating that the "Privacy Act prohibits the FBI from disclosing information about a living third party without a written privacy waiver, unless FOIA requires disclosure," and upholding the FBI's refusal to confirm or deny the existence of investigative records related to third parties in response to a FOIA request); see also FOIA Update, Vol. X, No. 2, at 6, available at http://www.justice.gov/oip/foia_updates/Vol_X_2/page3.html ("Privacy Protection Under the Supreme Court's Reporters Committee Decision"). As a result of Reporters Committee, agencies depend more on the subsection (b)(3) routine use exception to make compatible disclosures of records that are no

OVERVIEW OF THE PRIVACY ACT

longer required by the FOIA to be disclosed. See, e.g., USDA v. FLRA, 876 F.2d 50, 51 (8th Cir. 1989); see also FLRA v. U.S. Dep't of the Treasury, 884 F.2d 1446, 1450 & n.2 (D.C. Cir. 1989).

It should be noted that President Barack Obama's FOIA policy on openness in government, see Memorandum for the Heads of Executive Departments and Agencies, Subject: Freedom of Information Act (Jan. 21, 2009), available at http://whitehouse.gov/the_press_office/Freedom_of_Information_Act, as implemented by Attorney General Eric Holder's Memorandum for the Heads of Executive Departments and Agencies, Subject: The Freedom of Information Act (FOIA) (Mar. 19, 2009), available at http://www.justice.gov/ag/foia-memo-march2009.pdf, is inapplicable to information covered by the Privacy Act that also falls under one or more of the FOIA exemptions. See Department of Justice Office of Information Policy Guidance, President Obama's FOIA Memorandum and Attorney General Holder's FOIA Guidelines Creating a "New Era of Open Government," posted April 17, 2009, available at http://www.justice.gov/oip/foiapost/2009foiapost8.htm ("For information falling within Exemptions 6 and 7(C), if the information is also protected by the Privacy Act of 1974, it is not possible to make a discretionary release, as the Privacy Act contains a prohibition on disclosure of information not 'required' to be released under the FOIA.").

The Court of Appeals for the District of Columbia Circuit significantly limited the utility of subsection (b)(2) in Bartel v. FAA, 725 F.2d 1403 (D.C. Cir. 1984). In Bartel, the D.C. Circuit held that subsection (b)(2) cannot be invoked unless an agency actually has a FOIA request in hand. 725 F.2d at 1411-13; see also Chang v. Dep't of the Navy, 314 F. Supp. 2d 35, 41-42 (D.D.C. 2004) (citing Bartel, and noting that defendant agency conceded that it "had no FOIA request in hand"). In one case prior to Bartel, it similarly had been held that subsection (b)(2) was not available as a defense for the disclosure of information in the absence of a FOIA request. Zeller v. United States, 467 F. Supp. 487, 503 (E.D.N.Y. 1979) (finding subsection (b)(2) inapplicable to the "voluntary re-release" of a prior press release (that had been made prior to the effective date of the Privacy Act) as "nothing in the FOIA appears to require such information to be released in the absence of a request therefor").

Other courts have not taken the approach articulated by the D.C. Circuit in Bartel. See Cochran v. United States, 770 F.2d 949, 957-58 & n.14 (11th Cir. 1985) (applying subsection (b)(2) – in absence of written FOIA request – because requested records would not be withholdable under any FOIA exemption); Jafari v. Dep't of the Navy, 728 F.2d 247, 249-50 (4th Cir. 1984) (same); Russo v. United States, 576 F. Supp. 2d 662, 671-72 (D.N.J. 2008) (alternative holding) (expressing reluctance to follow Bartel because subsection (b)'s conditional language of "would be" rather than "is" casts "serious doubt upon Plaintiff's argument that the exception only applies where the agency is faced with a written FOIA request"); Mudd v. U.S. Army, No. 2:05-cv-137, 2007 WL 4358262, at *6 (M.D. Fla. Dec. 10, 2002) (agreeing with agency that "under the circumstances of this case, the balance of plaintiff's privacy against the public's right to disclosure weighs in favor of public disclosure, and that the FOIA exception was applicable even without a formal FOIA request"); see also Fla. Med. Ass'n, 479 F. Supp. at 1301, 1305-07. However, because the D.C. Circuit is the jurisdiction of "universal venue" under the Privacy Act (which means that any Privacy Act lawsuit for wrongful disclosure could be filed within that judicial circuit), see 5 U.S.C. § 552a(g)(5), its holding in Bartel is of paramount importance. See FOIA Update, Vol. V, No. 3, at 2, available at http://www.justice.gov/oip/foia_updates/Vol_V_3/page2.htm ("FOIA Counselor Q & A") (discussing Bartel).

Note also, though, that the Bartel decision left open the possibility that certain types of information "traditionally released by an agency to the public" might properly be disclosed even in the absence of an actual FOIA request. 725 F.2d at 1413 (dictum). Reacting to Bartel, OMB issued guidance indicating that records that have "traditionally" been considered to be in the public domain, and those that are required to be disclosed to the public – such as final opinions of agencies and press releases – can be released without waiting for an actual FOIA request. OMB Guidelines, 52 Fed. Reg. 12,990, 12,992-93 (Apr. 20, 1987), available at http://www.whitehouse.gov/sites/default/files/omb/assets/omb/inforeg/guidance_privacy_act.pdf (discussing Bartel, in context of guidance on "call detail" programs, and referring to OMB Memorandum For The Senior Agency Officials For Information Resources Management (May 24, 1985) at 4-6 (unpublished)). The District Court for the District of Columbia twice has applied this aspect of Bartel. In Tripp v. DOD, 193 F. Supp. 2d 229, 236 (D.D.C. 2002), the D.C. District Court held that "the names, titles, salaries, and salary-levels of public employees are information generally in the public domain" and thus that they are not prohibited from disclosure under subsection (b)(2). In Chang v. Dep't of the Navy, 314 F. Supp. 2d 42, the District Court found that the Privacy Act was not violated where the Navy disclosed

OVERVIEW OF THE PRIVACY ACT

information to the media about plaintiff's nonjudicial punishment, because the information was "releasable" under the FOIA, and the Navy had asserted that it "traditionally releases information that would be releasable under the FOIA to the press without a formal FOIA request," and was able to point to a Navy regulation to that effect. Id; see also Russo, 576 F. Supp. 2d at 670-73 (D.N.J. 2008) (alternative holding) (though declining to expressly adopt D.C. Circuit's holding in Bartel, concluding that "GS-level and salaries of public officials are 'information . . . traditionally released by an agency to the public without a FOIA request,'" and thus that agency may properly disclose plaintiff's active duty military status under the Privacy Act (quoting Bartel, 725 F.2d at 1413)). At least one pre-Bartel case also appears to support this idea. Owens v. MSPB, No. 3-83-0449-R, slip op. at 3 (N.D. Tex. Sept. 14, 1983) (finding that inadvertent disclosure to plaintiff's former attorney of initial decision rendered by MSPB did not violate Privacy Act, because "the Board's proper treatment of its initial decisions as final decisions for purposes of FOIA makes these decisions part of the public domain – and the release of public information simply cannot be an unlawful disclosure under the Privacy Act"). But see Zeller v. United States, 467 F. Supp. 487, 503 (E.D.N.Y. 1979) (finding subsection (b)(2) inapplicable to the "voluntary re-release" of a press release that had been made four years earlier, as "nothing in the FOIA appears to require such information to be released in the absence of a request therefor").

3. **5 U.S.C. § 552a(b)(3) (routine uses)**

"for a routine use as defined in subsection (a)(7) of this section and described under subsection (e)(4)(D)."

Cross-references:

Subsection (e)(4)(D) requires Federal Register publication of "each routine use of the records contained in the system, including the categories of users and the purpose of such use."

Subsection (a)(7) defines the term "routine use" to mean "with respect to the disclosure of a record, the use of such record for a purpose which is compatible with the purpose for which it was collected."

OVERVIEW OF THE PRIVACY ACT

Comment:

The routine use exception, because of its potential breadth, is one of the most controversial provisions in the Act. See Privacy Commission Report at 517-18, available at http://epic.org/privacy/ppsc1977report. The trend in recent cases is toward a narrower construction of the exception. The White House directed the Office of Management and Budget to issue additional guidance regarding the routine use exception in an executive memorandum on privacy sent to the heads of executive departments and agencies in 1998. Memorandum on Privacy and Personal Information in Federal Records, 34 Weekly Comp. Pres. Doc. 870 (May 14, 1998), available at http://www.whitehouse.gov/omb/memoranda/m99-05-a.html. See also FOIA Update, Vol. XIX, No. 2, at 1, available at http://www.whitehouse.gov/omb/memoranda_m99-05-a ("President Issues Privacy Act-Related Memorandum to All Federal Agencies") (providing summary of executive memorandum).

It should be noted that the routine use exception "was developed to permit other than intra-agency disclosures" and that therefore "[i]t is not necessary . . . to include intra-agency transfers in the portion of the system notice covering routine uses." OMB Guidelines, 40 Fed. Reg. 56,741, 56,742 (Dec. 4, 1975), available at http://www.whitehouse.gov/sites/default/files/omb/assets/omb/inforeg/implementation1974.pdf. But see O'Donnell v. DOD, No. 04-00101, 2006 WL 166531, at *8 n.8 (E.D. Pa. Jan. 20, 2006) (disagreeing with plaintiff that "routine use" should be defined as "the disclosure of a record outside of [DOD]" and explaining that "the 'routine use' exception specifically states that disclosure is allowed 'for a routine use as defined in subsection (a)(7) of [the Act]'"); cf. Shayesteh v. Raty, No. 02:05-CV-85TC, 2007 WL 2317435, at *5 (D. Utah Aug. 7, 2007) (although concluding that disclosures were proper under subsection (b)(1), nevertheless explaining that purpose of disclosures was compatible with purpose of collection under subsection (b)(3)).

By its terms, this exception sets forth two requirements for a proper routine use disclosure: (1) Federal Register publication, thereby providing constructive notice; and (2) compatibility. See, e.g., Britt v. Naval Investigative Serv., 886 F.2d 544, 547-50 (3d Cir. 1989); Shannon v. Gen. Elec. Co., 812 F. Supp. 308, 316 (N.D.N.Y. 1993).

However, the Court of Appeals for the Ninth Circuit has engrafted a third requirement onto this exception: Actual notice of the routine use under subsection (e)(3)(C) (i.e., at the time of information

OVERVIEW OF THE PRIVACY ACT

collection from the individual). Covert v. Harrington, 876 F.2d 751, 754-56 (9th Cir. 1989) (discussed below); accord Puerta v. HHS, No. 99-55497, 2000 WL 863974, at *1-2 (9th Cir. June 28, 2000), aff'g No. EDCV 94-0148, slip op. at 7 (C.D. Cal. Jan. 5, 1999); cf. Stafford v. SSA, 437 F. Supp. 2d 1113, 1119-20 (N.D. Cal. 2006) (adhering to Covert and finding that SSA notified plaintiff of potential uses "on three occasions when collecting her information"; explaining that notice need not "anticipate and list every single potential permutation of a routine use in order to invoke this exception"; "The Court is not persuaded that Congress intended to place such an impractical burden on federal agencies, which would in effect severely curtail the very exception that Congress sought to carve out in the interest of practicality."). Subsequently, the Court of Appeals for the District of Columbia Circuit cited this aspect of Covert with approval and remanded a case for determination as to whether (e)(3)(C) notice was provided, stating that "[a]lthough the statute itself does not provide, in so many terms, that an agency's failure to provide employees with actual notice of its routine uses would prevent a disclosure from qualifying as a 'routine use,' that conclusion seems implicit in the structure and purpose of the Act." USPS v. Nat'l Ass'n of Letter Carriers, 9 F.3d 138, 146 (D.C. Cir. 1993). But cf. Thompson v. Dep't of State, 400 F. Supp. 2d 1, 16-17 (D.D.C. 2005) (discussed below under "5 U.S.C. § 552a(e)(3)").

Federal Register Constructive Notice

The routine use exception's notice requirement "is intended to serve as a caution to agencies to think out in advance what uses [they] will make of information." 120 Cong. Rec. 40,881 (1974), reprinted in Source Book at 987, available at http://www.loc.gov/rr/frd/Military_Law/pdf/LH_privacy_act-1974.pdf. Indeed, it is possible for a routine use to be deemed facially invalid if it fails to satisfy subsection (e)(4)(D) – i.e., if it does not specify "the categories of users and the purpose of such use." See Britt, 886 F.2d at 547-48 (dictum) (suggesting that routine use (50 Fed. Reg. 22,802-03 (May 29, 1985)) permitting disclosure to "federal regulatory agencies with investigative units" is overbroad as it "does not provide adequate notice to individuals as to what information concerning them will be released and the purposes of such release"); cf. Krohn v. DOJ, No. 78-1536, slip op. at 4-7 (D.D.C. Mar. 19, 1984) ("to qualify as a 'routine use,' the agency must . . . publish in the Federal Register . . . 'each routine use of the records contained in the system, including the categories of users and the purpose of such use'"), reconsideration granted & vacated in nonpertinent part (D.D.C. Nov.

29, 1984) (discussed below).

It is well settled that the "scope of [a] routine use is confined to the published definition." Doe v. Naval Air Station, Pensacola, Fla., 768 F.2d 1229, 1231 (11th Cir. 1985); see also Parks v. IRS, 618 F.2d 677, 681-82 (10th Cir. 1980); Quilico v. U.S. Navy, No. 80-C-3568, 1983 U.S. Dist. LEXIS 14090, at *9-12 (N.D. Ill. Sept. 2, 1983); Local 2047, AFGE v. Def. Gen. Supply Ctr., 423 F. Supp. 481, 484-86 (E.D. Va. 1976), aff'd, 573 F.2d 184 (4th Cir. 1978). In other words, a particular disclosure is unauthorized if it does not fall within the clear terms of the routine use. See, e.g., Swenson v. USPS, 890 F.2d 1075, 1078 (9th Cir. 1989) (47 Fed. Reg. 1203 (Jan. 11, 1982) held inapplicable to agency's disclosure of record referencing employee's EEO complaints to her congressmen as their inquiries were not "made at the request of" employee); Tijerina v. Walters, 821 F.2d 789, 798 (D.C. Cir. 1987) (47 Fed. Reg. 24,012 (June 2, 1982) held inapplicable to VA's unsolicited letter notifying state board of bar examiners of possible fraud committed by bar applicant because no violation of state law was "reasonably imminent," and letter was not in response to "official request"); Doe v. DiGenova, 779 F.2d 74, 86 (D.C. Cir. 1985) (43 Fed. Reg. 44,743 (1978) held inapplicable to VA psychiatric report because disclosed record itself did not "indicate a potential violation of law"); Shearson v. DHS, No. 1:06 CV 1478, 2012 WL 398444, at *3 (N.D. Ohio Feb. 6, 2012) (where published routine use required agency to first be "aware of an indication of a violation or potential violation of" law and individual alleged that she had no criminal record, finding that plaintiff "fairly alleges that defendants did not meet the 'routine use' exception because the disclosing agency could not have been aware of any wrongful behavior"); Cooper v. FAA, No. 3:07-cv-01383, slip op. at 14-15 (N.D. Cal. Aug. 22, 2008) (concluding that "when DOT-OIG sent the name, social security number, date of birth and gender of approximately 45,000 pilots to SSA-OIG, it was not because those records indicated a violation or potential violation of the law," as required by language of DOT routine use), rev'd on other grounds, 596 F.3d 538 (9th Cir. 2010), rev'd on other grounds, 131 S. Ct. 3025 (2012); Bechhoefer v. DOJ, 179 F. Supp. 2d 93, 101-02 (W.D.N.Y. 2001) (although granting agency summary judgment on other grounds, finding that where a letter was collected by the agency due to its initial interest in investigating plaintiff's allegations of illegal drug activity by a local law enforcement agency, and was disclosed to that agency's investigator whose interest was in investigating possible unlawful, non-drug-related activity by plaintiff himself, such disclosure was not proper pursuant to a routine use providing for the

OVERVIEW OF THE PRIVACY ACT

disclosure to state and local law enforcement and regulatory agencies for law enforcement and regulatory purposes and stating that "it is difficult to see how [the] disclosure could be said to have been compatible with the purpose for which the letter was collected"), aff'd on other grounds, 312 F.3d 563 (2002), cert. denied sub nom. Bechhoefer v. DEA, 539 U.S. 514 (2003); Kvech v. Holder, No. 10-cv-545, 2011 WL 4369452, at *3-4 (D.D.C. Sept. 19, 2011) (ruling that dismissal was not yet warranted where "the record does not contain any evidence regarding precisely what information was disclosed . . . and the extent to which the disclosures fell inside or outside the confines of" the routine use); Pontecorvo v. FBI, No. 00-1511, slip op. at 13-15 (D.D.C. Sept. 30, 2001) (denying agency summary judgment and ordering discovery to determine whether the agency "overstepped [the] explicit restrictions" contained in its routine use); Vargas v. Reno, No. 99-2725, slip op. at 3, 12-13 (W.D. Tenn. Mar. 31, 2000) (routine uses permitting disclosure to appropriate agency when record indicates potential violation of law and to investigating agency in response to its request when information is relevant and necessary to investigation did not apply to disclosure of plaintiff's record, which was "'owned' by the Office of Personnel Management," to Department of Justice Inspector General agent conducting investigation of another employee; "The mere existence of an investigation at a facility is not sufficient to allow an investigating agent access to the records of every employee who is employed at that facility."); Greene v. VA, No. C-76-461-S, slip op. at 3-6 (M.D.N.C. July 3, 1978) (40 Fed. Reg. 38,105 (1975) held inapplicable to VA's disclosure of medical evaluation to state licensing bureau because routine use permitted disclosure only to facilitate VA decision); see also Covert, 667 F. Supp. at 736-39 (discussed below).

Note that an agency's construction of its routine use should be entitled to deference. See Dep't of the Air Force, Scott Air Force Base, Ill. v. FLRA, 104 F.3d 1396, 1402 (D.C. Cir. 1997); FLRA v. U.S. Dep't of the Treasury, 884 F.2d 1446, 1455-56 (D.C. Cir. 1989); Radack v. DOJ, 402 F. Supp. 2d 99, 106 n.7 (D.D.C. 2005). Cf. Stafford, 437 F. Supp. 2d at 1119 (relying on SSA regulations for proposition that "SSA generally would consider a use to be compatible if it relates to determining eligibility for needs-based income maintenance . . . or related medical benefits for low-income people" and concluding that SSA's disclosure of child abuse suspect's "precise medical diagnosis to [California Child Protective Services] . . . was not compatible with the purpose for which the information was collected"). But see NLRB v. USPS, 790 F. Supp.

OVERVIEW OF THE PRIVACY ACT

31, 33 (D.D.C. 1992) (rejecting Postal Service's interpretation of its own routine use).

Compatibility

The precise meaning of the term "compatible" is quite uncertain and must be assessed on a case-by-case basis. According to OMB, the "compatibility" concept encompasses (1) functionally equivalent uses, and (2) other uses that are necessary and proper. OMB Guidelines, 52 Fed. Reg. 12,990, 12,993 (Apr. 20, 1987), available at http://www.whitehouse.gov/sites/default/files/omb/assets/omb/inforeg/guidance_privacy_act.pdf.

An early leading case on "compatibility" is Britt v. Naval Investigative Service, 886 F.2d at 547-50, in which the Court of Appeals for the Third Circuit in 1989 ruled that the Naval Investigative Service's gratuitous disclosure of records, describing a then-pending criminal investigation of a Marine Corps reservist, to that individual's civilian employer (the Immigration and Naturalization Service), was not "compatible" with the "case-specific purpose for collecting" such records. Id. In holding that the employment/suitability purpose for disclosure was incompatible with the criminal law enforcement purpose for collection, the Third Circuit deemed it significant that "the [Immigration and Naturalization Service] was not conducting its own criminal investigation of the same activity or any other activity" by the subject, and that the records at issue concerned "merely a preliminary investigation with no inculpatory findings." Id. at 549-50. Employing especially broad language, the Third Circuit pointedly condemned the agency's equating of "compatibility" with mere "relevance" to the recipient entity, observing that "[t]here must be a more concrete relationship or similarity, some meaningful degree of convergence, between the disclosing agency's purpose in gathering the information and in its disclosure." Id. (citing Covert, 876 F.2d at 755 (dictum); Mazaleski v. Truesdale, 562 F.2d 701, 713 n.31 (D.C. Cir. 1977) (dictum)); accord Swenson, 890 F.2d at 1078; cf. Quinn v. Stone, 978 F.2d 126, 139 (3d Cir. 1992) (Nygaard, J., dissenting) (concluding that disclosure was authorized by routine use because disclosure was compatible with one of the purposes for collection, even if not with main purpose for collection).

The D.C. Circuit has also interpreted the term "compatibility" in considering a routine use providing for disclosure to labor organizations as part of the collective bargaining process. The court stated that application of the "common usage" of the word would require simply that "a proposed disclosure would not actually frustrate the purposes for which the information was gathered." USPS v. Nat'l Ass'n of Letter Carriers, 9 F.3d 138, 144 (D.C. Cir. 1993). The D.C. Circuit recognized the "far tighter nexus" that was required by the Third and Ninth Circuits in Britt and Swenson, and that is consistent with the legislative history, but stated:

> Whatever the merit of the decisions of prior courts that have held . . . that a finding of a substantial similarity of purpose might be appropriate in the non-labor law context in order to effectuate congressional intent, the compatibility requirement imposed by section 552a(a)(7) cannot be understood to prevent an agency from disclosing to a union information as part of the collective bargaining process.

Id. at 145. In a concurring opinion, Judge Williams agreed with the disposition of the case, but noted that he did not share the "belief that the meaning of 'compatible' . . . may depend on the identity of the entity to which the information is being disclosed." Id. at 147 n.1 (Williams, J., concurring). Rather, seeing "no conflict between the purposes for which the information was collected and those for which it will be disclosed," he found the disclosure to be compatible without further inquiry. Id. at 146-47. But cf. Pontecorvo v. FBI, No. 00-1511, slip op. at 10-11 (D.D.C. Sept. 30, 2001) (recognizing the D.C. Circuit's holding in USPS case, but finding "the test articulated by the Third and Ninth circuits to be controlling" in the non-labor law context).

There are two examples of "compatible" routine uses that frequently occur in the law enforcement context. First, in the context of investigations/prosecutions, law enforcement agencies may routinely share law enforcement records with one another. See OMB Guidelines, 40 Fed. Reg. at 28,955, available at http://www.whitehouse.gov/sites/default/files/omb/assets/omb/inforeg/implementation_guidelines.pdf (proper routine use is "transfer by a law enforcement agency of protective intelligence information to the Secret Service"); see also, e.g., 28 U.S.C. § 534 (2006) (authorizing Attorney General to exchange criminal records with "authorized officials of the Federal Government, the States, cities, and penal and other institutions"). Second, agencies may routinely disclose any records indicating a possible violation of law (regardless of the purpose for collection) to law enforcement agencies for purposes of investigation/prosecution. See OMB Guidelines, 40 Fed. Reg. at

28,953, 28,955; 120 Cong. Rec. 36,967, 40,884 (1974), reprinted in Source Book at 957-58, 995, available at http://www.loc.gov/rr/frd/Military_Law/pdf/LH_privacy_act-1974.pdf (remarks of Congressman Moorhead); see also, e.g., 28 U.S.C. § 535(b) (2006) (requiring agencies of the executive branch to expeditiously report "[a]ny information, allegation, or complaint" relating to crimes involving government officers and employees to United States Attorney General). These kinds of routine uses have been criticized on the ground that they circumvent the more restrictive requirements of subsection (b)(7). See Privacy Commission Report at 517-18, available at http://epic.org/privacy/ppsc1977report; see also Britt, 886 F.2d at 548 n.1 (dictum); Covert, 667 F. Supp. at 739, 742 (dictum). Yet, they have never been successfully challenged on that basis. Indeed, courts have routinely upheld disclosures made pursuant to such routine uses. See, e.g., Bansal v. Pavlock, 352 F. App'x 611, 613-14 (3d Cir. 2009) (upholding disclosure of detainee's recorded telephone conversations by Marshals Service to government case agent, who disclosed recording to interpreter, who disclosed recording to second interpreter); Weinberger v. Grimes, No. 07-6461, 2009 WL 331632, at *8 (6th Cir. Feb. 10, 2009) (BOP routine use "includes disclosure to federal law enforcement agencies for 'court-related purposes' including 'civil court actions'"); Shearson v. Holder, No. 1:10 CV 1492, 2011 WL 4102152, at *17 (N.D. Ohio Sept. 9, 2011) (ruling that FBI "dissemination of watchlist information to CBP officers to facilitate their border security responsibilities" fell within published routine use to agencies "engaged in terrorist screening"); Ray v. DHS, No. H-07-2967, 2008 WL 3263550, at *12-13 (S.D. Tex. Aug. 7, 2008) (disclosure by IG of results of investigation concerning plaintiff's SF 85P to U.S. Attorney's Office was proper because it was covered by published routine use); Freeman v. EPA, No. 02-0387, 2004 WL 2451409, at *6-7 (D.D.C. Oct. 25, 2004) (concluding that "disclosure [by a DOD investigator hired by EPA] of the plaintiff's records concerning drug testing schedules and test results to AUSA . . . for the purposes of [AUSA's] investigation of potentially criminal activity is a disclosure that is 'compatible with the purpose for which [those records were] collected'"); Nwangoro v. Dep't of the Army, 952 F. Supp. 394, 398 (N.D. Tex. 1996) (disclosure by Military Police of financial records obtained in an ongoing criminal investigation to foreign customs officials likewise involved in an investigation of possible infractions of foreign tax and customs laws was "permitted by the 'routine use' exception and d[id] not constitute a violation of the Privacy Act"); Little v. FBI, 793 F. Supp. 652, 655 (D. Md. 1992) (disclosure did not violate Privacy Act prohibition because it was made pursuant to

OVERVIEW OF THE PRIVACY ACT

routine use that allows disclosure of personnel matters to other government agencies when directly related to enforcement function of recipient agency), aff'd on other grounds, 1 F.3d 255 (4th Cir. 1993).

In Covert v. Harrington, 667 F. Supp. at 736-39, however, the district court held that a routine use permitting the Department of Energy's Inspector General to disclose to the Justice Department relevant records when "a record" indicates a potential violation of law, 47 Fed. Reg. 14,333 (Apr. 2, 1982), did not permit the disclosure of personnel security questionnaires submitted by the plaintiffs because such questionnaires did not on their face reveal potential violations of law. The court rejected the agency's argument that disclosure was proper because each questionnaire was disclosed as part of a prosecutive report that (when viewed as a whole) did reveal a potential violation of law. Id. at 736-37. Further, the court found that the Inspector General's disclosure of the questionnaires to the Justice Department (for a criminal fraud prosecution) was not compatible with the purpose for which they were originally collected by the Department of Energy (for a security-clearance eligibility determination), notwithstanding the fact that the questionnaires were subsequently acquired by the Inspector General – on an intra-agency "need to know" basis pursuant to 5 U.S.C. § 552a(b)(1) – for the purpose of a fraud investigation. Id. at 737-39.

On cross-appeals, a divided panel of the Court of Appeals for the Ninth Circuit affirmed the district court's judgment on other grounds. Covert, 876 F.2d at 754-56. The panel majority held that the Department of Energy's failure to provide actual notice of the routine use on the questionnaires at the time of original collection, under subsection (e)(3)(C), precluded the Department of Energy from later invoking that routine use under subsection (b)(3). Id. at 755-56; see also Puerta v. HHS, No. 99-55497, 2000 WL 863974, at *1-2 (9th Cir. June 28, 2000) (following Covert, but finding that agency had provided notice of routine use on form used to collect information), aff'g No. EDCV 94-0148, slip op. at 7 (C.D. Cal. Jan. 5, 1999); USPS v. Nat'l Ass'n of Letter Carriers, 9 F.3d at 146 (citing Covert with approval and remanding case for factual determination as to whether subsection (e)(3)(C) notice was given); Stafford v. SSA, 437 F. Supp. 2d 1113, 1119-20 (N.D. Cal. 2006) (adhering to Covert and finding that SSA notified plaintiff of potential uses "on three occasions when collecting information from her," even though these notifications were non-specific references to the Federal Register); Pontecorvo, No. 00-1511, slip op. at 12 (D.D.C. Sept. 30, 2001) (stating that agency must comply with subsection (e)(3)(C) "in order to substantiate an exception for 'routine use'"). Prior to Covert, no other court had ever so held. See the additional discussion under subsection (e)(3), below.

In Doe v. Stephens, 851 F.2d 1457, 1465-67 (D.C. Cir. 1988), the Court of Appeals for the District of Columbia Circuit held that a VA routine use – permitting disclosure of records "in order for the VA to respond to and comply with the issuance of a federal subpoena [47 Fed. Reg. 51,841 (Nov. 17, 1982)]" – was invalid under the Administrative Procedure Act because it was inconsistent with the Privacy Act as interpreted in Doe v. DiGenova, 779 F.2d at 78-84 – where the court had found that disclosures pursuant to subpoenas were not permitted by the subsection (b)(11) court order exception. In light of Doe v. Stephens, the decision in Fields v. Leuver, No. 83-0967, slip op. at 5-7 (D.D.C. Sept. 22, 1983) (upholding routine use permitting disclosure of payroll records "in response to a court subpoena"), is unreliable. But cf. Osborne v. USPS, No. 94-30353, slip op. at 6-9 (N.D. Fla. May 18, 1995) (holding on alternative ground that disclosure of plaintiff's injury-compensation file to retired employee who had prepared file and who had been subpoenaed by plaintiff and was expecting to be deposed on matters documented in file was proper pursuant to routine use that "'specifically contemplates that information may be released in response to relevant discovery and that any manner of response allowed by the rules of the forum may be employed'").

The Act's legislative history recognizes the "compatibility" of a routine use invoked to publicly file records in court. See 120 Cong. Rec. 40,405, 40,884 (1974), reprinted in Source Book at 858, 995, available at http://www.loc.gov/rr/frd/Military_Law/pdf/LH_privacy_act-1974.pdf (routine use appropriate where Justice Department "presents evidence [(tax information from IRS)] against the individual" in court); see also Schuenemeyer v. United States, No. SA-85-773, slip op. at 1-2, 4 (W.D. Tex. Mar. 31, 1988) (finding no violation of Privacy Act for disclosure of litigant's medical records to Justice Department and U.S. Claims Court, as the information was used "in preparing the position of the USAF before the [court]," and was authorized under agency routine use).

In Krohn v. U.S. Department of Justice, No. 78-1536, slip op. at 4-7 (D.D.C. Mar. 19, 1984), however, the court invalidated an FBI routine use allowing for "dissemination [of records] during appropriate legal proceedings," finding that such a routine use was

OVERVIEW OF THE PRIVACY ACT

impermissibly "vague" and was "capable of being construed so broadly as to encompass all legal proceedings." In response to Krohn, OMB issued guidance to agencies in which it suggested a model routine use – employing a "relevant and necessary to the litigation" standard – to permit the public filing of protected records with a court. OMB Memorandum for the Senior Agency Officials for Information Resources Management 2-4 (May 24, 1985), available at http://www.whitehouse.gov/sites/default/files/omb/assets/omb/inforeg/guidance1985.pdf. Many agencies, including the Justice Department, have adopted "post-Krohn" routine uses designed to authorize the public filing of relevant records in court. See, e.g., 66 Fed. Reg. 36,593, 36,594 (July 12, 2001), available at http://frwebgate.access.gpo.gov/cgi-bin/getdoc.cgi?dbname=2001_register&docid=01-17475-filed (routine use [number 7] applicable to records in Justice Department's "Civil Division Case File System"); 63 Fed. Reg. 8,666, 8,667-68 (Feb. 20, 1998), available at http://frwebgate.access.gpo.gov/cgibin/getdoc.cgi?dbname=1998_register&docid=98-4206-filed.pdf (routine uses [letters "o" and "p"] applicable to records in U.S. Attorney's Office's "Civil Case Files").

It should be noted that none of the "post-Krohn" routine uses – such as the ones cited above which employ an "arguably relevant to the litigation" standard – have been successfully challenged in the courts. See Jackson v. FBI, No. 02-C-3957, 2007 WL 2492069, at *8 (N.D. Ill. Aug. 28, 2007) (allowing U.S. Attorney's filing with court of plaintiff's unsuccessful application for employment with FBI during pendency of plaintiff's Title VII suit against FBI because application was "at the very heart of his civil suit"); Russell v. GSA, 935 F. Supp. 1142, 1145-46 (D. Colo. 1996) (without analyzing propriety of routine use, finding disclosure in public pleadings of information regarding investigation of plaintiff was permissible under routine use providing for disclosure in proceeding before court where agency is party and records are determined "to be arguably relevant to the litigation"); Osborne v. USPS, No. 94-30353, slip op. at 6-9 (N.D. Fla. May 18, 1995) (holding on alternative ground that disclosure of plaintiff's injury-compensation file to retired employee who had prepared file and who had been subpoenaed by plaintiff and was expecting to be deposed on matters documented in file was proper pursuant to routine use providing for disclosures "incident to litigation" and "in a proceeding before a court" because "deposition was a proceeding before [the] Court"); Sheptin v. DOJ, No. 91-2806, 1992 U.S. Dist. LEXIS 6221, at *6-7 (D.D.C. Apr. 30, 1992) (no wrongful disclosure where agency routine uses permit use of presentence report during course of habeas proceeding). Such challenges could arise, either based upon an argument that the routine use does not satisfy the "compatibility" requirement of subsection (a)(7) of the Act, cf. Britt, 886 F.2d at 547-50 (mere "relevance" to recipient entity held to be improper standard for a "compatible" routine use disclosure), or based upon an argument that the routine use effectively circumvents the more restrictive, privacy-protective requirements of subsection (b)(11), cf. Doe v. Stephens, 851 F.2d at 1465-67 (agency cannot use routine use exception to disclose records in response to subpoena where court had earlier ruled that such disclosure was improper under subsection (b)(11)).

Numerous types of information sharing between agencies and with organizations or individuals have been upheld as valid routine uses. See, e.g., Burnett v. DOJ, 213 F. App'x 526, 528 (9th Cir. 2006) (disclosure by U.S. Attorney's Office of administrative law judge's finding that plaintiff was not credible to criminal defendant against whom plaintiff was to testify as expert witness); Puerta v. HHS, No. 99-55497, 2000 WL 863974, at *1-2 (9th Cir. June 28, 2000) (disclosure of grant proposal to qualified expert who was member of peer review group for evaluation of proposal), aff'g No. EDCV 94-0148, slip op. at 7 (C.D. Cal. Jan. 5, 1999); Pippinger v. Rubin, 129 F.3d 519, 531-32 (10th Cir. 1997) (disclosure of plaintiff's personnel information to MSPB in deposition testimony in another individual's related MSPB proceeding, and to the other individual, his attorney, and court reporter in conjunction with MSPB proceeding); Taylor v. United States, 106 F.3d 833, 836-37 (8th Cir. 1997) (disclosure of federal taxpayer information collected for purpose of federal tax administration to state tax officials for purpose of state tax administration), aff'g Taylor v. IRS, 186 B.R. 441, 446-47, 453-54 (N.D. Iowa 1995); Mount v. USPS, 79 F.3d 531, 534 (6th Cir. 1996) (disclosure of plaintiff's medical information to union official representing him in administrative action in which his mental health was central issue); Alphin v. FAA, No. 89-2405, 1990 WL 52830, at *1 (4th Cir. Apr. 13, 1990) (disclosure of enforcement investigation final report to subject's customers); Hastings v. Judicial Conference of the United States, 770 F.2d 1093, 1104 (D.C. Cir. 1985) (disclosure of criminal investigative records to judicial committee investigating judge); United States v. Miller, 643 F.2d 713, 715 (10th Cir. 1981) (records submitted by individual to parole officer became part of Justice Department files and Department's use in criminal investigation constitutes routine use); United States v. Collins, 596 F.2d 166, 168 (6th Cir. 1979) (HEW's disclosure of plaintiff's Medicaid cost reports to Justice Department for use in criminal case

OVERVIEW OF THE PRIVACY ACT

against plaintiff); Middlebrooks v. Mabus, No. 1:11cv46, 2011 WL 4478686, at *7 (E.D. Va. Sept. 23, 2011) (disclosure of personnel records about plaintiff, a nurse, to state nursing board, HHS, and other healthcare reporting entities fell within routine use); Feldman v. CIA, 797 F. Supp. 2d 29, 38-39 (D.D.C. 2011) (disclosure to Congressional oversight committee to comply with statutory reporting requirements); Alexander v. FBI, 691 F. Supp. 2d 182, 191 (D.D.C. 2010) (disclosure of individuals' background reports to White House to determine trustworthiness for granting White House access); Doe v. DOJ, 660 F. Supp. 2d 31, 47-48 (D.D.C. 2009) (disclosure of information regarding employee's mental state, collected for purpose of coordinating his reasonable accommodation request, to state unemployment commission and to contractor in order to help determine employee's eligibility for benefits, where contractor appealed from plaintiff's award of benefits on agency's behalf); Lucido v. Mueller, No. 08-15269, 2009 WL 3190368, at *5-6 (E.D. Mich. Sept. 29, 2009) (FBI's disclosure of plaintiff's arrest and indictment on white-collar crimes to financial self-regulatory body where disclosure was required by federal law); Benham v. Rice, No. 0301127, 2005 WL 691871, at *5-6 (D.D.C. Mar. 24, 2005) (disclosure of agency employee's transfer request to AUSA, who had represented agency in prior discrimination suit brought by employee against agency, so that AUSA would "be informed of [the employee's] wishes to transfer offices" and so that AUSA "could attempt to settle the pending litigation with [the employee]"); Chang v. Dep't of the Navy, 314 F. Supp. 2d 35, 45-46 (D.D.C. 2004) (disclosure to Members of Congress for purposes of responding to constituent inquiries where, if constituent is other than record subject, only information releasable under FOIA could be disclosed); Mandel v. OPM, 244 F. Supp. 2d 146, 152 (E.D.N.Y. 2003) (alternative holding) (disclosure of information about plaintiff – including summary of charges, supporting information, and copy of OPM's investigation – to his former supervisors in connection with their testimony at plaintiff's MSPB hearing following determination that plaintiff was unsuitable for federal employment due to prior employment record and failure to disclose history), aff'd on other grounds, 79 F. App'x 479 (2d Cir. 2003); Fattahi v. ATF, 186 F. Supp. 2d 656, 661-64 (E.D. Va. 2002) (disclosure of fact that plaintiff had applied for federal firearms license to condominium association's counsel for purposes of determining whether firearms dealer could operate out of plaintiff's specific residential unit), aff'd, 328 F.3d 176, 181 (4th Cir. 2003) (agreeing with the district court "that ATF's routine use must be given 'a practical reading' such that disclosures are in accordance with the routine use when they are

OVERVIEW OF THE PRIVACY ACT

'reasonably necessary to verify pertinent information, [and] not just [when] verification cannot conceivably be obtained by any other means'"); Mumme v. U.S. Dep't of Labor, 150 F. Supp. 2d 162, 174 (D. Me. 2001) (alleged disclosure to agency's examining physician from investigation file detailing possible health care fraud by former government worker who was being examined regarding continuing eligibility for disability benefits), aff'd, No. 01-2256 (1st Cir. June 12, 2002); Contursi v. USPS, No. 98CV112, slip op. at 2-3 (S.D. Cal. July 6, 1999) (disclosure to county agency in response to its request in connection with investigation of employee), aff'd, 238 F.3d 428 (9th Cir. 2000) (unpublished table decision); Jones v. Runyon, 32 F. Supp. 2d 873, 876 (N.D. W. Va. 1998) (disclosure to credit reporting service of information about plaintiff when requesting employment reports in course of routine investigation of possible workers' compensation fraud), aff'd, 173 F.3d 850 (4th Cir. 1999) (unpublished table decision); Blazy v. Tenet, 979 F. Supp. 10, 26 (D.D.C. 1997) (CIA's disclosure of information about employee to FBI while FBI was investigating employee's application for FBI employment), summary affirmance granted, No. 97-5330, 1998 WL 315583 (D.C. Cir. May 12, 1998); Magee v. USPS, 903 F. Supp. 1022, 1029 (W.D. La. 1995) (disclosure of employee's medical records to clinical psychologist hired by agency to perform fitness-for-duty examination on employee), aff'd, 79 F.3d 1145 (5th Cir. 1996) (unpublished table decision); McNeill v. IRS, No. 93-2204, 1995 U.S. Dist. LEXIS 2372, at *6 (D.D.C. Feb. 7, 1995) (disclosure of IRS personnel records to prospective federal agency employer); Harry v. USPS, 867 F. Supp. 1199, 1206-07 (M.D. Pa. 1994) (disclosure of documents regarding individual's employment history, including details of settlement agreement, in response to congressional inquiries "made at the prompting of that individual"), aff'd sub nom. Harry v. USPS, Marvin T. Runyon, 60 F.3d 815 (3d Cir. 1995) (unpublished table decision); Lachenmyer v. Frank, No. 88-2414, slip op. at 4 (C.D. Ill. July 16, 1990) (disclosure of investigative report to persons at arbitration hearing held proper under routine use permitting disclosure of "record relating to a case or matter" in a "hearing in accordance with the procedures governing such proceeding or hearing"); Choe v. Smith, No. C-87-1764R, slip op. at 10-11 (W.D. Wash. Apr. 20, 1989) (INS's disclosure to its informant during investigation "to elicit information required by the Service to carry out its functions and statutory mandates"), aff'd, 935 F.2d 274 (9th Cir. 1991) (unpublished table decision); Brown v. FBI, No. 87-C-9982, 1988 WL 79653, at *1 (N.D. Ill. July 25, 1988) (disclosure of rap sheet to local police department); Ely v. DOJ, 610 F. Supp. 942, 945-46 (N.D. Ill. 1985) (disclosure to plaintiff's

OVERVIEW OF THE PRIVACY ACT

lawyer), aff'd, 792 F.2d 142 (7th Cir. 1986) (unpublished table decision); Kimberlin v. DOJ, 605 F. Supp. 79, 82-83 (N.D. Ill. 1985) (Bureau of Prisons' disclosure of prisoner's commissary account record to probation officer), aff'd, 788 F.2d 434 (7th Cir. 1986); Burley v. DEA, 443 F. Supp. 619, 623-24 (M.D. Tenn. 1977) (transmittal of DEA records to state pharmacy board); Harper v. United States, 423 F. Supp. 192, 198-99 (D.S.C. 1976) (IRS's disclosure of plaintiff's identity to other targets of investigation); see also Gowan v. U.S. Dep't of the Air Force, 148 F.3d 1182, 1187, 1194 (10th Cir. 1998) (disclosure of information regarding individual to Members of Congress in response to inquiries made pursuant to individual's letters requesting assistance; stating that such disclosure is not "incompatible" and thus "would likely be protected under the routine use exception"). But cf. Sussman v. U.S. Marshals Serv., 494 F.3d 1106, 1122-23 (D.C. Cir. 2007) (vacating grant of summary judgment to Marshals Service because plaintiff's allegations that agents were "'yelling and screaming [their allegations and theories in an effort to intimidate]' suggests disclosures went beyond what was 'necessary to obtain information or cooperation'" within terms of published routine use).

Four courts have required an agency to invoke its routine use to permit disclosure to unions of names of employees on the theory that refusal to so disclose was an unfair labor practice under the National Labor Relations Act. See NLRB v. USPS, No. 92-2358, 1994 WL 47743, at *3-4 (4th Cir. Feb. 16, 1994); NLRB v. USPS, 888 F.2d 1568, 1572-73 (11th Cir. 1989); NLRB v. USPS, 841 F.2d 141, 144-45 & n.3 (6th Cir. 1988); NLRB v. USPS, 790 F. Supp. 31, 33 (D.D.C. 1992); see also USPS v. Nat'l Ass'n of Letter Carriers, 9 F.3d at 141-46 (holding that "if Postal Service could disclose the information under [its routine use] then it must disclose that information, because in the absence of a Privacy Act defense the arbitrator's award must be enforced," but remanding case for determination as to whether proper (e)(3)(C) notice was given before requiring invocation of routine use); FLRA v. U.S. Dep't of the Navy, 966 F.2d 747, 761-65 (3d Cir. 1992) (alternative holding) (en banc) (release to union of home addresses of bargaining unit employees pursuant to routine use was required under Federal Service Labor-Management Relations Act). But cf. NLRB v. USPS, 660 F.3d 65, 70-72 (1st Cir. 2011) (ruling that USPS routine use for disclosure "[a]s required by applicable law . . . to a labor organization" did not require automatic disclosure of aptitude tests to union because National Labor Relations Act did not require that disclosure, but instead NLRB was required to balance "the interests

OVERVIEW OF THE PRIVACY ACT

of the union in the information against the privacy interests of the employees").

In addition, the Court of Appeals for the District of Columbia Circuit, in <u>Department of the Air Force v. FLRA</u>, granted enforcement of a Federal Labor Relations Authority decision requiring the Air Force to disclose to a union a disciplinary letter that was issued to a bargaining unit employee's supervisor. 104 F.3d 1396, 1399, 1401-02 (D.C. Cir. 1997). The court held that the Federal Labor-Management Relations Statute required disclosure of the letter, and that because the "union's request f[ell] within the Act's 'routine use' exception, the Privacy Act d[id] not bar disclosure," and that the union therefore was entitled to disclosure of the letter. <u>Id.</u> at 1401-02.

Apart from the FOIA (see subsection (b)(2)) and the Debt Collection Act (see subsection (b)(12)), the Privacy Act makes no provision for any nonconsensual disclosures that are provided for by other statutes. <u>See, e.g.</u>, 42 U.S.C. § 653 (2006) (establishing "Parent Locator Service" and requiring agencies to comply with requests from Secretary of HHS for addresses and places of employment of absent parents "[n]otwithstanding any other provision of law"). Recognizing this difficulty, the OMB Guidelines advise that "[s]uch disclosures, which are in effect congressionally mandated 'routine uses,' should still be established as 'routine uses' pursuant to subsections (e)(11) and (e)(4)(D)." OMB Guidelines, 40 Fed. Reg. at 28,954, available at http://www.whitehouse.gov/sites/default/files/omb/assets/omb/inforeg/implementation_guidelines.pdf; cf. <u>Zahedi v. DOJ</u>, No. 10-694, 2011 WL 1872206, at *5-6 (D. Or. May 16, 2011) (holding that plaintiff's "claim, for improper dissemination, fails both because the disclosure was authorized by [a foreign-intelligence sharing] statute and because the dissemination [falls] within the published routine uses" of the agencies).

4. **5 U.S.C. § 552a(b)(4) (Bureau of the Census)**

"to the Bureau of the Census for purposes of planning or carrying out a census or survey or related activity pursuant to the provisions of Title 13."

<u>Comment</u>:

For a discussion of this provision, see OMB Guidelines, 40 Fed. Reg. 28,948, 28,954 (July 9, 1975), available at http://www.whitehouse.

OVERVIEW OF THE PRIVACY ACT

gov/sites/default/files/omb/assets/omb/inforeg/implementation_guidelines.pdf.

5. **5 U.S.C. § 552a(b)(5) (statistical research)**

   "to a recipient who has provided the agency with advance adequate written assurance that the record will be used solely as a statistical research or reporting record, and the record is to be transferred in a form that is not individually identifiable."

   Comment:

   The term "statistical record" is defined in the Act as a record that is not used in making individual determinations. 5 U.S.C. § 552a(a)(6). One might question whether this exception to subsection (b) is anomalous: The information it permits to be released is arguably not a "record," see 5 U.S.C. § 552a(a)(4), or a "disclosure," see 5 U.S.C. § 552a(b), in the first place as it is not identifiable to any individual. However, the OMB Guidelines provide a plausible explanation for this unique provision: "One may infer from the legislative history and other portions of the Act that an objective of this provision is to reduce the possibility of matching and analysis of statistical records with other records to reconstruct individually identifiable records." OMB Guidelines, 40 Fed. Reg. 28,948, 28,954 (July 9, 1975), available at http://www.whitehouse.gov/sites/default/files/omb/assets/omb/inforeg/implementation_guidelines.pdf.

6. **5 U.S.C. § 552a(b)(6) (National Archives)**

   "to the National Archives and Records Administration as a record which has sufficient historical or other value to warrant its continued preservation by the United States Government, or for evaluation by the Archivist of the United States or the designee of the Archivist to determine whether the record has such value."

   Comment:

   For a discussion of this provision, see OMB Guidelines, 40 Fed. Reg. 28,948, 28,955 (July 9, 1975), available at http://www.whitehouse.gov/sites/default/files/omb/assets/omb/inforeg/implementation_guidelines.pdf.

OVERVIEW OF THE PRIVACY ACT

7. **5 U.S.C. § 552a(b)(7) (law enforcement request)**

"to another agency or to an instrumentality of any governmental jurisdiction within or under the control of the United States for a civil or criminal law enforcement activity if the activity is authorized by law, and if the head of the agency or instrumentality has made a written request to the agency which maintains the record specifying the particular portion desired and the law enforcement activity for which the record is sought."

Comment:

This provision, in addition to providing for disclosures to federal law enforcement agencies, also allows an agency, "upon receipt of a written request, [to] disclose a record to another agency or unit of State or local government for a civil or criminal law enforcement activity." OMB Guidelines, 40 Fed. Reg. 28,948, 28,955 (July 9, 1975), available at http://www.whitehouse.gov/sites/default/files/omb/assets/omb/inforeg/implementation_guidelines.pdf.

Note that the request must be submitted in writing and generally must be from the head of the agency or instrumentality. See Doe v. DiGenova, 779 F.2d 74, 85 (D.C. Cir. 1985); Doe v. Naval Air Station, 768 F.2d 1229, 1232-33 (11th Cir. 1985); see also Reyes v. Supervisor of DEA, 834 F.2d 1093, 1095 (1st Cir. 1987); United States v. Collins, 596 F.2d 166, 168 (6th Cir. 1979); Stafford v. SSA, 437 F. Supp. 2d 1113, 1121 (N.D. Cal. 2006); SEC v. Dimensional Entm't Corp., 518 F. Supp. 773, 775 (S.D.N.Y. 1981).

Record-requesting authority may be delegated down to lower-level agency officials when necessary, but not below the "section chief" level. See OMB Guidelines, 40 Fed. Reg. at 28,955; see also 120 Cong. Rec. 36,967 (1974), reprinted in Source Book at 958, available at http://www.loc.gov/rr/frd/Military_Law/pdf/LH_privacy_act-1974.pdf. The Department of Justice has delegated record-requesting authority to the "head of a component or a United States Attorney, or either's designee." 28 C.F.R. § 16.40(c) (2012); cf. Lora v. INS, No. 2:02cv756, 2002 WL 32488472, at *2 (E.D. Va. Oct. 8, 2002) (applying subsection (b)(7) to disclosure of information from INS file upon request of Assistant United States Attorney), aff'd per curiam, 61 F. App'x 80 (4th Cir. 2003).

OVERVIEW OF THE PRIVACY ACT

8. **5 U.S.C. § 552a(b)(8) (health or safety of an individual)**

"to a person pursuant to a showing of compelling circumstances affecting the health or safety of an individual if upon such disclosure notification is transmitted to the last known address of such individual."

Comment:

For cases discussing this provision, see Schwarz v. INTERPOL, No. 94-4111, 1995 U.S. App. LEXIS 3987, at *6 n.2 (10th Cir. Feb. 28, 1995) (unsubstantiated allegations alone do not constitute "showing of compelling circumstances"); Stafford v. SSA, 437 F. Supp. 2d 1113, 1121 (N.D. Cal. 2006) (exception not satisfied because agency did not provide requisite notice to plaintiff after disclosing reason that plaintiff received disability benefits to state child protective services for purpose of investigating possible child abuse); Schwarz v. U.S. Dep't of Treasury, 131 F. Supp. 2d 142, 146-47 (D.D.C. 2000) (citing and agreeing with Schwarz v. INTERPOL), summary affirmance granted, No. 00-5453 (D.C. Cir. May 10, 2001); and DePlanche v. Califano, 549 F. Supp. 685, 703-04 (W.D. Mich. 1982) (emphasizing emergency nature of exception).

According to the OMB Guidelines, the individual about whom records are disclosed "need not necessarily be the individual whose health or safety is at peril; e.g., release of dental records on several individuals in order to identify an individual who was injured in an accident." OMB Guidelines, 40 Fed. Reg. 28,948, 28,955 (July 9, 1975), available at http://www.whitehouse.gov/sites/default/files/omb/assets/omb/inforeg/implementation_guidelines.pdf. This construction, while certainly sensible as a policy matter, appears to conflict somewhat with the actual wording of subsection (b)(8).

9. **5 U.S.C. § 552a(b)(9) (Congress)**

"to either House of Congress, or, to the extent of matter within its jurisdiction, any committee or subcommittee thereof, any joint committee of Congress or subcommittee of any such joint committee."

Comment:

This exception does not authorize the disclosure of a Privacy Act-protected record to an individual Member of Congress acting on his

OVERVIEW OF THE PRIVACY ACT

or her own behalf or on behalf of a constituent. See OMB Guidelines, 40 Fed. Reg. 28,948, 28,955 (July 9, 1975), available at http://www.whitehouse.gov/sites/default/files/omb/assets/omb/inforeg/implementation_guidelines.pdf; 40 Fed. Reg. 56,741, 56,742 (Nov. 21, 1975), available at http://www.whitehouse.gov/sites/default/files/omb/assets/omb/inforeg/implementation1974.pdf; see also Swenson v. USPS, 890 F.2d 1075, 1077 (9th Cir. 1989); Lee v. Dearment, No. 91-2175, 1992 WL 119855, at *2 (4th Cir. June 3, 1992); cf. Chang v. Dep't of the Navy, 314 F. Supp. 2d 35, 45-47 (D.D.C. 2004) (discussing subsection (b)(9), but ultimately finding disclosure to be proper pursuant to routine use permitting disclosure to Members of Congress making inquiries on behalf of constituents). See generally FOIA Update, Vol. V, No. 1, at 3-4, available at http://www.justice.gov/oip/foia_updates/Vol_V_1/page3.htm ("Congressional Access Under FOIA") (interpreting counterpart provision of FOIA).

The Court of Appeals for the Second Circuit in Devine v. United States, in holding that the unsolicited disclosure of an Inspector General letter to a congressional subcommittee chairman and member fell "squarely within the ambit of § 552a(b)(9)," rejected the appellant's argument that subsection (b)(9) should not apply if the government agency knew or should have known that the information would eventually be released to the public. 202 F.3d 547, 551-53 (2d Cir. 2000).

10.   5 U.S.C. § 552a(b)(10) (Government Accountability Office)

"to the Comptroller General, or any of his authorized representatives, in the course of the performance of the duties of the G[overnment] Account[ability] Office."

11.   5 U.S.C. § 552a(b)(11) (court order)

"pursuant to the order of a court of competent jurisdiction."

Comment:

This exception – like the subsection (b)(3) routine use exception – has generated a great deal of uncertainty. Unfortunately, neither the Act's legislative history, see 120 Cong. Rec. 36,959 (1974), reprinted in Source Book at 936, available at http://www.loc.gov/rr/frd/Military_Law/pdf/LH_privacy_act-1974.pdf, nor the OMB Guidelines, see 40 Fed. Reg. 28,948, 28,955 (July 9, 1975), available

OVERVIEW OF THE PRIVACY ACT

at http://www.whitehouse.gov/sites/default/files/omb/assets/omb/inforeg/implementation_guidelines.pdf shed light in its meaning.

As a general proposition, it appears that the essential point of this exception is that the Privacy Act "cannot be used to block the normal course of court proceedings, including court-ordered discovery." Clavir v. United States, 84 F.R.D. 612, 614 (S.D.N.Y. 1979); see also, e.g., United States v. Revland, No. 5:05-2212, 2011 U.S. Dist. LEXIS 137756, at *3 (E.D.N.C. Nov. 30, 2011); Vinzant v. United States, No. 2:06-cv-10561, 2010 WL 2674609, at *7 (E.D. La. June 30, 2010) (stating that where the defendant agency objected to disclosing Privacy Act records requested in discovery, "the 'court order exception' to the Privacy Act will preclude any future liability for disclosure, thereby alleviating the government's concern and nullifying its objection"); Rogers v. England, 246 F.R.D. 1, 3 n.6 (D.D.C. 2007); In re Katrina Canal Breaches Consol. Litig., No. 05-4182, 2007 WL 1959193, at *6 (E.D. La. June 27, 2007); Martin v. United States, 1 Cl. Ct. 775, 780-82 (Cl. Ct. 1983); Newman v. United States, No. 81-2480, slip op. at 3 (D.D.C. Sept. 13, 1982); B & H Towing, 2006 WL 1728044, at *5 (S.D. W. Va. June 23, 2006).

5 U.S.C. § 552a(b)(11) permits disclosure of information by a court order. "However, [it] does not provide a basis for federal jurisdiction. Rather, it identifies an exception to the general rule under the Privacy Act" that no record may be disclosed except with the consent of the individual to whom the record pertains. Sheetz v. Marti, No. 10-10844, 2010 WL 2034775, at *1 (D. Mass. May 19, 2010) (stating that "in the absence of federal question jurisdiction . . . , diversity jurisdiction . . . , or some other statutory grant of jurisdiction, this court lacks authority to issue a subpoena" against a federal agency for records the plaintiff sought in connection with his divorce proceedings); see also Haydon Bros. Contracting, Inc. v. SSA, No. 7:11-96, 2012 WL 38608, at *2-4 (E.D. Ky. Jan. 9, 2012) (where plaintiff was seeking a (b)(11) order to require an agency to disclose a third party's records, stating that, "While the Privacy Act permits disclosure of an individual's records pursuant to a court order, it does not provide expressly for a private right of action to obtain such an order," and "implying a civil remedy . . . is not consistent with the legislative scheme of the Privacy Act.").

What Does "Court Order" Mean?

In Doe v. DiGenova, 779 F.2d 74, 77-85 (D.C. Cir. 1985), the Court of Appeals for the District of Columbia Circuit decisively ruled that a

OVERVIEW OF THE PRIVACY ACT

subpoena routinely issued by a court clerk – such as a federal grand jury subpoena – is not a "court order" within the meaning of this exception because it is not "specifically approved" by a judge. Cf. Hoffman v. Astrue, No. 3:10-CV-00214, 2011 WL 195617, at *4 (W.D. Ky. Jan. 18, 2011) (ruling that agency need not comply with state court subpoena to disclose records because all 12 exceptions under Privacy Act are "inapposite"). Prior to Doe v. DiGenova, a split of authority existed on this point. Compare Bruce v. United States, 621 F.2d 914, 916 (8th Cir. 1980) (dictum) (subpoena is not court order), and Stiles v. Atlanta Gas Light Co., 453 F. Supp. 798, 800 (N.D. Ga. 1978) (same), with Adams v. United States Lines, No. 80-0952, slip op. at 2-3 (E.D. La. Mar. 16, 1981) (subpoena is court order). Cf. Moore v. USPS, 609 F. Supp. 681, 682 (E.D.N.Y. 1985) (subpoena is court order where it is required to be approved by judge under state law).

Note that an agency cannot avoid the result in Doe v. DiGenova by relying on a routine use that seeks to authorize disclosure pursuant to a subpoena. See Doe v. Stephens, 851 F.2d 1457, 1465-67 (D.C. Cir. 1988) (discussed above under routine use exception).

What is the Standard for Issuance of a Court Order?

Unlike similar provisions in other federal confidentiality statutes, see, e.g., 42 U.S.C. § 290dd-2 (2006) (listing "good cause" factors to be weighed by court in evaluating applications for orders permitting disclosure of records pertaining to substance abuse), subsection (b)(11) contains no standard governing the issuance of an order authorizing the disclosure of otherwise protected Privacy Act information. However, several courts have addressed the issue with varying degrees of clarity. It has been held, for example, that because the Privacy Act does not itself create a qualified discovery "privilege," a showing of "need" is not a prerequisite to initiating discovery of protected records. See Laxalt v. McClatchy, 809 F.2d 885, 888-90 (D.C. Cir. 1987); see also Weahkee v. Norton, 621 F.2d 1080, 1082 (10th Cir. 1980) (noting that objection to discovery of protected records "does not state a claim of privilege"); Ala. & Gulf Coast Ry., LLC v. United States, No. CA 10-0352, 2011 WL 1838882, at *3-5 (S.D. Ala. May 13, 2011) (citing Laxalt in determining relevance of personnel files); Bosaw v. NTEU, 887 F. Supp. 1199, 1215-17 (S.D. Ind. 1995) (citing Laxalt with approval, although ultimately determining that court did not have jurisdiction to rule on merits of case); Ford Motor Co. v. United States, 825 F. Supp. 1081, 1083 (Ct. Int'l Trade 1993) ("[T]he Privacy Act does not

OVERVIEW OF THE PRIVACY ACT

establish a qualified discovery privilege that requires a party seeking disclosure under 5 U.S.C. § 552a(b)(11) to prove that its need for the information outweighs the privacy interest of the individual to whom the information relates."); Clavir v. United States, 84 F.R.D. at 614 ("it has never been suggested that the Privacy Act was intended to serve as a limiting amendment to . . . the Federal Rules of Civil Procedure"); cf. Baldrige v. Shapiro, 455 U.S. 345, 360-62 (1981) (Census Act held to constitute statutorily created discovery "privilege" because it precludes all disclosure of raw census data despite need demonstrated by litigant).

Rather, the D.C. Circuit's decision in Laxalt v. McClatchy establishes that the only test for discovery of Privacy Act-protected records is "relevance" under Rule 26(b)(1) of the Federal Rules of Civil Procedure. 809 F.2d at 888-90; see also, e.g., Riascos-Hurtado v. United States, No. 09-CV-0003, 2011 U.S. Dist. LEXIS 28008, at *1 (E.D.N.Y. Mar. 17, 2011) (citing Laxalt and granting plaintiff's motion to compel production of background investigation of former agency employee, which was "relevant to the action and may be relied upon by Plaintiffs in opposing the Government's motion" to dismiss); Buechel v. United States, No. 08-132, 2010 WL 3310243, at *1 (S.D. Ill. Aug. 19, 2010); R.T. Vanderbilt Co. v. United States, No. 95-283, 2010 WL 2706282, at *6 (Fed. Cl. July 8, 2010); SEC v. Gowrish, No. C 09-05883, 2010 WL 1929498, at *2 (N.D. Cal. May 12, 2010); Stiward v. United States, No. 05-1926, 2007 WL 2417382, at *1 (E.D. La. Aug. 24, 2007); Ezell v. Potter, No. 2:01 CV 637, 2006 WL 1094558, at *2 (N.D. Ind. Mar. 16, 2006); Hassan v. United States, No. C05-1066C, 2006 WL 681038, at *2 (W.D. Wash. Mar. 15, 2006); Snyder v. United States, No. 02-0976, 2003 WL 21088123, at *2-3 (E.D. La. May 12, 2003); Lynn v. Radford, No. 99-71007, 2001 WL 514360, at *3 (E.D. Mich. Mar. 16, 2001); Anderson v. Cornejo, No. 97 C 7556, 2001 WL 219639, at *3 (N.D. Ill. Mar. 6, 2001); Hernandez v. United States, No. 97-3367, 1998 WL 230200, at *2-3 (E.D. La. May 6, 1998); Forrest v. United States, No. 95-3889, 1996 WL 171539, at *2 (E.D. Pa. Apr. 11, 1996); Bosaw, 887 F. Supp. at 1216-17 (citing Laxalt with approval, although ultimately determining that court did not have jurisdiction to rule on merits of case); Ford Motor Co., 825 F. Supp. at 1083-84; Mary Imogene Bassett Hosp. v. Sullivan, 136 F.R.D. 42, 49 (N.D.N.Y. 1991); O'Neill v. Engels, 125 F.R.D. 518, 520 (S.D. Fla. 1989); Murray v. United States, No. 84-2364, slip op. at 1-3 (D. Kan. Feb. 21, 1988); Broderick v. Shad, 117 F.R.D. 306, 312 (D.D.C. 1987); Smith v. Regan, No. 81-1401, slip op. at 1-2 (D.D.C. Jan. 9, 1984); In re Grand Jury Subpoenas Issued to USPS, 535 F. Supp. 31,

OVERVIEW OF THE PRIVACY ACT

33 (E.D. Tenn. 1981); Christy v. United States, 68 F.R.D. 375, 378 (N.D. Tex. 1975). But see Perry v. State Farm Fire & Cas. Co., 734 F.2d 1441, 1447 (11th Cir. 1984) (requests for court orders "should be evaluated by balancing the need for the disclosure against the potential harm to the subject of the disclosure"); United States v. Meyer, No. 2:11-cr-43, 2011 U.S. Dist. LEXIS 94270, at *1 (M.D. Fla. Aug. 23, 2011) (granting an order after "balanc[ing] the need for disclosure against the potential harm from disclosure"); In re Becker v. Becker, No. 09-70173, 2010 WL 3119903, at *4 (Bnkr. W.D. Tex. Aug. 6, 2010) (ruling that although the court was "authorized to order discovery of confidential records, it must balance the public interest in avoiding harm from disclosure against the benefits of providing relevant evidence"); Newman, No. 81-2480, slip op. at 3 (D.D.C. Sept. 13, 1982) (evaluating "legitimacy" of discovery requests and "need" for records as factors governing issuance of court order).

However, it is important to note that a protective order limiting discovery under Rule 26(c) of the Federal Rules of Civil Procedure (based, if appropriate, upon a court's careful in camera inspection) is a proper procedural device for protecting particularly sensitive Privacy Act-protected records when subsection (b)(11) court orders are sought. See Laxalt, 809 F.2d at 889-90; see also, e.g., Nguyen v. Winter, 756 F. Supp. 2d 128, 129 (D.D.C. 2010) (stating that "[p]ersonnel files cannot be produced without a Privacy Act protective order"); Buechel v. United States, 2010 WL 3310243, at *3-4 (issuing protective order to address defendant's concern that "institutional safety militates against disclosure of information regarding exposure to MRSA within [Federal correctional institution]"); SEC v. Gowrish, 2010 WL 1929498, at *3 (ordering production of Privacy Act-protected documents, but fashioning protective order permitting redaction of information disclosure of which "may compromise any ongoing, unrelated criminal investigation," while simultaneously requiring submission of unredacted copies for in camera review); United States v. Chromatex, Inc., No. 91-1501, 2010 WL 2696759, at *5 (M.D. Pa. July 6, 2010) (ordering disclosure in camera to "allow the court to determine whether a protected order pursuant to the Privacy Act may properly be issued"); Sala v. Hawk, No. 1:008-cv-63, 2009 U.S. Dist. LEXIS 82176, at *1-7 (D.V.I. Sept. 4, 2009) (order "[p]ursuant to 5 U.S.C. § 552a(b)(11) and Fed. R. Civ. P. 26(c)" establishing rules to be followed in order to protect privacy of DEA employees and to facilitate discovery); Sattar v. Gonzales, No. 07-cv-02698, 2009 WL 2207691, at *1-2 (D. Colo. July 20, 2009) (granting defendants' motion for a protective order where plaintiff sought discovery of

OVERVIEW OF THE PRIVACY ACT

documents that defendants claimed were protected by the Act); Lopez v. Chula Vista Police Dep't, No. 07 CV 01272, 2008 WL 8178681, at *1 (S.D. Cal. Oct. 21, 2008) (issuing a (b)(11) protective order to govern disclosure of Privacy Act records concerning ongoing investigations of certain immigration crimes and that may reveal confidential informant and investigatory techniques and methods); In re Katrina Canal Breaches Consol. Litig., No. 05-4182, 2007 WL 1959193, at *6 (E.D. La. June 27, 2007) (ordering that materials containing "sensitive personal information" protected by Privacy Act be treated as "'CONFIDENTIAL INFORMATION' pursuant to the Master Protective Order"); Boudreaux v. United States, No. 97-1592, 1999 WL 499911, at *1-2 (E.D. La. July 14, 1999) (recognizing relevancy of subsection (b)(11) to court's resolution of dispute over motion to compel responses to production of documents subject to Privacy Act, but ordering in camera review of documents so that legitimacy of agency objections may be determined "in the considered and cautious manner contemplated by the Privacy Act"); Gary v. United States, No. 3:97-cv-658, 1998 U.S. Dist. LEXIS 16722, at *10-11 (E.D. Tenn. Sept. 4, 1998) (finding that while third party's personnel file may contain relevant information, disclosure of that file must be made pursuant to protective order); Bustillo v. Hawk, No. 97-WM-445, 1998 WL 299980, at *4-6 (D. Colo. May 28, 1998) (ordering defendant to provide United States Marshals Service with addresses of individually named defendants for service of process on behalf of inmate and ordering that addresses be safeguarded by Marshals Service); Hernandez, No. 97-3367, 1998 WL 230200, at *2-3 (E.D. La. May 6, 1998) (granting motion to compel agency to produce individual's personnel file "which is likely to contain information 'relevant to the subject matter involved in the pending action,'" but accommodating "legitimate privacy and confidentiality concerns" with protective order); Wright v. United States, No. 95-0274, 1996 WL 525324 (D.D.C. Sept. 10, 1996) (order "pursuant to the Privacy Act and Rule 26 of the Federal Rules of Civil Procedure" establishing procedures to be followed by parties "[i]n order to permit the parties to use information relevant to th[e] case without undermining the legislative purposes underlying the Privacy Act"); Bosaw, 887 F. Supp. at 1216-17 (citing Laxalt with approval, although ultimately determining that court did not have jurisdiction to rule on merits of case); PHE, Inc. v. DOJ, No. 90-0693, slip op. at 13 & accompanying order (D.D.C. Nov. 14, 1991); Mary Imogene Bassett Hosp. v. Sullivan, 136 F.R.D. at 49; Avirgan v. Hull, Misc. No. 88-0112, slip op. at 1-3 (Bankr. D.D.C. May 2, 1988); Baron & Assocs. v. U.S. Dep't of the Army, No. 84-2021, slip op. at 2-4

OVERVIEW OF THE PRIVACY ACT

(D.D.C. Apr. 1, 1985); Granton v. HHS, No. 83-C-3538, 1984 U.S. Dist. LEXIS 19113, at *2-3 (N.D. Ill. Feb. 27, 1984); White House Vigil for the ERA Comm. v. Watt, No. 83-1243, slip op. at 1-3 (D.D.C. Oct. 14, 1983); LaBuguen v. Bolger, No. 82-C-6803, 1983 U.S. Dist. LEXIS 13559, at *1-3 (N.D. Ill. Sept. 21, 1983) (order); Clymer v. Grzegorek, 515 F. Supp. 938, 942 (E.D. Va. 1981); cf. Brown v. Narvais, No. CIV-06-228-F, 2009 WL 2230774, at *3 (W.D. Okla. July 22, 2009) (where plaintiff served subpoena on BOP seeking disclosure of Privacy Act-protected information, recommending that parties agree to a protective order to protect privacy interests of subject of information); Forrest, 1996 WL 171539, at *2-3 (parties ordered to "explore the possibility of entering into a voluntary confidentiality agreement regarding protecting the privacy interests of those individuals affected by disclosure"); Loma Linda Cmty. Hosp. v. Shalala, 907 F. Supp. 1399, 1405 (C.D. Cal. 1995) ("Even if release of the data . . . had unexpectedly included information not already known to [the recipient], a confidentiality order could have been imposed to protect the privacy interests in issue."); Williams v. McCausland, No. 90 Civ. 7563, 1992 WL 309826, at *3 (S.D.N.Y. Oct. 15, 1992) (parties directed to agree on and execute appropriate protective stipulation for information sought in discovery that, under Privacy Act's subsection (b)(2) standard, would not be required to be disclosed under FOIA). But cf. Jacobs v. Schiffer, 204 F.3d 259, 264-66 & n.5 (D.C. Cir. 2000) (where the information that an employee wished to disclose to his private attorney was covered by the Privacy Act, inter alia, recognizing superiority of First Amendment rights and "[o]bserving that there is a "critical distinction between disclosures in the attorney-client context and public disclosures," and pointing to the attorney's "willingness to enter into a protective order" as relevant to the balancing of "the employee's interests in communication with the government's interests in preventing communication").

In some instances, it even may be appropriate for a court to entirely deny discovery. See, e.g., Farnsworth v. Proctor & Gamble Co., 758 F.2d 1545, 1546-48 (11th Cir. 1985); In re Becker, 2010 WL 3119903, at *4; Weems v. Corr. Corp. of Am., No. CIV-09-443, 2010 WL 2640114, at *2 (E.D. Okla. June 30, 2010); Oslund v. United States, 125 F.R.D. 110, 114-15 (D. Minn. 1989); cf. Padberg v. McGrath-McKenchnie, No. 00-3355, 2007 WL 2295402, at *2 (E.D.N.Y. Aug. 9, 2007) (declining to decide "whether a court may ever order a government agency to disclose social security numbers despite the provisions of [the Social Security Act]," and refusing to order disclosure of social security numbers of class members who

OVERVIEW OF THE PRIVACY ACT

have not submitted claim forms pursuant to settlement agreement); Barnett v. Dillon, 890 F. Supp. 83, 88 (N.D.N.Y. 1995) (declining to order disclosure of FBI investigative records protected by Privacy Act to arrestees despite their assertion that records were essential to proper prosecution and presentment of claims in their civil rights lawsuit).

In Redland Soccer Club, Inc. v. Department of the Army of the United States, No. 1:CV-90-1072, slip op. 1-3 & accompanying order (M.D. Pa. Jan. 14, 1991), aff'd, rev'd & remanded on other grounds, 55 F.3d 827 (3d Cir. 1995), the district court, recognizing the "defendants' initial reluctance to respond to plaintiffs' [discovery] requests without a specific order of court [as] a reasonable precaution in light of the terms of the Privacy Act," solved the dilemma by ordering the Army to respond to "all properly framed discovery requests in th[e] proceeding" and that such responses were to "be deemed made pursuant to an order of court." Id. See also Long Island Savings Bank v. United States, 63 Fed. Cl. 157, 159-160 (Fed. Cl. 2004) (concluding that "[t]he exception in the Privacy Act for actions taken under court order is satisfied here" because scheduling order "specifically incorporated [a provision of the local rules]" requiring parties to exchange "witness lists containing the addresses and telephone numbers of each witness").

Must an Agency Obtain a Court Order to Publicly File Protected Records with the Court?

As noted above, the Act's legislative history indicates that a court is not a "person" or "agency" within the meaning of subsection (b), and that the Act was "not designed to interfere with access to information by the courts." 120 Cong. Rec. 36,967 (1974), reprinted in Source Book at 958-59, available at http://www.loc.gov/rr/frd/Military_Law/pdf/LH_privacy_act-1974.pdf.

However, the nonconsensual public filing of protected records with a court, during the course of litigation, does constitute a subsection (b) disclosure. See Laningham v. U.S. Navy, No. 83-3238, slip op. at 2-3 (D.D.C. Sept. 25, 1984), summary judgment granted (D.D.C. Jan. 7, 1985), aff'd per curiam, 813 F.2d 1236 (D.C. Cir. 1987); Citizens Bureau of Investigation v. FBI, No. 78-60, slip op. at 3 (N.D. Ohio Dec. 14, 1979). Thus, such public filing is proper only if it is undertaken pursuant to: (1) the subsection (b)(3) routine use exception (previously discussed), or (2) the subsection (b)(11) court order exception. See generally Krohn v. DOJ, No. 78-1536, slip op.

OVERVIEW OF THE PRIVACY ACT

at 3-11 (D.D.C. Mar. 19, 1984) (finding violation of Privacy Act where agency's disclosure of records as attachments to affidavit in FOIA lawsuit "did not fall within any of the exceptions listed in Section 552a"), reconsideration granted & vacated in nonpertinent part (D.D.C. Nov. 29, 1984).

Where the routine use exception is unavailable, an agency should obtain a subsection (b)(11) court order permitting such public filing. Cf. Doe v. DiGenova, 779 F.2d at 85 n.20 ("This is not to say that a prosecutor, a defendant, or a civil litigant, cannot submit an in camera ex parte application for a [subsection (b)(11)] court order."). However, in light of Laningham, No. 83-3238, slip op. at 2-3 (D.D.C. Sept. 25, 1984), agencies should take care to apprise the court of the Privacy Act-related basis for seeking the order. In Laningham, the district court ruled that the government's nonconsensual disclosure of plaintiff's "disability evaluation" records to the United States Claims Court was improper – even though such records were filed only after the agency's motion for leave to file "out of time" was granted. Id. The court held that subsection (b)(11) applies only when "for compelling reasons, the court specifically orders that a document be disclosed," and it rejected the agency's argument that the exception applies whenever records happen to be filed with leave of court. Id. at 4.

One unique solution to the problem of filing Privacy Act-protected records in court is illustrated by In re A Motion for a Standing Order, in which the Court of Veterans Appeals issued a "standing order" permitting the Secretary of Veterans Affairs to routinely file relevant records from veterans' case files in all future proceedings with that court. 1 Vet. App. 555, 558-59 (Ct. Vet. App. 1990) (per curiam); cf. Perkins v. United States, No. 99-3031, 2001 WL 194928, at *3 (D.D.C. Feb. 21, 2001) (pursuant to subsection (b)(11), authorizing parties to seek admission into evidence at trial in that case of any materials subject to stipulated protective order).

What Does "Competent Jurisdiction" Mean?

One of the few Privacy Act decisions to even mention this oft-overlooked requirement is Laxalt v. McClatchy, 809 F.2d at 890-91. In that case, the Court of Appeals for the District of Columbia Circuit appeared to equate the term "competent jurisdiction" with personal jurisdiction, noting that the requests for discovery of the nonparty agency's records "were within the jurisdiction of the District Court for the District of Columbia" as "[n]either party contends that the

OVERVIEW OF THE PRIVACY ACT

District Court lacked personal jurisdiction over the FBI's custodian of records." Id.

Of course, where an agency is a proper party in a federal case, the district court's personal jurisdiction over the agency presumably exists and thus court-ordered discovery of the agency's records is clearly proper under subsection (b)(11).

However, where a party seeks discovery of a nonparty agency's records – pursuant to a subpoena duces tecum issued under Rule 45 of the Federal Rules of Civil Procedure – Laxalt suggests that the district court issuing the discovery order must have personal jurisdiction over the nonparty agency in order to be regarded as a court of "competent jurisdiction" within the meaning of subsection (b)(11). See 809 F.2d at 890-91; cf. Mason v. S. Bend Cmty. Sch. Corp., 990 F. Supp. 1096, 1097-99 (N.D. Ind. 1997) (determining that Social Security Administration's regulations "generally do not authorize the release of . . . records upon order of a court, even a federal court, in the absence of a special circumstance as defined by the statutes and regulations" and thus finding SSA not to be in contempt of court for failure to comply with prior order compelling SSA, a nonparty, to produce documents). But cf. Lohrenz v. Donnelly, 187 F.R.D. 1, 8-9 (D.D.C. 1999) (finding that requisite showing of good cause had been made by nonparty agency, and providing for entry of protective order with no discussion of jurisdiction over nonparty agency). The issue of whether personal jurisdiction exists in this kind of situation is not always a clear-cut one – particularly where the nonparty agency's records are kept at a place beyond the territorial jurisdiction of the district court that issued the discovery order. Indeed, this very issue was apparently raised but not decided in Laxalt, 809 F.2d at 890-91 (finding it unnecessary to decide whether federal district court in Nevada would have had jurisdiction to order discovery of FBI records located in District of Columbia).

The existence of "competent jurisdiction" is likewise questionable whenever a state court orders the disclosure of a nonparty federal agency's records – because ordinarily the doctrine of "sovereign immunity" will preclude state court jurisdiction over a federal agency or official. See, e.g., Bosaw, 887 F. Supp. at 1210-17 (state court lacked jurisdiction to order federal officers to produce documents because government did not explicitly waive its sovereign immunity and, because federal court's jurisdiction in this case was derivative of state court's jurisdiction, federal court was likewise barred from

OVERVIEW OF THE PRIVACY ACT

ordering officers to produce documents); Boron Oil Co. v. Downie, 873 F.2d 67, 70-71 (4th Cir. 1989) (state court subpoena held to constitute "action" against United States and thus sovereign immunity applied even though EPA was not party in suit); Sharon Lease Oil Co. v. FERC, 691 F. Supp. 381, 383-85 (D.D.C. 1988) (state court subpoena quashed as state court lacked jurisdiction to compel nonparty federal official to testify or produce documents absent waiver of sovereign immunity); see also Moore v. Armour Pharm. Co., 129 F.R.D. 551, 555 (N.D. Ga. 1990) (citing additional cases on point); cf. Louisiana v. Sparks, 978 F.2d 226, 235 n.15 (5th Cir. 1992) (noting that "[t]here is no indication that [subsection (b)(11)] evinces congressional intent to broadly waive the sovereign immunity of [federal] agencies . . . when ordered to comply with state court subpoenas"); Longtin v. DOJ, No. 06-1302, 2006 WL 2223999, at *2-3 (D.D.C. Aug. 3, 2006) (citing Sparks and rejecting plaintiff's argument that subsection (b)(11) is a "sweeping waiver of sovereign immunity"; concluding that "neither the Superior Court of the District of Columbia nor the Circuit Court for Prince George's County, Maryland constitute[s] a 'court of competent jurisdiction' . . . to issue an order compelling a federal official to comply with a state court subpoena").

Nevertheless, in Robinett v. State Farm Mutual Automobile Insurance Company, No. 02-0842, 2002 WL 31498992, at *3-4 (E.D. La. Nov. 7, 2002), aff'd per curiam, 83 F. App'x 638 (5th Cir. 2003), the district court looked to subsection (b)(11) and held that State Farm "properly obtained" an order from the state court for release of plaintiff's medical records where "plaintiff's medical condition was relevant to the litigation," and that the Department of Veterans Affairs' "determination that plaintiff's records were subject to release based on the court order . . . was therefore correct." The district court's holding in Robinett was affirmed per curiam by the Court of Appeals for the Fifth Circuit, which specifically stated that the medical records were "released pursuant to the exception for orders of a court of competent jurisdiction contained in 5 U.S.C. § 552a(b)(11)." 83 F. App'x at 639; see also Moore v. USPS, 609 F. Supp. 681, 682 (E.D.N.Y. 1985) (assuming without explanation that state court subpoena, required by state law to be approved by judge, constituted proper subsection (b)(11) court order; issue of "competent jurisdiction" was not addressed); cf. Henson v. Brown, No. 95-213, slip op. at 4-5 (D. Md. June 23, 1995) (although not disputed by parties, stating that judge's signature elevated subpoena to court order within meaning of subsection (b)(11) in context of determining whether defendant complied with order).

OVERVIEW OF THE PRIVACY ACT

In addition, at least one state court has ruled that it has "competent jurisdiction" to issue a subsection (b)(11) court order permitting the disclosure of a Privacy Act-protected record. Tootle v. Seaboard Coast Line R.R., 468 So. 2d 237, 239 (Fla. Dist. Ct. App. 1984); cf. Saulter v. Mun. Court for the Oakland-Piedmont Judicial Dist., 142 Cal. App. 3d 266, 275 (Cal. Ct. App. 1977) (suggesting that state court can order state prosecutor to subpoena federal records for purpose of disclosing them to criminal defendant in discovery).

Agencies that construe state court orders as providing authority to disclose under subsection (b)(11) should be aware that compliance with such an order might be taken by a court as acquiescence to the court's jurisdiction, notwithstanding applicable principles of sovereign immunity.

12. **5 U.S.C. § 552a(b)(12) (Debt Collection Act)**

"to a consumer reporting agency in accordance with section 3711(e) of Title 31."

Comment:

This disclosure exception was added to the original eleven exceptions by the Debt Collection Act of 1982. It authorizes agencies to disclose bad-debt information to credit bureaus. Before doing so, however, agencies must complete a series of due process steps designed to validate the debt and to offer the individual an opportunity to repay it. See OMB Guidelines, 48 Fed. Reg. 15,556-60 (Apr. 11, 1983), available at http://www.whitehouse.gov/sites/default/files/omb/assets/omb/inforeg/guidance1983.pdf.

ACCOUNTING OF CERTAIN DISCLOSURES

(1) Each agency, with respect to each system of records under its control, must keep a record of the date, nature, and purpose of each disclosure of a record to any person or to another agency under subsection (b) and the name and address of the person or agency to whom the disclosure is made. See 5 U.S.C. § 552a(c)(1). An accounting need not be kept of intra-agency disclosures (5 U.S.C. § 552a(b)(1)) or FOIA disclosures (5 U.S.C. § 552a(b)(2)). See 5 U.S.C. § 552a(c)(1).

(2) This accounting of disclosures must be kept for five years or the life of the record, whichever is longer, after the disclosure for which the accounting is made. See 5 U.S.C. § 552a(c)(2).

OVERVIEW OF THE PRIVACY ACT

(3)   Except for disclosures made under subsection (b)(7), an individual is entitled, upon request, to get access to this accounting of disclosures of his record. See 5 U.S.C. § 552a(c)(3).

(4)   An agency must inform any person or other agency about any correction or notation of dispute made by the agency in accordance with subsection (d) of any record that has been disclosed to the person or agency if an accounting of the disclosure was made. See 5 U.S.C. § 552a(c)(4).

Comment:

The language of subsection (c)(1) explicitly excepts both intra-agency "need to know" disclosures and FOIA disclosures from its coverage. See, e.g., Quinn v. U.S. Navy, No. 94-56067, 1995 WL 341513, at *1 (9th Cir. June 8, 1995) (only disclosure of records was within Navy and thus was exempt from accounting requirements); Clarkson v. IRS, 811 F.2d 1396, 1397-98 (11th Cir. 1987) (per curiam) (IRS's internal disclosure of records to its criminal investigation units does not require accounting). It should be noted, however, that the OMB Guidelines specifically state that an accounting of disclosure is required "even when such disclosure is . . . with the written consent or at the request of the individual." OMB Guidelines, 40 Fed. Reg. 28,948, 28,955 (July 9, 1975), available at http://www.whitehouse.gov/sites/default/files/omb/assets/omb/inforeg/implementation_guidelines.pdf.

Additionally, OMB has stated that "[w]hile an agency need not keep a running tabulation of every disclosure at the time it is made, the agency must be able to reconstruct an accurate and complete accounting of disclosures so as to be able to respond to requests in a timely fashion." OMB Memorandum for Heads of Departments and Agencies, Attachment B – Instructions for Complying with the President's Memorandum of May 14, 1998, "Privacy and Personal Information in Federal Records" 4 (January 7, 1999), available at http://georgewbush-whitehouse.archives.gov/omb/memoranda/m99-05-b.html; see also OMB Guidelines, 40 Fed. Reg. at 28,956, available at http://www.whitehouse.gov/sites/default/files/omb/assets/omb/inforeg/implementation_guidelines.pdf.

In one case, a district court noted that although an agency is required pursuant to 5 U.S.C. § 552a(c) to keep an accurate accounting of each disclosure, there is no requirement that the "disclosed records themselves contain 'the date, nature and purpose' of each disclosure." Sieverding v. DOJ, 693 F. Supp. 2d 93, 106 (D.D.C. 2010), summary affirmance granted, No. 10-5149, 2010 WL 4340348 (D.C. Cir. Oct. 19, 2010). The district court also went on to state that the accounting requirement only "requires agencies to keep accurate accountings of their disclosures of records; they need not account for conversations or personal visits." Id.

It is important to recognize that subsection (c)(3) grants individuals a right of access similar to the access right provided by subsection (d)(1). See Standley v. DOJ, 835 F.2d 216, 219 (9th Cir. 1987) (plaintiff entitled to gain access to list, compiled by U.S. Attorney, of persons in IRS to whom disclosures of grand jury materials about plaintiff were made); Ray v. DOJ, 558

OVERVIEW OF THE PRIVACY ACT

F. Supp. 226, 228 (D.D.C. 1982) (addresses of private persons who requested plaintiff's records required to be released to plaintiff notwithstanding that "concern about possible harrassment [sic] of these individuals may be legitimate"), aff'd, 720 F.2d 216 (D.C. Cir. 1983) (unpublished table decision); cf. Quinn, 1995 WL 341513, at *1 (no records to disclose in response to request for accounting because there were no disclosures that required accounting); Beaven v. DOJ, No. 03-84, 2007 WL 1032301, at *23 (E.D. Ky. March 30, 2007) (finding accounting provisions not applicable for unauthorized disclosures because provisions only cover disclosures made under subsection (b)). However, subsection (c)(3) makes an explicit exception "for disclosures made under subsection (b)(7)." 5 U.S.C. § 552a(c)(3); see also Lora v. INS, No. 2:02cv756, 2002 WL 32488472, at *2 (E.D. Va. Oct. 8, 2002) (where the court found that the agency had disclosed information to an AUSA pursuant to subsection (b)(7) and plaintiff claimed that the agency failed to keep accounting records (given that plaintiff had requested information about disclosures from the agency and the agency had responded that plaintiff's file contained no record of disclosure), citing subsection (c)(3) and holding that "to the extent plaintiff alleges that defendant's failure to give him information about disclosures from his . . . file violated his rights under [the Privacy Act], plaintiff's complaint fails to state a claim"), aff'd per curiam, 61 F. App'x 80 (4th Cir. 2003).

Of course, it should not be overlooked that certain Privacy Act exemptions – 5 U.S.C. § 552a(j) and (k) – are potentially available to shield an "accounting of disclosures" record from release to the subject thereof under subsection (c)(3). See Vazquez v. DOJ, 764 F. Supp. 2d 117, 120 (D.D.C. 2011) (ruling that "DOJ properly denied plaintiff's request under the Privacy Act on the basis that such records are" in a system "which the FBI has exempted" from the accounting provision pursuant to (j)(2)); Zahedi v. DOJ, No. 10-694, 2011 WL 1872206, at *4 (D. Or. May 16, 2011) ("Plaintiff seeks an accounting of information obtained pursuant to a search warrant in the context of a criminal investigation, which falls squarely within the exemptions [(j)(2) and (k)(2)] to the Privacy Act's accounting provision."); Standley, 835 F.2d at 219 (remanding case for consideration of whether exemptions are applicable); Hornes v. EOUSA, No. 04-2190, 2006 WL 2792680, at *4 (D.D.C. Sept. 27, 2006) (finding, pursuant to exemption (j)(2), that "EOUSA has specifically exempted its system of 'Criminal Case Files' from the disclosure requirements of subsection (c)(3)"); Maydak v. DOJ, 254 F. Supp. 2d 23, 34-35 (D.D.C. 2003) (although noting that the agency's "conten[tion] that it 'is exempt from [the accounting provision] with respect to logs of disclosure' . . . is incorrect," and that "[e]xemption from the accounting requirement of § 552a(c) is not as expansive as seemingly being suggested by [the agency]," nevertheless finding that plaintiff had failed to state a claim and had no right of access where the system was exempt from the provisions of subsection (c)(3) pursuant to subsection (j)); Mittleman v. U.S. Dep't of the Treasury, 919 F. Supp. 461, 469 (D.D.C. 1995) (finding that "application of exemption (k)(2) . . . is valid" and that Department of the Treasury IG's "General Allegations and Investigative Records System" is exempt "because, inter alia, application of the accounting-of-disclosures provision . . . would alert the subject to the existence of an investigation, possibly resulting in hindrance of an investigation"), aff'd in part & remanded in part on other grounds, 104 F.3d 410 (D.C. Cir. 1997); Bagley v. FBI, No. 88-4075, slip op. at 2-4 (N.D. Iowa Aug. 28, 1989) (applying subsection (j)(2)); see also Hart v. FBI, No. 94 C

OVERVIEW OF THE PRIVACY ACT

6010, 1995 U.S. Dist. LEXIS 4542, at *6 n.1 (N.D. Ill. Apr. 7, 1995) (noting exemption of FBI's Criminal Justice Information Services Division Records System), aff'd, 91 F.3d 146 (7th Cir. 1996) (unpublished table decision).

For a further discussion of this provision, see OMB Guidelines, 40 Fed. Reg. 28,948, 28,955-56 (July 9, 1975), available at http://www.whitehouse.gov/sites/default/files/omb/assets/omb/inforeg/implementation_guidelines.pdf.

Finally, a plaintiff may seek damages for an agency's failure to maintain adequate accounting of disclosures. See Sussman v. U.S. Marshals Serv., 734 F. Supp.2d 138, 149 (D.D.C. 2010) (stating that "[t]he core elements of the claim are (1) failure . . . to maintain an accurate accounting of disclosures, and (2) a resultant adverse effect." Sussman v. U.S. Marshals Serv., 494 F.3d 1106, 1124 (D.C. Cir. 2007). Finally, it should be noted that the Privacy Act permits an individual to recover damages for accounting failures regarding disclosures "only to the extent those disclosures involved materials in his records." Id.

INDIVIDUAL'S RIGHT OF ACCESS

"Each agency that maintains a system of records shall . . . upon request by any individual to gain access to his record or to any information pertaining to him which is contained in the system, permit him and upon his request, a person of his own choosing to accompany him, to review the record and have a copy made of all or any portion thereof in a form comprehensible to him, except that the agency may require the individual to furnish a written statement authorizing discussion of that individual's record in the accompanying person's presence." 5 U.S.C. § 552a(d)(1).

Comment:

The Privacy Act provides individuals with a means of access similar to that of the Freedom of Information Act. The statutes do overlap, but not entirely. See generally Greentree v. U.S. Customs Serv., 674 F.2d 74, 76-80 (D.C. Cir. 1982). The FOIA is entirely an access statute; it permits "any person" to seek access to any "agency record" that is not subject to any of its nine exemptions or its three exclusions. By comparison, the Privacy Act permits only an "individual" to seek access to only his own "record," and only if that record is maintained by the agency within a "system of records" – i.e., is retrieved by that individual requester's name or personal identifier – subject to ten Privacy Act exemptions (see the discussion of Privacy Act exemptions, below). Thus, the primary difference between the FOIA and the access provision of the Privacy Act is in the scope of information accessible under each statute.

An individual's access request for his own record maintained in a system of records should be processed under both the Privacy Act and the FOIA, regardless of the statute(s) cited. See 5 U.S.C. § 552a(t)(1) and (2) (prohibiting reliance on FOIA exemptions to withhold under Privacy Act, and vice versa); H.R. Rep. No. 98-726, pt. 2, at 16-17 (1984), reprinted in 1984 U.S.C.C.A.N. 3741, 3790-91 (regarding amendment of Privacy Act in 1984 to include

OVERVIEW OF THE PRIVACY ACT

subsection (t)(2) and stating: "Agencies that had made it a practice to treat a request made under either [the Privacy Act or the FOIA] as if the request had been made under both laws should continue to do so."); FOIA Update, Vol. VII, No. 1, at 6, available at http://www.justice.gov/oip/foia_updates/Vol_VII_1/page5.htm ("FOIA Counselor Q & A"); see also Martin v. Office of Special Counsel, 819 F.2d 1181, 1184 (D.C. Cir. 1987) ("[A]ccess to records under [FOIA and Privacy Act] is available without regard to exemptions under the other."); Shapiro v. DEA, 762 F.2d 611, 612 (7th Cir. 1985) ("Congress intends that the courts construe the Privacy Act and the Freedom of Information Act separately and independently so that exemption from disclosure under the Privacy Act does not exempt disclosure under the Freedom of Information Act, and vice versa."); Blazy v. Tenet, 979 F. Supp. 10, 16 (D.D.C. 1997) (quoting subsection (t)(2) and stating that "[d]ocument requests therefore must be analyzed under both Acts"), summary affirmance granted, No. 97-5330, 1998 WL 315593 (D.C. Cir. May 12, 1998); Sussman v. DOJ, No. 03-3618, 2006 WL 2850608, at *4 (E.D.N.Y. Sept. 30, 2006) ("[A]n exemption under the FOIA is not a bar to release files under the Privacy Act and . . . a Privacy Act exemption is not a bar to release of files under the FOIA."); Brown v. DOJ, No. 02-2662, slip op. at 18 n.36 (D. Ala. June 21, 2005) (following Blazy and concluding that plaintiff's request must be analyzed under both FOIA and Privacy Act because "access to documents under these statutes [is] dissimilar"); Bogan v. FBI, No. 04-C-532-C, 2005 WL 1367214, at *6 (W.D. Wis. June 7, 2005) (explaining that if records are requested under both FOIA and Privacy Act, requester can gain access to those records by showing that they were accessible under either statute); Harvey v. DOJ, No. 92-176-BLG, slip op. at 8 (D. Mont. Jan. 9, 1996) ("Even though information may be withheld under the [Privacy Act], the inquiry does not end. The agency must also process requests under the FOIA, since the agency may not rely upon an exemption under the [Privacy Act] to justify nondisclosure of records that would otherwise be accessible under the FOIA. 5 U.S.C. § 552a(t)(2)."), aff'd, 116 F.3d 484 (9th Cir. 1997) (unpublished table decision); cf. Wren v. Harris, 675 F.2d 1144, 1146 & n.5 (10th Cir. 1982) (per curiam) (construing pro se complaint to seek information under either Privacy Act or FOIA even though only FOIA was referenced by name); Hunsberger v. DOJ, No. 92-2587, slip op. at 2 n.2 (D.D.C. July 22, 1997) (system of records from which documents at issue were retrieved was exempt pursuant to Privacy Act exemption (j)(2); "[c]onsequently, the records were processed for release under the FOIA"); Kitchen v. FBI, No. 93-2382, slip op. at 7 (D.D.C. Mar. 18, 1996) (although all requested documents were exempt under Privacy Act, they "were also processed under FOIA in the interest of full disclosure"); Kitchen v. DEA, No. 93-2035, slip op. at 9 (D.D.C. Oct. 12, 1995) (same), appeal dismissed for failure to prosecute, No. 95-5380 (D.C. Cir. Dec. 11, 1996); Freeman v. DOJ, 822 F. Supp. 1064, 1066 (S.D.N.Y. 1993) (implicitly accepting agency's rationale that "because documents releasable pursuant to FOIA may not be withheld as exempt under the Privacy Act," it is proper for the agency not to distinguish between FOIA and Privacy Act requests when assigning numbers to establish the order of processing, and quoting Report of House Committee on Government Operations, H.R. Rep. No. 98-726, which was cited by the agency as "mandat[ing]" such practice); Pearson v. DEA, No. 84-2740, slip op. at 2 (D.D.C. Jan. 31, 1986) (same as Wren).

In addition, unlike the FOIA, see 5 U.S.C. § 552(a)(6)(A), the Privacy Act does not speak of a

OVERVIEW OF THE PRIVACY ACT

requester's right to administratively appeal any adverse determination that an agency makes on his access request. However, because agencies should process an individual's access request under both statutes – which includes processing the request through any administrative appeal – there is no practical effect of this distinction. See, e.g., 28 C.F.R. § 16.45 (2012) (Department of Justice Privacy Act regulation regarding appeals from denials of requests for access to records).

It should be noted that the Privacy Act – like the FOIA – does not require agencies to create records that do not exist. See DeBold v. Stimson, 735 F.2d 1037, 1041 (7th Cir. 1984); Schoenman v. FBI, 764 F. Supp. 2d 40, 48 (D.D.C. 2011); Harter v. IRS, No. 02-00325, 2002 WL 31689533, at *5 (D. Haw. Oct. 16, 2002); Perkins v. IRS, No. 86-CV-71551, slip op. at 4 (E.D. Mich. Dec. 16, 1986); see also, e.g., Villanueva v. DOJ, 782 F.2d 528, 532 (5th Cir. 1986) (rejecting argument that FBI was required to "find a way to provide a brief but intelligible explanation for its decision without [revealing exempt information]"). But compare May v. Dep't of the Air Force, 777 F.2d 1012, 1015-17 (5th Cir. 1985) ("reasonable segregation requirement" obligates agency to create and release typewritten version of handwritten evaluation forms so as not to reveal identity of evaluator under exemption (k)(7)), with Church of Scientology W. United States v. IRS, No. CV-89-5894, slip op. at 4 (C.D. Cal. Mar. 5, 1991) (FOIA decision rejecting argument based upon May and holding that agency not required to create records).

The Court of Appeals for the District of Columbia Circuit has addressed the issue of the adequacy of an agency's search in response to an access request under the Privacy Act. See Chambers v. U.S. Dep't of the Interior, 568 F.3d 998 (D.C. Cir. 2009). In Chambers, the Court of Appeals applied the standard articulated by courts for adequacy of search for records under the Freedom of Information Act to an access claim brought under the Privacy Act. See id. at 1003. The Court of Appeals stated: "In a suit seeking agency documents – whether under the Privacy Act or FOIA – '"[a]t the summary judgment stage, where the agency has the burden to show that it acted in accordance with the statute, the court may rely on a reasonably detailed affidavit, setting forth the search terms and the type of search performed, and averring that all files likely to contain responsive materials (if such records exist) were searched."'" Id. (quoting McCready v. Nicholson, 465 F.3d 1, 14 (D.C. Cir. 2006), which in turn quotes Valencia-Lucena v. U.S. Coast Guard, 180 F.3d 321, 326 (D.C. Cir. 1999), a FOIA case addressing agency adequacy of search obligations); cf. Schulze v. FBI, No. 1:05-CV-0180, 2010 WL 2902518, at *15 (E.D. Cal. July 22, 2010) ("While the court is of the opinion that there exists some doubt that Congress intended that the Privacy Act provide civil remedies for an agency's failure to adequately search its files, . . . [t]he court, in the interests of giving fullest consideration to Plaintiff's claims, will follow Chambers and apply FOIA standards to Plaintiff's failure to search claims to the extent those claims are asserted under the Privacy Act.").

In Chambers, the Court of Appeals was also presented with the question of "whether [the agency] intentionally destroyed the [record sought] after [plaintiff] requested access to it." Chambers, 568 F.3d at 1000. The court of appeals reversed the district court's grant of

OVERVIEW OF THE PRIVACY ACT

summary judgment to the agency, reasoning that the agency's "search would not be adequate under the Privacy Act if [agency] officials, aware of Chambers's document requests, deliberately destroyed her performance appraisal before completing the search in order to avoid providing the document to her. . . . Such a search would not be '"reasonably calculated to uncover all relevant documents'" – which is what the Privacy Act, like FOIA, requires." Id. at 1005. In remanding the case back to the district court, the Court of Appeals noted that "should Chambers prevail on [her access claim], the available remedies may be limited given that additional searches at this late date would likely prove futile," but went on to state that "nonetheless, she may be entitled at a minimum to 'reasonable attorney fees and other litigation costs.'" Id. at 1008. On remand, the district court concluded that it "need not reach" the question of whether the agency intentionally destroyed the record at issue because the plaintiff "failed to sustain her burden of proof" on the question of "whether the document in question ever existed." Chambers v. U.S. Dep't of the Interior, No. 05-0380, 2010 WL 2293262, at *2-3 (D.D.C. May 28, 2010).

For a discussion of the unique procedures involved in processing first-party requests for medical records, see the discussion below under 5 U.S.C. § 552a(f)(3).

FOIA/PRIVACY ACT INTERFACE EXAMPLE: ACCESS

Suppose John Q. Citizen writes to Agency: "Please send to me all records that you have on me."

For purposes of this example, assume that the only responsive records are contained in a system of records retrieved by Mr. Citizen's own name or personal identifier. Thus, both the Privacy Act and the FOIA potentially apply to the records.

(1) IF NO PRIVACY ACT EXEMPTION APPLIES

Result: Mr. Citizen should receive access to his Privacy Act records where Agency can invoke no Privacy Act exemption.

The Agency cannot rely upon a FOIA exemption alone to deny Mr. Citizen access to any of his records under the Privacy Act. See 5 U.S.C. § 552a(t)(1) (FOIA exemptions cannot defeat Privacy Act access); see also Martin v. Office of Special Counsel, 819 F.2d 1181, 1184 (D.C. Cir. 1987) ("If a FOIA exemption covers the documents, but a Privacy Act exemption does not, the documents must be released under the Privacy Act." (emphasis added)); Hoffman v. Brown, No. 1:96cv53-C, slip op. at 4 (W.D.N.C. Nov. 26, 1996) (agreeing with plaintiff that "no provision of the Privacy Act allows the government to withhold or redact records concerning [his] own personnel records" and ordering production of e-

OVERVIEW OF THE PRIVACY ACT

mail and other correspondence regarding plaintiff's employment), aff'd, 145 F.3d 1324 (4th Cir. 1998) (unpublished table decision); Viotti v. U.S. Air Force, 902 F. Supp. 1331, 1336-37 (D. Colo. 1995) ("If the records are accessible under the Privacy Act, the exemptions from disclosure in the FOIA are inapplicable."), aff'd, 153 F.3d 730 (10th Cir. 1998) (unpublished table decision); Savada v. DOD, 755 F. Supp. 6, 9 (D.D.C. 1991) (citing Martin for the proposition that "[i]f an individual is entitled to a document under FOIA and the Privacy Act, to withhold this document an agency must prove that the document is exempt from release under both statutes"); cf. Stone v. Def. Investigative Serv., 816 F. Supp. 782, 788 (D.D.C. 1993) ("[T]he Court must determine separately [from the FOIA] whether plaintiff is entitled to any of the withheld information under the Privacy Act."); Rojem v. DOJ, 775 F. Supp. 6, 13 (D.D.C. 1991) ("[T]here are instances in which the FOIA denies access and the Privacy Act compels release."), appeal dismissed for failure to timely file, No. 92-5088 (D.C. Cir. Nov. 4, 1992); Ray v. DOJ, 558 F. Supp. 226, 228 (D.D.C. 1982) (requester is entitled, under subsection (c)(3), to receive the addresses of private persons who requested information about him, as "defendant is unable to cite a specific [Privacy Act] exemption that justifies non-disclosure of this information"), aff'd, 720 F.2d 216 (D.C. Cir. 1983) (unpublished table decision).

In other words, a requester is entitled to the combined total of what both statutes provide. See Clarkson v. IRS, 678 F.2d 1368, 1376 (11th Cir. 1982); Wren v. Harris, 675 F.2d 1144, 1147 (10th Cir. 1982) (per curiam); Searcy v. SSA, No. 91-C-26 J, slip op. at 7-8 (D. Utah June 25, 1991) (magistrate's recommendation), adopted (D. Utah Sept. 19, 1991), aff'd, No. 91-4181 (10th Cir. Mar. 2, 1992); Whittle v. Moschella, 756 F. Supp. 589, 595 (D.D.C. 1991); Fagot v. FDIC, 584 F. Supp. 1168, 1173-74 (D.P.R. 1984), aff'd in part & rev'd in part, 760 F.2d 252 (1st Cir. 1985) (unpublished table decision); see also 120 Cong. Rec. 40,406 (1974), reprinted in Source Book at 861, available at http://www.loc.gov/rr/frd/Military_Law/pdf/LH_privacy_act-1974.pdf. For access purposes, the two statutes work completely independently of one another.

(2)   IF A PRIVACY ACT EXEMPTION APPLIES

Result: Where a Privacy Act exemption applies, Mr. Citizen is not entitled to obtain access to his records under the Privacy Act.

But he may still be able to obtain access to his records (or portions thereof) under the FOIA. See 5 U.S.C. § 552a(t)(2) (Privacy Act exemption(s) cannot defeat FOIA access); Martin, 819 F.2d at 1184 ("[I]f a Privacy Act exemption but not a FOIA exemption applies, the

OVERVIEW OF THE PRIVACY ACT

documents <u>must be released</u> under FOIA.") (emphasis added); <u>Savada</u>, 755 F. Supp. at 9 (citing <u>Martin</u> and holding that agency must prove that document is exempt from release under both FOIA and Privacy Act); <u>see also</u> <u>Shapiro v. DEA</u>, 762 F.2d 611, 612 (7th Cir. 1985); <u>Vazquez v. DOJ</u>, 764 F. Supp. 2d 117, 120 (D.D.C. 2011); <u>Riser v. U.S. Dep't of State</u>, No. 09-3273, 2010 WL 4284925, at *6 (S.D. Tex. Oct. 22, 2010) (explaining that even if Privacy Act applied to record, "that statute cannot be used to withhold any record 'which is otherwise accessible to [an] individual' under FOIA"); <u>Grove v. CIA</u>, 752 F. Supp. 28, 30 (D.D.C. 1990); <u>Simon v. DOJ</u>, 752 F. Supp. 14, 22 (D.D.C. 1990), <u>aff'd</u>, 980 F.2d 782 (D.C. Cir. 1992); <u>Miller v. United States</u>, 630 F. Supp. 347, 348-49 (E.D.N.Y. 1986); <u>Nunez v. DEA</u>, 497 F. Supp. 209, 211 (S.D.N.Y. 1980). The outcome will depend upon FOIA exemption applicability.

(3) IF NO PRIVACY ACT EXEMPTION AND NO FOIA EXEMPTION APPLY

<u>Result</u>: The information should be disclosed.

(4) IF BOTH PRIVACY ACT AND FOIA EXEMPTIONS APPLY

<u>Result</u>: The record should be withheld, unless the agency, after careful consideration, decides to disclose the record to the first-party requester as a matter of administrative discretion. <u>See</u> Attorney General's Memorandum for Heads of Departments and Agencies, Subject: The Freedom of Information Act (Mar. 19, 2009), <u>available at</u> http://www.justice.gov/ag/foia-memo-march2009.pdf (encouraging agencies "to make discretionary disclosures of information" when they may legally do so). But remember: When an individual requests access to his own record (i.e., a first-party request) that is maintained in a system of records, an agency must be able to invoke properly <u>both</u> a Privacy Act exemption and a FOIA exemption in order to withhold that record.

<u>Rule</u>: ALL PRIVACY ACT ACCESS REQUESTS SHOULD ALSO BE TREATED AS FOIA REQUESTS.

Note also that Mr. Citizen's first-party request – because it is a FOIA request as well – additionally obligates Agency to search for any records on him that are <u>not</u> maintained in a Privacy Act system of records. With respect to those records, only the FOIA's exemptions are relevant; the Privacy Act's access provision and exemptions are <u>entirely inapplicable</u> to any records not maintained in a system of records.

OVERVIEW OF THE PRIVACY ACT

Comment:

A particularly troubling and unsettled problem under the Privacy Act arises where a file indexed and retrieved by the requester's name or personal identifier contains information pertaining to a third party that, if released, would invade that third party's privacy.

As a preliminary matter, it should be noted that this problem arises only when a requester seeks access to his record contained in a non-law enforcement system of records – typically a personnel or background security investigative system – inasmuch as agencies are generally permitted to exempt the entirety of their criminal and civil law enforcement systems of records from the subsection (d)(1) access provision pursuant to 5 U.S.C. § 552a(j)(2) and (k)(2).

The problem stems from the fact that unlike under the FOIA, see 5 U.S.C. § 552(b)(6), (7)(C), the Privacy Act (ironically) does not contain any exemption that protects a third party's privacy. Cf. 5 U.S.C. § 552a(k)(5) (protecting only confidential source-identifying information in background security investigative systems). The Privacy Act's access provision simply permits an individual to gain access to "his record or to any information pertaining to him" that is contained in a system of records indexed and retrieved by his name or personal identifier. 5 U.S.C. § 552a(d)(1).

The only two courts of appeals to have squarely addressed this issue have reached different conclusions. Compare Voelker v. IRS, 646 F.2d 332, 333-35 (8th Cir. 1981), with Sussman v. U.S. Marshals Serv., 494 F.3d 1106, 1120-21 (D.C. Cir. 2007).

In Voelker v. IRS, the Court of Appeals for the Eighth Circuit held that where the requested information – contained in a system of records indexed and retrieved by the requester's name – is "about" that requester within the meaning of subsection (a)(4)'s definition of "record," all such information is subject to the subsection (d)(1) access provision. 646 F.2d at 334. In construing subsection (d)(1), the Eighth Circuit noted that there is "no justification for requiring that information in a requesting individual's record meet some separate 'pertaining to' standard before disclosure is authorized [and i]n any event, it defies logic to say that information properly contained in a person's record does not pertain to that person, even if it may also pertain to another individual." Id. Relying on the importance of the access provision to the enforcement of other provisions of the Privacy Act, and the lack of any provision in the exemption portion of the statute to protect a third party's privacy, the Eighth Circuit rejected the government's argument that subsection (b) prohibited disclosure to the requester of the information about a third party. Id. at 334-35. A careful reading of Voelker reveals that the Eighth Circuit appeared to equate the term "record" with "file" for subsection (d)(1) access purposes. Cf. Wren v. Harris, 675 F.2d 1144, 1147 (10th Cir. 1982) (per curiam) (reversing district court's judgment that FOIA Exemption 6 protected certain third-party information requested under the Privacy Act; stating "[o]n remand, should the district court find that the documents requested by Mr. Wren consist of 'his record' or 'any information pertaining to him,' and that they are 'records' contained in a 'system of records,' § 552a(a)(4),

OVERVIEW OF THE PRIVACY ACT

(5), (d)(1), then the court must grant him access to those documents as provided in § 552a(d)(1), unless the court finds that they are exempt from disclosure under [Privacy Act exemptions]"; "the [district] court's reliance on [FOIA Exemption 6] to withhold the documents would be improper if the court determines that the [Privacy Act] permits disclosure"); Henke v. U.S. Dep't of Commerce, No. 94-0189, 1996 WL 692020, at *4 (D.D.C. Aug. 19, 1994) (rejecting government's argument that information contained in one individual's records is exempt from the disclosure requirements of the Privacy Act simply because the same information is also contained in another individual's records, and further stating that it would "not create an exemption to the Privacy Act that [C]ongress did not see fit to include itself"), aff'd on other grounds, 83 F.3d 1445 (D.C. Cir. 1996); Ray v. DOJ, 558 F. Supp. 226, 228 (D.D.C. 1982) (ruling that requester was entitled to access, under subsection (c)(3), to addresses of private persons who had requested information about him because no Privacy Act exemption justified withholding such information, notwithstanding that agency's "concern about possible harrassment [sic] of these individuals may be legitimate"), aff'd, 720 F.2d 216 (D.C. Cir. 1983) (unpublished table decision).

Voelker's rationale was purportedly distinguished (but in actuality was rejected) in DePlanche v. Califano, 549 F. Supp. 685, 693-98 (W.D. Mich. 1982), a case involving a father's request for access to a social security benefits file indexed and retrieved by his social security number which contained the address of his two minor children. In denying the father access to the children's address, the court reasoned that such third-party information, although contained in the father's file, was not "about" the father, and therefore by definition was not his "record" within the meaning of subsection (a)(4), nor was it information "pertaining" to him within the meaning of the subsection (d)(1) access provision. Id. at 694-96. In distinguishing Voelker, the court relied upon an array of facts suggesting that the father might harass or harm his children if their location were to be disclosed. Id. at 693, 696-98.

Other courts, too, have made findings that certain items of information, although contained in a file or document retrieved by an individual's name, did not qualify as Privacy Act records "about" that individual. See Riser v. U.S. Dep't of State, No. 09-3273, 2010 WL 4284925, at *6 (S.D. Tex. Oct. 22, 2010) (OPM document describing "background investigations generally, with no reference to or identifying information about any individual" does "not constitute a 'record' for Privacy Act purposes"); Murray v. BOP, 741 F. Supp. 2d 156, 161 (D.D.C. 2010) (names of individuals who visited plaintiff in prison and dates and times of their visits "certainly pertain[] to him in a generic sense – the visitors came to see him at the various BOP facilities where he had been incarcerated, and these visitors necessarily are linked to plaintiff"; However, "[e]ven if the information he seeks includes his name and identifying number . . . , the balance of the information requested pertains to the third party visitors personally; the information is not 'about' the plaintiff and therefore is not a 'record.'"); Nolan v. DOJ, No. 89-A-2035, 1991 WL 36547, at *10 (D. Colo. Mar. 18, 1991) (names of FBI agents and other personnel held not requester's "record" and therefore "outside the scope of the [Privacy Act]"), aff'd, 973 F.2d 843 (10th Cir. 1992); Haddon v. Freeh, 31 F. Supp. 2d 16, 22 (D.D.C. 1998) (applying Nolan and Doe, infra, to hold that identities and telephone extensions of FBI agents and personnel were not "about" plaintiff and thus were properly withheld); Springmann v. U.S. Dep't of State, No. 93-1238, slip op. at 8 & n.1 (D.D.C. Apr. 21, 1997) (citing Nolan and holding that name of foreign official who provided information to State Department and names of foreign service officers (other than plaintiff) who were denied tenure were "not accessible to plaintiff under the Privacy Act because the identities of these individuals d[id] not constitute information 'about' plaintiff, and therefore [we]re not 'records' with respect to plaintiff under the Privacy Act"); Hunsberger v. CIA, No. 92-2186, slip op. at 3-4 (D.D.C. Apr. 5, 1995) (citing Nolan and holding that names of employees of private insurance company used by Director of Central Intelligence and Director's unique professional liability insurance certificate number maintained in litigation file created as result of plaintiff's prior suit against CIA Director were not "about" plaintiff and therefore were not "record[s]" within meaning of Privacy Act); Doe v. DOJ, 790 F. Supp. 17, 22 (D.D.C. 1992) (citing Nolan and alternatively holding that "names of agents involved in the investigation are properly protected from disclosure"); cf. Allard v. HHS, No. 4:90-CV-156, slip op. at 9-11 (W.D. Mich. Feb. 14, 1992) (citing DePlanche with approval and arriving at same result, but conducting analysis solely under FOIA Exemption 6), aff'd, 972 F.2d 346 (6th Cir. 1992) (unpublished table decision).

The District Court for the District of Columbia was confronted with a more complex version of this issue in Topuridze v. USIA, 772 F. Supp. 662 (D.D.C. 1991), reconsidering Topuridze v. FBI, No. 86-3120, 1989 WL 11709 (D.D.C. Feb. 6, 1989), when the subject of a letter requested access to it and the agencies withheld it to protect the author's privacy interests. In Topuridze, the issue of access to third-party information in a requester's file was further complicated by the fact that the information was "retrievable" by both the requester's identifier and the third party's identifier, Topuridze v. FBI, No. 86-3120, 1989 WL 11709, at *1 (D.D.C. Feb. 6, 1989) – the record was subject to "dual retrieval." In apparent contradiction to the subsection (d)(1) access provision, subsection (b) prohibits the nonconsensual disclosure of an individual's record contained in a system of records indexed and retrieved by his name or personal identifier to any third party. See 5 U.S.C. § 552a(b). Because the letter was both the requester's and the third party's Privacy Act record, the government argued that subsection (b), though technically not an "exemption," nevertheless restricts first-party access under subsection (d)(1) where the record is about both the requester and the third-party author, and is located in a system of records that is "retrievable" by both their names. See Topuridze v. FBI, No. 86-3120, 1989 WL 11709, at *1 (D.D.C. Feb. 6, 1989); Topuridze v. USIA, 772 F. Supp. at 665-66. Although the court had previously ruled that the document was not about the author, see Topuridze v. FBI, No. 86-3120, 1989 WL 11709, at *2-3 (D.D.C. Feb. 6, 1989), on reconsideration it ruled that it need not reach that issue, finding that "[b]ecause the document is without dispute about the [requester], it must be released to him in any event." 772 F. Supp. at 665. On reconsideration, the court embraced Voelker and rejected the government's argument that subsection (b) created a "dual record exemption" to Privacy Act access. Id. at 665-66.

However, more recently, the Court of Appeals for the District of Columbia Circuit reached a result different from those reached in Voelker and Topuridze, although the court did not mention either of those cases. See Sussman, 494 F.3d 1106. The U.S. Marshals Service

OVERVIEW OF THE PRIVACY ACT

processed Sussman's subsection (d)(1) request "by searching for records indexed to his name" and found only one document. Sussman v. U.S. Marshall Serv., No. Civ. A. 03-610, 2005 WL 3213912, at *1 (D.D.C. Oct. 13, 2005). Sussman argued that the Marshals Service performed an inadequate search and identified a "Wanted Poster" that the Marshals Service had issued for Keith Maydak, which listed "Michael Sussman" as an alias for "Keith Maydak." 494 F.3d 1109. The Marshals Service conducted a second search, "now taking into account Sussman's connections to Maydak." Id. at 1110. The second search yielded more than 800 pages of documents "relating to Sussman." Id. The district court stated that "the [Marshals Service] searched Keith Maydak's files for records related to or pertaining to [Sussman] or that mentioned [Sussman] by name." 2005 WL 3213912, at *2. The Marshals service disclosed only some of these records to Sussman. 494 F.3d at 1110. Sussman brought a subsection (d)(1) claim against the Marshals Service. Id. The D.C. Circuit "interpret[ed] 5 U.S.C. § 552a(d)(1) to give parties access only to their own records, not to all information pertaining to them that happens to be contained in a system of records." Id. at 1121. The court explained that "[f]or an assemblage of data to qualify as one of Sussman's records, it must not only contain his name or other identifying particular but also be 'about' him. . . . That is, it must actually describe him in some way." Id.; see also Aguirre v. SEC, 671 F. Supp. 2d 113, 122 (D.D.C. 2009) (declining to dismiss claim seeking access to record that "clearly contains plaintiff's name and describes him, his history at the SEC and details related to his termination" because record "sufficiently describes plaintiff to satisfy the standard established by Sussman"). Thus, the court held, "the Marshals Service must disclose to Sussman those materials – and only those materials – contained in records about him, the release of which would not violate 5 U.S.C. § 552a(b)." Id. In a footnote, the court explained that "[i]f certain materials pertain to both Sussman and other individuals, from whom the Marshals Service has received no written consent permitting disclosure, the Privacy Act would both require (5 U.S.C. § 552a(d)(1)) and forbid (id. § 552a(b)) their disclosure." Id. at n.9. In such a situation, subsection (d)(1) must give way because "the consent requirement in § 552a(b) is one of the most important, if not the most important, provisions in the Privacy Act." Id.; see also Anderson v. U.S. Dep't of the Treasury, No. 76-1404, slip op. at 13 (D.D.C. July 19, 1977) (presaging Sussman by finding name of third-party complainant in requester's file to be "about" complainant and, therefore, denying requester access to complainant's name).

The D.C. Circuit's opinion in Sussman seriously calls into question the validity of Topuridze, insofar as Topuridze could be read to require an agency to disclose to a requester "those materials . . . contained in records about him" even if the release of those materials would violate the subsection (b) rights of the non-requesting party. See Sussman, 494 F.3d at 1121. While Sussman controls in the D.C. Circuit, which has universal venue for Privacy Act matters, the holding in Voelker remains undisturbed in the Eighth Circuit.

A requester need not state his reason for seeking access to records under the Privacy Act, but an agency should verify the identity of the requester in order to avoid violating subsection (b). See OMB Guidelines, 40 Fed. Reg. 28,948, 28,957-58 (July 9, 1975), available at http://www.whitehouse.gov/sites/default/files/omb/assets/omb/inforeg/implementation_guidel

OVERVIEW OF THE PRIVACY ACT

ines.pdf; see also 5 U.S.C. § 552a(i)(1) (criminal penalties for disclosure of information to parties not entitled to receive it); 5 U.S.C. § 552a(i)(3) (criminal penalties for obtaining records about an individual under false pretenses); cf., e.g., 28 C.F.R. § 16.41(d) (2012) (Department of Justice regulation regarding verification of identity).

Also, although it has been observed that subsection (d)(1) "carries no prospective obligation to turn over new documents that come into existence after the date of the request," Crichton v. Cmty. Servs. Admin., 567 F. Supp. 322, 325 (S.D.N.Y. 1983), the D.C. Circuit has held that under the FOIA a date-of-request cut-off policy – as opposed to a date-of-search cut-off policy – was unreasonable under the facts of that case. Public Citizen v. Dep't of State, 276 F.3d 634, 644 (D.C. Cir. 2002). See generally FOIA Post, "Use of 'Cut-Off' Dates for FOIA Searches," available at http://www.justice.gov/oip/foiapost/2004foiapost14.htm.

INDIVIDUAL'S RIGHT OF AMENDMENT

(1) An individual can request amendment of his own record. 5 U.S.C. § 552a(d)(2).

(2) Ten "working" days after receipt of an amendment request, an agency must acknowledge it in writing and promptly either:

    (a) correct any information which the individual asserts is not accurate, relevant, timely, or complete; or

    (b) inform the individual of its refusal to amend in accordance with the request, the reason for refusal, and the procedures for administrative appeal. 5 U.S.C. § 552a(d)(2).

(3) The agency must permit an individual who disagrees with its refusal to amend his record to request review of such refusal, and not later than 30 "working" days from the date the individual requests such review, the agency must complete it. If the reviewing official also refuses to amend in accordance with the request, the individual must be permitted to file with the agency a concise statement setting forth the reasons for disagreement with the agency. 5 U.S.C. § 552a(d)(3). The individual's statement of disagreement must be included with any subsequent disclosure of the record. 5 U.S.C. § 552a(d)(4). In addition, where the agency has made prior disclosures of the record and an accounting of those disclosures was made, the agency must inform the prior recipients of the record of any correction or notation of dispute that concerns the disclosed record. 5 U.S.C. § 552a(c)(4).

Comment:

For a discussion of subsections (d)(2)-(4), see OMB Guidelines, 40 Fed. Reg. 28,948, 28,958-60 (July 9, 1975), available at http://www.whitehouse.gov/sites/default/files/omb/assets/

OVERVIEW OF THE PRIVACY ACT

omb/inforeg/implementation_guidelines.pdf. For a discussion of amendment lawsuits, see the section entitled "Civil Remedies," below. For cases discussing statements of disagreement, see Strong v. OPM, 92 F. App'x 285, 288 (6th Cir. 2004) ("As [plaintiff] remains free to supplement his file to disprove [the reference's] opinion, OPM did not violate the Privacy Act by refusing to remove [the reference's] statement from [plaintiff's] file."), Gowan v. U.S. Dep't of the Air Force, 148 F.3d 1182, 1188-89 (10th Cir. 1998) (concluding that although plaintiff "does not have a Privacy Act cause of action to require Air Force to amend records or attach a statement of disagreement" to records maintained in a properly exempt system of records, agency may "voluntarily comply" with the statement of disagreement provision), and Middlebrooks v. Mabus, No. 1:11cv46, 2011 WL 4478686, at *5 (E.D. Va. Sept. 23, 2011) ("Plaintiff's allegations clearly challenge opinions. Specifically, she complains of her colleagues' and supervisors' assessments of her performance. Yet, if [plaintiff] believed that her evaluations were misleading or unfair, her proper recourse was to place a concise statement in [her] records which sets forth [her] disagreement with the opinions contained therein." (quoting Subh v. Dep't of Army, No. 1:10cv433, 2010 WL 4961613, at *3-4 (E.D. Va. Nov. 30, 2010)).

AGENCY REQUIREMENTS

Each agency that maintains a system of records shall –

    A.   5 U.S.C. § 552a(e)(1)

"maintain in its records only such information about an individual as is relevant and necessary to accomplish a purpose of the agency required to be accomplished by statute or by executive order of the President."

Comment:

This subsection is not violated so long as the maintenance of the information at issue is relevant and necessary to accomplish a legal purpose of the agency. See, e.g., Reuber v. United States, 829 F.2d 133, 139-40 (D.C. Cir. 1987); Kalderon v. Finkelstein, No. 1:08 Civ. 09440, slip op. at 72-73 (S.D.N.Y. Mar. 10, 2010) (magistrate's recommendation), adopted in pertinent part, 2010 WL 3359473 (S.D.N.Y. Aug. 25, 2010); Azmat v. Shalala, 186 F. Supp. 2d 744, 751 (W.D. Ky. 2001), aff'd per curiam sub nom. Azmat v. Thompson, No. 01-5282 (6th Cir. Oct. 15, 2002); Nat'l Fed'n of Fed. Employees v. Greenberg, 789 F. Supp. 430, 433-34 (D.D.C. 1992), vacated & remanded on other grounds, 983 F.2d 286 (D.C. Cir. 1993); Beckette v. USPS, No. 88-802, slip op. at 9-10 (E.D. Va. July 3, 1989); NTEU v. IRS, 601 F. Supp. 1268, 1271 (D.D.C. 1985); Chocallo v. Bureau of Hearings & Appeals, 548 F. Supp. 1349, 1368 (E.D. Pa. 1982), aff'd, 716 F.2d 889 (3d Cir. 1983) (unpublished table decision); see also AFGE v. HUD, 118 F.3d 786, 794 (D.C. Cir. 1997) (holding agency use of release

OVERVIEW OF THE PRIVACY ACT

form on employment suitability questionnaire constitutional in light of Privacy Act's subsection (e)(1) requirement and "relying on the limitation that the release form authorizes the government to obtain only relevant information used to verify representations made by the employee"); Barlow v. VA, No. 92-16744, 1993 WL 355099, at *1 (9th Cir. Sept. 13, 1993) (VA's request for appellant's medical records did not violate Privacy Act because VA is authorized to request such information and it is "relevant and necessary" to appellant's claim for benefits; citing subsection (e)(1)); Crummey v. SSA, 794 F. Supp. 2d 46, 56-57 (D.D.C. 2011) (where plaintiff – who believed that the Social Security Administration created a trust when it assigned him a Social Security Number and a Social Security Card and who had "drafted an agreement designed to reflect the alleged creation of the Trust" – requested amendment of his records "to include a copy of the Trust Agreement, or to reflect its contents," ruling that SSA need not amend the records because doing so "would require the SSA to maintain information about [plaintiff] that is neither relevant nor necessary to accomplishing any purpose of the SSA"), summary affirmance granted, No. 11-5231, 2012 WL 556317 (D.C. Cir. Feb. 6, 2012); Thompson v. Dep't of State, 400 F. Supp. 2d 1, 18 (D.D.C. 2005) ("While an agency normally would have no reason to maintain information on an employee's personal relationships, in these circumstances plaintiff's relationship was inextricably linked with allegations of favoritism by her supervisor."); Felsen v. HHS, No. 95-975, slip op. at 59-61 (D. Md. Sept. 30, 1998) (subsection (e)(1) "refers to the types of information maintained and whether they are germane to the agency's statutory mission," and "does not incorporate [an] accuracy standard"); Jones v. U.S. Dep't of the Treasury, No. 82-2420, slip op. at 2 (D.D.C. Oct. 18, 1983) (ruling that maintenance of record concerning unsubstantiated allegation that ATF Special Agent committed crime was "relevant and necessary"), aff'd, 744 F.2d 878 (D.C. Cir. 1984) (unpublished table decision). See also OMB Guidelines, 40 Fed. Reg. 28,948, 28,960-61 (July 9, 1975), available at http://www.whitehouse.gov/sites/default/files/omb/assets/omb/inforeg/implementation_guidelines.pdf; 120 Cong. Rec. 40,407 (1974), reprinted in Source Book at 863, available at http://www.loc.gov/rr/frd/Military_Law/pdf/LH_privacy_act-1974.pdf.

B. 5 U.S.C. § 552a(e)(2)

"collect information to the greatest extent practicable directly from the subject individual when the information may result in adverse determinations about an individual's rights, benefits, and privileges under Federal programs."

OVERVIEW OF THE PRIVACY ACT

Comment:

The leading cases under this provision are Waters v. Thornburgh, 888 F.2d 870 (D.C. Cir. 1989), and Brune v. IRS, 861 F.2d 1284 (D.C. Cir. 1988). Waters involved a Justice Department employee whose supervisor became aware of information that raised suspicions concerning the employee's unauthorized use of administrative leave. 888 F.2d at 871-72. Without first approaching the employee for clarification, the supervisor sought and received from a state board of law examiners verification of the employee's attendance at a bar examination. Id. at 872. In finding a violation of subsection (e)(2) on these facts, the Court of Appeals for the District of Columbia Circuit ruled that "[i]n the context of an investigation that is seeking objective, unalterable information, reasonable questions about a subject's credibility cannot relieve an agency from its responsibility to collect that information first from the subject." Id. at 873 (emphasis added); accord Dong v. Smithsonian Inst., 943 F. Supp. 69, 72-73 (D.D.C. 1996) ("concern over Plaintiff's possible reaction to an unpleasant rumor" did not warrant Smithsonian Institution's "fail[ure] to elicit information regarding alleged unauthorized trip directly from her"), rev'd on grounds of statutory inapplicability, 125 F.3d 877 (D.C. Cir. 1997) (ruling that "Smithsonian is not an agency for Privacy Act purposes"). The D.C. Circuit in Waters distinguished its earlier decision in Brune, which had permitted an IRS supervisor to contact taxpayers to check on an agent's visits to them without first interviewing the agent, based upon the "special nature of the investigation in that case – possible false statements by an IRS agent" and the concomitant risk that the agent, if contacted first, could coerce the taxpayers to falsify or secret evidence. Waters, 888 F.2d at 874; see also Velikonja v. Mueller, 362 F. Supp. 2d 1, 19-20 (D.D.C. 2004) ("seeking records from an electronic door log is very different from asking [plaintiff's] colleagues, rather than her, about her schedule" as "[t]he door log provided the most objective source of information about her actual entry times to the building, and unlike the proof of bar exam attendance in Waters, the records could not be obtained from plaintiff"), aff'd in pertinent part & rev'd in part sub nom. Velikonja v. Gonzales, 466 F.3d 122 (D.C. Cir. 2006) (per curiam).

Consistent with Brune, two other decisions have upheld the IRS's practice of contacting taxpayers prior to confronting agents who were under internal investigations. See Alexander v. IRS, No. 86-0414, 1987 WL 13958, at *6-7 (D.D.C. June 30, 1987); Merola v. Dep't of the Treasury, No. 83-3323, slip op. at 5-9 (D.D.C. Oct. 24, 1986).

In addition, the Court of Appeals for the Sixth Circuit relied on Brune and the OMB Guidelines, referenced below, to hold that subsection (e)(2) had

OVERVIEW OF THE PRIVACY ACT

not been violated by an investigator looking into charges of misconduct by an Assistant U.S. Attorney who had interviewed others before interviewing her. Hudson v. Reno, 130 F.3d 1193, 1205 (6th Cir. 1997). Given that the district court had found that the AUSA "was suspected of making false statements and she was allegedly intimidating and threatening people and otherwise dividing the U.S. Attorney's office," the Sixth Circuit held that "[a]ll of these practical considerations demonstrate that [the investigator] did not violate the Privacy Act when he interviewed others before interviewing [her]." 130 F.3d at 1205. Moreover, in a case involving a misconduct investigation into whether an agency employee had been intoxicated on the job, the Court of Appeals for the Fourth Circuit went so far as to observe that "[s]o long as the agency inevitably will need to interview both [the employee] and others, the Act takes no position on the order in which they were approached." Hogan v. England, 159 F. App'x 534, 537 (4th Cir. 2005). See also Carton v. Reno, 310 F.3d 108, 112-13 (2d Cir. 2002) (permitting "a preference to interview [plaintiff] last" when investigating a misconduct complaint against him because of plaintiff's "authority as an INS agent" and the existing "specific allegations that [plaintiff] had already terrorized and intimidated the complainants"); Cardamone v. Cohen, 241 F.3d 520, 527-28 (6th Cir. 2001) (finding it "impracticable to think that charges of employee mistreatment and harassment could be resolved by interviewing [the plaintiff] before others" because the plaintiff "could not have verified any conclusions" as to the "subjective allegations of employee mistreatment"); Carlson v. GSA, No. 04-C-7937, 2006 WL 3409150, at *6 (N.D. Ill. Nov. 21, 2006) (ruling that agency did not violate subsection (e)(2) "by not interviewing [an agency employee] first" since "[t]he issues under investigation [regarding the employee's undisclosed arrest] could not have been resolved by objective evidence within [the employee's] possession"; and concluding that "[t]he Act does not require the agency to undertake a piecemeal investigation by obtaining objective evidence first and then interviewing third party witnesses as to the more subjective claims"); Thompson v. Dep't of State, 400 F. Supp. 2d 1, 10-11 (D.D.C. 2005) (finding that agency "sought information directly from plaintiff 'to the extent practicable'" where agency interviewed plaintiff's coworkers before interviewing her in the context of an investigation into allegations made by some of plaintiff's coworkers that plaintiff helped create a hostile work environment; and further stating that "[t]he order of interviews therefore would not have altered the investigation's impact on plaintiff's reputation"); Mumme v. U.S. Dep't of Labor, 150 F. Supp. 2d 162, 173 (D. Me. 2001) (observing that "[w]hen conducting a criminal investigation of an individual . . . however, it may not be practicable for the investigating officers to collect information via direct questioning of the individual"), aff'd, No. 01-2256 (1st Cir. June 12, 2002); Jacobs v. Reno, No. 3:97-CV-2698-D, 1999 U.S. Dist. LEXIS 3104, at *19-22, 29-35 (N.D. Tex. Mar. 11, 1999) (finding no

OVERVIEW OF THE PRIVACY ACT

subsection (e)(2) violation in agency's "extensive, multifaceted investigation of an entire district office" where plaintiff was "both a charging party in several complaints and an accused in several others," as it "was not always practical" for agency to interview plaintiff first, given nature of allegations against him), subsequent decision, 1999 WL 493056, at *1 (N.D. Tex. July 9, 1999) (denying motion for relief from March 11, 1999 order because "newly-discovered evidence" would not have produced different result), aff'd, 208 F.3d 1006 (5th Cir. 2000) (unpublished table decision).

The Court of Appeals for the Eighth Circuit has examined the issue of whether a "collection" subject to the requirements of subsection (e)(2) occurs when an agency reviews its own files to obtain information. Darst v. SSA, 172 F.3d 1065 (8th Cir. 1999). The Eighth Circuit held that because the "situation merely involved a review of the agency's files," the agency "did not contact third party sources to gather information," and because "the indications of impropriety were apparent from the face of the documents and the sequence of events" reflected in the file, there was "no need to interview Darst about the sequence of events," and thus no violation of subsection (e)(2). Id. at 1068. The Eighth Circuit further stated that "[a]s the district court noted, the Privacy Act does not require that the information be collected directly from the individual in all circumstances," and that "[h]ere the information in the [agency] file obviated the need to interview Darst or third persons." Id.; see also Brune v. IRS, 861 F.2d 1284, 1287 (D.C. Cir. 1988) (stating that "investigations of false statement charges, by their nature, involve a suspect who has already given the government his version of the facts"); Velikonja, 362 F. Supp. 2d at 20 (holding that agency was not required to interview plaintiff before examining "electronic door logs" to compare them with her sworn attendance sheets because objective proof – the "electronic door logs" – could not be obtained from plaintiff).

For other decisions concerning this provision, see Olivares v. NASA, No. 95-2343, 1996 WL 690065, at *2-3 (4th Cir. Dec. 3, 1996), aff'g per curiam 882 F. Supp. 1545 (D. Md. 1995); Hubbard v. EPA, 809 F.2d 1, 11 n.8 (D.C. Cir.), vacated in nonpertinent part & reh'g en banc granted (due to conflict within circuit), 809 F.2d 1 (D.C. Cir. 1986), resolved on reh'g en banc sub nom. Spagnola v. Mathis, 859 F.2d 223 (D.C. Cir. 1988); Augustus v. McHugh, 825 F. Supp. 2d 245, 257-58 (D.D.C. 2011); Ramey v. U.S. Marshals Serv., 755 F. Supp. 2d 88, 97 (D.D.C. 2010); Kalderon v. Finkelstein, No. 08 Civ. 9440, slip op. at 73-77 (S.D.N.Y. Mar. 10, 2010) (magistrate's recommendation), adopted in pertinent part, 2010 WL 3359473 (S.D.N.Y. Aug. 25, 2010); Doe v. Goss, No. 04-2122, 2007 WL 106523, at *12-14 (D.D.C. Jan 12, 2007); McCready v. Principi, 297 F. Supp. 2d 178, 199-200 (D.D.C. 2003), aff'd in pertinent part & rev'd in part sub nom. McCready v. Nicholson, 465 F.3d 1 (D.C. Cir. 2006); Jones v. Runyon, 32

OVERVIEW OF THE PRIVACY ACT

F. Supp. 2d 873, 876 (N.D. W. Va. 1998), aff'd, 173 F.3d 850 (4th Cir. 1999) (unpublished table decision); Magee v. USPS, 903 F. Supp. 1022, 1028-29 (W.D. La. 1995), aff'd, 79 F.3d 1145 (5th Cir. 1996) (unpublished table decision); and Kassel v. VA, 709 F. Supp. 1194, 1203 (D.N.H. 1989); cf. Felsen v. HHS, No. CCB-95-975, slip op. at 62-65 (D. Md. Sept. 30, 1998) (granting defendants summary judgment on alternative ground on subsection (e)(2) claim due to "lack of a 'practicable' need to collect information directly from the plaintiffs"); Beckette v. USPS, No. 88-802, slip op. at 10 (E.D. Va. July 3, 1989) (subsection (e)(2) requirements satisfied where information contained in records was derived from other records containing information collected directly from individual).

The OMB Guidelines suggest several factors to be evaluated in determining whether it is impractical to contact the subject first. OMB Guidelines, 40 Fed. Reg. 28,948, 28,961 (July 9, 1975), available at http://www.whitehouse.gov/sites/default/files/omb/assets/omb/inforeg/implementation_guidelines.pdf; see also 120 Cong. Rec. 40,407 (1974), reprinted in Source Book at 863, available at http://www.loc.gov/rr/frd/Military_Law/pdf/LH_privacy_act-1974.pdf.

C.   5 U.S.C. § 552a(e)(3)

"inform each individual whom it asks to supply information, on the form which it uses to collect the information or on a separate form that can be retained by the individual – (A) the authority (whether granted by statute, or by executive order of the President) which authorizes the solicitation of the information and whether disclosure of such information is mandatory or voluntary; (B) the principal purpose or purposes for which the information is intended to be used; (C) the routine uses which may be made of the information as published pursuant to paragraph (4)(D) of this subsection; and (D) the effects on him, if any, of not providing all or any part of the requested information."

Comment:

The OMB Guidelines note that "[i]mplicit in this subsection is the notion of informed consent since an individual should be provided with sufficient information about the request for information to make an informed decision on whether or not to respond." OMB Guidelines, 40 Fed. Reg. 28,948, 28,961 (July 9, 1975), available at http://www.whitehouse.gov/sites/default/files/omb/assets/omb/inforeg/implementation_guidelines.pdf. The OMB Guidelines also note that subsection (e)(3) is applicable to both written and oral (i.e., interview) solicitations of personal information. Id.

OVERVIEW OF THE PRIVACY ACT

There is some authority for the proposition that subsection (e)(3) is inapplicable when an agency solicits information about an individual from a third party. See Truxal v. Casey, 2 Gov't Disclosure Serv. (P-H) ¶ 81,391, at 82,043 (S.D. Ohio Apr. 3, 1981); see also Gardner v. United States, No. 96-1467, 1999 U.S. Dist. LEXIS 2195, at *19 (D.D.C. Jan. 29, 1999) (noting that although it is correct that the Privacy Act mandates actual notice of routine uses, "information in the instant case was not gathered from Plaintiff, but from third parties"), summary affirmance granted on other grounds, No. 99-5089, 1999 WL 728359 (D.C. Cir. Aug. 4, 1999); McTaggart v. United States, 570 F. Supp. 547, 550 (E.D. Mich. 1983) (individual lacks standing to complain of insufficient Privacy Act notice to third party). The OMB Guidelines support this view, but suggest that "agencies should, where feasible, inform third-party sources of the purposes for which information they are asked to provide will be used." OMB Guidelines, 40 Fed. Reg. at 28,961. The practice of not providing notice to third parties was condemned by the Privacy Protection Study Commission, see Privacy Commission Report at 514, available at http://epic.org/privacy/ppsc1977report, and, indeed, several courts have disagreed with Truxal and the OMB Guidelines on this point. See Usher v. Sec'y of HHS, 721 F.2d 854, 856 (1st Cir. 1983) (costs awarded to plaintiff due to agency "intransigence" in refusing to provide information specified in subsection (e)(3) to third party); Kassel v. VA, No. 87-217-S, slip op. at 24-25 (D.N.H. Mar. 30, 1992) (in light of "the express language of § (e)(3) and the Privacy Act's overall purposes . . . § (e)(3) applies to information supplied by third-parties"); Saunders v. Schweiker, 508 F. Supp. 305, 309 (W.D.N.Y. 1981) (plain language of subsection (e)(3) "does not in any way distinguish between first-party and third-party contacts").

Generally, an agency does not need to explain "all of [its] rules and regulations" on "one small form" to meet the substantive requirements of subsection (e)(3). Glasgold v. Sec'y of HHS, 558 F. Supp. 129, 150 (E.D.N.Y. 1982); see also Field v. Brown, 610 F.2d 981, 987 (D.C. Cir. 1979) (holding that the agency's form "contained all the elements required by 5 U.S.C. § 552a(e)(3)").

In evaluating the requirements of subsection (e)(3)(A), it has been held that "[n]othing in the Privacy Act requires agencies to employ the exact language of the statute to give effective notice." United States v. Wilber, 696 F.2d 79, 80 (8th Cir. 1982) (per curiam) (finding that an IRS notice was in compliance with subsection (e)(3)(A) even though it did not use the word "mandatory"); see also Bartoli v. Richmond, No. 00-1043, 2000 WL 687155, at *3 (7th Cir. May 23, 2000) (finding that the IRS sufficiently gave notice pursuant to subsection (e)(3)(A) by citing section 6001 of the Internal Revenue Code as authority for its field examination); cf. Thompson v. Dep't

OVERVIEW OF THE PRIVACY ACT

of State, 400 F. Supp. 2d 1, 17 (D.D.C. 2005) (finding that "[t]he very uses of the information to which plaintiff specifically objects (i.e., giving it to [other offices within the agency] and placing it in her security file) . . . can be reasonably inferred from the warning given," which stated that the information was being collected for an "administrative inquiry regarding misconduct or improper performance"; further stating that plaintiff could infer from this warning that "if she provided information revealing misconduct by her, the agency might use it to make a determination adverse to her").

The Court of Appeals for the Fifth Circuit has gone so far as to rule in favor of an agency even though the agency "clearly did not follow the Act's requirements because the [form] did not indicate whether filling out the form was voluntary or mandatory or, alternatively, because [plaintiff's] supervisors ordered him to fill out the form even though filling it out was voluntary." Sweeney v. Chertoff, 178 F. App'x 354, 357 (5th Cir. 2006). The court reasoned that the Privacy Act did not provide the remedy for the plaintiff's damages – which arose from his punishment for insubordination based on his refusal to fill out the form – because "the Privacy Act is not the proper channel by which to challenge internal agency disciplinary actions with which one disagrees." Id. at 358 & n.3.

One court has held that a notice that informed witnesses of an investigation into allegations of misconduct but did not warn of the investigation subject's possible termination as an outcome, met the requirements of subsection (e)(3)(B) because the "text of the statute clearly requires" that the witnesses be notified of the "purpose" of the interview "not [its] possible results." Cardamone v. Cohen, No. 3:97CV540H, slip op. at 4-5 (W.D. Ky. Sept. 30, 1999), aff'd, 241 F.3d 520, 529-30 (6th Cir. 2001); cf. Beller v. Middendorf, 632 F.2d 788, 798 n.6 (9th Cir. 1980) (noting that when plaintiff provided information to the agency "albeit originally in connection with a check for a top secret security clearance," he "must have known that information which disclosed grounds for being discharged could be used in discharge proceedings"); Thompson, 400 F. Supp. 2d at 16 (where agency notified employee that purpose of collection was to assess her "suitability for continued employment," ruling that an agency need not "tell an individual that she is the subject of an investigation" in order to provide her with "informed consent").

In Covert v. Harrington, a divided panel of the Court of Appeals for the Ninth Circuit held that an agency component's failure to provide actual notice of a routine use under subsection (e)(3)(C), at the time at which information was submitted, precluded a separate component of the agency (the Inspector General) from later invoking that routine use as a basis for

OVERVIEW OF THE PRIVACY ACT

disclosing such information. 876 F.2d 751, 755-56 (9th Cir. 1989); see also Puerta v. HHS, No. 99-55497, 2000 WL 863974, at *1-2 (9th Cir. June 28, 2000) (following Covert, but finding that agency had provided notice of routine use on form used to collect information), aff'g No. EDCV 94-0148, slip op. at 7 (C.D. Cal. Jan. 5, 1999); USPS v. Nat'l Ass'n of Letter Carriers, 9 F.3d 138, 146 (D.C. Cir. 1993) (citing Covert with approval and remanding case for factual determination as to whether subsection (e)(3)(C) notice was given); Cooper v. FAA, No. 3:07-cv-01383, slip op. at 15-19 (N.D. Cal. Aug. 22, 2008) (holding that disclosure of social security records to Transportation Department by SSA was improper because "the notice provided on the form [plaintiff] used to submit his information to SSA was insufficient"); Pontecorvo v. FBI, No. 00-1511, slip op. at 12 (D.D.C. Sept. 30, 2001) (stating that agency must comply with subsection (e)(3)(C) "in order to substantiate an exception for 'routine use'"). But see OMB Guidelines at 28,961-62 (July 9, 1975), available at http://www.whitehouse.gov/sites/default/files/omb/assets/omb/inforeg/implementation_guidelines.pdf ("It was not the intent of [subsection (e)(3)] to create a right the nonobservance of which would preclude the use of the information or void an action taken on the basis of that information.").

In addition, it has been held in many criminal cases that subsection (e)(3)(D) does not require an agency to provide notice of the specific criminal penalty that may be imposed for failure to provide information. See, e.g., United States v. Bishop, No. 90-4077, 1991 WL 213755, at *4 (6th Cir. Oct. 23, 1991) (per curiam); United States v. Bressler, 772 F.2d 287, 292-93 (7th Cir. 1985); United States v. Bell, 734 F.2d 1315, 1318 (8th Cir. 1984) (per curiam); United States v. Wilber, 696 F.2d 79, 80 (8th Cir. 1982) (per curiam); United States v. Annunziato, 643 F.2d 676, 678 (9th Cir. 1981); United States v. Rickman, 638 F.2d 182, 183 (10th Cir. 1980); United States v. Gillotti, 822 F. Supp. 984, 988 (W.D.N.Y. 1993).

D. 5 U.S.C. § 552a(e)(4)

"[subject to notice and comment], publish in the Federal Register upon establishment or revision a notice of the existence and character of the system of records, which notice shall include – (A) the name and location of the system; (B) the categories of individuals on whom records are maintained in the system; (C) the categories of records maintained in the system; (D) each routine use of the records contained in the system, including the categories of users and the purpose of such use; (E) the policies and practices of the agency regarding storage, retrievability, access controls, retention, and disposal of the records; (F) the title and business address of the agency official who is responsible for the system of records; (G) the agency procedures whereby an individual can be notified at his request if the

OVERVIEW OF THE PRIVACY ACT

system of records contains a record pertaining to him; (H) the agency procedures whereby an individual can be notified at his request how he can gain access to any record pertaining to him contained in the system of records, and how he can contest its contents; and (I) the categories of sources of records in the system."

Comment:

For a discussion of this provision, see OMB Guidelines, 40 Fed. Reg. 28,948, 28,962-64 (July 9, 1975), available at http://www.whitehouse.gov/sites/default/files/omb/assets/omb/inforeg/implementation_guidelines.pdf. Although Privacy Act system notices are spread throughout the Federal Register, the Office of the Federal Register publishes a biennial compilation of all such system notices. See 5 U.S.C. § 552a(f). These "Privacy Act Compilation Issuances" are available on the Government Printing Office's Web site, which can be accessed at: http://www.gpoaccess.gov/privacyact/index.html. In order to provide more current and convenient access to system notices, OMB has required each agency to "provide the URL of the centrally located page on the agency web site listing working links to the published [system notices]." Memorandum for Heads of Executive Departments and Agencies, Subject: FY 2009 Reporting Instructions for the Federal Information Security Management Act and Agency Privacy Management (Aug. 20, 2009), SAOP Questions Attachment, at 1, available at http://www.whitehouse.gov/sites/default/files/omb/assets/memoranda_fy2009/m09-29.pdf. See also, e.g., DOJ Privacy Act Systems of Records, available at http://www.justice.gov/opcl/privacyact.html.

The only case to discuss the requirements of subsection (e)(4) in any depth is Pippinger v. Rubin, 129 F.3d 519 (10th Cir. 1997). In that case, the Court of Appeals for the Tenth Circuit addressed whether the Internal Revenue Service had complied with several of the requirements of subsection (e)(4) with regard to a computer database known as the "Automated Labor Employee Relations Tracking System [(ALERTS)]." Id. at 524-28. The database was used by the IRS to record all disciplinary action proposed or taken against any IRS employee and contained a limited subset of information from two existing Privacy Act systems that the IRS had properly noticed in the Federal Register. See id. at 524-25. Of particular note is that the Tenth Circuit found that ALERTS, being an "abstraction of certain individual records" from other systems of records, did not constitute a new system of records requiring Federal Register publication, because it could be accessed only by the same users and only for the same purposes as those published in the Federal Register for the original systems of records. Id. at 526-27.

OVERVIEW OF THE PRIVACY ACT

E. **5 U.S.C. § 552a(e)(5)**

"maintain all records which are used by the agency in making any determination about any individual with such accuracy, relevance, timeliness, and completeness as is reasonably necessary to assure fairness to the individual in the determination."

Comment:

This provision (along with subsections (e)(1) and (e)(7)) sets forth the standard to which records must conform in the context of an amendment lawsuit, as well as in the context of a lawsuit brought under subsection (g)(1)(C) for damages. See 5 U.S.C. § 552a(g)(1)(A); 5 U.S.C. § 552a(g)(1)(C). As the Court of Appeals for the District of Columbia Circuit has held, "whether the nature of the relief sought is injunctive or monetary, the standard against which the accuracy of the record is measured remains constant [and] that standard is found in 5 U.S.C. § 552a(e)(5) and reiterated in 5 U.S.C. § 552a(g)(1)(C)." Doe v. United States, 821 F.2d 694, 697 n.8 (D.C. Cir. 1987) (en banc).

In theory, a violation of this provision (or any other part of the Act) could also give rise to a damages action under 5 U.S.C. § 552a(g)(1)(D). Cf. Perry v. FBI, 759 F.2d 1271, 1275 (7th Cir. 1985), rev'd en banc on other grounds, 781 F.2d 1294 (7th Cir. 1986). However, the Court of Appeals for the District of Columbia Circuit has held that "a plaintiff seeking damages for noncompliance with the standard set out in subsection (e)(5) must sue under subsection (g)(1)(C) and not subsection (g)(1)(D)." Deters v. U.S. Parole Comm'n, 85 F.3d 655, 660-61 & n.5 (D.C. Cir. 1996) (noting that although court had suggested in Dickson v. OPM, 828 F.2d 32, 39 (D.C. Cir. 1987), that subsection (g)(1)(D) could cover a violation of subsection (e)(5), "the holding in that case is limited to the scope of subsection (g)(1)(C)").

Among the most frequently litigated subsection (e)(5)/(g)(1)(C) claims are those brought by federal inmates against the Bureau of Prisons. The discussion of subsection (e)(5), below, includes citations to numerous cases involving such claims. Note, though, that it was not until 2002 that the Bureau of Prisons exempted many of its systems of records – among them, notably, the Inmate Central Records System – from subsection (e)(5) pursuant to subsection (j)(2). See 28 C.F.R. § 16.97(j) (codifying 67 Fed. Reg. 51,754 (Aug. 9, 2002)). This came about as a result of Sellers v. Bureau of Prisons, 959 F.2d 307, 309-312 (D.C. Cir. 1992), in which the Court of Appeals for the District of Columbia Circuit noted that "regulations governing the Bureau of Prisons . . . do not exempt [the agency's] records from section (e)(5) of the Act" and, accordingly, remanded the case for a

OVERVIEW OF THE PRIVACY ACT

determination of "whether the [agency] met the requirements of sections (e)(5) and (g)(1)(C)" with regard to the items of information at issue. While the subsection (e)(5) analyses contained in cases decided prior to the promulgation of that exemption regulation remain useful resources in interpreting subsection (e)(5), it should be noted that inmates' subsection (e)(5)/(g)(1)(C) claims arising subsequent to August 9, 2002, should not succeed. See, e.g., Blackshear v. Lockett, 411 F. App'x 906, 907-08 (7th Cir. 2011) ("[A]fter Sellers the [Bureau of Prisons] availed itself of a Privacy Act exemption that frees it from an obligation to keep accurate inmate files. . . . Accordingly, the damages remedy available to the plaintiff in Sellers is no longer applicable."); Lane v. BOP, No. 09-5228, 2010 WL 288816, at *1 (D.C. Cir. Jan. 7, 2010) ("Sellers v. Bureau of Prisons, 959 F.2d 307 (D.C. Cir. 1992), does not control here, as it was decided before the Bureau of Prisons exempted the relevant system of records from the accuracy provision."), aff'g per curiam No. 08-1269, 2009 WL 1636422, (D.D.C. June 9, 2009); Fisher v. BOP, No. 06-5088, 2007 U.S. App. LEXIS 5140, at *1 (D.C. Cir. Mar. 1, 2007) ("[T]he statement in Sellers v. Bureau of Prisons, 959 F.2d 307, 309 (D.C. Cir. 1992), that the 'regulations governing the Bureau of Prisons . . . do not exempt those agenc[y's] records from section (e)(5) of the Act' is no longer accurate."), denying reh'g to 2006 U.S. App. LEXIS 28532 (D.C. Cir. Nov. 16, 2006), aff'g per curiam No. 05-0851, 2006 U.S. Dist. LEXIS 9738 (D.D.C. Feb. 21, 2006); Earle v. Holder, 815 F. Supp. 2d 176, 182-83 (D.D.C. 2011), aff'd per curiam, No. 11-5280, 2012 WL 1450574 (D.C. Cir. Apr. 20, 2012); Kates v. King, No. 3:11-CV-00951, 2011 WL 6937553, at *3 & n.1 (M.D. Pa. June 3, 2011), adopted, 2012 WL 10667 (M.D. Pa. Jan. 3, 2012); Davis v. United States, No. CIV-10-1136, 2011 WL 704894, at *5 (W.D. Okla. Jan. 4, 2011) (magistrate's recommendation), adopted, 2011 WL 693639 (W.D. Okla. Feb. 18, 2011), appeal dismissed, 426 F. App'x 648 (10th Cir. June 14, 2011). Courts have disagreed, however, on whether to permit claims that arose before August 9, 2002, but were filed after that date to go forward. Compare Patel v. United States, No. 08-1168, 2009 WL 1377530, at *1-2 (W.D. Okla. May 14, 2009) (declining to dismiss claim on ground that record was exempt from subsection (e)(5) because "the exemption . . . post-dates the allegedly false record"), aff'd, 399 F. App'x 355, 360 (10th Cir. 2010), with Truesdale v. DOJ, 731 F. Supp. 2d 3, 9 (D.D.C. 2010) (rejecting argument that "[b]ecause [plaintiff] had been allowed to contest the accuracy of sentencing-related information before 28 C.F.R. § 16.97(j) and (k) became effective . . . he should be allowed to pursue his Privacy Act claims"; "Plaintiff cites no authority for the proposition that he need not be subjected to a duly promulgated and published administrative regulation simply because he demands amendment of records in existence before the effective date of that regulation."). See also generally Skinner v. BOP, 584 F.3d 1093, 1097 (D.C. Cir. 2009) (declining to decide whether "it would be impermissibly

OVERVIEW OF THE PRIVACY ACT

retroactive to apply [the exemption] to [prisoner's] lawsuit" where claim arose before date of exemption but was filed after that date). This issue is discussed further under "5 U.S.C. § 552a(j)(2)," below.

Perfect records are not required by subsection (e)(5); instead, "reasonableness" is the standard. See Johnston v. Horne, 875 F.2d 1415, 1421 (9th Cir. 1989); DeBold v. Stimson, 735 F.2d 1037, 1041 (7th Cir. 1984); Edison v. Dep't of the Army, 672 F.2d 840, 843 (11th Cir. 1982); Vymetalik v. FBI, No. 82-3495, slip op. at 3-5 (D.D.C. Jan. 30, 1987); Marcotte v. Sec'y of Def., 618 F. Supp. 756, 762 (D. Kan. 1985); Smiertka v. U.S. Dep't of the Treasury, 447 F. Supp. 221, 225-26 & n.35 (D.D.C. 1978), remanded on other grounds, 604 F.2d 698 (D.C. Cir. 1979); see also, e.g., Kvech v. Holder, No. 10-cv-545, 2011 WL 4369452, at *5-6 (D.D.C. Sept. 19, 2011) (where plaintiff "admit[ted] that she defended herself against the charges by submitting the very evidence she claims would have 'corrected' the records," concluding that plaintiff "has not asserted any facts to support a claim that the FBI failed to maintain accurate or complete records with reasonable fairness"); Crummey v. SSA, 794 F. Supp. 2d 46, 56-57 (D.D.C. 2011) (finding that "there can be no genuine dispute that the SSA has maintained its records 'with the accuracy necessary to assure fairness'" where plaintiff had "failed to present even a scintilla of competent evidence suggesting that the SSA's records are, in actuality, materially inaccurate or incomplete," and where "in order to reach that conclusion, the fact finder would first have to accept two premises, neither of which is tenable"), summary affirmance granted, No. 11-5231, 2012 WL 556317 (D.C. Cir. Feb. 6, 2012); Wilson v. CIA, No. 01-1758, slip op. at 6 (D.D.C. Aug. 29, 2002) ("No reasonable fact finder could accept plaintiff's denial of a meeting having occurred twenty-five years ago over an official record prepared 'less than two weeks' after the meeting which memorialized the event."), summary affirmance granted, No. 02-5282, 2003 U.S. App. LEXIS 1290 (D.C. Cir. Jan. 24, 2003); Halus v. U.S. Dep't of the Army, No. 87-4133, 1990 WL 121507, at *11 (E.D. Pa. Aug. 15, 1990) (erroneous information held not subject to amendment if it is merely a "picayune" and immaterial error); Jones v. U.S. Dep't of the Treasury, No. 82-2420, slip op. at 2-3 (D.D.C. Oct. 18, 1983) (ruling it reasonable for agency – without conducting its own investigation – to maintain record concerning unsubstantiated allegation of sexual misconduct by ATF agent conveyed to it by state and local authorities), aff'd, 744 F.2d 878 (D.C. Cir. 1984) (unpublished table decision); cf. Ramey v. U.S. Marshals Serv., 755 F. Supp. 2d 88, 97 (D.D.C. 2010) (finding that plaintiff who claimed that "the U.S. Marshals's records which concluded that she [abandoned her post] are not accurate" had "not set forth specific facts showing a genuine issue for trial on the question of whether the U.S. Marshals relied on inaccurate information"); Griffin v. Ashcroft, No. 02-5399, 2003 WL 22097940, at *1

OVERVIEW OF THE PRIVACY ACT

(D.C. Cir. Sept. 3, 2003) (per curiam) (finding that appellant had made no showing that the facts regarding information in his presentence investigation report were inaccurate, and "even if the information were inaccurate, appellant [had] not shown the BOP either had no grounds to believe maintaining the information was lawful or that it flagrantly disregarded his rights under the Privacy Act"); Sullivan v. BOP, No. 94-5218, 1995 WL 66711, at *1 (D.C. Cir. Jan. 17, 1995) (even if plaintiff's subsection (e)(5) claim were not time-barred, the "Parole Commission met the requirements of the Act by providing [plaintiff] with a parole revocation hearing at which he was represented by counsel and given the opportunity to refute the validity of his continued confinement"); Kirkland v. Gess-Valagobar, No. 1:08-CV-0239, 2008 WL 504394, at *4 (N.D. Ga. Feb. 21, 2008) (explaining that BOP properly included juvenile record in presentence report because Sentencing Guidelines permit consideration of juvenile adjudications in some cases); Holz v. Westphal, 217 F. Supp. 2d 50, 56-57 (D.D.C. 2002) (finding that report of investigation was not "accurate or complete as to ensure its fairness to [individual]," and requiring removal of individual's name from report of investigation when report contained notations of "Fatal Traffic Accident" and "Negligent Homicide" without further explanation, which thus suggested commission of crime even though individual was never found guilty of offense); Pons v. U.S. Dep't of the Treasury, No. 94-2250, 1998 U.S. Dist. LEXIS 5809, at *11-15 (D.D.C. Apr. 21, 1998) (entering judgment in favor of agency where agency presented "substantial evidence to suggest that [it] acted in the reasonable belief that there were no grounds to amend plaintiff's records"; plaintiff failed to identify any records that contained alleged false statements and even if file did contain those statements, plaintiff never presented any evidence from which to conclude that statements were false); Smith v. BOP, No. 94-1798, 1996 WL 43556, at *3-4 (D.D.C. Jan. 31, 1996) (finding that plaintiff's record was not inaccurate with respect to his pre-commitment status in light of Bureau of Prisons' "full authority to promulgate rules governing the treatment and classification of prisoners" and "broad discretionary power," and because there was "no evidence that the BOP's interpretation of its own regulations was an abuse of discretion or discriminatorily administered," "BOP officials reconsidered their decision at least once," and "the determination of which plaintiff complains ha[d] been resolved in his favor"); Hampton v. FBI, No. 93-0816, slip op. at 3-6, 13-17 (D.D.C. June 30, 1995) (although not mentioning subsection (e)(5), finding that FBI "acted lawfully under the Privacy Act in the maintenance of the plaintiff's arrest record" when FBI refused to expunge challenged entries of arrests that did not result in conviction absent authorization by local law enforcement agencies that had originally submitted the information); Buxton v. U.S. Parole Comm'n, 844 F. Supp. 642, 644 (D. Or. 1994) (subsection (e)(5) fairness standard satisfied where Parole Commission complied with statutory procedures regarding

OVERVIEW OF THE PRIVACY ACT

parole hearings even though it did not investigate or correct alleged inaccuracies in presentence report).

Erroneous facts – as well as opinions, evaluations, and subjective judgments based entirely on erroneous facts – can be amended. See, e.g., Hewitt v. Grabicki, 794 F.2d 1373, 1378 (9th Cir. 1986); Holz, 217 F. Supp. 2d at 56-57; Douglas v. Farmers Home Admin., 778 F. Supp. 584, 585 (D.D.C. 1991); Rodgers v. Dep't of the Army, 676 F. Supp. 858, 860-61 (N.D. Ill. 1988); Ertell v. Dep't of the Army, 626 F. Supp. 903, 910-12 (C.D. Ill. 1986); R.R. v. Dep't of the Army, 482 F. Supp. 770, 773-74 (D.D.C. 1980); Murphy v. NSA, 2 Gov't Disclosure Serv. (P-H) ¶ 81,389, at 82,036 (D.D.C. Sept. 29, 1981); Trinidad v. U.S. Civil Serv. Comm'n, 2 Gov't Disclosure Serv. (P-H) ¶ 81,322, at 81,870-71 (N.D. Ill. Apr. 7, 1980); Turner v. Dep't of the Army, 447 F. Supp. 1207, 1213 (D.D.C. 1978), aff'd, 593 F.2d 1372 (D.C. Cir. 1979). As the Court of Appeals for the Seventh Circuit has noted, "[t]he Privacy Act merely requires an agency to attempt to keep accurate records, and provides a remedy to a claimant who demonstrates that facts underlying judgments contained in his records have been discredited." DeBold, 735 F.2d at 1040-41.

In addition, one court has held that where records contain disputed hearsay and reports from informants and unnamed parties, "the records are maintained with adequate fairness if they accurately reflect the nature of the evidence" (i.e., indicate that the information is a hearsay report from an unnamed informant). Graham v. Hawk, 857 F. Supp. 38, 40 (W.D. Tenn. 1994), aff'd, 59 F.3d 170 (6th Cir. 1995) (unpublished table decision); cf. Hass v. U.S. Air Force, 848 F. Supp. 926, 931 (D. Kan. 1994) (although acknowledging possibility that agency relied upon incorrect information in making determination about plaintiff, finding no Privacy Act violation because no evidence was suggested that information was recorded inaccurately).

As a general rule, courts are reluctant to disturb judgmental matters in an individual's record when such judgments are based on a number of factors or when the factual predicates for a judgment or evaluation are diverse. As the D.C. Circuit has ruled, where a subjective evaluation is "based on a multitude of factors" and "there are various ways of characterizing some of the underlying [factual] events," it is proper to retain and rely on the record. White v. OPM, 787 F.2d 660, 662 (D.C. Cir. 1986); see also Mueller v. Winter, 485 F.3d 1191, 1197 (D.C. Cir. 2007) (holding amendment claim to be "doom[ed]" where "subjective evaluation [was] based on a multitude of factors" and where "there [were] various ways of characterizing some of the underlying events"); Webb v. Magaw, 880 F. Supp. 20, 25 (D.D.C. 1995) (records were not based on demonstrably false premise, but rather on

OVERVIEW OF THE PRIVACY ACT

subjective evaluation "'based on a multitude of factors'" (quoting White, 787 F.2d at 662)); Bernson v. ICC, 625 F. Supp. 10, 13 (D. Mass. 1984) (court cannot order amendment of opinions "to reflect the plaintiffs' version of the facts"); cf. Phillips v. Widnall, No. 96-2099, 1997 WL 176394, at *2-3 (10th Cir. Apr. 14, 1997) (although not mentioning subsection (e)(5), holding that appellant was not entitled to court-ordered amendment, nor award of damages, concerning record in her medical files that contained "physician's notation to the effect that [appellant] was probably dependent upon a prescription medication," as such notation "reflected the physician's medical conclusion, which he based upon a number of objective factors and [appellant's] own complaints of neck and low back pain," and "Privacy Act does not permit a court to alter documents that accurately reflect an agency decision, no matter how contestable the conclusion may be").

Many courts have held that pure opinions and judgments are not subject to amendment. See, e.g., Baker v. Winter, 210 F. App'x 16, 18 (D.C. Cir. 2006); Reinbold v. Evers, 187 F.3d 348, 361 (4th Cir. 1999); Hewitt, 794 F.2d at 1378-79; Blevins v. Plummer, 613 F.2d 767, 768 (9th Cir. 1980) (per curiam); Middlebrooks v. Mabus, No. 1:11cv46, 2011 WL 4478686, at *5 (E.D. Va. Sept. 23, 2011); Feldman v. CIA, 797 F. Supp. 2d 29, 46-47 (D.D.C. 2011); Washington v. Donley, 802 F. Supp. 2d 539, 553-54 (D. Del. 2011); Kursar, 751 F. Supp. 2d at 170-71, aff'd per curiam, 442 F. App'x 565; Hardy v. McHugh, 692 F. Supp. 2d 76, 80 (D.D.C. 2010); Patel v. United States, No. CIV-08-1168, slip op. at 14-17 (W.D. Okla. Oct. 9, 2009) (magistrate's recommendation), adopted, 2009 WL 5168306 (W.D. Okla. Dec. 18, 2009), aff'd, 399 F. App'x 355, 360 (10th Cir. 2010); Register v. Lappin, No. 07-CV-136, 2007 WL 2020243, at *3 (E.D. Ky. July 6, 2007); Enigwe v. BOP, No. 06-457, 2006 WL 3791379, at *2 (D.D.C. Dec. 22, 2006); Toolasprashad v. BOP, No. 04-3219, 2006 WL 2627931, *4 (D.N.J. Sept. 13, 2006); Doyon v. DOJ, 304 F. Supp. 2d 32, 35 (D.D.C. 2004); Fields v. NRC, No. 98-1714, slip op. at 5-7 (D.D.C. May 12, 1999); Blazy v. Tenet, 979 F. Supp. 10, 20-21 (D.D.C. 1997), summary affirmance granted, No. 97-5330, 1998 WL 315583 (D.C. Cir. May 12, 1998); Gowan v. Dep't of the Air Force, No. 90-94, slip op. at 28-30 (D.N.M. Sept. 1, 1995), aff'd, 148 F.3d 1182 (10th Cir. 1998); Webb, 880 F. Supp. at 25; Linneman v. FBI, No. 89-505, slip op. at 14 (D.D.C. July 13, 1992); Nolan v. DOJ, No. 89-A-2035, 1991 WL 134803, at *3 (D. Colo. July 17, 1991), appeal dismissed in pertinent part on procedural grounds, 973 F.2d 843 (10th Cir. 1992); Frobish v. U.S. Army, 766 F. Supp. 919, 926-27 (D. Kan. 1988); Daigneau v. United States, No. 88-54-D, slip op. at 3-4 (D.N.H. July 8, 1988); Brumley v. U.S. Dep't of Labor, No. LR-C-87-437, slip op. at 4 (E.D. Ark. June 15, 1988), aff'd, 881 F.2d 1081 (8th Cir. 1989) (unpublished table decision); Tannehill v. U.S. Dep't of the Air Force, No. 87-M-1395, slip op. at 2 (D. Colo. May 23, 1988); Rogers v. U.S. Dep't of Labor, 607 F. Supp. 697, 699-700 (N.D.

Cal. 1985); Fagot v. FDIC, 584 F. Supp. 1168, 1176 (D.P.R. 1984), aff'd in part & rev'd in part, 760 F.2d 252 (1st Cir. 1985) (unpublished table decision); DeSha v. Sec'y of the Navy, 3 Gov't Disclosure Serv. (P-H) ¶ 82,496, at 82,251 (C.D. Cal. Feb. 26, 1982), aff'd, 780 F.2d 1025 (9th Cir. 1985) (unpublished table decision); Lee v. U.S. Dep't of Labor, 2 Gov't Disclosure Serv. (P-H) ¶ 81,335, at 81,891 (D. Va. Apr. 17, 1980); Hacopian v. Marshall, 2 Gov't Disclosure Serv. (P-H) ¶ 81,312, at 81,856 (C.D. Cal. Apr. 16, 1980); Castle v. U.S. Civil Serv. Comm'n, No. 77-1544, slip op. at 5 (D.D.C. Jan. 23, 1979); Rowe v. Dep't of the Air Force, No. 3-77-220, slip op. at 5 (E.D. Tenn. Mar. 20, 1978); cf. Strong v. OPM, 92 F. App'x 285, 289 (6th Cir. Mar. 16, 2004) (finding that OPM did not violate Privacy Act by refusing to remove reference's statement as plaintiff failed to offer any evidence that reference's statement was inaccurate or irrelevant); Davidson v. Daniels, No. 07-960, 2007 WL 3232608, at *2 (D. Or. Oct. 28, 2007) ("Respondent has no authority to alter court judgments. The correction of judgments i[s] the providence of the court."); Doe v. DOJ, 660 F. Supp. 2d 31, 43 (D.D.C. 2009) ("[P]laintiff's complaint objects to inaccurate 'conclusions drawn by lay employees' that were based on accurate records. . . . Thus, plaintiff objects not to erroneous . . . records but to misinterpretation of the records by DOJ employees, for which there is no remedy under the Privacy Act."); Turner, 447 F. Supp. at 1212-13 (where a negative rating had been expunged and plaintiff's prayer was "in essence" that the court "determine de novo 'a fair and accurate' rating as to the 'quality' of his service," the court declined to add its opinion, stating that such a rating "is a highly subjective process which requires the opinions and judgments of military professionals").

In determining what steps an agency must take in order to satisfy the accuracy standard of subsection (e)(5), the Court of Appeals for the District of Columbia Circuit has looked to whether the information at issue is capable of being verified. In Doe v. United States, 821 F.2d 694, 697-701 (D.C. Cir. 1987), the D.C. Circuit, sitting en banc, in a seven-to-four decision, held that the inclusion in a job applicant's record of both the applicant's and agency interviewer's conflicting versions of an interview (in which only they were present) satisfies subsection (e)(5)'s requirement of maintaining reasonably accurate records. In rejecting the argument that the agency and reviewing court must themselves make a credibility determination of which version of the interview to believe, the D.C. Circuit ruled that subsections (e)(5) and (g)(1)(C) "establish as the record-keeper's polestar, 'fairness' to the individual about whom information is gathered," and that "the 'fairness' criterion does not demand a credibility determination in the atypical circumstances of this case." Id. at 699 (emphasis added); see also Harris v USDA, No. 96-5783, 1997 WL 528498, at *2-3 (6th Cir. Aug. 26, 1997) (ruling that the agency "reasonably excluded" information from the plaintiff's record where there was "substantial evidence that the [information] was unreliable," and in the absence of "verifiable information which contradicted its investigators' records," the agency "reasonably kept and relied on the information gathered by its investigators when it terminated plaintiff"); Graham, 857 F. Supp. at 40 (agency was under no obligation to resolve whether hearsay contained in report is true, so long as that information was characterized as hearsay); Doe v. FBI, No. 91-1252, slip op. at 6-7 (D.N.J. Feb. 27, 1992) (following Doe v. United States, 821 F.2d at 699, and holding that FBI fulfilled its obligations under Privacy Act by including plaintiff's objections to statements contained in FBI polygrapher's memorandum and by verifying to extent possible that polygraph was properly conducted).

Subsequently, the D.C. Circuit held that in a "typical" case, where the records at issue are "not ambivalent" and the facts described therein are "susceptible of proof," the agency and reviewing court must determine accuracy as to each filed item of information. Strang v. U.S. Arms Control & Disarmament Agency, 864 F.2d 859, 866 (D.C. Cir. 1989). In order to "assure fairness" and render the record "complete" under subsection (e)(5), an agency may even be required to include contrary or qualifying information. See Strang v. U.S. Arms Control & Disarmament Agency, 920 F.2d 30, 32 (D.C. Cir. 1990); Kassel v. VA, 709 F. Supp. 1194, 1204-05 (D.N.H. 1989).

Adhering to its holding in Strang, the D.C. Circuit later held:

> As long as the information contained in an agency's files is capable of being verified, then, under sections (e)(5) and (g)(1)(C) of the Act, the agency must take reasonable steps to maintain the accuracy of the information to assure fairness to the individual. If the agency wilfully or intentionally fails to maintain its records in that way and, as a result, it makes a determination adverse to an individual, then it will be liable to that person for money damages. . . . [T]he agency did not satisfy the requirements of the Privacy Act simply by noting in [the individual's] files that he disputed some of the information the files contained.

Sellers, 959 F.2d at 312. (It is worth noting that Sellers was solely a subsection (e)(5)/(g)(1)(C) case; the system of records at issue was exempt from subsection (d).) See also McCready v. Nicholson, 465 F.3d 1, 19 (D.C. Cir. 2006) (citing Sellers and Doe and remanding because court "fail[ed] to see how [plaintiff's] presence at a meeting is not a 'fact' capable of

OVERVIEW OF THE PRIVACY ACT

verification and why the [agency] need not correct that fact or show that it took reasonable steps to verify its accuracy"); Martinez v. BOP, 444 F.3d 620, 624 (D.C. Cir. 2006) (dicta) (explaining that BOP had contacted U.S. Parole Commission and U.S. Probation Office and was advised that BOP's records were accurate); Toolasprashad v. BOP, 286 F.3d 576, 583 (D.C. Cir. 2002) (citing Sellers and Doe and remanding so that "typicality issue" may be resolved and so that agency can prove inmate had a "significant documented history of harassing and demeaning staff members"); Griffin v. U.S. Parole Comm'n, No. 97-5084, 1997 U.S. App. LEXIS 22401, at *3-5 (D.C. Cir. July 16, 1997) (citing Doe and Deters, and finding itself presented with "typical" case in which information was capable of verification; therefore vacating district court opinion that had characterized case as "atypical"), vacating & remanding No. 96-0342, 1997 U.S. Dist. LEXIS 2846 (D.D.C. Mar. 11, 1997); Deters, 85 F.3d at 658-59 (quoting Sellers and Doe, and although finding itself presented with "an atypical case because the 'truth' . . . is not readily ascertainable . . . assum[ing] without concluding that the Commission failed to maintain Deters's records with sufficient accuracy," because Commission had "not argued that this was an atypical case"); Lopez v. Huff, 508 F. Supp. 2d 71, 77-78 (D.D.C. 2007) (finding that "BOP satisfied its [Privacy Act] obligations by contacting the appropriate [U.S. Probation Office] to verify the accuracy of the challenged information"); Brown v. U.S. Prob. Office, No. 03-872, 2005 WL 2284207, at *3 (E.D. Tex. Aug. 15, 2005) (concluding that BOP's maintenance of inmate's presentence report satisfied subsection (e)(5) because BOP "took affirmative steps to verify the information by contacting the state court and the probation officer who prepared the [report]"); Blazy, 979 F. Supp. at 20-21 (citing Sellers and Doe, and finding that alleged inaccuracies were either nonexistent, corrected, or "unverifiable opinions of supervisors, other employees and/or informants"); Bayless v. U.S. Parole Comm'n, No. 94CV0686, 1996 WL 525325, at *5 (D.D.C. Sept. 11, 1996) (citing Sellers and Doe, and finding itself presented with an "atypical" case because "truth concerning plaintiff[']s culpability in the conspiracy and the weight of drugs attributed to him involves credibility determinations of trial witnesses and government informants and, therefore, is not 'clearly provable'"); Webb, 880 F. Supp. at 25 (finding that record at issue contained "justified statements of opinion, not fact" and "[c]onsequently, they were not 'capable of being verified' as false and cannot be considered inaccurate statements" (quoting Sellers, 959 F.2d at 312, and citing Doe, 821 F.2d at 699)); Thomas v. U.S. Parole Comm'n, No. 94-0174, 1994 WL 487139, at *4-6 (D.D.C. Sept. 7, 1994) (discussing Doe, Strang, and Sellers, but finding that the Parole Commission "verified the external 'verifiable' facts"; further holding that the plaintiff should not be allowed to use the Privacy Act "to collaterally attack the contents of his presentence report," as he "originally had the opportunity to challenge the accuracy . . . before the judge who sentenced

OVERVIEW OF THE PRIVACY ACT

him"); Linneman, No. 89-505, slip op. at 11-22 (D.D.C. July 13, 1992) (applying Sellers and Doe to variety of items of which plaintiff sought amendment).

The D.C. Circuit has noted that where "an agency has no subsection (d) duty to amend, upon request, it is not clear what residual duty subsection (e)(5) imposes when an individual challenges the accuracy of a record." Deters, 85 F.3d at 658 n.2. It went on to question whether subsection (e)(5) would still require an agency to amend or expunge upon the individual's request, or whether the agency merely must "address the accuracy of the records at some point before using it to make a determination of consequence to the individual." Id. Although stating that the Sellers opinion was "not entirely clear on this point," the D.C. Circuit reasoned that "the language of subsection (e)(5) . . . suggests the latter course." Id. (citing OMB Guidelines, 40 Fed. Reg. 28,948, 28,964 (July 9, 1975), available at http://www.whitehouse.gov/sites/default/files/omb/assets/omb/inforeg/implementation_guidelines.pdf. The court went on to state that subsection (e)(5) suggests that an agency has "no duty to act on an [individual's] challenge and verify his record until the agency uses the record in making a determination affecting his rights, benefits, entitlements or opportunities," 85 F.3d at 660; see also Bayless, 1996 WL 525325, at *6 n.19 (quoting Deters and determining that the agency "fulfilled its requisite duty by 'addressing' plaintiff's allegations prior to rendering a parole determination"); cf. Bassiouni v. FBI, No. 02-8918, 2003 WL 22227189, at *5 (N.D. Ill. Sept. 26, 2003) (holding that agency's denial to amend alleged inaccurate records about plaintiff was in and of itself a "determination" under subsection (e)(5)), aff'd on other grounds, 436 F.3d 712 (7th Cir. 2006).

The Court of Appeals for the Ninth Circuit has held that an agency can comply with subsection (e)(5) by simply including a complainant's rebuttal statement with an allegedly inaccurate record. Fendler v. BOP, 846 F.2d 550, 554 (9th Cir. 1988) (subsections (e)(5) and (g)(1)(C) lawsuit); see also Graham, 857 F. Supp. at 40 (citing Fendler and holding that where individual disputes accuracy of information that agency has characterized as hearsay, agency satisfies subsection (e)(5) by permitting individual to place rebuttal in file); cf. Harris, No. 96-5783, 1997 WL 528498, at *2 (6th Cir. Aug. 26, 1997) (although holding that exclusion of information from appellant's record due to unreliability of information was reasonable, finding it "notabl[e]" that the appellant had not contested the district court's finding that the agency "did not prevent him from adding to the file his disagreement with the [agency] investigators' conclusions"). Fendler thus appears to conflict with both Doe and Strang, as well as with the D.C. Circuit's earlier decision in Vymetalik v. FBI, 785 F.2d 1090, 1098 n.12 (D.C. Cir. 1986) (noting that subsection (d)(2) "guarantees an individual the right to demand

OVERVIEW OF THE PRIVACY ACT

that his or her records be amended if inaccurate" and that mere inclusion of rebuttal statement was not "intended to be [the] exclusive [remedy]").

The District Court for the District of Columbia has considered a subsection (e)(5)/(g)(1)(C) claim alleging not inaccuracy, but irrelevancy. Gerlich v. DOJ, 659 F. Supp. 2d 1 (D.D.C. 2009). The plaintiffs, who had applied to work for the Justice Department, alleged that two members of the selection committee had taken the plaintiffs' political and ideological associations into account in deselecting them for interviews. Id. at 6. Specifically, the plaintiffs alleged that one official "conducted Internet searches regarding candidates' political and ideological affiliations, printed out such information when it revealed liberal associations and then attached the printouts and her own handwritten comments to the candidates' applications in support of her recommendations to deselect them." Id. The court noted that "[m]ost 'adverse determination' claims hinge on inaccurate or incomplete records." Id. at 15. Here, however, the plaintiffs alleged that "irrelevant records (i.e., the records of their First Amendment activities) led to an adverse determination against them (i.e., deselection by the Screening Committee)." Id. The court rejected the Department's argument that the plaintiffs' failure to allege any inaccuracy was grounds for dismissal of plaintiffs' (e)(5) claim: "By the plain language of (g)(1)(C), relevance stands on equal footing with accuracy, timeliness and completeness as a basis for pursuing money damages for an adverse determination." Id. at 15-16. The court then concluded that "plaintiffs have met their pleading burden with respect to their subsection (e)(5) claim" because they alleged "that they suffered an adverse determination (deselection/non-hiring), that DOJ maintained irrelevant records (regarding plaintiffs' First Amendment activities) which undermined the fairness of the hiring process, that DOJ's reliance on those records (or the reliance of its employees . . .) proximately caused the adverse determination, and that DOJ (again, through its employees . . .) acted intentionally or willfully in maintaining such records." Id. at 16.

In Chapman v. NASA, 682 F.2d 526, 528-30 (5th Cir. 1982), the Court of Appeals for the Fifth Circuit recognized a "timely incorporation" duty under subsection (e)(5). It ruled that a supervisor's personal notes "evanesced" into Privacy Act records when they were used by the agency to effect an adverse disciplinary action, and that such records must be placed into the employee's file "at the time of the next evaluation or report on the employee's work status or performance." Id. at 529. In reversing the district court's ruling that such notes were not records within a system of records, the Fifth Circuit noted that such incorporation ensures fairness by allowing employees a meaningful opportunity to make refutatory notations, and avoids an "ambush" approach to maintaining records. Id.; see also

OVERVIEW OF THE PRIVACY ACT

Thompson v. Dep't of Transp. U.S. Coast Guard, 547 F. Supp. 274, 283-84 (S.D. Fla. 1982) (explaining Chapman). Chapman's "timely incorporation" doctrine has been followed in several other cases. See, e.g., MacDonald v. VA, No. 87-544-CIV-T-15A, slip op. at 2-5 (M.D. Fla. Feb. 8, 1988) (counseling memorandum used in preparation of proficiency report "became" part of VA system of records); Lawrence v. Dole, No. 83-2876, slip op. at 5-6 (D.D.C. Dec. 12, 1985) (notes not incorporated in timely manner cannot be used as basis for adverse employment action); Waldrop v. U.S. Dep't of the Air Force, 3 Gov't Disclosure Serv. (P-H) ¶ 83,016, at 83,453 (S.D. Ill. Aug. 5, 1981) (certain records at issue became Privacy Act "records"; others were merely "memory joggers"); Nelson v. EEOC, No. 83-C-983, slip op. at 6-11 (E.D. Wis. Feb. 14, 1984) (memorandum was used in making determination about an individual and therefore must be included in system of records and made available to individual); cf. Hudson v. Reno, 103 F.3d 1193, 1205-06 & n.9 (6th Cir. 1997) (distinguishing facts in Chapman and holding that supervisor's "notes about [p]laintiff's misconduct which were kept in a locked drawer and labeled the 'First Assistant's' files do not fall within th[e system of records] definition," as they "were not used to make any determination with respect to [p]laintiff"); Manuel v. VA, 857 F.2d 1112, 1117-19 (6th Cir. 1988) (no duty to place records within system of records where records "are not part of an official agency investigation into activities of the individual requesting the records, and where the records requested do not have an adverse effect on the individual"); Magee v. United States, 903 F. Supp. 1022, 1029-30 (W.D. La. 1995) (plaintiff's file kept in a supervisor's desk, separate from other employee files, because of plaintiff's concerns about access to it and with plaintiff's acquiescence, did "not fall within the proscriptions of maintaining a 'secret file' under the Act"), aff'd, 79 F.3d 1145 (5th Cir. 1996) (unpublished table decision).

Also note that subsection (e)(5)'s "timeliness" requirement does not require that agency records contain only information that is "hot off the presses." White v. OPM, 787 F.2d 660, 663 (D.C. Cir. 1986) (rejecting argument that use of year-old evaluation violates Act, as it "would be an unwarranted intrusion on the agency's freedom to shape employment application procedures"); see also Beckette v. USPS, No. 88-802, slip op. at 12-14 (E.D. Va. July 3, 1989) (stating that "[a]ll of the record maintenance requirements of subsection 552a(e)(5), including timeliness, concern fairness," and finding that as to records regarding "restricted sick leave," "[w]iping the . . . slate clean after an employee has remained off the listing for only six months is not required to assure fairness to the individual"; also finding that maintenance of those records for six months after restricted sick leave had been rescinded "did not violate the relevancy requirement of subsection 552a(e)(5)").

OVERVIEW OF THE PRIVACY ACT

Finally, the Court of Appeals for the Fourth Circuit has held that subsection (e)(5) is "not violated by the destruction of [a] record" that is destroyed "pursuant to [agency] records retention policy." Vaughn v. Danzig, 18 F. App'x 122, 124-25 (4th Cir. 2001) (per curiam) (where Navy maintained the record at issue in its files "at the time of the adverse action," the subsequent routine destruction of the record was proper and, indeed, plaintiff "cited no authority" to show that "the Privacy Act requires that records be maintained in perpetuity").

For a further discussion of subsection (e)(5), see OMB Guidelines, 40 Fed. Reg. 28,948, 28,964-65 (July 9, 1975), available at http://www.whitehouse.gov/sites/default/files/omb/assets/omb/inforeg/implementation_guidelines.pdf.

F. 5 U.S.C. § 552a(e)(6)

"prior to disseminating any record about an individual to any person other than an agency, unless the dissemination is made pursuant to subsection (b)(2) of this section [FOIA], make reasonable efforts to assure that such records are accurate, complete, timely, and relevant for agency purposes."

Comment:

This provision requires a reasonable effort by the agency to review records prior to their dissemination. See NTEU v. IRS, 601 F. Supp. 1268, 1272 (D.D.C. 1985); see also Stewart v. FBI, No. 97-1595, slip op. at 4 (D. Or. Mar. 12, 1999) (provision violated where agency failed to establish that it conducted reasonable efforts to ensure the accuracy of information "'of a factual nature'" that was "'capable of being verified'"), withdrawn by stipulation as part of settlement, No. 97-1595, 2000 WL 739253 (D. Or. May 12, 2000); Gang v. Civil Serv. Comm'n, No. 76-1263, slip op. at 2-5 (D.D.C. May 10, 1977) (provision violated where agency failed to review personnel file to determine relevance and timeliness of dated material concerning political activities before disseminating it to Library of Congress).

The District Court for the District of Columbia has held that an agency was not liable under subsection (e)(6) for damages for the dissemination of information that plaintiff had claimed was inaccurate but that the court determined consisted of statements of opinion and subjective evaluation that were not subject to amendment. Webb v. Magaw, 880 F. Supp. 20, 25 (D.D.C. 1995); see also Pontecorvo v. FBI, No. 00-1511, slip op. at 20 (D.D.C. Sept. 30, 2001) (finding that "if the information gathered and contained within an individual's background records is the subjective opinion of witnesses, it is incapable of being verified as false and cannot

OVERVIEW OF THE PRIVACY ACT

constitute inaccurate statements under the Privacy Act"); cf. Bhatia v. Office of the U.S. Attorney, N. Dist. Of Cal., No. C 09-5581, 2011 WL 1298763, at *6-7 (N.D. Cal. Mar. 29, 2011) (plaintiff failed to state a claim under § 552a(e)(6) because "the documents cited by [plaintiff] [do] not establish that the allegations in the pending criminal indictment are inaccurate"); Doe v. DOJ, 660 F. Supp. 2d 31, 43 (D.D.C. 2009) (concluding that "[b]ecause plaintiff has failed to show that there was an 'error in the records,' . . . he cannot succeed under . . . (e)(6)").

The District Court for the Southern District of California has also considered a claim under subsection (e)(6), and in doing so took into account the requirements of causation and intentional and willful wrongdoing in Privacy Act damages actions, discussed below. Guccione v. Nat'l Indian Gaming Comm'n, No. 98-CV-164, 1999 U.S. Dist. LEXIS 15475, at *14-19 (S.D. Cal. Aug. 5, 1999). The court found that an administrative hearing concerning inconsistencies in plaintiff's employment application "smacked generally of reprimand even though no talismanic phrases akin to reprimand were used," and that therefore "there was no 'intentional' or 'willful' misconduct in the [agency's] use of the term reprimand," nor was there sufficient causation where the recipients of the information also had reviewed the transcript of the administrative hearing and could draw their own conclusions. Id. at *16-19.

In addition, the District Court for the District of Columbia has concluded that regulations promulgated by the Department of Health and Human Services pursuant to the Health Care Quality Improvement Act, which concern collection and dissemination of information contained in the National Practitioners' Data Bank, do not supercede the more stringent protections provided by subsection (e)(6) of the Privacy Act. Doe v. Thompson, 332 F. Supp. 2d 124, 129-32 (D.D.C. 2004).

By its terms, this provision does not apply to intra- or inter-agency disclosures, see Thompson v. Dep't of State, 400 F. Supp. 2d 1, 21-22 (D.D.C. 2005), or to mandatory FOIA disclosures, see Smith v. United States, 817 F.2d 86, 87 (10th Cir. 1987); Kassel v. VA, 709 F. Supp. 1194, 1205 & n.5 (D.N.H. 1989); see also OMB Guidelines, 40 Fed. Reg. 28,948, 28,965 (July 9, 1975), available at http://www.whitehouse.gov/sites/default/files/omb/assets/omb/inforeg/implementation_guidelines.pdf.

G.   5 U.S.C. § 552a(e)(7)

"maintain no record describing how any individual exercises rights guaranteed by the First Amendment unless expressly authorized by statute or by the individual about whom the record is maintained or unless pertinent to

OVERVIEW OF THE PRIVACY ACT

and within the scope of an authorized law enforcement activity."

Comment:

The OMB Guidelines advise agencies in determining whether a particular activity constitutes exercise of a right guaranteed by the First Amendment to "apply the broadest reasonable interpretation." 40 Fed. Reg. 28,948, 28,965 (July 9, 1975), available at http://www.whitehouse.gov/sites/default/files/omb/assets/omb/inforeg/implementation_guidelines.pdf; see also 120 Cong. Rec. 40,406 (1974), reprinted in Source Book at 860, available at http://www.loc.gov/rr/frd/Military_Law/pdf/LH_privacy_act-1974.pdf. As noted above, Albright v. United States establishes that the record at issue need not be within a system of records to violate subsection (e)(7). 631 F.2d 915, 918-20 (D.C. Cir. 1980); see also Maydak v. United States, 363 F.3d 512, 516-20 (D.C. Cir. 2004); MacPherson v. IRS, 803 F.2d 479, 481 (9th Cir. 1986); Boyd v. Sec'y of the Navy, 709 F.2d 684, 687 (11th Cir. 1983) (per curiam); Clarkson v. IRS, 678 F.2d 1368, 1373-77 (11th Cir. 1982); Gerlich v. DOJ, 659 F. Supp. 2d 1, 13-15 (D.D.C. 2009); McCready v. Principi, 297 F. Supp. 2d 178, 187 (D.D.C. 2003), aff'd in part & rev'd in part on other grounds sub nom. McCready v. Nicholson, 465 F.3d 1 (D.C. Cir. 2006); Fagot v. FDIC, 584 F. Supp. 1168, 1175 (D.P.R. 1984), aff'd in part & rev'd in part, 760 F.2d 252 (1st Cir. 1985) (unpublished table decision). See also the discussion under "System of Records: Other Aspects," above. However, the record at issue does need to be considered a "record" under the Privacy Act for subsection (e)(7) to be applicable. See e.g., Houghton v. U.S. Dep't of State, No. 11-0869, 2012 WL 2855868, at *12 (D.D.C. July 12, 2012) (finding that transcripts containing reference to plaintiff's work were not "about" plaintiff, and therefore, not a record under Privacy Act to implicate application of subsection (e)(7)); Iqbal v. FBI, No. 3:11-cv-369, 2012 WL 2366634, at *5 (M.D. Fla. June 21, 2012) (finding allegation in complaint that stated "the agents [took] notes to aid the creation of official reports" sufficient to "satisfy the requirement that the agency maintain[ed] a record" in order to invoke application of subsection (e)(7)).

The record at issue also "must implicate an individual's First Amendment rights." Boyd, 709 F.2d at 684; accord Banks v. Garrett, 901 F.2d 1084, 1089 (Fed. Cir. 1990); see also Elnashar v. DOJ, 446 F.3d 792, 794-95 (8th Cir. 2006) (explaining that plaintiff "failed to identify how his First Amendment rights were implicated" when FBI contacted him "to determine whether he had expertise with chemical weapons"); Reuber v. United States, 829 F.2d 133, 142-43 (D.C. Cir. 1987) (noting threshold requirement that record itself must describe First Amendment-protected activity); Iqbal, 2012 WL 2366634, at *5 (same); Gerlich, 659 F. Supp. 2d at 13-15 (same); Pototsky v. Dep't of the Navy, 717 F. Supp. 20, 22 (D. Mass. 1989) (same),

OVERVIEW OF THE PRIVACY ACT

aff'd, 907 F.2d 142 (1st Cir. 1990) (unpublished table decision). Thus, subsection (e)(7) is not triggered in the first place unless the record describes First Amendment-protected activity. See, e.g., Maydak, 363 F.3d at 516 (finding "it obvious that photographs of prisoners visiting with family, friends, and associates depict the exercise of associational rights protected by the First Amendment"); England v. Comm'r, 798 F.2d 350, 352-53 (9th Cir. 1986) (record identifying individual as having "tax protester" status does not describe how individual exercises First Amendment rights); Iqbal, 2012 WL 2366634, at *5 (allegation that FBI "agents were monitoring [plaintiff] during prayer and later commented on those prayers" was "sufficient (if barely so) to support an inference that the notes maintained by the FBI implicated [plaintiff's] exercise of his First Amendment rights."); Kvech v. Holder, No. 10-cv-545, 2011 WL 4369452, at *6 (D.D.C. Sept. 19, 2011) (citing Maydak and finding argument that "the non-marital, non-familial relationship between [plaintiff] and the detective is not the type protected as freedom of expression under the First Amendment" to be "contrary to precedent"); Ramey v. U.S. Marshals Serv., 755 F. Supp. 2d 88, 97-98 (D.D.C. 2010) ("[Plaintiff's] statements to the Chief Judge were made in the course of her duties as a [court security officer] and receive no First Amendment protection."); Gerlich, 659 F. Supp. 2d at 13 (holding that plaintiff job applicants "met their pleading burden" where they alleged that agency official "conducted Internet searches regarding applicants' political and ideological affiliations" and "either created printouts of such information or made written comments on the applications throughout the process concerning the liberal affiliations of candidates"); Krieger v. DOJ, 529 F. Supp. 2d 29, 51-52 (D.D.C. 2008) (finding that documents announcing speeches to be given by plaintiff and complaints filed by plaintiff against his former law firm described how plaintiff exercises First Amendment rights); Weeden v. Frank, No. 1:91CV0016, slip op. at 7-8 (N.D. Ohio Apr. 10, 1992) (to read subsection (e)(7) as requiring a privacy waiver for the agency to even file plaintiff's request for religious accommodation is "a broad and unreasonable interpretation of subsection (e)(7)"; however, agency would need to obtain waiver to collect information in order to verify plaintiff's exercise of religious beliefs), aff'd, 16 F.3d 1223 (6th Cir. 1994) (unpublished table decision); Cloud v. Heckler, 3 Gov't Disclosure Serv. (P-H) ¶ 83,230, at 83,962 (W.D. Ark. Apr. 21, 1983) (maintenance of employee's letters criticizing agency – written while on duty – does not violate subsection (e)(7) because "[p]oor judgment is not protected by the First Amendment").

Assuming that the challenged record itself describes activity protected by the First Amendment, subsection (e)(7) is violated unless maintenance of the record is:

OVERVIEW OF THE PRIVACY ACT

(1) expressly authorized by statute, see, e.g., Abernethy v. IRS, 909 F. Supp. 1562, 1570 (N.D. Ga. 1995) (IRS "authorized by statute" to maintain copies of documents relevant to processing of plaintiff's requests under FOIA and Privacy Act, which both "provide implied authorization to federal agencies to maintain copies for their own records of the documents which are released to requesters under those Acts"), aff'd per curiam, No. 95-9489 (11th Cir. Feb. 13, 1997); Hass v. U.S. Air Force, 848 F. Supp. 926, 930-31 (D. Kan. 1994) (agency's maintenance of FOIA and Privacy Act requests "cannot logically violate the Privacy Act"); Attorney Gen. of the United States v. Irish N. Aid Comm., No. 77-708, 1977 U.S. Dist. LEXIS 13581, at *14 (S.D.N.Y. Oct. 7, 1977) (Foreign Agents Registration Act); OMB Guidelines, 40 Fed. Reg. at 28,965, available at http://www.whitehouse.gov/sites/default/files/omb/assets/omb/inforeg/implementation_guidelines.pdf (Immigration and Nationality Act); cf. Abernethy, 909 F. Supp. at 1570 (maintenance of documents in congressional communications files "does not violate the Privacy Act" because IRS "must respond to Congressional inquiries" and maintenance was necessary to carry out that responsibility (citing Internal Revenue Manual 1(15)29, Chapter 500, Congressional Communications)); Gang v. U.S. Civil Serv. Comm'n, No. 76-1263, slip op. at 5-7 & n.5 (D.D.C. May 10, 1977) (recognizing that 5 U.S.C. § 7311, which prohibits individual from holding position with federal government if he advocates – or is member of organization that he knows advocates – overthrow of government, may be read together with subsection (e)(7) as permitting maintenance of files relating to membership in such groups, but ruling that "it cannot fairly be read to permit wholesale maintenance of all materials relating to political beliefs, association, and religion"; nor does 5 U.S.C. § 3301, which authorizes President to ascertain fitness of federal applicants for employment as to character, provide authorization for maintenance of such information); or

(2) expressly authorized by the individual about whom the record is maintained, see Abernethy, 909 F. Supp. at 1570 ("Plaintiff authorized the maintenance of the documents at issue by submitting copies to various components of the Defendant IRS."); OMB Guidelines, 40 Fed. Reg. at 28,965, available at http://www.whitehouse.gov/sites/default/files/omb/assets/omb/inforeg/implementation_guidelines.pdf ("volunteered" information is properly maintained); see also Radford v. SSA, No. 81-4099, slip op. at 4-5 (D. Kan. July 11, 1985) (plaintiff's publication of contents of offending record does not constitute "express authorization"); Murphy v. NSA, 2 Gov't Disclosure Serv. (P-H) ¶ 81,389, at 82,036 (D.D.C. Sept. 29, 1981) (consent to maintain may be withdrawn); cf. Weeden v. Frank, No. 93-3681, 1994 WL 47137, at *2

OVERVIEW OF THE PRIVACY ACT

(6th Cir. Feb. 16, 1994) (Postal Service's procedure requiring individual to expressly waive subsection (e)(7) Privacy Act rights in order to allow agency to collect information regarding employee's exercise of religious beliefs so that accommodation could be established held not unreasonable); or

(3) pertinent to and within the scope of an authorized law enforcement activity. Perhaps the leading precedent in the early case law on the "law enforcement activity" exception is <u>Patterson v. FBI</u>, 893 F.2d 595, 602-03 (3d Cir. 1990), a case that attracted national media attention because of its unusual factual background. An elementary school student, in the lawful exercise of his constitutional rights to write an encyclopedia of the world based upon requests to 169 countries for information, became the subject of an FBI national security investigation. The Court of Appeals for the Third Circuit, in affirming the dismissal of the student's subsection (e)(7) claim, ruled that a standard of "relevance" to a lawful law enforcement activity is "more consistent with Congress's intent and will prove to be a more manageable standard than employing one based on ad-hoc review." <u>Id.</u> at 603.

The "relevance" standard articulated in <u>Patterson</u> had earlier been recognized by the Court of Appeals for the Sixth Circuit in <u>Jabara v. Webster</u>, 691 F.2d 272, 279-80 (6th Cir. 1982), a case involving a challenge to the FBI's maintenance of investigative records regarding surveillance of the plaintiff's overseas communications. In <u>Jabara</u>, the Sixth Circuit vacated as "too narrow" the district court's ruling that the exception is limited to "investigation of past, present or future criminal activity." <u>Id.</u> It held that the exception applies where the record is "relevant to an authorized criminal investigation or to an authorized intelligence or administrative one." <u>Id.</u> at 280.

In <u>MacPherson v. IRS</u>, 803 F.2d at 482-85, the Court of Appeals for the Ninth Circuit ruled that the applicability of the exception could be assessed only on an "individual, case-by-case basis" and that a "hard and fast standard" was inappropriate. On the facts before it, however, the Ninth Circuit upheld the maintenance of notes and purchased tapes of a tax protester's speech as "necessary to give the IRS [and Justice Department] a complete and representative picture of the events," notwithstanding that no investigation of a specific violation of law was involved and no past, present or anticipated illegal conduct was revealed or even suspected. <u>Id.</u> The Ninth Circuit cautioned, though, that its holding was a narrow one tied to the specific facts before it. <u>Id.</u> at 485 n.9.

OVERVIEW OF THE PRIVACY ACT

In Clarkson v. IRS, 678 F.2d at 1374-75 – a case involving facts similar to those of MacPherson in that it likewise involved a challenge to the IRS's maintenance of records regarding surveillance of a tax protester's speech – the Court of Appeals for the Eleventh Circuit quoted with approval the standard set forth by the district court decision in Jabara (subsequently vacated and remanded by the Sixth Circuit) and held that the exception does not apply if the record is "unconnected to any investigation of past, present or anticipated violations of statutes [the agency] is authorized to enforce." On remand, the district court upheld the IRS's maintenance of the surveillance records as "connected to anticipated violations of the tax statutes" inasmuch as such records "provide information relating to suggested methods of avoiding tax liability" and aid in the "identification of potential tax violators." Clarkson v. IRS, No. C79-642A, slip op. at 6-10 (N.D. Ga. Dec. 27, 1984), aff'd per curiam, 811 F.2d 1396 (11th Cir. 1987); accord Tate v. Bindseil, 2 Gov't Disclosure Serv. (P-H) ¶ 82,114, at 82,427 (D.S.C. Aug. 4, 1981) ("[An] IRS investigation of activist organizations and individuals prominently associated with those organizations which advocate resistance to the tax laws by refusing to file returns or filing blank returns is a legitimate law enforcement activity.").

In initially addressing the law enforcement exception, the Court of Appeals for the Seventh Circuit, although recognizing the "varying views" adopted by other courts of appeals, had adopted what seems to be the most strict application of the law enforcement exception to date. The Seventh Circuit ordered the IRS to expunge information in a closed investigative file, based upon its determination, through in camera inspection, that it could not "be helpful in future enforcement activity." Becker v. IRS, 34 F.3d 398, 408-09 (7th Cir. 1994); cf. J. Roderick MacArthur Found. v. FBI, 102 F.3d 600, 607 (D.C. Cir. 1996) (Tatel, J., dissenting) (opining in favor of requirement that information be maintained only if pertinent to current law enforcement activity). In so ruling, the Seventh Circuit appeared to confusingly engraft the timeliness requirement of subsection (e)(5) onto subsection (e)(7). See Becker, 34 F.3d at 409 & n.28. Additionally, the Seventh Circuit appeared to confuse the district court's determination that the information was exempt from access under subsection (k)(2) with the district court's further ruling that the information also satisfied the requirements of subsection (e)(7). See id. at 407-08; see also Becker v. IRS, No. 91 C 1203, 1993 WL 114612, at *1 (N.D. Ill. Apr. 13, 1993).

The Court of Appeals for the District of Columbia Circuit was faced with interpreting the law enforcement exception in J. Roderick MacArthur Found. v. FBI, 102 F.3d 600 (D.C. Cir. 1996). In MacArthur, the D.C. Circuit rejected the appellants' arguments, which were based on Becker, stating that "the court's analysis of § (e)(7) in Becker is neither clear nor compelling," and that the Seventh Circuit had "set out to determine the meaning 'of the "law enforcement purpose" phrase of § 552a(e)(7)' not realizing that the phrase used in the Privacy Act is 'authorized law enforcement activity'" and that the Seventh Circuit "appears to have confused § 552a(e)(7) with § 552a(k)(2)." 102 F.3d at 603. In MacArthur, the appellant did not challenge the FBI's having collected the information about him, but rather claimed that the FBI could not maintain or retain such information unless there was a "current law enforcement necessity to do so." Id. at 602. The D.C. Circuit, however, realizing that "[m]aterial may continue to be relevant to a law enforcement activity long after a particular investigation undertaken pursuant to that activity has been closed," id. at 602-03, ruled that "[i]nformation that was pertinent to an authorized law enforcement activity when collected does not later lose its pertinence to that activity simply because the information is not of current interest (let alone 'necessity') to the agency," id. at 603. The panel majority went on to hold:

> [T]he Privacy Act does not prohibit an agency from maintaining records about an individual's [F]irst [A]mendment activities if the information was pertinent to an authorized law enforcement activity when the agency collected the information. The Act does not require an agency to expunge records when they are no longer pertinent to a current law enforcement activity.

Id. at 605. In its conclusion, the D.C. Circuit stated that subsection (e)(7) "does not by its terms" require an agency to show that information is pertinent to a "currently" authorized law enforcement activity, and that it found "nothing in the structure or purpose of the Act that would suggest such a reading." Id. at 607.

More recently, the Court of Appeals for the Seventh Circuit again addressed the law enforcement exception, but in the context of national security, and reached a conclusion similar to that in MacArthur. See Bassiouni v. FBI, 436 F.3d 712, 723-25 (7th Cir. 2006). At issue in Bassiouni was whether the law enforcement exception covered the FBI's maintenance of records pertaining to a law professor who once presided over two Arab-American associations. Id. at 724. The court noted that "the realm of national security belongs to the executive branch, and we owe considerable deference to that branch's assessment of matters of national security." Id. at 724. The court then rejected the plaintiff's argument that the FBI must be "currently involved in a law enforcement investigation" for the exception to apply to the records at issue, concluding that the FBI was not "required to purge, on a continuous basis, properly collected information with respect to individuals that the agency has good reason to believe may be relevant on a continuing

OVERVIEW OF THE PRIVACY ACT

basis in the fulfillment of the agency's statutory responsibilities." Id. at 724-25.

Several other courts have upheld the exception's applicability in a variety of contexts. See Doe v. FBI, 936 F.2d 1346, 1354-55, 1360-61 (D.C. Cir. 1991) (although holding that appellant was foreclosed from obtaining relief because he had "not suffered any adverse effect," stating that to extent appellant's argument as to violation of subsection (e)(7) was directed to underlying FBI records concerning investigation of appellant's "unauthorized possession of an explosive device" and reported advocacy of "violent overthrow of the Government," subsection (e)(7) was not violated as "'law enforcement activity' exception applies"); Wabun-Inini v. Sessions, 900 F.2d 1231, 1245-46 (8th Cir. 1990) (FBI maintenance of photographs seized with probable cause); Jochen v. VA, No. 88-6138, slip op. at 6-7 (9th Cir. Apr. 5, 1989) (VA evaluative report concerning operation of VA facility and job performance of public employee that contained remarks by plaintiff); Nagel v. HEW, 725 F.2d 1438, 1441 & n.3 (D.C. Cir. 1984) (citing Jabara with approval and holding that records describing statements made by employees while at work were properly maintained "for evaluative or disciplinary purposes"); Iqbal, 2012 WL 2366634, at *5 (finding "any records connected to FBI's question" regarding an email sent to TSA where agents threatened to charge plaintiff with a crime "would be pertinent to and within the scope of an authorized law enforcement activity"); Falwell v. Executive Office of the President, 158 F. Supp. 2d 734, 742-43 (W.D. Va. 2001) (holding that the FBI did not violate subsection (e)(7) by maintaining a document entitled "The New Right Humanitarians" in its files, "because the document pertained to and was within the scope of a duly authorized FBI counterintelligence investigation" of the Communist Party USA); Abernethy, 909 F. Supp. at 1566, 1570 (holding that maintenance of newspaper article that quoted plaintiff on subject of reverse discrimination and "Notice of Potential Class Action Complaint" were "relevant to and pertinent to authorized law enforcement activities" as they appeared in file pertaining to EEO complaint in which plaintiff was complainant's representative and was kept due to belief that a conflict of interest might exist through plaintiff's representation of complainant and, citing Nagel, holding that maintenance was also "valid" in files concerning possible disciplinary action against plaintiff); Maki v. Sessions, No. 1:90-CV-587, 1991 U.S. Dist. LEXIS 7103, at *27-28 (W.D. Mich. May 29, 1991) (holding that, although plaintiff claimed FBI investigation was illegal, the uncontested evidence was that plaintiff was the subject of an authorized investigation by FBI); Kassel v. VA, No. 87-217-S, slip op. at 27-28 (D.N.H. Mar. 30, 1992) (citing Nagel and Jabara, inter alia, and holding that information about plaintiff's statements to media fell within ambit of administrative investigation); Pacheco v. FBI, 470 F. Supp. 1091, 1108 n.21

OVERVIEW OF THE PRIVACY ACT

(D.P.R. 1979) ("all investigative files of the FBI fall under the exception"); AFGE v. Schlesinger, 443 F. Supp. 431, 435 (D.D.C. 1978) (reasonable steps taken by agencies to prevent conflicts of interest are within exception); see also Felsen v. HHS, No. 95-975, slip op. at 68-72 (D. Md. Sept. 30, 1998) (although not deciding whether report described First Amendment activity, finding no violation of subsection (e)(7) where report was relevant to authorized law enforcement activity of HHS and also was related to possible past violation of statute that HHS is empowered to enforce). But see Maydak, 363 F.3d at 516-17 (remanding to district court to determine whether portions of BOP's declarations stating that certain institutions maintained and reviewed "photographs of prisoners visiting with family, friends and associates" for "investigative and informative value" is consistent with subsection (e)(7)'s law enforcement exception); Levering v. Hinton, No. 2:07-CV-989, 2008 WL 4425961, at *8 (S.D. Ohio Sept. 25, 2008) (refusing to apply law enforcement exception to maintenance of "running record of practically all of Plaintiff's speech at work").

Finally, even if records are found to be maintained in violation of subsection (e)(7), it does not follow that those records must be disclosed. See Bassiouni v. CIA, 392 F.3d. 244, 247-48 (7th Cir. 2004); see also Irons v. Bell, 596 F.2d 468, 470-71 & n.4 (1st Cir. 1979).

H.   5 U.S.C. § 552a(e)(8)

"make reasonable efforts to serve notice on an individual when any record on such individual is made available to any person under compulsory legal process when such process becomes a matter of public record."

Comment:

This provision becomes applicable when subsection (b)(11) "court order" disclosures occur. See, e.g., Robinett v. State Farm Mut. Auto. Ins. Co., No. 02-0842, 2002 WL 31498992, at *3-4 (E.D. La. Nov. 7, 2002), aff'd per curiam, 83 F. App'x 638 (5th Cir. 2003); Moore v. USPS, 609 F. Supp. 681, 682 (E.D.N.Y. 1985); see also OMB Guidelines, 40 Fed. Reg. 28,948, 28,965 (July 9, 1975), available at http://www.whitehouse.gov/sites/default/files/omb/assets/omb/inforeg/implementation_guidelines.pdf. By its terms, it requires notice not prior to the making of a legally compelled disclosure, but rather at the time that the process becomes a matter of public record. See Kassel v. VA, No. 87-217-S, slip op. at 30 (D.N.H. Mar. 30, 1992); see also Moore, 609 F. Supp. at 682 ("§ 552a(e)(8) does not speak of advance notice of release"); cf. Mangino v. Dep't of the Army, No. 94-2067, 1994 WL 477260, at *11-12 (D. Kan. Aug. 24, 1994) (citing Moore for proposition that subsection (e)(8) does not require advance notice, although finding no

OVERVIEW OF THE PRIVACY ACT

allegation that disclosure at issue was made "under compulsory legal process").

I. **5 U.S.C. § 552a(e)(9)**

"establish rules of conduct for persons involved in the design, development, operation, or maintenance of any system of records, or in maintaining any record, and instruct each such person with respect to such rules and the requirements of this section, including any other rules and procedures adopted pursuant to this section and the penalties for noncompliance."

Comment:

For a discussion of this provision, see OMB Guidelines, 40 Fed. Reg. 28,948, 28,965 (July 9, 1975), available at http://www.whitehouse.gov/sites/default/files/omb/assets/omb/inforeg/implementation_guidelines.pdf, Convertino v. DOJ, 769 F. Supp. 2d 139, 153-54 (D.D.C. 2011) ("[T]he Privacy Act does not require DOJ officials to understand the Privacy Act. It only requires that each covered employee understand the proper handling of systems of records over which he or she has responsibility as well as records that he or she is responsible for maintaining. Just because certain DOJ employees did not associate their knowledge and training regarding records system management with the words 'Privacy Act' does not mean that they were not, in fact, properly instructed in records system management."), rev'd and remanded on other grounds, No. 11-5133, 2012 WL 2362591 (D.C. Cir. June 22, 2012) (reversing district court's summary judgment and ruling that district court committed abuse of discretion in denying appellant's motion to stay summary judgment to allow for further discovery), Doe v. DOJ, 660 F. Supp. 2d 31, 43 (D.D.C. 2009) ("[A]lthough plaintiff suggests that DOJ violated (e)(9) by failing to formally train [an agency employee], the Privacy Act does not specify how the agency must 'instruct' its personnel, and plaintiff has provided no support for his suggestion that listing rules and requirements on the Internet is inappropriate." (citations omitted)), and Fleury v. USPS, No. 00-5550, 2001 WL 964147, at *2 (E.D. Pa. Aug. 21, 2001) (finding that plaintiff's "proof" that confidential information did not reach the intended recipient "would not establish that defendant failed to instruct supervisors and managers regarding Privacy Act requirements in violation of 552a(e)(9)").

J. **5 U.S.C. § 552a(e)(10)**

"establish appropriate administrative, technical and physical safeguards to insure the security and confidentiality of records and to protect against any anticipated threats or hazards to their security or integrity which could result

OVERVIEW OF THE PRIVACY ACT

in substantial harm, embarrassment, inconvenience, or unfairness to any individual on whom information is maintained."

Comment:

This provision may come into play when documents are allegedly "leaked." See, e.g., Pilon v. DOJ, 796 F. Supp. 7, 13 (D.D.C. 1992) (because subsection (e)(10) is more specific than subsection (b), it governs with regard to allegedly inadequate safeguards that resulted in disclosure); Kostyu v. United States, 742 F. Supp. 413, 414-17 (E.D. Mich. 1990) (alleged lapses in IRS document-security safeguards were not willful and intentional); cf. Paige v. DEA, 665 F.3d 1355, 1361 (D.C. Cir. 2012) (although plaintiff did not raise subsection (e)(10) claim at district court and finding no violation of subsection (b), stating "the widespread circulation of the accidental discharge video demonstrates the need for every federal agency to safeguard video records with extreme diligence in this internet age of iPhones and YouTube with their instantaneous and universal reach. The DEA's treatment of the video-recording – particularly the creation of so many different versions and copies – undoubtedly increased the likelihood of disclosure and, although not an abuse of a system of records, is far from a model of agency treatment of private data.").

One district court has found that disclosures that are the result of "official decisions" by an agency, "cannot be the basis for a claim under subsection (e)(10)." Chasse v. DOJ, No. 1:98-CV-207, slip op. at 16-17 (D. Vt. Jan. 14, 1999) (magistrate's recommendation), adopted (D. Vt. Feb. 9, 1999), aff'd on other grounds sub nom. Devine v. United States, 202 F.3d 547 (2d Cir. 2000).

Another district court has held that conclusory allegations predicated on the fact that confidential information was forwarded to an unintended recipient are not sufficient to establish a subsection (e)(10) violation. See Fleury v. USPS, No. 00-5550, 2001 WL 964147, at *2 (E.D. Pa. Aug. 21, 2001); cf. Doe v. DOJ, 660 F. Supp. 2d 31, 43 (D.D.C. 2009) (rejecting argument that "DOJ's violations of the Privacy Act imply that its rules and safeguards are 'illusory,'" because "'DOJ has promulgated extensive regulations that safeguard its Privacy Act-protected records, notwithstanding the allegations of a single violation against one individual.'" (quoting Krieger v. DOJ, 529 F. Supp. 2d 29, 54-55 (D.D.C. 2008))); Thompson v. Dep't of State, 400 F. Supp. 2d 1, 23 (D.D.C. 2005) (where agency kept record "in a sealed envelope that was addressed to [plaintiff] and clearly marked 'To Be Opened Only by Addressee,'" but did not "take the further precaution of keeping confidential information in a locked file cabinet," concluding that "a reasonable jury could not find that this failure amounted to a reckless

OVERVIEW OF THE PRIVACY ACT

disregard of plaintiff's rights" (internal quotation marks omitted)). By contrast, another district court held that a genuine issue of material fact existed as to whether the Department of Veterans Affairs intentionally or willfully violated subsection (e)(10) by failing to install "patches" on its computer system to allow tracing of a user's access to the social security numbers of certain employees. See Schmidt v. VA, 218 F.R.D. 619, 634-35 (E.D. Wis. 2003). For a further discussion of this provision, see OMB Guidelines, 40 Fed. Reg. 28,948, 28,966 (July 9, 1975), available at http://www.whitehouse.gov/sites/default/files/omb/assets/omb/inforeg/implementation_guidelines.pdf.

K. 5 U.S.C. § 552a(e)(11)

"at least 30 days prior to publication of information under paragraph (4)(D) of this subsection [routine uses], publish in the Federal Register notice of any new use or intended use of the information in the system, and provide an opportunity for interested persons to submit written data, views, or arguments to the agency."

Comment:

For a discussion of this provision, see OMB Guidelines, 40 Fed. Reg. 28,948, 28,966 (July 9, 1975), available at http://www.whitehouse.gov/sites/default/files/omb/assets/omb/inforeg/implementation_guidelines.pdf.

AGENCY RULES

To implement the Act, an agency that maintains a system of records "shall promulgate rules, in accordance with [notice and comment rulemaking, see 5 U.S.C. § 553]," which shall –

A. 5 U.S.C. § 552a(f)(1)

"establish procedures whereby an individual can be notified in response to his request if any system of records named by the individual contains a record pertaining to him."

Comment:

For a discussion of this provision, see OMB Guidelines, 40 Fed. Reg. 28,948, 28,967 (July 9, 1975), available at http://www.whitehouse.gov/sites/default/files/omb/assets/omb/inforeg/implementation_guidelines.pdf.

OVERVIEW OF THE PRIVACY ACT

B.   5 U.S.C. § 552a(f)(2)

"define reasonable times, places, and requirements for identifying an individual who requests his record or information pertaining to him before the agency shall make the record or information available to the individual."

Comment:

For a discussion of this provision, see OMB Guidelines, 40 Fed. Reg. 28,948, 28,967 (July 9, 1975), available at http://www.whitehouse.gov/sites/default/files/omb/assets/omb/inforeg/implementation_guidelines.pdf.

C.   5 U.S.C. § 552a(f)(3)

"establish procedures for the disclosure to an individual upon his request of his record or information pertaining to him, including special procedure, if deemed necessary, for the disclosure to an individual of medical records, including psychological records pertaining to him."

Comment:

In the past, a typical regulation consistent with this provision would allow an agency to advise an individual requester that his medical records would be provided only to a physician, designated by the individual, who requested the records and established his identity in writing, and that the designated physician would determine which records should be provided to the individual and which should not be disclosed because of the possible harm to the individual or another person.

However, as a result of the opinion by the Court of Appeals for the District of Columbia Circuit in <u>Benavides v. BOP</u>, 995 F.2d 269 (D.C. Cir. 1993), such regulations are no longer valid. In <u>Benavides</u>, the D.C. Circuit held that subsection (f)(3) is "strictly procedural . . . merely authoriz[ing] agencies to devise the manner in which they will disclose properly requested <u>non-exempt</u> records" and that "[a] regulation that expressly contemplates that the requesting individual may never see certain medical records [as a result of the discretion of the designated physician] is simply not a special procedure for disclosure to that person." <u>Id.</u> at 272. The D.C. Circuit went on to state that the Justice Department's subsection (f)(3) regulation at issue, 28 C.F.R. § 16.43(d) (1992), "in effect, create[d] another substantive exemption" to Privacy Act access, and it accordingly held the regulation to be "ultra vires." 995 F.2d at 272-73.

Nevertheless, the D.C. Circuit in <u>Benavides</u> rejected the argument that the

OVERVIEW OF THE PRIVACY ACT

Privacy Act requires <u>direct</u> disclosure of medical records to the individual. Recognizing the "potential harm that could result from unfettered access to medical and psychological records," the court provided that "as long as agencies guarantee the ultimate disclosure of the medical records to the requesting individual . . . they should have freedom to craft special procedures to limit the potential harm." <u>Id.</u> at 273; <u>accord</u> <u>Bavido v. Apfel</u>, 215 F.3d 743, 748-50 (7th Cir. 2000) (finding that "Privacy Act clearly directs agencies to devise special procedures for disclosure of medical records in cases in which direct transmission could adversely affect a requesting individual," but that "these procedures eventually must lead to disclosure of the records to the requesting individual"; further finding exhaustion "not required" because agency's regulations "trapped" plaintiff by requiring him to "formally [designate] a representative" and "[t]o name such a representative would amount to conceding his case"); <u>Melvin v. SSA</u>, No. 5:09-CV-235, 2010 WL 1979880, at *5 & n.3 (E.D.N.C. May 13, 2010) (explaining that "SSA amended the regulation [at issue in <u>Bavido</u>] in such a way that ensures the ultimate disclosure of records" and, therefore, allowing plaintiff to proceed with her Privacy Act claims), <u>aff'd per curiam</u>, 442 F. App'x 870 (4th Cir. 2011); <u>cf.</u> <u>Simmons v. Reno</u>, No. 97-2167, 1998 WL 964228, at *1 (6th Cir. Dec. 29, 1998) (citing <u>Benavides</u> and questioning district court's reliance on SSA regulation that required designation of medical representative for receipt of all medical records), <u>vacating & remanding</u> No. 4:96CV214 (W.D. Mich. Sept. 30, 1997); <u>Waldron v. SSA</u>, No. CS-92-334, slip op. at 9-10 (E.D. Wash. July 21, 1993) (holding claim not ripe because plaintiff had not designated representative and had not been denied information (only direct access), but stating that portion of regulation granting representative discretion in providing access to medical records "is troubling because it could be applied in such a manner as to totally deny an individual access to his medical records").

As a result of the <u>Benavides</u> decision, prior case law applying (and thus implicitly upholding) subsection (f)(3) regulations, such as the Justice Department's former regulation on this point, is unreliable. <u>See, e.g.</u>, <u>Cowsen-El v. DOJ</u>, 826 F. Supp. 532, 535-37 (D.D.C. 1992) (although recognizing that "the Privacy Act does not authorize government agencies to create new disclosure exemptions by virtue of their regulatory powers under the Privacy Act," nevertheless upholding the DOJ regulation); <u>Becher v. Demers</u>, No. 91-C-99-S, 1991 WL 333708, at *4 (W.D. Wis. May 28, 1991) (where plaintiff failed to designate medical representative and agency determined that direct access would have adverse effect on plaintiff, request was properly denied); <u>Sweatt v. U.S. Navy</u>, 2 Gov't Disclosure Serv. (P-H) ¶ 81,038, at 81,102 (D.D.C. Dec. 19, 1980) (withholding of "raw psychological data" in accordance with regulation, on ground that disclosure would adversely affect requester's health, deemed not denial of request), aff'd per curiam, 683 F.2d 420 (D.C. Cir. 1982). Nevertheless, some courts, without addressing the holding in Benavides, have upheld the denial of access pursuant to agency regulations that require the designation of a representative to review medical records. See Hill v. Blevins, No. 3-CV-92-0859, slip op. at 5-7 (M.D. Pa. Apr. 12, 1993) (finding SSA procedure requiring designation of representative other than family member for receipt and review of medical and psychological information valid), aff'd, 19 F.3d 643 (3d Cir. 1994) (unpublished table decision); Besecker v. SSA, No. 91-C-4818, 1992 WL 32243, at *2 (N.D. Ill. Feb. 18, 1992) (dismissal for failure to exhaust administrative remedies where plaintiff failed to designate representative to receive medical records), aff'd, 48 F.3d 1221 (7th Cir. 1995) (unpublished table decision); cf. Polewsky v. SSA, No. 95-6125, 1996 WL 110179, at *1-2 (2d Cir. Mar. 12, 1996) (affirming lower court decision which held that plaintiff's access claims were moot because he had ultimately designated representative to receive medical records and had been provided with them (even though prior to filing suit, plaintiff had refused to designate representative); stating further that plaintiff decided voluntarily to designate representative and thus although issue was "capable of repetition" it had "not been shown to evade review").

Although there is no counterpart provision qualifying a requester's independent right of access to his medical records under the FOIA, the D.C. Circuit found it unnecessary in Benavides to confront this issue. See 995 F.2d at 273. In fact, only two courts have addressed the matter of separate FOIA access and the possible applicability of 5 U.S.C. § 552a(t)(2) (addressing access interplay between Privacy Act and FOIA), one of which was the lower court in a companion case to Benavides. See Smith v. Quinlan, No. 91-1187, 1992 WL 25689, at *4 (D.D.C. Jan. 13, 1992) (court did "not find Section 552a(f)(3) as implemented [by 28 C.F.R. § 16.43(d)] and Section 552a(t)(2) to be incompatible"; reasoning that "if Congress had intended Section 552a(t) to disallow or narrow the scope of special procedures that agencies may deem necessary in releasing medical and psychological records, it would have so indicated by legislation"), rev'd & remanded sub nom. Benavides v. BOP, 995 F.2d 269 (D.C. Cir. 1993); Waldron v. SSA, No. CS-92-334, slip op. at 10-15 (E.D. Wash. June 1, 1993) (same as Smith, but with regard to SSA regulation); cf. Hill, No. 3-CV-92-0859, slip op. at 7 (M.D. Pa. Apr. 12, 1993) (incorrectly interpreting subsection (f)(3) as constituting an "exempting statute" under FOIA).

For further discussion of this provision, see OMB Guidelines, 40 Fed. Reg. 28,948, 28,957, 28,967 (July 9, 1975), available at http://www.whitehouse.gov/sites/default/files/omb/assets/omb/inforeg/implementation_guidelines.pdf, and the Report of the House Committee on Government Operations, H.R. Rep. No. 1416, 93d Cong., 2d Sess., at 16-17 (1974), reprinted in Source

OVERVIEW OF THE PRIVACY ACT

Book at 309-10, available at http://www.loc.gov/rr/frd/Military_Law/pdf/LH_privacy_act-1974.pdf.

D.   5 U.S.C. § 552a(f)(4)

"establish procedures for reviewing a request from an individual concerning the amendment of any record or information pertaining to the individual, for making a determination on the request, for an appeal within the agency of an initial adverse agency determination, and for whatever additional means may be necessary for each individual to be able to exercise fully his rights under [the Act]."

Comment:

For a discussion of this provision, see OMB Guidelines, 40 Fed. Reg. 28,948, 28,967 (July 9, 1975), available at http://www.whitehouse.gov/sites/default/files/omb/assets/omb/inforeg/implementation_guidelines.pdf.

E.   5 U.S.C. § 552a(f)(5)

"establish fees to be charged, if any, to any individual for making copies of his record, excluding the cost of any search for and review of the record."

Comment:

Unlike under the FOIA, search and review costs are never chargeable under the Privacy Act. See OMB Guidelines, 40 Fed. Reg. 28,948, 28,968 (July 9, 1975), available at http://www.whitehouse.gov/sites/default/files/omb/assets/omb/inforeg/implementation_guidelines.pdf.

Note also that subsection (f) provides that the Office of the Federal Register shall biennially compile and publish the rules outlined above and agency notices published under subsection (e)(4) in a form available to the public at low cost.

CIVIL REMEDIES

The Privacy Act provides for four separate and distinct civil causes of action, see 5 U.S.C. § 552a(g), two of which provide for injunctive relief – amendment lawsuits under (g)(1)(A) and access lawsuits under (g)(1)(B) – and two of which provide for compensatory relief in the form of monetary damages – damages lawsuits under (g)(1)(C) and (g)(1)(D).

It is worth noting that several courts have stated that the remedies provided for by the Privacy Act are exclusive, in that a violation of the Act does not provide for any relief in the course of

OVERVIEW OF THE PRIVACY ACT

a federal criminal prosecution, see United States v. Bressler, 772 F.2d 287, 293 (7th Cir. 1985) ("[E]ven if the defendant had made a sustainable argument [under 5 U.S.C. § 552a(e)(3)], the proper remedy is a civil action under Section 552a(g)(1) of the Privacy Act, not dismissal of the indictment."); United States v. Bell, 734 F.2d 1315, 1318 (8th Cir. 1984) (Even if appellant's (e)(3) argument was sufficiently raised at trial, "it cannot be a basis for reversing his conviction."); United States v. Gillotti, 822 F. Supp. 984, 989 (W.D.N.Y. 1993) ("[T]he appropriate relief for a violation of Section 552a(e)(7) is found in the statute and allows for damages as well as amendment or expungement of the unlawful records.... [T]here is nothing in the statute itself, nor in any judicial authority, which suggests that its violation may provide any form of relief in a federal criminal prosecution."), nor is failure to comply with the Privacy Act a proper defense to summons enforcement, see, e.g., United States v. McAnlis, 721 F.2d 334, 337 (11th Cir. 1983) (compliance with 5 U.S.C. § 552a(e)(3) held not prerequisite to enforcement of summons); United States v. Berney, 713 F.2d 568, 572 (10th Cir. 1983) (Privacy Act "contains its own remedies for noncompliance"); United States v. Harris, No. 98-3117, 1998 WL 870351, at *2 (7th Cir. Dec. 11, 1998) (citing McAnlis and Berney and rejecting "irrelevant argument that . . . the Privacy Act . . . guarantee[s] [appellant] answers to his questions before he has to comply with the IRS summons"); Hernandez v. United States, No. CV-10-MC-9181, 2010 WL 5292339, at *3 (D. Or. Dec. 17, 2010) ("[T]he IRS is not required to comply with section 552a(e)(3) as a prerequisite to issuing or enforcing a summons. . . . Additionally, the Privacy Act does not contain any provision allowing the quashing of an IRS summons as a remedy for any alleged failure to provide information as required by that Act."); Adams v. IRS, No. 2:98 MC 9, 1999 U.S. Dist. LEXIS 16018, at *15 (N.D. Ind. Sept. 29, 1999) (compliance with Privacy Act not prerequisite to enforcement of IRS summons); Reimer v. United States, 43 F. Supp. 2d 232, 237 (N.D.N.Y. 1999) (rejecting argument to quash summons on (e)(3) grounds because requirements of subsection (e)(3) "are not applicable to summons issued pursuant to 26 U.S.C. §§ 7602, 7609"); Connell v. United States, No. 1:98 CV 2094, 1998 U.S. Dist. LEXIS 20149, at *9 (N.D. Ohio Dec. 7, 1998) (citing McAnlis and stating: "That the Respondent did not comply with the Privacy Act, 5 U.S.C. § 552a(e)(3)(A)-(D), is not a basis upon which to quash the summonses at issue."); see also Phillips v. United States, No. 98-3128, 1999 WL 228585, at *2 (6th Cir. Mar. 10, 1999) (holding Privacy Act notice requirements inapplicable to issuance of IRS summons, as 26 U.S.C. § 7852(e) "plainly states that the provisions of the Privacy Act do not apply, directly or indirectly, to assessing the possibility of a tax liability"); Schwartz v. Kempf, No. 4:02-cv-198, 2004 U.S. Dist. LEXIS 2238, at *11 (W.D. Mich. Jan. 22, 2004) (same); Reimer v. United States, No. CV-F-99-5685, 1999 U.S. Dist. LEXIS 15282, at *10 (E.D. Cal. Sept. 8, 1999) (same); cf. Estate of Myers v. United States, 842 F. Supp. 1297, 1300-02 (E.D. Wash. 1993) (although ultimately applying § 7852(e)'s jurisdictional bar to dismiss Privacy Act claim, nevertheless recognizing applicability of subsection (e)(3) to IRS summons, and possibility "that a summons may be judicially enforceable yet not meet the disclosure requirements of the Privacy Act"). It has also been held that "[b]ecause the Privacy Act provides its own remedy for an agency's improper refusal to process a proper request for information, [a plaintiff] is not entitled to mandamus relief." Kotmair v. Netsch, No. 93-490, 1993 U.S. Dist. LEXIS 10781, at *5 (D. Md. July 21, 1993); see also Christian v. Sec'y of the Army, No. 11-0276, 2011 WL 345945, at *1 (D.D.C. Jan. 31, 2011) (rejecting pro se

OVERVIEW OF THE PRIVACY ACT

plaintiff's attempt "to correct his military records via a writ of mandamus" on ground that the Privacy Act "provides an adequate remedy for addressing plaintiff's claims"); Carrick v. Disclosure Specialist Brenda Spencer, IRS, No. 3:02MC95-V, 2003 U.S. Dist. LEXIS 11706, at *3-4 (W.D.N.C. June 6, 2003) (magistrate's recommendation) (denying petition for writ of mandamus as "the Privacy Act establishes a procedure for filing suit in federal court if an agency refuses to comply with a request" and petitioner has not "shown, or attempted to show, that this procedure is inadequate to obtain the relief requested"), adopted 2003 U.S. Dist. LEXIS 17189 (W.D.N.C. Sept. 2, 2003); cf. Graham v. Hawk, 857 F. Supp. 38, 41 (W.D. Tenn. 1994) ("[T]he existence of remedies under the Privacy Act [for alleged inaccuracy] preclude plaintiff's entitlement to mandamus, even though his claim under that act is substantively meritless."), aff'd, 59 F.3d 170 (6th Cir. 1995) (unpublished table decision).

In the context of civil remedies, the only court of appeals to consider the issue has held that the Privacy Act "does not limit the remedial rights of persons to pursue whatever remedies they may have under the [Federal Tort Claims Act]" for privacy violations consisting of record disclosures. O'Donnell v. United States, 891 F.2d 1079, 1084-85 (3d Cir. 1989); see also Beaven v. DOJ, No. 03-84, 2007 WL 1032301, at *21-25 (E.D. Ky. Mar. 30, 2007) (assuming jurisdiction over claims of invasion of privacy brought under FTCA and based on conduct held to violate Privacy Act, but determining that plaintiffs failed to prove the elements of those claims), aff'd in part, rev'd in part & remanded, on other grounds, 622 F.3d 540 (6th Cir. 2010); cf. Alexander v. FBI, 971 F. Supp. 603, 610-11 (D.D.C. 1997) (citing O'Donnell and holding that Privacy Act does not preempt causes of action under local or state law for common law invasion of privacy tort), modified in nonpertinent part, 691 F. Supp. 2d 182 (D.D.C. 2010), aff'd on other grounds, 456 F. App'x 1 (D.C. Cir. 2011). But see Hager v. United States, No. 86-3555, slip op. at 7-8 (N.D. Ohio Oct. 20, 1987) ("Because the Privacy Act does have its own enforcement mechanism" for plaintiff's claims relating to the disclosure of confidential information, "it preempts the FTCA."); cf. Tripp v. United States, 257 F. Supp. 2d 37, 45 (D.D.C. 2003) (dismissing plaintiff's claim under the FTCA for negligent disclosure of private information, as plaintiff could point to no "duty analogous to that created by the federal Privacy Act under local law to state a claim upon which relief [could] be granted"); Fort Hall Landowners Alliance, Inc. v. BIA, No. 99-052, slip op. at 16 (D. Idaho Mar. 29, 2001) (finding that common law obligations "not to disclose personal information" were "preempted by the Privacy Act").

It should also be noted that the Court of Appeals for the District of Columbia Circuit has held that the Feres doctrine, which holds that "'the [g]overnment is not liable under the Federal Tort Claims Act for injuries to servicemen where the injuries arise out of or are in the course of activity incident to service'" does not apply to the Privacy Act. Cummings v. Dep't of the Navy, 279 F.3d 1051, 1053-58 (D.C. Cir. 2002) (quoting Feres v. United States, 340 U.S. 135, 146 (1950), and concluding that "without regard to the identity of the plaintiff or the agency she is suing, the [Privacy Act] plainly authorizes injunctive relief . . . and monetary relief," which remains "the best evidence of congressional intent" that the Feres doctrine "does not extend to Privacy Act lawsuits brought by military personnel against the military departments"), rev'g 116 F. Supp. 2d 76 (D.D.C. 2000); see also Chang v. U.S. Dep't of the

OVERVIEW OF THE PRIVACY ACT

Navy, No. 01-5240, slip op. at 1 (D.C. Cir. July 8, 2002) (citing Cummings to vacate district court opinion), vacating & remanding per curiam No. 00-0783 (D.D.C. May 17, 2001) (holding suit to be barred by Feres doctrine); Gamble v. Dep't of Army, 567 F. Supp. 2d 150, 155 n.9 (D.D.C. 2008), abrogated on other grounds by In re Sealed Case, 551 F.2d 1047, 1049-50 (D.C. Cir. 2009). But cf. Duggan v. Dep't of Air Force, No. H-11-2556, 2012 WL 1884144, at *4 (S.D. Tex. May 21, 2012) ("plaintiff's claim that the Feres doctrine does not bar his Privacy Act claim also fails" as "plaintiff's medical information was released within the military command structure."). In an earlier decision, however, the Court of Appeals for the Eighth Circuit held that the plaintiff's Privacy Act claims were barred under the Feres doctrine. See Uhl v. Swanstrom, 79 F.3d 751, 755-56 (8th Cir. 1996); cf. Walsh v. United States, No. 1:05-CV-0818, 2006 WL 1617273, at *5 (M.D. Pa. June 9, 2006) (dicta) (comparing Uhl and Cummings and noting that "[t]here is a split of authority as to whether the Feres doctrine bars Privacy Act claims"), aff'd on other grounds, 328 F. App'x 806 (3d Cir. 2009), cert. denied, 130 S. Ct. 502 (2009). The Cummings opinion did not reference Uhl, the only other appellate decision on this issue.

Several courts of appeals have held that the Privacy Act's remedies do preclude an action against individual employees for damages under the Constitution in a "Bivens" suit. See Djenasevic v. EOUSA, No. 08-5509, 2009 U.S. App. LEXIS 15424, at *2 (D.C. Cir. July 8, 2009) ("[T]o the extent appellant attempts to state a Bivens claim, the comprehensive remedial scheme of the Privacy Act precludes creation of a Bivens remedy for any of his constitutional claims."); Wilson v. Libby, 535 F.3d 697, 707 (D.C. Cir. 2008) (concluding that the Privacy Act's comprehensive remedial scheme precludes a Bivens claim even though that scheme does not necessarily provide plaintiffs with full relief); Griffin v. Ashcroft, No. 02-5399, 2003 WL 22097940, at *2 (D.C. Cir. Sept. 3, 2003) (per curiam) (affirming "district court's dismissal of appellant's constitutional claims based on the BOP's alleged maintenance and use of inaccurate information because such claims are encompassed within the Privacy Act's comprehensive remedial scheme"); Chung v. DOJ, 333 F.3d 273, 274 (D.C. Cir. 2003) (affirming district court's dismissal of plaintiff's Bivens claims "because . . . they are encompassed within the remedial scheme of the Privacy Act"); Downie v. City of Middleburg Hts., 301 F.3d 688, 696 (6th Cir. 2002) (agreeing with district court that "because the Privacy Act is a comprehensive legislative scheme that provides a meaningful remedy for the kind of wrong [plaintiff] alleges that he suffered, we should not imply a Bivens remedy"); see also Lange v. Taylor, 5:10-CT-3097, 2012 WL 255333, at *2-3 (E.D.N.C. Jan. 27, 2012); Lim v. United States, No. 10-2574, 2011 WL 2650889, at *8 (D. Md. July 5, 2011); Lewis v. U.S. Parole Comm'n, 770 F. Supp. 2d 246, 251-52 (D.D.C. 2011); Melvin v. SSA, No. 5:09-CV-235, 2010 WL 1979880, at *4 (E.D.N.C. May 13, 2010); Hurt v. D.C. Court Servs., 612 F. Supp. 2d 54, 56 (D.D.C. 2009), aff'd in pertinent part per curiam sub nom. Hurt v. Cromer, No. 09-5224, 2010 WL 604863 (D.C. Cir. Jan. 21, 2010); Roggio v. FBI, No. 08-4991, 2009 WL 2460780, at *2 (D.N.J. Aug. 11, 2009); Al-Beshrawi v. Arney, No. 5:06CV2114, 2007 WL 1245845, at *3-4 (N.D. Ohio Apr. 27, 2007); Sudnick v. DOD, 474 F. Supp. 2d 91, 100 (D.D.C. 2007); Hatfill v. Ashcroft, 404 F. Supp. 2d 104, 116-17 (D.D.C. 2005); Clark v. BOP, 407 F. Supp. 2d 127, 131 (D.D.C. 2005); Newmark v. Principi, 262 F. Supp. 2d 509, 518-19 (E.D. Pa. 2003); Khalfani v. Sec'y, VA, No. 94-CV-5720, 1999 WL 138247, at *7 (E.D.N.Y.

OVERVIEW OF THE PRIVACY ACT

Mar. 10, 1999), appeal dismissed for appellant's failure to comply with scheduling order, No. 99-6140 (2d Cir. Oct. 10, 2000); Fares v. INS, 29 F. Supp. 2d 259, 262 (W.D.N.C. 1998); Sullivan v. USPS, 944 F. Supp. 191, 195-96 (W.D.N.Y. 1996); Hughley v. BOP, No. 94-1048, slip op. at 5 (D.D.C. Apr. 30, 1996), aff'd sub nom. Hughley v. Hawks, No. 96-5159, 1997 WL 362725 (D.C. Cir. May 6, 1997); Blazy v. Woolsey, No. 93-2424, 1996 WL 43554, at *1 (D.D.C. Jan. 31, 1996), subsequent decision sub nom. Blazy v. Tenet, 979 F. Supp. 10, 27 (D.D.C. 1997), summary affirmance granted, No. 97-5330, 1998 WL 315583 (D.C. Cir. May 12, 1998); Williams v. VA, 879 F. Supp. 578, 585-87 (E.D. Va. 1995); Mangino v. Dep't of the Army, No. 94-2067, 1994 WL 477260, at *9 (D. Kan. Aug. 24, 1994); Mittleman v. U.S. Treasury, 773 F. Supp. 442, 454 (D.D.C. 1991); cf. Royer v. BOP, No. 1:10-cv-0146, 2010 WL 4827727, at *5 (E.D. Va. Nov. 19, 2010) (in transferring case to different venue, stating that plaintiff's Bivens claims "may simply collapse into [his] Privacy Act claims, at least insofar as they merely repeat the allegations that the BOP has maintained inaccurate records about [his] affiliation with terrorist groups"); Patterson v. FBI, 705 F. Supp. 1033, 1045 n.16 (D.N.J. 1989) (to extent that First Amendment claim involves damages resulting from maintenance of records, "such an action is apt to be foreclosed by the existence of the Privacy Act"), aff'd, 893 F.2d 595 (3d Cir. 1990). But see Doe v. U.S. Civil Serv. Comm'n, 483 F. Supp. 539, 564-75 (S.D.N.Y. 1980) (permitting Bivens claim, but relying on fact that plaintiff's claims related in part to events predating effective date of Privacy Act and, more significantly, so holding without benefit of subsequent Supreme Court precedent bearing on issue); see also Alexander, 971 F. Supp. at 610-11 (agreeing with outcome in Blazy and Mittleman, but concluding that their logic does not extend to prohibit recovery under local law for torts committed by individuals who, although government employees, were acting outside scope of their employment; holding that "Privacy Act does not preempt the common law invasion of privacy tort").

In the context of equitable relief under the judicial review provisions of the Administrative Procedure Act, 5 U.S.C. §§ 701-706 (2006), for claims governed by the Privacy Act, the Supreme Court has recently stated that "[t]he Privacy Act says nothing about standards of proof governing equitable relief that may be open to victims of adverse determinations or effects, although it may be that this inattention is explained by the general provisions for equitable relief within the [APA]." Doe v. Chao, 540 U.S. 614, 619 n.1 (2004); cf. OMB Guidelines, 40 Fed. Reg. 28,948, 28,968 (July 9, 1975), available at http://www.whitehouse.gov/sites/default/files/omb/assets/omb/inforeg/implementation_guidelines.pdf (stating in its Civil Remedies section that "[a]n individual may seek judicial review under other provisions of the Administrative Procedure Act (APA)"). Indeed, under the APA, the Court of Appeals for the District of Columbia Circuit enjoined the Veterans Administration from disclosing medical records about an individual pursuant to a routine use that "would permit routine disclosure pursuant to a grand jury subpoena" as that would "circumvent the mandates of the Privacy Act." Doe v. Stephens, 851 F.2d 1457, 1466-67 (D.C. Cir. 1988) (although plaintiff did "not premise his claim for equitable relief on the APA," the court considered the claim under the APA, rather than resolving the plaintiff's constitutional claims, in order to further the principle of "avoiding constitutional questions if at all possible") (discussed above under subsections (b)(3) and (b)(11)); see also Recticel Foam Corp. v. DOJ, No. 98-2523, slip op. at

OVERVIEW OF THE PRIVACY ACT

9 (D.D.C. Jan. 31, 2002), appeal dismissed, No. 02-5118 (D.C. Cir. Apr. 25, 2002) (holding that court had jurisdiction under APA to enjoin FBI from disclosing investigative records in order to prevent future violation of subsection (b) of Privacy Act); Doe v. Herman, No. 97-0043, 1998 WL 34194937, at *4-7 (W.D. Va. Mar. 18, 1998) (invoking APA to issue preventative injunction in response to Privacy Act claim); cf. Haase v. Sessions, 893 F.2d 370, 374 n.6 (D.C. Cir. 1990) (stating in dicta that "[i]t is not at all clear to us that Congress intended to preclude broad equitable relief (injunctions) to prevent (e)(7) violations . . . [a]nd in the absence of such explicit intention, by creating a general cause of action (under (g)(1)(D)) for violations of the Privacy Act, Congress presumably intended the district court to use inherent equitable powers"); Rice v. United States, 245 F.R.D. 3, 7 (D.D.C. 2007) (noting that "there is some authority for awarding [declaratory] relief under the APA" for claims arising under the Privacy Act); Doe v. Veneman, 230 F. Supp. 2d 739, 752 (W.D. Tex. 2002) (enjoining release of records in system of records because release would be violation of FOIA and Privacy Act) (reverse FOIA suit), aff'd in part & rev'd in part on other grounds, 380 F.3d 807 (5th Cir. 2004); AFL-CIO v. FEC, 177 F. Supp. 2d 48, 61-64 (D.D.C. 2001) (although not reaching merits of Privacy Act claims, finding disclosure contrary to law where Exemption 7(C) "bar[s] release" of information under APA), aff'd on other grounds, 333 F.3d 168 (D.C. Cir. 2003). However, courts in other cases have refused to allow claims brought under the Administrative Procedure Act where the relief sought is expressly provided by the Privacy Act. See Andreozzi v. DOD, No. 03-5304, 2004 WL 1083036, at *2 (D.C. Cir. May 13, 2004) (per curiam) (holding that plaintiff's APA claim for expunction of records "lacked merit"; denying plaintiff's Privacy Act claim for expunction or amendment of records as the agency had exempted "the relevant system of records from the access, amendment, and civil penalty provisions of the Act," and plaintiff failed to "request expunction or amendment at the agency level prior to filing suit"); Wilson v. McHugh, No. 11-303, 2012 WL 403282, at *9 (D.D.C. Feb. 9, 2012) ("To the extent [plaintiff] relies on the Privacy Act and believes the Privacy Act provides him a legal remedy, . . . [plaintiff] cannot seek review in this Court under the APA."); Reid v. BOP, No. 04-1845, 2005 WL 1699425, at *2 (D.D.C. July 20, 2005) (reasoning that "[b]ecause there is an adequate remedy available to plaintiff under the Privacy Act, he cannot resort to the APA for relief"); Tripp v. DOD, 193 F. Supp. 2d 229, 238-40 (D.D.C. 2002) (holding that a "plaintiff [cannot] bring an independent APA claim predicated on a Privacy Act violation"); Mittleman v. U.S. Treasury, 773 F. Supp. 442, 449 (D.D.C. 1991) (finding that plaintiff's APA claim for failure to follow agency regulations and to provide plaintiff with hearing or other opportunity to rebut allegations against her in various government reports "is, in part, simply a restatement of her Privacy Act claim . . . [for which] Congress has provided plaintiff with statutory schemes and remedies through which she may seek relief").

It also has been held that a court may order equitable relief in the form of the expungement of records either in an action under the Privacy Act or in a direct action under the Constitution. See, e.g., Doe v. U.S. Air Force, 812 F.2d 738, 741 (D.C. Cir. 1987); Smith v. Nixon, 807 F.2d 197, 204 (D.C. Cir. 1986); Hobson v. Wilson, 737 F.2d 1, 65-66 (D.C. Cir. 1984); Ezenwa v. Gallen, 906 F. Supp. 978, 986 (M.D. Pa. 1995); cf. Dickson v. OPM, 828 F.2d 32, 41 (D.C. Cir. 1987) (suggesting that it is not resolved "whether as a general proposition, the

OVERVIEW OF THE PRIVACY ACT

Privacy Act defines the scope of remedies available under the Constitution"). See also the discussion of expungement of records under "Amendment Lawsuits under (g)(1)(A)," below.

The District Court for the District of Columbia has analyzed the relationship between the Privacy Act and the Health Care Quality Improvement Act ("HCQIA"), Pub. L. No. 99-660, 100 Stat. 3784, which "protect[s] patients from incompetent physicians by establishing a database to collect information related to professional competence or conduct which could adversely affect the health or welfare of patients." Doe v. Thompson, 332 F. Supp. 2d 124, 125 (D.D.C. 2004). In Doe, a dentist filed a subsection (g)(1)(B) claim against the Department of Health and Human Services. Id. at 127. However, "instead of reviewing the plaintiff's request pursuant to the Privacy Act, the [Department] responded by informing the plaintiff that the sole administrative remedy available to him was the procedures promulgated by the [Department]" pursuant to HCQIA. Id. The court concluded that because the procedures promulgated by the Department pursuant to HCQUIA "provide less protection than the procedures required by the Privacy Act," it held that the Department "must adhere to the requirements of the Privacy Act when considering a dispute to a record in the" database established by HCQIA. Id. at 130, 132-33.

The District Court for the District of Columbia has also analyzed the relationship between the Privacy Act and the Health Insurance Portability and Accountability Act ("HIPAA"), 42 U.S.C. § 1320d-1320d-8 (2006), which "prohibits both the improper disclosure of individually identifiable health information and the improper acquisition of such information." Cacho v. Chertoff, No. 06-00292, 2006 WL 3422548, *2 (D.D.C. Nov. 28, 2006). In Cacho, the plaintiff brought a subsection (b)/(g)(1)(D) claim against the Department of Homeland Security "on the theory that [a Department employee] improperly accessed [the plaintiff's] medical record." Id. at *5. The court dismissed this claim on the ground that it "would be inconsistent with both HIPAA and the Privacy Act's plain language" to "recognize under the Privacy Act a private right of action that Congress has expressly denied under HIPAA." Id.

In addition, the District Court for the District of Columbia has dismissed a plaintiff's subsection (b)/(g)(1)(D) claims where the Attorney General invoked the State Secrets Privilege. Edmonds v. DOJ, 323 F. Supp. 2d 65, 80-82 (D.D.C. 2004). Specifically, the court explained that "because the . . . documents related to the plaintiff's employment, termination and security review that comprise the system of records are privileged, and because the plaintiff would be unable to depose witnesses whose identities are privileged or to otherwise identify through discovery the individual or individuals who purportedly released the privileged information, the plaintiff is . . . unable to proceed with her Privacy Act claims." Id. at 81.

Finally, for discussions of class certifications for claims brought under the Privacy Act, see Rice v. United States, 211 F.R.D. 10, 14 (D.D.C. 2002), Fort Hall Landowners Alliance, Inc. v. BIA, No. 99-052, slip op. at 10 (D. Idaho Aug. 16, 2002), Baker v. Runyon, No. 96-2619, 1997 WL 232606, at *4 (N.D. Ill. May 2, 1997), and Ingerman v. IRS, No. 89-5396, 1990 WL 10029523, at *2 (D.N.J. July 16, 1990), for examples of cases granting class certification, and

OVERVIEW OF THE PRIVACY ACT

Doe v. Chao, 306 F.3d 170, 184 (4th Cir. 2002), aff'd on other grounds, 540 U.S. 614 (2004), Fort Hall Landowners Alliance, Inc. V. BIA, No. 99-052, 2007 WL 218725, at *3 (D. Idaho July 16, 2007), Schmidt v. VA, 218 F.R.D. 619, 637 (E.D. Wis. 2003), and Lyon v. United States, 94 F.R.D. 69, 76 (W.D. Okla. 1982), for examples of cases limiting or denying class certification. Compare also Covert v. Harrington, 876 F.2d 751, 752 (9th Cir. 1989), Andrews v. VA, 838 F.2d 418, 419 (10th Cir. 1988), Parks v. IRS, 618 F.2d 677, 679 (10th Cir. 1980), and Romero-Vargas v. Shalala, 907 F. Supp. 1128, 1131 (N.D. Ohio Oct. 13, 1995), for cases involving multiple plaintiffs.

A. Amendment Lawsuits under (g)(1)(A)

"Whenever any agency . . . makes a determination under subsection (d)(3) . . . not to amend an individual's record in accordance with his request, or fails to make such review in conformity with that subsection [the individual may bring a civil action against the agency]." 5 U.S.C. § 552a(g)(1)(A).

– Exhaustion of administrative remedies – through pursuit of an amendment request to the agency and a request for administrative review, see 5 U.S.C. § 552a(d)(2)-(3) – is a prerequisite to a civil action for amendment of records. As explained in greater detail below under "Access Lawsuits under (g)(1)(B)," this requirement is jurisdictional in nature because it is imposed by the Act itself, whereas the requirement of exhaustion in access lawsuits is only jurisprudential in nature, as it is not imposed by the Act itself.

Comment:

The exhaustion principle is well established in the Privacy Act case law. For cases in which the court has required the individual to file a request for amendment of his or her records, in conformity with the agency's regulations, before commencing a subsection (g)(1)(A) lawsuit, see, e.g., Quinn v. Stone, 978 F.2d 126, 137-38 (3d Cir. 1992); Hill v. U.S. Air Force, 795 F.2d 1067, 1069 (D.C. Cir. 1986) (per curiam); Nagel v. HEW, 725 F.2d 1438, 1441 (D.C. Cir. 1984); Middlebrooks v. Mabus, No. 1:11cv46, 2011 WL 4478686, at *5 n.10 (E.D. Va. Sept. 23, 2011); Kvech v. Holder, No. 10-cv-545, 2011 WL 4369452, at *4 n.10 (D.D.C. Sept. 19, 2011); Washington v. Donley, 802 F. Supp. 2d 539, 553-54 (D. Del. 2011); Reitz v. USDA, No. 08-4131, 2010 WL 786586, at *10 (D. Kan. Mar. 4, 2010); Pailes v. U.S. Peace Corps, 783 F. Supp. 2d 1, 7-8 (D.D.C. 2009), summary affirmance granted on other grounds, No. 09-5400, 2010 WL 2160012 (D.C. Cir. May 27, 2010); Pototsky v. DHS, No. CV 07-144, slip op. at 4 (D. Ariz. Jan. 15, 2009), aff'd, 368 F. App'x 832 (9th Cir. 2010); Watson v. Mineta, No. 4:05-CV-007, 2007 WL 3102196, at *2 (M.D. Ga. Oct. 23, 2007) (dicta); Brown v. DOJ, No. 02-2662, slip op. at 24-26 (D. Ala. June 21,

OVERVIEW OF THE PRIVACY ACT

2005); Pontecorvo v. FBI, No. 00-1511, slip op. at 21-22 (D.D.C. Sept. 30, 2001); Murphy v. United States, 121 F. Supp. 2d 21, 28 (D.D.C. 2000), aff'd per curiam, 64 F. App'x 250 (D.C. Cir. 2003); M.K. v. Tenet, 99 F. Supp. 2d 12, 20 (D.D.C. 2000); Blazy v. Tenet, 979 F. Supp. 10, 18-19 (D.D.C. 1997), summary affirmance granted, No. 97-5330, 1998 WL 315583 (D.C. Cir. May 12, 1998); Olivares v. NASA, 882 F. Supp. 1545, 1552 (D. Md. 1995), aff'd, 103 F.3d 119 (4th Cir. 1996) (unpublished table decision); Jerez v. DOJ, No. 94-100, slip op. at 8-9 (D. Ariz. Feb. 2, 1995); Gergick v. Austin, No. 89-0838-CV-W-2, 1992 U.S. Dist. LEXIS 7338, at *13-16 (W.D. Mo. Apr. 29, 1992), aff'd, No. 92-3210 (8th Cir. July 9, 1993); Simon v. DOJ, 752 F. Supp. 14, 23 n.6 (D.D.C. 1990), aff'd, 980 F.2d 782 (D.C. Cir. 1992); Campbell v. USPS, No. 86-3609, 1990 WL 36132, at *4 (E.D. La. Mar. 28, 1990); Green v. USPS, No. 88-0539, 1989 U.S. Dist. LEXIS 6846, at *6-7 (S.D.N.Y. June 19, 1989); Tracy v. SSA, No. 88-C-570-S, slip op. at 3-4 (W.D. Wis. Sept. 23, 1988); and Ross v. USPS, 556 F. Supp. 729, 735 (N.D. Ala. 1983). Cf. New-Howard v. Shinseki, No. 09-5350, 2012 WL 2362546, at *6 (E.D. Pa. June 21, 2012) (finding plaintiff's amendment request "flawed [] as she asserts her claim against an entity that no longer has control of the documents" because at the time plaintiff filed her amendment request, she had filed an MSPB action, and thus, records that would "ordinarily be under the control of OPM" were "covered by the appropriate MSPB or EEOC system of records"). For cases in which the court has required the individual to administratively appeal an agency's denial of his or her amendment request before commencing a subsection (g)(1)(A) lawsuit, see Jernigan v. Dep't of the Air Force, No. 97-35930, 1998 WL 658662, at *2 (9th Cir. Sept. 17, 1998); Dickson v. OPM, 828 F.2d 32, 40 (D.C. Cir 1987); Hewitt v. Grabicki, 794 F. 2d 1373, 1377-78 (9th Cir. 1986); Conley v. United States, No. 2:10-cv-444, 2011 WL 1256611, at *7 (S.D. Ohio Mar. 31, 2011); Pearson v. DHS, No. 3:08-CV-1885-B, 2009 WL 4016414, at *8 (N.D. Tex. Nov. 17, 2009); Leighton v. CIA., 412 F. Supp. 2d 30, 34-35 (D.D.C. 2006); Finnerty v. USPS, No. 03-558, 2006 WL 54345, at *6-8 (D.N.J. Jan. 9, 2006); Hass v. U.S. Air Force, 848 F. Supp. 926, 930 (D. Kan. 1994); Freude v. McSteen, No. 4-85-882, slip op. at 4-5 (D. Minn. Oct. 23, 1985), aff'd, 786 F.2d 1171 (8th Cir. 1986) (unpublished table decision); and Beaver v. VA, No. 1-82-477, slip op. at 2 (E.D. Tenn. Apr. 6, 1983). Cf. Williams v. Bezy, 97 F. App'x 573, 574 (6th Cir. 2004) (affirming district court's dismissal of plaintiff's subsection (e)(5) claim for failure to exhaust administrative remedies without specifically discussing whether claim was brought under subsection (g)(1)(A) or subsection (g)(1)(C)); Doe v. Goss, No. 04-2122, 2007 WL 106523, at *8 n.14 (D.D.C. Jan. 12, 2007) ("Plaintiff cannot circumvent the exhaustion requirement by styling his 'equitable right' as a constitutional claim where, as here, Congress has provided administrative machinery for the resolution of the statutory claim."). But cf. Duke v. United States, 305 F. Supp. 2d 478, 488

OVERVIEW OF THE PRIVACY ACT

(E.D. Pa. 2004) (finding that "although plaintiff [had] not exhausted administrative remedies" court had "subject matter jurisdiction over this claim" because "this exhaustion requirement is not a jurisdictional requirement" but a "practical" one). It also has been held that a plaintiff cannot "boot-strap" an access claim under (g)(1)(B) into a (g)(1)(A) amendment violation, even though she argued that by denying her request for access the agency had prevented her from exercising her right to request amendment. See Smith v. Cont'l Assurance Co., No. 91 C 0963, 1991 WL 164348, at *2 (N.D. Ill. Aug. 22, 1991); accord Mumme v. U.S. Dep't of Labor, 150 F. Supp. 2d 162, 173 (D. Me. 2001), aff'd, No. 01-2256 (1st Cir. June 12, 2002); see also M.K., 99 F. Supp. 2d at 20 n.15 (holding that plaintiffs must exhaust administrative remedies by requesting amendment of records even though they argued that "they cannot ask the CIA[] to amend that which the CIA refuses to admit exists").

Although subsection (d)(2)(A) requires an agency to "acknowledge in writing such receipt" of an amendment request within ten working days, subsection (d)(2)(B) merely requires an agency to "promptly" make the requested correction or inform the individual of its refusal to amend. In construing this language, the Court of Appeals for the District of Columbia Circuit has held that "[t]he statute provides no exemption from administrative review when an agency fails, even by several months, to abide by a deadline, and none is reasonably implied." Dickson v. OPM, 828 F.2d 32, 40 (D.C. Cir. 1987) (requiring exhaustion of subsection (d)(3) administrative appeal remedy even when agency did not respond to initial amendment request for 90 days (citing Nagel, 725 F.2d at 1440-41)). But see Schaeuble v. Reno, 87 F. Supp. 2d 383, 389-90 (D.N.J. 2000) (not requiring further exhaustion of administrative remedies where plaintiff had requested amendment and agency had not responded for six months; stating that "[a] six month delay is not a 'prompt' response," and that "[m]oreover, not only has the [agency] not indicated that it will make a final determination . . . by any certain date, the Privacy Act does not bind the [agency] to any definite timeframe for administrative action, which weighs in favor of waiving the exhaustion requirement").

However, in contrast to subsection (d)(2)(B), subsection (d)(3) requires an agency to make a final determination on administrative appeal from an initial denial of an amendment request within 30 working days (unless, for good cause shown, the head of the agency extends this 30-day period). Thus, court jurisdiction exists as soon as an agency fails to comply with the time requirements of subsection (d)(3); "[t]o require further exhaustion would not only contradict the plain words of the statute but also would undercut [C]ongress's clear intent to provide speedy disposition of these claims." Diederich v. Dep't of the Army, 878 F.2d 646, 648 (2d Cir. 1989).

OVERVIEW OF THE PRIVACY ACT

In Harper v. Kobelinski, 589 F.2d 721 (D.C. Cir. 1978) (per curiam), and Liguori v. Alexander, 495 F. Supp. 641 (S.D.N.Y. 1980), the agencies denied amendment requests but failed to inform the plaintiffs of their rights to administratively appeal those decisions. In light of the Act's requirement that agencies inform complainants whose amendment requests have been denied of the available administrative remedies, 5 U.S.C. § 552a(d)(2)(B)(ii), the courts in Harper and Liguori refused to penalize the plaintiffs for their failures to exhaust. Harper, 589 F.2d at 723; Liguori, 495 F. Supp. at 646-47; see also Germane v. Heckler, 804 F.2d 366, 369 (7th Cir. 1986) (discussing Harper and Liguori with approval); Mahar v. Nat'l Parks Serv., No. 86-0398, slip op. at 7-11 (D.D.C. Dec. 23, 1987) (same); cf. Ertell v. Dep't of Army, 626 F. Supp. 903, 909-10 (C.D. Ill. 1986) (rejecting agency's exhaustion defense where it first told employee, in response to his amendment request, that it had destroyed the record but later used same record against him, and ruling that employee was not required to make new request or appeal initial action).

In White v. U.S. Civil Service Commission, 589 F.2d 713, 715-16 (D.C. Cir. 1978) (per curiam), the D.C. Circuit held that, notwithstanding any exhaustion of administrative remedies, an amendment action is "inappropriate and premature" where the individual had not yet sought judicial review (under the Administrative Procedure Act) of adverse employment decisions, because granting Privacy Act relief "would tend to undermine the established and proven method by which individuals . . . have obtained review from the courts." Cf. Douglas v. Farmers Home Admin., No. 91-1969, 1992 U.S. Dist. LEXIS 9159, at *4-5 (D.D.C. June 26, 1992) (dismissing damages action under Privacy Act where plaintiff had not sought review under Administrative Procedure Act of allegedly inaccurate property appraisal). But see Churchwell v. United States, 545 F.2d 59, 61 (8th Cir. 1976) (probationary employee need not pursue Privacy Act remedy prior to proceeding with due process claim for hearing).

In Crummey v. SSA, 794 F. Supp. 2d 46, 58 (D.D.C. 2011), aff'd per curiam, No. 11-5231, 2012 WL 556317 (D.C. Cir. Feb. 6, 2012), the District Court for the District of Columbia explained that "an individual's request for amendment must relate to an existing record that is maintained within one of the agency's systems of records." The plaintiff – who "believe[d] that the Social Security Administration created a trust . . . when it assigned him a Social Security Number and a Social Security Card" – had "draft[ed] an agreement designed to reflect the alleged creation of the Trust." 794 F. Supp. 2d at 49. The plaintiff brought a subsection (g)(1)(A) claim seeking a court order requiring the SSA "to amend its records to add the Trust Agreement to the SSA's Master Files, or to somehow incorporate its

OVERVIEW OF THE PRIVACY ACT

contents therein." Id. at 52. The court reviewed the categories of records listed in the applicable system of records notice, see 75 Fed. Reg. 82,123 (Dec. 29, 2010), and determined that "[n]one of the information set forth in the Trust Agreement falls within this universe." 794 F. Supp. 2d at 58. "In short," the court concluded, "the Trust Agreement and the information contained therein do not correspond to an 'item, collection, or grouping' of information in the Master Files," and granted summary judgment to the SSA. Id. at 59.

It has also been recognized that jurisdiction to consider a Privacy Act amendment claim exists only if the government has failed to comply with a request for amendment; once a request is complied with and the identified records have been amended, an amendment claim is moot. See, e.g., Conley, 2011 WL 1256611, at *7; Blanton v. Warden, No. 7:10-cv-00552, 2011 WL 1226010, at *2-3 (W.D. Va. Mar. 30, 2011); Garza v. Pearson, No. 5:08-cv-300, 2009 WL 2500116, at *1 (S.D. Miss. Aug. 13, 2009); Blazy v. Tenet, 979 F. Supp. 10, 19 (D.D.C. 1997), summary affirmance granted, No. 97-5330, 1998 WL 315583 (D.C. Cir. May 12, 1998).

– Courts "shall determine the matter de novo." 5 U.S.C. § 552(g)(2)(A).

Comment:

"De novo review does not contemplate that the court will substitute its judgment for the [agency's], but rather that the court will undertake an independent determination of whether the amendment request should be denied." Nolan v. DOJ, No. 89-A-2035, 1991 WL 134803, at *3 (D. Colo. July 17, 1991), appeal dismissed in pertinent part on procedural grounds, 973 F.2d 843 (10th Cir. 1992); see also Doe v. United States, 821 F.2d 694, 697-98 (D.C. Cir. 1987) (holding that "[d]e novo means . . . a fresh, independent determination of 'the matter' at stake"). The applicable standards in amendment lawsuits are accuracy, relevancy, timeliness, and completeness. 5 U.S.C. § 552a(d)(2)(B)(i). But see Doe v. United States, 821 F.2d at 697 n.8, 699 (without explanation, stating that "whether the nature of the relief sought is injunctive or monetary, the standard against which the accuracy of the record is measured remains constant" and "[t]hat standard is found in 5 U.S.C. § 552a(e)(5) and reiterated in 5 U.S.C. § 552a(g)(1)(C)"). The burden of proof is on the individual. See Mervin v. FTC, 591 F.2d 821, 827 (D.C. Cir. 1978) (per curiam); Thompson v. Dep't of Transp. U.S. Coast Guard, 547 F. Supp. 274, 282 (S.D. Fla. 1982); OMB Guidelines, 40 Fed. Reg. 28,948, 28,969 (July 9, 1975), available at http://www.whitehouse.gov/sites/default/files/omb/assets/omb/inforeg/implementation_guidelines.pdf.

OVERVIEW OF THE PRIVACY ACT

Note that in a unique statutory displacement action, Congress has expressly removed the jurisdiction of the district courts to order the amendment of IRS records concerning tax liability. 26 U.S.C. § 7852(e) (2006). See, e.g., Gardner v. United States, 213 F.3d 735, 740-41 & n.5 (D.C. Cir. 2000); Gogert v. IRS, No. 86-1674, slip op. at 3 (9th Cir. Apr. 7, 1987); England v. Comm'r, 798 F.2d 350, 351-52 (9th Cir. 1986); Meyer v. Comm'r, No. 10-767, 2010 WL 4157173, at *8 (D. Minn. Sept. 27, 2010) (magistrate's recommendation), adopted 2010 WL 4134958 (D. Minn. Oct. 19, 2010); Schlabach v. IRS, No. CV-09-298, 2010 WL 2682281, at *1-2 (E.D. Wash. July 2, 2010), related subsequent opinion 2010 WL 3789074, at *2 (E.D. Wash. Sept. 23, 2010); Gulden v. United States, No. 8:06-CV-2327-T-27MSS, 2007 WL 3202480, at *3 (M.D. Fla. Oct. 29, 2007); MacLeod v. IRS, No. 01-2320, 2002 U.S. Dist. LEXIS 14975, at *9-10 (S.D. Cal. June 7, 2002); Singer v. IRS, No. 98-0024, 1998 U.S. Dist. LEXIS 13301, at *10-11 (E.D. Pa. Aug. 10, 1998); Chandler v. United States, No. 93-C-812A, 1994 WL 315759, at *1 (D. Utah Mar. 8, 1994); Fuselier v. IRS, No. 90-0300, slip op. at 1 (W.D. La. Oct. 25, 1990); Mallas v. Kolak, 721 F. Supp. 748, 751 (M.D.N.C. 1989); Schandl v. Heye, No. 86-6219, slip op. at 2 (S.D. Fla. Sept. 30, 1986); Dyrdra v. Comm'r, No. 85-0-41, slip op. at 2 (D. Neb. Oct. 28, 1985); Conklin v. United States, No. 83-C-587, slip op. at 2-3 (D. Colo. Feb. 26, 1985); Green v. IRS, 556 F. Supp. 79, 80 (N.D. Ill. 1982), aff'd, 734 F.2d 18 (7th Cir. 1984) (unpublished table decision); see also Gardner v. United States, No. 96-1467, 1999 U.S. Dist. LEXIS 2195, at *18 (D.D.C. Jan. 29, 1999) (finding that by virtue of § 7852(e) IRS is "exempt" from amendment provisions of Privacy Act), summary affirmance granted on other grounds, No. 99-5089, 1999 WL 728359 (D.C. Cir. Aug. 4, 1999).

Consistent with the OMB Guidelines, 40 Fed. Reg. at 28,958, 28,969 (July 9, 1975), available at http://www.whitehouse.gov/sites/default/files/omb/assets/omb/inforeg/implementation_guidelines.pdf, courts have routinely expressed disfavor toward litigants who attempt to invoke the subsection (g)(1)(A) amendment remedy as a basis for collateral attacks on judicial or quasi-judicial determinations recorded in agency records. See, e.g., Sydnor v. OPM, 336 F. App'x 175, 180 (3d Cir. 2009) (concluding that "a collateral attack upon that which has been or could have been the subject of a judicial, quasi-judicial or administrative proceeding" lies "outside the scope of the Privacy Act"); Jones v. MSPB, 216 F. App'x 608, 609 (8th Cir. 2007) (affirming dismissal of amendment claim because "the statements accurately reflect administrative decisions"); Cooper v. U.S. Dep't of Treasury, No. 05-0314, 2006 WL 637817, at *2-3 (11th Cir. Mar. 15, 2006) (law-of-the-case doctrine bars relitigation of claim under Privacy Act that had been decided against plaintiff in district court and affirmed by court of appeals); Reinbold v. Evers, 187 F.3d 348, 361 (4th Cir. 1999) ("[T]he Privacy Act does not allow a court to alter records that accurately reflect an administrative decision, or the opinions behind that administrative decision."); Milhous v. EEOC, No. 97-5242, 1998 WL 152784, at *1 (6th Cir. Mar. 24, 1998) ("The Privacy Act may not be used to challenge unfavorable agency decisions. It is intended solely to be used to correct factual or historical errors."); Douglas v. Agric. Stabilization & Conservation Serv., 33 F.3d 784, 785 (7th Cir. 1994) ("Privacy Act does not authorize relitigation of the substance of agency decisions"; "the right response . . . is to correct the disposition under the Administrative Procedure Act"); Bailey v. VA, No. 94-55092, 1994 WL 417423, at *1 (9th Cir. Aug. 10, 1994) (plaintiff may not use Privacy Act to collaterally attack grant or denial of benefits); Sugrue v. Derwinski, 26 F.3d 8, 11 (2d Cir. 1994) (Privacy Act may not be used "as a rhetorical cover to attack VA benefits determinations"); Edwards v. Rozzi, No. 92-3008, 1992 WL 133035, at *1 (6th Cir. June 12, 1992) ("[T]he Privacy Act may not be used to challenge unfavorable agency decisions."); Geurin v. Dep't of the Army, No. 90-16783, 1992 WL 2781, at *2 (9th Cir. Jan. 6, 1992) (doctrine of res judicata bars relitigation of claims under Privacy Act that had been decided against plaintiff by United States Claims Court in prior action under 28 U.S.C. § 1491); Pellerin v. VA, 790 F.2d 1553, 1555 (11th Cir. 1986) (amendment lawsuit challenging VA disability benefits determination dismissed on ground that 38 U.S.C. § 211(a) (later repealed, now see 38 U.S.C. § 511 (2006)) limits judicial review of VA's determinations; noting that Privacy Act "'may not be employed as a skeleton key for reopening consideration of unfavorable federal agency decisions'" (quoting Rogers v. U.S. Dep't of Labor, 607 F. Supp. 697, 699 (N.D. Cal. 1985))); New-Howard v. Shinseki, No. 09-5350, 2012 WL 2362546, at *7 (E.D. Pa. June 21, 2012) ("Plaintiff's placement in the position of Office Automation Clerk and her placement in the FERS system may have been substantively incorrect, to the extent that such placement occurred, the records in her file accurately reflect what occurred in August 2005. As a result, the proper procedure for Plaintiff to employ in order to correct the error is to pursue the matter before the MSPB."); Hardy v. McHugh, 692 F. Supp. 2d 76, 80-81 (D.D.C. 2010) (rejecting claim seeking correction of Army memorandum of reprimand including "implication that [plaintiff] intentionally misrepresented his educational credentials" because "the Army's judgment is based on accurate facts" and because plaintiff "presents the same facts that have been considered by various Army boards [including Army Board for Correction of Military Records] and asks [the court] to substitute [its] judgment for theirs"); Jackson v. U.S. Dep't of Labor, No. 2:06-CV-02157, 2008 WL 539925, at *4 (E.D. Cal. Feb. 25, 2008) (ruling that plaintiff may not bring amendment lawsuit under Privacy Act to re-litigate determination of Federal Employees' Compensation Act benefits); Davenport v. Harvey, No. 06-CV-02669, slip op. at 8 (S.D. Cal. May 3, 2007) (rejecting claim "seek[ing] to alter factual findings and conclusion made by the [DOD Office of Hearings and Appeals] [administrative judge] as part of Plaintiff's appeal of the denial

OVERVIEW OF THE PRIVACY ACT

of his security clearance"), aff'd in pertinent part, vacated in part, & remanded sub nom. Davenport v. McHugh, 372 F. App'x 820 (9th Cir. 2010); Lee v. Geren, 480 F. Supp. 2d 198, 209 (D.D.C. Mar. 29, 2007) (finding that plaintiff "is not seeking to correct any true errors in his records" but instead "is hoping that this Court will expunge all references in his records to an adverse personnel action that he could not challenge directly because the CSRA precludes such review"); Lechliter v. Dep't of Army, No. 04-814, 2006 WL 462750, at *2-3 (D. Del. Feb. 27, 2006) ("To the extent that [plaintiff] is asking [the court] to alter the ultimate determination by the Department that he is not disabled, rather than to correct factual errors recited in his records, such relief is outside that provided by the Privacy Act."); Levant v. Roche, 384 F. Supp. 2d 262, 270 (D.D.C. 2005) (concluding that plaintiff's "true complaint is not about the accuracy of his records, but about the underlying decision [not to promote him to the rank of major general, which those records] reflect"); Byrnes v. MSPB, No. 04-742, 2005 WL 486156, at *2-3 (D.D.C. Mar. 2, 2005) (ruling that plaintiff could not collaterally attack "an inartfully drafted settlement agreement" terminating a lawsuit by seeking to amend agreement to include a provision requiring MSPB to "depublish" its prior decision); Bernard v. DOD, 362 F. Supp. 2d 272, 280-81 (D.D.C. 2005) (dismissing plaintiff's amendment claim because plaintiff did not "seek to correct a factual or historical error" but rather challenged agency's substantive judgments or decisions); Fields v. NRC, No. 98-1714, slip op. at 1-2, 5-7 (D.D.C. May 12, 1999) (stating that Privacy Act may not be used to collaterally attack NRC conclusion, as Act is not vehicle for amending judgments of federal officials); Gowan v. Dep't of the Air Force, No. 90-94, slip op. at 26, 33 (D.N.M. Sept. 1, 1995) (commenting that "Privacy Act, unfortunately, may not be used as a collateral attack on the improper preferral of charges [for court martial], nor may the Privacy Act be used as a method for the Court to oversee the activities of the armed services"), aff'd, 148 F.3d 1182 (10th Cir. 1998); Williams v. McCausland, 90 Civ. 7563, 1994 WL 18510, at *17 (S.D.N.Y. Jan. 18, 1994) (MSPB properly denied plaintiff's request to supplement record of his administrative proceeding before MSPB because request "constitutes an attempt to contest the MSPB's determination on the merits of his request for a stay of his removal"); Smith v. VA, No. CV-93-B-2158-S, slip op. at 4-5 (N.D. Ala. Jan. 13, 1994) (following Pellerin and holding that plaintiff could not use Privacy Act to challenge dishonorable discharge or denial of VA disability benefits); Smith v. Cont'l Assurance Co., No. 91 C 0963, 1991 WL 164348, at *5 (N.D. Ill. Aug. 22, 1991) (plaintiff cannot use Privacy Act to collaterally attack agency decision regarding her Federal Employees Health Benefit Act claim); Rowan v. USPS, No. 82-C-6550, 1984 U.S. Dist. LEXIS 17042, at *6 (N.D. Ill. May 2, 1984) (Privacy Act not "a means for all governmental employees to have unflattering appraisals removed from their personnel files or shaded according to their own whims

OVERVIEW OF THE PRIVACY ACT

or preferences"); Leib v. VA, 546 F. Supp. 758, 762 (D.D.C. 1982) ("The Privacy Act was not intended to be and should not be allowed to become a 'backdoor mechanism' to subvert the finality of agency determinations."); Lyon v. United States, 94 F.R.D. 69, 72 (W.D. Okla. 1982) (Privacy Act claim cannot be "a backdoor mechanism to subvert authority bestowed upon the Secretary of Labor to handle employee compensation claims"; the FECA "provides the exclusive method of presenting compensation claims resulting from on-the-job injuries of federal employees"); Allen v. Henefin, 2 Gov't Disclosure Serv. (P-H) ¶ 81,056, at 81,147 (D.D.C. Dec. 10, 1980) (dismissing lawsuit seeking amendment of supervisor evaluation forms and comments, for failure to exhaust, but noting that "there is considerable doubt as to the permissibility of a Privacy Act suit to collaterally attack a final agency personnel determination of this type"); Weber v. Dep't of the Air Force, No. C-3-78-146, slip op. at 3-4 (S.D. Ohio Mar. 19, 1979) (Privacy Act not proper means "to arbitrate and determine a dispute over job classification"); Bashaw v. U.S. Dep't of the Treasury, 468 F. Supp. 1195, 1196-97 (E.D. Wis. 1979) (citing OMB Guidelines with approval and holding that amendment remedy is "neither a necessary nor an appropriate vehicle for resolving the merits of the plaintiff's [discrimination] claims"); Kennedy v. Andrus, 459 F. Supp. 240, 242 (D.D.C. 1978) (noting that OMB Guidelines "clearly forbid collateral attack in the case of final judicial or quasi-judicial actions" and observing that "the same considerations would seem to apply to agency personnel actions, such as the reprimand here, for collateral attack under the Privacy Act could undermine the effectiveness of agency grievance systems"), aff'd, 612 F.2d 586 (D.C. Cir. 1980) (unpublished table decision); cf. Subh v. Dep't of Army, No. 1:10cv433, 2010 WL 4961613, at *4 (E.D. Va. Nov. 30, 2010) (rejecting plaintiff's attempt "to rewrite history to pretend that he correctly answered 'yes' to question 22 [on Standard Form 86, the 'Questionnaire for National Security Positions,'] when in fact he falsely answered 'no'" because "[t]he Privacy Act plainly does not exist to allow applicants to obtain such a 'do-over' of their security forms in the guise of an administrative 'correction'"); Doe v. HHS, 871 F. Supp. 808, 814-15 (E.D. Pa. 1994) ("[T]he specific reporting provisions encompassed in the [Health Care Quality Improvement] Act supersede[] any claims [plaintiff] might have under the Privacy Act."), aff'd, 66 F.3d 310 (3d Cir. 1995) (unpublished table decision).

Federal prisoners frequently attempt to invoke the subsection (g)(1)(A) amendment remedy as a basis for a collateral attack on a conviction or the duration of a sentence. Just as in the damages context (see "Damages Lawsuits under (g)(1)(C)," below), courts have frequently ruled that unless the conviction or sentence has been invalidated in a prior proceeding, the prisoner's exclusive remedy is a writ of habeas corpus. See, e.g., King v. Johns, No. 4:10cv1835, 2010 WL 4065405, at *1 (N.D. Ohio Oct. 14, 2010)

OVERVIEW OF THE PRIVACY ACT

("[A] complaint seeking relief under . . . § 552a is not a permissible alternative to a petition for a writ of habeas corpus if the plaintiff essentially challenges the legality of his confinement."); Truesdale v. DOJ, 731 F. Supp. 2d 3, 11 (D.D.C. 2010) (dismissing Privacy Act claims because a ruling in plaintiff's favor would impact the duration of his confinement, and should be brought in a petition for a writ of habeas corpus "not by way of a suit brought under the Privacy Act"); Davis v. United States, No. 09-1961, 2010 WL 2011549, at *1 n.1 (D. Md. May 18, 2010) ("[T]o the extent Petitioner believes that his sentence should be modified, such claims may only be made in the context of a habeas petition."); Brown v. BOP, 498 F. Supp. 2d 298, 303-04 (D.D.C. 2007) ("The Privacy Act is not the proper means by which a prisoner may collaterally attack his sentence absent a showing that his sentence has been invalidated in a prior proceeding."); Forrester v. U.S. Parole Comm'n, 310 F. Supp. 2d 162, 168-70 (D.D.C. 2004) (concluding that reaching plaintiff's Privacy Act claim seeking an order to expunge information "would have a probabilistic impact on his confinement . . . and therefore plaintiff may only raise [such a claim] in a petition for a writ of habeas corpus"); Graham v. Hawk, 857 F. Supp. 38, 40-41 (W.D. Tenn. 1994) ("The Privacy Act is not a means of circumventing [habeas] exhaustion requirement."), aff'd, 59 F.3d 170 (6th Cir. 1995) (unpublished table decision).

In addition, the Court of Appeals for the Fifth Circuit has held that a plaintiff had no right to amend the record at issue even though that record was only "exempt from the <u>access</u> requirements of the Act." Smith v. United States, 142 F. App'x 209, 210 (5th Cir. 2005) (per curiam) (emphasis added). In other words, the court explained, "the scope of accessibility and the scope of amendment under the Privacy Act are the same." Id. (agreeing with Baker v. Dep't of the Navy, 814 F.2d 1381, 1384-85 (9th Cir. 1987), which involved a record that the plaintiff had obtained through a FOIA request but that was not contained in a system of records as required by subsection (d)(1), and with Wentz v. DOJ, 772 F.2d 335, 338 (7th Cir. 1985) (alternative holding), which involved a record that had been exempted from subsection (d)(1) pursuant to subsection (j)(2)). In Smith, the plaintiff sought to amend a report that was "prepared in response to [his Federal Tort Claims Act] claim." 142 F. App'x at 210. Interestingly, the court explained that because this report "was prepared in reasonable anticipation of a civil suit or proceeding" within the meaning of subsection (d)(5), "[t]he report is . . . also exempt from the amendment requirements of the Act." Id. Thus, the court concluded, the amendment claim was "barred by exemption." Id. Subsection (d)(5) is discussed below under "Ten Exemptions."

It has even been held that the Civil Service Reform Act's (CSRA) comprehensive remedial scheme operates to deprive a court of subsection

OVERVIEW OF THE PRIVACY ACT

(g)(1)(A) jurisdiction to order the amendment of an allegedly inaccurate job description in a former federal employee's personnel file. See Kleiman v. Dep't of Energy, 956 F.2d 335, 338 (D.C. Cir. 1992) (refusing to allow exhaustive remedial scheme of CSRA to be "impermissibly frustrated" by granting review of personnel decisions under Privacy Act); see also Wills v. OPM, No. 93-2079, slip op. at 3-4 (4th Cir. Jan. 28, 1994) (alternative holding) (per curiam) (where challenge to merits of statement on SF-50 was actually complaint regarding adverse employment decision, jurisdiction was proper under CSRA); Vessella v. Dep't of the Air Force, No. 92-2195, 1993 WL 230172, at *2 (1st Cir. June 28, 1993) (citing Kleiman and holding that plaintiff could not "bypass the CSRA's regulatory scheme" by bringing a Privacy Act claim for the same alleged impermissible adverse personnel practices that he challenged before the MSPB, even though the MSPB dismissed his claims as untimely); Lee v. Geren, 480 F. Supp. 2d 198, 206, 208 (D.D.C. 2007) (following "the course set by [Kleiman]" by "evaluat[ing] the merits of plaintiff's claims . . . in a way that does not do violence to the CSRA" but ultimately finding that "[t]here is simply nothing inaccurate about" plaintiff's records).

Similarly, the D.C. Circuit has held that "[t]he proper means by which to seek a change to military records is through a proceeding before the . . . Board for Correction of Military Records," not under the Privacy Act. Glick v. Dep't of the Army, No. 91-5213, 1992 WL 168004, at *1 (D.C. Cir. June 5, 1992) (per curiam); see also Cargill v. Marsh, 902 F.2d 1006, 1007-08 (D.C. Cir. 1990) (per curiam) (affirming dismissal of Privacy Act claim; proper means to seek substantive change in military records is through proceeding before the Boards for Correction of Records for the various services under 10 U.S.C. § 1552(a) (2006) (amended 2003 to take into account establishment of DHS)); Doe v. Dep't of the Navy, 764 F. Supp. 1324, 1327 (N.D. Ind. 1991) ("plaintiff is not free to choose to attempt amendment of his military records under the Privacy Act alone without resort to the records correction board remedy"); cf. Hardy v. McHugh, 692 F. Supp. 2d 76, 80-81 (D.D.C. 2010) (rejecting claim seeking correction of Army memorandum of reprimand including "implication that [plaintiff] intentionally misrepresented his educational credentials" because "the Army's judgment is based on accurate facts" and because plaintiff "presents the same facts that have been considered by various Army boards [including Army Board for Correction of Military Records] and asks [the court] to substitute [its] judgment for theirs"); Walker v. United States, No. 93-2728, 1998 WL 637360, at *14 (E.D. La. Sept. 16, 1998) (citing Cargill and finding plaintiff's claim "unavailing" to extent that he "is attempting to use the Privacy Act as a vehicle for his collateral attack on the Army's allegedly improper failure to correct his military records"), aff'd, 184 F.3d 816 (5th Cir. 1999) (unpublished table decision). But see Diederich v. Dep't of the

OVERVIEW OF THE PRIVACY ACT

Army, 878 F.2d 646, 647-48 (2d Cir. 1989) (holding that "Privacy Act claims were properly before the district court" and that plaintiff was not required to further exhaust administrative remedies before asserting claim for amendment of military records where his direct request to Army for correction had been stalled before appeals board for several months); see also Corrections of Military Records Under the Privacy Act, Defense Privacy Board Advisory Opinion 4, available at http://dpclo.defense.gov/privacy/About_The_Office/opinions/04.html (affording review under Privacy Act for factual matters only but noting that challenges to judgmental decisions may be made to the Boards for Correction of Military or Naval Records).

It should be noted that several courts have ruled that statutes that provide other avenues of redress, such as the CSRA, can bar certain kinds of subsection (g)(1)(C) damages actions. These cases are discussed below under "Damages Lawsuits under (g)(1)(C)."

— Courts can order an agency to amend records in accordance with a request "or in such other way as the court may direct." 5 U.S.C. § 552a(g)(2)(A).

Comment:

The Act contemplates "expungement [of inaccuracies] and not merely redress by supplement." R.R. v. Dep't of the Army, 482 F. Supp. 770, 774 (D.D.C. 1980); see also Smith v. Nixon, 807 F.2d 197, 204 (D.C. Cir. 1986); Hobson v. Wilson, 737 F.2d 1, 65-66 (D.C. Cir. 1984). In addition, several courts have concluded that judges have the equitable power, even apart from the Privacy Act, to order the expungement of records when the affected individual's privacy interest greatly outweighs the government's interest in maintaining the records. See, e.g., Doe v. U.S. Air Force, 812 F.2d 738, 740-41 (D.C. Cir. 1987); Fendler v. U.S. Parole Comm'n, 774 F.2d 975, 979 (9th Cir. 1985); Chastain v. Kelley, 510 F.2d 1232, 1235-38 (D.C. Cir. 1975); Ezenwa v. Gallen, 906 F. Supp. 978, 986 (M.D. Pa. 1995); NTEU v. IRS, 601 F. Supp. 1268, 1273 (D.D.C. 1985); cf. Johnson v. Sessions, No. 92-201, 1992 WL 212408, at *2 (D.D.C. Aug. 19, 1992) (refusing to invoke equitable powers to expunge plaintiff's arrest record because court did not have jurisdiction to order FBI to violate its own regulations which require FBI to wait for authorization from appropriate judicial authority before expunging arrest record). But see Scruggs v. United States, 929 F.2d 305, 307 (7th Cir. 1991) (questioning jurisdictional power of courts to order expungement of records that satisfy Privacy Act's requirements).

OVERVIEW OF THE PRIVACY ACT

Once an agency offers to destroy a record in response to an expungement request, the lawsuit is at an end and the agency cannot be compelled to affirmatively determine and announce that the challenged record violated the Act. See Reuber v. United States, 829 F.2d 133, 144-49 (D.C. Cir. 1987); see also Comm. in Solidarity v. Sessions, 929 F.2d 742, 745 n.2 (D.C. Cir. 1991); Metadure Corp. v. United States, 490 F. Supp. 1368, 1375 (S.D.N.Y. 1980). But see Doe v. U.S. Civil Serv. Comm'n, 483 F. Supp. 539, 551 (S.D.N.Y. 1980).

B.   Access Lawsuits under (g)(1)(B)

"Whenever any agency . . . refuses to comply with an individual request under subsection (d)(1) of this section [the individual may bring a civil action against the agency]." 5 U.S.C. § 552a(g)(1)(B).

– Courts can enjoin the agency from withholding records and order their production to the individual. See 5 U.S.C. § 552a(g)(3)(A).

Comment:

Just as under the FOIA, a requester must comply with agency procedures and exhaust all available administrative remedies – through pursuit of an access request to the agency and, if that request is denied, through an administrative appeal – prior to bringing a subsection (g)(1)(B) action.

Because "[t]he language in [subsections (d)(1) and (g)] does not expressly require exhaustion of particular administrative remedies," Taylor v. U.S. Treasury Dep't, 127 F.3d 470, 476 (5th Cir. 1997), "[t]here is no statutory requirement of exhaustion related to a request for access to records. To the extent exhaustion of administrative remedies is required, it is not a jurisdictional prerequisite," Wadhwa v. VA, 342 F. App'x 860, 862-63 (3d Cir. 2009) (per curiam) (citing Taylor, 127 F.3d at 475-76) (emphases added). Rather, courts have required plaintiffs seeking access to records to exhaust administrative remedies pursuant to the "jurisprudential exhaustion doctrine." See, e.g., id. Thus, in Taylor the Court of Appeals for the Fifth Circuit concluded: "[Plaintiff's] failure to exhaust administrative remedies did not constitute a jurisdictional bar to assertion of his claim [for access to records.] . . . However, our inquiry does not end here because . . . application of the jurisprudential exhaustion doctrine in this case indicates that . . . [plaintiff's] claims under the Privacy Act must be dismissed for failure to state a claim upon which relief can be granted." Id. at 476-77. Likewise, in Wadhwa the Court of Appeals for the Third Circuit "disagree[d] with the District Court's conclusion that it lacks jurisdiction to entertain [plaintiff's] claim [for access to records] under the Privacy Act because [plaintiff] failed to exhaust his administrative remedies." 342 F. App'x at 862; see also Buckley v. Schaul, 135 F. App'x 960, 960 (9th Cir. 2005) (holding that "even in the absence of an explicit exhaustion requirement, a district court may in its discretion require such exhaustion"). As noted above, access lawsuits differ in this respect from amendment lawsuits. See also, e.g., Kvech v. Holder, No. 10-cv-545, 2011 WL 4369452, at *8 (D.D.C. Sept. 19, 2011) ("While the Privacy Act requires that plaintiffs first resort to administrative remedies for denials of requests to amend records, . . . the statute does not contain a similar requirement with respect to an access claim."). Because subsection (d)(2) regarding amendment by its terms requires exhaustion, 5 U.S.C. § 552a(d)(2); see also Quinn v. Stone, 978 F.2d 126, 137-38 (3d Cir. 1992) ("These provisions entail a requirement that the plaintiff exhaust her administrative remedies before she can take advantage of [subsection (g)(1)(A)]." (citing Dickson v. OPM, 828 F.2d 32, 40-41 (D.C. Cir. 1987))), that requirement is jurisdictional in nature, id. See also Taylor, 127 F.3d at 475 ("Whenever the Congress statutorily mandates that a claimant exhaust administrative remedies, the exhaustion requirement is jurisdictional because it is tantamount to a legislative investiture of exclusive original jurisdiction in the agency. However, in the absence of a statutory requirement of exhaustion . . . the jurisprudential doctrine of exhaustion controls. The jurisprudential exhaustion doctrine is not jurisdictional in nature." (citations omitted)).

For cases in which the court ruled that the plaintiff failed to exhaust administrative remedies by not making an access request in conformity with agency regulations, see Vaughn v. Danzig, 18 F. App'x 122, 125 (4th Cir. 2001) (per curiam); Taylor, 127 F.3d at 473-78; Godaire v. Napolitano, No. 3:10cv01266, 2010 WL 6634572, at *7 (D. Conn. Nov. 17, 2010); Ioane v. Comm'r of IRS, No. 3:09-CV-00243, 2010 WL 2600689, at *4 (D. Nev. Mar. 11, 2010); Sterrett v. Dep't of the Navy, No. 09-CV-2083, 2010 WL 330086, at *3-4 (S.D. Cal. Jan. 20, 2010); Gadd v. United States, No. 4:08CV04229, 2010 WL 60953, at *12 (E.D. Ark. Jan. 5, 2010), aff'd, 392 F. App'x 503 (8th Cir. 2010); Ramstack v. Dep't of the Army, 607 F. Supp. 2d 94, 102-03 (D.D.C. 2009); Willis v. DOJ, 581 F. Supp. 2d 57, 69-70 (D.D.C. 2008); Mulhern v. Gates, 525 F. Supp. 2d 174, 187 (D.D.C. 2007); Brown v. DOJ, No. 02-2662, slip op. at 20-24 (N.D. Ala. June 21, 2005); MacLeod v. IRS, No. 99-1088, 2001 U.S. Dist. LEXIS 9327, at *3-4 (S.D. Cal. June 4, 2001); Broaddrick v. Executive Office of the President, 139 F. Supp. 2d 55, 61 (D.D.C. 2001), aff'd per curiam, No. 01-5178 (D.C. Cir. May 1, 2002); Scaife v. IRS, No. 02-1805, 2003 U.S. Dist. LEXIS 22661, at *8 (D.D.C. Nov. 20, 2003); Flowers v. Executive Office of the President, 142 F. Supp. 2d 38, 44 (D.D.C. 2001); Walker v. Henderson, No. 98 C 3824, 1999 WL 39545, at *9 (N.D. Ill. Jan. 20, 1999), appeal voluntarily dismissed, No. 99-1615 (7th Cir. May 27, 1999); Reeves v. United States,

OVERVIEW OF THE PRIVACY ACT

No. 94-1291, 1994 WL 782235, at *2 (E.D. Cal. Nov. 16, 1994), aff'd, 108 F.3d 338 (9th Cir. 1997) (unpublished table decision); Guzman v. United States, No. S-93-1949, slip op. at 3-5 (E.D. Cal. Oct. 5, 1994); Hass v. U.S. Air Force, 848 F. Supp. 926, 930 (D. Kan. 1994); Gergick v. Austin, No. 89-0838-CV-W-2, 1992 U.S. Dist. LEXIS 7338, at *13-16 (W.D. Mo. Apr. 29, 1992), aff'd, No. 92-3210 (8th Cir. July 9, 1993); Wood v. IRS, No. 1:90-CV-2614, 1991 U.S. Dist. LEXIS 19707, at *8 (N.D. Ga. July 26, 1991); Searcy v. SSA, No. 91-C-26 J, slip op. at 8-11 (D. Utah June 25, 1991) (magistrate's recommendation), adopted (D. Utah Sept. 19, 1991), aff'd, No. 91-4181 (10th Cir. Mar. 2, 1992); Crooker v. U.S. Marshals Serv., 577 F. Supp. 1217, 1217-18 (D.D.C. 1983); Lilienthal v. Parks, 574 F. Supp. 14, 18 & n.7 (E.D. Ark. 1983); Gibbs v. Rauch, No. 77-59, slip op. at 2-3 (E.D. Ky. Feb. 9, 1978); Larsen v. Hoffman, 444 F. Supp. 245, 256 (D.D.C. 1977); cf. Banks v. DOJ, 605 F. Supp. 2d 131, 139 (D.D.C. 2009) (concluding that plaintiff failed to exhaust administrative remedies with respect to instant request because he did not pay record duplication fees for earlier request); Nurse v. Sec'y of the Air Force, 231 F. Supp. 2d 323, 331 (D.D.C. 2002) ("[W]hile the FOIA requires that a request must '[reasonably] describe' the records, Privacy Act requests require greater specificity.").

For cases in which the court ruled that the plaintiff failed to exhaust administrative remedies by not filing an administrative appeal after receiving a denial of the access request, see Yee v. Solis, No. C-08-4259, 2010 WL 1655816, at *14 (N.D. Cal. Apr. 22, 2010), aff'd on other grounds, No. 10-16376, 2012 WL 902895 (9th Cir. Mar. 19, 2012); Gadd, 2010 WL 60953, at *12; Bettweiser v. Lucas, No. 06-CIV-0142, 2007 WL 2601089, at *2 (D. Idaho Sept. 10, 2007); Clemmons v. DOJ, No. 06-00305, 2007 WL 1020796, at *5 (D.D.C. Mar. 30, 2007); Sussman v. DOJ, No. 03-3618, 2006 WL 2850608, at *5 (E.D.N.Y. Sept. 30, 2006); Glenn v. Rumsfeld, No. C 05-01787, 2006 WL 515626, at *6-7 (N.D. Cal. Feb. 28, 2006); Biondo v. Dep't of the Navy, 928 F. Supp. 626, 630-33 (D.S.C. 1995), aff'd, 86 F.3d 1148 (4th Cir. 1996) (unpublished table decision); Hass v. U.S. Air Force, 848 F. Supp. 926, 930 (D. Kan. 1994); cf. Ramstack, 607 F. Supp. 2d at 104 (defendant bears burden of proving affirmative defense of failure to exhaust administrative remedies). But see Fischer v. FBI, No. 07-2037, 2008 WL 2248711, at *2 (D.D.C. May 29, 2008) (excusing failure to file an administrative appeal where agency had previously remanded request on administrative appeal and requester apparently did not understand that he had to file a second appeal after agency reprocessed the request); Mumme v. U.S. Dep't of Labor, 150 F. Supp. 2d 162, 171 (D. Me. 2001) (refusing to "strictly apply formalistic procedural rules against [p]laintiff" because "[p]rocedural rules . . . cut both ways," and it was not clear that agency's response letter "included any written explanation of the partial grant of

OVERVIEW OF THE PRIVACY ACT

[p]laintiff's appeal as required by [its] regulation"), aff'd, No. 01-2256 (1st Cir. June 12, 2002).

The Court of Appeals for the Fourth Circuit has also noted that an individual cannot "constructively exhaust" his administrative remedies under the Privacy Act, as "the Privacy Act contains no equivalent to FOIA's 'constructive exhaustion' provision [5 U.S.C. § 552(a)(6)(C)]." Pollack v. DOJ, 49 F.3d 115, 116 n.1 (4th Cir. 1995) (only FOIA claim was properly before district court); see also Gadd, 2010 WL 60953, at *12 (citing Pollack and dismissing access claim for failure to exhaust administrative remedies); Sussman v. DOJ, No. 03-3618, 2006 WL 2850608, at *5 (E.D.N.Y. Sept. 30, 2006) ("The Privacy Act . . . does not allow for 'constructive exhaustion,' and prohibits a requester from filing an action without having obtained a response from the agency."); Anderson v. USPS, 7 F. Supp. 2d 583, 586 n.3 (E.D. Pa. 1998) (citing Pollack for proposition that "Privacy Act contains no section equivalent to the 'constructive exhaustion' provision of the FOIA," but alternatively finding that access suit must be dismissed for failure to exhaust administrative remedies), aff'd, 187 F.3d 625 (3d Cir. 1999) (unpublished table decision); cf. Johnson v. FBI, No. 94-1741, slip op. at 6 (D.D.C. Aug. 31, 1995) (citing Pollack but determining that "since plaintiff has sought an action in equity, and has not exhausted his administrative remedies through administrative appeal . . . plaintiff is barred from seeking injunctive relief under the Privacy Act"). However, an agency's failure to comply with its own regulations can undercut an exhaustion defense. See Jonsson v. IRS, No. 90-2519, 1992 WL 115607, at *1 (D.D.C. May 4, 1992); Haldane v. Comm'r, No. 90-654M, 1990 U.S. Dist. LEXIS 11612, at *4-6 (W.D. Wash. Aug. 23, 1990).

Several courts have recognized that jurisdiction to consider a Privacy Act access claim exists only if the government has failed to comply with a request for records; once a request is complied with and the responsive records have been disclosed, a Privacy Act access claim is moot. See Campbell v. SSA, 446 F. App'x 477, 480 (3d Cir. 2011); Yonemoto v. VA, 305 F. App'x 333, 334 (9th Cir. 2008); Crummey v. SSA, 794 F. Supp. 2d 46, 61 (D.D.C. June 30, 2011), aff'd per curiam, No. 11-5231, 2012 WL 556317 (D.C. Cir. Feb. 6, 2012); Sterrett, 2010 WL 330086, at *2-3; Jordan v. DOJ, No. 07-cv-02303, 2009 WL 2913223, at *26 (D. Colo. Sept. 8, 2009); Van Allen v. HUD, No. G-07-315, 2009 WL 1636303, at *1 (S.D. Tex. June 9, 2009); Falwell v. Executive Office of the President, 158 F. Supp. 2d 734, 740 (W.D. Va. 2001); Mumme, 150 F. Supp. 2d at 171-72; Fisher v. FBI, 94 F. Supp. 2d at 216; Biondo, 928 F. Supp. at 631; Letscher v. IRS, No. 95-0077, 1995 WL 555476, at *1 (D.D.C. July 6, 1995); Polewsky v. SSA, No. 5:93-CV-200, slip op. at 9-10 (D. Vt. Mar. 31, 1995) (magistrate's recommendation), adopted (D. Vt. Apr. 13, 1995), aff'd, No.

OVERVIEW OF THE PRIVACY ACT

95-6125, 1996 WL 110179, at *2 (2d Cir. Mar. 12, 1996); Smith v. Cont'l Assurance Co., No. 91 C 0963, 1991 WL 164348, at *3 (N.D. Ill. Aug. 22, 1991); see also Jacobs v. Reno, No. 3:97-CV-2698-D, 1999 U.S. Dist. LEXIS 3104, at *14-15 (N.D. Tex. Mar. 11, 1999) (dismissing access claim as moot where plaintiff had received access to records and finding no eligibility for award of attorney fees and costs based on plaintiff's assertion that his lawsuit may have caused agency to comply with Privacy Act when it would not otherwise have done so, "particularly when § 552a(d)(1) imposes no deadline for agency compliance and absent evidence of extended and unjustified delay"), aff'd, 208 F.3d 1006 (5th Cir. 2000) (unpublished table decision); cf. Riser v. U.S. Dep't of State, No. 09-3273, 2010 WL 4284925, at *7 (S.D. Tex. Oct. 22, 2010) (dismissing claim "seek[ing] a declaratory judgment that the agencies' earlier withholding of his records . . . was improper" as moot "because the documents have now been produced"); Yee, 2010 WL 1655816, at *14 (Privacy Act claim for access was moot where magistrate judge in prior order had found that agency complied with his order to produce the record at issue to plaintiff); Lundy v. VA, 142 F. Supp. 2d 776, 779 (W.D. La. 2001) (finding that "the VA conducted an adequate search" and, "in the absence of any improperly withheld records, [plaintiff's] claim must be dismissed for lack of subject matter jurisdiction").

The Court of Appeals for the District of Columbia Circuit has ruled that "the specific provisions of [26 U.S.C.] § 6103 rather than the general provisions of the Privacy Act govern the disclosure of . . . tax information" and that "individuals seeking 'return information' . . . must do so pursuant to § 6103 of the Internal Revenue Code, rather than the Privacy Act." Lake v. Rubin, 162 F.3d 113, 115-16 (D.C. Cir. 1998). In reaching this conclusion, the D.C. Circuit looked to the legislative history of § 6103 and embraced an earlier ruling by the Court of Appeals for the Seventh Circuit, Cheek v. IRS, 703 F.2d 271 (7th Cir. 1983) (per curiam), that similarly had held that § 6103 "displaces" the Privacy Act and shields tax return information from release to a first-party requester, id. at 272; see also Lake, 162 F.3d at 115-16; Kendrick v. Wayne County, No. 10-13752, 2011 WL 2580675, at *1-2 (E.D. Mich. June 29, 2011); Paige v. IRS, No. 1P-85-64-C, slip op. at 3-4 (S.D. Ind. Jan. 13, 1986); cf. Maxwell v. O'Neill, No. 00-01953, 2002 WL 31367754, at *4 (D.D.C. Sept. 12, 2002) ("while [section] 6103 may supersede the Privacy Act, it does not supersede the FOIA"), aff'd, No. 04-5082 (D.C. Cir. May 27, 2005). But cf. Sinicki v. U.S. Dep't of Treasury, No. 97 CIV. 0901, 1998 WL 80188, at *3-5 (S.D.N.Y. Feb. 24, 1998) (finding Cheek unpersuasive in context of wrongful disclosure claim and denying motion to dismiss Privacy Act claim, stating that "the language, structure, purpose and legislative history of Section 6103 do not make manifest and clear a legislative intent to repeal the Privacy Act as it applies to tax return information").

OVERVIEW OF THE PRIVACY ACT

The Court of Appeals for the Ninth Circuit has confusingly interpreted 26 U.S.C. § 7852(e) (2006) to likewise prevent Privacy Act access to records pertaining to tax liability. Jacques v. IRS, No. 91-15992, 1992 WL 185449, at *2 (9th Cir. Aug. 5, 1992); O'Connor v. United States, No. 89-15321, slip op. at 5 (9th Cir. June 4, 1991); see also Prince v. Comm'r, No. 98-17183, 1999 WL 511185, at *1 (9th Cir. July 15, 1999) (concluding that district court lacked subject matter jurisdiction over claim for attorney fees in Privacy Act suit for access to tax return records due to 26 U.S.C. § 7852(e)'s prohibition against application of subsection (g) of Privacy Act to determinations of tax liability); Hart v. United States, No. 00-2158, 2000 WL 1727737, at *1-2 (E.D. Pa. Sept. 27, 2000) (following Maxwell v. Rubin, infra, and dismissing access claim for lack of subject matter jurisdiction for records relating "directly and indirectly[] to tax disputes with the IRS concerning liability," because although § 7852(e) does not exempt the IRS from the access provision, it does exempt it from the civil remedy provision), aff'd, 275 F.3d 35 (3d Cir. 2001) (unpublished table decision); Weiss v. Sawyer, 28 F. Supp. 2d 1221, 1227-28 (W.D. Okla. 1997) (applying 26 U.S.C. § 7852 to prevent apparent access claim); cf. Baker v. Matson, No. 98 M 1675, 1998 U.S. Dist. LEXIS 21312, at *8-9 (D. Colo. Dec. 7, 1998) (ruling that court had no jurisdiction over Privacy Act access claim) (magistrate's recommendation), adopted (D. Colo. Jan. 12, 1999). The Ninth Circuit's interpretation of 26 U.S.C. § 7852(e), however, seems to go beyond that statute's objective of exempting determinations of tax liability from the Privacy Act's amendment provisions. Cf. Lake v. Rubin, 162 F.3d at 114-16 (discussing § 7852(e) – which had been interpreted by district court to deprive it of jurisdiction in access cases, see Maxwell v. Rubin, 3 F. Supp. 2d 45, 47-49 (D.D.C. 1998) – but affirming judgments of district court "not on the jurisdictional rationale contained in its opinions" but on basis of § 6103); Wood v. IRS, No. 1:90-CV-2614, 1991 U.S. Dist. LEXIS 19707, at *1, 8 (N.D. Ga. July 29, 1991) (denying plaintiff summary judgment on other grounds, but not barring Privacy Act request for access to records concerning plaintiff's tax liability).

Lastly, damages are not recoverable in an access case. See Benoist v. United States, No. 87-1028, slip op. at 3 (8th Cir. Nov. 4, 1987); Thurston v. United States, 810 F.2d 438, 447 (4th Cir. 1987); Kvech, 2011 WL 4369452, at *8 n.13; Brown v. DOJ, No. 02-2662, slip op. at 27 (D. Ala. June 21, 2005); Haddon v. Freeh, 31 F. Supp. 2d 16, 22 (D.D.C. 1998); Vennes v. IRS, No. 5-88-36, slip op. at 6-7 (D. Minn. Oct. 14, 1988) (magistrate's recommendation), adopted (D. Minn. Feb. 14, 1989), aff'd, No. 89-5136MN (8th Cir. Oct. 13, 1989); Bentson v. Comm'r, No. 83-048-GLO-WDB, slip op. at 2 (D. Ariz. Sept. 14, 1984); see also Quinn v. HHS, 838 F. Supp. 70, 76 (W.D.N.Y. 1993) (citing Thurston in dictum). But cf. Beattie v. Astrue, No. 01-2493, 2012 WL 628346, at *7 (D.D.C. Feb. 28, 2012) (in context of

OVERVIEW OF THE PRIVACY ACT

access claim ruling that plaintiff "failed to make out a claim under the Privacy Act" because agency's responses did not meet the intentional and willful standard); Robinson v. Watkins, No. 4:11cv89, 2011 WL 6029969, at *5 (E.D. Va. Oct. 13, 2011) ("The relief provided [under the Privacy Act] is that the plaintiff will be given access to the record, and for monetary damages if an agency's persistent refusal to allow access is 'intentional and willful.'"); Riser, 2010 WL 4284925, at *7 ("Plaintiff's factual assertions about his repeated Privacy Act requests and the delay in receiving records are insufficient to raise an inference of willful or intentional withholding of records about him."); Fischer v. DOJ, 723 F. Supp. 2d 104, 115 (D.D.C. 2010) (where plaintiff sought damages pursuant to subsection (g)(1)(D) in connection with his access request, refusing to award damages on ground that agency "neither inappropriately withheld information nor acted in bad faith").

– Courts "shall determine the matter de novo." 5 U.S.C. § 552a(g)(3)(A).

– Courts may review records in camera to determine whether any of the exemptions set forth in subsection (k) apply. See 5 U.S.C. § 552a(g)(3)(A).

C. Damages Lawsuits under (g)(1)(C)

"Whenever any agency . . . fails to maintain any record concerning any individual with such accuracy, relevance, timeliness, and completeness as is necessary to assure fairness in any determination relating to the qualifications, character, rights, or opportunities of, or benefits to the individual that may be made on the basis of such record, and consequently a determination is made which is adverse to the individual [the individual may bring a civil action against the agency]." 5 U.S.C. § 552a(g)(1)(C).

Comment:

The standard of accuracy under this provision is the same as under subsection (e)(5), which requires agencies to maintain records used in making determinations about individuals "with such accuracy, relevance, timeliness, and completeness as is reasonably necessary to assure fairness to the individual in the determination." See, e.g., Bettersworth v. FDIC, 248 F.3d 386, 390 n.3 (5th Cir. 2001) (explaining that the "statutory obligation" imposed by subsection (e)(5) "is made enforceable by substantively identical language in subsection 552a(g)(1)(C)"); Doe v. United States, 821 F.2d 694, 698 n.10 (D.C. Cir. 1987) (en banc) ("[Subsection (e)(5)] uses the phrase 'reasonably necessary to assure fairness'; [subsection (g)(1)(C)] does not

OVERVIEW OF THE PRIVACY ACT

include the word 'reasonably.' We attribute no substantive significance, for the issue at hand, to the omission of the word 'reasonably' in § 552a(g)(1)(C). The key element of the standard – the necessity 'to assure fairness in any determination' – calls for a balanced judgment, one inherently involving a reasonableness criterion."); Edison v. Dep't of the Army, 672 F.2d 840, 843 (11th Cir. 1982) ("If we accepted [the argument that 'it is not sufficient for the Court to find that the Army took reasonable steps to maintain its personnel files since subsection (g)(1)(C) of the Act does not use the word "reasonable,"'] it would render subsection (e)(5) of the Act meaningless. The Army would be strictly liable for any inaccuracy, no matter how small or how reasonably the agency acted. . . . Subsection (g)(1) must be read in pari materia with subsection (e)(5). If the court determines that the agency has done what is reasonable in assuring the accuracy of the information, no more is required."); Gard v. U.S. Dep't of Educ., 789 F. Supp. 2d 96, 106 (D.D.C. 2011) (explaining that claim alleging violation of subsection (e)(5) "is entirely duplicative" of claim alleging violation of subsection (g)(1)(C) because "[c]laims predicated upon violations of Section 552a(e)(5) . . . must be brought under 552a(g)(1)(C)").

Exhaustion of administrative remedies is not a prerequisite to a civil action for damages under subsection (g)(1)(C). See Phillips v. Widnall, No. 96-2099, 1997 WL 176394, at *2-3 (10th Cir. Apr. 14, 1997); Hubbard v. EPA, 809 F.2d 1, 7 (D.C. Cir. 1986), vacated in nonpertinent part & reh'g en banc granted (due to conflict within circuit), 809 F.2d 1 (D.C. Cir. 1986), resolved on reh'g en banc sub nom. Spagnola v. Mathis, 859 F.2d 223 (D.C. Cir. 1988); Hewitt v. Grabicki, 794 F.2d 1373, 1379 (9th Cir. 1986); Nagel v. HEW, 725 F.2d 1438, 1441 & n.2 (D.C. Cir. 1984); Johnson v. U.S. Air Force, No. CV F 09-0281, 2010 WL 1780231, at *6 (E.D. Cal. Apr. 30, 2010) (citing Hewitt), aff'd on other grounds, No. 10-16450, 2012 WL 32132 (9th Cir. Jan. 6, 2012); Reitz v. USDA, No. 08-4131, 2010 WL 786586, at *11 n.12 (D. Kan. Mar. 4, 2010); Murphy v. United States, 121 F. Supp. 2d 21, 28 (D.D.C. 2000), aff'd per curiam, 64 F. App'x 250 (D.C. Cir. 2003); M.K. v. Tenet, 99 F. Supp. 2d 12, 20 (D.D.C. 2000) (quoting Nagel); Gergick v. Austin, No. 89-0838-CV-W-2, 1992 U.S. Dist. LEXIS 7338, at *13-16 (W.D. Mo. Apr. 29, 1992), aff'd, No. 92-3210 (8th Cir. July 9, 1993). But see Moore v. Potter, No. 3:04-CV-1057, 2006 WL 2092277, at *8 (M.D. Fla. July 26, 2006) (requiring plaintiff to exhaust administrative remedies before bringing an (e)(5) claim under (g)(1)(C)); Olivares v. NASA, 882 F. Supp. 1545, 1546, 1552 (D. Md. 1995) (apparently confusingly concluding that plaintiff's failure to exhaust administrative remedies precludes damages claim under subsection (e)(5)), aff'd, 103 F.3d 119 (4th Cir. 1996) (unpublished table decision); Graham v. Hawk, 857 F. Supp. 38, 40 (W.D. Tenn. 1994) (heedlessly stating that "[e]ach paragraph of 5 U.S.C. § 552a(g) . . . requires as a prerequisite to any action that the agency refuse an individual's request to take some corrective action regarding his file"), aff'd, 59 F.3d 170 (6th Cir. 1995) (unpublished table decision).

Note, though, that 42 U.S.C. § 1997e(a) (2006), a provision of the Prison Litigation Reform Act of 1996 ("PLRA"), imposes an exhaustion requirement on inmates prior to bringing an "action . . . with respect to prison conditions." 42 U.S.C. § 1997e(a). Because the Bureau of Prisons has exempted its Inmate Central Record System from subsection (e)(5) pursuant to subsection (j)(2), 28 C.F.R. § 16.97(j), this provision of the PLRA would seem to have minimal practical effect on subsection (e)(5)/(g)(1)(C) claims brought by inmates against the Bureau of Prisons. But cf. McCulough v. BOP, No. 1:06-cv-00563, 2011 WL 3568800, at *3-4 (E.D. Cal. Aug. 12, 2011) (recommending dismissal of claim that "BOP violated the Privacy Act through its maintenance of inaccurate records and use of those records as the basis for decisions that adversely affected Plaintiff" on ground that plaintiff failed to satisfy exhaustion requirement of PLRA) (magistrate's recommendation), adopted 2011 WL 4373939 (E.D. Cal. Sept. 19, 2011).

For a discussion of the exhaustion requirement imposed by the PLRA on claims for damages brought by prisoners under subsection (g)(1)(D), see the discussion below under "Damages Lawsuits under (g)(1)(D)."

In addition, de novo review is not provided for in (g)(1)(C) actions, see 5 U.S.C. § 552a(g)(4); rather, the court is to determine whether the standards set forth in subsection (g)(1)(C) have been met. See Sellers v. BOP, 959 F.2d 307, 312-13 (D.C. Cir. 1992); White v. OPM, 787 F.2d 660, 663 (D.C. Cir. 1986); Reitz, 2010 WL 786586, at *10; Nolan v. DOJ, No. 89-A-2035, 1991 WL 134803, at *3 (D. Colo. July 17, 1991), appeal dismissed in pertinent part on procedural grounds, 973 F.2d 843 (10th Cir. 1992); see also Doe v. United States, 821 F.2d 694, 712 (D.C. Cir. 1987) (en banc) (Mikva, J., joined by Robinson and Edwards, JJ., dissenting).

However, in order to bring a damages action under subsection (g)(1)(C), an individual has the burden of proving that (1) a defective record (2) proximately caused (3) an adverse determination concerning him. See, e.g., Chambers v. U.S. Dep't of the Interior, 568 F.3d 998, 1007 (D.C. Cir. 2009); Rogers v. BOP, 105 F. App'x 980, 983-84 (10th Cir. 2004); Perry v. BOP, 371 F.3d 1304, 1305 (11th Cir. 2004); Deters v. U.S. Parole Comm'n, 85 F.3d 655, 657 (D.C. Cir. 1996); Rose v. United States, 905 F.2d 1257, 1259 (9th Cir. 1990); Johnston v. Horne, 875 F.2d 1415, 1422 (9th Cir. 1989); White v. OPM, 840 F.2d 85, 87 (D.C. Cir. 1988); Hubbard, 809 F.2d at 4-6; Hewitt v. Grabicki, 794 F.2d 1373, 1379 (9th Cir. 1986); Perry v. FBI, 759

OVERVIEW OF THE PRIVACY ACT

F.2d 1271, 1275, rev'd en banc on other grounds, 781 F.2d 1294 (7th Cir. 1986); Molerio v. FBI, 749 F.2d 815, 826 (D.C. Cir. 1984); Clarkson v. IRS, 678 F.2d 1368, 1377 (11th Cir. 1982) (citing Edison v. Dep't of the Army, 672 F.2d 840, 845 (11th Cir. 1982)); Feldman v. CIA, Civ. No. 09-02080, 797 F. Supp. 2d 29, 44-47 (D.D.C. 2011); Ajaj v. BOP, No. 08-cv-02006, 2011 WL 902440, at *15 (D. Colo. Mar. 10, 2011); Ramey v. U.S. Marshals Serv., 755 F. Supp. 2d 88, 96 (D.D.C. 2010); Kalderon v. Finkelstein, No. 08 Civ. 9440, slip op. at 63-70 (S.D.N.Y. Mar. 10, 2010) (magistrate's recommendation), adopted in pertinent part, 2010 WL 3359473 (S.D.N.Y. Aug. 25, 2010); Reitz, 2010 WL 786586, at *11; Ramirez v. DOJ, 594 F. Supp. 2d 58, 66-67 (D.D.C. 2009), aff'd per curiam on other grounds, No. 10-5016, 2010 WL 4340408 (D.C. Cir. Oct. 19, 2010); Peter B. v. CIA, 620 F. Supp. 2d 58, 77-78 (D.D.C. 2009); De la Cruz-Jimenez v. DOJ, 566 F. Supp. 2d 7, 9-10 (D.D.C. 2008); Brown v. U.S. Prob. Office, No. 03-872, 2005 WL 2284207, at *2 (E.D. Tex. Aug. 15, 2005); Kellett v. United States, 856 F. Supp. 65, 70-71 (D.N.H. 1994), aff'd, 66 F.3d 306 (1st Cir. 1995) (unpublished table decision); McGregor v. Greer, 748 F. Supp. 881, 886 (D.D.C. 1990); Mobley v. Doyle, No. JH-87-3300, slip op. at 3-5 (D. Md. Nov. 8, 1988); Wirth v. SSA, No. JH-85-1060, slip op. at 6 (D. Md. Jan. 20, 1988); NTEU v. IRS, 601 F. Supp. 1268, 1271-72 (D.D.C. 1985). See also Jones v. Luis, 372 F. App'x 967, 969-70 (11th Cir. 2010) (per curiam) (ruling that district court properly dismissed Privacy Act claim where plaintiff "does not allege any errors in the BOP's record keeping" but rather merely "alleges that [a BOP official] misused the information in the records to make an adverse determination against" plaintiff); Hutchinson v. CIA, 393 F.3d 226, 229-30 (D.C. Cir. 2005) (concluding that plaintiff failed to show that alleged inaccuracies proximately caused adverse determination because record demonstrates that she was dismissed for sustained poor performance spanning three years); Toolasprashad v. BOP, 286 F.3d 576, 583-86 (D.C. Cir. 2002) (holding that transfer of prisoner in alleged retaliation for exercise of his First Amendment rights constitutes assertion of "'adverse determination'" under Privacy Act, sufficient to "survive [agency's] motion to dismiss"); Treadwell v. BOP, 32 F. App'x 519, 520-21 (10th Cir. 2002) (plaintiff's claim that Bureau of Prisons erroneously based his security classification in part on nonviolent juvenile robbery offense does not amount to violation of Privacy Act where plaintiff agreed that conviction accurately appeared on his record but disagreed with way Bureau of Prisons used that information); Bettersworth v. FDIC, 248 F.3d 386, 392-93 (5th Cir. 2001) (holding that Federal Reserve Bank letter informing company that its Bank Holding Company Act (BHCA) application was unlikely to be approved without further information being provided did not constitute "adverse determination" against plaintiff, who held controlling interest in company, as there were "diverse grounds relied upon in the Reserve Bank's letter" (other than information about plaintiff's experience in banking

OVERVIEW OF THE PRIVACY ACT

industry) and entity applying for BHCA status was company, not plaintiff; further stating that "informal oral or written statements made in the deliberative process about a particular administrative determination do not constitute the determination itself"); Gowan v. U.S. Dep't of the Air Force, 148 F.3d 1182, 1194 (10th Cir. 1998) (no adverse effect from Air Force's informing Wyoming Bar of court martial charges preferred against plaintiff where plaintiff himself later informed Wyoming Bar without knowing Air Force had already done so); Williams v. BOP, No. 94-5098, 1994 WL 676801, at *1 (D.C. Cir. Oct. 21, 1994) (appellant did not establish either that agency "maintained an inaccurate record or that it made a determination adverse to him in reliance on inaccurate information capable of verification, the statutory prerequisites to maintaining an action pursuant to the Privacy Act"); Hadley v. Moon, No. 94-1212, 1994 WL 582907, at *1-2 (10th Cir. Oct. 21, 1994) (plaintiff must allege actual detriment or adverse determination in order to maintain claim under Privacy Act); New-Howard v. Shinseki, No. 09-5350, 2012 WL 2362546, at *9 (E.D. Pa. June 21, 2012) ("Plaintiff presents absolutely no evidence of instances in which she was denied leave due to an absence of accrued leave" and " [a]s a consequence, Plaintiff can maintain no cause of action for damages on the basis of the failure to maintain records regarding her leave."); Radakovic v. OPM, No. 11-10706, 2012 WL 1900037, at *3 (D. Mass. May 23, 2012) ("Plaintiff does not allege at the time of the 'adverse determination' . . . [agency] had any information available to it that contradicted any of the negative information provided directly to it by [his former employer] and verified by [his supervisor]" as letter explaining reasons for plaintiff's separation from former employer was not provided to agency until "two years and one month after plaintiff's termination" and therefore plaintiff, "as a matter of law, does not allege a § 552a(g)(1)(C) violation"); Gerlich v. DOJ, 828 F. Supp. 2d 284, 294-97 (D.D.C. 2011) (ruling that plaintiffs failed to prove that agency's maintenance of allegedly irrelevant information about them caused agency to deselect them for job interviews because "the Department has made plausible arguments that each of the applications could have been rejected on its face" – "for reasons ranging from typographical errors to unimpressive academic credentials to 'liberal' affiliations reflected on plaintiffs' resumes" – and because "there is no evidence that [a member of the selection committee] made annotations or printouts about these three plaintiffs"); Kvech v. Holder, No. 10-cv-545, 2011 WL 4369452, at *5-6 (D.D.C. Sept. 19, 2011) (Plaintiff asserted facts "sufficient to support only two of the four required elements."); Conley v. United States, No. 2:10-cv-444, 2011 WL 1256611, at *6-7 (S.D. Ohio Mar. 31, 2011) ("[A]ny possible recovery under [(g)(1)(C)] is precluded because [plaintiff] has failed to adequately plead that an adverse determination resulted from any of the [agency's] alleged violations of the Privacy Act."); Hollins v. Cross, No. 1:09cv75, 2010 WL 1439430, at *5 (N.D. W. Va. Mar. 17, 2010)

OVERVIEW OF THE PRIVACY ACT

("[B]ecause the plaintiff has failed to show that his [presentence investigation report] is actually erroneous, he cannot show that the BOP's use of that document to make . . . administrative decisions, has had an adverse effect on him."); Doe v. DOJ, 660 F. Supp. 2d 31, 43 (D.D.C. 2009) (concluding that plaintiff "failed to show that there was an error in the records" by objecting only to "misinterpretation of [accurate] records by DOJ employees, for which there is no remedy under the Privacy Act"); Krieger v. DOJ, 529 F. Supp. 2d 29, 49-50 (D.D.C. 2008) (explaining that even if former agency employee's performance appraisal reports were missing from his file, he "has adduced no evidence that his missing [reports] were the proximate cause of his failure to obtain job offers"); Elliott v. BOP, 521 F. Supp. 2d 41, 56 (D.D.C. 2007) ("The fact that Plaintiff was kept at [a particular institution] during [the period during which plaintiff alleged that BOP relied upon inaccurate or incomplete medical records] does not mean that the BOP actually made a 'determination' to do so."); Lee v. Geren, 480 F. Supp. 2d 198, 209-10 (D.D.C. Mar. 29, 2007) (where plaintiff received notice of proposed termination but was only suspended for two weeks, concluding that "[t]he mere issuance of a notice of proposed termination does not constitute an 'adverse determination' under the Privacy Act" and that "[t]he only 'adverse determination' at issue in this case is plaintiff's fourteen-day suspension"); Brown v. DOJ, No. 02-2662, slip op. at 27 (D. Ala. June 21, 2005) (explaining that "plaintiff fails to allege that there was any adverse determination made against her[;] instead she alleges that a threat of such action exists"); Wilson v. CIA, No. 01-1758, slip op. at 5 (D.D.C. Aug. 29, 2002) ("A claim for damages under the Privacy Act cannot survive without some evidence, not presented here, that the challenged record was used in reaching an adverse decision."), summary affirmance granted, No. 02-5282, 2003 U.S. App. LEXIS 1290 (D.C. Cir. Jan. 24, 2003); Murphy v. United States, 167 F. Supp. 2d 94, 97-98 (D.D.C. 2001) (although documents delayed plaintiff's transfer and thus played a part in transfer process, plaintiff "has neither shown that they caused the transfer nor identified a genuine issue of fact that is material to the dispositive issue of causation"), aff'd per curiam, 64 F. App'x 250 (D.C. Cir. 2003); Hughley v. BOP, No. 94-1048, slip op. at 4-5 (D.D.C. Apr. 30, 1996) (admitted inaccuracy in plaintiff's presentence investigation report regarding length of prior sentence did not result in "any cognizable injury that would give rise to an action under [subs]ection (g)(1)(C) because no adverse determination was made based on the inaccurate statement"; report correctly calculated plaintiff's criminal history points regardless of error), aff'd sub nom. Hughley v. Hawk, No. 96-5159, 1997 WL 362725 (D.C. Cir. May 6, 1997); Schwartz v. DOJ, No. 94 CIV. 7476, 1995 WL 675462, at *7-8 (S.D.N.Y. Nov. 14, 1995) (alleged inaccuracy in presentence report "cannot have caused an adverse determination" where sentencing judge was made aware of error and stated that fact at issue was not material for sentencing, nor did

OVERVIEW OF THE PRIVACY ACT

any omission of additional facts in report result in plaintiff's "not receiving a fair determination relating to his rights"), aff'd, 101 F.3d 686 (2d Cir. 1996) (unpublished table decision); Gowan v. Dep't of the Air Force, No. 90-94, slip op. at 34 (D.N.M. Sept. 1, 1995) (inaccuracy in report, i.e., listing of witnesses who were not interviewed, did not cause adverse agency action), aff'd, 148 F.3d 1182 (10th Cir. 1998).

As discussed above under "5 U.S.C. § 552a(e)(5)," the District Court for the District of Columbia recently has considered a subsection (e)(5)/(g)(1)(C) claim alleging not inaccuracy, but irrelevancy. Gerlich v. DOJ, 659 F. Supp. 2d 1 (D.D.C. 2009). The court noted that "[m]ost 'adverse determination' claims hinge on inaccurate or incomplete records." Id. at 15. Here, however, the plaintiffs alleged that "irrelevant records (i.e., the records of their First Amendment activities) led to an adverse [hiring] determination against them (i.e., deselection by the Screening Committee)." Id. In denying the Department's motion to dismiss, the court stated: "By the plain language of (g)(1)(C), relevance stands on equal footing with accuracy, timeliness and completeness as a basis for pursuing money damages for an adverse determination." Id. at 15-16. For a more complete discussion of Gerlich, see the discussion above.

In addition, an agency must be found to have acted in an "intentional or willful" manner in order for a damages action to succeed. See 5 U.S.C. § 552a(g)(4). This standard is discussed below under "Intentional/ Willful Standard."

Just as in the amendment context (see the discussion above), many courts have expressed disfavor toward litigants who attempt to invoke the subsection (g)(1)(C) damages remedy as a basis for collateral attacks on judicial and quasi-judicial agency determinations, such as benefit and employment decisions. See, e.g., Middlebrooks v. Mabus, No. 1:11cv46, 2011 WL 4478686, at *5 (E.D. Va. Sept. 23, 2011) ("Even if these claims were not untimely, . . . plaintiff's challenge to the accuracy of her record is a veiled attempt to relitigate her discrimination claim, which is . . . beyond the scope of the [Privacy] Act" because "[t]he Act is a vehicle for correcting facts in agency records if those facts are erroneously recorded but not for altering records that reflect an administrative decision or assessments, such as incident reports and evaluations."); Feldman v. CIA, 797 F. Supp. 2d at 47 (dismissing Privacy Act claim and stating: "It is [the] fully informed judgment of the CIA director that, at bottom, the plaintiff's Privacy Act claim attempts to challenge. The plaintiff's Complaint has not identified any discrete factual inaccuracies that this decision relied upon."); Doe v. DOJ, 660 F. Supp. 2d at 42-43 ("[P]laintiff's arguments that defendants lacked a basis to terminate him because his job did not require a security clearance or

OVERVIEW OF THE PRIVACY ACT

because they failed to follow the correct procedures . . . or that DOJ gave too much weight to his psychologist's . . . letter are impermissible attacks on DOJ's personnel decisions and administrative actions." (citations omitted)); Allmon v. BOP, 605 F. Supp. 2d 1, 7 (D.D.C. 2009) (ruling that a prisoner may not "us[e] [a] Privacy Act suit as a means to effect his transfer to a less-secure facility"); Ray v. DHS, No. H-07-2967, 2008 WL 3263550, at *10-11 (S.D. Tex. Aug. 7, 2008) ("To the extent that [plaintiff's] section 552a(g)(1)(C) claim seeks review of the TSA's decision to suspend him indefinitely without pay based on his failure to disclose his previous offenses," it must be dismissed because "[t]he Privacy Act . . . does not authorize relitigation of the substance of agency decisions."); Brown v. U.S. Prob. Office, No. 03-872, 2005 WL 2284207, at *3 (E.D. Tex. Aug. 15, 2005) (magistrate's recommendation) (rejecting plaintiff's claim as essentially a "challeng[e to] the application of the classification guidelines, not the accuracy or completeness of the information"), adopted, No. 03-872 (E.D. Tex. Sept. 9, 2005); Compro-Tax v. IRS, No. H-98-2471, 1999 U.S. Dist. LEXIS 5972, at *11-12 (S.D. Tex. Apr. 9, 1999) (magistrate's recommendation) (finding no intentional or willful agency action, and stating that the "Privacy Act may not be used to collaterally attack a final agency decision as 'inaccurate,' or 'incomplete' merely because the individual contests the decision"), adopted (S.D. Tex. May 12, 1999); Douglas v. Farmers Home Admin., No. 91-1969, 1992 U.S. Dist. LEXIS 9159, at *2-3 (D.D.C. June 26, 1992) (applying principles of White v. U.S. Civil Serv. Comm'n, 589 F.2d 713 (D.C. Cir. 1978) (per curiam) (holding that (g)(1)(A) plaintiff was not entitled to bring Privacy Act damages action for allegedly inaccurate appraisal of his property where he had not sought judicial review under APA); Castella v. Long, 701 F. Supp. 578, 584-85 (N.D. Tex. 1988) ("collateral attack on correctness of the finding supporting the discharge decision" improper under Act), aff'd, 862 F.2d 872 (5th Cir. 1988) (unpublished table decision); Holmberg v. United States, No. 85-2052, slip op. at 2-3 (D.D.C. Dec. 10, 1985) (Privacy Act "cannot be used to attack the outcome of adjudicatory-type proceedings by alleging that the underlying record was erroneous"); cf. Bhatia, 2011 WL 1298763, at *4-5 (dismissing as "unripe" plaintiff's "attempt[] to collaterally attack the validity of the criminal indictment . . . under the guise of Privacy Act claims" because "[t]he validity or invalidity of the criminal charges contained in the indictment cannot be determined until the criminal action is finally resolved"; because his "injury, if any, is dependent upon the outcome of his criminal case, his claims . . . will not ripen (if at all) until that action is finally concluded"). The OMB Guidelines, 40 Fed. Reg. 28,948, 28,969 (July 9, 1975), available at http://www.whitehouse.gov/sites/default/files/omb/assets/omb/inforeg/implementation_guidelines.pdf, also address this issue.

OVERVIEW OF THE PRIVACY ACT

Federal prisoners frequently attempt to invoke the subsection (g)(1)(C) damages remedy as a basis for a collateral attack on a conviction or the duration of a sentence. The Court of Appeals for the D.C. Circuit has explained that "such a claim is not cognizable" unless the conviction or sentence "has been invalidated in a prior proceeding." White v. U.S. Prob. Office, 148 F.3d 1124, 1125-26 (D.C. Cir. 1998) (per curiam). In White, the D.C. Circuit held that a Privacy Act claim for damages could not be brought "collaterally to attack" a federal prisoner's sentence, stating that: "Because a judgment in favor of [plaintiff] on his challenge to the legal conclusions in his presentence report would necessarily imply the invalidity of his sentence, which has not been invalidated in a prior proceeding, his complaint for damages under the Privacy Act must be dismissed." Id. at 1125-26. See also, e.g., Skinner v. BOP, 584 F.3d 1093, 1098, 1101 (D.C. Cir. 2009) (explaining that federal inmate's subsection (g)(1)(C) claim "is barred unless and until he successfully challenges the disciplinary hearing on which it is based through an action in habeas corpus"); Wattleton v. Lappin, 94 F. App'x 844, 845 (D.C. Cir. 2004) (per curiam) (Because "success on [the] Privacy Act claim would, at a minimum, have a 'probabilistic impact' on the duration of [the prisoner's] custody, appellant is required to proceed by way of a habeas petition."); Razzoli v. BOP, 230 F.3d 371, 373, 376 (D.C. Cir. 2000) (holding that "habeas is indeed exclusive even when a non-habeas claim would have a merely probabilistic impact on the duration of custody" and, therefore, finding "not cognizable" prisoner's claim that agency violated Privacy Act by relying on inaccurate information in postponing his eligibility for parole); Lewis v. U.S. Parole Comm'n, 770 F. Supp. 2d 246, 249-51 (D.D.C. 2011) (dismissing claim that agency's reliance on allegedly inaccurate information adversely affected plaintiff in parole hearings because "it is 'probabilistic' that the plaintiff's claim, if successful, would result in a decreased sentence or a more favorable parole decision" and such claims must be brought in habeas); Cargill v. U.S. Prob. Office for the Middle Dist. of N.C., No. 10-0388, 2010 WL 917010, at *1 (D.D.C. Mar. 9, 2010) (citing White v. U.S. Prob. Office and stating that "plaintiff cannot maintain his Privacy Act claim for damages based on the premise that his sentence is unlawful unless he can also show that his sentence was invalidated by an appropriate court"); Corley v. U.S. Parole Comm'n, 709 F. Supp. 2d 1, 5 (D.D.C. 2009) ("To the extent that this Privacy Act case is a disguised collateral attack on the plaintiff's conviction and sentence by denying that an indictment ever issued or that a conviction was ever obtained . . . this court must dismiss the case."); Brown v. BOP, 498 F. Supp. 2d. 298, 303-04 (D.D.C. 2007) ("The Privacy Act is not the proper means by which a prisoner may collaterally attack his sentence absent a showing that his sentence has been invalidated in a prior proceeding."); Doyon v. DOJ, 304 F. Supp. 2d 32, 35 (D.D.C. 2004) ("A challenge to the professional judgment of [BOP] officials in assessing points for purposes of establishing a prisoner's custody classification is not properly mounted by means of a Privacy Act suit."); Thomas v. U.S. Parole Comm'n, No. 94-0174, 1994 WL 487139, at *6 (D.D.C. Sept. 7, 1994) (plaintiff should not be allowed to use Privacy Act "to collaterally attack the contents of his presentence report," as he "originally had the opportunity to challenge the accuracy . . . before the judge who sentenced him"). Other courts have rejected these types of claims on similar grounds. See, e.g., Whitley v. Hunt, 158 F.3d 882, 889-90 (5th Cir. 1998) (affirming district court's conclusion that there was "no factual or legal basis" for claim that "prison officials abused their discretion by relying upon the sentence imposed against Whitley to determine his classification"; "Whitley is essentially claiming that his sentence itself was incorrectly entered. That is an issue that should have been resolved on direct appeal from his criminal conviction."); Hurley v. BOP, No. 95-1696, 1995 U.S. App. LEXIS 30148, at *4 (1st Cir. Oct. 24, 1995) (any alleged inaccuracy in plaintiff's presentence report, which agency relied on, "should have been brought to the attention of the district court at sentencing; or, at the very least, on appeal from his conviction and sentence"); Eubanks v. United States, No. 2:09cv126, 2010 WL 1141436, at *2 (N.D. W. Va. Jan. 12, 2010) (magistrate's recommendation) (claim "seeking damages for the alleged miscalculation of [plaintiff's] sentence should be dismissed" because his "sentence calculation has never been invalidated"), adopted 2010 WL 1141437 (N.D. W. Va. Mar. 22, 2010), aff'd per curiam, 405 F. App'x 796 (4th Cir. 2010); Blanton v. Schultz, No. 105CV0001, 2005 WL 3507969, at *3 (E.D. Cal. Dec. 21, 2005) (prisoner's argument that BOP is using "false information" to assign him less favorable custody and security classifications "is nothing more than an attempt to resurrect an otherwise improper [petition for writ of habeas corpus]").

As in the amendment context, 26 U.S.C. § 7852(e) (2006) (a provision of the Internal Revenue Code) also displaces the Privacy Act's damages remedy for inaccurate records in matters concerning tax liability. See, e.g., Ford v. United States, No. 91-36319, 1992 WL 387154, at *2 (9th Cir. Dec. 24, 1992); McMillen v. U.S. Dep't of Treasury, 960 F.2d 187, 188 (1st Cir. 1991); Swartz v. IRS, No. 05-72215, 2006 WL 1374472, at *2 (May 18, 2006); Sherwood v. United States, No. 96-2223, 1996 WL 732512, at *9 (N.D. Cal. Dec. 9, 1996).

In Hubbard v. EPA, the leading D.C. Circuit case concerning the causation requirement of subsection (g)(1)(C), the D.C. Circuit's finding of a lack of causation was heavily influenced by the Civil Service Reform Act's (CSRA) jurisdictional bar to district court review of government personnel practices. See 809 F.2d at 5. Although the D.C. Circuit stopped short of holding that the CSRA's comprehensive remedial scheme constitutes a jurisdictional bar to a subsection (g)(1)(C) action, it noted that "it would be anomalous to

OVERVIEW OF THE PRIVACY ACT

construe the pre-existing Privacy Act to grant the district court power to do indirectly that which Congress precluded directly: 'the Privacy Act was not intended to shield [federal] employees from the vicissitudes of federal personnel management decisions.'" Id. (quoting Albright v. United States, 732 F.2d 181, 190 (D.C. Cir. 1984)); cf. Biondo v. Dep't of the Navy, No. 2:92-0184-18, slip op. at 21-23 (D.S.C. June 29, 1993) (finding, based upon Hubbard, "that the 'collateral attack' argument complements the causation requirement of the Privacy Act"). The concurring opinion in Hubbard objected to this "canon of niggardliness" in construing subsection (g)(1)(C) and noted that circuit precedents since the passage of the CSRA have "without a hint of the majority's caution, reviewed the Privacy Act claims of federal employees or applicants embroiled in personnel disputes." 809 F.2d at 12-13 (Wald, J., concurring) (citing Molerio v. FBI, 749 F.2d 815, 826 (D.C. Cir. 1984), Albright, 732 F.2d at 188, and Borrell v. U.S. Int'l Commc'n Agency, 682 F.2d 981, 992-93 (D.C. Cir. 1982)).

Although Hubbard merely applied a strict causation test where a government personnel determination was being challenged, several more recent cases have construed the CSRA's comprehensive remedial scheme to constitute a jurisdictional bar to subsection (g)(1)(C) damages lawsuits challenging federal employment determinations. See Orsay v. DOJ, 289 F.3d 1125, 1128-31 (9th Cir. 2002); Houlihan v. OPM, 909 F.2d 383, 384-85 (9th Cir. 1990) (per curiam); Henderson v. SSA, 908 F.2d 559, 560-61 (10th Cir. 1990), aff'g 716 F. Supp. 15, 16-17 (D. Kan. 1989)); Miller v. Hart, No. PB-C-91-249, slip op. at 6-8 (E.D. Ark. Feb. 25, 1993); Kassel v. VA, No. 87-217-S, slip op. at 7-8 (D.N.H. Mar. 30, 1992); Holly v. HHS, No. 89-0137, slip op. at 1 (D.D.C. Aug. 9, 1991), aff'd, 968 F.2d 92 (D.C. Cir. 1992) (unpublished table decision); Barhorst v. Marsh, 765 F. Supp. 995, 999 (E.D. Mo. 1991); Barkley v. USPS, 745 F. Supp. 892, 893-94 (W.D.N.Y. 1990); McDowell v. Cheney, 718 F. Supp. 1531, 1543 (M.D. Ga. 1989); Holly v. HHS, No. 87-3205, slip op. at 4-6 (D.D.C. Aug. 22, 1988), aff'd, 895 F.2d 809 (D.C. Cir. 1990) (unpublished table decision); Tuesburg v. HUD, 652 F. Supp. 1044, 1049 (E.D. Mo. 1987); see also Phillips v. Widnall, No. 96-2099, 1997 WL 176394, at *3 (10th Cir. Apr. 14, 1997) (citing Henderson to hold that claim concerning alleged inaccuracies and omissions in appellant's employment file that formed basis of her claim for damages to remedy loss of promotion and other benefits of employment "is not a recognizable claim under the Privacy Act," as "CSRA provides the exclusive remedial scheme for review of [appellant's] claims related to her position as a nonappropriated fund instrumentality employee"); Vessella v. Dep't of the Air Force, No. 92-2195, 1993 WL 230172, at *2 (1st Cir. June 28, 1993) (citing Hubbard and Henderson v. SSA for the proposition that the Privacy Act "cannot be used . . . to frustrate the exclusive, comprehensive scheme provided by the CSRA"); Doe v. FDIC, No. 11 Civ. 307, 2012 WL 612461,

OVERVIEW OF THE PRIVACY ACT

at *5 (S.D.N.Y. Feb. 27, 2012) ("To the extent [plaintiff] has alleged that the disclosures underlying her Privacy Act claims were personnel actions taken in response to her reporting violations of banking laws and regulations, the Court finds that these claims are precluded by the CSRA."); Yu v. VA, No. 08-933, 2011 WL 2634095, at *10 (W.D. Pa. July 5, 2011) ("find[ing] that [plaintiff's] Privacy Act claims . . . are precluded under the CSRA" because plaintiff's claims, "in essence, challenge Defendant's employment decisions for which he seeks remedies that are normally within the purview of the MSPB"); Lim v. United States, No. 10-2574, 2011 WL 2650889, at *8 (D. Md. July 5, 2011) ("[W]hile labeled as a Privacy Act violation, [plaintiff] is ultimately challenging the basis for his discharge, a personnel decision which cannot be challenged outside the framework of the CSRA."); Pippinger v. Sec'y of the U.S. Treasury, No. 95-CV-017, 1996 U.S. Dist. LEXIS 5485, at *15 (D. Wyo. Apr. 10, 1996) (citing Henderson and stating that to the extent plaintiff challenges the accuracy of his personnel records, an action cannot be maintained, because the court does not have jurisdiction "to review errors in judgment that occur during the course of an employment/personnel decision where the CSRA precludes such review"), aff'd sub nom. Pippinger v. Rubin, 129 F.3d 519 (10th Cir. 1997); Edwards v. Baker, No. 83-2642, slip op. at 4-6 (D.D.C. July 16, 1986) (plaintiff's Privacy Act challenge to an "employee performance appraisal system" rejected on the ground that "plaintiffs may not use that Act as an alternative route for obtaining judicial review of alleged violations of the CSRA"). Other cases have declined to go that far. See Doe v. FBI, 718 F. Supp. 90, 100-01 n.14 (D.D.C. 1989) (rejecting contention that CSRA limited subsection (g)(1)(C) action), aff'd in part, rev'd in part & remanded, on other grounds, 936 F.2d 1346 (D.C. Cir. 1991); see also Halus v. U.S. Dep't of the Army, No. 87-4133, 1990 WL 121507, at *5 n.8 (E.D. Pa. Aug. 15, 1990) ("court may determine whether a Privacy Act violation caused the plaintiff damage (here, the loss of his job)"); Hay v. Sec'y of the Army, 739 F. Supp. 609, 612-13 (S.D. Ga. 1990) (similar).

As yet, the D.C. Circuit has declined to rule that the CSRA bars a Privacy Act claim for damages. See Kleiman v. Dep't of Energy, 956 F.2d 335, 337-39 & n.5 (D.C. Cir. 1992) (holding that Privacy Act does not afford relief where plaintiff did not contest that record accurately reflected his assigned job title, but rather challenged his position classification – a personnel decision judicially unreviewable under the CSRA – but noting that nothing in opinion "should be taken to cast doubt on Hubbard's statement that 'the Privacy Act permits a federal job applicant to recover damages for an adverse personnel action actually caused by an inaccurate or incomplete record'" (quoting Hubbard, 809 F.2d at 5)); Holly v. HHS, No. 88-5372, 1990 WL 13096, at *1 (D.C. Cir. Feb. 7, 1990) (declining to decide whether CSRA in all events precludes Privacy Act claim challenging federal

OVERVIEW OF THE PRIVACY ACT

employment determination; instead applying doctrine of "issue preclusion" to bar individual "from relitigating an agency's maintenance of the challenged records" where an arbitrator – in a negotiated grievance proceeding that included review of such records – had previously found that no "[agency] manager acted arbitrarily, capriciously or unreasonably in determining [that plaintiff] was not qualified"); see also Gard v. U.S. Dep't of Educ., 789 F. Supp. 2d 96, 106 (D.D.C. 2011) (citing and quoting Hubbard, but finding that plaintiff's "claims must fail to the extent that he has not produced any evidence supporting a reasonable inference that a Privacy Act violation itself actually caused the adverse events of which he complains"); Gerlich, 659 F. Supp. 2d at 14 (observing that the D.C. Circuit has "taken a rather narrow view of CSRA preclusion in Privacy Act cases" and finding that plaintiff job applicants, who had been "deselected" for interviews based on their political and ideological associations, sufficiently pleaded actual causation because "it is plain from [Hubbard and Kleiman] that but-for causation . . . is sufficient"); Peter B. v. CIA, 620 F. Supp. 2d 58, 76 (D.D.C. 2009) (explaining that if plaintiff "seeks to correct factually inaccurate records," then his claim "would not be precluded by the CSRA," but concluding that "[i]t is premature to determine whether [plaintiff] seeks to [do this], or if [plaintiff] disagrees with the [agency's] judgments contained in his records" because "the documents at issue are not yet in the record"); Lee v. Geren, 480 F. Supp. 2d at 210-12 (following Hubbard and Kleiman and concluding that allegedly inaccurate documents produced during investigation of plaintiff did not actually cause his suspension but rather "merely memorialized" that determination and thus "had no independent effect of their own"); Doe v. Goss, No. 04-2122, 2007 WL 106523, at *8-9 (D.D.C. Jan. 12, 2007) (citing Hubbard and finding that CSRA did not preclude plaintiff's accuracy claim or his "information-gathering" claim because plaintiff alleged actual causation with respect to both claims). But see Holly v. HHS, No. 89-0137, slip op. at 1 (D.D.C. Aug. 9, 1991) (citing Kleiman for proposition that court lacks subject matter jurisdiction in Privacy Act damages action in which plaintiff challenges a personnel action governed by CSRA), aff'd, 968 F.2d 92 (D.C. Cir. 1992) (unpublished table decision).

In Rosen v. Walters, 719 F.2d 1422, 1424-25 (9th Cir. 1983), the Court of Appeals for the Ninth Circuit held that 38 U.S.C. § 211(a) (later repealed, now see 38 U.S.C. § 511 (2006)) – a statute that broadly precludes judicial review of VA disability benefit decisions – operated to bar a subsection (g)(1)(C) damages action. In Rosen, the plaintiff contended that the VA deliberately destroyed medical records pertinent to his disability claim, thereby preventing him from presenting all the evidence in his favor. Id. at 1424. The Ninth Circuit ruled that such a damages claim would "necessarily run counter to the purposes of § 211(a)" because it would require a

OVERVIEW OF THE PRIVACY ACT

determination as to whether "but for the missing records, Rosen should have been awarded disability benefits." Id. at 1425. Further, it declined to find that the Privacy Act "repealed by implication" 38 U.S.C. § 211(a). Id.; see also Thomas v. Principi, 265 F. Supp. 2d 35, 39-40 (D.D.C. 2003) (holding a claim for failure to maintain accurate and complete records to be barred by 38 U.S.C. § 511 "because the injuries that allegedly resulted from defendants' failure to maintain [plaintiff's] records all ultimately concern the adverse benefits determination made by the [VA]"), aff'd in pertinent part, rev'd in part, 394 F.3d 970 (D.C. Cir. 2005); R.R. v. Dep't of the Army, 482 F. Supp. 770, 775-76 (D.D.C. 1980) (rejecting damages claim for lack of causation and noting that "[w]hat plaintiff apparently seeks to accomplish is to circumvent the statutory provisions making the VA's determinations of benefits final and not subject to judicial review"); cf. Kaswan v. VA, No. 81-3805, 1988 WL 98334, at *12 (E.D.N.Y. Sept. 15, 1988) (Privacy Act "not available to collaterally attack factual and legal decisions to grant or deny veterans benefits"), aff'd, 875 F.2d 856 (2d Cir. 1989) (unpublished table decision); Leib v. VA, 546 F. Supp. 758, 761-62 (D.D.C. 1982) ("The Privacy Act was not intended to be and should not be allowed to become a 'backdoor mechanism' to subvert the finality of agency determinations." (quoting Lyon v. United States, 94 F.R.D. 69, 72 (W.D. Okla. 1982))). Relying on Rosen, the District Court for the District of Idaho similarly held that the statutory scheme regarding the awarding of retirement benefits and "Congress's intent that OPM, MSPB and the Federal Circuit review decisions regarding the denial of disability retirement benefits" prohibited it from reviewing a Privacy Act damages claim where the plaintiff alleged that the VA's failure to maintain a file resulted in his being denied disability retirement benefits by OPM. Braun v. Brown, No. CV 97-0063-S, slip op. at 7-11 (D. Idaho June 22, 1998).

Several courts have held that the provision of the Federal Employees' Compensation Act (FECA), 5 U.S.C. § 8116(c) (2006), that provides that the liability of the United States under FECA with respect to the injury of an employee is exclusive, operates to preclude a cause of action under the Privacy Act, and deprives the court of subject matter jurisdiction. Vogrin v. ATF, No. 598CV117, 2001 WL 777427, at *7-8 (N.D. W. Va. Mar. 30, 2001), aff'd per curiam, No. 01-1491 (4th Cir. July 3, 2001). The court ruled that the FECA's exclusivity provision "precludes a suit under the Privacy Act even if FECA does not provide benefits for all of the injuries that [the plaintiff] claims." Id. at *7; see also Scott v. USPS, No. 05-0002, 2006 WL 2787832, at *3-4 (D.D.C. Sept. 26, 2006) (explaining that "even though [plaintiff] was ultimately denied compensation under FECA based on a lack of competent medical evidence" establishing that agency's disclosure of records caused her alleged emotional injury, "that is immaterial to the issue of the Court's jurisdiction"); Lyon v. United States, 94 F.R.D. 69, 72

OVERVIEW OF THE PRIVACY ACT

(W.D. Okla. 1982) (Privacy Act claim cannot be "a backdoor mechanism to subvert authority bestowed upon the Secretary of Labor to handle employee compensation claims"; the FECA "provides the exclusive method of presenting compensation claims resulting from on-the-job injuries of federal employees"); cf. Weber v. Henderson, 33 F. App'x 610, 612 (3d Cir. 2002) (holding that Privacy Act claim was barred by res judicata where plaintiff could have raised Privacy Act claim in prior suit when he brought claim against same defendants as cause of action under FECA); Jackson v. U.S. Dep't of Labor, No. 2:06-CV-02157, 2008 WL 539925, at *4 (E.D. Cal. Feb. 25, 2008) (ruling that plaintiff may not bring amendment lawsuit under Privacy Act to re-litigate determination of Federal Employees' Compensation Act benefits).

The District Court for the District of Columbia denied a motion by the government to dismiss a Privacy Act claim where the government argued that the Privacy Act claim was precluded by the exclusivity of relief under Title VII of the Civil Rights Act of 1964, 42 U.S.C. § 2000e, et seq. (2006). See Velikonja v. Mueller, 315 F. Supp. 2d 66, 77 (D.D.C. 2004) (noting that agency "failed to cite any cases in which a Privacy Act claim is precluded by Title VII" and that "the court is not aware of any"), subsequent opinion, 362 F. Supp. 2d 1, 13-19 (D.D.C. 2004) (finding no inaccuracies, adverse determination, or intentional or willful conduct), aff'd in part & rev'd in part sub nom. Velikonja v. Gonzales, 466 F.3d 122 (D.C. Cir. 2006) (affirming on ground of finding of no inaccuracies, adverse determination, or intentional or willful conduct).

In Perry v. FBI, 759 F.2d 1271, 1275-76 (7th Cir.), reh'g en banc granted on other grounds, 769 F.2d 450 (7th Cir. 1985), the Court of Appeals for the Seventh Circuit, without discussing subsection (g)(1)(C), adopted a comparatively narrower construction of subsection (e)(5), holding that "when one federal agency sends records to another agency to be used by the latter in making a decision about someone, the responsibility for ensuring that the information is accurate, relevant, timely, and complete lies with the receiving agency – the agency making 'the determination' about the person in question – not the sending agency."

Subsequently, though, in Dickson v. OPM, 828 F.2d 32, 36-40 (D.C. Cir. 1987), the D.C. Circuit held that a subsection (g)(1)(C) damages lawsuit is proper against any agency maintaining a record violating the standard of fairness mandated by the Act, regardless of whether that agency is the one making the adverse determination. See also Blazy v. Tenet, 979 F. Supp. 10, 19 (D.D.C. 1997) ("The adverse determination need not be made by the agency that actually maintains the record so long as it flowed from the inaccurate record." (citing Dickson)), summary affirmance granted, No. 97-

OVERVIEW OF THE PRIVACY ACT

5330, 1998 WL 315583 (D.C. Cir. May 12, 1998); Doe v. U.S. Civil Serv. Comm'n, 483 F. Supp. 539, 556 (S.D.N.Y. 1980) (applying subsection (e)(5) to agency whose records were used by another agency in making determination about individual); R.R. v. Dep't of the Army, 482 F. Supp. at 773 (same). In so holding, the D.C. Circuit noted that "the structure of the Act makes it abundantly clear that [sub]section (g) civil remedy actions operate independently of the obligations imposed on agency recordkeeping pursuant to [sub]section (e)(5)." Dickson, 828 F.2d at 38. In Dickson, the D.C. Circuit distinguished Perry on the grounds that "[a]ppellant is not proceeding under [sub]section (e)(5), Perry does not discuss [sub]section (g)(1)(C), and the construction of (e)(5) does not migrate by logic or statutory mandate to a separate [sub]section on civil remedies." 828 F.2d at 38; see also Doe v. FBI, 718 F. Supp. at 95 n.15 (noting conflict in cases but finding that Dickson's holding obviated need "to enter that thicket").

Assuming that causation is proven, "actual damages" sustained by the individual as a result of the failure, but in no case less than $1000, are recoverable. See 5 U.S.C. § 552a(g)(4)(A). The meaning of "actual damages" and the $1000 minimum recovery provision are discussed below under "Damages Lawsuits under (g)(1)(D)."

D. Damages Lawsuits under (g)(1)(D)

"Whenever any agency . . . fails to comply with any other provision of this section, or any rule promulgated thereunder, in such a way as to have an adverse effect on an individual [the individual may bring a civil action]." 5 U.S.C. § 552a(g)(1)(D).

Comment:

Exhaustion of administrative remedies is not a prerequisite to a civil action for damages under subsection (g)(1)(D). Diederich v. Dep't of the Army, 878 F.2d 646, 648 (2d Cir. 1989); Nagel v. HEW, 725 F.2d 1438, 1441 & n.2 (D.C. Cir. 1984); Gergick v. Austin, No. 89-0838-CV-W-2, 1992 U.S. Dist. LEXIS 7338, at *13-16 (W.D. Mo. Apr. 29, 1992), aff'd, No. 92-3210 (8th Cir. July 9, 1993); Pope v. Bond, 641 F. Supp. 489, 500 (D.D.C. 1986). But see Graham v. Hawk, 857 F. Supp. 38, 40 (W.D. Tenn. 1994) (heedlessly stating that "[e]ach paragraph of 5 U.S.C. § 552a(g) . . . requires as a prerequisite to any action that the agency refuse an individual's request to take some corrective action regarding his file"), aff'd, 59 F.3d 170 (6th Cir. 1995) (unpublished table decision).

While "exhaustion is normally not required for damages actions under the Privacy Act," note that 42 U.S.C. § 1997e(a) (2006), a provision of the

OVERVIEW OF THE PRIVACY ACT

Prison Litigation Reform Act of 1996 ("PLRA"), "imposes additional procedural requirements with respect to prisoners." Reid v. BOP, No. 04-1845, 2005 WL 1699425, at *3 (D.D.C. July 20, 2005). Specifically, § 1997e(a) provides that "[n]o action shall be brought with respect to prison conditions under [any Federal law] by a prisoner confined in any jail, prison, or other correctional facility until such administrative remedies as are available are exhausted." 42 U.S.C. § 1997e(a). The Supreme Court "has read the exhaustion requirements [of § 1997e(a)] broadly to include 'all inmate suits about prison life, whether they involve general circumstances or particular episodes, and whether they allege excessive force or some other wrong.'" Reid, 2005 WL 1699425, at *3 (quoting Porter v. Nussle, 534 U.S. 516, 532 (2002)). In McGee v. Bureau of Prisons, for example, the prisoner sued the Bureau of Prisons alleging unlawful disclosure. 118 F. App'x 471, 474 (10th Cir. 2004). The Court of Appeals for the Tenth Circuit concluded that the prisoner "failed to exhaust his administrative remedies with respect to his Privacy Act claim" pursuant to § 1997e(a). Id. at 475; see also Lugo-Vazquez v. Grondolsky, No. 08-986, 2010 WL 2287556, at *2-3 (D.N.J. June 2, 2010) (granting summary judgment to agency on Privacy Act claim because plaintiff failed to exhaust administrative remedies under § 1997e(a)); cf. Lee v. DOJ, 235 F.R.D. 274, 289-91 (W.D. Pa. 2006) (concluding that PLRA did not apply to allegation that "pertain[ed] to the disclosure of the [record] to a private bank, not to the means by which it was obtained," because allegation "did not relate to prison life").

A complaint is subject to dismissal, for failure to state a subsection (g)(1)(D) damages claim, if no "adverse effect" is alleged. See, e.g., Doe v. Chao, 540 U.S. 614, 624 (2004) ("'[A]dverse effect' acts as a term of art identifying a potential plaintiff who satisfies the injury-in-fact and causation requirements of Article III standing, and who may consequently bring a civil action without suffering dismissal for want of standing to sue."); Shearson v. DHS, 638 F.3d 498, 505-06 (6th Cir. 2011) ("[Plaintiff's] request to pursue a claim under § 552a(e)(4) was properly denied because she failed to allege or show the requisite 'adverse effect' from Defendants' alleged failure to provide notice specifically regarding the [system of records] at an earlier date."); McCready v. Nicholson, 465 F.3d 1 (D.C. Cir. 2006) (remanding case for district court to determine whether plaintiff suffered an "adverse effect" by being denied a bonus); Quinn v. Stone, 978 F.2d 126, 135 (3d Cir. 1992) ("[T]he adverse effect requirement of (g)(1)(D) is, in effect, a standing requirement."); Mata v. McHugh, No. 10-cv-838, 2012 WL 2376285, at *6 (W.D. Tex. June 22, 2012); Mauldin v. Napolitano, No. 10-12826, 2011 WL 3113104, at *3 (E.D. Mich. July 26, 2011); Conley v. United States, No. 2:10-cv-444, 2011 WL 1256611, at *7 (S.D. Ohio Mar. 31, 2011); Shope v. Dep't of Navy, No. 1:CV-09-2400, 2010 WL 2766638, at *3 (M.D. Pa. July 13, 2010); Sieverding v. DOJ, 693 F. Supp. 2d 93, 106 (D.D.C. 2010), aff'd

OVERVIEW OF THE PRIVACY ACT

per curiam, No. 10-5149, 2010 WL 4340348 (D.C. Cir. Oct. 19, 2010); Ciralsky v. CIA, 689 F. Supp. 2d 141, 155-56 (D.D.C. 2010); Sutera v. TSA, 708 F. Supp. 2d 304, 318-19 (E.D.N.Y. 2010); Goodwin v. Johnson, No. 8:10CV40, 2010 WL 1500872, at *3 (D. Neb. Apr. 14, 2010); Doe v. DOJ, 660 F. Supp. 2d 31, 49 (D.D.C. 2009); Fort Hall Landowners Alliance, Inc. v. BIA, No. CV-99-00052-E, slip op. at 12 (D. Idaho Mar. 29, 2001); Hass v. U.S. Air Force, 848 F. Supp. 926, 932 (D. Kan. 1994); Swenson v. USPS, No. S-87-1282, 1994 U.S. Dist. LEXIS 16524, at *30 (E.D. Cal. Mar. 10, 1994); Green v. USPS, No. 88-0539, 1989 U.S. Dist. LEXIS 6846, at *6-8 (S.D.N.Y. June 19, 1989); Tracy v. SSA, No. 88-C-570-S, slip op. at 4-5 (W.D. Wis. Sept. 23, 1988); Bryant v. Dep't of the Air Force, No. 85-4096, slip op. at 5 (D.D.C. Mar. 31, 1986); Harper v. United States, 423 F. Supp. 192, 196-97 (D.S.C. 1976); see also Raley v. Astrue, No. 2:11cv555, 2012 WL 2368609, at *7 (M.D. Ala. June 21, 2012) ("Plaintiff presents no evidence to establish that receiving someone else's information did in fact adversely affect her."); Philippeaux v. United States, No. 10 Civ. 6143, 2011 WL 4472064, at *9 (S.D.N.Y. Sept. 27, 2011) (plaintiff failed to allege that "any pertinent records have been removed" and, "[a]s a result, . . . he fails to adequately show that he was adversely affected by any disclosure"); Bhatia v. Office of the U.S. Attorney, N. Dist. of Cal., No. C 09-5581, 2011 WL 1298763, at *4 (N.D. Cal. Mar. 29, 2011) (finding that plaintiff who was "wrongly indicted" lacked standing because he "cannot show, at this juncture, that he was injured by the return of the criminal indictment" because "those charges are currently pending"); Baker v. United States, No. 5:05-221, 2006 WL 1635634, at *4 (E.D. Ky. June 8, 2006) (finding that plaintiff failed to allege any adverse effect resulting from disclosure to press of reasons for his medical discharge); Robinett v. State Farm Mut. Auto. Ins. Co., No. 02-0842, 2002 WL 31498992, at *4 (E.D. La. Nov. 7, 2002) (stating that "[e]ven if [the agency's] communication did not technically satisfy the notice requirement of [subsection (e)(8)], plaintiff was not adversely affected by a failure to receive notice after the records were disclosed," because "plaintiff had no legal basis to prevent [the agency] from releasing his records" and in fact knew of the possible release and tried to prevent it), aff'd per curiam, 83 F. App'x 638 (5th Cir. 2003); Crichton v. Cmty. Servs. Admin., 567 F. Supp. 322, 324 (S.D.N.Y. 1983) (mere maintenance of allegedly "secret file" insufficient to warrant damages where no showing of adverse effect); Church v. United States, 2 Gov't Disclosure Serv. (P-H) ¶ 81,350, at 81,911 (D. Md. Jan. 5, 1981) (no adverse effect from failure to provide subsection (e)(3) notice); cf. Banks v. Butler, No. 5:08CV336, 2010 WL 4537902, at *6 (S.D. Miss. Sept. 23, 2010) (magistrate's recommendation) (statements about plaintiff by staff members were "at most – innocuous statements of opinion, rather than disclosures of records and create no real adverse effect"), adopted 2010 WL 4537909 (S.D. Miss. Nov. 2, 2010); Nunez v. Lindsay, No. 3:CV005-1763, 2007 WL

517754, at *1-2 (M.D. Pa. Feb. 12, 2007) (concluding that inmate lacked standing to bring Privacy Act claim against BOP based on prison's "practice of photographing friends and family who chose to visit" him because "[a]ny invasion of privacy interests concerns the visitors, not the inmates"); Clark v. BOP, 407 F. Supp. 2d 127, 129-131 (D.D.C. 2005) (concluding that disclosure of inmate's medical records to second inmate so that he could decipher word on first inmate's chart presented triable issue of whether first inmate's HIV status was disclosed, but dismissing claim because "plaintiff has not shown that the disclosure caused him to suffer an adverse effect or to sustain actual damages").

An "adverse effect" includes not only monetary damages, but also nonpecuniary and nonphysical harm, such as mental distress, embarrassment, or emotional trauma. See, e.g., Speaker v. HHS Ctrs. for Disease Control & Prevention, 623 F.3d 1371, 1382-83 (11th Cir. 2010); Doe v. Chao, 306 F.3d 170, 187 (4th Cir. 2002) (Michael, J., dissenting) ("The majority and I . . . also agree that emotional distress can qualify as an adverse effect."), aff'd, 540 U.S. 614 (2004); Quinn, 978 F.2d at 135-36; Albright v. United States, 732 F.2d 181, 186 (D.C. Cir. 1984); Usher v. Sec'y of HHS, 721 F.2d 854, 856 (1st Cir. 1983); Parks v. IRS, 618 F.2d 677, 682-83 & n.2 (10th Cir. 1980); Iqbal v. FBI, No. 3:11-cv-369, 2012 WL 2366634, at *6 n.10 (M.D. Fla. June 21, 2012); Kvech v. Holder, No. 10-cv-545, 2011 WL 4369452, at *4 (D.D.C. Sept. 19, 2011); Rice v. United States, 245 F.R.D. 3, 5-6 (D.D.C. 2007); Schmidt v. VA, 218 F.R.D. 619, 632 (E.D. Wis. 2003); Romero-Vargas v. Shalala, 907 F. Supp. 1128, 1134 (N.D. Ohio 1995); see also Englerius v. VA, 837 F.2d 895, 897 (9th Cir. 1988); Lechliter v. Dep't of Army, No. 04-814, 2006 WL 462750, at *5 (D. Del. Feb. 27, 2006); cf. Tarullo v. Def. Contract Audit Agency, 600 F. Supp. 2d 352, 359 (D. Conn. 2009) (dismissing case where "the disclosures of [plaintiff's] [social security number] had [no] adverse effect on [him] other than the displeasure he felt because these disclosures were against his wishes"); Clark v. BOP, 407 F. Supp. 2d 127, 131 (D.D.C. 2005) ("Nothing in the record . . . connects the alleged adverse effect, i.e., plaintiff's maltreatment, with the disclosure at issue."); Doyon v. DOJ, 304 F. Supp. 2d 32, 35 (D.D.C. 2004) ("assum[ing] without deciding that [BOP's] decision 'to restrict [plaintiff] from a transfer and many Institutional programs' . . . is an adverse determination," but finding the claim to have been rendered moot). But see Risch v. Henderson, 128 F. Supp. 2d 437, 441 (E.D. Mich. 1999) (conflating the concepts of "adverse effect" and "actual damages," and stating that even assuming that there had been a violation of the Privacy Act for the maintenance of alleged "secret files," because plaintiff claimed only "'extreme mental anguish and mental concern and worry,'" she had "failed to demonstrate [an] 'adverse effect'"), aff'd sub nom. Risch v. USPS, 244 F.3d 510 (6th Cir. 2001).

OVERVIEW OF THE PRIVACY ACT

For a novel interpretation of "adverse effect," see <u>Bagwell v. Brannon</u>, No. 82-8711, slip op. at 5-6 (11th Cir. Feb. 22, 1984), in which the Court of Appeals for the Eleventh Circuit found that no "adverse effect" was caused by the government's disclosure of an employee's personnel file (during cross-examination) while defending against the employee's tort lawsuit, because the "employee created the risk that pertinent but embarrassing aspects of his work record would be publicized" and "disclosure was consistent with the purpose for which the information was originally collected."

The threshold showing of "adverse effect," which typically is not difficult for a plaintiff to satisfy, should carefully be distinguished from the conceptually separate requirement of "actual damages," discussed below. <u>See, e.g.</u>, <u>Fort Hall Landowners Alliance, Inc. v. BIA</u>, 407 F. Supp. 2d 1220, 1225 (D. Idaho 2006) (explaining that "[i]t is important not to confuse this standing requirement with the entirely separate element that requires proof of actual damages" and that "to satisfy the Privacy Act's adverse effect and causation requirements, plaintiffs need not show actual damages from the disclosure, but must merely satisfy the traditional 'injury-in-fact and causation requirements of Article III'"). As one district court has explained, "[t]he requirement of an 'adverse effect' requires more" than a "statement of 'damages' [that] merely summarizes the alleged violations of law." <u>Foncello v. U.S. Dep't of the Army</u>, No. 04-604, 2005 WL 2994011, at *4 (D. Conn. Nov. 7, 2005). This distinct nature of these two elements is demonstrated by the Supreme Court's review in <u>FAA v. Cooper</u>, 132 S. Ct. 1441 (2012), of an opinion by the Court of Appeals for the Ninth Circuit, <u>Cooper v. FAA</u>, 622 F.3d 1016 (9th Cir. 2010). In <u>Cooper</u>, the Ninth Circuit in construing the Privacy Act to allow for the recovery of nonpecuniary damages, reasoned that because "mental distress or emotional harm is sufficient to constitute an adverse effect," a construction of the Act that allowed a plaintiff to establish standing for an injury that results in nonpecuniary harm, but that would not allow the plaintiff to seek actual damages for such a nonpecuniary injury would "frustrate the intent of Congress." <u>Id.</u> at 1021. The Ninth Circuit majority went on to state that "[i]n contrast, our opinion is true to the overall objective of the Act, allowing a plaintiff who demonstrates a nonpecuniary adverse effect to have the opportunity to recover nonpecuniary damages." <u>Id.</u> However, on writ of certiorari a majority of the Supreme Court reversed the Ninth Circuit's opinion and held that the Privacy Act does not authorize damages for nonpecuniary injuries such as mental or emotional distress. The Supreme Court did not so much as consider the separate issue of "adverse effect" in its ruling. <u>See</u> <u>FAA v. Cooper</u>, 132 S. Ct. at 1453.

OVERVIEW OF THE PRIVACY ACT

A showing of causation – that the violation caused an adverse effect, and that the violation caused "actual damages," as discussed below – is also required. See, e.g., Beaven v. DOJ, 622 F. 3d 540, 558 (6th Cir. 2010); Sweeney v. Chertoff, 178 F. App'x 354, 357-58 (5th Cir. 2006); Mandel v. OPM, 79 F. App'x 479, 481-82 (2d Cir. 2003), aff'g 244 F. Supp. 2d 146, 153 (E.D.N.Y. 2003); Orekoya v. Mooney, 330 F.3d 1, 10 (1st Cir. 2003); Quinn, 978 F.2d at 135; Hewitt v. Grabicki, 794 F.2d 1373, 1379 (9th Cir. 1986); Albright, 732 F.2d at 186-87; Edison v. Dep't of the Army, 672 F.2d 840, 842, 845 (11th Cir. 1982); York v. McHugh, 698 F. Supp. 2d 101, 108 (D.D.C. 2010); Thompson v. Dep't of State, 400 F. Supp. 2d 1, 14 (D.D.C. 2005); Harmer v. Perry, No. 95-4197, 1998 WL 229637, at *3 (E.D. Pa. Apr. 28, 1998), aff'd, No. 98-1532 (3d Cir. Jan. 29, 1999); Swenson, No. S-87-1282, 1994 U.S. Dist. LEXIS 16524, at *30 (E.D. Cal. Mar. 10, 1994); Connelly v. Comptroller of the Currency, No. H-84-3783, slip op. at 4 (S.D. Tex. June 3, 1991); Rodgers v. Dep't of the Army, 676 F. Supp. 858, 862 (N.D. Ill. 1988); Tuesburg v. HUD, 652 F. Supp. 1044, 1048 (E.D. Mo. 1987); Ely v. DOJ, 610 F. Supp. 942, 946 (N.D. Ill. 1985), aff'd, 792 F.2d 142 (7th Cir. 1986) (unpublished table decision). But see Rickles v. Marsh, No. 3:88-100, slip op. at 8-9 (N.D. Ga. Jan. 10, 1990) (aberrational decision awarding minimum damages even in absence of causation).

It also has been held that "[f]or there to be a causal link between the injury and the violation of the Act, the injury necessarily must be distinct and independent from the violation of the Act itself." Schmidt v. VA, 218 F.R.D. at 632; see also Doe v. Chao, 306 F.3d at 186 (Michaels, J., dissenting) ("The causal prong makes it especially clear that an adverse effect must be something distinct from the intentional and willful violation itself. For if a violation of the Privacy Act was sufficient to constitute an adverse effect, there could be no question of whether the violation caused the adverse effect, and hence the causal prong would be superfluous."); Quinn, 978 F.2d at 135 (stating that in addition to establishing an adverse effect sufficient to confer standing, "plaintiff must also allege a causal connection between the agency violation and the adverse effect"); cf. Doe v. Chao, 540 U.S. 614, 627 (2004) ("The 'entitle[ment] to recovery' necessary to qualify for the $1,000 minimum is not shown merely by an intentional or willful violation of the Act producing some adverse effect."). But cf. Romero-Vargas v. Shalala, 907 F. Supp. 1128, 1134-35 (N.D. Ohio 1995) (stating, prior to Supreme Court's decision in Doe v. Chao, that "emotional distress caused by the fact that the plaintiff's privacy has been violated is itself an adverse effect, and that statutory damages can be awarded without an independent showing of adverse effects"; stating further in memorandum on motion to alter or amend judgment that "[i]t is eminently reasonable to infer that plaintiffs suffered mental distress by the fact of knowing their personal information had been disclosed").

OVERVIEW OF THE PRIVACY ACT

In addition, an agency must be found to have acted in an "intentional or willful" manner in order for a damages action to succeed. See 5 U.S.C. § 552a(g)(4). This standard is discussed below under "Intentional/Willful Standard."

The issue of the Privacy Act's applicability to disclosures of tax information has been analyzed most recently by the Court of Appeals for the District of Columbia Circuit in Gardner v. United States, 213 F.3d 735 (D.C. Cir. 2000), aff'g No. 96-1467, 1999 U.S. Dist. LEXIS 2195, at *14-17 (D.D.C. Jan. 29, 1999). In Gardner, the D.C. Circuit concluded that the Internal Revenue Code preempts the Privacy Act for remedies for disclosures of tax information, holding that 26 U.S.C. § 6103 is "the exclusive remedy for a taxpayer claiming unlawful disclosure of his or her tax returns and tax information." 213 F.3d at 741-42. Similarly, although not going quite as far, the Court of Appeals for the Fifth Circuit had previously held that "[26 U.S.C.] § 6103 is a more detailed statute that should preempt the more general remedies of the Privacy Act, at least where . . . those remedies are in conflict." Hobbs v. United States, 209 F.3d 408, 412 (5th Cir. 2000) (finding § 6103 and the Privacy Act to be "in conflict" where disclosure fell within one of the exceptions in § 6103, and holding that "[t]o the extent that the Privacy Act would recognize a cause of action for unauthorized disclosure of tax return information even where § 6103 would provide an exception for the particular disclosure, § 6103 trumps the Privacy Act"). Other courts, too, have found the provisions of the tax code to be exclusive as to wrongful disclosures of tax information. See Ross v. United States, 460 F. Supp. 2d 139, 151 (D.D.C. 2006) ("[Section] 6103 is the exclusive remedy for a taxpayer claiming unlawful disclosure of his or her tax returns and information."); Schwartz v. Kempf, No. 4:02-cv-198, 2004 U.S. Dist. LEXIS 2238, at *10-12 (W.D. Mich. Jan. 22, 2004) (citing Gardner and finding the provisions of the Privacy Act to be "trumped by the more specific provisions of the Internal Revenue Code found in 26 U.S.C. § 6103"); Berridge v. Heiser, 993 F. Supp. 1136, 1144-45 (S.D. Ohio 1997) (holding that 26 U.S.C. § 7431(a)(1), which provides a mechanism for the award of civil damages for unauthorized disclosure of tax return information (as defined in 26 U.S.C. § 6103), is the "exclusive remedy by which [plaintiff] may bring a cause of action for improper disclosure of return information"); Gov't Nat'l Mortgage, Ass'n v. Lunsford, No. 95-273, 1996 U.S. Dist. LEXIS 1591, at *8 (E.D. Ky. Feb. 2, 1996) (dismissing a Privacy Act claim for wrongful disclosure (presumably brought under subsection (g)(1)(D)) and stating that "26 U.S.C. § 7852(e) precludes the maintenance of Privacy Act damages remedies in matters concerning federal tax liabilities").

OVERVIEW OF THE PRIVACY ACT

Nevertheless, the Courts of Appeals for the Fourth and the Eighth Circuits, as well as the United States Tax Court, have readily applied the Privacy Act as well as the provisions of the tax code to disclosures of tax return information, with no discussion of the issue of preemption. Scrimgeour v. IRS, 149 F.3d 318, 325-26 (4th Cir. 1998) (affirming denial of damages and finding that the agency had not acted with gross negligence under 26 U.S.C. § 7431 or greater than gross negligence under the Privacy Act for wrongful disclosure claims resting upon identical factual allegations); Taylor v. United States, 106 F.3d 833, 835-37 (8th Cir. 1997) (affirming finding that disclosures did not violate 26 U.S.C. § 6103 or Privacy Act); Stone v. Comm'r of IRS, No. 3812-97, 1998 WL 547043 (T.C. Aug. 31, 1998) (finding that disclosures did not violate either 26 U.S.C. § 6103 or Privacy Act). In addition, one district court specifically considered the issue and arrived at the conclusion that the Privacy Act's remedies are available for the wrongful disclosure of tax return information. Sinicki v. U.S. Dep't of Treasury, No. 97 CIV. 0901, 1998 WL 80188, at *3-5 (S.D.N.Y. Feb. 24, 1998) (denying motion to dismiss Privacy Act wrongful disclosure claim and stating that "the language, structure, purpose and legislative history of Section 6103 do not make manifest and clear a legislative intent to repeal the Privacy Act as it applies to tax return information").

Several district courts have held that various sections of the Internal Revenue Code prevent their exercise of subject matter jurisdiction over Privacy Act claims brought under subsection (g)(1)(D) for alleged violations of other provisions of the Privacy Act. See Schwartz v. Kempf, 2004 U.S. Dist. LEXIS 2238, at *10-12 (where plaintiffs alleged that the IRS violated the Privacy Act by contacting persons regarding plaintiffs' tax situation, citing 26 U.S.C. § 7852(e) and stating that the "provisions of the Privacy Act do not apply, either directly or indirectly, to assessing the possibility of a tax liability"); Berridge v. Heiser, 993 F. Supp. 1136, 1145 (S.D. Ohio 1997) (holding that 26 U.S.C. § 7852(e) prevented it from exercising jurisdiction over plaintiff's Privacy Act claims under subsections (e)(2), (e)(5), and (e)(6) related to tax liability); Estate of Myers v. United States, 842 F. Supp. 1297, 1302-04 (E.D. Wash. 1993) (dismissing Privacy Act subsection (g)(1)(D) damages claim and applying § 7852(e)'s jurisdictional bar to preclude subject matter jurisdiction to consider action against IRS for alleged violation of subsection (e)(3) concerning summons issued to assist in determination of foreign tax liability); cf. Smilde v. Richardson, Comm'r, No. 97-568, 1997 U.S. Dist. LEXIS 15050, at *6-7 (D. Minn. Aug. 28, 1997) (relying on limitation of Privacy Act applicability pursuant to sections 6103 and 7852(e), and finding that "Privacy Act does not support subject matter jurisdiction" to enjoin IRS from contracting out processing of tax returns), aff'd per curiam, 141 F.3d 1170 (8th Cir. 1998) (unpublished table decision); Trimble v. United States, No. 92-74219, 1993 WL 288295, at *1 (E.D.

OVERVIEW OF THE PRIVACY ACT

Mich. May 18, 1993) (citing 26 U.S.C. § 7852(e) for Privacy Act's inapplicability and dismissing unspecified Privacy Act claim), aff'd, 28 F.3d 1214 (6th Cir. 1994) (unpublished table decision).

Consistent with case law under subsection (g)(1)(C), the District Court for the District of Columbia has stated that a plaintiff "cannot rely on any arguable violation of the Privacy Act" – in that case an alleged wrongful disclosure – to "collaterally attack" an agency personnel decision. Hanna v. Herman, 121 F. Supp. 2d 113, 123-24 (D.D.C. 2000) (appeal of MSPB decision upholding plaintiff's demotion; finding that MSPB did not err in refusing to address plaintiff's Privacy Act argument, but, "assuming arguendo that [he] preserved [it]," discussing merits of plaintiff's "Privacy Act defense to the demotion"), summary affirmance granted sub nom. Hanna v. Chao, No. 00-5433 (D.C. Cir. Apr. 11, 2001). See also Doe v. DOJ, 660 F. Supp. 2d at 50-51 (concluding that plaintiff's subsection (b)/(g)(1)(D) claim against MSPB for refusing to allow him to proceed under a pseudonym was a "collateral attack" of that decision because plaintiff's claim "attempts to achieve the same forbidden objective" as prototypical collateral attacks – "relitigating issues already decided by the ALJ").

Note also that some courts have held that the exclusivity provision of the Federal Employees' Compensation Act, 5 U.S.C. § 8116(c) (2006), precludes a cause of action under the Privacy Act. See, e.g., Smith v. Nicholson, 287 F. App'x 402, 403-05 (5th Cir. 2008) (per curiam) (where Labor Secretary denied plaintiff's FECA claim alleging that VA injured him by disclosing his records "not for lack of coverage, but for insufficient proof," holding that "such a denial is conclusive as to FECA coverage"; "the Secretary found FECA applicable" and "[t]hat decision precludes any further action on [plaintiff's] Privacy Act claim"); Richards v. CIA, No. 1:11-cv-784, 2011 WL 5593166, at *4-5 (E.D. Va. Nov. 16, 2011) (dismissing Privacy Act claim because "[t]he disclosures and the subsequent harm came exclusively in the context of [plaintiff's] employment at the CIA" and stating that "absent a determination by the Secretary of Labor that FECA does not cover [plaintiff's] Privacy Act claim, this Court has no jurisdiction to entertain the Privacy Act claim"); Carte v. United States, No. 2:07-0515, 2010 WL 3259420, at *7-8 (S.D. W. Va. Aug. 18, 2010) (where plaintiff attempted to recover for injury allegedly caused by agency's disclosure of his medical information by filing both a FECA claim and a Privacy Act claim, concluding that "whether viewed as being precluded by a meritsbased DOL decision or a decision of lesser quantum leaving open the substantial question of whether [plaintiff's] injuries, if any, were sustained while performing his duties, section 8116(c) bars a Privacy Act claim from being pursued in this action"); Vogrin v. ATF, No. 598CV117, 2001 WL 777427, at *7-8 (N.D. W. Va. Mar. 30, 2001) (ruling that FECA's exclusivity

OVERVIEW OF THE PRIVACY ACT

provision "precludes a suit under the Privacy Act even if FECA does not provide benefits for all of the injuries that [the plaintiff] claims"), aff'd per curiam, No. 01-1491 (4th Cir. July 3, 2001).

Similarly, it has been held that the Civil Service Reform Act deprives a court of subject matter jurisdiction over a Privacy Act claim brought under subsection (g)(1)(D). See Henderson v. U.S. Air Force, No. 06-323, 2008 WL 4542761, at *2-3 (D. Ariz. Oct. 10, 2008), aff'd, 370 F. App'x 807 (9th Cir. 2010). This issue is discussed more fully above in the context of damages lawsuits brought under subsection (g)(1)(C).

E. Principles Applicable to Damages Lawsuits

"In any suit brought under the provisions of subsection (g)(1)(C) or (D) of this section in which the court determines that the agency acted in a manner which was intentional or willful, the United States shall be liable to the individual in an amount equal to the sum of . . . actual damages sustained by the individual as a result of the refusal or failure, but in no case shall a person entitled to recovery receive less than the sum of $1,000." 5 U.S.C. § 552a(g)(4).

1. Intentional/Willful Standard

Comment:

In order for there to be any liability in a subsection (g)(1)(C) or (D) damages lawsuit, the agency must have acted in an "intentional or willful" manner. 5 U.S.C. § 552a(g)(4). It is important to understand that the words "intentional" and "willful" in subsection (g)(4) do not have their vernacular meanings; instead, they are "terms of art." White v. OPM, 840 F.2d 85, 87 (D.C. Cir. 1988) (per curiam); see also Convertino v. DOJ, 769 F. Supp. 2d 139, 145-46 (D.D.C. 2011) (noting that "[s]tandards of intentionality and willfulness are anything but rare in the law" but explaining that "the Privacy Act's intent or willfulness requirement is peculiar to the Act and must not be confused with less exacting standards parading under the same name from other common law or statutory sources" (citing White)), rev'd and remanded on other grounds, No. 11-5133, 2012 WL 2362591 (D.C. Cir. June 22, 2012) (reversing district court's summary judgment and ruling that district court committed abuse of discretion in denying appellant's motion to stay summary judgment to allow for further discovery). The Act's legislative history indicates that this unique standard is "[o]n a continuum between negligence and the very high standard of willful, arbitrary, or

OVERVIEW OF THE PRIVACY ACT

capricious conduct," and that it "is viewed as only somewhat greater than gross negligence." 120 Cong. Rec. 40,406 (1974), reprinted in Source Book at 862, available at http://www.loc.gov/rr/frd/Military_Law/pdf/LH_privacy_act-1974.pdf.

While not requiring premeditated malice, see Parks v. IRS, 618 F.2d 677, 683 (10th Cir. 1980), the voluminous case law construing this standard makes clear that it is a formidable barrier for a plaintiff seeking damages. See, e.g., Luster v. Vilsack, 667 F.3d 1089, 1098 (10th Cir. 2011) ("[G]iven the lack of any authority in support of [plaintiff's] contention that it is a violation of the Privacy Act to transmit confidential materials (all but one of which was covered by a transmittal cover sheet) to an unsecured fax machine, we agree with the district court that [plaintiff] has not demonstrated that any actual disclosure by [defendant] was willful and intentional."); Campbell v. SSA, 446 F. App'x 477, 479, 481 (3d Cir. 2011) (upholding district court conclusion that "there was no record evidence to support an assertion of willful or intentional conduct" where district court found that plaintiff's "assertion that his wife discovered some documents in her SSA file that should have been in his file, if true, established nothing more than negligence"); Maydak v. United States, 630 F. 3d 166, 179-83 (D.C. Cir. 2010) ("assum[ing], without deciding, that BOP's review and retention of the duplicate photos [of prisoners] constituted a system of records," holding that BOP did not intentionally or willfully commit Privacy Act violations because, among other reasons, "the photographs . . . were used only for legitimate law enforcement purposes" and notwithstanding the court's "critical discussion of the review and retention policies" in prior opinions, "BOP officials were still never placed on clear notice that their practices violated the Act"); Wilkerson v. Shinseki, 606 F. 3d 1256, 1268 (10th Cir. 2010) (standard not met where VA physician accessed plaintiff's medical records because physician testified that "he thought he could access the record so long as he had a 'need to know'" and, "given that [plaintiff's] health records were relevant to whether he could continue working at the VA, [that] belief was reasonable"); Powers v. U.S. Parole Comm'n, 296 F. App'x 86, 87 (D.C. Cir. 2008) (where plaintiff "claim[ed] only that the Commission acted 'intentionally'" in "'not maintain[ing] correct records'" and that "its 'negligence' violated his Privacy Act rights," his complaint "imputes at most 'gross negligence' to the Commission with regard to its maintenance and use of inaccurate records"); Puerta v. HHS, No. 99-55497, 2000 WL 863974, at *3 (9th Cir. June 28, 2000) (where agency, upon advice of its general counsel's office, disclosed documents in response to grand jury subpoena, agency "may have intentionally produced [the] documents, but it does not necessarily follow that [it] intentionally violated . . . the Privacy Act"); Scrimgeour v. IRS, 149 F.3d 318, 326 (4th Cir. 1998) (plaintiff did not "demonstrate the higher standard of culpability required for recovery under the Privacy Act" where court had already determined that IRS's release of his tax returns did not meet lower standard of gross negligence for recovery under provision of Internal Revenue Code); Deters v. U.S. Parole Comm'n, 85 F.3d 655, 660 (D.C. Cir. 1996) (Parole Commission did not "'flagrantly disregard'" plaintiff's privacy when it supplemented his file with rebuttal quantity of drugs attributed to him in presentence investigation report (PSI) and offered inmate hearing concerning accuracy of disputed report and "[e]ven if the Commission inadvertently or negligently violated [plaintiff's] Privacy Act rights by not examining the accuracy of the PSI before preparing a preliminary assessment . . . such a violation (if any) could in no sense be deemed 'patently egregious and unlawful'" (quoting Albright and Laningham, infra)); Bailey v. Clay, No. 95-7533, 1996 WL 155160, at *1 (4th Cir. Mar. 29, 1996) (stating that because appellant had alleged mere negligence, he had not stated claim under Privacy Act); Nathanson v. FDIC, No. 95-1604, 1996 U.S. App. LEXIS 3111, at *3-6 (1st Cir. Feb. 22, 1996) (per curiam) (although declining to affirm district court opinion on basis that disclosure pursuant to routine use was proper given that published agency commentary conflicted with such routine use, nevertheless affirming on grounds that disclosure was not intentional and willful because routine use "afforded reasonable grounds for belie[f] that [agency employee's] conduct was lawful"); Kellett v. BOP, No. 94-1898, 1995 U.S. App. LEXIS 26746, at *8-10 (1st Cir. Sept. 18, 1995) (per curiam) (standard requires "showing that the agency acted without grounds for believing its action to be lawful, or in 'flagrant disregard' for rights under the Act" (quoting Wilborn v. HHS, infra)); Rose v. United States, 905 F.2d 1257, 1260 (9th Cir. 1990) ("conduct amounting to more than gross negligence" is required); Johnston v. Horne, 875 F.2d 1415, 1422-23 (9th Cir. 1989) (same); Scullion v. VA, No. 87-2405, slip op. at 4-8 (7th Cir. June 22, 1988) (no damages where agency relied upon apparently valid and unrevoked written consent to disclose records); Andrews v. VA, 838 F.2d 418, 424-25 (10th Cir. 1988) (standard "clearly requires conduct amounting to more than gross negligence" and that "must amount to, at the very least, reckless behavior"); Reuber v. United States, 829 F.2d 133, 144 (D.C. Cir. 1987) (standard not met as no evidence showed maintenance of record "was anything other than a good-faith effort to preserve an unsolicited and possibly useful piece of information"); Laningham v. U.S. Navy, 813 F.2d 1236,

OVERVIEW OF THE PRIVACY ACT

1242-43 (D.C. Cir. 1987) (per curiam) (violation must be so "'patently egregious and unlawful'" that anyone undertaking the conduct "'should have known it unlawful'" (quoting Wisdom v. HUD, infra)); Hill v. U.S. Air Force, 795 F.2d 1067, 1070 (D.C. Cir. 1986) (per curiam) (no damages where no evidence of conduct greater than gross negligence); Moskiewicz v. USDA, 791 F.2d 561, 564 (7th Cir. 1986) (noting that "elements of recklessness often have been a key characteristic incorporated into a definition of willful and intentional conduct" (citing Sorenson v. United States, 521 F.2d 325 (9th Cir. 1975); South v. FBI, 508 F. Supp. 1104 (N.D. Ill. 1981))); Dowd v. IRS, 776 F.2d 1083, 1084 (2d Cir. 1985) (per curiam) ("mere administrative error" in negligently destroying files not a predicate for liability); Chapman v. NASA, 736 F.2d 238, 242-43 (5th Cir. 1984) (per curiam) (standard not met where agency "reasonably could have thought" untimely filing of evaluations was proper; "before our previous opinion 'timely' had no precise legal meaning in this circuit"); Albright v. United States, 732 F.2d 181, 189-90 (D.C. Cir. 1984) (standard requires that agency "act without grounds for believing it to be lawful, or by flagrantly disregarding others' rights under the Act"); Wisdom v. HUD, 713 F.2d 422, 424-25 (8th Cir. 1983) (good faith release of loan default records pursuant to unchallenged "Handbook" not willful violation of Act); Perry v. Block, 684 F.2d 121, 129 (D.C. Cir. 1982) (delayed disclosure of documents through administrative oversight not intentional or willful); Edison v. Dep't of the Army, 672 F.2d 840, 846 (11th Cir. 1982) (failure to prove agency acted "unreasonably" in maintaining records precludes finding intentional or willful conduct); Bruce v. United States, 621 F.2d 914, 917 (8th Cir. 1980) (standard not met where agency relied on regulations permitting disclosure of records pursuant to subpoena, as there were "at that time no regulations or other authority to the contrary"); Hurt v. D.C. Court Servs. & Offender Supervision Agency, No. 07-1167, 2011 WL 6098010, at *3-4 (D.D.C. Dec. 8, 2011) (standard not met where agency officials "believed that under [agency] policy they could disclose public information, such as the plaintiff's conviction, to a third party without running afoul of the Privacy Act"); Del Fuoco v. O'Neill, No. 8:09-CV-1262, 2011 WL 601645, at *10 (M.D. Fla. Feb. 11, 2011) ("DOJ's compliance with the regulation mandating disclosure to the [MSPB] effectively negates the requisite element of intent or willfulness for a Privacy Act claim, which did not require Plaintiff's consent, which is implied by virtue of his appeal."); Alexander v. FBI, 691 F. Supp. 2d 182, 191 (D.D.C. 2010) (standard not met where agency disclosed records in response to "facially ordinary requests submitted according to unchallenged procedures that had

OVERVIEW OF THE PRIVACY ACT

been in place for thirty years" and "pursuant to its unchallenged regulations"), aff'd per curiam on other grounds, 456 F. App'x 1 (D.C. Cir. 2011); Tungjunyatham v. Johanns, No. 1:06-cv-1764, 2009 WL 3823920, at *23 (E.D. Cal. Nov. 13, 2009) (where agency representative faxed to office of plaintiff's EEO representative records concerning plaintiff while latter representative was out of town and, as a result, "numerous agency employees had the chance to see the documents," standard not met "[i]n light of the two representatives' established practice of communication by [fax] in such a fashion"); Walker v. Gambrell, 647 F. Supp. 2d 529, 537-38 (D. Md. July 16, 2009) (alternative holding) (standard not met where plaintiff agency employee missed work due to a miscarriage, her husband called agency to inform office of reason for plaintiff's absence, employee who received call reacted in disruptive manner, and agency official sent e-mail to staff regarding miscarriage to inform it of reason for disruption; "disclosure may show negligence or a lack of tact and sensitivity; however, evidence of negligence is not sufficient to show that the agency acted willfully or intentionally"); Baptiste v. BOP, 585 F. Supp. 2d 133, 135 (D.D.C. 2008) (concluding that ICE's failure to confirm receipt of a faxed notice regarding plaintiff's citizenship is no worse than negligence); Trice v. U.S. Parole Comm'n, 530 F. Supp. 2d 213, 215 (D.D.C. 2008) ("Although plaintiff disagreed with the victim's version of the circumstances surrounding the assault, he was able to provide his version of events at the revocation hearing. Plaintiff therefore cannot demonstrate to a reasonable fact finder that the Commission acted with the requisite level of intent [by considering only plaintiff's version.]"); Mulhern v. Gates, 525 F. Supp. 2d 174, 185-86 (D.D.C. 2007) (holding inadvertent disclosure "while attempting to assist plaintiff" not sufficient to satisfy standard); Elliott v. BOP, 521 F. Supp. 2d 41, 48 (D.D.C. 2007) (standard not met where BOP based plaintiff's designation on inaccurate presentence report because "BOP was [not] aware of any potential inaccuracy in [that] report"); Doe v. U.S. Dep't of Labor, 451 F. Supp. 2d 156, 176-80 (D.D.C. 2006) (ruling that agency's Internet posting of plaintiff's employee compensation appeal decision, which contained his name and detailed medical facts, was not willful and intentional because agency incorrectly believed that it was required by the FOIA and permitted by a routine use), vacated by settlement, 2007 WL 1321116 (D.D.C. Mar. 22, 2007); Cooper v. BOP, No. 02-1844, 2006 WL 751341, at *3-4 (D.D.C. Mar. 23, 2006) (concluding that plaintiff failed to show that BOP "either acted without grounds for believing its actions lawful, or flagrantly disregarded plaintiff's rights under the Privacy Act" where "[t]he record demonstrate[d] that BOP staff acted on plaintiff's claims by contacting the author of the [presentence report]"); Thompson v. Dep't of State, 400 F. Supp. 2d 1, 12-13 (D.D.C. 2005) (standard not met in subsection (e)(2) claim where agency "assumed that it would be appropriate to correspond with [plaintiff's doctor] about [plaintiff's] medical condition" because "it was plaintiff's doctor who made the first contact with the [agency], offering unsolicited medical information on plaintiff's behalf"); Pontecorvo v. FBI, No. 00-1511, slip op. at 4, 10-15 (D.D.C. Mar. 5, 2004) (finding that the "greater than gross negligence" standard was not met where an FBI Special Agent disclosed information about plaintiff's prior arrest and altercation in the course of conducting background interviews, and stating that the "disclosures that occurred . . . were intended to ferret out potentially relevant information about Plaintiff's suitability for a security clearance"); Wiley v. VA, 176 F. Supp. 2d 747, 756-57 (E.D. Mich. 2001) (Even if the agency violated the Privacy Act by disclosing a VA claims file to an employer pursuant to a broadly written release, the agency's actions were not "beyond grossly negligent," as "reasonable minds clearly could differ on the scope of the release," and thus the agency's reliance on it "cannot be deemed wholly groundless."); Mallory v. DOD, No. 97-2377, slip op. at 9-14 (D.D.C. Sept. 30, 1999) (although DOD disclosure of record of plaintiff's rifle purchase to corporation was unlawful, intentional and willful standard was not met because statute gave DOD officials grounds to believe that transfer of such records was implicitly required by statute); Wesley v. Don Stein Buick, Inc., 985 F. Supp. 1288, 1305-06 (D. Kan. 1997) (standard not met where, although disclosure was "unlawful," employee acted with belief that disclosure was proper, and it would have been proper if procedures set forth in routine use had been followed); Armstrong v. BOP, 976 F. Supp. 17, 22 (D.D.C. 1997) (standard not met where Bureau of Prisons refused to amend prison records to incorporate favorable information from inmate's prior incarceration in accordance with Bureau of Prisons guidelines), summary affirmance granted, Armstrong v. BOP, No. 97-5208, 1998 WL 65543 (D.C. Cir. Jan. 30, 1998); Porter v. USPS, No. CV595-30, slip op. at 10, 13, 21-22 (S.D. Ga. July 24, 1997) (concluding that Postal Service acted with "mere negligence" when it disclosed letter from plaintiff's attorney written as response to plaintiff's proposed termination to two union officials with belief that they had "a right and duty to know the disciplinary affairs of a fellow postal worker" even though plaintiff had not filed a grievance through union and "had specifically instructed the management that he did not want anyone from the [union] representing his interests"), aff'd, 166 F.3d 352 (11th Cir. 1998) (unpublished table decision);

OVERVIEW OF THE PRIVACY ACT

Harris v. USDA, No. 3:92CV-283-H, slip op. at 1-2, 4-5 (W.D. Ky. May 14, 1996) (standard not met where agency acted pursuant to Correspondence Management Handbook in maintaining supporting documentation for plaintiff's 1975 suspension), aff'd, 124 F.3d 197 (6th Cir. 1997) (unpublished table decision); Purrier v. HHS, No. 95-CV-6203, slip op. at 6-7 (W.D.N.Y. Mar. 15, 1996) ("given [defendant's] knowledge that she was subject to a grand jury subpoena," disclosure of limited information "even if [it] did violate the Act (which, with respect to plaintiff at least, [it] did not), fell far short of the kind of flagrant disregard of plaintiff's rights that is required"); Smith v. BOP, No. 94-1798, 1996 WL 43556, at *2 (D.D.C. Jan. 31, 1996) (standard not met where adverse determination had been rectified; fact that certain forms were corrected immediately, even though another form may not have been, "indicates that BOP officials did not intend to maintain plaintiff[']s records incorrectly"); Henson v. Brown, No. 95-213, slip op. at 5-7 (D. Md. June 23, 1995) (disclosure of medical records in response to subpoena signed by judge to attorney for plaintiff's ex-wife, rather than to court, did not "constitute an extreme departure from the standard of ordinary care"); Baitey v. VA, No. 8:CV89-706, slip op. at 8 (D. Neb. June 21, 1995) (standard not met where plaintiff failed to prove that VA acted in "flagrant or reckless disregard of [plaintiff's] rights under the Privacy Act" when it disclosed his medical records in response to incomplete and unsigned medical authorization); Olivares v. NASA, 882 F. Supp. 1545, 1549-50 (D. Md. 1995) (NASA's actions in contacting educational institutions to verify and correct discrepancies in plaintiff's record, even assuming initial consent to contact those institutions was limited, were not even negligent and do not "come close" to meeting standard), aff'd, 103 F.3d 119 (4th Cir. 1996) (unpublished table decision); Webb v. Magaw, 880 F. Supp. 20, 25 (D.D.C. 1995) (stating that even if court had found Privacy Act violation, agency conduct "at worst . . . would only amount to negligence . . . and would not amount to willful, intentional or even reckless disregard"); Sterling v. United States, 826 F. Supp. 570, 572 (D.D.C. 1993) (standard not met where agency's "efforts both before and after the release of information . . . indicate a sensitivity to the potential harm the release might cause and represent attempts to avert that harm"), summary affirmance granted, No. 93-5264 (D.C. Cir. Mar. 11, 1994); Dickson v. OPM, No. 83-3503, 1991 WL 423968, at *16-17 (D.D.C. Aug. 27, 1991) ("mere negligence" due to failure to follow internal guidelines not enough to show willfulness), summary affirmance granted, No. 91-5363 (D.C. Cir. Aug. 31, 1992); Stephens v. TVA, 754 F. Supp. 579, 582 (E.D. Tenn. 1990) (no damages where "some authority" existed

OVERVIEW OF THE PRIVACY ACT

for proposition that retrieval not initially and directly from system of records was not a "disclosure," and agency attempted to sanitize disclosed records); Brumley v. U.S. Dep't of Labor, No. 87-2220, 1990 WL 640002, at *2-3 (D.D.C. Dec. 5, 1990) (no damages for delayed response to amendment request); Alexander v. IRS, No. 86-0414, 1987 WL 13958, at *6 (D.D.C. June 30, 1987) (standard not met where agency relied on OMB Guidelines and internal manual in interviewing third parties prior to contacting plaintiff); Blanton v. DOJ, No. 82-0452, slip op. at 6-8 (D.D.C. Feb. 17, 1984) (unauthorized "leak" of record not intentional or willful agency conduct); Krohn v. DOJ, No. 78-1536, slip op. at 3-7 (D.D.C. Nov. 29, 1984) (standard not met where agency relied in good faith on previously unchallenged routine use to publicly file records with court); Daniels v. St. Louis VA Reg'l Office, 561 F. Supp. 250, 252 (E.D. Mo. 1983) (mere delay in disclosure due in part to plaintiff's failure to pay fees not intentional or willful); Doe v. GSA, 544 F. Supp. 530, 541-42 (D. Md. 1982) (disclosure not "wholly unreasonable" where "some kind of consent" given for release of psychiatric records and where agency employees believed that release was authorized under GSA's interpretation of its own guidelines, even though court concluded that such interpretation was erroneous); cf. Stokes v. Barnhart, 257 F. Supp. 2d 288, 299-300 (D. Me. 2003) (rejecting argument that leave to amend complaint would be futile because employee who made disclosure did not believe that her conduct violated any law or regulation, and, citing Andrews and Albright, stating that employee's "belief does not establish that anyone engaging in the same conduct should not have known that the conduct was unlawful or that it did not constitute flagrant disregard for the plaintiff's rights under the Act, if any").

In the context of a claim for unlawful disclosure, several courts have ruled that a plaintiff cannot show intentional or willful conduct without identifying the individual or individuals who disclosed the information. See, e.g., Convertino v. DOJ, 769 F. Supp. 2d 139, 146 (D.D.C. 2011) ("To meet the Privacy Act's high standard for a showing of willfulness or intentionality, [plaintiff] must know the leaker's identity. . . . [L]acking any evidence of the leaker's identity, no reasonable fact-finder could find that DOJ acted willfully or intentionally with regard to any leak in this case."), rev'd and remanded on other grounds, No. 11-5133, 2012 WL 2362591 (D.C. Cir. June 22, 2012) (reversing district court's summary judgment and ruling that district court committed abuse of discretion in denying appellant's motion to stay summary judgment to allow for further discovery to determine leaker's identity); Paige v. DEA, 818 F. Supp.

OVERVIEW OF THE PRIVACY ACT

2d 4, 14 (D.D.C. 2010) ("In order to prove that [the agency] acted willfully and intentionally, it is essential that Plaintiff identify the source of the disclosure."), aff'd, 665 F. 3d 1355 (D.C. Cir. 2012); Convertino v. DOJ, No. 07-cv-13842, 2008 WL 4104347, at *7 (E.D. Mich. Aug. 28, 2008) ("To establish that the DOJ committed a willful or intentional violation, [plaintiff] must present evidence of the disclosing person's state of mind, which requires him to identify and question those who perpetrated the allegedly improper disclosure."); cf. Lee v. DOJ, 413 F. 3d 53, 55, 60 (D.C. Cir. 2005) (upholding district court order "holding [journalists] in contempt of court for refusing to answer questions regarding confidential sources" because "[i]f [plaintiff] cannot show the identities of the leakers, [plaintiff's] ability to show the other elements of the Privacy Act claim, such as willfulness and intent, will be compromised"); Hatfill v. Gonzales, 505 F. Supp. 2d 33, 43 (D.D.C. 2007) (granting motion to compel reporters to disclose identity of individuals who disclosed information protected by Privacy Act because "the identity of DOJ and FBI sources will be an integral component of the plaintiff's attempt to prove the requisite agency mens rea").

Several district court decisions have found "intentional or willful" violations of the statute. See, e.g., Carlson v. GSA, No. 04-C-7937, 2006 WL 3409150, at *5 (N.D. Ill. Nov. 21, 2006) (e-mail sent by agency employee's supervisor to other agency personnel and to individuals outside agency regarding plaintiff's termination settlement agreement, which included "unnecessary details concerning [employee's] personal information" and which supervisor encouraged recipients to disseminate); Johnson v. BOP, No. 03-2047, slip op. at 11-12 (D. Colo. June 17, 2005) (statements made by BOP health systems specialist in violation of BOP regulations and policy regarding medical privacy); Doe v. Herman, No. 297CV00043, 1999 WL 1000212, at *1, *13-14 (W.D. Va. Oct. 29, 1999) (magistrate's recommendation) (unnecessary disclosure of claimant's social security number on multi-captioned hearing form to twenty other claimants, coal companies, and insurance companies), adopted in pertinent part & rev'd in other part, 2000 WL 34204432 (W.D. Va. July 24, 2000), aff'd in part, rev'd in part, & remanded, on other grounds sub nom. Doe v. Chao, 306 F.3d 170 (4th Cir. 2002), aff'd, 540 U.S. 614 (2004); Stewart v. FBI, No. 97-1595, slip op. at 5-8 (D. Or. Mar. 12, 1999) (violations of subsections (b) and (e)(6) based on dissemination of an incorrect report containing criminal allegations concerning plaintiff), withdrawn by stipulation as part of settlement, 2000 WL 739253 (D. Or. May 12, 2000); Tomasello v. Rubin, No. 93-1326, slip op. at 17-19 (D.D.C. Aug. 19, 1997) (disclosure to "60

OVERVIEW OF THE PRIVACY ACT

Minutes" and all 4,500 ATF employees of details concerning plaintiff's EEO complaint), aff'd on other grounds, 167 F.3d 612 (D.C. Cir. 1999); Porter, No. CV595-30, slip op. at 22-23 (S.D. Ga. July 24, 1997) (disclosure by Postmaster to USPS personnel who had no "need to know" of plaintiff's two-week suspension for impersonating a postal inspector); Romero-Vargas v. Shalala, 907 F. Supp. 1128, 1133-34 (N.D. Ohio 1995) (telephonic verification or non-verification of plaintiffs' social security number provided by agency to their employers in violation of regulations and agency employee manual); Louis v. VA, No. C95-5606, slip op. at 4-5 (W.D. Wash. Oct. 31, 1996) (failure to remove record as required and use of that record in subsequent determination); Swenson v. USPS, No. S-87-1282, 1994 U.S. Dist. LEXIS 16524, at *33-45 (E.D. Cal. Mar. 10, 1994) (disclosure to Members of Congress, who were seeking to assist constituent with complaint regarding rural mail delivery, of irrelevant information concerning plaintiff's EEO complaints and grievances); Connelly v. Comptroller of the Currency, No. H-84-3783, slip op. at 25-27 (S.D. Tex. June 3, 1991) (violation of subsection (e)(5) by disapproving of plaintiff's appointment as president of a new bank without first obtaining evaluations of prominent bankers who knew plaintiff); MacDonald v. VA, No. 87-544-CIV-T-15A, slip op. at 4, 7 (M.D. Fla. July 28, 1989) (disclosure of "counseling memorandum" to plaintiff's employer "with malicious intent and with the purpose to injure Plaintiff"); Fitzpatrick v. IRS, 1 Gov't Disclosure Serv. (P-H) ¶ 80,232, at 80,580 (N.D. Ga. Aug. 22, 1980) (disclosure to plaintiff's co-workers and former co-worker that he had retired for "mental" reasons, even though purpose of disclosure was to "quell[] rumors and gossip"), aff'd in part, vacated & remanded in part, on other grounds, 655 F.2d 327 (11th Cir. 1982). Cf. Feldman v. CIA, 797 F. Supp. 2d 29, 40 (D.D.C. 2011) (finding that "plaintiff adequately alleged intentional or willful conduct at this stage of the litigation" and denying agency's motion to dismiss); McCullough v. BOP, No. 1:06-cv-00563, 2010 WL 5136133, at *6-7 (E.D. Cal. Dec. 6, 2010) (magistrate's recommendation) ("Plaintiff's allegation that [BOP] employees falsified reports and his central file and used those records to convict him of a rule violation is sufficient to state a cognizable claim against [BOP]."), adopted 2010 WL 5476701 (E.D. Cal. Dec. 29, 2010); Tolbert-Smith v. Chu, 714 F. Supp. 2d 37, 43-44 (D.D.C. 2010) (declining to dismiss allegation that agency employee "placed records referring and relating to [plaintiff's] disability on a server accessible by other federal employees and members of the public . . . to retaliate against her for filing an administrative complaint"); Doe v. Goss, No. 04-2122, 2007 WL 106523, at *12 (D.D.C. Jan. 12,

OVERVIEW OF THE PRIVACY ACT

2007) ("If proven, Defendants' calculated recording of false information pursuant to these allegedly sham investigations would certainly meet <u>Deters</u>' definition of willful or intentional conduct.").

As yet, however, only two courts of appeals have found "intentional or willful" violations of the statute – the Court of Appeals for the Sixth Circuit and the Court of Appeals for the Ninth Circuit. See Beaven v. DOJ, 622 F.3d 540, 547-53 (6th Cir. 2010); Louis v. U.S. Dep't of Labor, 19 F. App'x 487, 488-89 (9th Cir. 2001); Wilborn v. HHS, 49 F.3d 597, 602-03 (9th Cir. 1995); Covert v. Harrington, 876 F.2d 751, 756-57 (9th Cir. 1989); cf. Oja v. U.S. Army Corps of Engineers, 440 F.3d 1122, 1136 (9th Cir. 2006) (concluding that "it was clear . . . that the [agency's] disclosures were intentional or willful" where agency posted information about former employee on its Web site, but dismissing claim as untimely). But see generally Downie v. City of Middleburg Hts., 301 F.3d 688, 697-99 (6th Cir. 2002) (in course of ruling that remedial scheme of Privacy Act barred Bivens action, citing Toolasprashad, infra, and stating that "[w]hile the Privacy Act does not provide a <u>separate</u> damages remedy for the intentional or willful creation, maintenance, or dissemination of false records in retaliation for an individual's First Amendment rights, we believe that retaliation on any basis clearly constitutes intentional or willful action"); Toolasprashad v. BOP, 286 F.3d 576, 584 (D.C. Cir. 2002) (remanding case where district court had found that record would not support finding of intentional and willful action, and stating that, "[i]f proven, retaliatory fabrication of prison records would certainly meet [our] definition [as articulated in Deters] of a willful or intentional Privacy Act violation").

In <u>Beaven</u>, a group of individuals employed by the Bureau of Prisons sued the agency for unlawful disclosure after a BOP investigator left an "employee roster" containing their "sensitive personal information" on a desk in an area to which prisoners had access. See 622 F.3d at 544-45. The district court had "found that [the investigator's] <u>course of conduct</u> resulted in a disclosure under the Privacy Act . . . and that his actions were 'intentional or willful' within the meaning of § 552a(g)(4), although his <u>final act</u> of leaving the folder unsecured was 'inadvertent.'" 622 F.3d at 547; see Beaven v. DOJ, No. 03-84, 2007 WL 1032301, at *2, *14-17 (E.D. Ky. Mar. 30, 2007) (noting that investigator "was aware of the security guidelines and the importance of maintaining the confidentiality of sensitive information"; that investigator made "conscious decision to ignore the risks associated with bringing unmarked confidential information into an area to which inmates have access," which "was

OVERVIEW OF THE PRIVACY ACT

in flagrant disregard for [the plaintiffs'] right to protect that information from improper disclosure"; and that "[a]lthough leaving the folder unsecured on [the] desk was inadvertent, [the investigator's] failure to account for the potential for human error and minimize the potential harm from such possible errors demonstrates flagrant disregard for the plaintiffs' rights under the Privacy Act"). Thus, the Court of Appeals for the Sixth Circuit framed the "main issue" as "whether the requirement under § 552a(g)(4) that the district court find that 'the agency acted in a manner which was intentional or willful' requires the court to find that the final act that resulted in the disclosure was 'intentional or willful' or whether the court may find that the entire course of conduct that resulted in the disclosure was 'intentional or willful.'" 622 F.3d at 547. In holding the latter to be correct, the Sixth Circuit pointed out that "[n]o court has specifically interpreted § 552a(g)(4) in the light this panel must address" but observed, after reviewing the case law, that courts "in determining whether a Privacy Act violation occurred have not differentiated between the final act and the course of action that results in the final act, but rather courts generally look to the entire course of conduct in context." Id. at 548-50. The Sixth Circuit went on to conclude that "the facts in the instant case support[] the district court's conclusion" and that the district court "did not commit clear error in finding that [the investigator's] course of conduct was 'willful.'" Id. at 552. In support of this conclusion, the court noted that the investigator "carried the folder, which he knew contain[ed] confidential and sensitive information, into an inmate-accessible work area for the purpose of carrying out his own investigative work should he need to call a . . . computer administrator at home. Yet the roster [in the folder] not only listed the home telephone numbers of . . . computer administrators but also included detailed private and personal information related to all [of the prison facility] employees"; and that the roster was not marked "[Limited Official Use]-Sensitive," as required by a BOP Program Statement, among other violations of BOP policy. Id. The Court went on to state that the investigator's "need for some of the information . . . did not provide a legitimate basis for him to have the entire contents of the folder with him at the time" and that his "course of conduct that resulted in his having the unmarked file in an inmate-accessible area . . . could properly be viewed as 'the intentional or willful failure of the agency to abide by the Act.'" Id. at 552-53.

In Louis, the plaintiff had sought reconsideration of the denial of his claim for Federal Employees Compensation benefits by the

OVERVIEW OF THE PRIVACY ACT

Department of Labor. See 19 F. App'x at 488. In denying the plaintiff's request for reconsideration, the Department of Labor's rationale indicated that it had considered the entirety of its prior decision, including a portion of that prior decision that impermissibly relied on a memorandum that had been the subject of prior litigation by the plaintiff. See id.; see also Louis v. Dep't of Labor, No. C99-5195, slip op. at 1-2 (W.D. Wash. Oct. 15, 1999), aff'd in part, rev'd in part & remanded sub nom. Louis v. U.S. Dep't of Labor, 19 F. App'x 487 (9th Cir. 2001); Louis v. Dep't of Labor, No. C97-5521 (W.D. Wash. Feb. 27, 1998) (magistrate's recommendation), adopted (W.D. Wash. Mar. 23, 1998); Louis v. VA, No. C95-5606 (W.D. Wash. Oct. 31, 1996). Specifically, the district court in a prior action had ordered that the agency "destroy all but one known copy of the document" and that it "maintain that single copy in a sealed envelope to be revealed to no person, agency, or entity." Louis v. Dep't of Labor, No. C97-5521, slip op. at 3 (W.D. Wash. Feb. 27, 1998). The Ninth Circuit ruled that the Department of Labor violated the Privacy Act when it failed "to maintain its records in such a way as to indicate to the claims examiner that it could not rely on [that memorandum] in reviewing Louis' request for reconsideration." 19 F. App'x at 489. The court stated that the agency's "disregard of both the district court's prior decision rendering reliance on [the memorandum] impermissible and its own assurance that it would annotate the memo in its files 'to reflect that it was not to be considered in any future action related to Dr. Louis' claim' constitutes a willful failure on the part of the government to abide by its obligations, and proximately resulted in the government's refusal to reconsider its earlier decision, thereby adversely affecting [plaintiff]." Id.

In Wilborn, the plaintiff, an attorney who previously had been employed by the Department of Health and Human Services, sought damages under the Privacy Act for the disclosure of adverse personnel information about him that was disclosed in an opinion by an Administrative Law Judge before whom he had presented a case. 49 F.3d at 599-602. The court ruled that the "uncontroverted facts plainly establish that the ALJ disclosed the information . . . without any ground for believing it to be lawful and in flagrant disregard of the rights of Wilborn under the Privacy Act." Id. at 602. The Ninth Circuit noted that not only was the ALJ personally familiar with the Privacy Act and had advised his staff concerning the Act's disclosure prohibition, but further, that the ALJ had been informed by an agency attorney that the language at issue was "inappropriate and should not be included in the decision." Id. Particularly troubling in this case is

OVERVIEW OF THE PRIVACY ACT

the additional fact that all information pertaining to the adverse personnel record was required to, and in fact had been, removed from the system of records by the ALJ as a result of a grievance action filed by the plaintiff. Id.

In Covert, the Ninth Circuit ruled that the Department of Energy Inspector General's routine use disclosure of prosecutive reports, showing possible criminal fraud, to the Justice Department violated subsection (e)(3)(C) because, at the time of their original collection by another component of the agency, portions of those reports – consisting of personnel security questionnaires submitted by the plaintiffs – did not provide actual notice of the routine use. 876 F.2d 751, 754-57 (9th Cir. 1989). The Ninth Circuit held that the failure to comply with subsection (e)(3)(C) was "greater than grossly negligent" even though the Inspector General was relying on statutes, regulations and disclosure practices that appeared to permit disclosure, and no prior court had ever suggested that noncompliance with subsection (e)(3)(C) would render a subsequent subsection (b)(3) routine use disclosure improper. See id. Though it paid lip service to the correct standard, the Ninth Circuit in Covert actually applied a strict liability standard – one based upon the government's failure to anticipate its novel "linkage" between subsection (e)(3)(C) and subsection (b)(3) – a standard which markedly departs from settled precedent. Compare Covert, 876 F.2d at 756-57, with Chapman, 736 F.2d at 243, Wisdom, 713 F.2d at 424-25, and Bruce, 621 F.2d at 917. See also Doe v. Stephens, 851 F.2d 1457, 1462 (D.C. Cir. 1988) ("We cannot, in short, fairly predicate negligence liability on the basis of the VA's failure to predict the precise statutory interpretation that led this court in [Doe v. DiGenova, 779 F.2d 74, 79-85 (D.C. Cir. 1985)] to reject the agency's reliance on the [law indicating that a subpoena constituted a subsection (b)(11) court order].").

The Court of Appeals for the Third Circuit has held that the Privacy Act – with its stringent "greater than gross negligence" standard for liability – does not indicate a congressional intent to limit an individual's right under state law to recover damages caused by the merely negligent disclosure of a psychiatric report. See O'Donnell v. United States, 891 F.2d 1079, 1083-87 (3d Cir. 1989) (Federal Tort Claims Act case). But see Hager v. United States, No. 86-3555, slip op. at 7-8 (N.D. Ohio Oct. 20, 1987) (Privacy Act preempts FTCA action alleging wrongful disclosure); cf. Doe v. DiGenova, 642 F. Supp. 624, 629-30, 632 (D.D.C. 1986) (holding state law/FTCA claim preempted by Veterans' Records Statute, 38 U.S.C. §§ 3301-

OVERVIEW OF THE PRIVACY ACT

3302 (renumbered as 38 U.S.C. §§ 5701-5702 (2006))), aff'd in pertinent part, rev'd in part & remanded sub nom. Doe v. Stephens, 851 F.2d 1457 (D.C. Cir. 1988).

2. **Actual Damages**

Assuming that a Privacy Act plaintiff can show: (1) a violation; (2) an adverse effect; (3) causation; and (4) intentional or willful agency conduct, then "actual damages sustained by the [plaintiff are recoverable], but in no case shall a person [who is] entitled to recovery receive less than the sum of $1,000." 5 U.S.C. § 552a(g)(4)(A).

The Court of Appeals for the District of Columbia Circuit has ruled that a plaintiff was not entitled to $1000 for each copy of a letter that was disclosed in violation of the Privacy Act to 4500 individuals. See Tomasello v. Rubin, 167 F.3d 612, 617-18 (D.C. Cir. 1999). The D.C. Circuit stated that "[w]hile it may be linguistically possible to read the language [of § 552a(g)(4)] so as to forbid the aggregation of several more-or-less contemporaneous transmissions of the same record into one 'act[]' or 'failure [to comply with the Privacy Act],' the result [sought in this case] shows that such a reading defies common sense." Id. at 618. In reaching its determination "that each letter disclosure was not independently compensable," the D.C. Circuit also reasoned that as a waiver of sovereign immunity, subsection (g)(4) "'must be construed strictly in favor of the sovereign, and not enlarge[d] . . . beyond what the language requires.'" Id. (quoting United States v. Nordic Vill., Inc., 503 U.S. 30, 34 (1992)); cf. Siddiqui v. United States, 359 F.3d 1200, 1201-03 (9th Cir. 2004) (non-Privacy Act case, finding that disclosure of tax information by IRS agent to 100 people in one room at one time constituted one act of disclosure for purposes of determining statutory damages under Internal Revenue Code).

The issue of what needs to be shown in order to recover damages under subsection (g)(4)(A) historically had engendered some inconsistent and confusing case law. See, e.g., Orekoya v. Mooney, 330 F.3d 1, 7-8 (1st Cir. 2003) (holding that "statutory damages [of $1000], if not actual damages, are available to individuals who suffer adverse effects from intentional and willful violations of the act and that provable emotional distress may constitute an adverse effect"); Wilborn v. HHS, 49 F.3d 597, 603 (9th Cir. 1995) (seemingly not requiring "proven injuries"; finding no need to remand to district court for determination of amount of damages because plaintiff had limited damages sought to statutory minimum); Quinn v. Stone, 978 F.2d 126, 135 (3d Cir. 1992) (stating that subsection (g)(1)(D) "gives an individual adversely affected by any agency violation of the Act a judicial remedy whereby the individual may seek damages"); Waters v. Thornburg, 888 F.2d 870, 872 (D.C. Cir. 1989) (stating that to obtain relief under the Privacy Act plaintiff must establish that (1) the agency violated a provision of the Act; "(2) the violation of the Act was 'intentional or willful,'" and "(3) this action had an 'adverse effect' on the plaintiff" and that "[i]f these three factors are satisfied, the plaintiff is entitled to the greater of $1,000 or the actual damages sustained"); Johnson v. Dep't of Treasury, IRS, 700 F.2d 971, 977 & n.12, 986 (5th Cir. 1983) (recognizing entitlement to statutory minimum for proven physical and mental injuries even if "actual damages" were interpreted to include only pecuniary harm, but going on to hold that "actual damages" includes "proven mental and physical injuries"); Fitzpatrick v. IRS, 665 F.2d 327, 329-31 (11th Cir. 1982) (awarding statutory minimum $1000 damages, but denying recovery beyond the statutory minimum because "appellant proved only that he suffered a general mental injury"). See generally OMB Guidelines, 40 Fed. Reg. 28,948, 28,970 (July 9, 1975), available at http://www.whitehouse.gov/sites/default/files/omb/ assets/omb/inforeg/implementation_guidelines.pdf (stating that "[a]ctual damages or $1,000, whichever is greater," are/is recoverable (emphasis added)).

However, in issuing its first purely Privacy Act decision in the history of the Act, the Supreme Court in Doe v. Chao resolved much of the confusion in this area. 540 U.S. 614 (2004) (6-3 decision), aff'g 306 F.3d 170 (4th Cir. 2002). In Doe, the Supreme Court was petitioned to review a decision by the Court of Appeals for the Fourth Circuit in which a divided panel of the Fourth Circuit held that in order to be entitled to a statutory minimum damages award for violation of the Privacy Act, a complainant must prove actual damages. Doe v. Chao, 306 F.3d at 177-79. Recognizing that the Fourth Circuit's opinion in Doe "conflicted with the views of other Circuits," 540 U.S. at 614 (citing Orekoya, Wilborn, Waters, Johnson, and Fitzpatrick), the Supreme Court granted certiorari. The majority conducted "a straightforward textual analysis," looked to the Privacy Act's legislative history, and ultimately concluded that the Fourth Circuit's view was correct. Id. at 620-29. The Court held that the "'entitle[ment] to recovery' necessary to qualify for the $1,000 minimum is not shown merely by an intentional or willful violation of the Act producing some adverse effect. The statute guarantees $1,000 only to plaintiffs who have suffered some actual damages."

Id. at 627 (alteration in original). As a result, any prior case law that suggests that anything less than proven actual damages is sufficient to entitle an individual to an award of the statutory minimum $1000 damages has been abrogated. Cf., e.g., Pinkney v. VA, No. 1:07-CV-00142, 2008 WL 4272749, at *5-6 (S.D. Ohio Sept. 11, 2008) (stating that "the Supreme Court in Doe carefully reviewed the statutory language and legislative history and held that the minimum guarantee goes only to victims who prove some actual damages").

Although as a result of the Supreme Court's decision in Doe v. Chao it is now settled that proof of actual damages is required in order to recover either the statutory minimum or damages beyond the minimum, and it is well established that actual damages include out-of-pocket expenses, the Supreme Court in Doe explicitly did not rule on the issue of whether nonpecuniary damages for mental injury – such as emotional trauma, anger, fear, or fright – satisfy the definition of actual damages. Doe v. Chao, 540 U.S. at 627 n.12 (noting division amongst Courts of Appeal on "the precise definition of actual damages," and stating that "[t]hat issue is not before us, however, since the petition for certiorari did not raise it for our review"; "We do not suggest that out-of-pocket expenses are necessary for recovery of the $1,000 minimum; only that they suffice to qualify under any view of actual damages.") Until the Supreme Court answered this question eight years later in FAA v. Cooper, 132 S. Ct. 1441 (2012), discussed below, lower courts were divided on the issue. Compare, e.g., Jacobs v. Nat'l Drug Intelligence Ctr., 548 F.3d 375, 378 (5th Cir. 2008) (following Johnson and holding that emotional damages are recoverable); Johnson v. Dep't of the Treasury, IRS, 700 F.2d at 974-80 (nonpecuniary damages recoverable); Parks v. IRS, 618 F.2d 677, 682-83, 685 (10th Cir. 1980) (stating that plaintiffs had "alleged viable claims for damages" where only alleged adverse effect was "psychological harm"); Mulhern v. Gates, 525 F. Supp. 2d 174, 186 (D.D.C. 2007) ("To defeat a motion for summary judgment, a plaintiff must offer evidence sufficient for a jury to find that the emotional harm he claims to have suffered was acute, tangible, and severe enough to give rise to actual damages."); Papse v. BIA, No. 99-0052, 2007 WL 1189369, at *2 (D. Idaho Apr. 20, 2007) (concluding that "the term 'actual damages' in the Privacy Act includes damages for emotional distress"); Boyd v. Snow, 335 F. Supp. 2d 28, 38-39 (D.D.C. 2004) (allowing claims of actual damages that included "severe emotional and physical harm, stress, sleeplessness and nightmares" to be proven at trial); Dong v. Smithsonian Inst., 943 F. Supp. 69, 74-75 (D.D.C. Oct. 31, 1996) (following Johnson and awarding damages for injury

OVERVIEW OF THE PRIVACY ACT

to reputation), rev'd on grounds of statutory inapplicability, 125 F.3d 877 (D.C. Cir. 1997) (ruling that "Smithsonian is not an agency for Privacy Act purposes"); Louis v. VA, No. C95-5606, slip op. at 5 (W.D. Wash. Oct. 31, 1996) (awarding damages for "emotional suffering"); Swenson v. USPS, No. S-87-1282, 1994 U.S. Dist. LEXIS 16524, at *46-52 (E.D. Cal. Mar. 10, 1994) (following Johnson); and Kassel v. VA, No. 87-217-S, slip op. at 38 (D.N.H. Mar. 30, 1992) (same); with Fanin v. VA, 572 F.3d 868, 872 (11th Cir. 2009) (following Fitzpatrick in requiring pecuniary losses), cert. denied sub nom. Perkins v. VA, 130 S. Ct. 1755 (2010); Mitchell v. VA, 310 F. App'x 351, 353-54 (11th Cir. 2009) (same); Hudson v. Reno, 130 F.3d 1193, 1207 & n.11 (6th Cir. 1997) (citing plaintiff's failure to show "actual damages" as additional basis for affirming district court decision and stating that "the weight of authority suggests that actual damages under the Privacy Act do not include recovery for 'mental injuries, loss of reputation, embarrassment or other non-quantifiable injuries'" (citing Fitzpatrick)); Fitzpatrick, 665 F.2d at 329-31 (damages for generalized mental injuries, loss of reputation, embarrassment or other nonquantifiable injuries not recoverable); Wiley v. VA, 176 F. Supp. 2d 747, 757 (E.D. Mich. 2001) (citing Hudson and stating that even if there had been violation of Privacy Act, evidence "consisting solely of claimed emotional injuries, does not suffice"); Mallory v. DOD, No. 97-2377, slip op. at 15-16 n.3 (D.D.C. Sept. 30, 1999) (holding that actual damages limited to out-of-pocket losses); Gowan v. Dep't of the Air Force, No. 90-94, slip op. at 31 (D.N.M. Sept. 1, 1995) (adopting analysis of DiMura, infra, that emotional damages would not be recoverable), aff'd, 148 F.3d 1182 (10th Cir. 1998); DiMura v. FBI, 823 F. Supp. 45, 47-48 (D. Mass. 1993) ("'actual damages' does not include emotional damages"); Pope v. Bond, 641 F. Supp. 489, 500-01 (D.D.C. 1986) (only out-of-pocket expenses recoverable); and Houston v. U.S. Dep't of Treasury, 494 F. Supp. 24, 30 (D.D.C. 1979) (same). See generally Doe v. Chao, 306 F.3d at 181-82 (where plaintiff "did not produce any evidence of tangible consequences stemming from his alleged angst over the disclosure of his [social security number]" to corroborate his "conclusory allegations" of emotional distress, finding that plaintiff had "utterly failed to produce evidence sufficient to permit a rational trier of fact to conclude that he suffered any 'actual damages,'" and thus stating that "we need not reach the issue of whether the term 'actual damages' as used in the Act encompasses damages for non-pecuniary emotional distress because, regardless of the disposition of that issue, [appellant's] claims fail for lack of evidentiary support"); Doe v. Chao, 306 F.3d at 198 n.13 (Michael, J., dissenting) (also "need[ing] not reach the difficult question of the meaning of 'actual damages,'" but stating "belie[f] that the majority's holding commits this circuit to the position that the term 'actual damages' includes at least emotional distress that would qualify as 'demonstrable' under Price [v. City of Charlotte, 93 F.3d 1241 (4th Cir. 1996)]").

In Cooper, the Supreme Court settled this confusion by "adopt[ing] an interpretation of 'actual damages' limited to proven pecuniary or economic harm." 132 S. Ct. at 1453; see also Iqbal v. FBI, No. 3:11-cv-369, 2012 WL 2366634, at *6 (M.D. Fla. June 21, 2012) (citing Cooper and dismissing plaintiff's subsection (e)(7) claim as plaintiff's contention that he "suffered severe mental and emotional distress as a result of his treatment by the FBI . . . cannot be recovered under the Privacy Act"). The plaintiff in Cooper had alleged that the agency's "unlawful disclosure . . . of his confidential medical information, including his HIV status, had caused him 'humiliation, embarrassment, mental anguish, fear of social ostracism, and other severe emotional distress,'" but he "did not allege any pecuniary or economic loss." Id. at 1447. In framing the issue, the Court stated: "Because respondent seeks to recover monetary compensation from the Government for mental and emotional harm, we must decide whether the civil remedies provision of the Privacy Act waives the Government's sovereign immunity with respect to such a recovery." Id. at 1448. The Court explained that any ambiguities in the scope of the waiver must be construed "in favor of the sovereign." Id. In reaching its conclusion, the Court first observed that "'actual damages' is a legal term of art" that has a "chameleon-like quality" because its "precise meaning . . . 'changes with the specific statute in which it is found.'" Id. at 1449, 1450. The Court also picked up on its observation in Doe v. Chao, see 540 U.S. at 625-26, that the civil remedies provision "'parallels' the remedial scheme for the common-law torts of libel per quod and slander, under which plaintiffs can recover 'general damages'" – which "cover 'loss of reputation, shame, mortification, injury to the feelings and the like and need not be alleged in detail and require no proof'" – "but only if they prove 'special harm' (also known as 'special damages')" – which "are limited to actual pecuniary loss, which must be specially pleaded and proved." Id. at 1451. "This parallel," the Court reasoned, "suggests the possibility that Congress intended the term 'actual damages' in the Act to mean special damages. The basic idea is that Privacy Act victims, like victims of libel per quod or slander, are barred from any recovery unless they can first show actual – that is, pecuniary or material – harm." Id. Finally, the Court placed considerable emphasis on the fact that the

OVERVIEW OF THE PRIVACY ACT

Privacy Protection Study Commission (discussed above under "Role of the Privacy Protection Study Commission"), which Congress established "to consider, among its other jobs, 'whether the Federal Government should be liable for general damages,'" recommended that general damages be allowed; however, Congress "never amended the Act to include them." Id. at 1452. As a result, any prior case law suggesting that actual damages are not limited to proven pecuniary or economic harm has been abrogated.

One district court has applied the doctrine of mitigation to certain Privacy Act claims, holding that "an individual whose information is disclosed in violation of the Privacy Act may recover for costs incurred to prevent harm from that disclosure." Beaven v. DOJ, No. 03-84, 2007 WL 1032301, at *28 (E.D. Ky. Mar. 30, 2007) (concluding that "plaintiffs' out-of-pocket expenses [incurred in monitoring their financial information] to protect themselves from potential harm were caused by the instant Privacy Act violation"), aff'd in part, rev'd in part & remanded, on other grounds, 622 F. 3d 540 (6th Cir. 2010).

It is well settled that injunctive relief as provided for in the Privacy Act is available only under subsections (g)(1)(A) (amendment) and (g)(1)(B) (access) – both of which, incidentally, require exhaustion – and that it is not available under subsections (g)(1)(C) or (g)(1)(D). See, e.g., Doe v. Chao, 540 U.S. at 635 (Ginsburg, J., dissenting); McLeod v. VA, 43 F. App'x 70, 71 (9th Cir. 2002) (quoting Cell Assocs. v. NIH, infra); Locklear v. Holland, No. 98-6407, 1999 WL 1000835, at *1 (6th Cir. Oct. 28, 1999); Risley v. Hawk, 108 F.3d 1396, 1397 (D.C. Cir. 1997) (per curiam); Doe v. Stephens, 851 F.2d at 1463; Hastings v. Judicial Conference of the United States, 770 F.2d 1093, 1104 (D.C. Cir. 1985); Edison, 672 F.2d at 846; Hanley v. DOJ, 623 F.2d 1138, 1139 (6th Cir. 1980) (per curiam); Parks, 618 F.2d at 684; Cell Assocs. v. NIH, 579 F.2d 1155, 1161-62 (9th Cir. 1978); Kursar v. TSA, 581 F. Supp. 2d 7, 19 (D.D.C. 2008), aff'd per curiam on other grounds, 442 F. App'x 565 (D.C. Cir. 2011); Tarullo v. Def. Contract Audit Agency, 600 F. Supp. 2d 352, 358 (D. Conn. 2009); Purrier, No. 95-CV-6203, slip op. at 5 (W.D.N.Y. Mar. 15, 1996); AFGE v. HUD, 924 F. Supp. 225, 228 n.7 (D.D.C. 1996), rev'd on other grounds, 118 F.3d 786 (D.C. Cir. 1997); Robinson v. VA, No. 89-1156-B(M), slip op. at 2 (S.D. Cal. Dec. 14, 1989); Houston, 494 F. Supp. at 29; see also Word v. United States, 604 F.2d 1127, 1130 (8th Cir. 1979) (no "exclusionary rule" for subsection (b) violations; "No need and no authority exists to design or grant a remedy exceeding that established in the statutory

OVERVIEW OF THE PRIVACY ACT

scheme."); Shields v. Shetler, 682 F. Supp. 1172, 1176 (D. Colo. 1988) (Act "does not create a private right of action to enjoin agency disclosures"); 120 Cong. Rec. 40,406 (1974), reprinted in Source Book at 862, available at http://www.loc.gov/rr/frd/Military_Law/pdf/LH_privacy_act-1974.pdf; cf. New-Howard v. Shinseki, No. 09-5350, 2012 WL 2362546, at *8 (E.D. Pa. June 21, 2012) ("To the extent that Plaintiff seeks to enjoin Defendant from using the allegedly altered records in the course of further litigation, the statute in question does not authorize the relief requested."). But see Fla. Med. Ass'n v. HEW, 479 F. Supp. 1291, 1299 & n.8 (M.D. Fla. 1979) (aberrational decision construing subsection (g)(1)(D) to confer jurisdiction to enjoin agency's disclosure of Privacy Act-protected record). However, courts have recognized the availability of equitable relief under the Administrative Procedure Act for claims governed by the Privacy Act. See the discussion above under "Civil Remedies."

There should be no reason for regarding this settled law concerning injunctive relief under the Privacy Act as inapplicable where a subsection (e)(7) claim is involved. See Wabun-Inini v. Sessions, 900 F.2d 1234, 1245 (8th Cir. 1990); Clarkson v. IRS, 678 F.2d 1368, 1375 n.11 (11th Cir. 1982); Comm. in Solidarity v. Sessions, 738 F. Supp. 544, 548 (D.D.C. 1990), aff'd, 929 F.2d 742 (D.C. Cir. 1991); see also Socialist Workers Party v. Attorney Gen., 642 F. Supp. 1357, 1431 (S.D.N.Y. 1986) (in absence of exhaustion, only damages remedy, rather than injunctive relief, is available for violation of subsection (e)(7)). In Haase v. Sessions, 893 F.2d 370, 373-75 (D.C. Cir. 1990), however, the D.C. Circuit, in dictum, suggested that its decision in Nagel v. HEW, 725 F.2d 1438, 1441 (D.C. Cir. 1984), could be read to recognize the availability of injunctive relief to remedy a subsection (e)(7) violation, under subsection (g)(1)(D); cf. Becker v. IRS, 34 F.3d 398, 409 (7th Cir. 1994) (finding that the IRS had not justified maintenance of documents under subsection (e)(7), and stating that thus "the documents should be expunged"). Such a view is somewhat difficult to reconcile with the structure of subsection (g) and with the case law mentioned above.

There is a split of authority on the issue of whether destruction of a Privacy Act record gives rise to a damages action. Compare Tufts v. Dep't of the Air Force, 793 F.2d 259, 261-62 (10th Cir. 1986) (no), with Rosen v. Walters, 719 F.2d 1422, 1424 (9th Cir. 1983) (assuming action exists), and Waldrop v. U.S. Dep't of the Air Force, 3 Gov't Disclosure Serv. (P-H) ¶ 83,016, at 83,453 (S.D. Ill. Aug. 5,

OVERVIEW OF THE PRIVACY ACT

1981) (yes). See also Vaughn v. Danzig, 18 F. App'x 122, 124-25 (4th Cir. 2001) (per curiam) (finding no Privacy Act violation where record of nonjudicial punishment was maintained in files of plaintiff's military unit at time of his discharge, but later was destroyed pursuant to records retention policy; "Although [plaintiff] seems to argue that the Privacy Act requires that records be maintained in perpetuity, he has cited no authority for that proposition."; "[A]gencies are not required to retain records on the possibility that a . . . Privacy Act request may be submitted."); Dowd v. IRS, 776 F.2d 1083, 1084 (2d Cir. 1985) (per curiam) (expressly declining to decide issue). Cf. Beaven, 2007 WL 1032301, at *16-17 (applying adverse inference because agency "destroyed the [records] intentionally and in bad faith" and concluding that "[t]he inference is conclusive as to disclosure, and the defendants' conduct therefore constitutes a violation of the Privacy Act"), aff'd, 622 F. 3d 540.

F. Principles Applicable to All Privacy Act Civil Actions

1. Attorney Fees and Costs

In amendment lawsuits brought under subsection (g)(1)(A), and access lawsuits brought under subsection (g)(1)(B), attorney fees and costs that are "reasonably incurred" are recoverable, in the court's discretion, if the plaintiff "has substantially prevailed." 5 U.S.C. § 552a(g)(2)(B) (amendment), (g)(3)(B) (access).

In damages lawsuits brought under subsection (g)(1)(C) or subsection (g)(1)(D), "the costs of the action together with reasonable attorney fees as determined by the court" are recoverable by the prevailing plaintiff. 5 U.S.C. § 552a(g)(4)(B). Such an award is not discretionary. See OMB Guidelines, 40 Fed. Reg. 28,948, 28,970 (July 9, 1975), available at http://www.whitehouse.gov/sites/default/files/omb/assets/omb/inforeg/implementation_guidelines.pdf.

Comment:

The Privacy Act is one of many federal statutes containing a "fee-shifting" provision allowing a prevailing plaintiff to recover attorney fees and costs from the government.

The Supreme Court has held that a pro se attorney may not recover attorney fees under the fee-shifting provision of 42 U.S.C. § 1988 (2006). See Kay v. Ehrler, 499 U.S. 432, 437 (1991). The Court's reasoning in Kay calls into question the propriety of Cazalas v. DOJ,

OVERVIEW OF THE PRIVACY ACT

709 F.2d 1051 (5th Cir. 1983), which addressed the award of attorney fees under the Privacy Act and held that a pro se attorney may recover attorney fees. Id. at 1052 n.3, 1057.

Although the Supreme Court in Kay did not expressly rule on the issue of the award of attorney fees to non-attorney pro se litigants, the Court recognized that "the Circuits are in agreement . . . that a pro se litigant who is not a lawyer is not entitled to attorney's fees" and was "satisfied that [those cases so holding] were correctly decided." 499 U.S. at 435. Furthermore, the Court's rationale in Kay would seem to preclude an award of fees to any pro se Privacy Act litigant, as the Court observed that "awards of counsel fees to pro se litigants – even if limited to those who are members of the bar – would create a disincentive to employ counsel" and that "[t]he statutory policy of furthering the successful prosecution of meritorious claims is better served by a rule that creates an incentive to retain counsel in every such case." Id. at 438; see also Wilborn v. HHS, No. 91-538, slip op. at 14-16 (D. Or. Mar. 5, 1996) (rejecting argument that rationale in Kay should be construed as applying only to district court stage of litigation; "policy of the Privacy Act . . . would be better served by a rule that creates an incentive to retain counsel at all stages of the litigation, including appeals"), appeal voluntarily dismissed, No. 96-35569 (9th Cir. June 3, 1996).

Indeed, the Court of Appeals for the District of Columbia Circuit granted summary affirmance to a district court decision which held that a "nonattorney pro se litigant cannot recover attorney's fees under the Privacy Act." Sellers v. BOP, No. 87-2048, 1993 U.S. Dist. LEXIS 787, at *1 (D.D.C. Jan. 26, 1993), summary affirmance granted, No. 93-5090 (D.C. Cir. July 27, 1993). The district court in Sellers was "persuaded by the Fifth Circuit's opinion in Barrett v. Bureau of Customs, 651 F.2d 1087, 1089 (5th Cir. 1981)," an earlier Privacy Act decision also denying a non-attorney pro se litigant fees, and noted that "[t]he rationale utilized by the Supreme Court in Kay . . . is in accord." Sellers, No. 87-2048, 1993 U.S. Dist. LEXIS 787, at *1 (D.D.C. Jan. 26, 1993); see also Smith v. O'Brien, No. 94-41371, slip op. at 4 (5th Cir. June 19, 1995) (per curiam) (citing Barrett and stating: "Pro se litigants are not entitled to attorney fees under either the FOIA or the Privacy Act unless the litigant is also an attorney."); Riser v. U.S. Dep't of State, No. 09-3273, 2010 WL 4284925, at *8 (S.D. Tex. Oct. 22, 2010) (citing Barrett and Smith and denying non-attorney pro se plaintiff's request for attorney fees); Westendorf v. IRS, No. 3:92-cv-761WS, 1994 WL 714011, at *2 (S.D. Miss. July 7, 1994) (citing Barrett and holding that non-attorney pro se plaintiff is

OVERVIEW OF THE PRIVACY ACT

not entitled to attorney fees), <u>appeal dismissed</u>, No. 94-60503, slip op. at 2-3 (5th Cir. Nov. 17, 1994) (stating that district court's holding is correct under <u>Barrett</u>). The D.C. Circuit has further ruled, however, that a plaintiff's pro se status does not preclude the recovery of fees for "consultations" with outside counsel. <u>Blazy v. Tenet</u>, 194 F.3d 90, 94 (D.C. Cir. 1999); <u>see also id.</u> at 98-99 (Sentelle, J., concurring but "writing separately only to distance [him]self from the majority's determination that a pro se litigant is entitled to recover counsel fees for consultations with attorneys not appearing or connected with appearances in the pro se litigation").

It has also been held that a plaintiff does not substantially prevail in an access case merely because the agency produced the records in question subsequent to the filing of the lawsuit. <u>See</u> <u>Reinbold v. Evers</u>, 187 F.3d 348, 363 (4th Cir. 1999) (upholding denial of interim fees where plaintiff had "not proved that his lawsuit was a catalyst for the [agency's] action," and evidence showed that delay was caused by staffing shortage); <u>Jacobs v. Reno</u>, No. 3:97-CV-2698-D, 1999 U.S. Dist. LEXIS 3104, at *14-15 (N.D. Tex. Mar. 11, 1999) (denying plaintiff's request for attorney fees and costs, and stating that plaintiff's argument was "too slim a reed on which to rest a § 552a(g)(1)(B) claim, particularly when § 552a(d)(1) imposes no deadline for agency compliance and absent evidence of extended and unjustified delay"), <u>aff'd</u>, 208 F.3d 1006 (5th Cir. 2000) (unpublished table decision).

Subsection (g)(3)(B) is similar to 5 U.S.C. § 552(a)(4)(E), the FOIA's attorney fees provision, and FOIA decisions concerning a plaintiff's eligibility for attorney fees may be consulted in this area. However, the Court of Appeals for the District of Columbia Circuit has expressly ruled that the FOIA's criteria for determining the additional factor of entitlement to attorney fees are inapplicable to a claim for fees under the Privacy Act. <u>Blazy v. Tenet</u>, 194 F.3d at 95-97 ("Even a cursory examination of these factors makes it clear that they have little or no relevance in the context of the Privacy Act."); <u>see also</u> <u>Herring v. VA</u>, No. 94-55955, 1996 WL 32147, at *5-6 (9th Cir. Jan. 26, 1996) (finding plaintiff to be "prevailing party" on access claim for her medical record with no mention or application of FOIA criteria). Nevertheless, two other courts of appeals have held the FOIA's entitlement criteria to be applicable to Privacy Act claims for attorney fees. <u>See</u> <u>Gowan v. U.S. Dep't of the Air Force</u>, 148 F.3d 1182, 1194-95 (10th Cir. 1998) (applying the FOIA's criteria and determining that the plaintiff was not entitled to fees because his "suit was for his personal benefit rather than for the benefit of the

OVERVIEW OF THE PRIVACY ACT

public interest"); Barrett v. Bureau of Customs, 651 F.2d at 1088 (stating that FOIA's guidelines apply to claims for attorney fees under Privacy Act); see also Reinbold v. Evers, 187 F.3d 348, 362 (4th Cir. 1999) (citing Gowan and stating in dicta that if determination is made that plaintiff substantially prevailed, court must evaluate FOIA factors to determine entitlement); Sweatt v. U.S. Navy, 683 F.2d 420, 423 (D.C. Cir. 1982) (stating in dicta that cases construing attorney fee provision in FOIA are apposite in Privacy Act context).

Note also that in 2002 the D.C. Circuit held that "in order for plaintiffs in FOIA actions to become eligible for an award of attorney's fees, they must have 'been awarded some relief by [a] court,' either in a judgment on the merits or in a court-ordered consent decree." Oil, Chem. & Atomic Workers Int'l Union v. Dep't of Energy, 288 F.3d 452, 455-56 (D.C. Cir. May 10, 2002) (quoting, and applying to FOIA cases, Supreme Court's holding in Buckhannon Bd. & Care Home, Inc. v. W. Va. Dep't of Health & Human Res., 532 U.S. 598, 603 (2001), which concerned attorney fees under other fee-shifting statutes). This interpretation of Buckhannon was widely followed, with the result that plaintiffs were denied attorney fees in FOIA cases in which the agency voluntarily disclosed the records at issue. See, e.g., Union of Needletrades, Indus. and Textile Employees v. INS, 336 F.3d 200, 206 (2d Cir. 2003); McBride v. U.S. Dep't of the Army, No. 06-4082, 2007 WL 1017328, at *3-4 (E.D. La. Mar. 30, 2007); Poulsen v. U.S. Customs & Border Prot., No. 06-1743, 2007 WL 160945, at *1 (N.D. Cal. Jan. 17, 2007); Martinez v. EEOC, No. 04-CA-0271, 2005 U.S. Dist. LEXIS 3864, at *19 (W.D. Tex. Mar. 3, 2005); Landers v. Dep't of the Air Force, 257 F. Supp. 2d 1011, 1012 (S.D. Ohio 2003). However, the OPEN Government Act of 2007, Pub. L. No. 110-175, 121 Stat. 2524, amended the FOIA to provide that a plaintiff is eligible to obtain attorney fees if records are obtained as a result of "(I) a judicial order, or an enforceable written agreement or consent decree; or (II) a voluntary or unilateral change in position by the agency, if the complainant's claim is not insubstantial." 5 U.S.C. § 552(a)(4)(E)(ii), as amended. This statutory change should not have any impact on the awarding of attorney fees under the Privacy Act in the context of access lawsuits; since all withholdings must be based on exemptions under both the FOIA and the Privacy Act, the FOIA's more generous provisions permit attorney fees for any voluntary disclosure in litigation. However, the Buckhannon requirement – that attorney fees be available only if the relief sought results from a court order or enforceable consent decree – still appears to apply to any case brought under subsection (g)(1)(A) where the agency voluntarily amends the record during the pendency of litigation.

Although under the FOIA it had previously been held that a fee enhancement as compensation for the risk in a contingency fee arrangement might be available in limited circumstances, see, e.g., Weisberg v. DOJ, 848 F.2d 1265, 1272 (D.C. Cir. 1988), the Supreme Court has clarified that such enhancements are not available under statutes authorizing an award of reasonable attorney fees to a prevailing or substantially prevailing party, City of Burlington v. Dague, 505 U.S. 557, 561-66 (1992) (prohibiting contingency enhancement in environmental fee-shifting statutes); see also King v. Palmer, 950 F.2d 771, 775 (D.C. Cir. 1991) (en banc) (pre-City of Burlington case anticipating result later reached by Supreme Court). In light of the Court's further observation that case law "construing what is a 'reasonable' fee applies uniformly to all [federal fee-shifting statutes], there seems to be little doubt that the same principle also prohibits fee enhancements under the Privacy Act.

The Court of Appeals for the Fourth Circuit has held that in a damages lawsuit brought under the Privacy Act, subsection (g)(4) "does not require a showing of actual damages . . . in order to receive costs and reasonable attorneys fee." Doe v. Chao, 435 F.3d 492, 495-96 (4th Cir. 2006) (explaining that "the word 'sum' – as it is used in [subsection (g)(4)] – requires a court to fulfill the simple act of adding actual damages and fees and costs once the preceding elements of the statute are satisfied" and that, therefore, a plaintiff who establishes a violation but does not recover damages is eligible for attorney fees). But cf. Rice v. United States, 245 F.R.D. 3, 7 n.6 (D.D.C. 2007) ("There is some question as to whether plaintiffs could recover costs and reasonable attorney fees under section 552a(g)(4) even without showing actual damages. . . . [H]owever, the Supreme Court's [opinion in Doe v. Chao, 540 U.S. 614, 625 n.9 (2004),] appears to foreclose such a recovery.").

Attorney fees are not recoverable for services rendered at the administrative level. See Kennedy v. Andrus, 459 F. Supp. 240, 244 (D.D.C. 1978), aff'd, 612 F.2d 586 (D.C. Cir. 1980) (unpublished table decision).

The D.C. Circuit has held that attorney fees are not available in a subsection (g)(1)(A) amendment case unless the plaintiff has exhausted his administrative remedies. See Haase v. Sessions, 893 F.2d 370, 373-75 (D.C. Cir. 1990). Relying on Haase in a subsection

OVERVIEW OF THE PRIVACY ACT

(g)(1)(B) access case, the District Court for the Southern District of California concluded that "a fee award would be improper because Plaintiff failed to exhaust her administrative remedies." Sterrett v. Dep't of the Navy, No. 09-CV-2083, 2010 WL 330086, at *6 (S.D. Cal. Jan. 20, 2010).

Litigation costs (if reasonably incurred) can be recovered by all plaintiffs who substantially prevail. See Parkinson v. Comm'r, No. 87-3219, 1988 WL 12121, at *3 (6th Cir. Feb. 17, 1988); Walker v. DOJ, No. 00-0106, slip op. at 5-6 (D.D.C. July 14, 2000); Young v. CIA, No. 91-527-A, slip op. at 2 (E.D. Va. Nov. 30, 1992), aff'd, 1 F.3d 1235 (4th Cir. 1993) (unpublished table decision). Compare Herring v. VA, No. 94-55955, 1996 WL 32147, at *5-6 (9th Cir. Jan. 26, 1996) (although ruling in favor of VA on plaintiff's access claim, nonetheless finding that plaintiff was "a prevailing party with respect to her access claim" because "the VA did not provide her access to all her records until she filed her lawsuit"), with Abernethy v. IRS, 909 F. Supp. 1562, 1567-69 (N.D. Ga. 1995) ("[T]he fact that records were released after the lawsuit was filed, in and of itself, is insufficient to establish Plaintiff's eligibility for an award of attorneys' fees."), aff'd per curiam, No. 95-9489 (11th Cir. Feb. 13, 1997). Further, the D.C. Circuit has held that a pro se plaintiff's claim for litigation costs under the Privacy Act is not limited by 28 U.S.C. § 1920 (governing litigation costs generally). Blazy v. Tenet, 194 F.3d at 94-95 (embracing reasoning of Kuzma v. IRS, 821 F.2d 930 (2d Cir. 1987) (FOIA case)).

"Judgments, costs, and attorney's fees assessed against the United States under [subsection (g) of the Privacy Act] would appear to be payable from the public funds rather than from agency funds." OMB Guidelines, 40 Fed. Reg. 28,948, 28,968 (July 9, 1975), available at http://www.whitehouse.gov/sites/default/files/omb/assets/omb/inforeg/implementation_guidelines.pdf (citing 28 U.S.C. § 2414 (2006); 31 U.S.C. § 724a (later replaced during enactment of revised Title 31, now see 31 U.S.C. § 1304 (2006) (first sentence of former § 724a) and 39 U.S.C. § 409(e) (2006) (last sentence of former § 724a)); and 28 U.S.C. § 1924 (2006)).

3. **Jurisdiction and Venue**

"An action to enforce any liability created under this section may be brought in the district court of the United States in the district in which the complainant resides, or has his principal place of business,

OVERVIEW OF THE PRIVACY ACT

or in which the agency records are situated, or in the District of Columbia." 5 U.S.C. § 552a(g)(5).

Comment:

By its very terms, this section limits jurisdiction over Privacy Act matters to the federal district courts. 5 U.S.C. § 552a(g)(5). Accordingly, it has been held that the U.S. Court of Federal Claims does not have jurisdiction over Privacy Act claims, see, e.g., Parker v. United States, 280 F. App'x 957, 958 (Fed. Cir. 2008); Frasier v. United States, No. 94-5131, 1994 U.S. App. LEXIS 35392, at *3 (Fed. Cir. Dec. 6, 1994); Madison v. United States, 98 Fed. Cl. 393, 395 (Fed Cl. 2011); Treece v. United States, 96 Fed. Cl. 226, 232 (Fed. Cl. 2010); Addington v. United States, 94 Fed. Cl. 779, 784 (Fed. Cl. 2010); Stephanatos v. United States, 81 Fed. Cl. 440, 444 (Fed. Cl. 2008); Agee v. United States, 72 Fed. Cl. 284, 290 (Fed. Cl. 2006); Doe v. United States, 74 Fed. Cl. 794, 798 (Fed. Cl. 2006), that the Merit Systems Protection Board does not have jurisdiction over Privacy Act claims, see, e.g., Carell v. MSPB, 131 F. App'x 296, 299 (Fed. Cir. 2005); Martin v. Dep't of the Army, No. 00-3302, 2000 WL 1807419, at *2 (Fed. Cir. Dec. 8, 2000) (per curiam); Minnich v. MSPB, No. 94-3587, 1995 U.S. App. LEXIS 5768, at *3 (Fed. Cir. Mar. 21, 1995) (per curiam), and that the U.S. Tax Court does not have jurisdiction over Privacy Act claims, see, e.g., Strickland v. Comm'r, No. 9799-95, 2000 WL 274077, at *1 (T.C. Mar. 14, 2000).

In Creed v. National Transportation Safety Board, the District Court for the District of Columbia ruled that the judicial review provision of the Independent Safety Board Act, 49 U.S.C. § 1153(a), operates to give exclusive jurisdiction to the appropriate U.S. Court of Appeals or the Court of Appeals for the District of Columbia Circuit, to review final orders of the National Transportation Safety Board (NTSB). 758 F. Supp. 2d 1, 4-8 (D.D.C. 2011). In Creed, the plaintiff, a commercial truck driver, alleged that the NTSB violated the Privacy Act by "post[ing] summaries of [his] medical information, which it had obtained while investigating a serious multi-vehicle accident in which he was involved, on its public website." Id. at 2. Section 1153(a) provides that only a federal court of appeals "may review a final order of the [NTSB] under this chapter." 49 U.S.C. § 1153(a). The district court agreed with the NTSB that "its denials of [plaintiff's] requests to prevent the public disclosure of his medical information constitute final orders pursuant to the Act, such that any judicial review of those denials would fall

OVERVIEW OF THE PRIVACY ACT

squarely within the language of section 1153(a)." 758 F. Supp. 2d at 4-8. The district court acknowledged "[t]he Privacy Act's grant of original jurisdiction to the district courts" but stated that it "does not change this conclusion" and that "section 1153(a) still governs the judicial review of Creed's claims." Id. at 6 n.6.

Because venue is always proper in the District of Columbia, the Privacy Act decisions of the Court of Appeals for the District of Columbia Circuit are of great importance.

For cases involving this provision, see Akutowicz v. United States, 859 F.2d 1122, 1126 (2d Cir. 1988) (venue proper only in District of Columbia for plaintiff who resided and worked continuously in France); Budik v. United States, No. 09-3079, 2011 U.S. Dist. LEXIS 74655, at *4 (D. Md. July 11, 2011) (transferring Privacy Act claim to District of Columbia, where plaintiff resided and "where the records at issue were created and stored"; adding that "the United States District Court for the District of Columbia is surely more thoroughly vested in the complex issues surrounding suits brought against the United States under the Privacy Act than is this Court"); Pickard v. DOJ, No. C 10-05253, 2011 WL 2199297, at *2-3 (N.D. Cal. June 7, 2011) (acknowledging that some courts "conclude that residence is where the now-incarcerated defendant was last domiciled" but "find[ing] more persuasive the cases holding that an individual resides where he is incarcerated, at least for purposes of FOIA and the Privacy Act"); Royer v. BOP, No. 1:10-cv-0146, 2010 WL 4827727, at *4 (E.D. Va. Nov. 19, 2010) ("Royer's domicile may well be in the Eastern District of Virginia. However, in light of the fact that he is presently serving a 20-year sentence and is confined in a federal facility in Colorado, Royer has failed to set forth sufficient information establishing that he resides in this District for FOIA and Privacy Act purposes."); Tildon v. Alexander, 587 F. Supp. 2d 242, 243 n.1 (D.D.C. 2008) (transferring multi-claim cause of action to another district, even though plaintiff was able to bring Privacy Act claim in District of Columbia, because "judicial economy . . . will be served by transferring this action in its entirety"); Dehaemers v. Wynne, 522 F. Supp. 2d 240, 248-49 (D.D.C. 2007) (where plaintiff's Privacy Act claims were properly venued in District of Columbia, declining to assume pendent venue over plaintiff's Rehabilitation Act and Title VII claims; concluding, therefore, that plaintiff must either transfer Privacy Act claim or have court consider it alone); In re Dep't of VA Data Theft Litigation v. Nicholson, 461 F. Supp. 2d 1367, 1368-69 (E.D. Ky. 2006) (explaining that District of District of Columbia "is a preferable

OVERVIEW OF THE PRIVACY ACT

transferee forum for this litigation" because it is "where likely relevant documents and witnesses may be found, inasmuch as many of the defendants are located in this district and the theft occurred in the Washington, D.C., metropolitan area"); Roberts v. DOT, No. 02-829, 2002 U.S. Dist. LEXIS 14116, at *1-2 (E.D. Pa. July 3, 2003) (finding venue improper in Eastern District of Pennsylvania, and transferring the case to Eastern District of New York, as "both plaintiff and the records are located within [that district]"); Troupe v. O'Neill, No. 02-4157, 2003 WL 21289977, at *3 (D. Kan. May 9, 2003) (transferring case to Northern District of Georgia as "agency records would be situated there"); Boers v. United States, 133 F. Supp. 2d 64, 65 (D.D.C. 2001) (transferring case under 28 U.S.C. § 1404(a) to plaintiff's "home forum," even though "venue is proper" in District of Columbia, given that "[a]ll the operative facts occurred in Arizona" and "it cannot be said that forcing a plaintiff to litigate in his home district will prejudice or burden the plaintiff in any way"), mandamus denied per curiam sub nom. In re Howard L. Boers, No. 01-5192 (D.C. Cir. Aug. 28, 2001); Warg v. Reno, 19 F. Supp. 2d 776, 785 (N.D. Ohio 1998) ("find[ing] the Northern District of Ohio to be an improper venue" and transferring case to District of Columbia in interest of justice where plaintiff resided in Maryland and records were located in Washington, D.C.); Harton v. BOP, No. 97-0638, slip op. at 3, 6-7 (D.D.C. Nov. 12, 1997) (stating that "the fact that the Privacy Act provides for venue in the District of Columbia does not, by itself, establish that each and every Privacy Act claim involves issues of national policy," and granting agency's motion to transfer to jurisdiction where plaintiff was incarcerated, as complaint focused primarily on issues specific to plaintiff); and Finley v. NEA, 795 F. Supp. 1457, 1467 (C.D. Cal. 1992) ("[I]n a multi-plaintiff Privacy Act action, if any plaintiff satisfies the venue requirement of 5 U.S.C. § 552a(g)(5), the venue requirement is satisfied as to the remaining plaintiffs.").

3. Statute of Limitations

"An action to enforce any liability created under this section may be brought . . . within two years from the date on which the cause of action arises, except that where an agency has materially and willfully misrepresented any information required under this section to be disclosed to an individual and the information so misrepresented is material to establishment of the liability of the agency to the individual under this section, the action may be brought at any time within two years after discovery by the individual of the misrepresentation. Nothing in this section shall be construed to

OVERVIEW OF THE PRIVACY ACT

authorize any civil action by reason of any injury sustained as the result of a disclosure of a record prior to September 27, 1975." 5 U.S.C. § 552a(g)(5).

Comment:

The statute of limitations has been held to be jurisdictional in nature and has been strictly construed as it is an "'integral condition of the sovereign's consent to be sued under the Privacy Act.'" Bowyer v. U.S. Dep't of the Air Force, 875 F.2d 632, 635 (7th Cir. 1989) (quoting Diliberti v. United States, 817 F.2d 1259, 1262 (7th Cir. 1987)); accord Harrell v. Fleming, 282 F.3d 1292, 1293-94 (10th Cir. 2002); Weber v. Henderson, 33 F. App'x 610, 611 (3d Cir. 2002) (per curiam); Davis v. DOJ, 204 F.3d 723, 726 (7th Cir. 2000) (per curiam); Akutowicz v. United States, 859 F.2d 1122, 1126 (2d Cir. 1988); Davis v. Gross, No. 83-5223, 1984 U.S. App. LEXIS 14279, at *2-3 (6th Cir. May 10, 1984); Doe v. FDIC, No. 11 Civ. 307, 2012 WL 612461, at *4 (S.D.N.Y. Feb. 27, 2012); Mauldin v. Napolitano, No. 10-12826, 2011 WL 3113104, at *2 (E.D. Mich. July 26, 2011); Bassiouni v. FBI, No. 02-8918, 2003 WL 22227189, at *2 (N.D. Ill. Sept. 26, 2003), aff'd on other grounds, 436 F.3d 712 (7th Cir. 2006); Logan v. United States, 272 F. Supp. 2d 1182, 1187 (D. Kan. 2003); Mangino v. Dep't of the Army, 818 F. Supp. 1432, 1437 (D. Kan. 1993), aff'd, 17 F.3d 1437 (10th Cir. 1994) (unpublished table decision). Consequently, a plaintiff's failure to file suit within the specified time period has been held to "[deprive] the federal courts of subject matter jurisdiction over the action." Diliberti, 817 F.2d at 1262. But compare M.K. v. Tenet, 196 F. Supp. 2d 8, 13 (D.D.C. 2001) (finding that "statute of limitations is an affirmative defense that does not need to be anticipated and rebutted by the complaint . . . [a]s such, even if the plaintiffs have not alleged illegal conduct of the defendants that the plaintiffs first knew or should have known within the limitations period, the Privacy Act claim should not be dismissed for lack of subject matter jurisdiction"), with Fort Hall Landowners Alliance, Inc. v. BIA, No. 99-052, slip op. at 3-4 (D. Idaho Mar. 14, 2003) (stating that the court "may grant a motion to dismiss based on the running of a statute of limitations period only 'if the assertions of the complaint, read with the required liberality, would not permit the plaintiff to prove that the statute was tolled'" (quoting Supermail Cargo, Inc. v. United States, 68 F.3d 1204, 1207 (9th Cir. 1995))).

In the past, the Court of Appeals for the District of Columbia Circuit also had held that the Privacy Act's statute of limitations is jurisdictional. See, e.g., Griffin v. U.S. Parole Comm'n, 192 F.3d

OVERVIEW OF THE PRIVACY ACT

1081, 1082 (D.C. Cir. 1999), overruled by Chung v. DOJ, 333 F.3d 273, 278 n.1 (D.C. Cir. 2003); Williams v. Reno, No. 95-5155, 1996 WL 460093, at *1 (D.C. Cir. Aug. 7, 1996); see also Farrero v. NASA, 180 F. Supp. 2d 92, 97 (D.D.C. 2001). Subsequently, however, the District of Columbia Circuit has held that the Privacy Act's statute of limitations for a damages "claim for unlawful disclosure of personal information" need not be strictly construed and that a "'rebuttable presumption' in favor of equitable tolling applies." Chung v. DOJ, 333 F.3d 273, 277 (D.C. Cir. 2003). Relying on the Supreme Court's decision in Irwin v. VA, 498 U.S. 89, 95 (1990), which announced a "'general rule' establishing a presumption in favor of equitable tolling in 'suits against the Government,'" the D.C. Circuit concluded that "a Privacy Act claim for unlawful disclosure of personal information is sufficiently similar to a traditional tort claim for invasion of privacy to render the Irwin presumption applicable." Chung, 333 F.3d at 276-77; see also Fort Hall Landowners Alliance, Inc., No. 99-052, slip op. at 6-7 (citing Irwin and finding that the Privacy Act "does not use such language [of jurisdiction], and therefore does not present a jurisdictional bar"); cf. Freeman v. EPA, No. 02-0387, 2004 WL 2451409, at *9 n.8 (D.D.C. Oct. 25, 2004) ("prefer[ring] to dismiss" for failure to state a claim on which relief can be granted rather than for lack of subject matter jurisdiction). Although the D.C. Circuit appeared to limit its holding in Chung to "claim[s] for unlawful disclosure of personal information," 333 F.3d at 277, the District Court for the District of Columbia has relied on Chung in considering equitable tolling in other types of Privacy Act claims without conducting the "similarity inquiry" articulated in Chung, 333 F.3d at 277, with respect to the individual claims. See, e.g., Earle v. Holder, 815 F. Supp. 2d 176, 180 (D.D.C. 2011) (quoting Chung in apparent (g)(1)(A) and (g)(1)(C) claim, and applying principle that statute of limitations is subject to equitable tolling "'when the plaintiff "despite all due diligence . . . is unable to obtain vital information bearing on the existence of his claim"'"), aff'd per curiam, No. 11-5280, 2012 WL 1450574 (D.C. Cir. Apr. 20, 2012); Bailey v. Fulwood, 780 F. Supp. 2d 20, 22, 27-28 (D.D.C. 2011) (citing Kursar and Chung for proposition that the statute of limitations of the Privacy Act "is not a jurisdictional bar," but ultimately dismissing apparent (g)(1)(C) claim – not for lack of subject matter jurisdiction – because "there is no reason in this case to toll the running of the statute of limitations"); Kursar v. TSA, 751 F. Supp. 2d 154, 165-69 (D.D.C. 2010) (citing Chung and considering equitable tolling with respect to claims under subsections (e)(2) and (g)(1)(C) but declining to apply equitable tolling), aff'd per curiam, 442 F. App'x 565 (D.C. Cir. 2011).

Other courts have also adopted the Irwin approach. The Court of Appeals for the Ninth Circuit has held that Privacy Act claims brought under subsection (g)(1)(D) and based on alleged violations of subsections (e)(5) and (e)(6) "are sufficiently similar to traditional tort actions such as misrepresentation and false light to warrant the application of Irwin's rebuttable presumption." Rouse v. U.S. Dep't of State, 567 F.3d 408, 416 (9th Cir. 2009) (amended opinion) (citing Chung, 333 F.3d at 277). Because the Ninth Circuit agreed with Chung that no aspect of the Privacy Act "militate[s] against tolling," the court concluded that "the Irwin presumption has not been rebutted." Rouse, 567 F.3d at *416-17. However, the court "decline[d] to decide whether equitable tolling is warranted on the facts of this case." Id. at 417. See also Shearson v. Holder, No. 1:10 CV 1492, 2011 WL 4102152, at *15 (N.D. Ohio Sept. 9, 2011) (noting the "split in the circuits as to whether the Privacy Act's statute of limitations is jurisdictional in nature" but "agree[ing] with the courts that have adopted the Irwin approach and have held that Privacy Act claims are sufficiently similar to privacy tort claims to trigger the application of the Irwin rule").

Amendment

In a subsection (g)(1)(A) amendment action, the limitations period begins when the agency denies the plaintiff's request to amend. See Englerius v. VA, 837 F.2d 895, 897-98 (9th Cir. 1988) (holding that the statute of limitations "commences at the time that a person knows or has reason to know that the request has been denied," rather than as of the date of the request letter); see also Bassiouni, 2003 WL 22227189, at *3-4 (explicitly acknowledging distinction as to when a claim arises among the four distinct Privacy Act causes of actions and finding that in an amendment cause of action, a claim arises "when an individual knows or has reason to know that his request to amend has been denied"); Kursar, 751 F. Supp. 2d at 167 ("Since the statute of limitations began running when the TSA denied [plaintiff's] amendment request in January 2009, and he filed his amended complaint approximately two months later on March 16, 2009, [plaintiff's] claim seeking amendment of his records is timely."), aff'd per curiam on other grounds, 442 F. App'x 565; Blazy v. Tenet, 979 F. Supp. 10, 18 (D.D.C. 1997) (although ultimately finding plaintiff's amendment claim moot due to remedial action taken by CIA, citing Englerius and finding that claim for

OVERVIEW OF THE PRIVACY ACT

amendment of sexual harassment allegations in personnel file did not begin to run until employee discovered that FBI, where plaintiff had applied for employment, never received corrective letter from CIA, prior to which time plaintiff did not and could not have known of CIA's failure to amend), summary affirmance granted, No. 97-5330, 1998 WL 315583 (D.C. Cir. May 12, 1998). But see Wills v. OPM, No. 93-2079, slip op. at 2-3 (4th Cir. Jan. 28, 1994) (per curiam) (alternatively holding that cause of action triggers statute of limitations when plaintiff knows or should have known of alleged violation, which in this case was when plaintiff sent his first letter requesting amendment); Alexander v. Mich. Adjutant Gen., No. 1:10-cv-192, 2012 WL 925955, at *7-8 (W.D. Mich. Mar. 16, 2012) (ruling that limitations period began when plaintiff was terminated "approximately fifteen years prior to filing this action," or "[g]iving plaintiff every benefit of the doubt" considering several "other dates that plaintiff could have claimed to have first 'known,'" under any of which "plaintiff's complaint would have been untimely"); cf. Foulke v. Potter, No. 10-CV-4061, 2011 WL 127119, at *3 n.4 (E.D.N.Y. Jan. 10, 2011) (where plaintiff never submitted an amendment request, noting, though "mak[ing] no determination," that a subsection (g)(1)(A) claim would likely fail "[s]ince the documents which plaintiff seeks to have corrected were created in 2008, and plaintiff was clearly aware of the purported inaccuracies in such documents in 2008"); Reitz v. USDA, No. 08-4131, 2010 WL 786586, at *9-10 (D. Kan. Mar. 4, 2010) (dismissing amendment claim where plaintiffs had not "specifie[d] any date for the alleged Privacy Act violations," and working back from date of court filing, finding that plaintiffs had "not raised a material question of fact that any Privacy Act violation occurred" within the two years prior); Evans v. United States, No. 99-1268, 2000 WL 1595748, at *2 (D. Kan. Oct. 16, 2000) (finding that "plaintiff neither knew nor had reason to know of the alleged error in his records until the receipt of information provided by those witnesses who claimed the [Equal Opportunity] complaint Summary inaccurately reported their testimony," which prompted him to request a "reconsideration and reinvestigation" of the information). One district court has "f[ound] it troubling that [a plaintiff] was aware of the existence of allegedly incorrect records in 2002, but waited until 2009 to request amendment of his records." Kursar, 751 F. Supp. 2d at 167 n.11. "Nonetheless, the court [was] not aware of any limitations period for seeking an amendment in a statute or otherwise compelled by binding case authority." Id. (adding that "an equitable defense such as laches may be applicable in this instance" but declining to "consider the defense as it was not raised by" defendant).

OVERVIEW OF THE PRIVACY ACT

In determining what constitutes the agency's denial, it has been held that the agency's initial denial should govern, rather than the date of the agency's administrative appeal determination. See Quarry v. DOJ, 3 Gov't Disclosure Serv. (P-H) ¶ 82,407, at 83,020-21 (D.D.C. Feb. 2, 1982); see also Singer v. OPM, No. 83-1095, slip op. at 2 (D.N.J. Mar. 8, 1984) (rejecting claim that limitations period began on date plaintiff's appeal was dismissed as time-barred under agency regulation); cf. Shannon v. Gen. Elec. Co., 812 F. Supp. 308, 320 & n.10 (N.D.N.Y. 1993) (finding that cause of action for damages claim arose when plaintiff's amendment request was partially denied and noting that "no caselaw can be found to support a finding that the pendency of the appeal has any affect upon the running of the statute of limitations").

In cases "[w]here the agency has not issued an express denial of the request, the question of when a person learns of the denial requires a factual inquiry and cannot ordinarily be decided on a motion to dismiss." Englerius, 837 F.2d at 897; see also Jarrell v. USPS, 753 F.2d 1088, 1092 (D.C. Cir. 1985) (holding that issue of material fact existed and therefore summary judgment was inappropriate where agency contended that cause of action arose when it issued final denial of expungement request but requester argued that due to agency's excision of certain parts of documents, he was unaware of information until later point in time); Conklin v. BOP, 514 F. Supp. 2d 1, 5 (D.D.C. 2007) (denying motion to dismiss as "the date on which plaintiff knew or had reason to know of the alleged Privacy Act violations is unclear"); Lechliter v. Dep't of Army, No. 04-814, 2006 WL 462750, at *3-4 (D. Del. Feb. 27, 2006) (denying motion to dismiss because "[t]here does not appear to have been a final denial of [plaintiff's] request" and "there [was] some question regarding what was said" during a telephone call concerning status of request); cf. Bowles v. BOP, No. 08 CV 9591, 2010 WL 23326, at *3 (S.D.N.Y. Jan. 5, 2010) (where prisoner's amendment request was subject of administrative review "and the BOP failed to notify [him] one way or the other" of the action on his final appeal, stating that "[t]he troubling failure of the BOP to do their job and respond to Plaintiff's claim, as well as the Plaintiff's right to be made aware of these deadlines by those that maintain complete control over him are serious, factual questions that would need to be addressed before the statute of limitations issue could be resolved" but determining that it need not reach these considerations and dismissing claim on other grounds).

OVERVIEW OF THE PRIVACY ACT

Access

The two-year statute of limitations set forth in subsection (g)(5) applies to the access provision of the Privacy Act as well. 5 U.S.C. § 552a(g)(5). However, because an individual's Privacy Act access request should be processed under the FOIA as well – see H.R. Rep. No. 98-726, pt. 2, at 16-17 (1984), reprinted in 1984 U.S.C.C.A.N. 3741, 3790-91 (regarding amendment of Privacy Act in 1984 to include subsection (t)(2) and stating: "Agencies that had made it a practice to treat a request made under either [the Privacy Act or the FOIA] as if the request had been made under both laws should continue to do so."); FOIA Update, Vol. VII, No. 1, at 6, available at http://www.justice.gov/oip/foia_updates/Vol_VII_1/page5.htm ("FOIA Counselor Q & A") – and because the FOIA is subject to the general six-year statute of limitations, see Spannaus v. DOJ, 824 F.2d 52, 55-56 (D.C. Cir. 1987) (applying 28 U.S.C. § 2401(a) to FOIA actions), the Privacy Act's "two-year bar" may be of little, if any, consequence. The ramifications of these arguably conflicting provisions have not been explored.

For cases involving application of the statute of limitations in the context of subsection (g)(1)(B) access lawsuits, see Zied v. Barnhart, 418 F. App'x 109, 113-14 (3d Cir. 2011) (per curiam) (concluding that plaintiff "knew of the agency's alleged errors when defendant . . . sent her a letter that was unresponsive to her Privacy Act requests and she responded to it"); Willis v. DOJ, 581 F. Supp. 2d 57, 69 (D.D.C. 2008) (ruling that "[a]pplication of the tolling doctrine is inappropriate in this case" because plaintiff "had sufficient knowledge" to bring an action within the limitations period); Levant v. Roche, 384 F. Supp. 2d 262, 270 (D.D.C. 2005) (concluding that plaintiff knew or should have known that his access request was denied when Air Force issued a final decision on his Privacy Act and FOIA requests for documents); Bernard v. DOD, 362 F. Supp. 2d 272, 278-79 (D.D.C. 2005) (determining that it was "clear from the administrative record that the plaintiff knew or should have known about his ability to request his medical records . . . when he alleged he was denied them in the hospital at that time"); Logan v. United States, 272 F. Supp. 2d 1182, 1187 (D. Kan. 2003) (finding that plaintiff's access claim was untimely as the claim arose "when [the agency] disclosed the records to plaintiff," and observing that plaintiff brought the action after "two years from the date on which the cause of action arose"); McClain v. DOJ, No. 97-0385, 1999 WL 759505, at *4 (N.D. Ill. Sept. 1, 1999) (finding that the action "would have accrued when [plaintiff] knew or should have known that his

OVERVIEW OF THE PRIVACY ACT

request for access to his IRS records had been denied," which was more than nine years before he filed suit), aff'd on other grounds, 17 F. App'x 471 (7th Cir. 2001); Biondo v. Dep't of the Navy, 928 F. Supp. 626, 632, 634-35 (D.S.C. 1995) (summarily stating that 1987 request "cannot serve as a basis for relief for a suit brought in 1992 because the Privacy Act has a two-year statute of limitations"; similar statements made as to undocumented requests for information made in mid-80s and in 1976-77), aff'd, 86 F.3d 1148 (4th Cir. 1996) (unpublished table decision); Burkins v. United States, 865 F. Supp. 1480, 1496 (D. Colo. 1994) (cause of action "should not be time-barred" because it would have accrued when plaintiff knew his request for access had been denied); Mittleman v. U.S. Treasury, 773 F. Supp. 442, 448, 450-51 n.7 (D.D.C. 1991) (where claims are barred by statute of limitations, plaintiff "cannot attempt to resurrect" them by making subsequent request more than three years after she had first received information and almost six months after complaint had been filed), related subsequent case, Mittleman v. OPM, No. 92-158, slip op. at 1 n.1 (D.D.C. Jan. 18, 1995), summary affirmance granted, 76 F.3d 1240, 1242 (D.C. Cir. 1996).

The only judicial discussion of the Supreme Court's Irwin presumption of equitable tolling in the context of an access lawsuit is found in Rouse v. U.S. Department of State, 548 F.3d 871, 876-77 (9th Cir. 2008), amended and superseded by 567 F.3d 408 (9th Cir. 2009). Although the opinion was superseded (apparently on mootness grounds, see id. at 410 & n.1), the Ninth Circuit determined that the Irwin rebuttable presumption did not apply to an access claim because it "has no analog in private litigation." 548 F.3d at 877-78.

Damages

The statute of limitations for a damages cause of action begins when the plaintiff knew or should have known of the Privacy Act violation. See Burnham v. Mayberry, 313 F. App'x 455, 456 (3d Cir. 2009); Shehee v. DEA, No. 05-5276, 2006 U.S. App. LEXIS 15586, at *2 (D.C. Cir. June 14, 2006); Duncan v. EPA, 89 F. App'x 635, 635 (9th Cir. 2004); Williams v. Reno, No. 95-5155, 1996 WL 460093, at *1 (D.C. Cir. Aug. 7, 1996); Tijerina v. Walters, 821 F.2d 789, 797 (D.C. Cir. 1987); see also Smith v. United States, 142 F. App'x 209, 210 (5th Cir. 2005) (per curiam) ("agree[ing] with the majority of other circuits that, under section 552a(g)(5) of the Privacy Act, . . . a cause of action accrues when the plaintiff knew or should have known of the alleged violation"); Green v. Westphal, 94 F. App'x 902, 904 (3d Cir. 2004) ("A cause of action arises under the Privacy

OVERVIEW OF THE PRIVACY ACT

Act when the individual knows or has reason to know of the alleged error in the individual's record and the individual is harmed by the alleged error."); Bergman v. United States, 751 F.2d 314, 316-17 (10th Cir. 1984) (holding that limitations period for damages action under subsection (g)(1)(C) commences at time three conditions are met: (1) an error was made in maintaining plaintiff's records; (2) plaintiff was wronged by such error; and (3) plaintiff either knew or had reason to know of such error); Brockway v. VA Conn. Healthcare Sys., No. 3:10-CV-719, 2012 WL 2154263, at *13-14 (D. Conn. June 13, 2012) (dismissing claim as time-barred as plaintiff "was [] on notice that a possible disclosure of his VA medical records had occurred" when "a non-VA doctor" called "asking if [plaintiff] would like to receive psychotherapy from him" "well outside the requisite two-year statute of limitations"); Toolasprashad v. BOP, No. 09-0317, 2009 WL 3163068, at *2 (D.D.C. Sept. 29, 2009) (finding Privacy Act claim time-barred because plaintiff filed it more than two years after final agency action); cf. Bowyer v. U.S. Dep't of the Air Force, 875 F.2d 632, 636 (7th Cir. 1989) (applying stricter standard and holding that the limitations period begins to run when "plaintiff first knew or had reason to know that the private records were being maintained"); Diliberti v. United States, 817 F.2d 1259, 1262-64 (7th Cir. 1987) (same); Leibenguth v. United States, No. 08-CV-6008, 2009 WL 3165846, at *3 (W.D.N.Y. Sept. 29, 2009) (concluding that plaintiff's claim for damages "based on the VA's failure to disclose his medical records in a timely fashion" was time-barred because he filed it more than two years after he became aware of the denial of his claim for disability benefits).

Some courts have held that once the plaintiff knows or has reason to know of a record's existence, even if based upon hearsay or rumors, the plaintiff has a "duty to inquire" into the matter – i.e., "two years from that time to investigate whether sufficient factual and legal bases existed for bringing suit." See Bowyer, 875 F.2d at 637; see also Diliberti, 817 F.2d at 1263-64 (stating that "the hearsay and rumors which the plaintiff described in his affidavit were enough to put him on notice" and "impose a duty to inquire into the veracity of those rumors"); Munson, No. 96-CV-70920-DT, slip op. at 2-3 (E.D. Mich. July 2, 1996); Strang v. Indahl, No. 93-97, slip op. at 2-4 (M.D. Ga. Apr. 13, 1995) ("The statute does not await confirmation or actual access to the records; hearsay and rumor are sufficient to begin running the statute of limitations."); Mangino, 818 F. Supp. at 1438 (quoting Diliberti); Rickard v. USPS, No. 87-1212, slip op. at 5 (C.D. Ill. Feb. 16, 1990) (recognizing "duty to inquire" established by Diliberti, and stating that "[e]ven unsubstantiated hearsay and rumor suffice to give a plaintiff notice of alleged inaccuracies in a record").

Generally, the plaintiff knows or has reason to know of records in violation of the Privacy Act when the plaintiff suspects there is a violation rather than when the plaintiff actually possesses those records or when the government creates those records. See Diliberti, 817 F.2d at 1262 (stating that the "relevant fact is not when the plaintiff first had physical possession of the particular records, but rather when he first knew of the existence of the records"); see also Duncan, 89 F. App'x at 635 (quoting Rose v. United States, 905 F.2d 1257, 1259 (9th Cir. 1990), and reasoning that "a certainty, or testimony under oath, is not required to begin the running of the limitations period, but rather 'what a reasonable person should have known'"). If the plaintiff has constructive notice of the possible violation, the statute of limitations is triggered. See id. at 1262-63; see also Bowyer, 875 F. 2d at 632, 636 (stating that when agency employee confirmed that agency maintained private records on plaintiff relating to previous conflict with his supervisor, he had sufficient notice of possibly erroneous records). In the context of a damages action for wrongful disclosure, the D.C. Circuit rejected the government's argument that the limitations period commenced when the contested disclosure occurred, and observed that such an unauthorized disclosure "is unlikely to come to the subject's attention until it affects him adversely, if then." Tijerina, 821 F.2d at 797. But cf. Hill v. N.Y. Post, No. 08 Civ. 5777, 2010 WL 2985906, at *3 (S.D.N.Y. July 29, 2010) (explaining that claim brought "against the unnamed BOP staff for revealing private information regarding [plaintiff] contained in his records . . . accrued . . . upon the publication of the articles describing [plaintiff's] affair").

Consistent with the constructive notice theory, other courts have similarly found that the statute of limitations began to run where the evidence or circumstances indicated that the plaintiff knew of the violation or had been affected by it. See Zied, 418 F. App'x at 113-14 (ruling that plaintiff "knew of the harm caused by" alleged inaccuracies in her SSA records, at the very latest, "when her eligible child benefits were stopped"); Lockett v. Potter, 259 F. App'x 784, 787 (6th Cir. 2008) ("EEOC hearings that took place in March 2002 and April 2003, which addressed [plaintiff's] complaints that the Postal Service's manner of storing and disseminating his records violated the Privacy Act . . . demonstrate that he knew about the alleged Privacy Act violation more than two years before his March 2006 filing of his complaint."); Harrell v. Fleming, 285 F.3d 1292,

OVERVIEW OF THE PRIVACY ACT

1293-94 (10th Cir. Apr. 10, 2002) (finding that the "limitations period began to run when [plaintiff] first became aware of the alleged errors in his presentence investigation reports" and that it was not "extended either by the government's subsequent actions or by his receipt of documents allegedly corroborating his assertions of error"); Weber v. Henderson, No. 01-1049, 2002 WL 538508, at *2 (3d Cir. Mar. 18, 2002) (per curiam) (plaintiff should have known that the entire file had been lost "when he was informed by the defendants in writing that the record had been misplaced"); Seldowitz v. Office of IG, No. 00-1142, 2000 WL 1742098, at *3 (4th Cir. Nov. 13, 2000) (per curiam) (following Tijerina and finding that plaintiff "was aware of the alleged inaccuracies when the AUSA showed him the unannotated receipts" of his housing expenses, even though he did not possess a copy of them to make a side-by-side comparison with annotated ones); Todd v. Holder, No. 11-AR-3811-S, 2012 WL 1542212, at *2, 6 (N.D. Ala. May 7, 2012) ("[plaintiff] filed this action . . . approximately three and a half years after" alleged violations of wrongful disclosures to Office of Inspector General); Doe v. FDIC, No. 11 Civ. 307, 2012 WL 612461, at *5 (S.D.N.Y. Feb. 27, 2012) (dismissing claims for unlawful disclosure as time-barred where plaintiff had sent e-mail to her supervisor more than two years before filing suit in which she stated that agency had disclosed her medical information in possible violation of Privacy Act); Shearson, 2011 WL 4102152, at *15-16 (where plaintiff had submitted brief in prior case, concluding that "filings in [that case] demonstrate that Plaintiff should have known of alleged violations" at that time); Jackson v. Shinseki, No. 10-cv-02596, 2011 WL 3568025, at *5-7 (D. Colo. Aug. 9, 2011) (dismissing as "clearly untimely" claim filed in 2010 "alleg[ing] that [plaintiff's] 1994 termination from the VA was based on the VA having inaccurate records concerning his psychiatric status" because "[t]he termination put [plaintiff] on notice that the VA considered him to be of unsuitable psychiatric disposition" and plaintiff "had reason to promptly investigate the basis of the VA's decision and thus to learn of any error in the VA's records"); Bailey v. Fulwood, 780 F. Supp. 2d 20, 28 (D.D.C. 2011) (concluding that plaintiff knew or should have known that agency had relied on a "subsequently dismissed" warrant in determining whether to grant him parole when plaintiff received "denial notice" that "specifically informed Plaintiff that [the agency's] decision was partially based on" that warrant); Jones v. BOP, No. 5:09-cv-216, 2011 WL 554080, at *2 (S.D. Miss. Feb. 7, 2011) (reasoning that federal prisoner "must have known no later than 2006 that his [presentence investigation report] included the [disputed] charge" because "he began pursuing his administrative

OVERVIEW OF THE PRIVACY ACT

remedies with respect to the [report] in 2006"); Ramey v. U.S. Marshals Serv., 755 F. Supp. 2d 88, 97-98 (D.D.C. 2010) (dismissing as time-barred claim alleging violation of subsection (e)(7) "to the extent [it] encompasses the Defendant's collection and maintenance of information regarding [contractor's] 2003 investigation" of plaintiff, during which plaintiff was interviewed by contractor); Kursar, 751 F. Supp. 2d at 167-68 ("[P]laintiff knew, or should have known, of the purported inaccuracies by as early as April 25, 2002," because he "received notification on April 25, 2002, that the TSA intended to terminate him for 'submitting false or incorrect information on his employment application and Standard Form 86'" and because he "acknowledged receipt of this [notification] when he replied on April 29, 2002, denying the allegations."), aff'd per curiam, 442 F. App'x 565; Reitz v. USDA, No. 08-4131, 2010 WL 786586, at *9, 11 (D. Kan. Mar. 4, 2010) (dismissing claims filed in 2008 because "[m]ost of the plaintiffs' letters in the record allege continuing ill effects from [Privacy Act] violations occurring in 1997 or other dates before 2006"); Gard v. U.S. Dep't of Educ., 691 F. Supp. 2d 93, 99 (D.D.C. 2010) (finding that plaintiff "became aware of the alleged violation" when he "expressed his belief that his . . . records had been destroyed in a declaration to the U.S. Office of Special Counsel"), summary affirmance granted, No. 11-5020, 2011 WL 2148585 (D.C. Cir. May 25, 2011); Ramirez v. DOJ, 594 F. Supp. 2d 58, 62-64 (D.D.C. 2009) (dismissing complaint filed in 2007 as time-barred because in 2004 plaintiff "notified the prosecutors, the probation officer, and the presiding judge at sentencing of inaccuracies in the [presentence investigation report]"), aff'd on other grounds, No. 10-5016, 2010 WL 4340408 (D.C. Cir. Oct. 19, 2010); Sims v. New, No. 08-cv-00794, 2009 WL 3234225, at *4 (D. Colo. Sept. 30, 2009) (concluding that clock began in April 2002 even though plaintiff did not receive letter containing inaccuracy until December 2005, where plaintiff learned of inaccuracy in April 2002 and was informed shortly thereafter that the inaccuracy was the basis for adverse determination); Joseph v. Cole, No. 5:07-CV-225, 2007 WL 2480171, at *2 (M.D. Ga. Aug. 27, 2007) (barring accuracy lawsuit where plaintiff inmate admitted that he knew of errors in his presentence report when it was adopted by court thirteen years prior to filing of suit); Ingram v. Gonzales, 501 F. Supp. 2d 180, 184-85 (D.D.C. 2007) (finding that prisoner's claim accrued "when he discovered that the erroneous career offender finding [in his presentence report] was being used by BOP to determine his custody classification," not at time of his sentencing); Counce v. Nicholson, No. 3:06cv00171, 2007 WL 1191013, at *15 (M.D. Tenn. Apr. 18, 2007) (barring subsection (b)/(g)(1)(D) claim

OVERVIEW OF THE PRIVACY ACT

where plaintiff first complained of Privacy Act violations to an EEO counselor in November 2003 but did not file suit until February 2006); Kenney v. Barnhart, No. 05-426, 2006 WL 2092607, at *11-12 (C.D. Cal. July 26, 2006) (finding claim untimely because plaintiff filed it more than two years after he complained to SSA of inaccuracies in his credit reports, which were allegedly based on inaccuracies in SSA records); Peterson v. Tomaselli, No. 02-6325, 2003 WL 22213125, at *8 (S.D.N.Y. Sept. 29, 2003) (finding that plaintiff's claim arose when he "knew that the false documents existed"); Fort Hall Landowners Alliance, Inc. v. BIA, No. 99-052, slip op. at 5 (finding that plaintiff's "claim accrued as soon as Plaintiffs either were aware, or should have been aware, of the existence of and source of injury, not when the Plaintiffs knew or should have known that the injury constituted a legal wrong"); Farrero, 180 F. Supp. 2d at 97 (finding that plaintiff should have known of potential violation when agency specifically informed him that it was maintaining certain documents regarding his alleged misconduct); Walker v. Ashcroft, No. 99-2385, slip op. at 15 (D.D.C. Apr. 30, 2001) ("Contrary to [p]laintiffs' contention, the record establishes that [p]laintiffs were aware of the FBI's actions well before they received this report."), summary affirmance granted, No. 01-5222, 2002 U.S. App. LEXIS 2485 (D.C. Cir. Jan. 25, 2002); Villescas v. Richardson, 124 F. Supp. 2d 647, 659 (D. Colo. 2000) (statute of limitations began to run when plaintiff received declaration in another lawsuit describing disclosure of records, even though he did not receive actual documents), appeal dismissed per stipulation sub nom. Villescas v. Abraham, No. 03-1503, slip op. at 1 (10th Cir. Feb. 24, 2004); Armstrong v. BOP, 976 F. Supp. 17, 21 (D.D.C. 1997) (following Tijerina and finding plaintiff's claim barred by statute of limitations where plaintiff had written letter more than two and one-half years earlier indicating that her prison file was lacking favorable information), summary affirmance granted, Armstrong v. BOP, No. 97-5208, 1998 WL 65543 (D.C. Cir. Jan. 30. 1998); Nwangoro v. Dep't of the Army, 952 F. Supp. 394, 397-98 (N.D. Tex. 1996) ("[T]he limitation period commences not when the plaintiff first obtains possession of the particular records at issue, but rather when he first knew of their existence."); Brown v. VA, No. 94-1119, 1996 WL 263636, at *1-2 (D.D.C. May 15, 1996) (Privacy Act claim barred by statute of limitations because plaintiff "knew or should have known that the Privacy Act may have been violated" when he submitted federal tort claim to VA concerning same matter "over two and a half years" before suit filed); Gordon v. DOJ, No. 94-2636, 1995 WL 472360, at *2 (D.D.C. Aug. 3, 1995) (statute of limitations ran from time of plaintiff's receipt of letter from

OVERVIEW OF THE PRIVACY ACT

sentencing judge rejecting information contained in presentencing report, at which point plaintiff "knew or . . . should have known what became inaccuracies in his presentencing report"); Rice v. Hawk, No. 94-1519, slip op. at 2-3 & n.1 (D.D.C. Dec. 30, 1994) (plaintiff knew of contents of presentence report at time he filed "Objection to Presentence Investigation Report," at which time statute of limitations began to run), summary affirmance granted, No. 95-5027, 1995 WL 551148 (D.C. Cir. Aug. 2, 1995); Szymanski, 870 F. Supp. at 378-79 (citing Bergman and Tijerina, and stating that "[b]ecause plaintiff was given the opportunity to review the documents he now maintains contain incorrect information and waived that opportunity, the Court finds that he should have known about any errors at the time of this waiver" but that, additionally, plaintiff had complained about same information in his appeal to Parole Commission more than two years previously); Malewich v. USPS, No. 91-4871, slip op. at 21-22 (D.N.J. Apr. 8, 1993) (statute began to run when plaintiff was aware that file was being used in investigation of plaintiff and when he was notified of proposed termination of employment), aff'd, 27 F.3d 557 (3d Cir. 1994) (unpublished table decision); Mangino, 818 F. Supp. at 1437-38 (applying Bergman, Bowyer, and Diliberti, and finding that cause of action accrued on date of letter in which plaintiff indicated knowledge of records being used by agency as basis for revoking his security clearance, rather than upon his receipt of records); Ertell v. Dep't of the Army, 626 F. Supp. 903, 908 (C.D. Ill. 1986) (limitations period commenced when plaintiff "knew" that there "had been negative evaluations in his file which may explain why he is not being selected," rather than upon actual discovery of such records); cf. Doe v. NSA, No. 97-2650, 1998 WL 743665, at *1-3 (4th Cir. Oct. 23, 1998) (per curiam) (citing Rose and Diliberti, and holding that appellant's wrongful disclosure claim was time-barred because in accordance with principles of agency law, Privacy Act action accrued from time her attorney received her records).

In contrast to the constructive notice theory adopted by many courts, some courts have suggested that the limitations period for a subsection (g)(1)(C) damages action would commence when a plaintiff actually receives his record – i.e., when he actually discovers the inaccuracy. See Akutowicz v. United States, 859 F.2d 1122, 1126 (2d Cir. 1988) (holding that the limitations period "began to run, at the very latest, when the citizen received a copy of his records from the State Department"); see also Rose v. United States, 905 F.2d 1257, 1259 (9th Cir. 1990) (subsection (g)(1)(C) action accrues when reasonable person "knows or has reason to know of the alleged violation" and that period commenced when plaintiff received copy

OVERVIEW OF THE PRIVACY ACT

of her file); Lepkowski v. U.S. Dep't of the Treasury, 804 F.2d 1310, 1322-23 (D.C. Cir. 1986) (Robinson, J., concurring) (subsection (g)(1)(C) action "accrued no later than the date upon which [plaintiff] received IRS' letter . . . apprising him of destruction of the photographs and associated workpapers"); Middlebrooks v. Mabus, No. 1:11cv46, 2011 WL 4478686, at *4 (E.D. Va. Sept. 23, 2011) (finding that plaintiff "first learned of the alleged inaccuracies in her personnel record on . . . the date she received the Notice of her termination," which "contained extensive factual recitals of the specific grounds for plaintiff's termination"); Ciralsky v. CIA, 689 F. Supp. 2d 141, 158 (D.D.C. 2010) (concluding that statute of limitations "was triggered . . . when the CIA passed the [memorandum] and investigative file to Plaintiff" where claim was "based in whole or in part on the information contained in those documents"); Off, 2010 WL 3862097, at *3 ("Because Plaintiff attached the SF-50 to at least one of the complaints he filed on November 12, 1998, Plaintiff knew or had reason to know of the allegedly incorrect SF-50 at that time."); Brooks v. BOP, No. 04-0055, 2005 WL 623229, at *2 (D.D.C. Mar. 17, 2005) (claim barred where plaintiff inmate "has known of incorrect information in BOP records pertaining to him" since he received response from regional director, which "incorrectly stated that plaintiff had been found to have committed [a more serious offense]," but plaintiff did not file suit until four years later); Harry v. USPS, 867 F. Supp. 1199, 1205 (M.D. Pa. 1994) (although exact date when plaintiff should have known about alleged improper file maintenance was unclear, date of actual discovery was "sterling clear" – when plaintiff physically reviewed his files), aff'd sub nom. Harry v. USPS, Marvin T. Runyon, 60 F.3d 815 (3d Cir. 1995) (unpublished table decision); Shannon, 812 F. Supp. at 319-20 (causes of action arose when plaintiff learned of wrongs allegedly committed against him which was when he received documents that were allegedly inaccurate or wrongfully maintained); Fiorella v. HEW, 2 Gov't Disclosure Serv. (P-H) ¶ 81,363, at 81,944 (W.D. Wash. Mar. 9, 1981); cf. Steele v. Cochran, No. 95-35373, 1996 WL 285651, at *1 (9th Cir. May 29, 1996) (citing Rose and holding that Privacy Act claim filed in 1994 was time-barred because plaintiff wrote letter to agency questioning validity of information disclosed to State Bar in 1991 and was formally informed by State Bar that he was denied admission in 1991).

One district court decision has also considered the statute of limitations in connection with a Privacy Act claim under subsection (e)(3) concerning the collection of information from individuals.

OVERVIEW OF THE PRIVACY ACT

Darby v. Jensen, No. 94-S-569, 1995 U.S. Dist. LEXIS 7007, at *7-8 (D. Colo. May 15, 1995). In that case, the court determined that the claim was time-barred, as more than two years had passed since the date upon which the plaintiff had received the request for information. Id.

Several courts have considered whether a Privacy Act claim not apparently raised in the initial complaint filed within the limitations period could be found to "relate back" to the date of that earlier complaint under Rule 15(c) of the Federal Rules of Civil Procedure. See Oja v. U.S. Army Corps of Engineers, 440 F.3d 1122, 1134-35 (9th Cir. 2006) (where agency posted information pertaining to plaintiff on Web site in November 2000 and posted same information on second Web site in December 2000, holding that amended complaint did not relate back to filing date of initial complaint because "[t]he fact that the language in the two disclosures is identical is inapposite because [plaintiff's] claims . . . are based on the acts of disclosure themselves, each of which is distinct in time and place"); Freeman v. EPA, No. 02-0387, 2004 WL 2451409, at *8-9 (D.D.C. Oct. 25, 2004) (concluding that even though "the new claim is similar in that it also involves disclosure of information . . . it is hardly conceivable that the defendants would have had notice regarding the new" claim, nor "does the new claim build on facts the plaintiffs previously alleged other than the very general factual context of the case," and that, therefore, the claim fails to relate back); Fort Hall Landowners Alliance, Inc., No. 99-052, slip op. at 15 (finding that Privacy Act wrongful disclosure claims first brought in amended and second amended complaints related back to original complaint); Tripp v. DOD, 219 F. Supp. 2d 85, 91-92 (D.D.C. 2002) (holding that plaintiff's subsequent Privacy Act accounting claim was not barred by the two-year statute of limitations because plaintiff's subsequent claim arose "out of the same conduct and occurrences alleged in the initial Complaint," which dealt with the improper disclosures of Privacy Act-protected records); cf. Yee v. Solis, No. C 08-4259, 2009 WL 5064980, at *2 (N.D. Cal. Dec. 23, 2009) (rejecting argument that motion for leave to amend complaint to add Privacy Act claim "should be denied because the proposed claim does not 'relate back' to plaintiff's original claims" on ground that defendant "does not contend, let alone demonstrate, such additional claim is, in the absence of relation back, time-barred"), aff'd on other grounds, No. 10-16376, 2012 WL 902895 (9th Cir. Mar. 19, 2012).

OVERVIEW OF THE PRIVACY ACT

As discussed above, the Court of Appeals for the District of Columbia Circuit has held that the rebuttable presumption in favor of equitable tolling that was established in the Supreme Court case, Irwin v. VA, 498 U.S. 89, 95-96 (1990), applies to the Privacy Act's statute of limitations for a damages claim for unlawful disclosure. Chung v. DOJ, 333 F.3d 273, 276-77 (D.C. Cir. 2003). Further, because the D.C. Circuit could find no reason to think that Congress did not intend to equitably toll the Privacy Act's statute of limitations, it held that the government did not overcome this presumption. Id. at 278; see also Doe v. Winter, No. 1:04-CV-2170, 2007 WL 1074206, at *10-11 (M.D. Pa. Apr. 5, 2007) (noting that equitable tolling doctrine has been recognized by Third Circuit but finding that plaintiff failed to provide evidence for its application); Cannon-Harper v. U.S. Postmaster Gen., No. 06-10520, 2006 WL 2975492, at *1 (E.D. Mich. Oct. 17, 2006) (declining to apply equitable tolling to statute of limitations for subsection (b)/(g)(1)(C) claim where plaintiff had initially filed claim in state court); Cooper v. BOP, No. 02-1844, 2006 WL 751341, at *3 (D.D.C. Mar. 23, 2006) (applying equitable tolling where court had sealed inmate's presentence report because he "was unable to obtain vital information on the existence of his claim until he could review the [report]"); Freeman v. EPA, 2004 WL 2451409, at *9 (concluding that plaintiffs' argument that they "have not had the opportunity to support [their] allegation" due to lack of discovery was "insufficient justification for this court to countenance any equitable adjustment to the statute of limitations"); Fort Hall Landowners Alliance, Inc., No. 99-052, slip op. at 7 (finding "Privacy Act's statute of limitations subject to a rebuttable presumption of equitable tolling" but holding that statute of limitations was not tolled based on the facts before the court).

In addition, the statute's own terms provide that if the plaintiff remains unaware of his cause of action because of the agency's material and willful misrepresentations of information required by the statute to be disclosed to him and the information is material to establishment of the liability of the agency to the individual, then the limitations period runs from the date upon which the plaintiff discovers the misrepresentation. 5 U.S.C. § 552a(g)(5); see also Ciralsky, 689 F. Supp. 2d at 154 (where plaintiff argued that "by allegedly denying [the plaintiff's] request . . . for pertinent information confirming his suspicion . . . the CIA committed a material and willful misrepresentation of information required to be disclosed to Plaintiff and material to establishing the liability of the Agency to him. . . . Taking the factual allegations of the complaint as true, such misrepresentation delays the start of the limitations period."); Lacey v. United States, 74 F. Supp. 2d 13, 15-16 (D.D.C. 1999) (concluding that defendants made material and willful misrepresentations to plaintiffs by telling them that they lacked evidence and should wait for agency to finish its own investigation of claim before bringing suit, which tolled statute of limitations until agency "confirmed that there was substance to plaintiffs' claim of violations"); Burkins, 865 F. Supp. at 1496 ("Accepting plaintiff's claims of agency misrepresentation as true, the statute may have been tolled."); Pope v. Bond, 641 F. Supp. 489, 500 (D.D.C. 1986) (holding that the FAA's actions constituted willful and material representation because of its repeated denials of plaintiff's request for access, which "prevents the statute of limitations from running until the misrepresentation is discovered"); cf. Weber v. Henderson, 22 F. App'x 610, 612 (3d Cir. 2002) (per curiam) (finding that even if the court were to consider the claim not properly raised on the appeal, "[t]here is no evidence in the record to show that the failure to disclose [a memorandum that plaintiff claims would have avoided much of the pending litigation] was the result of willful misrepresentation"); Sims v. New, 2009 WL 3234225, at *4-5 (concluding that "[e]ven if Defendants concealed the actual contents of the [letter at issue] from Plaintiffs [for more than three years], Defendants did not fraudulently conceal the facts giving rise to Plaintiff's claims" because plaintiff knew of the inaccuracy contained in the letter when he requested it); Leibenguth, 2009 WL 3165846, at *3 ("Because the alleged misrepresentation was made with respect to when a rehearing would be held, and did not pertain to information required to be disclosed under the Privacy Act, plaintiffs have failed to establish that the alternative statute of limitations period applies."); Mudd v. U.S. Army, No. 2:05-CV-137, 2007 WL 4358262, at *7 (M.D. Fla. Dec. 10, 2007) (concluding that plaintiff failed to establish that "information allegedly undermining the accuracy of the [record] was materially and willfully misrepresented, or that it was information required under the Privacy Act to be disclosed to plaintiff, or that the allegedly misrepresented information was material to establishment of the liability"); Doe v. Thompson, 332 F. Supp. 2d 124, 134 (D.D.C. 2004) (finding no material and willful misrepresentation where agency "notified the plaintiff about the record and its contents . . . when the record was first created" and "changed the record twice [at plaintiff's request] in an effort to produce an accurate record"); Marin v. DOD, No. 95-2175, 1998 WL 779101, at *1 (D.D.C. Oct. 23, 1998) (denying defendants' motion to dismiss on ground that claim was time-barred and accepting plaintiff's claim regarding timing of agency misrepresentation),

OVERVIEW OF THE PRIVACY ACT

summary affirmance granted, No. 99-5102, 1999 WL 1006404 (D.C. Cir. Oct. 8, 1999); Munson, No. 96-CV-70920-DT, slip op. at 4-5 (E.D. Mich. July 2, 1996) (statement that agency could find no record of disclosure of report to state police but that it would check further "does not provide any evidence of a willful and material misrepresentation"); Strang v. Indahl, No. 93-97, slip op. at 2-4 (M.D. Ga. Apr. 13, 1995) (agency's denial of allegations in plaintiff's complaint did not equate as material misrepresentation; by voluntarily dismissing suit on belief that reliance on circumstantial evidence was insufficient, plaintiff "elected to forego the very lawsuit which would have . . . substantiated her suspicions").

Note that the Seventh Circuit has stated that this special relief provision is necessarily incorporated into tests, such as the one set forth in Bergman, which focus on when a plaintiff first knew or had reason to know of an error in maintaining his records. Diliberti, 817 F.2d at 1262 n.1; see also Malewich, No. 91-4871, slip op. at 25-27 (D.N.J. Apr. 8, 1993) (following Diliberti and precluding "the plaintiff from utilizing the discovery rule as a basis for extending the permissible filing date"). The government argued to the Court of Appeals for the District of Columbia Circuit in Tijerina v. Walters that subsection (g)(5) "makes sense only if Congress intended the normal statutory period to commence at the time of the alleged violation, regardless of whether the potential plaintiff is or should be aware of the agency's action." See 821 F.2d at 797-98. The D.C. Circuit, however, rejected that argument and stated that in order to ensure that the government cannot escape liability by purposefully misrepresenting information, "the Act allows the period to commence upon actual discovery of the misrepresentation, whereas . . . for other actions under the Act, the period begins when the plaintiff knew or should have known of the violation . . . thus in no way affect[ing] the special treatment Congress provided for the particularly egregious cases of government misconduct singled out in the Act's statute of limitations." Id. at 798.

Additionally, it has been held that "[a] Privacy Act claim is not tolled by continuing violations." Davis v. DOJ, 204 F.3d 723, 726 (7th Cir. 2000); see also Bowyer, 875 F.2d at 638 (citing Bergman and Diliberti, and rejecting argument that continuing violation doctrine should toll statute of limitations); Diliberti, 817 F.2d at 1264 (citing Bergman for same proposition); Bergman, 751 F.2d at 316-17 (ruling that limitations period commenced when agency first notified plaintiff in writing that it would not reconsider his discharge or correct his job classification records and rejecting argument "that a

OVERVIEW OF THE PRIVACY ACT

new cause of action arose upon each and every subsequent adverse determination based on erroneous records"); Reitz, 2010 WL 786586, at *9-10 (dismissing as time-barred claims filed in 2008 "alleg[ing] continuing ill effects from violations occurring in 1997 or other dates before 2006" because "'[a] new cause of action does not arise' 'upon each and every subsequent adverse determination based on erroneous records'" (quoting Harrell, 285 F.3d at 1293)); Blaylock v. Snow, No. 4:06-CV-142-A, 2006 WL 3751308, at *7 (N.D. Tex. Dec. 21, 2006) (ruling that "continuing violations do not toll limitations period" in case involving several allegedly improper disclosures over course of three years); Thompson, 332 F. Supp. 2d at 132-33 (rejecting argument that "a new cause of action was created each time [the agency] disseminated [plaintiff's] revised Report after [the agency] had been placed on notice of a potential problem and before it reviewed the revised Report for accuracy, relevance, completeness, and timeliness"); Jarrett v. White, No. 01-800, 2002 WL 1348304, at *6 (D. Del. June 17, 2002), aff'd per curiam sub nom. Jarrett v. Brownlee, 80 F. App'x 107 (Fed. Cir. 2003) (rejecting argument that continuing violation doctrine should toll statute of limitations); Malewich, No. 91-4871, slip op. at 23-25 (D.N.J. Apr. 8, 1993) (same); Shannon, 812 F. Supp. at 319-20 (plaintiff "cannot revive a potential cause of action simply because the violation continued to occur; he can allege subsequent violations only if there are subsequent events that occurred in violation of the Privacy Act"); cf. Baker v. United States, 943 F. Supp. 270, 273 (W.D.N.Y. 1996) (citing Shannon with approval). But cf. Burkins v. United States, 865 F. Supp. 1480, 1496 (D. Colo. 1994) (citing Bergman and viewing plaintiff's harm as "continuing transaction").

The Court of Appeals for the Ninth Circuit in Oja v. U.S. Army Corps of Engineers, 440 F.3d 1122 (9th Cir. 2006), applied the single publication rule in a case involving a subsection (b)/(g)(1)(D) claim based on multiple postings to two agency Web sites of information pertaining to the plaintiff. 440 F.3d at 1130-33. The court rejected the argument that "the continuous hosting of private information on an Internet Web site [is] a series of discrete and ongoing acts of publication, each giving rise to a cause of action with its own statute of limitations." Id. at 1132. Applying the single publication rule, the court held that the claim was time-barred because the plaintiff filed it more than two years from when plaintiff became aware of the first posting. Id. at 1133.

Moreover, a plaintiff's voluntary pursuit of administrative procedures should not toll the running of the statute of limitations, because no

OVERVIEW OF THE PRIVACY ACT

administrative exhaustion requirement exists before a damages action can be brought. See Uhl v. Swanstrom, 876 F. Supp. 1545, 1560-61 (N.D. Iowa 1995), aff'd on other grounds, 79 F.3d 751 (8th Cir. 1996); see also Majied v. United States, No. 7:05CV00077, 2007 WL 1170628, at *3 (W.D. Va. Apr. 18, 2007); Molzen v. BOP, No. 05-2360, 2007 WL 779059, at *3 (D.D.C. Mar. 8, 2007); Mitchell v. BOP, No. 05-0443, 2005 WL 3275803, at *3 (D.D.C. Sept. 30, 2005); cf. Kursar, 751 F. Supp. 2d at 168-69 (stating that it was "not persuaded" by plaintiff's argument that "equitable tolling should apply to his claim because he first sought relief before the MSPB" but finding that "[i]n any event, tolling is inappropriate here because [plaintiff's] pursuit of a remedy before the MSPB was in regards to her termination . . . and not the maintenance of his . . . records"), aff'd per curiam, 442 F. App'x 565; Christensen v. U.S. Dep't of the Interior, 109 F. App'x 373, 375 (10th Cir. 2004) ("[T]here is no basis for tolling the limitations period while Plaintiff pursued his administrative claim [under the Federal Tort Claims Act], because there is no administrative exhaustion requirement when a plaintiff seeks damages under the Privacy Act.").

Finally, one district court has applied a provision of the Servicemember's Civil Relief Act to toll the statute of limitations for a Privacy Act claim brought by an active duty member of the U.S. Marine Corps. See Baker v. England, 397 F. Supp. 2d 18, 23-24 (D.D.C. 2005), aff'd on other grounds, 210 F. App'x 16 (D.C. Cir. 2006). Under that statute, "the period of a servicemember's military service may not be included in computing any period limited by law, regulation, or order for the bringing of any action or proceeding in court." 50 U.S.C. App. § 526(a).

4. **Jury Trial**

Generally, the Seventh Amendment does not grant a plaintiff the right to trial by jury in actions against the federal government. U.S. Const. amend. VII. Under sovereign immunity principles, a plaintiff has a right to a jury trial only when the right has been "unequivocally expressed" by Congress. Lehman v. Nakshian, 453 U.S. 156, 160-61 (1981). The Privacy Act is silent on this point and, therefore, there is no right to a jury trial under the statute. Every court to have considered the issue has ruled accordingly. See Payne v. EEOC, No. 00-2021, 2000 WL 1862659, at *2 (10th Cir. Dec. 20, 2000); Harris v. USDA, No. 96-5783, 1997 WL 528498, at *3 (6th Cir. Aug. 26, 1997); Buckles v. Indian Health Serv./Belcourt Serv. Unit, 268 F. Supp. 2d 1101, 1102-03 (D.N.D. 2003); Stewart v. FBI, No. 97-1595,

OVERVIEW OF THE PRIVACY ACT

1999 U.S. Dist. LEXIS 18773, at *7-9 (D. Or. Sept. 29, 1999) (magistrate's recommendation), adopted, No. 97-1595, 1999 U.S. Dist. LEXIS 18785 (D. Or. Nov. 24, 1999); Flanagan v. Reno, 8 F. Supp. 2d 1049, 1053 n.3 (N.D. Ill. 1998); Clarkson v. IRS, No. 8:88-3036-3K, slip op. at 8 (D.S.C. May 10, 1990), aff'd, 935 F.2d 1285 (4th Cir. 1991) (unpublished table decision); Williams v. United States, No. H-80-249, slip op. at 13-14 (D. Conn. Apr. 10, 1984); Calhoun v. Wells, 3 Gov't Disclosure Serv. (P-H) ¶ 83,272, at 84,059 n.2 (D.S.C. July 30, 1980); Henson v. U.S. Army, No. 76-45-C5, 1977 U.S. Dist. LEXIS 16868 (D. Kan. Mar. 16, 1977). But cf. Tomasello v. Rubin, No. 93-1326, slip op. at 3-5, 19 (D.D.C. Aug. 19, 1997) (noting that court was "guided by" advisory jury verdict in awarding Privacy Act damages in case also involving non-Privacy Act claims), aff'd, 167 F.3d 612, 616-17 (D.C. Cir. 1999) (recounting fact of advisory jury verdict as to Privacy Act claims).

CRIMINAL PENALTIES

"Any officer or employee of an agency, who by virtue of his employment or official position, has possession of, or access to, agency records which contain individually identifiable information the disclosure of which is prohibited by this section or by rules or regulations established thereunder, and who knowing that disclosure of the specific material is so prohibited, willfully discloses the material in any manner to any person or agency not entitled to receive it, shall be guilty of a misdemeanor and fined not more than $5,000." 5 U.S.C. § 552a(i)(1).

"Any officer or employee of any agency who willfully maintains a system of records without meeting the notice requirements of subsection (e)(4) of this section shall be guilty of a misdemeanor and fined not more than $5,000." 5 U.S.C. § 552a(i)(2).

"Any person who knowingly and willfully requests or obtains any record concerning an individual from an agency under false pretenses shall be guilty of a misdemeanor and fined not more than $5,000." 5 U.S.C. § 552a(i)(3).

Comment:

These provisions are solely penal and create no private right of action. See Jones v. Farm Credit Admin., No. 86-2243, slip op. at 3 (8th Cir. Apr. 13, 1987); Unt v. Aerospace Corp., 765 F.2d 1440, 1448 (9th Cir. 1985); McNeill v. IRS, No. 93-2204, 1995 U.S. Dist. LEXIS 2372, at *9-10 (D.D.C. Feb. 7, 1995); Lapin v. Taylor, 475 F. Supp. 446, 448 (D. Haw. 1979); see also FLRA v. DOD, 977 F.2d 545, 549 n.6 (11th Cir. 1992) (dictum); Beckette v. USPS, No. 88-802, slip op. at 14 n.14 (E.D. Va. July 3, 1989); Kassel v. VA, 682 F. Supp. 646, 657 (D.N.H. 1988); Bernson v. ICC, 625 F. Supp. 10, 13 (D. Mass. 1984); cf. Thomas v. Reno, No. 97-1155, 1998 WL 33923, at *2 (10th Cir. Jan. 29, 1998) (finding that plaintiff's request

OVERVIEW OF THE PRIVACY ACT

for criminal sanctions did "not allege sufficient facts to raise the issue of whether there exists a private right of action to enforce the Privacy Act's provision for criminal penalties," and citing Unt and FLRA v. DOD); Study v. United States, No. 3:08cv493, 2009 WL 2340649, at *4 (N.D. Fla. July 24, 2009) (granting plaintiff's motion to amend his complaint but directing him to "delete his request [made pursuant to subsection (i)] that criminal charges be initiated against any Defendant" because "a private citizen has no authority to initiate a criminal prosecution").

There have been at least two criminal prosecutions for unlawful disclosure of Privacy Act-protected records. See United States v. Trabert, 978 F. Supp. 1368 (D. Colo. 1997) (defendant found not guilty; prosecution did not prove "beyond a reasonable doubt that defendant 'willfully disclosed' protected material"; evidence presented constituted, "at best, gross negligence" and thus was "insufficient for purposes of prosecution under § 552a(i)(1)"); United States v. Gonzales, No. 76-132 (M.D. La. Dec. 21, 1976) (guilty plea entered). See generally In re Mullins (Tamposi Fee Application), 84 F.3d 1439, 1441 (D.C. Cir. 1996) (per curiam) (case concerning application for reimbursement of attorney fees where Independent Counsel found that no prosecution was warranted under Privacy Act because there was no conclusive evidence of improper disclosure of information).

TEN EXEMPTIONS

A. One Special Exemption – 5 U.S.C. § 552a(d)(5)

"nothing in this [Act] shall allow an individual access to any information compiled in reasonable anticipation of a civil action or proceeding."

Comment:

The subsection (d)(5) provision is sometimes mistakenly overlooked because it is not located with the other exemptions in sections (j) and (k). It is an exemption from only the access provision of the Privacy Act. But cf. Smith v. United States, 142 F. App'x 209, 210 (5th Cir. 2005) (per curiam) (holding that plaintiff had no right to amend record that was "prepared in response to [his] [Federal Tort Claims Act] claim" because it fell within coverage of subsection (d)(5) and, therefore, it was "also exempt from the amendment requirements of the Act" (emphases added)).

This exemption provision reflects Congress's intent to exclude civil litigation files from access under subsection (d)(1). See 120 Cong. Rec. 36,959-60 (1974), reprinted in Source Book at 936-38, available at http://www.loc.gov/rr/frd/Military_Law/pdf/LH_privacy_act-1974.pdf. Indeed, this Privacy Act provision has been held to be similar to the attorney work-product privilege, see, e.g., Martin v. Office of Special Counsel, 819 F.2d 1181, 1187-89 (D.C. Cir. 1987); Hernandez v. Alexander, 671 F.2d

OVERVIEW OF THE PRIVACY ACT

402, 408 (10th Cir. 1982); Barber v. INS, No. 90-0067C, slip op. at 4-6 (W.D. Wash. May 15, 1990), and to extend even to information prepared by non-attorneys, see Varville v. Rubin, No. 3:96CV00629, 1998 U.S. Dist. LEXIS 14006, at *9-12 (D. Conn. Aug. 18, 1998) (citing Martin and Smiertka, infra, for proposition that courts "have interpreted the exemption in accordance with its plain language and have not read the requirements of the attorney work product doctrine into Exemption (d)(5)," and broadly construing subsection (d)(5) to protect report prepared pursuant to ethics inquiry into alleged hiring improprieties, finding "that the fact that the documents at issue were not prepared by or at the direction of an attorney is not determinative in deciding whether Exemption (d)(5) exempts the documents from disclosure"); Blazy v. Tenet, 979 F. Supp. 10, 24 (D.D.C. 1997) (broadly construing subsection (d)(5) to protect communications between CIA's Office of General Counsel and members of plaintiff's Employee Review Panel while panel was deciding whether to recommend retaining plaintiff), summary affirmance granted, No. 97-5330, 1998 WL 315583 (D.C. Cir. May 12, 1998); Smiertka v. U.S. Dep't of the Treasury, 447 F. Supp. 221, 227-28 (D.D.C. 1978) (broadly construing subsection (d)(5) to cover documents prepared by and at direction of lay agency staff persons during period prior to plaintiff's firing), remanded on other grounds, 604 F.2d 698 (D.C. Cir. 1979); see also Nazimuddin v. IRS, No. 99-2476, 2001 WL 112274, at *3-4 (S.D. Tex. Jan. 10, 2001) (applying subsection (d)(5) to internal memorandum from anonymous informant to plaintiff's supervisor prepared in anticipation of disciplinary action of plaintiff); Taylor v. U.S. Dep't of Educ., No. 91 N 837, slip op. at 3, 6 (D. Colo. Feb. 25, 1994) (applying subsection (d)(5) to private citizen's complaint letter maintained by plaintiff's supervisor in anticipation of plaintiff's termination); Gov't Accountability Project v. Office of Special Counsel, No. 87-0235, 1988 WL 21394, at *5 (D.D.C. Feb. 22, 1988) (subsection (d)(5) "extends to any records compiled in anticipation of civil proceedings, whether prepared by attorneys or lay investigators"); Crooker v. Marshals Serv., No. 85-2599, slip op. at 2-3 (D.D.C. Dec. 16, 1985) (subsection (d)(5) protects information "regardless of whether it was prepared by an attorney"); Barrett v. Customs Serv., No. 77-3033, slip op. at 2-3 (E.D. La. Feb. 22, 1979) (applying subsection (d)(5) to "policy recommendations regarding plaintiff['s] separation from the Customs Service and the possibility of a sex discrimination action").

This provision shields information that is compiled in anticipation of court proceedings or quasi-judicial administrative hearings. See, e.g., Martin, 819 F.2d at 1188-89; Louis v. U.S. Dep't of Labor, No. 03-5534, slip op. at 7 (W.D. Wash. Mar. 8, 2004); McCready v. Principi, 297 F. Supp. 2d 178, 189-90 (D.D.C. 2003), aff'd in part & rev'd in part on other grounds sub nom. McCready v. Nicholson, 465 F.3d 1 (D.C. Cir. 2006); Nazimuddin,

OVERVIEW OF THE PRIVACY ACT

2001 WL 112274, at *3-4; Frets v. DOT, No. 88-0404-CV-W-9, slip op. at 11 (W.D. Mo. Dec. 14, 1988); see also OMB Guidelines, 40 Fed. Reg. 28,948, 28,960 (July 9, 1975), available at http://www.whitehouse.gov/sites/default/files/omb/assets/omb/inforeg/implementation_guidelines.pdf ("civil proceeding" term intended to cover "quasi-judicial and preliminary judicial steps").

It should be noted, however, that this provision is in certain respects not as broad as Exemption 5 of the Freedom of Information Act, 5 U.S.C. § 552(b)(5) (2006). For example, by its terms it does not cover information compiled in anticipation of criminal actions. (Of course, subsection (j)(2), discussed below, may provide protection for such information.) Also, subsection (d)(5) does not incorporate other Exemption 5 privileges, such as the deliberative process privilege. See, e.g., Savada v. DOD, 755 F. Supp. 6, 9 (D.D.C. 1991). But see Blazy, 979 F. Supp. at 24 (incorrectly stating that "FOIA Exemption 5 and Privacy Act Exemption (d)(5) permit the agency to withhold information that qualifies as attorney work product or falls under the attorney-client or deliberative process privilege"). This means that deliberative information regularly withheld under the FOIA can be required to be disclosed under the Privacy Act. See, e.g., Savada, 755 F. Supp. at 9.

In addition, one court has held that an agency had not waived the applicability of subsection (d)(5) to preclude access despite plaintiffs' arguments that the agency waived its common law attorney-client and attorney work-product privileges. McCready, 297 F. Supp. 2d at 189-90 (concluding that "[s]ubsection (d)(5) states that 'nothing in this section shall allow' access to information compiled in anticipation of a civil action" and that "[s]ince 'shall' is a mandatory word," the agency had not waived its right to invoke subsection (d)(5)), aff'd in part & rev'd in part on other grounds sub nom. McCready v. Nicholson, 465 F.3d 1.

Unlike all of the other Privacy Act exemptions discussed below, however, subsection (d)(5) is entirely "self-executing," inasmuch as it does not require an implementing regulation in order to be effective. Cf. Mervin v. Bonfanti, 410 F. Supp. 1205, 1207 (D.D.C. 1976) ("[A]n absolute prerequisite for taking advantage of [exemption (k)(5)] is that the head of the particular agency promulgate a rule.").

B. Two General Exemptions – 5 U.S.C. § 552a(j)(1) and (j)(2)

"The head of any agency may promulgate rules, in accordance with the requirements (including general notice) of sections 553(b)(1), (2), and (3), (c), and (e) of this title, to exempt any system of records within the agency from any part of this section except subsections (b), (c)(1) and (2), (e)(4)(A)

OVERVIEW OF THE PRIVACY ACT

through (F), (e)(6), (7), (9), (10), and (11), and (i) if the system of records is

(1) maintained by the Central Intelligence Agency; or

(2) maintained by an agency or component thereof which performs as its principal function any activity pertaining to the enforcement of criminal laws, including police efforts to prevent, control, or reduce crime or to apprehend criminals, and the activities of prosecutors, courts, correctional, probation, pardon, or parole authorities, and which consists of

(A) information compiled for the purpose of identifying individual criminal offenders and alleged offenders and consisting only of identifying data and notations of arrests, the nature and disposition of criminal charges, sentencing, confinement, release, and parole and probation status;

(B) information compiled for the purpose of a criminal investigation, including reports of informants and investigators, and associated with an identifiable individual; or

(C) reports identifiable to an individual compiled at any stage of the process of enforcement of the criminal laws from arrest or indictment through release from supervision.

At the time rules are adopted under this subsection, the agency shall include in the statement required under section 553(c) of this title, the reasons why the system of records is to be exempted from a provision of this section."

Comment:

One district court has described subsection (j) as follows: "Put in the simplest terms, what Congress gave Congress can take away, which it did here by conferring on agencies the power to exempt certain records from the Privacy Act." Williams v. Farrior, 334 F. Supp. 2d 898, 905 (E.D. Va. 2004). The court went on to explain that "Congress, at most, granted" an "inchoate right" to individuals. Id. "[B]y specifically granting agencies . . . the power to exempt certain records from the Privacy Act," moreover, "Congress conditioned any right [an individual] might have to assert a Privacy Act claim on whether [a particular agency] exercises this power." Id. Thus, "[w]hen [an agency] exercise[s] this exemption power, any inchoate claim [an individual] may once have had [is] extinguished." Id.

For cases involving subsection (j)(1), see Alford v. CIA, 610 F.2d 348, 348-

OVERVIEW OF THE PRIVACY ACT

49 (5th Cir. 1980); Bassiouni v. CIA, No. 02-4049, 2004 U.S. Dist. LEXIS 5290, at *13-24 (N.D. Ill. Mar. 30, 2004), aff'd, 392 F.3d 244 (7th Cir. 2005); Pipko v. CIA, 312 F. Supp. 2d 669, 678-79 (D.N.J. 2004); Blazy v. Tenet, 979 F. Supp. 10, 23-25 (D.D.C. 1997), summary affirmance granted, No. 97-5330, 1998 WL 315583 (D.C. Cir. May 12, 1998); Hunsberger v. CIA, No. 92-2186, slip op. at 2-3 (D.D.C. Apr. 5, 1995); Wilson v. CIA, No. 89-3356, 1991 WL 226682, at *1 (D.D.C. Oct. 15, 1991); Bryant v. CIA, No. 90-1163, 1991 U.S. Dist. LEXIS 8964, at *2 (D.D.C. June 28, 1991); and Anthony v. CIA, 1 Gov't Disclosure Serv. (P-H) ¶ 79,196, at 79,371 (E.D. Va. Sept. 19, 1979).

Subsection (j)(2)'s threshold requirement is that the system of records be maintained by "an agency or component thereof which performs as its principal function any activity pertaining to the enforcement of criminal laws." This requirement is usually met by such obvious law enforcement components as the FBI, DEA, and ATF. In addition, Department of Justice components such as the Federal Bureau of Prisons, see, e.g., Skinner v. BOP, 584 F.3d 1093, 1096 (D.C. Cir. 2009); White v. U.S. Prob. Office, 148 F.3d 1124, 1125 (D.C. Cir. 1998); Kellett v. BOP, No. 94-1898, 1995 U.S. App. LEXIS 26746, at *10-11 (1st Cir. Sept. 18, 1995) (per curiam); Duffin v. Carlson, 636 F.2d 709, 711 (D.C. Cir. 1980), the U.S. Attorney's Office, see, e.g., Holub v. EOUSA, No. 09-347, 2009 WL 3247000, at *5-6 (D.D.C. Oct. 12, 2009); Foster v. EOUSA, No. 4:05CV658, 2006 WL 1045762, at *2 (E.D. Mo. Apr. 19, 2006); Hatcher v. DOJ, 910 F. Supp. 1, 2-3 (D.D.C. 1995), the Office of the Pardon Attorney, see, e.g., Binion v. DOJ, 695 F.2d 1189, 1191 (9th Cir. 1983), the U.S. Marshals Service, see, e.g., Boyer v. U.S. Marshals Serv., No. 04-1472, 2005 WL 599971, at *2-3 (D.D.C. Mar. 14, 2005), and the U.S. Parole Commission, see, e.g., Fendler v. U.S. Parole Comm'n, 774 F.2d 975, 979 (9th Cir. 1985); James v. Baer, No. 89-2841, 1990 U.S. Dist. LEXIS 5702, at *2 (D.D.C. May 11, 1990), qualify to use subsection (j)(2). Other entities that have been held to meet the threshold requirement include the Criminal Investigation Division of the Internal Revenue Service, see Carp v. IRS, No. 00-5992, 2002 U.S. Dist. LEXIS 2921, at *17 (D.N.J. Jan. 28, 2002), the U.S. Secret Service, a component of the Department of Homeland Security, see Arnold v. U.S. Secret Serv., 524 F. Supp. 2d 65, 66 (D.D.C. 2007), the Postal Inspection Service, a U.S. Postal Service component, see Anderson v. USPS, 7 F. Supp. 2d 583, 586 n.3 (E.D. Pa. 1998), aff'd, 187 F.3d 625 (3d Cir. 1999) (unpublished table decision); Dorman v. Mulligan, No. 92 C 3230 (N.D. Ill. Sept. 23, 1992), and the Air Force Office of Special Investigations, see, e.g., Gowan v. U.S. Dep't of the Air Force, 148 F.3d 1182, 1189-90 (10th Cir. 1998); Butler v. Dep't of the Air Force, 888 F. Supp. 174, 179 (D.D.C. 1995), aff'd per curiam, No. 96-5111 (D.C. Cir. May 6, 1997).

OVERVIEW OF THE PRIVACY ACT

However, it has been held that the threshold requirement is not met where only one of the principal functions of the component maintaining the system is criminal law enforcement. See Alexander v. IRS, No. 86-0414, 1987 WL 13958, at *4 (D.D.C. June 30, 1987) (IRS Inspection Service's internal "conduct investigation" system); Anderson v. U.S. Dep't of the Treasury, No. 76-1404, slip op. at 6-7 (D.D.C. July 19, 1977) (same). Several courts have held that an Inspector General's Office qualifies as a "principal function" criminal law enforcement component. See Seldowitz v. Office of IG, No. 00-1142, 2000 WL 1742098, at *4 (4th Cir. Nov. 13, 2000) (per curiam); Mumme v. U.S. Dep't of Labor, 150 F. Supp. 2d 162, 172 (D. Me. 2001), aff'd, No. 01-2256 (1st Cir. June 12, 2002); Smith v. Treasury Inspector Gen. for Tax Admin., No. 11-2033, 2011 WL 6026040, at *2 (D. Md. Dec. 1, 2011); Taylor v. U.S. Dep't of Educ., No. 91 N 837, slip op. at 5 (D. Colo. Feb. 25, 1994); Von Tempske v. HHS, 2 Gov't Disclosure Serv. (P-H) ¶ 82,091, at 82,385 (W.D. Mo. Nov. 11, 1981).

Once the threshold requirement is satisfied, it must be shown that the system of records at issue consists of information compiled for one of the criminal law enforcement purposes listed in subsection (j)(2)(A)-(C). See, e.g., Jordan v. DOJ, 668 F. 3d 1188, 1201-02 (10th Cir. 2011) (rejecting argument that "the district court reached its conclusion based on the simple fact that the BOP has by regulation exempted from Privacy Act disclosure the file systems in which it keeps his psychological records and the copied mail" because the magistrate judge explicitly considered § 552a(j), stating that 'because [the psychological records and copied mail] were generated during [plaintiff's] incarceration in federal prison, they are subject to exemption'"; noting also that records at issue "are exempt under § 552a(j)(2)(C) because they are 'identifiable' to [plaintiff] and were 'compiled' during his incarceration"); Taccetta v. FBI, No. 10-6194, 2012 WL 2523075, at *5 (D.N.J. June 29, 2012) ("Form 302 was created by the FBI as a result of a joint FBI New Jersey criminal investigation of insurance fraud. All records created by the FBI in its investigation of violation of criminal law are exempt from disclosure under the Privacy Act."); Smith v. Treasury Inspector Gen. for Tax Admin., 2011 WL 6026040, at *3 (rejecting argument that report of investigation "cannot be properly exempted because any claim that [plaintiff] violated a criminal law ceased to be 'colorable' once the AUSA declined to prosecute him" on ground that "whether or not an investigation is 'criminal' depends on what is being investigated and not the ultimate conclusion of the investigators or the decision of a prosecutor"); Shearson v. DHS, No. 1:06 CV 1478, 2007 WL 764026, at *11 (N.D. Ohio Mar. 9, 2007) (concluding that agency had properly exempted records at issue pursuant to subsection (j)(2) because "a review of the records indicates that plaintiff is considered a 'lookout and/or a suspected terrorist'" and, therefore, "the records properly qualify as 'information compiled for the

OVERVIEW OF THE PRIVACY ACT

purpose of a criminal investigation . . . and associated with an identifiable individual'"), aff'd in pertinent part, rev'd in part, & remanded, on other grounds, 638 F. 3d 498 (6th Cir. 2011); Holz v. Westphal, 217 F. Supp. 2d 50, 54-56 (D.D.C. 2002) (finding subsection (j)(2) inapplicable to report of investigation even though report was maintained in exempt system of records, because agency's operating regulations provided that investigation underlying report was never within agency's purview and therefore was not compiled for criminal law enforcement purpose); cf. Kates v. King, No. 12-1835, 2012 WL 2583374, at *1-2 (3d Cir. July 5, 2012) (per curiam) ("Indeed, the BOP has exempted its central record system, where an inmate's PSI is located," which was used in plaintiff's sentencing). Given the breadth of this exemption, an agency's burden of proof is generally less stringent than under the FOIA, at least in the access context. See Binion, 695 F.2d at 1192-93 (9th Cir. 1983) (referencing legislative history in support of "a broad exemption" because these records "contain particularly sensitive information" (quoting H.R. Rep. No. 1416, 93d Cong., 2d Sess. 18 (1974))). Indeed, several courts have observed that "the Vaughn rationale [requiring itemized indices of withheld records] is probably inapplicable to Privacy Act cases where a general exemption has been established." Restrepo v. DOJ, No. 5-86-294, slip op. at 6 (D. Minn. June 23, 1987) (citing Shapiro v. DEA, 721 F.2d 215, 218 (7th Cir. 1983), vacated as moot, 469 U.S. 14 (1984)); see also Schulze v. FBI, No. 1:05-CV-0180, 2010 WL 2902518, at *15 (E.D. Cal. July 22, 2010) (The (j)(2) "exemption is both categorical and enduring."); Miller v. FBI, No. 77-C-3331, 1987 WL 18331, at *2 (N.D. Ill. Oct. 7, 1987); Welsh v. IRS, No. 85-1024, slip op. at 3-4 (D.N.M. Oct. 21, 1986). Moreover, in access cases the Act does not grant courts the authority to review the information at issue in camera to determine whether subsection (j)(2)(A)-(C) is applicable. See 5 U.S.C. § 552a(g)(3)(A) (in camera review only where subsection (k) exemptions are invoked); see also Exner v. FBI, 612 F.2d 1202, 1206 (9th Cir. 1980); Reyes v. DEA, 647 F. Supp. 1509, 1512 (D.P.R. 1986), vacated & remanded on other grounds, 834 F.2d 1093 (1st Cir. 1987). However, this may be a rather academic point in light of the FOIA's grant of in camera review authority under 5 U.S.C. § 552(a)(4)(B). See, e.g., Von Tempske v. HHS, 2 Gov't Disclosure Serv. at 82,385 (rejecting claim that "administrative inquiry" investigative file fell within subsection (j)(2)(B), following in camera review under FOIA).

An important requirement of subsection (j) is that an agency must state in the Federal Register "the reasons why the system of records is to be exempted" from a particular subsection of the Act. 5 U.S.C. § 552a(j) (final sentence); see also 5 U.S.C. § 552a(k) (final sentence). It is unclear whether an agency's stated reasons for exemption – typically, a list of the adverse effects that would occur if the exemption were not available – limit the scope

OVERVIEW OF THE PRIVACY ACT

of the exemption when it is applied to specific records in the exempt system in particular cases. See Exner, 612 F.2d at 1206 (framing issue but declining to decide it). As discussed below, a confusing mass of case law in this area illustrates the struggle to give legal effect to this requirement.

Most courts have permitted agencies to claim subsection (j)(2) as a defense in access and/or amendment cases – usually without regard to the specific records at issue or the regulation's stated reasons for the exemption. See, e.g., Castaneda v. Henman, 914 F.2d 981, 986 (7th Cir. 1990) (amendment); Wentz v. DOJ, 772 F.2d 335, 337-39 (7th Cir. 1985) (amendment); Fendler, 774 F.2d at 979 (amendment); Shapiro, 721 F.2d at 217-18 (access and amendment); Binion, 695 F.2d at 1192-93 (access); Duffin, 636 F.2d at 711 (access); Exner, 612 F.2d at 1204-07 (access); Ryan v. DOJ, 595 F.2d 954, 956-57 (4th Cir. 1979) (access); Marshall v. FBI, 802 F. Supp. 2d 125, 133-34 (D.D.C. 2011) (access); Bhatia v. Office of the U.S. Attorney, N. Dist. of Cal., No. C 09-5581, 2011 WL 1298763, at *6 (N.D. Cal. Mar. 29, 2011) (amendment); Vazquez v. DOJ, 764 F. Supp. 2d 117, 120 (D.D.C. 2011) (access to accounting of disclosures); Murray v. BOP, 741 F. Supp. 2d 156, 162 (D.D.C. 2010) (access); Blackwell v. FBI, 680 F. Supp. 2d 79, 91 (D.D.C. 2010) (access); Study v. United States, No. 3:08cv493, 2010 WL 1257655, at *4 (N.D. Fla. Mar. 4, 2010) (amendment); Holt v. DOJ, 734 F. Supp. 2d 28, 39 (D.D.C. 2010) (access); Jordan v. DOJ, No. 07-cv-02303, 2009 WL 2913223, at *26-27 (D. Colo. Sept. 8, 2009) (access); Davis v. BOP, No. 06-1698, 2007 WL 1830863, at *2 (D.D.C. June 26, 2007) (amendment); Enigwe v. BOP, No. 06-457, 2006 WL 3791379, at *3 n.2 (D.D.C. Dec. 22, 2006) (amendment); Cooper v. BOP, No. 02-1844, 2006 WL 751341, at *3 (D.D.C. Mar. 23, 2006) (amendment); Fisher v. BOP, No. 05-0851, 2006 WL 401819, at *1 (D.D.C. Feb. 21, 2006) (amendment); Maydak v. DOJ, 254 F. Supp. 2d 23, 34-35 (D.D.C. 2003) (access to accounting of disclosures); Anderson v. U.S. Marshals Serv., 943 F. Supp. 37, 39-40 (D.D.C. 1996) (access); Hatcher, 910 F. Supp. at 2-3 (access); Aquino v. Stone, 768 F. Supp. 529, 530-31 (E.D. Va. 1991) (amendment), aff'd, 957 F.2d 139 (4th Cir. 1992); Whittle v. Moschella, 756 F. Supp. 589, 595-96 (D.D.C. 1991) (access); Simon v. DOJ, 752 F. Supp. 14, 23 (D.D.C. 1990) (access), aff'd, 980 F.2d 782 (D.C. Cir. 1992); Bagley v. FBI, No. C88-4075, slip op. at 2-4 (N.D. Iowa Aug. 28, 1989) (access to accounting of disclosures); Anderson v. DOJ, No. 87-5959, 1988 WL 50372, at *1 (E.D. Pa. May 16, 1988) (amendment); Yon v. IRS, 671 F. Supp. 1344, 1347 (S.D. Fla. 1987) (access); Burks v. DOJ, No. 83-CV-189, slip op. at 2 n.1 (N.D.N.Y. Aug. 9, 1985) (access); Stimac v. Dep't of the Treasury, 586 F. Supp. 34, 35-37 (N.D. Ill. 1984) (access); Cooper v. DOJ, 578 F. Supp. 546, 547 (D.D.C. 1983) (access); Stimac v. FBI, 577 F. Supp. 923, 924-25 (N.D. Ill. 1984) (access); Turner v. Ralston, 567 F. Supp. 606, 607-08 (W.D. Mo. 1983) (access), superseded by statute on other grounds, Central Intelligence

OVERVIEW OF THE PRIVACY ACT

Agency Information Act, Pub. L. No. 98-477, codified at 5 U.S.C. § 552a(t); Smith v. DOJ, No. 81-CV-813, 1983 U.S. Dist. Lexis 10878, at *15-20 (N.D.N.Y. Dec. 13, 1983) (amendment); Wilson v. Bell, 3 Gov't Disclosure Serv. (P-H) ¶ 83,025, at 83,471 (S.D. Tex. Nov. 2, 1982) (amendment); Nunez v. DEA, 497 F. Supp. 209, 211 (S.D.N.Y. 1980) (access); Bambulas v. Chief, U.S. Marshal, No. 77-3229, slip op. at 2 (D. Kan. Jan. 3, 1979) (amendment); Pacheco v. FBI, 470 F. Supp. 1091, 1107 (D.P.R. 1979) (amendment); Varona Pacheco v. FBI, 456 F. Supp. 1024, 1034-35 (D.P.R. 1978) (amendment). But cf. Zahedi v. DOJ, No. 10-694, 2011 WL 1872206, at *3 (D. Or. May 16, 2011) (explaining that "an accounting of information obtained pursuant to a search warrant in the context of a criminal investigation . . . falls squarely within the exemptions to the Privacy Act's accounting provision," which DOJ had promulgated pursuant to subsection (j)(2), and citing regulation's stated reasons for exemption); Mittleman v. U.S. Dep't of the Treasury, 919 F. Supp. 461, 469 (D.D.C. 1995) (finding subsection (k)(2) applicable and citing regulation's stated reasons for exemption of Department of Treasury Inspector General system of records from accounting of disclosures provision pursuant to subsections (j) and (k)(2)), aff'd in part & remanded in part on other grounds, 104 F.3d 410 (D.C. Cir. 1997).

Indeed, the Court of Appeals for the Seventh Circuit has gone so far as to hold that subsection (j)(2) "'does not require that a regulation's rationale for exempting a record from [access] apply in each particular case.'" Wentz, 772 F.2d at 337-38 (quoting Shapiro, 721 F.2d at 218). This appears also to be the view of the Court of Appeals for the First Circuit. See Irons v. Bell, 596 F.2d 468, 471 (1st Cir. 1979) ("None of the additional conditions found in Exemption 7 of the FOIA, such as disclosure of a confidential source, need be met before the Privacy Act exemption applies."); see also Reyes, 647 F. Supp. at 1512 (noting that "justification need not apply to every record and every piece of a record as long as the system is properly exempted" and that "[t]he general exemption applies to the whole system regardless of the content of individual records within it").

Some courts have construed subsection (j)(2) regulations to permit exemption of systems of records from provisions of the Act even where the stated reasons do not appear to be applicable in the particular case. See, e.g., Alexander v. United States, 787 F.2d 1349, 1351-52 & n.2 (9th Cir. 1986) (dismissing subsection (g)(1)(C) damages action – alleging violation of subsection (e)(5) – on ground that system of records was exempt from subsection (g) even though implementing regulation mentioned only "access" as rationale for exemption); Wentz, 772 F.2d at 336-39 (dismissing amendment action on ground that system of records was exempt from subsection (d) even though implementing regulation mentioned only

OVERVIEW OF THE PRIVACY ACT

"access" as rationale for exemption and record at issue had been disclosed to plaintiff). Note, however, that the Ninth Circuit's decision in Fendler v. U.S. Bureau of Prisons significantly narrowed the breadth of its earlier holding in Alexander. See 846 F.2d at 554 n.3 (observing that agency in Alexander "had clearly and expressly exempted its system of records from both subsection (e)(5) and subsection (g) . . . [but that for] some unexplained reason, the Bureau of Prisons, unlike the agency involved in Alexander, did not exempt itself from [subsection] (e)(5)").

In contrast to these cases, a concurring opinion in the decision by the Court of Appeals for the Ninth Circuit in Exner v. FBI articulated a narrower view of subsection (j)(2). See 612 F.2d 1202, 1207-08 (9th Cir. 1980) (construing subsection (j)(2)(B) as "coextensive" with FOIA Exemption 7 and noting that "reason for withholding the document must be consistent with at least one of the adverse effects listed in the [regulation]"). This narrower view of the exemption finds support in two decisions – Powell v. U.S. Department of Justice, 851 F.2d 394, 395 (D.C. Cir. 1988) (per curiam), and Rosenberg v. Meese, 622 F. Supp. 1451, 1460 (S.D.N.Y. 1985). In Powell, the Court of Appeals for the District of Columbia Circuit ruled that "no legitimate reason" can exist for an agency to refuse to amend a record (in an exempt system of records) already made public with regard only to the requester's correct residence address, and that subsection (j)(2) does not permit an agency to refuse "disclosure or amendment of objective, noncontroversial information" such as race, sex, and correct addresses). 851 F.2d at 395. In Rosenberg, a district court ordered access to a sentencing transcript contained in the same exempt system of records on the ground that the "proffered reasons are simply inapplicable when the particular document requested is a matter of public record." 622 F. Supp. at 1460. The system of records at issue in both Powell and Rosenberg had been exempted from subsection (d), the Act's access and amendment provision. Powell, 851 F.2d at 395; Rosenberg, 622 F. Supp. at 1459-60. However, the agency's regulation failed to specifically state any reason for exempting the system from amendment and its reasons for exempting the system from access were limited. Powell, 851 F.2d at 395; Rosenberg, 622 F. Supp. at 1460. Apparently, because the contents of the particular records at issue were viewed as innocuous – i.e., they had previously been made public – each court found that the agency had lost its exemption (j)(2) claim. Powell, 851 F.2d at 395; Rosenberg, 622 F. Supp. at 1460.

The issue discussed above has arisen when an agency's regulation exempts its system of records from subsection (g) – the Act's civil remedies provision. Oddly, the language of subsection (j) appears to permit this. See OMB Guidelines, 40 Fed. Reg. 28,948, 28,971, available at http://www.whitehouse.gov/sites/default/files/omb/assets/omb/inforeg/implementation_

guidelines.pdf. However, in Tijerina v. Walters, 821 F.2d 789, 795-97 (D.C. Cir. 1987), the D.C. Circuit held that an agency cannot insulate itself from a wrongful disclosure damages action (see 5 U.S.C. § 552a(b), (g)(1)(D)) in such a manner. It construed subsection (j) to permit an agency to exempt only a system of records – and not the agency itself – from other provisions of the Act. See 821 F.2d at 796-97. The result in Tijerina was heavily and understandably influenced by the fact that subsection (j) by its terms does not permit exemption from the subsection (b) restriction-on-disclosure provision. Id. In Tijerina, the government argued that "subsection (g) is 'conspicuously absent' from the list" of specific provisions that are not eligible for exemption under (j)(2), and that that "omission demonstrates that Congress intended agencies to be able to elude civil liability for any violation of the Act," including subsection (b)'s disclosure prohibition. Id. at 795. While the D.C. Circuit noted that "some other courts ha[d] indicated in dicta" to the contrary, "[h]aving considered the issue at length [in Tijerina], in which it [wa]s squarely presented, [the Court] declined to follow that view." Id. (citing Kimberlin v. DOJ, 788 F.2d 434, 436 n.2 (7th Cir. 1986), and Ryan v. DOJ, 595 F.2d 954, 958 (5th Cir. 1979)). In ruling that the exemption does not operate in this manner the Court stated: "The Act's statutory language, framework, and legislative history persuade us that the government is urging a completely anomalous use of the exemption provision that makes the Act a foolishness. The interpretation offered by the government would give agencies license to defang completely the strict limitations on disclosure that Congress intended to impose." Tijerina, 821 F.2d at 797. See also Doe v. FBI, 936 F.2d 1346, 1351-52 (D.C. Cir. 1991) (explaining that "the touchstone for an agency's liability to suit under the Act is the substantive obligation underlying the plaintiff's claim"; holding that a cause of action under (g)(1)(A) could "not lie with regard to records that the agency had properly exempted from the Act's amendment requirements," because "Tijerina merely held that an agency cannot escape liability for violating non-exemptible Privacy Act obligations simply by exempting itself from the Act's remedial provisions"). The Court of Appeals for the Sixth Circuit has considered this issue as well. See Shearson v. DHS, 638 F.3d 498 (6th Cir. 2011). Although viewing the cases that the D.C. Circuit in Tijerina had characterized as dicta, instead, as "implicat[ing] a Circuit split in authority," the Sixth Circuit nonetheless determined that the D.C. Circuit "expresses the better view . . . [that] an agency is permitted to exempt a system of records from the civil remedies provision if the underlying substantive duty is exemptible." Id. at 503-04 (remanding claims brought under (b) and (e)(7)); Nakash v. DOJ, 708 F. Supp. 1354, 1358-65 (S.D.N.Y. 1988) (agreeing with Tijerina after extensive discussion of case law and legislative history). But see Saleh v. United States, No. 09-cv-02563, 2011 WL 2682803, at *6 (D. Colo. Mar. 8, 2011) (magistrate's recommendation) (concluding that "Plaintiff has no private right of action

OVERVIEW OF THE PRIVACY ACT

pursuant to the Privacy Act with respect to the alleged dissemination of one of his grievances" because agency had exempted system of records from subsection (g)), adopted in pertinent part, 2011 WL 2682728 (D. Colo. July 8, 2011).

While other courts have indicated that agencies may employ subsection (j)(2) to exempt their systems of records from the subsection (g) civil remedies provision, generally, these cases suggest that the regulation's statement of reasons for exempting a system of records from the subsection (g) civil remedies provision itself constitutes a limitation on the scope of the exemption. See Fendler, 846 F.2d at 553-54 & n.3 (declining to dismiss subsection (g)(1)(C) damages action – alleging violation of subsection (e)(5) – on ground that agency's "stated justification for exemption from subsection (g) bears no relation to subsection (e)(5)"); Ryan v. DOJ, 595 F.2d 954, 957-58 (4th Cir. 1979) (dismissing access claim, but not wrongful disclosure claim, on ground that record system was exempt from subsection (g) because regulation mentioned only "access" as reason for exemption); Nakash, 708 F. Supp. at 1365 (alternative holding) (declining to dismiss wrongful disclosure action for same reason); Kimberlin v. DOJ, 605 F. Supp. 79, 82 (N.D. Ill. 1985) (same), aff'd, 788 F.2d 434 (7th Cir. 1986); Nutter v. VA, No. 84-2392, slip op. at 2-4 (D.D.C. July 9, 1985) (same); see also Alford v. CIA, 610 F.2d 348, 349 (5th Cir. 1980) (declining to decide whether agency may, by regulation, deprive district courts of jurisdiction to review decisions to deny access). Cf. Shearson v. DHS, 638 F.3d 498, 503 (6th Cir. 2011) (although holding that an agency may not claim exemption from (g) unless "the underlying substantive duty is exemptible," going on to "question whether [the agency's] efforts to exempt the system of records from § 552a(g) were procedurally adequate" because "[t]he agency's stated justification for exempting the [system of records] from § 552a(g) is ambiguous regarding the extent to which the rule exempts the [system of records] from the civil-remedies provision").

The Bureau of Prisons has promulgated rules exempting a number of its systems of records – among them, notably, the Inmate Central Records System – from various subsections of the Act, including (d), (e)(5), and (g). See 28 C.F.R. § 16.97 (2012). Among the most frequently litigated Privacy Act claims are those brought by federal inmates against BOP based on one or more allegedly inaccurate records. In a typical case, an inmate sues BOP seeking amendment of or damages arising out of an allegedly inaccurate record contained in a BOP system of records – usually the Inmate Central Records System. Courts have consistently dismissed these claims on the ground that BOP has exempted the system of records containing the allegedly inaccurate record from the pertinent subsection of the Act. See, e.g., Kates v. King, No. 12-1835, 2012 WL 2583374, at *2, (3d Cir. July 5,

OVERVIEW OF THE PRIVACY ACT

2012) (per curiam); Blackshear v. Lockett, 411 F. App'x 906, 907-08 (7th Cir. 2011); Flores v. Fox, 394 F. App'x 170, 172 (5th Cir. 2010); Davis v. United States, 353 F. App'x 864, 864 (4th Cir. 2009) (per curiam); Skinner, 584 F.3d at 1096; Martinez v. BOP, 444 F.3d 620, 624 (D.C. Cir. 2006); Scaff-Martinez v. BOP, 160 F. App'x 955, 956 (11th Cir. 2005); Barbour v. U.S. Parole Comm'n, No. 04-5114, 2005 WL 79041, at *1 (D.C. Cir. Jan. 13, 2005); Williams v. BOP, 85 F. App'x 299, 306 n.14 (3d Cir. 2004); Locklear v. Holland, 194 F.3d 1313, 1313 (6th Cir. 1999); Duffin, 636 F.2d at 711; Lange v. Taylor, 5:10-CT-3097, 2012 WL 255333, at *3 (E.D.N.C. Jan. 27, 2012); Earle v. Holder, 815 F. Supp. 2d 176, 181-83 (D.D.C. 2011), aff'd per curiam, No. 11-5280, 2012 WL 1450574 (D.C. Cir. Apr. 20, 2012); Thomas v. Caraway, No. 10-2031, 2011 WL 2416643, at *3 (D. Md. June 10, 2011); Blanton v. Warden, No. 7:10-cv-552, 2011 WL 1226010, at *3 (W.D. Va. Mar. 30, 2011); Keyes v. Krick, No. 09-cv-02380, 2011 WL 1100128, at *7 (D. Colo. Mar. 23, 2011); Davis v. United States, No. CIV-10-1136, 2011 WL 704894, at *5 (W.D. Okla. Jan. 4, 2011) (magistrate's recommendation), adopted 2011 WL 693639 (W.D. Okla. Feb. 18, 2011), aff'd, 426 F. App'x 648 (10th Cir. 2011); Lee v. BOP, 751 F. Supp. 2d 101, 103-04 (D.D.C. 2010); Sheppard v. Revell, No. 5:09-CT-3044, 2010 WL 3672261, at *3 (E.D.N.C. Sept. 20, 2010); Cruel v. BOP, No. 2:09CV00189, 2010 WL 3655644, at *3 (E.D. Ark. Sept. 9, 2010); James v. Tejera, No. 5:10-cv-048, 2010 WL 3324833, at *1 (M.D. Fla. Aug. 23, 2010); Banks v. BOP, No. 5:09cv147, 2010 WL 3737923, at *6 (S.D. Miss. Aug. 19, 2010) (magistrate's recommendation), adopted 2010 WL 3767112 (S.D. Miss. Sept. 17, 2010); Jones v. BOP, No. 5:09cv216, 2010 WL 6117082, at *2 (S.D. Miss. July 21, 2010); Davis v. United States, No. 09-1961, 2010 WL 2011549, at *2 (D. Md. May 18, 2010); Mosby v. Hunt, No. 09-1917, 2010 WL 1783536, at *5 (D.D.C. May 5, 2010), aff'd per curiam, No. 10-5296, 2011 WL 3240492 (D.C. Cir. July 6, 2011); Razzoli v. U.S. Navy, No. 09 Civ. 4323, 2010 WL 1438999, at *2 n.6 (S.D.N.Y. Apr. 12, 2010); Gosier v. Mitchell, No. 3:09-931, 2010 WL 619175, at *4 (D.S.C. Feb. 18, 2010); Bowles v. BOP, No. 08 CV 9591, 2010 WL 23326, at *4-5 (S.D.N.Y. Jan. 5, 2010); Jackson v. DOJ, No. 09-0846, 2009 WL 5205421, at *4 (D. Minn. Dec. 23, 2009); Ramirez v. DOJ, 594 F. Supp. 2d 58, 65-66 (D.D.C. 2009), aff'd per curiam, No. 10-5016, 2010 WL 4340408 (D.C. Cir. Oct. 19, 2010); Lane v. BOP, No. 08-1269, 2009 WL 1636422, at *1 (D.D.C. June 9, 2009), aff'd per curiam, No. 09-5228, 2010 WL 288816 (D.C. Cir. Jan. 7, 2010); Jordan, 2009 WL 2913223, at *26-27; Brown v. BOP, 498 F. Supp. 2d 298, 301-03 (D.D.C. 2007); Robinson v. Vazquez, No. CV207-082, 2007 WL 4209370, at *1 (S.D. Ga. Nov. 26, 2007); Reuter v. BOP, No. C-06-00259, 2007 WL 1521544, at *5 (S.D. Tex. May 24, 2007); Elliott v. BOP, 521 F. Supp. 2d 41, 56 (D.D.C. 2007); Collins v. BOP, No. 5:06CV129, 2007 WL 2433967, at *3-4 (S.D. Miss. Aug. 2, 2007); Edwards v. Lewis, No. 06-5044, 2007 WL 1035029, at *6 (D.N.J. Mar. 30, 2007); Simpson v. BOP,

OVERVIEW OF THE PRIVACY ACT

No. 05-2295, 2007 WL 666517, at *2-3 (D.D.C. Mar. 2, 2007); Davis v. Driver, No. 1:05CV419, 2007 WL 2220997, at *3 (E.D. Tex. Aug. 2, 2007); Parks v. BOP, No. 7:06-CV-00131, 2006 WL 771718, at *1 (W.D. Va. Mar. 23, 2006); McClellan v. BOP, No. 5:05CV194, 2006 WL 2711631, at *5 (S.D. Miss. Aug. 2, 2006); Cerralla v. Lappin, No. 1:06CV2101, 2006 WL 2794624, at *3 (N.D. Ohio Sept. 27, 2006); Bryant v. BOP, No. 04-2263, 2005 WL 3275902, at *2 (D.D.C. Sept. 27, 2005); Anderson, 1988 WL 50372, at *1.

As discussed above under "5 U.S.C. § 552a(e)(5)," note that it was not until 2002 that BOP exempted many of its systems of records, including the Inmate Central Records System, from subsection (e)(5) pursuant to subsection (j)(2). See 28 C.F.R. § 16.97(j) (codifying 67 Fed. Reg. 51,754 (Aug. 9, 2002)). Thus, inmates' subsection (e)(5)/(g)(1)(C) claims arising subsequent to August 9, 2002, should not succeed. See, e.g., Fisher v. BOP, No. 06-5088, 2007 U.S. App. LEXIS 5140, at *1 (D.C. Cir. Mar. 1, 2007) (per curiam). See "5 U.S.C. § 552a(e)(5)," above, for a more complete discussion of this issue.

Another important issue can arise with regard to the recompilation of information originally compiled for law enforcement purposes into a non-law enforcement record. The D.C. Circuit confronted this issue in Doe v. FBI, 936 F.2d 1346 (D.C. Cir. 1991), in which it applied the principles of a Supreme Court FOIA decision concerning recompilation, FBI v. Abramson, 456 U.S. 615 (1982), to Privacy Act-protected records. It held that "information contained in a document qualifying for subsection (j) or (k) exemption as a law enforcement record does not lose its exempt status when recompiled in a non-law enforcement record if the purposes underlying the exemption of the original document pertain to the recompilation as well." Doe, 936 F.2d at 1356. As was held in Abramson, the D.C. Circuit determined that recompilation does not change the basic "nature" of the information. Id.; accord OMB Guidelines, 40 Fed. Reg. at 28,971, available at http://www.whitehouse.gov/sites/default/files/omb/assets/omb/inforeg/implementation_guidelines.pdf ("The public policy which dictates the need for exempting records . . . is based on the need to protect the contents of the records in the system – not the location of the records. Consequently, in responding to a request for access where documents of another agency are involved, the agency receiving the request should consult the originating agency to determine if the records in question have been exempted."). By the same token, law enforcement files recompiled into another agency's law enforcement files may retain the exemption of the prior agency's system of records. See Dupre v. FBI, No. 01-2431, 2002 WL 1042073, at *2 n.2 (E.D. La. May 22, 2002) (finding that Suspicious Activity Report maintained in exempt Department of the Treasury system of records remained exempt

OVERVIEW OF THE PRIVACY ACT

under that system of records when transferred to FBI for law enforcement purposes).

In the context of a subsection (g)(1)(B) access claim, the District Court for the Northern District of California has ruled that an agency "is entitled to rely on exemptions promulgated after the dates on which [the plaintiff] made his Privacy Act requests." Hasbrouck v. CBP, No. C 10-3793, 2012 WL 177563, at *3 (N.D. Cal. Jan. 23, 2012) ("'[R]etroactivity' simply is not implicated, because plaintiff's claim in essence seeks prospective injunctive relief – an order requiring CBP to turn over information now. As such, this is one of the many circumstances in which 'a court should apply the law in effect at the time it renders its decision,' notwithstanding the happenstance that [plaintiff] made his Privacy Act requests before the current exemptions were promulgated.").

Finally, note that in the context of a subsection (g)(1)(B) claim for access to records, some courts have recognized that "there is no requirement that an agency administratively invoke an exemption in order to later rely on it in federal court." Barnard v. DHS, 598 F. Supp. 2d 1, 24 (D.D.C. 2009); see also, e.g., Cuban v. SEC, 744 F. Supp. 2d 60, 89-90 (D.D.C. 2010).

C. **Seven Specific Exemptions – 5 U.S.C. § 552a(k)**

"The head of any agency may promulgate rules, in accordance with the requirements (including general notice) of sections 553(b)(1), (2), and (3), (c), and (e) of this title, to exempt any system of records within the agency from subsections (c)(3), (d), (e)(1), (e)(4)(G), (H), and (I) and (f) of this section if the system of records is –

[The seven specific exemptions are discussed in order below.]

At the time rules are adopted under this subsection, the agency shall include in the statement required under section 553(c) of this title, the reasons why the system of records is to be exempted from a provision of this section."

Comment:

As noted above, subsection (g)(3)(A) grants courts the authority to "examine the contents of any agency records in camera to determine whether the records or any portion thereof may be withheld under any of the exemptions set forth in subsection (k) of this section." 5 U.S.C. § 552a(g)(3)(A). Further, several courts have held that reasonable segregation is required under the Act whenever a subsection (k) exemption is invoked. See, e.g., May v. Dep't of the Air Force, 777 F.2d 1012, 1015-17 (5th Cir. 1985);

OVERVIEW OF THE PRIVACY ACT

Lorenz v. NRC, 516 F. Supp. 1151, 1153-55 (D. Colo. 1981); Nemetz v. Dep't of the Treasury, 446 F. Supp. 102, 105 (N.D. Ill. 1978).

The District Court for the District of Columbia has rejected the argument that an agency failed to comply with subsection (k) because the agency's statement of reasons for exempting the system of records "appears only in the Federal Register, and not in the Code of Federal Regulations where the rule was eventually codified." Nat'l Whistleblower Ctr. v. HHS, No. 10-2120, 2012 WL 1026725, at *5-6 (D.D.C. Mar. 28, 2012). The court first pointed out that "[s]ubsection (k)(2) requires only that an agency's rule exempting investigative materials comply with the Administrative Procedure Act's requirement that 'the agency shall incorporate in the rules adopted a concise general statement of their basis and purpose.'" Id. (quoting 5 U.S.C. § 553(c)). The court concluded that "§ 553(c) is satisfied when a statement of the rule's basis and purpose is included in the preamble to the Final Rule appearing in the Federal Register." 2012 WL 1026725, at *6.

1. **5 U.S.C. § 552a(k)(1)**

   "subject to the provisions of section 552(b)(1) of this title."

   Comment:

   Subsection (k)(1) simply incorporates FOIA Exemption 1, 5 U.S.C. § 552(b)(1). See Arnold v. U.S. Secret Serv., 524 F. Supp. 2d 65, 66 (D.D.C. 2007); Makky v. Chertoff, 489 F. Supp. 2d 421, 441 (D.N.J. 2007); Bassiouni v. CIA, No. 02-4049, 2004 WL 1125919, at *4 (N.D. Ill. Mar. 30, 2004), aff'd on other grounds, 392 F.3d 244 (7th Cir. 2004); Pipko v. CIA, 312 F. Supp. 2d 669, 677-78 (D.N.J. 2004); Snyder v. CIA, 230 F. Supp. 2d 17, 23 (D.D.C. 2003); Keenan v. DOJ, No. 94-1909, slip op. at 2 n.2, 7-9 (D.D.C. Dec. 17, 1997); Blazy v. Tenet, 979 F. Supp. 10, 23-25 (D.D.C. 1997), summary affirmance granted, No. 97-5330, 1998 WL 315583 (D.C. Cir. May 12, 1998); Laroque v. DOJ, No. 86-2677, 1988 WL 28334, at *2 (D.D.C. Mar. 16, 1988); Moessmer v. CIA, No. 86-948C(1), slip op. at 3-5 (E.D. Mo. Feb. 19, 1987); Demetracopoulos v. CIA, 3 Gov't Disclosure Serv. (P-H) ¶ 82,508, at 83,279 (D.D.C. Oct. 8, 1982); see also OMB Guidelines, 40 Fed. Reg. 28,948, 28,972 (July 9, 1975), available at http://www.whitehouse.gov/sites/default/files/omb/assets/omb/inforeg/implementation_guidelines.pdf. The exemption has been construed to permit the withholding of classified records from an agency employee with a security clearance who seeks only private access to records about him. See Martens v. U.S. Dep't of Commerce, No. 88-3334, 1990 U.S. Dist. LEXIS 10351, at *10-11

OVERVIEW OF THE PRIVACY ACT

(D.D.C. Aug. 6, 1990).

2. **5 U.S.C. § 552a(k)(2)**

"investigatory material compiled for law enforcement purposes, other than material within the scope of subsection (j)(2) of this section: Provided, however, That if any individual is denied any right, privilege, or benefit that he would otherwise be entitled by Federal law, or for which he would otherwise be eligible, as a result of the maintenance of such material, such material shall be provided to such individual, except to the extent that the disclosure of such material would reveal the identity of a source who furnished information to the Government under an express promise that the identity of the source would be held in confidence, or, prior to the effective date of this section [September 27, 1975], under an implied promise that the identity of the source would be held in confidence."

Comment:

This exemption covers: (1) material compiled for criminal investigative law enforcement purposes, by nonprincipal function criminal law enforcement entities; and (2) material compiled for other investigative law enforcement purposes, by any agency.

The material must be compiled for some investigative "law enforcement" purpose, such as a civil investigation or a criminal investigation by a nonprincipal function criminal law enforcement agency. See OMB Guidelines, 40 Fed. Reg. 28,948, 28,972-73 (July 9, 1975), available at http://www.whitehouse.gov/sites/default/ files/omb/assets/omb/inforeg/implementation_guidelines.pdf; see also, e.g., Gowan v. U.S. Dep't of the Air Force, 148 F.3d 1182, 1188-89 (10th Cir. 1998) (fraud, waste, and abuse complaint to IG); Berger v. IRS, 487 F. Supp. 2d 482, 497-98 (D.N.J. 2007) (civil trust fund recovery penalty investigation), aff'd 288 F. App'x 829 (3d Cir. 2008), cert. denied, 129 S. Ct. 2789 (2009); Melius v. Nat'l Indian Gaming Comm'n, No. 98-2210, 1999 U.S. Dist. LEXIS 17537, at *14-15, 18-19 (D.D.C. Nov. 3, 1999) (law enforcement investigation into suitability of person involved in gaming contracts); Shewchun v. INS, No. 95-1920, slip op. at 3, 8-9 (D.D.C. Dec. 10, 1996) (investigation into deportability pursuant to Immigration and Nationality Act), summary affirmance granted, No. 97-5044 (D.C. Cir. June 5, 1997); Viotti v. U.S. Air Force, 902 F. Supp. 1331, 1335 (D. Colo. 1995) (inspector general's fraud, waste, and abuse investigation into plaintiff's travel records), aff'd, 153 F.3d 730 (10th

OVERVIEW OF THE PRIVACY ACT

Cir. 1998) (unpublished table decision); Jaindl v. Dep't of State, No. 90-1489, slip op. at 3 (D.D.C. Jan. 31, 1991) (non-principal function law enforcement agency assisting in apprehension of plaintiff by revoking his passport), summary affirmance granted, No. 91-5034 (D.C. Cir. Jan. 8, 1992); Barber v. INS, No. 90-0067C, slip op. at 6-9 (W.D. Wash. May 15, 1990) (enforcement of Immigration and Nationality Act); Welsh v. IRS, No. 85-1024, slip op. at 2-3 (D.N.M. Oct. 21, 1986) (taxpayer audit); Spence v. IRS, No. 85-1076, slip op. at 2 (D.N.M. Mar. 27, 1986) (taxpayer audit); Nader v. ICC, No. 82-1037, 1983 U.S. Dist. LEXIS 11380, at *14 (D.D.C. Nov. 23, 1983) (investigation to determine whether to bar attorney from practicing before ICC for knowingly submitting false, inaccurate, and misleading statements to agency); Heinzl v. INS, 3 Gov't Disclosure Serv. (P-H) ¶ 83,121, at 83,725 (N.D. Cal. Dec. 18, 1981) (investigation regarding possible deportation); Lobosco v. IRS, No. 77-1464, 1981 WL 1780, at *3 (E.D.N.Y. Jan. 14, 1981) (taxpayer audit); Utah Gas & Oil, Inc. v. SEC, 1 Gov't Disclosure Serv. (P-H) ¶ 80,038, at 80,114 (D. Utah Jan. 9, 1980) (dictum) (SEC investigatory files). But cf. Louis v. U.S. Dep't of Labor, No. 03-5534, slip op. at 8 (W.D. Wash. Mar. 8, 2004) (inexplicably finding that records compiled for purposes of Federal Employee Compensation Act claim were properly exempt based on stated reasons for exemption in agency's regulation without discussing whether records were indeed compiled for investigative law enforcement purposes as is statutorily required).

Therefore, subsection (k)(2) does not include material compiled solely for the purpose of a routine background security investigation of a job applicant. See Vymetalik v. FBI, 785 F.2d 1090, 1093-98 (D.C. Cir. 1986) (noting applicability of narrower subsection (k)(5) to such material and ruling that "specific allegations of illegal activities" must be involved in order for subsection (k)(2) to apply); Bostic v. FBI, No. 1:94 CV 71, slip op. at 7-8 (W.D. Mich. Dec. 16, 1994) (following Vymetalik). However, material compiled for the purpose of investigating agency employees for suspected violations of law can fall within subsection (k)(2). See Strang v. U.S. Arms Control & Disarmament Agency, 864 F.2d 859, 862-63 n.2 (D.C. Cir. 1989) ("Unlike Vymetalik, this case involves not a job applicant undergoing a routine check of his background and his ability to perform the job, but an existing agency employee investigated for violating national security regulations."); Cohen v. FBI, No. 93-1701, slip op. at 4-6 (D.D.C. Oct. 3, 1995) (applying Vymetalik and finding that particular information within background investigation file qualified as "law enforcement" information "withheld out of a legitimate concern for national security," thus "satisf[ying] the standards set forth in Vymetalik," which recognized that "'[i]f specific allegations of illegal activities were involved, then th[e] investigation might well be characterized as a law enforcement investigation'" and that "'[s]o long as the investigation was "realistically based on a legitimate concern that federal laws have been or may be violated or that national security may be breached" the records may be considered law enforcement records'" (quoting Vymetalik, 785 F.2d at 1098, in turn quoting Pratt v. Webster, 673 F.2d 408, 421 (D.C. Cir. 1982))); see also Nazimuddin v. IRS, No. 99-2476, 2001 WL 112274, at *2, 4 (S.D. Tex. Jan. 10, 2001) (protecting identity of confidential source in document prepared in anticipation of disciplinary action resulting from investigation of employee's alleged misuse of Lexis/Nexis research account); Croskey v. U.S. Office of Special Counsel, 9 F. Supp. 2d 8, 11 (D.D.C. 1998) (finding Office of Special Counsel Report of Investigation, which was developed to determine whether plaintiff had been fired for legitimate or retaliatory reasons, exempt from access and amendment provisions of Privacy Act pursuant to subsection (k)(2)), summary affirmance granted, No. 98-5346, 1999 WL 58614 (D.C. Cir. Jan. 12, 1999); Viotti, 902 F. Supp. at 1335 (concluding, "as a matter of law, that [Report of Inquiry] was compiled for a law enforcement purpose as stated in 5 U.S.C. § 552a(k)(2)" where "original purpose of the investigation . . . was a complaint to the [Inspector General] of fraud, waste and abuse," even though "complaint was not sustained and no criminal charges were brought," because "plain language of the exemption states that it applies to the purpose of the investigation, not to the result"); Mittleman v. U.S. Dep't of the Treasury, 919 F. Supp. 461, 469 (D.D.C. 1995) (finding that Inspector General's report "pertain[ing] to plaintiff's grievance against Treasury officials and related matters . . . falls squarely within the reach of exemption (k)(2)"), aff'd in part & remanded in part on other grounds, 104 F.3d 410 (D.C. Cir. 1997); Fausto v. Watt, 3 Gov't Disclosure Serv. (P-H) ¶ 83,217, at 83,929-30 (4th Cir. June 7, 1983) (holding that investigation prompted by a "hotline" tip and conducted to avoid fraud, waste, and abuse qualified under (k)(2)); Frank v. DOJ, 480 F. Supp. 596, 597 (D.D.C. 1979).

However, in Doe v. U.S. Department of Justice, 790 F. Supp. 17, 19-21 (D.D.C. 1992), the District Court for the District of Columbia construed Vymetalik narrowly and determined that although subsection (k)(5) was "directly applicable," subsection (k)(2) also applied to records of an FBI background check on a prospective

OVERVIEW OF THE PRIVACY ACT

Department of Justice attorney. It determined that the Department of Justice, as "the nation's primary law enforcement and security agency," id. at 20, had a legitimate law enforcement purpose in ensuring that "officials like Doe . . . be 'reliable, trustworthy, of good conduct and character, and of complete and unswerving loyalty to the United States,'" id. (quoting Exec. Order No. 10,450, 18 Fed. Reg. 2489 (Apr. 29, 1953)). It would seem to follow that subsection (k)(2) would likewise apply to background investigations of prospective FBI/DEA special agents. See Putnam v. DOJ, 873 F. Supp. 705, 717 (D.D.C. 1995) (finding that subsection (k)(2) was properly invoked to withhold information that would reveal identities of individuals who provided information in connection with former FBI special agent's pre-employment investigation).

Subsequently, though, the District Court for the District of Columbia, when faced with the same issue concerning subsection (k)(2)/(k)(5) applicability, relied entirely on the D.C. Circuit's opinion in Vymetalik, with no mention whatsoever of Doe v. DOJ. Cohen v. FBI, No. 93-1701 (D.D.C. Oct. 3, 1995). Nevertheless, the District Court found subsection (k)(2) to be applicable to one document in the background investigation file because that document was "withheld out of a legitimate concern for national security" and it "satisfie[d] the standards set forth in Vymetalik," which recognized that "'[i]f specific allegations of illegal activities were involved, then th[e] investigation might well be characterized as a law enforcement investigation'" and that "'[s]o long as the investigation was "realistically based on a legitimate concern that federal laws have been or may be violated or that national security may be breached" the records may be considered law enforcement records.'" Cohen, No. 93-1701, slip op. at 3-6 (D.D.C. Oct. 3, 1995) (quoting Vymetalik, 785 F.2d at 1098, in turn quoting Pratt, 673 F.2d at 421). Another district court considered Doe but found "the rationale in Vymetalik more compelling," and held that "'law enforcement purposes' as that term is utilized in [subsection (k)(2) of] the Privacy Act, does not apply to documents and information gathered during a[n FBI agent applicant's] pre-employment background investigation." Bostic, No. 1:94 CV 71, slip op. at 7-8 (W.D. Mich. Dec. 16, 1994).

Unlike with Exemption 7(A) of the Freedom of Information Act, 5 U.S.C. § 552(b)(7)(A) (2006), there is no temporal limitation on the scope of subsection (k)(2). See Irons v. Bell, 596 F.2d 468, 471 (1st Cir. 1979); Lobosco, 1981 WL 1780, at *4. But see Anderson v. U.S. Dep't of the Treasury, No. 76-1404, slip op. at 9-11 (D.D.C.

OVERVIEW OF THE PRIVACY ACT

July 19, 1977) (subsection (k)(2) inapplicable to investigatory report regarding alleged wrongdoing by IRS agent where investigation was closed and no possibility of any future law enforcement proceedings existed).

Although the issue has not been the subject of much significant case law, the OMB Guidelines explain that the "Provided, however" provision of subsection (k)(2) means that "[t]o the extent that such an investigatory record is used as a basis for denying an individual any right, privilege, or benefit to which the individual would be entitled in the absence of that record, the individual must be granted access to that record except to the extent that access would reveal the identity of a confidential source." OMB Guidelines, 40 Fed. Reg. at 28,973, available at http://www.whitehouse.gov/sites/default/files/omb/ assets/omb/inforeg/implementation_guidelines.pdf; cf. Nazimuddin, 2001 WL 112274, at *4 (protecting identity of source under express promise of confidentiality pursuant to subsection (k)(2) without discussion of whether investigatory record was used to deny right, privilege, or benefit); Guccione v. Nat'l Indian Gaming Comm'n, No. 98-CV-164, 1999 U.S. Dist. LEXIS 15475, at *11-12 (S.D. Cal. Aug. 5, 1999) (approving agency invocation of subsection (k)(2) to protect third-party names of individuals who had not been given express promises of confidentiality where plaintiff did not contend any denial of right, privilege, or benefit).

Only two decisions have discussed this provision in any depth. In Viotti v. U.S. Air Force, 902 F. Supp. at 1335-36, the District Court for the District of Colorado determined that an Air Force Colonel's forced early retirement "resulted in a loss of a benefit, right or privilege for which he was eligible – the loss of six months to four years of the difference between his active duty pay and retirement pay," and "over his life expectancy . . . the difference in pay between the amount of his retirement pay for twenty-six years of active duty versus thirty years of active duty." Id. The court found that "as a matter of law, based on [a report of inquiry, plaintiff] lost benefits, rights, and privileges for which he was eligible" and thus he was entitled to an unredacted copy of the report "despite the fact that [it] was prepared pursuant to a law enforcement investigation." Id. It went on to find that "the 'express' promise requirement" of (k)(2) was not satisfied where a witness "merely expressed a 'fear of reprisal.'" Id. (citing Londrigan v. FBI, 670 F.2d 1164, 1170 (D.C. Cir. 1981)).

The Court of Appeals for the Tenth Circuit, in affirming Viotti, noted

OVERVIEW OF THE PRIVACY ACT

that subsection (k)(2)'s limiting exception applied only in the context of access requests and did not apply to limit the exemption's applicability with regard to amendment requests. Viotti v. U.S. Air Force, No. 97-1371, 1998 WL 453670, at *2 n.2 (10th Cir. Aug. 5, 1998). While the court's footnote in Viotti spoke in terms of the particular exempting regulations at issue, the more general proposition is in complete accord with the plain language of subsection (k)(2). See 5 U.S.C. § 552a(k)(2) (in provision limiting exemption's applicability requiring that "material shall be provided to [the] individual except to the extent that disclosure of such material would reveal the identity of a [confidential source]" (emphasis added)). Nevertheless, only a matter of weeks earlier, in its decision in Gowan v. U.S. Department of the Air Force, 148 F.3d 1182, 1189 (10th Cir. 1998), the Tenth Circuit, citing the Viotti district court decision in comparison, went through the exercise of determining whether subsection (k)(2)'s limiting exception applied in the context of the amendment claims before it. The Tenth Circuit stated that subsection (k)(2)'s limiting exception was inapplicable to an Inspector General complaint because "the charges contained in the complaint were deemed unworthy of further action." Gowan, 148 F.3d at 1189. Given the very limited case law interpreting subsection (k)(2)'s limiting exception and what constitutes denial of a "right, privilege, or benefit," it is worth noting the Tenth's Circuit's statement in Gowan, even though the court's subsequent footnote in Viotti certainly calls into question its relevance to the court's ultimate holding regarding subsection (k)(2)'s applicability.

More recently, the District Court for the District of Columbia considered this provision in Nat'l Whistleblower Ctr. v. HHS, No. 10-2120, 2012 WL 1026725 (D.D.C. Mar. 28, 2012). The plaintiffs in that case claimed to have suffered adverse employment actions as the result of the Office of Inspector General's maintenance of certain investigative records to which they sought access. Id. at *7. The OIG disputed that any employment actions "occurred as a result of the maintenance" of its investigative file, especially as the results of its investigation found no misconduct. Id. The OIG maintained that any action taken by the FDA against plaintiffs "was at FDA's discretion." Id. The court agreed, stating: "In sum, OIG's maintenance of its investigative files did not cause Plaintiffs to be denied rights or benefits; instead, FDA's maintenance of its own investigative files resulted in any adverse employment actions suffered by Plaintiffs." Id.

In Doe v. U.S. Department of Justice, 790 F. Supp. at 21 n.4, 22, the court noted this provision of subsection (k)(2), but determined that it was not applicable because the plaintiff "ha[d] no entitlement to a job with the Justice Department." Inexplicably, the court did not discuss whether the denial of a federal job would amount to the denial of a "privilege" or "benefit." See id.; see also Jaindl, No. 90-1489, slip op. at 2 n.1 (D.D.C. Jan. 31, 1991) (noting that "[b]ecause there is no general right to possess a passport," application of (k)(2) was not limited in that case). Another court refused to address the provision's applicability where the plaintiff failed to raise the issue at the administrative level. Comer v. IRS, No. 85-10503-BC, slip op. at 3-5 (E.D. Mich. Mar. 27, 1986), aff'd, 831 F.2d 294 (6th Cir. 1987) (unpublished table decision).

It should be noted that information that originally qualifies for subsection (k)(2) protection should retain that protection even if it subsequently is recompiled into a non-law enforcement record. See Doe v. FBI, 936 F.2d 1346, 1356 (D.C. Cir. 1991) (discussed under subsection (j)(2), above); accord OMB Guidelines, 40 Fed. Reg. at 28,971, available at http://www.whitehouse.gov/sites/default/ files/omb/assets/omb/inforeg/implementation_guidelines.pdf (same).

Finally, two courts have considered claims brought by individuals who allegedly provided information pursuant to a promise of confidentiality and sought damages resulting from disclosure of the information and failure to sufficiently protect their identities pursuant to subsection (k)(2). Bechhoefer v. DOJ, 934 F. Supp. 535, 538-39 (W.D.N.Y. 1996), vacated & remanded, 209 F.3d 57 (2d Cir. 2000) (finding that information at issue did qualify as "record" under Privacy Act); Sterling v. United States, 798 F. Supp. 47, 49 (D.D.C. 1992). In Sterling, the District Court for the District of Columbia stated that the plaintiff was "not barred from stating a claim for monetary damages [under (g)(1)(D)] merely because the record did not contain 'personal information' about him and was not retrieved through a search of indices bearing his name or other identifying characteristics," 798 F. Supp. at 49, but in a subsequent opinion the court ultimately ruled in favor of the agency, having been presented with no evidence that the agency had intentionally or willfully disclosed the plaintiff's identity. Sterling v. United States, 826 F. Supp. 570, 571-72 (D.D.C. 1993), summary affirmance granted, No. 93-5264 (D.C. Cir. Mar. 11, 1994). However, the District Court for the Western District of New York in Bechhoefer, when presented with an argument based on Sterling, stated that it did not "find the Sterling court's analysis persuasive." Bechhoefer, 934 F. Supp. at 538-39. Having already determined that the information at issue did

OVERVIEW OF THE PRIVACY ACT

not qualify as a record "about" the plaintiff, that court recognized that subsection (k)(2) "does not prohibit agencies from releasing material that would reveal the identity of a confidential source" but rather "allows agencies to promulgate rules to exempt certain types of documents from mandatory disclosure under other portions of the Act." Id. The court went on to state that "plaintiff's reliance on § 552a(k)(2) [wa]s misplaced," and that subsection (k) was "irrelevant" to the claim before it for wrongful disclosure. Id. at 539.

3. **5 U.S.C. § 552a(k)(3)**

"maintained in connection with providing protective services to the President of the United States or other individuals pursuant to section 3056 of Title 18."

Comment:

This exemption obviously is applicable to certain Secret Service record systems. For a discussion of this exemption, see OMB Guidelines, 40 Fed. Reg. 28,948, 28,973 (July 9, 1975), available at http://www.whitehouse.gov/sites/default/files/omb/assets/omb/inforeg/implementation_guidelines.pdf.

4. **5 U.S.C. § 552a(k)(4)**

"required by statute to be maintained and used solely as statistical records."

Comment:

For a discussion of this exemption, see OMB Guidelines, 40 Fed. Reg. 28,948, 28,973 (July 9, 1975), available at http://www.whitehouse.gov/sites/default/files/omb/assets/omb/inforeg/implementation_guidelines.pdf.

5. **5 U.S.C. § 552a(k)(5)**

"investigatory material compiled solely for the purpose of determining suitability, eligibility, or qualifications for Federal civilian employment, military service, Federal contracts, or access to classified information, but only to the extent that the disclosure of such material would reveal the identity of a source who furnished information to the Government under an express promise that the identity of the source would be held in confidence, or, prior to the effective date of this section [September 27, 1975], under an implied promise that the identity of the source would be held in confidence."

Comment:

This exemption is generally applicable to source-identifying material in background employment and personnel-type investigative files. See OMB Guidelines, 40 Fed. Reg. 28,948, 28,973-74 (July 9, 1975), available at http://www.whitehouse.gov/sites/default/files/omb/assets/omb/inforeg/implementation_guidelines.pdf; 120 Cong. Rec. 40,406, 40,884-85 (1974), reprinted in Source Book at 860, 996-97, available at http://www.loc.gov/rr/frd/Military_Law/pdf/LH_privacy_act-1974.pdf. The Court of Appeals for the District of Columbia Circuit has held that exemption (k)(5) is also applicable to source-identifying material compiled for determining eligibility for federal grants, stating that "the term 'Federal contracts' in Privacy Act exemption (k)(5) encompasses a federal grant agreement if the grant agreement includes the essential elements of a contract and establishes a contractual relationship between the government and the grantee." Henke v. U.S. Dep't of Commerce, 83 F.3d 1445, 1453 (D.C. Cir. 1996). In addition, exemption (k)(5) is applicable to information collected for continued as well as original employment. See Hernandez v. Alexander, 671 F.2d 402, 406 (10th Cir. 1982). In situations where "specific allegations of illegal activities" are being investigated, an agency may be able to invoke subsection (k)(2) – which is potentially broader in its coverage than subsection (k)(5). See, e.g., Vymetalik v. FBI, 785 F.2d 1090, 1093-98 (D.C. Cir. 1986).

Subsection (k)(5) – known as the "Erlenborn Amendment" – was among the most hotly debated of any the Act's provisions because it provides for absolute protection to those who qualify as confidential sources, regardless of the adverse effect that the material they provide may have on an individual. See 120 Cong. Rec. 36,655-58 (1974), reprinted in Source Book at 908-19, available at http://www.loc.gov/rr/frd/Military_Law/pdf/LH_privacy_act-1974.pdf.

That aside, though, subsection (k)(5) still is a narrow exemption in two respects. First, in contrast to Exemption 7(D) of the Freedom of Information Act, 5 U.S.C. § 552(b)(7)(D) (2006), it requires an express promise of confidentiality for source material acquired after the effective date of the Privacy Act (September 27, 1975). Cf. Viotti v. U.S. Air Force, 902 F. Supp. 1331, 1336 (D. Colo. 1995) (finding that "'express' promise requirement" of subsection (k)(2)

OVERVIEW OF THE PRIVACY ACT

was not satisfied when witness "merely expressed a 'fear of reprisal'"), aff'd, 153 F.3d 730 (10th Cir. 1998) (unpublished table decision). For source material acquired prior to the effective date of the Privacy Act, an implied promise of confidentiality will suffice. See 5 U.S.C. § 552a(k)(5); cf. Londrigan v. FBI, 722 F.2d 840, 844-45 (D.C. Cir. 1983) (no "automatic exemption" for FBI background interviews prior to effective date of Privacy Act; however, inference drawn that interviewees were impliedly promised confidentiality where FBI showed that it had pursued "policy of confidentiality" to which interviewing agents conformed their conduct). See generally DOJ v. Landano, 508 U.S. 165 (1993) (setting standards for demonstrating implied confidentiality under FOIA Exemption 7(D)). Second, in contrast to the second clause of FOIA Exemption 7(D), subsection (k)(5) protects only source-identifying material, not all source-supplied material.

Of course, where source-identifying material is exempt from Privacy Act access under subsection (k)(5), it typically is exempt under the broader exemptions of the FOIA as well. See, e.g., Keenan v. DOJ, No. 94-1909, slip op. at 16-17 (D.D.C. Mar. 25, 1997), subsequent decision, slip op. at 5-7 (D.D.C. Dec. 16, 1997); Bostic v. FBI, No. 1:94 CV 71, slip op. at 8-9, 12-13 (W.D. Mich. Dec. 16, 1994); Miller v. United States, 630 F. Supp. 347, 348-49 (E.D.N.Y. 1986); Patton v. FBI, 626 F. Supp. 445, 446-47 (M.D. Pa. 1985), aff'd, 782 F.2d 1030 (3d Cir. 1986) (unpublished table decision); Diamond v. FBI, 532 F. Supp. 216, 232 (S.D.N.Y. 1981), aff'd, 707 F.2d 75 (2d Cir. 1983). One court has held that subsection (k)(5) protects source-identifying material even where the identity of the source is known. See Volz v. DOJ, 619 F.2d 49, 50 (10th Cir. 1980). Another court has suggested to the contrary. Doe v. U.S. Civil Serv. Comm'n, 483 F. Supp. 539, 576-77 (S.D.N.Y. 1980) (aberrational decision holding the addresses of three named persons "not exempt from disclosure under (k)(5) . . . because they didn't serve as confidential sources and the plaintiff already knows their identity").

Subsection (k)(5) is not limited to those sources who provide derogatory comments, see Londrigan v. FBI, 670 F.2d 1164, 1170 (D.C. Cir. 1981); see also Voelker v. FBI, 638 F. Supp. 571, 572-73 (E.D. Mo. 1986). It has also been held that the exemption is not limited to information that would reveal the identity of the source in statements made by those confidential sources, but also protects information that would reveal the source's identity in statements provided by third parties. See Haddon v. Freeh, 31 F. Supp. 2d 16, 21 (D.D.C. 1998). Also, the exemption's applicability is not diminished by the age of the source-identifying material. See Diamond, 532 F. Supp. at 232-33.

However, an agency cannot rely upon subsection (k)(5) to bar a requester's amendment request, as the exemption applies only to the extent that disclosure of information would reveal the identity of a confidential source. See Vymetalik, 785 F.2d at 1096-98; see also Doe v. FBI, 936 F.2d at 1356 n.12 (although documents at issue were not limited to exemption pursuant to subsection (k)(5), noting that subsection (k)(5) would not apply where FBI refused to amend information that had already been disclosed to individual seeking amendment); Bostic, No. 1:94 CV 71, slip op. at 9 (W.D. Mich. Dec. 16, 1994) (application of exemption (k)(5) in this access case is not contrary to, but rather consistent with, Vymetalik and Doe because in those cases exemption (k)(5) did not apply because relief sought was amendment of records).

Note also that OMB's policy guidance indicates that promises of confidentiality are not to be made automatically. 40 Fed. Reg. 28,948, 28,974, available at http://www.whitehouse.gov/sites/default/files/omb/assets/omb/inforeg/implementation_guidelines.pdf. Consistent with the OMB Guidelines, the Office of Personnel Management has promulgated regulations establishing procedures for determining when a pledge of confidentiality is appropriate. See 5 C.F.R. § 736.102 (2012); see also Larry v. Lawler, 605 F.2d 954, 961 n.8 (7th Cir. 1978) (suggesting that finding of "good cause" is prerequisite for granting of confidentiality to sources).

Nevertheless, the District Court for the District of Columbia has held that in order to invoke exemption (k)(5) for sources that were in fact promised confidentiality, it is not necessary that the sources themselves affirmatively sought confidentiality, nor must the government make a showing that the sources would not have furnished information without a promise of confidentiality. Henke v. U.S. Dep't of Commerce, No. 94-0189, 1996 WL 692020, at *9-10 (D.D.C. Aug. 19, 1994). The court went on to state: "[T]he question of whether the reviewers expressed a desire to keep their identities confidential is wholly irrelevant to the Court's determination of whether they were in fact given promises of confidentiality." Id. at *10. On appeal, the Court of Appeals for the District of Columbia Circuit stated that while it "would not go quite that far," as agencies "must use subsection (k)(5) sparingly," agencies may make determinations that promises of confidentiality are necessary "categorically," as "[n]othing in either the statute or the case law

OVERVIEW OF THE PRIVACY ACT

requires that [an agency] apply subsection (k)(5) only to those particular reviewers who have expressly asked for an exemption and would otherwise have declined to participate in the peer review process." Henke v. U.S. Dep't of Commerce, 83 F.3d 1445, 1449 (D.C. Cir. 1996).

Finally, it should be noted that information that originally qualifies for subsection (k)(5) protection should retain that protection even if it subsequently is recompiled into a non-law enforcement record. See Doe v. FBI, 936 F.2d 1346, 1356 (D.C. Cir. 1991) (discussed under subsection (j)(2), above); accord OMB Guidelines, 40 Fed. Reg. at 28,971, available at http://www.whitehouse.gov/sites/default/files/omb/assets/omb/inforeg/implementation_guidelines.pdf (same).

6. **5 U.S.C. § 552a(k)(6)**

"testing or examination material used solely to determine individual qualifications for appointment or promotion in the Federal service the disclosure of which would compromise the objectivity or fairness of the testing or examination process."

Comment:

It should be noted that material exempt from Privacy Act access under subsection (k)(6) is also typically exempt from FOIA access under FOIA Exemption 2. See Kelly v. U.S. Census Bureau, No. C 10-04507, 2011 U.S. Dist. LEXIS 100279, at *6 (N.D. Cal. Sept. 7, 2011); Patton v. FBI, 626 F. Supp. 445, 447 (M.D. Pa. 1985), aff'd, 782 F.2d 1030 (3d Cir. 1986) (unpublished table decision); Oatley v. United States, 3 Gov't Disclosure Serv. (P-H) ¶ 83,274, at 84,065-66 (D.D.C. Aug. 16, 1983); see also Robinett v. USPS, No. 02-1094, slip op. at 15 & n.2, 16-18 (E.D. La. July 24, 2002) (finding that information showing "how much [the agency] reduced [the plaintiff's] application score because of [a traffic violation]" was "just the type of information that courts have found could compromise an agency's evaluation process" and thus was exempt from disclosure under subsection (k)(6), and further, noting that although the court did not need to address the agency's FOIA Exemption 2 argument "[i]n light of the Court's finding that the information fits under another FOIA exemption," FOIA Exemption 2 "has been read to reflect the same concerns and cover the same information as the exemption codified in Section 552a(k)(6)"). For a further discussion of this provision, see OMB Guidelines, 40 Fed. Reg. 28,948, 28,974 (July 9, 1975), available at http://www.

OVERVIEW OF THE PRIVACY ACT

whitehouse.gov/sites/default/files/omb/assets/omb/inforeg/implementation_guidelines.pdf.

7. 5 U.S.C. § 552a(k)(7)

"evaluation material used to determine potential for promotion in the armed services, but only to the extent that the disclosure of such material would reveal the identity of a source who furnished information to the government under an express promise that the identity of the source would be held in confidence, or, prior to the effective date of this section [9-25-75], under an implied promise that the identity of the source would be held in confidence."

Comment:

For an example of the application of this exemption, see May v. Dep't of the Air Force, 777 F.2d 1012, 1015-17 (5th Cir. 1985). For a further discussion of this provision, see OMB Guidelines, 40 Fed. Reg. 28,948, 28,974 (July 9, 1975), available at http://www.whitehouse.gov/sites/default/files/omb/assets/omb/inforeg/implementation_guidelines.pdf.

SOCIAL SECURITY NUMBER USAGE

Section 7 of the Privacy Act (found at 5 U.S.C. § 552a note (Disclosure of Social Security Number)) provides that:

"It shall be unlawful for any Federal, State or local government agency to deny to any individual any right, benefit, or privilege provided by law because of such individual's refusal to disclose his social security account number." Sec. 7(a)(1).

Comment:

Note that although this provision applies beyond federal agencies, it does not apply to: (1) any disclosure which is required by federal statute; or (2) any disclosure of a social security number to any federal, state, or local agency maintaining a system of records in existence and operating before January 1, 1975, if such disclosure was required under statute or regulation adopted prior to such date to verify the identity of an individual. See Sec. 7(a)(2)(A)-(B).

Note also that the Tax Reform Act of 1976, 42 U.S.C. § 405(c)(2)(C)(i), (iv) (2006), expressly exempts state agencies from this restriction to the extent that social security numbers are used "in the administration of any tax, general public assistance, driver's license, or motor vehicle registration law within its jurisdiction." See, e.g., Peterson v. City of Detroit, 76 F. App'x 601, 602 (6th Cir. 2003) (Because 42 U.S.C. § 405(c)(2)(C)(i) "permits states to require

OVERVIEW OF THE PRIVACY ACT

disclosure of social security numbers in the administration of its driver's license law[,] . . . § 7 of the Privacy Act, insofar as it relates to the 'privilege' at issue in this case [(denial of plaintiff's application for taxicab license)], has been superseded[.]"); Stoianoff v. Comm'r of the Dep't of Motor Vehicles, 12 F. App'x 33, 35 (2d Cir. 2001) (finding that plaintiff's Privacy Act claim would fail because § 405(c)(2)(C)(i) "expressly authorizes states to require the disclosure of social security numbers in the administration of driver's license programs" and further provides that "any federal law that conflicts with this section is 'null, void, and of no effect'"); Peterson v. Michigan, No. 11-12153, slip op. at 4 (E.D. Mich. May 27, 2011) (citing Peterson v. City of Detroit and stating that 42 U.S.C. § 405(c)(2)(C)(i) "supersedes § 7 of the Privacy Act"); Claugus v. Roosevelt Island Hous. Mgmt. Corp., No. 96CIV8155, 1999 WL 258275, at *4 (S.D.N.Y. Apr. 29, 1999) (considering housing management corporation to be state actor for Privacy Act purposes but finding that Privacy Act does not apply to income verification process for public housing program because of exception created by 42 U.S.C. § 405(c)(2)(C)(i)). Exemption from the social security number provisions of the Privacy Act is also provided for certain other government uses. See, e.g., 42 U.S.C. § 405(c)(2)(C)(ii) (authorizing state use of social security numbers in issuance of birth certificates and for purposes of enforcement of child support orders); 42 U.S.C. § 405(c)(2)(C)(iii) (authorizing use of social security numbers by Secretary of Agriculture in administration of Food Stamp Act of 1977 and by Federal Crop Insurance Corporation in administration of Federal Crop Insurance Act).

"Any Federal, State or local government agency which requests an individual to disclose his social security account number shall inform that individual whether that disclosure is mandatory or voluntary, by what statutory or other authority such number is solicited, and what uses will be made of it." Sec. 7(b).

Comment:

Jurisdiction to enforce the social security number provision might appear questionable inasmuch as the Privacy Act does not expressly provide for a civil remedy against a nonfederal agency, or for injunctive relief outside of the access and amendment contexts. In fact, two courts of appeals have held that section 7 of the Privacy Act applies exclusively to federal agencies and does not provide for causes of action against state and local entities. See Schmitt v. City of Detroit, 395 F.3d 327, 329-30 (6th Cir. 2005) (noting Privacy Act's "inherently inconsistent" treatment of "agencies" as only federal agencies in subsection (a)(1) and as including "Federal, State, or local government" bodies in section 7 and, after looking to legislative history, ultimately holding that Privacy Act applies only to federal agencies); Dittman v. Cal., 191 F.3d 1020, 1026 (9th Cir. 1999) (holding that Privacy Act provides no cause of action against a state licensing entity inasmuch as the private right of civil action created by subsection (g) "is specifically limited to actions against agencies of the United States Government"); see also Peterson v. Michigan, No. 11-12153, slip op. at 3-4; Dionicio v. Allison, No. 3:09-cv-00575, 2010 WL 3893816, at *18 (M.D. Tenn. Sept. 30, 2010); Treesh v. Cardaris, No. 2:10-CV-437, 2010 WL 3603553, at *3 (S.D. Ohio Sept. 9, 2010).

OVERVIEW OF THE PRIVACY ACT

However, the Courts of Appeals for the Eleventh Circuit and the Seventh Circuit, when faced with this issue, have both held that the remedial scheme of section 3 of the Privacy Act, which applies strictly to federal agencies, does not apply to section 7, which governs social security number usage. See Gonzalez v. Vill. of W. Milwaukee, 671 F.3d 649, 661-63 (7th Cir. 2012); Schwier v. Cox, 340 F.3d 1284, 1292 (11th Cir. 2003). In Schwier, the Eleventh Circuit concluded that "Congress created an 'unambiguously conferred right' in section 7 of the Privacy Act," and it reasoned that section 7 may be enforced under 42 U.S.C. § 1983, which "provides a private right of action whenever an individual has been deprived of any constitutional or statutory federal right under color of state law" as "the remedial scheme of section 3 provides no basis for concluding that Congress intended to preclude private remedies under § 1983 for violations of section 7." Schwier, 340 F.3d at 1289-90, 1292. Following the Eleventh Circuit's reasoning in Schwier, the Seventh Circuit in Gonzalez found "no conflict between §§ 3 and 7 [of the Privacy Act]" as "it seems clear that when § 3(a)(1) defines agencies as federal agencies 'for purposes of this section,' it refers only to § 3 . . . . Accordingly, there is no need to look beyond the unambiguous text of § 7 to determine its applicability. By its express terms, § 7 applies to federal, state, and local agencies." Gonzalez, 671 F.3d at 662. Cf. Lawson v. Shelby County, Tenn., 211 F.3d 311, 335 (6th Cir. 2000) (holding that "Congress never expressly abrogated state sovereign immunity under the Privacy Act"; however, permitting plaintiffs' request for prospective injunctive relief [to enforce section 7 of the Privacy Act] against [state] officials" under Ex Parte Young, 209 U.S. 123 (1908)); Warner v. Twp. of S. Harrison, Civ. No. 09-6095, 2010 WL 3001969, at *4 (D.N.J. July 26, 2010) (dismissing plaintiff's section 7(b) claim against Township because "Plaintiff's real complaint is Defendant's widespread, and apparently unjustifiable, dissemination of his social security number to the public . . . [which is] not covered by Section 7(b), but instead by Section 3. Section 3, however, does not apply to state and local agencies."); Ingerman v. Del. River Port Auth., 630 F. Supp. 2d 426, 445 (D.N.J. 2009) (ruling that Port Authority's requirement that social security number had to be submitted to receive a senior citizen "E-Z Pass" violated section 7, which was enforceable under Ex Parte Young); Szymecki v. Norfolk, No. 2:08cv142, 2008 WL 4223620, at *9 (E.D. Va. Sept. 11, 2008) (concluding that "because Section 7 confers a legal right on individuals and because Congress did not specifically foreclose a remedy under [42 U.S.C.] § 1983 for violations of Section 7 . . . violations of Section 7 are enforceable under § 1983"); Stollenwerk v. Miller, No. 04-5510, 2006 WL 463393, at *3-7 (E.D. Pa. Feb. 24, 2006) (concluding that state statute requiring submission of social security number to purchase a handgun was invalid, as section 7 is enforceable under 42 U.S.C. § 1983). But cf. Treesh, 2010 WL 3603553, at *3 ("[E]ven if disclosure of plaintiff's medical information somehow violated the Privacy Act, [plaintiff] still fails to state a federal claim" because "section 1983 cannot be used to redress violations of the Privacy Act."); Bush v. Lancaster Bureau of Police, No. 07-3172, 2008 WL 3930290, at *7-8 (E.D. Pa. Aug. 28, 2008) (concluding that "Plaintiff cannot state a claim under [42 U.S.C. § 1983] for a violation of subsection (b) of section 7 of the Privacy Act" because "[u]pon review of the th[e] statutory language, the court cannot conclude that Congress created an 'unambiguously conferred right'" for individuals).

Other courts also have recognized implied remedies for violations of this provision's

OVERVIEW OF THE PRIVACY ACT

requirements. See Ky. Rest. Concepts, Inc. v. City of Louisville, Jefferson County, Ky., 209 F. Supp. 2d 672, 687 (W.D. Ky. 2002); McKay v. Altobello, No. 96-3458, 1997 WL 266717, at *1-3, 5 (E.D. La. May 16, 1997); Yeager v. Hackensack Water Co., 615 F. Supp. 1087, 1090-92 (D.N.J. 1985); Wolman v. United States, 501 F. Supp. 310, 311 (D.D.C. 1980), remanded, 675 F.2d 1341 (D.C. Cir. 1982) (unpublished table decision), on remand, 542 F. Supp. 84, 85-86 (D.D.C. 1982); Greater Cleveland Welfare Rights Org. v. Bauer, 462 F. Supp. 1313, 1319-21 (N.D. Ohio 1978).

For other discussions of this provision, see Schwier v. Cox, 439 F.3d 1285, 1285-86 (11th Cir. 2006) (holding that section 7(a)(2)(B) grandfather exception did not apply to Georgia voter registration procedures), aff'g 412 F. Supp. 2d 1266 (N.D. Ga. 2005), remanded by 340 F.3d at 1288-89 (explaining that although section 7 is uncodified, it is still present in the Statutes at Large and therefore is not "a dead letter"); McKay v. Thompson, 226 F.3d 752, 755 (6th Cir. 2000) (finding that Tennessee law requiring disclosure of social security number for voter registration fell within section 7(a)(2)'s exception for systems of records in existence prior to January 1, 1975, where disclosure was required under statute or regulation); Crawford v. U.S. Tr., 194 F.3d 954, 961-62 (9th Cir. 1999) (rejecting government's argument that because disclosure of plaintiff's social security number was expressly required by federal statute, section 7 was wholly inapplicable, stating that "§ 7(a)(2)(A)'s exclusion for federal statutes only pertains to the limitation recited in § 7(a)(1)"; holding that section 7(b) had "no bearing on the public disclosure of [plaintiff's] social security number[] by the government," which was the only issue in dispute); Alcaraz v. Block, 746 F.2d 593, 608-09 (9th Cir. 1984) (section 7(b)'s notice provision satisfied where agency informed "participants of the voluntariness of the disclosure, the source of authority for it and the possible uses to which the disclosed numbers may be put"); Brookens v. United States, 627 F.2d 494, 496-99 (D.C. Cir. 1980) (agency did not violate Privacy Act because it maintained system of records "before January 1, 1975 and disclosure of a social security number to identify individuals was required under [executive order]"); McElrath v. Califano, 615 F.2d 434, 440 (7th Cir. 1980) (because disclosure of social security number required by Aid to Families with Dependent Children program under 42 U.S.C. § 602(a)(25) (2006), regulations that give effect to that requirement are not violative of Privacy Act); Green v. Philbrook, 576 F.2d 440, 445-46 (2d Cir. 1978) (same); Peterson v. Michigan, No. 11-12153, slip op. at 4 (dismissing claim that "the State of Michigan unlawfully denied [plaintiff's] application for renewal of his chauffeur license . . . because he refused to provide his social security number" on ground that REAL ID Act of 2005, 109 Pub. L. No. 109-13, § 202(c), 119 Stat. 312, "requires disclosure of social security numbers when obtaining drivers licenses, thereby exempting such request for disclosure from § 7(a)(1)") (alternative holding); White v. Cain, No. 2:10-cv-01182, 2011 WL 1087489, at *6-7 (S.D. W. Va. Mar. 21, 2011) (dismissing claim brought against police officer alleging that officer violated section 7 by "requesting the plaintiff's Social Security Number without providing the plaintiff with adequate information" on ground that "the Privacy Act is not applicable to individuals"); El-Bey v. N.C. Bd. of Nursing, No. 1:09CV753, 2009 WL 5220166, at *2 (M.D.N.C. Dec. 31, 2009) (dismissing plaintiff's "Privacy Act/Social Security Act claim" because "Plaintiff alleges only that Defendants requested his number, not that they denied him a legal right based on its non-disclosure so as to potentially violate the Privacy

OVERVIEW OF THE PRIVACY ACT

Act"); GeorgiaCarry.org, Inc. v. Metro. Atlanta Rapid Transit Auth., No. 1:09-CV-594, 2009 WL 5033444, at *9-10 (N.D. Ga. Dec. 14, 2009) (finding "one or both of the [transit authority police] officer Defendants violated section 7(b)" when officers "asked [plaintiff] for his identification, firearms license, and social security number . . . . But neither officer told [plaintiff] whether he had to provide his social security number, what authority they relied on in asking for the number, or what the number would be used for."); Ingerman, 630 F. Supp. 2d at 439-41 (ruling that because Port Authority was publicly created and sufficiently under the joint control and guidance of governments of New Jersey and Pennsylvania, it qualified as an "agency" under section 7); Szymecki, 2008 WL 4223620, at *9 (concluding that plaintiff stated claim under section 7 where he alleged that city threatened to arrest and incarcerate him if he did not provide his social security number and that city did not inform him why it needed number or how it would be used); Lynn v. Comm'r, 80 T.C.M. (CCH) 31 (2000) (holding that agency did not violate Privacy Act, because section 151(e) of the IRS code "is a Federal statute that requires the disclosure of a dependent's Social Security number"); Russell v. Bd. of Plumbing Exam'rs, 74 F. Supp. 2d 339, 347 (S.D.N.Y. 1999) (finding violation of section 7 and ordering injunctive relief where defendants neither informed applicants that providing social security number was optional nor provided statutory authority by which number was solicited, and no statutory authority existed); Johnson v. Fleming, No. 95 Civ. 1891, 1996 WL 502410, at *1, 3-4 (S.D.N.Y. Sept. 4, 1996) (no violation of either section 7(a)(1) or section 7(b) where, during course of seizure of property from plaintiff, an unlicensed street vendor, plaintiff refused to provide police officer with his social security number and officer "seized all of Plaintiff's records rather than only 'a bagful' as other officers allegedly had done" on previous occasions); In re Rausch, No. BK-S-95-23707, 1996 WL 333685, at *7 (Bankr. D. Nev. May 20, 1996) (Privacy Act "inapplicable" because 11 U.S.C. § 110 "requires placing the SSN upon 'documents for filing'"); In re Floyd, 193 B.R. 548, 552-53 (Bankr. N.D. Cal. 1996) (Bankruptcy Code, 11 U.S.C. § 110(c) (2006), required disclosure of social security number, thus section 7(a) inapplicable; further stating that section 7(b) also inapplicable "even assuming the [U.S. Trustee] or the clerk of the bankruptcy court were agencies" because no "request" had been made; rather, because disclosure of social security number is required by statute, "the [U.S. Trustee] is enforcing a Congressional directive, not 'requesting' anyone's SSN" and "[t]he clerk receives documents for filing but does not police their content or form or request that certain information be included"); Krebs v. Rutgers, 797 F. Supp. 1246, 1256 (D.N.J. 1992) (although state-chartered, Rutgers is not state agency or government-controlled corporation subject to Privacy Act); Greidinger v. Davis, 782 F. Supp. 1106, 1108-09 (E.D. Va. 1992) (Privacy Act violated where state did not provide timely notice in accordance with section 7(b) when collecting social security number for voter registration), rev'd & remanded on other grounds, 988 F.2d 1344 (4th Cir. 1993); Libertarian Party v. Bremer Ehrler, Etc., 776 F. Supp. 1200, 1209 (E.D. Ky. 1991) (requirement that voter include social security number on signature petition violates Privacy Act); Ingerman v. IRS, No. 89-5396, slip op. at 3-5 (D.N.J. Apr. 3, 1991) (section 7(b) not applicable to IRS request that taxpayers affix printed mailing label containing social security number on tax returns; no new disclosure occurs because IRS already was in possession of taxpayers' social security numbers), aff'd, 953 F.2d 1380 (3d Cir. 1992) (unpublished table decision); Oakes v. IRS, No. 86-2804, slip op. at 2-3 (D.D.C. Apr. 16, 1987) (section 7(b) does not require agency requesting individual to disclose

OVERVIEW OF THE PRIVACY ACT

his social security number to publish any notice in Federal Register); Doyle v. Wilson, 529 F. Supp. 1343, 1348-50 (D. Del. 1982) (section 7(b)'s requirements are not fulfilled when no affirmative effort is made to disclose information required under 7(b) "at or before the time the number is requested"); Doe v. Sharp, 491 F. Supp. 346, 347-50 (D. Mass. 1980) (same as Green and McElrath regarding section 7(a); section 7(b) creates affirmative duty for agencies to inform applicant of uses to be made of social security numbers – "after-the-fact explanations" not sufficient); and Chambers v. Klein, 419 F. Supp. 569, 580 (D.N.J. 1976) (same as Green, McElrath, and Doe regarding section 7(a); section 7(b) not violated where agency failed to notify applicants of use to be made of social security numbers as state had not begun using them pending full implementation of statute requiring their disclosure), aff'd, 564 F.2d 89 (3d Cir. 1977) (unpublished table decision). Cf. Gonzalez, 671 F.3d at 663-64 (concluding that qualified immunity shielded police officers from liability where officers had "asked [plaintiff] for his social security number" but "did not give him the information listed in § 7(b)," as "the officers' obligation to make the disclosures specified in § 7(b) was not clearly established" at time of plaintiff's arrest); Doe v. Herman, No. 297CV00043, 1999 WL 1000212, at *9 (W.D. Va. Oct. 29, 1999) (magistrate's recommendation) (although not citing section 7 with regard to issue, citing Doe v. Sharp and subsection (e)(3) for proposition that "when agency solicits a social security number it shall inform the individual of what use will be made of it"), adopted in pertinent part & rev'd in other part (W.D. Va. July 24, 2000), aff'd in part, rev'd in part, & remanded, on other grounds sub nom. Doe v. Chao, 306 F.3d 170 (4th Cir. 2002), aff'd, 540 U.S. 615 (2004).

GOVERNMENT CONTRACTORS

"When an agency provides by a contract for the operation by or on behalf of the agency of a system of records to accomplish an agency function, the agency shall, consistent with its authority, cause the requirements of this section to be applied to such system. For purposes of subsection (i) of this section any such contractor and any employee of such contractor, if such contract is agreed to on or after the effective date of this section [9-27-75], shall be considered to be an employee of an agency." 5 U.S.C. § 552a(m)(1).

"A consumer reporting agency to which a record is disclosed under section 3711(e) of Title 31 shall not be considered a contractor for the purposes of this section." 5 U.S.C. § 552a(m)(2).

Comment:

For guidance concerning this provision, see OMB Guidelines, 40 Fed. Reg. 28,948, 28,951, 28,975-76, (July 9, 1975), available at http://www.whitehouse.gov/sites/default/files/omb/assets/omb/inforeg/implementation_guidelines.pdf, and the legislative debate reported at 120 Cong. Rec. 40,408 (1974), reprinted in Source Book at 866, available at http://www.loc.gov/rr/frd/Military_Law/pdf/LH_privacy_act-1974.pdf. See generally Boggs v. Se. Tidewater Opportunity Project, No. 2:96cv196, U.S. Dist. LEXIS 6977, at *5 (E.D. Va. May 22, 1996) (subsection (m) inapplicable to community action agency that was not "in the business of keeping records for federal agencies").

OVERVIEW OF THE PRIVACY ACT

The Federal Acquisition Regulation sets forth the language that must be inserted in solicitations and contracts "[w]hen the design, development, or operation of a system of records on individuals is required to accomplish an agency function." 48 C.F.R. § 24.104 (2012); see also id. § 52.224-1 to -2. The regulation defines "operation of a system of records" as "performance of any of the activities associated with maintaining the system of records, including the collection, use, and dissemination of records." Id. at § 52.224-2(c)(1). But cf. Koch v. Schapiro, 777 F. Supp. 2d 86, 91 (D.D.C. 2011) (concluding, in context of claim brought under Rehabilitation Act, that "a contract to investigate complaints of discrimination by employees of the agency on behalf of the [agency's] EEO Office" is "not a contract for the design or development of a system of records" and therefore is "not the type of contract covered by 48 C.F.R. pt. 24").

Additionally, see the discussion regarding treatment of contractors as "employees" for purposes of subsection (b)(1) disclosures under "Conditions Of Disclosure To Third Parties," above.

Even when subsection (m) is applicable, the agency – not the contractor – remains the only proper party defendant in a Privacy Act civil lawsuit. See Campbell v. VA, 2 Gov't Disclosure Serv. (P-H) ¶ 82,076, at 82,355 (S.D. Iowa Dec. 21, 1981); see also Patterson v. Austin Med. Ctr., No. 97-1241, slip op. at 4-5 (D. Minn. Jan. 28, 1998) (Subsection (m) "does not create a private cause of action against a government contractor for violations of the Act."), aff'd, No. 98-1643, 1998 U.S. App. LEXIS 22371 (8th Cir. Sept. 11, 1998). But cf. Shannon v. Gen. Elec. Co., 812 F. Supp. 308, 311-15 & n.5 (N.D.N.Y. 1993) (although subsection (m) not mentioned, stating that "GE is subject to the requirements of the Privacy Act, inasmuch as it falls within the definition of 'agency'"). See generally Adelman v. Discover Card Servs., 915 F. Supp. 1163, 1166 (D. Utah 1996) (with no mention of subsection (m), finding no waiver of sovereign immunity for action brought for alleged violation by state agency working as independent contractor to administer federal program for Social Security Administration, even though procedures and standards governing relationship between SSA and state agency explicitly stated that in event of alleged violation of Privacy Act concerning operation of system of records to accomplish agency function, civil action could be brought against agency).

MAILING LISTS

"An individual's name and address may not be sold or rented by an agency unless such action is specifically authorized by law. This provision shall not be construed to require the withholding of names and addresses otherwise permitted to be made public." 5 U.S.C. § 552a(n).

Comment:

For a decision discussing this provision, see Disabled Officer's Ass'n v. Rumsfeld, 428 F. Supp. 454, 459 (D.D.C. 1977), aff'd, 574 F.2d 636 (D.C. Cir. 1978) (unpublished table

OVERVIEW OF THE PRIVACY ACT

decision). For a further discussion of this provision, see OMB Guidelines, 40 Fed. Reg. 28,948, 28,976 (July 9, 1975), <u>available at</u> http://www.whitehouse.gov/sites/default/files/omb/assets/omb/inforeg/implementation_guidelines.pdf.

MISCELLANEOUS PROVISIONS

Note that the Privacy Act also contains provisions concerning archival records, <u>see</u> 5 U.S.C. § 552a(l); <u>see also</u> OMB Guidelines, 40 Fed. Reg. 28,948, 28,974-75 (July 9, 1975), <u>available at</u> http://www.whitehouse.gov/sites/default/files/omb/assets/omb/inforeg/implementation_guidelines.pdf, and reporting requirements for new record systems, <u>see</u> 5 U.S.C. § 552a(r).

The Privacy Act of 1974
5 U.S.C. § 552a (2006)

THE PRIVACY ACT OF 1974

5 U.S.C. § 552a

As Amended

§ 552a. Records maintained on individuals

(a) Definitions

For purposes of this section—

(1) the term "agency" means agency as defined in section 552(e) of this title;

(2) the term "individual" means a citizen of the United States or an alien lawfully admitted for permanent residence;

(3) the term "maintain" includes maintain, collect, use, or disseminate;

(4) the term "record" means any item, collection, or grouping of information about an individual that is maintained by an agency, including, but not limited to, his education, financial transactions, medical history, and criminal or employment history and that contains his name, or the identifying number, symbol, or other identifying particular assigned to the individual, such as a finger or voice print or a photograph;

(5) the term "system of records" means a group of any records under the control of any agency from which information is retrieved by the name of the individual or by some identifying number, symbol, or other identifying particular assigned to the individual;

(6) the term "statistical record" means a record in a system of records maintained for statistical research or reporting purposes only and not used in whole or in part in making any determination about an identifiable individual, except as provided by section 8 of Title 13;

(7) the term "routine use" means, with respect to the disclosure of a record, the use of such record for a purpose which is compatible with the purpose for which it was collected;

(8) the term "matching program"—

(A) means any computerized comparison of—

(i) two or more automated systems of records or a system of records with non-Federal records for the purpose of—

(I) establishing or verifying the eligibility of, or continuing compliance with statutory and regulatory requirements by, applicants for, recipients or beneficiaries of, participants in, or providers of services with respect to, cash or in-kind assistance or payments under Federal benefit programs, or

(II) recouping payments or delinquent debts under such Federal benefit programs, or

(ii) two or more automated Federal personnel or payroll systems of records or a system of Federal personnel or payroll records with non-Federal records,

(B) but does not include—

(i) matches performed to produce aggregate statistical data without any personal identifiers;

(ii) matches performed to support any research or statistical project, the specific data of which may not be used to make decisions concerning the rights, benefits, or privileges of specific individuals;

(iii) matches performed, by an agency (or component thereof) which performs as its principal function any activity pertaining to the enforcement of criminal laws, subsequent to the initiation of a specific criminal or civil law enforcement investigation of a named person or persons for the purpose of gathering evidence against such person or persons;

(iv) matches of tax information (I) pursuant to section 6103(d) of the Internal Revenue Code of 1986, (II) for purposes of tax administration as defined in section 6103(b)(4) of such Code, (III) for the purpose of intercepting a tax refund due an individual under authority granted by section 404(e), 464, or 1137 of the Social Security Act; or (IV) for the purpose of intercepting a tax refund due an individual under any other tax refund intercept program authorized by statute which has been determined by the Director of the Office of Management and Budget to contain verification, notice, and hearing requirements that are substantially similar to the procedures in section 1137 of the Social Security Act;

(v) matches—

(I) using records predominantly relating to Federal personnel, that are performed for routine administrative purposes (subject to guidance provided by the Director of the Office of Management and Budget pursuant to subsection (v));

(II) conducted by an agency using only records from systems of records maintained by that agency; if the purpose of the match is not to take any adverse financial, personnel, disciplinary, or other adverse action against Federal personnel;

(vi) matches performed for foreign counterintelligence purposes or to produce background checks for security clearances of Federal personnel or Federal contractor personnel;

(vii) matches performed incident to a levy described in section 6103(k)(8) of the Internal Revenue Code of 1986;

(viii) matches performed pursuant to section 202(x)(3) or 1611(e)(1) of the Social Security Act (42 U.S.C. 402(x)(3), 1382(e)(1)); or

(ix) matches performed by the Secretary of Health and Human Services or the Inspector General of the Department of Health and Human Services with respect to potential fraud, waste, and abuse, including matches of a system of records with non-Federal records;

(9) the term "recipient agency" means any agency, or contractor thereof, receiving records contained in a system of records from a source agency for use in a matching program;

(10) the term "non-Federal agency" means any State or local government, or agency thereof, which receives records contained in a system of records from a source agency for use in a matching program;

(11) the term "source agency" means any agency which discloses records contained in a system of records to be used in a matching program, or any State or local government, or agency thereof, which discloses records to be used in a matching program;

(12) the term "Federal benefit program" means any program administered or funded by the Federal Government, or by any agent or State on behalf of the Federal Government, providing cash or in-kind assistance in the form of payments, grants, loans, or loan guarantees to individuals; and

(13) the term "Federal personnel" means officers and employees of the Government of the United States, members of the uniformed services (including members of the Reserve Components), individuals entitled to receive immediate or deferred retirement benefits under any retirement program of the Government of the United States (including survivor benefits).

(b) Conditions of disclosure

No agency shall disclose any record which is contained in a system of records by any means of communication to any person, or to another agency, except pursuant to a written request by, or with the prior written consent of, the individual to whom the record pertains, unless disclosure of the record would be—

(1) to those officers and employees of the agency which maintains the record who have a need for the record in the performance of their duties;

(2) required under section 552 of this title;

(3) for a routine use as defined in subsection (a)(7) of this section and described under subsection (e)(4)(D) of this section;

(4) to the Bureau of the Census for purposes of planning or carrying out a census or survey or related activity pursuant to the provisions of Title 13;

(5) to a recipient who has provided the agency with advance adequate written assurance that the record will be used solely as a statistical research or reporting record, and the record is to be transferred in a form that is not individually identifiable;

(6) to the National Archives and Records Administration as a record which has sufficient historical or other value to warrant its continued preservation by the United States Government, or for evaluation by the Archivist of the United States or the designee of the Archivist to determine whether the record has such value;

(7) to another agency or to an instrumentality of any governmental jurisdiction within or under the control of the United States for a civil or criminal law enforcement activity if the activity is authorized by law, and if the head of the agency or instrumentality has made a written request to the agency which maintains the record specifying the particular portion desired and the law enforcement activity for which the record is sought;

(8) to a person pursuant to a showing of compelling circumstances affecting the health or safety of an individual if upon such disclosure notification is transmitted to the last known address of such individual;

(9) to either House of Congress, or, to the extent of matter within its jurisdiction, any committee or subcommittee thereof, any joint committee of Congress or subcommittee of any such joint committee;

(10) to the Comptroller General, or any of his authorized representatives, in the course of the performance of the duties of the Government Accountability Office;

(11) pursuant to the order of a court of competent jurisdiction; or

(12) to a consumer reporting agency in accordance with section 3711(e) of Title 31.

(c) Accounting of certain disclosures

Each agency, with respect to each system of records under its control, shall—

(1) except for disclosures made under subsections (b)(1) or (b)(2) of this section, keep an accurate accounting of—

(A) the date, nature, and purpose of each disclosure of a record to any person or to another agency made under subsection (b) of this section; and

(B) the name and address of the person or agency to whom the disclosure is made;

(2) retain the accounting made under paragraph (1) of this subsection for at least five years or the life of the record, whichever is longer, after the disclosure for which the accounting is made;

(3) except for disclosures made under subsection (b)(7) of this section, make the accounting made under paragraph (1) of this subsection available to the individual named in the record at his request; and

(4) inform any person or other agency about any correction or notation of dispute made by the agency in accordance with subsection (d) of this section of any record that has been disclosed to the person or agency if an accounting of the disclosure was made.

(d) Access to records

Each agency that maintains a system of records shall—

(1) upon request by any individual to gain access to his record or to any information pertaining to him which is contained in the system, permit him and upon his request, a person of his own choosing to accompany him, to review the record and have a copy made of all or any portion thereof in a form comprehensible to him, except that the agency may require the individual to furnish a written statement authorizing discussion of that individual's record in the accompanying person's presence;

(2) permit the individual to request amendment of a record pertaining to him and—

> (A) not later than 10 days (excluding Saturdays, Sundays, and legal public holidays) after the date of receipt of such request, acknowledge in writing such receipt; and
>
> (B) promptly, either—
>
>> (i) make any correction of any portion thereof which the individual believes is not accurate, relevant, timely, or complete; or
>>
>> (ii) inform the individual of its refusal to amend the record in accordance with his request, the reason for the refusal, the procedures established by the agency for the individual to request a review of that refusal by the head of the agency or an officer designated by the head of the agency, and the name and business address of that official;

(3) permit the individual who disagrees with the refusal of the agency to amend his record to request a review of such refusal, and not later than 30 days (excluding Saturdays, Sundays, and legal public holidays) from the date on which the individual requests such review, complete such review and make a final determination unless, for good cause shown, the head of the agency extends such 30-day period; and if, after his review, the reviewing official also refuses to amend the record in accordance with the request, permit the individual to file with the agency a concise statement setting forth the reasons for his disagreement with the refusal of the agency, and notify the individual of the provisions for judicial review of the reviewing official's determination under subsection (g)(1)(A) of this section;

(4) in any disclosure, containing information about which the individual has filed a statement of disagreement, occurring after the filing of the statement under paragraph (3) of this subsection, clearly note any portion of the record which is disputed and provide copies of the statement and, if the agency deems it appropriate, copies of a concise statement of the reasons of the agency for not

making the amendments requested, to persons or other agencies to whom the disputed record has been disclosed; and

(5) nothing in this section shall allow an individual access to any information compiled in reasonable anticipation of a civil action or proceeding.

(e) Agency requirements

Each agency that maintains a system of records shall—

(1) maintain in its records only such information about an individual as is relevant and necessary to accomplish a purpose of the agency required to be accomplished by statute or by executive order of the President;

(2) collect information to the greatest extent practicable directly from the subject individual when the information may result in adverse determinations about an individual's rights, benefits, and privileges under Federal programs;

(3) inform each individual whom it asks to supply information, on the form which it uses to collect the information or on a separate form that can be retained by the individual—

(A) the authority (whether granted by statute, or by executive order of the President) which authorizes the solicitation of the information and whether disclosure of such information is mandatory or voluntary;

(B) the principal purpose or purposes for which the information is intended to be used;

(C) the routine uses which may be made of the information, as published pursuant to paragraph (4)(D) of this subsection; and

(D) the effects on him, if any, of not providing all or any part of the requested information;

(4) subject to the provisions of paragraph (11) of this subsection, publish in the Federal Register upon establishment or revision a notice of the existence and character of the system of records, which notice shall include—

(A) the name and location of the system;

(B) the categories of individuals on whom records are maintained in the system;

(C) the categories of records maintained in the system;

(D) each routine use of the records contained in the system, including the categories of users and the purpose of such use;

(E) the policies and practices of the agency regarding storage, retrievability, access controls, retention, and disposal of the records;

(F) the title and business address of the agency official who is responsible for the system of records;

(G) the agency procedures whereby an individual can be notified at his request if the system of records contains a record pertaining to him;

(H) the agency procedures whereby an individual can be notified at his request how he can gain access to any record pertaining to him contained in the system of records, and how he can contest its content; and

(I) the categories of sources of records in the system;

(5) maintain all records which are used by the agency in making any determination about any individual with such accuracy, relevance, timeliness, and completeness as is reasonably necessary to assure fairness to the individual in the determination;

(6) prior to disseminating any record about an individual to any person other than an agency, unless the dissemination is made pursuant to subsection (b)(2) of this section, make reasonable efforts to assure that such records are accurate, complete, timely, and relevant for agency purposes;

(7) maintain no record describing how any individual exercises rights guaranteed by the First Amendment unless expressly authorized by statute or by the individual about whom the record is maintained or unless pertinent to and within the scope of an authorized law enforcement activity;

(8) make reasonable efforts to serve notice on an individual when any record on such individual is made available to any person under compulsory legal process when such process becomes a matter of public record;

(9) establish rules of conduct for persons involved in the design, development, operation, or maintenance of any system of records, or in maintaining any record, and instruct each such person with respect to such rules and the requirements of this section, including any other rules and procedures adopted pursuant to this section and the penalties for noncompliance;

(10) establish appropriate administrative, technical, and physical safeguards to insure the security and confidentiality of records and to protect against any anticipated threats or hazards to their security or integrity which could result in substantial harm, embarrassment, inconvenience, or unfairness to any individual on whom information is maintained;

(11) at least 30 days prior to publication of information under paragraph (4)(D) of this subsection, publish in the Federal Register notice of any new use or intended use of the information in the system, and provide an opportunity for interested persons to submit written data, views, or arguments to the agency; and

(12) if such agency is a recipient agency or a source agency in a matching program with a non-Federal agency, with respect to any establishment or revision of a matching program, at least 30 days prior to conducting such program, publish in the Federal Register notice of such establishment or revision.

(f) Agency rules

In order to carry out the provisions of this section, each agency that maintains a system of records shall promulgate rules, in accordance with the requirements (including general notice) of section 553 of this title, which shall—

(1) establish procedures whereby an individual can be notified in response to his request if any system of records named by the individual contains a record pertaining to him;

(2) define reasonable times, places, and requirements for identifying an individual who requests his record or information pertaining to him before the agency shall make the record or information available to the individual;

(3) establish procedures for the disclosure to an individual upon his request of his record or information pertaining to him, including special procedure, if deemed necessary, for the disclosure to an individual of medical records, including psychological records, pertaining to him;

(4) establish procedures for reviewing a request from an individual concerning the amendment of any record or information pertaining to the individual, for making a determination on the request, for an appeal within the agency of an initial adverse agency determination, and for whatever additional means may be necessary for each individual to be able to exercise fully his rights under this section; and

(5) establish fees to be charged, if any, to any individual for making copies of his record, excluding the cost of any search for and review of the record.

The Office of the Federal Register shall biennially compile and publish the rules promulgated under this subsection and agency notices published under subsection (e)(4) of this section in a form available to the public at low cost.

(g)(1) Civil remedies

Whenever any agency

(A) makes a determination under subsection (d)(3) of this section not to amend an individual's record in accordance with his request, or fails to make such review in conformity with that subsection;

(B) refuses to comply with an individual request under subsection (d)(1) of this section;

(C) fails to maintain any record concerning any individual with such accuracy, relevance, timeliness, and completeness as is necessary to assure fairness in any determination relating to the qualifications, character, rights, or opportunities of, or benefits to the individual that may be made on the basis of such record, and consequently a determination is made which is adverse to the individual; or

(D) fails to comply with any other provision of this section, or any rule promulgated thereunder, in such a way as to have an adverse effect on an individual, the individual may bring a civil action against the agency, and the district courts of the United States shall have jurisdiction in the matters under the provisions of this subsection.

(2)(A) In any suit brought under the provisions of subsection (g)(1)(A) of this section, the court may order the agency to amend the individual's record in accordance with his request or in such other way as the court may direct. In such a case the court shall determine the matter de novo.

(B) The court may assess against the United States reasonable attorney fees and other litigation costs reasonably incurred in any case under this paragraph in which the complainant has substantially prevailed.

(3)(A) In any suit brought under the provisions of subsection (g)(1)(B) of this section, the court may enjoin the agency from withholding the records and order the production to the complainant of any agency records improperly withheld from him. In such a case the court shall determine the matter de novo, and may examine the contents of any agency records in camera to determine whether the records or any portion thereof may be withheld under any of the exemptions set forth in subsection (k) of this section, and the burden is on the agency to sustain its action.

> (B) The court may assess against the United States reasonable attorney fees and other litigation costs reasonably incurred in any case under this paragraph in which the complainant has substantially prevailed.

(4) In any suit brought under the provisions of subsection (g)(1)(C) or (D) of this section in which the court determines that the agency acted in a manner which was intentional or willful, the United States shall be liable to the individual in an amount equal to the sum of—

> (A) actual damages sustained by the individual as a result of the refusal or failure, but in no case shall a person entitled to recovery receive less than the sum of $1,000; and

> (B) the costs of the action together with reasonable attorney fees as determined by the court.

(5) An action to enforce any liability created under this section may be brought in the district court of the United States in the district in which the complainant resides, or has his principal place of business, or in which the agency records are situated, or in the District of Columbia, without regard to the amount in controversy, within two years from the date on which the cause of action arises, except that where an agency has materially and willfully misrepresented any information required under this section to be disclosed to an individual and the information so misrepresented is material to establishment of the liability of the agency to the individual under this section, the action may be brought at any time within two years after discovery by the individual of the misrepresentation. Nothing in this section shall be construed to authorize any civil action by reason of any injury sustained as the result of a disclosure of a record prior to September 27, 1975.

(h) Rights of legal guardians

> For the purposes of this section, the parent of any minor, or the legal guardian of any individual who has been declared to be incompetent due to physical or mental incapacity or age by a court of competent jurisdiction, may act on behalf of the individual.

(i)(1) Criminal penalties

> Any officer or employee of an agency, who by virtue of his employment or official position, has possession of, or access to, agency records which contain

individually identifiable information the disclosure of which is prohibited by this section or by rules or regulations established thereunder, and who knowing that disclosure of the specific material is so prohibited, willfully discloses the material in any manner to any person or agency not entitled to receive it, shall be guilty of a misdemeanor and fined not more than $5,000.

(2) Any officer or employee of any agency who willfully maintains a system of records without meeting the notice requirements of subsection (e)(4) of this section shall be guilty of a misdemeanor and fined not more than $5,000.

(3) Any person who knowingly and willfully requests or obtains any record concerning an individual from an agency under false pretenses shall be guilty of a misdemeanor and fined not more than $5,000.

(j) General exemptions

The head of any agency may promulgate rules, in accordance with the requirements (including general notice) of sections 553(b)(1), (2), and (3), (c), and (e) of this title, to exempt any system of records within the agency from any part of this section except subsections (b), (c)(1) and (2), (e)(4)(A) through (F), (e)(6), (7), (9), (10), and (11), and (i) if the system of records is—

(1) maintained by the Central Intelligence Agency; or

(2) maintained by an agency or component thereof which performs as its principal function any activity pertaining to the enforcement of criminal laws, including police efforts to prevent, control, or reduce crime or to apprehend criminals, and the activities of prosecutors, courts, correctional, probation, pardon, or parole authorities, and which consists of (A) information compiled for the purpose of identifying individual criminal offenders and alleged offenders and consisting only of identifying data and notations of arrests, the nature and disposition of criminal charges, sentencing, confinement, release, and parole and probation status; (B) information compiled for the purpose of a criminal investigation, including reports of informants and investigators, and associated with an identifiable individual; or (C) reports identifiable to an individual compiled at any stage of the process of enforcement of the criminal laws from arrest or indictment through release from supervision.

At the time rules are adopted under this subsection, the agency shall include in the statement required under section 553(c) of this title, the reasons why the system of records is to be exempted from a provision of this section.

(k) Specific exemptions

The head of any agency may promulgate rules, in accordance with the requirements (including general notice) of sections 553(b)(1), (2), and (3), (c), and (e) of this title, to exempt any system of records within the agency from subsections (c)(3), (d), (e)(1), (e)(4)(G), (H), and (I) and (f) of this section if the system of records is—

(1) subject to the provisions of section 552(b)(1) of this title;

(2) investigatory material compiled for law enforcement purposes, other than material within the scope of subsection (j)(2) of this section: Provided, however, That if any individual is denied any right, privilege, or benefit that he would otherwise be entitled by Federal law, or for which he would otherwise be eligible, as a result of the maintenance of such material, such material shall be provided to such individual, except to the extent that the disclosure of such material would reveal the identity of a source who furnished information to the Government under an express promise that the identity of the source would be held in confidence, or, prior to the effective date of this section, under an implied promise that the identity of the source would be held in confidence;

(3) maintained in connection with providing protective services to the President of the United States or other individuals pursuant to section 3056 of Title 18;

(4) required by statute to be maintained and used solely as statistical records;

(5) investigatory material compiled solely for the purpose of determining suitability, eligibility, or qualifications for Federal civilian employment, military service, Federal contracts, or access to classified information, but only to the extent that the disclosure of such material would reveal the identity of a source who furnished information to the Government under an express promise that the identity of the source would be held in confidence, or, prior to the effective date of this section, under an implied promise that the identity of the source would be held in confidence;

(6) testing or examination material used solely to determine individual qualifications for appointment or promotion in the Federal service the disclosure of which would compromise the objectivity or fairness of the testing or examination process; or

(7) evaluation material used to determine potential for promotion in the armed services, but only to the extent that the disclosure of such material would reveal the identity of a source who furnished information to the Government under an express promise that the identity of the source would be held in confidence, or, prior to the effective date of this section, under an implied promise that the identity of the source would be held in confidence.

At the time rules are adopted under this subsection, the agency shall include in the statement required under section 553(c) of this title, the reasons why the system of records is to be exempted from a provision of this section.

(l) Archival records

(1) Each agency record which is accepted by the Archivist of the United States for storage, processing, and servicing in accordance with section 3103 of Title 44 shall, for the purposes of this section, be considered to be maintained by the agency which deposited the record and shall be subject to the provisions of this section. The Archivist of the United States shall not disclose the record except to the agency which maintains the record, or under rules established by that agency which are not inconsistent with the provisions of this section.

(2) Each agency record pertaining to an identifiable individual which was transferred to the National Archives of the United States as a record which has sufficient historical or other value to warrant its continued preservation by the United States Government, prior to the effective date of this section, shall, for the purposes of this section, be considered to be maintained by the National Archives and shall not be subject to the provisions of this section, except that a statement generally describing such records (modeled after the requirements relating to records subject to subsections (e)(4)(A) through (G) of this section) shall be published in the Federal Register.

(3) Each agency record pertaining to an identifiable individual which is transferred to the National Archives of the United States as a record which has sufficient historical or other value to warrant its continued preservation by the United States Government, on or after the effective date of this section, shall, for the purposes of this section, be considered to be maintained by the National Archives and shall be exempt from the requirements of this section except subsections (e)(4)(A) through (G) and (e)(9) of this section.

(m) Government contractors

(1) When an agency provides by a contract for the operation by or on behalf of the agency of a system of records to accomplish an agency function, the agency shall, consistent with its authority, cause the requirements of this section to be applied to such system. For purposes of subsection (i) of this section any such contractor and any employee of such contractor, if such contract is agreed to on or after the effective date of this section, shall be considered to be an employee of an agency.

(2) A consumer reporting agency to which a record is disclosed under section 3711(e) of Title 31 shall not be considered a contractor for the purposes of this section.

(n) Mailing lists

An individual's name and address may not be sold or rented by an agency unless such action is specifically authorized by law. This provision shall not be construed to require the withholding of names and addresses otherwise permitted to be made public.

(o) Matching agreements

(1) No record which is contained in a system of records may be disclosed to a recipient agency or non-Federal agency for use in a computer matching program except pursuant to a written agreement between the source agency and the recipient agency or non-Federal agency specifying—

(A) the purpose and legal authority for conducting the program;

(B) the justification for the program and the anticipated results, including a specific estimate of any savings;

(C) a description of the records that will be matched, including each data element that will be used, the approximate number of records that will be matched, and the projected starting and completion dates of the matching program;

(D) procedures for providing individualized notice at the time of application, and notice periodically thereafter as directed by the Data Integrity Board of such agency (subject to guidance provided by the Director of the Office of Management and Budget pursuant to subsection (v)), to—

(i) applicants for and recipients of financial assistance or payments under Federal benefit programs, and

(ii) applicants for and holders of positions as Federal personnel, that any information provided by such applicants, recipients, holders, and individuals may be subject to verification through matching programs;

(E) procedures for verifying information produced in such matching program as required by subsection (p);

(F) procedures for the retention and timely destruction of identifiable records created by a recipient agency or non-Federal agency in such matching program;

(G) procedures for ensuring the administrative, technical, and physical security of the records matched and the results of such programs;

(H) prohibitions on duplication and redisclosure of records provided by the source agency within or outside the recipient agency or the non-Federal agency, except where required by law or essential to the conduct of the matching program;

(I) procedures governing the use by a recipient agency or non-Federal agency of records provided in a matching program by a source agency, including procedures governing return of the records to the source agency or destruction of records used in such program;

(J) information on assessments that have been made on the accuracy of the records that will be used in such matching program; and

(K) that the Comptroller General may have access to all records of a recipient agency or a non-Federal agency that the Comptroller General deems necessary in order to monitor or verify compliance with the agreement.

(2)(A) A copy of each agreement entered into pursuant to paragraph (1) shall—

> (i) be transmitted to the Committee on Governmental Affairs of the Senate and the Committee on Government Operations of the House of Representatives; and
>
> (ii) be available upon request to the public.

(B) No such agreement shall be effective until 30 days after the date on which such a copy is transmitted pursuant to subparagraph (A)(i).

(C) Such an agreement shall remain in effect only for such period, not to exceed 18 months, as the Data Integrity Board of the agency determines is appropriate in light of the purposes, and length of time necessary for the conduct, of the matching program.

(D) Within 3 months prior to the expiration of such an agreement pursuant to subparagraph (C), the Data Integrity Board of the agency may, without additional review, renew the matching agreement for a current, ongoing matching program for not more than one additional year if—

    (i) such program will be conducted without any change; and

    (ii) each party to the agreement certifies to the Board in writing that the program has been conducted in compliance with the agreement.

(p) Verification and opportunity to contest findings

    (1) In order to protect any individual whose records are used in a matching program, no recipient agency, non-Federal agency, or source agency may suspend, terminate, reduce, or make a final denial of any financial assistance or payment under a Federal benefit program to such individual, or take other adverse action against such individual, as a result of information produced by such matching program, until—

    (A)(i) the agency has independently verified the information; or

    (ii) the Data Integrity Board of the agency, or in the case of a non-Federal agency the Data Integrity Board of the source agency, determines in accordance with guidance issued by the Director of the Office of Management and Budget that—

        (I) the information is limited to identification and amount of benefits paid by the source agency under a Federal benefit program; and

        (II) there is a high degree of confidence that the information provided to the recipient agency is accurate;

    (B) the individual receives a notice from the agency containing a statement of its findings and informing the individual of the opportunity to contest such findings; and

    (C)(i) the expiration of any time period established for the program by statute or regulation for the individual to respond to that notice; or

    (ii) in the case of a program for which no such period is established, the end of the 30-day period beginning on the date on which notice under subparagraph (B) is mailed or otherwise provided to the individual.

    (2) Independent verification referred to in paragraph (1) requires investigation and confirmation of specific information relating to an individual that is used as

a basis for an adverse action against the individual, including where applicable investigation and confirmation of—

(A) the amount of any asset or income involved;

(B) whether such individual actually has or had access to such asset or income for such individual's own use; and

(C) the period or periods when the individual actually had such asset or income.

(3) Notwithstanding paragraph (1), an agency may take any appropriate action otherwise prohibited by such paragraph if the agency determines that the public health or public safety may be adversely affected or significantly threatened during any notice period required by such paragraph.

(q) Sanctions

(1) Notwithstanding any other provision of law, no source agency may disclose any record which is contained in a system of records to a recipient agency or non-Federal agency for a matching program if such source agency has reason to believe that the requirements of subsection (p), or any matching agreement entered into pursuant to subsection (o), or both, are not being met by such recipient agency.

(2) No source agency may renew a matching agreement unless--

(A) the recipient agency or non-Federal agency has certified that it has complied with the provisions of that agreement; and

(B) the source agency has no reason to believe that the certification is inaccurate.

(r) Report on new systems and matching programs

Each agency that proposes to establish or make a significant change in a system of records or a matching program shall provide adequate advance notice of any such proposal (in duplicate) to the Committee on Government Operations of the House of Representatives, the Committee on Governmental Affairs of the Senate, and the Office of Management and Budget in order to permit an evaluation of the probable or potential effect of such proposal on the privacy or other rights of individuals.

(s) [Biennial report] Repealed by the Federal Reports Elimination and Sunset Act of 1995, Pub. L. No. 104-66, § 3003, 109 Stat. 707, 734-36 (1995), amended by Pub. L.

No. 106-113, § 236, 113 Stat. 1501, 1501A-302 (1999) (changing effective date to May 15, 2000).

(t) Effect of other laws

> (1) No agency shall rely on any exemption contained in section 552 of this title to withhold from an individual any record which is otherwise accessible to such individual under the provisions of this section.
>
> (2) No agency shall rely on any exemption in this section to withhold from an individual any record which is otherwise accessible to such individual under the provisions of section 552 of this title.

(u) Data Integrity Boards

> (1) Every agency conducting or participating in a matching program shall establish a Data Integrity Board to oversee and coordinate among the various components of such agency the agency's implementation of this section.
>
> (2) Each Data Integrity Board shall consist of senior officials designated by the head of the agency, and shall include any senior official designated by the head of the agency as responsible for implementation of this section, and the inspector general of the agency, if any. The inspector general shall not serve as chairman of the Data Integrity Board.
>
> (3) Each Data Integrity Board—
>
>> (A) shall review, approve, and maintain all written agreements for receipt or disclosure of agency records for matching programs to ensure compliance with subsection (o), and all relevant statutes, regulations, and guidelines;
>>
>> (B) shall review all matching programs in which the agency has participated during the year, either as a source agency or recipient agency, determine compliance with applicable laws, regulations, guidelines, and agency agreements, and assess the costs and benefits of such programs;
>>
>> (C) shall review all recurring matching programs in which the agency has participated during the year, either as a source agency or recipient agency, for continued justification for such disclosures;
>>
>> (D) shall compile an annual report, which shall be submitted to the head of the agency and the Office of Management and Budget and made available to the public on request, describing the matching activities of the agency, including—

(i) matching programs in which the agency has participated as a source agency or recipient agency;

(ii) matching agreements proposed under subsection (o) that were disapproved by the Board;

(iii) any changes in membership or structure of the Board in the preceding year;

(iv) the reasons for any waiver of the requirement in paragraph (4) of this section for completion and submission of a cost-benefit analysis prior to the approval of a matching program;

(v) any violations of matching agreements that have been alleged or identified and any corrective action taken; and

(vi) any other information required by the Director of the Office of Management and Budget to be included in such report;

(E) shall serve as a clearinghouse for receiving and providing information on the accuracy, completeness, and reliability of records used in matching programs;

(F) shall provide interpretation and guidance to agency components and personnel on the requirements of this section for matching programs;

(G) shall review agency recordkeeping and disposal policies and practices for matching programs to assure compliance with this section; and

(H) may review and report on any agency matching activities that are not matching programs.

(4)(A) Except as provided in subparagraphs (B) and (C), a Data Integrity Board shall not approve any written agreement for a matching program unless the agency has completed and submitted to such Board a cost-benefit analysis of the proposed program and such analysis demonstrates that the program is likely to be cost effective.

(B) The Board may waive the requirements of subparagraph (A) of this paragraph if it determines in writing, in accordance with guidelines prescribed by the Director of the Office of Management and Budget, that a cost-benefit analysis is not required.

(C) A cost-benefit analysis shall not be required under subparagraph (A) prior to the initial approval of a written agreement for a matching program that is specifically required by statute. Any subsequent written agreement for such a program shall not be approved by the Data Integrity Board unless the agency has submitted a cost-benefit analysis of the program as conducted under the preceding approval of such agreement.

(5)(A) If a matching agreement is disapproved by a Data Integrity Board, any party to such agreement may appeal the disapproval to the Director of the Office of Management and Budget. Timely notice of the filing of such an appeal shall be provided by the Director of the Office of Management and Budget to the Committee on Governmental Affairs of the Senate and the Committee on Government Operations of the House of Representatives.

(B) The Director of the Office of Management and Budget may approve a matching agreement notwithstanding the disapproval of a Data Integrity Board if the Director determines that—

(i) the matching program will be consistent with all applicable legal, regulatory, and policy requirements;

(ii) there is adequate evidence that the matching agreement will be cost-effective; and

(iii) the matching program is in the public interest.

(C) The decision of the Director to approve a matching agreement shall not take effect until 30 days after it is reported to committees described in subparagraph (A).

(D) If the Data Integrity Board and the Director of the Office of Management and Budget disapprove a matching program proposed by the inspector general of an agency, the inspector general may report the disapproval to the head of the agency and to the Congress.

(6) In the reports required by paragraph (3)(D), agency matching activities that are not matching programs may be reported on an aggregate basis, if and to the extent necessary to protect ongoing law enforcement or counterintelligence investigations.

(v) Office of Management and Budget responsibilities

The Director of the Office of Management and Budget shall—

(1) develop and, after notice and opportunity for public comment, prescribe guidelines and regulations for the use of agencies in implementing the provisions of this section; and

(2) provide continuing assistance to and oversight of the implementation of this section by agencies.

(w) Applicability to Bureau of Consumer Financial Protection

Except as provided in the Consumer Financial Protection Act of 2010, this section shall apply with respect to the Bureau of Consumer Financial Protection.

The following section originally was part of the Privacy Act but was not codified; it may be found at § 552a (note).

Sec. 7(a) (1) It shall be unlawful for any Federal, State or local government agency to deny to any individual any right, benefit, or privilege provided by law because of such individual's refusal to disclose his social security account number.

(2) the provisions of paragraph (1) of this subsection shall not apply with respect to--

(A) any disclosure which is required by Federal statute, or

(B) the disclosure of a social security number to any Federal, State, or local agency maintaining a system of records in existence and operating before January 1, 1975, if such disclosure was required under statute or regulation adopted prior to such date to verify the identity of an individual.

(b) Any Federal, State, or local government agency which requests an individual to disclose his social security account number shall inform that individual whether that disclosure is mandatory or voluntary, by what statutory or other authority such number is solicited, and what uses will be made of it.

The following sections originally were part of Pub. L. No. 100-503, the Computer Matching and Privacy Protection Act of 1988; they may be found at § 552a (note).

Sec. 6 Functions of the Director of the Office of Management and Budget

(b) Implementation Guidance for Amendments – The Director shall, pursuant to section 552a(v) of Title 5, United States Code, develop guidelines and regulations for the use of agencies in implementing the amendments made by this Act not later than 8 months after the date of enactment of this Act.

Sec. 9 Rules of Construction

Nothing in the amendments made by this Act shall be construed to authorize

(1) the establishment or maintenance by any agency of a national data bank that combines, merges, or links information on individuals maintained in systems of records by other Federal agencies;

(2) the direct linking of computerized systems of records maintained by Federal agencies;

(3) the computer matching of records not otherwise authorized by law; or

(4) the disclosure of records for computer matching except to a Federal, State, or local agency.

Sec. 10 Effective Dates.

(a) In General – Except as provided in subsection (b), the amendments made by this Act shall take effect 9 months after the date of enactment of this Act.

(b) Exceptions – The amendment made by sections 3(b) [Notice of Matching Programs – Report to Congress and the Office of Management and Budget], 6 [Functions of the Director of the Office of Management and Budget], 7 [Compilation of Rules and Notices], and 8 [Annual Report] of this Act shall take effect upon enactment.